S0-AXB-453

MOON HANDBOOKS®
NEW ZEALAND

Lake Wakatipu

© ANDREW HEMPSTEAD

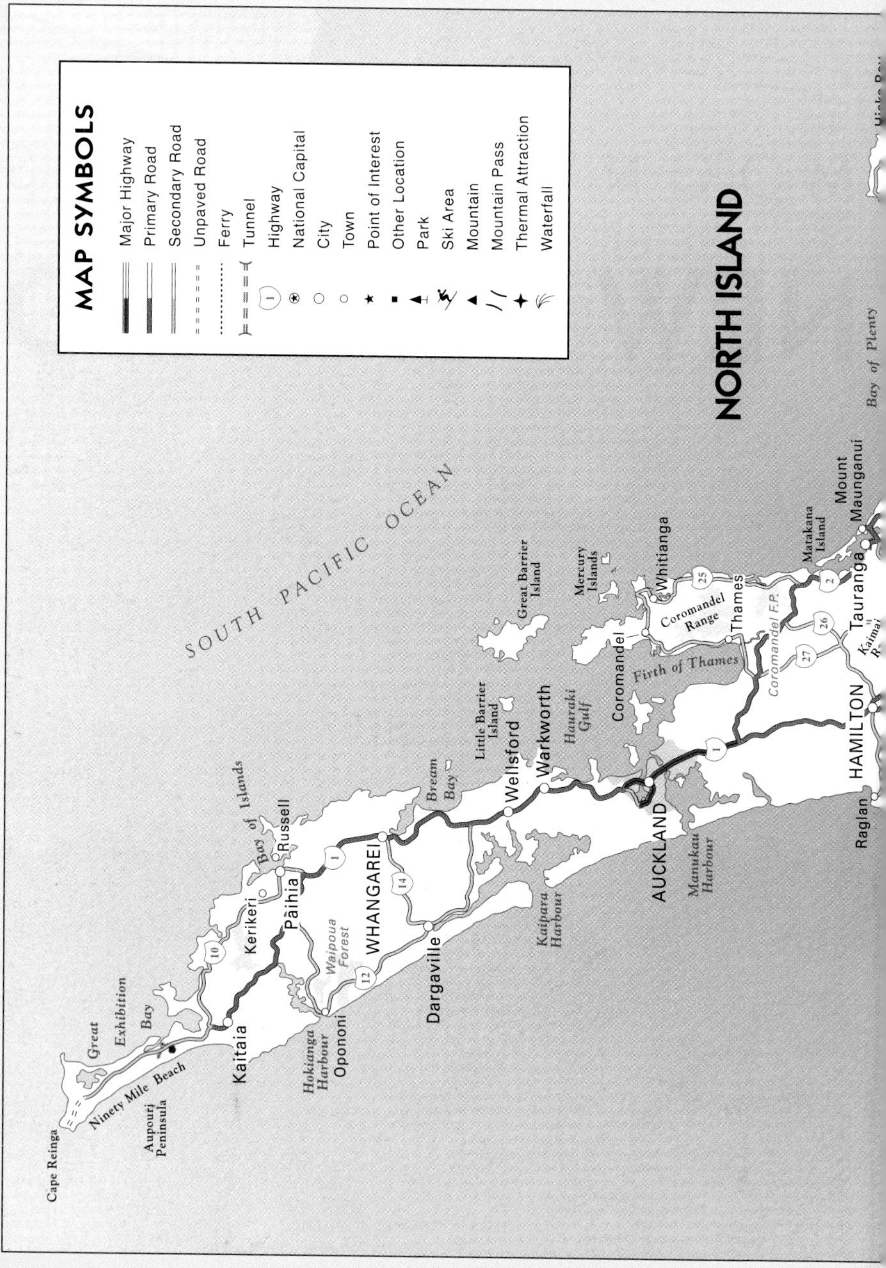

MAP SYMBOLS

	Major Highway
	Primary Road
	Secondary Road
	Unpaved Road
	Ferry
	Tunnel
	Highway
⊛	National Capital
○	City
○	Town
★	Point of Interest
■	Other Location
◄	Park
✗	Ski Area
▲	Mountain
/	Mountain Pass
✦	Thermal Attraction
✿	Waterfall

NORTH ISLAND

SOUTH PACIFIC OCEAN

Cape Reinga

Great Exhibition Bay

Ninety Mile Beach

Aupouri Peninsula

Kaitaia

Hokianga Harbour
Opononi

Waipoua Forest

Kerikeri

Bay of Islands

Russell

Paihia

WHANGAREI

Dargaville

Kaipara Harbour

Bream Bay

Little Barrier Island

Wellsford

Warkworth

Great Barrier Island

Mercury Islands

Whitianga

Coromandel

Coromandel Range

Coromandel F.P.

Thames

Firth of Thames

Hauraki Gulf

AUCKLAND

Manukau Harbour

Raglan

HAMILTON

Matakana Island

Mount Maunganui

Tauranga

Katmai

Bay of Plenty

Waihi Bay

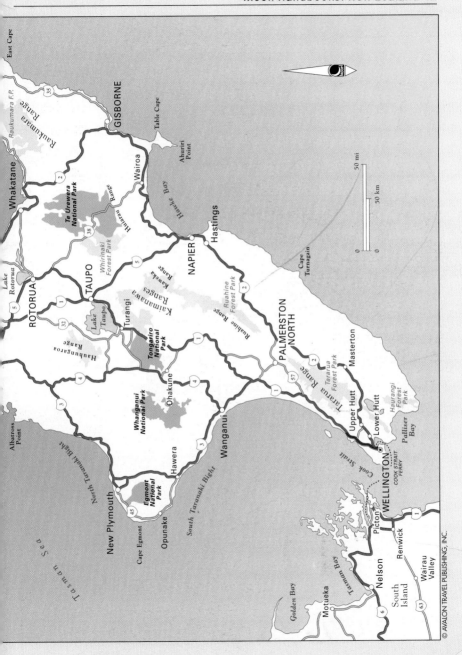

50 mi
50 km

East Cape
Whakatane
Raukumara F.P.
Raukumara Range
GISBORNE
Table Cape
Ahuriri Point
Wairoa
Te Urewera National Park
Huiarau Range
Hawke Bay
Lake Rotorua
ROTORUA
TAUPO
Whirinaki Forest Park
NAPIER
Hastings
Kaweka Range
Cape Turnagain
Turangi
Lake Taupo
Kaimanawa Ranges
Ruahine Range
Ruahine Forest Park
Hauhungaroa Range
Tongariro National Park
PALMERSTON NORTH
Masterton
Tararua Forest Park
Haurangi Forest Park
Ohakune
Whanganui National Park
Upper Hutt
Lower Hutt
Palliser Bay
North Taranaki Bight
Albatross Point
Hawera
Wanganui
Tararua Range
Cook Strait
New Plymouth
Egmont National Park
Cape Egmont
Opunake
South Taranaki Bight
WELLINGTON
COOK STRAIT FERRY
Picton
Renwick
Tasman Sea
Golden Bay
Motueka
Tasman Bay
Nelson
Wairau Valley
South Island

© AVALON TRAVEL PUBLISHING, INC.

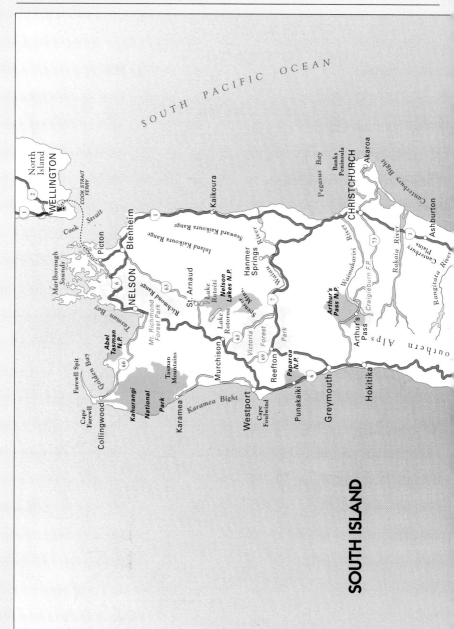

SOUTH ISLAND

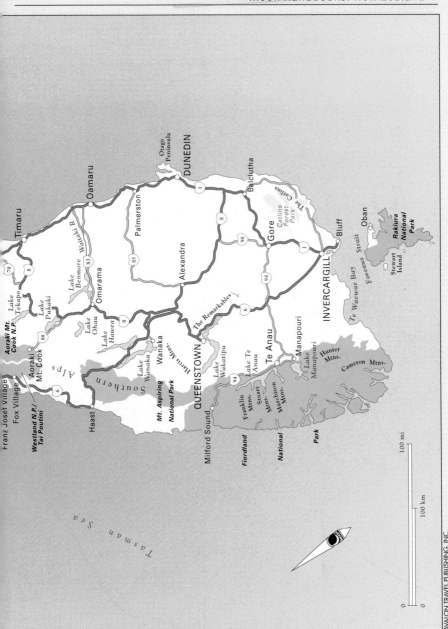

Tasman Sea

Franz Josef Village
Fox Village

**Westland N.P./
Tai Poutini**

**Aoraki Mt.
Cook N.P.**

Lake
Tekapo

Lake
Pukaki

Aoraki
Mt. Cook

Southern Alps

Haast

Timaru

Oamaru

Omarama

Lake
Benmore

Waitaki R

Lake
Ohau

Lake
Hawea

Lake
Wanaka

Wanaka

**Mt. Aspiring
National Park**

Harris Mtns.

Milford Sound

Fiordland

National

Park

Franklin
Mtns.

Stuart
Mtns.

Murchison
Mtns.

The Remarkables

QUEENSTOWN

Lake
Wakatipu

Lake Te
Anau

Te Anau

Manapouri

Lake
Manapouri

Hunter
Mtns.

Cameron Mtns.

Palmerston

Alexandra

DUNEDIN

Otago
Peninsula

Balclutha

The Catlins

Catlins
Forest
Park

Gore

INVERCARGILL

Bluff

Te Waewae Bay

Foveaux Strait

Stewart
Island

Oban

**Rakiura
National
Park**

70

8

80

6

8

85

83

8

1

8

90

1

6

94

94

100 mi

100 km

0

0

© AVALON TRAVEL PUBLISHING, INC.

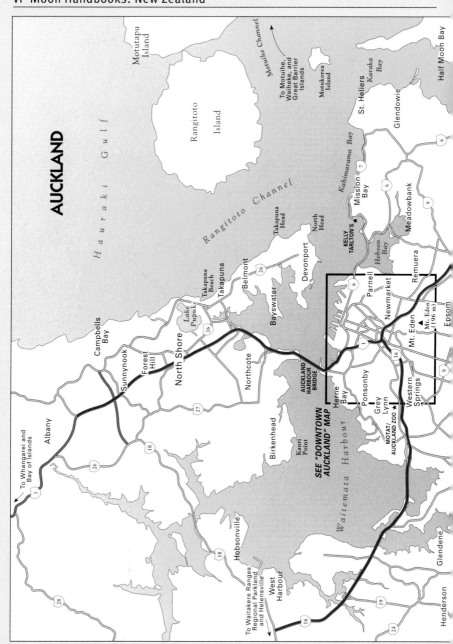

AUCKLAND

Hauraki Gulf

Motutapu Island

Rangitoto Island

Rangitoto Channel

Motuihe Channel

To Motuihe, Waiheke, and Great Barrier Islands

Motukorea Island

Half Moon Bay

Karaka Bay

St. Heliers

Glendowie

Kohimarama Bay

Mission Bay

6

7

6

KELLY TARLTON'S ★

Takapuna Head

North Head

Takapuna Beach

Takapuna

Belmont

26

Bayswater

Devonport

Meadowbank

9

Hobson Bay

Remuera

Parnell

Newmarket

6

Campbells Bay

North Shore

Sunnynook

Forest Hill

Lake Pupuke

26

Northcote

AUCKLAND HARBOUR BRIDGE

1

Mt. Eden (196 m) ▲

Mt. Eden

Epsom

9

16

Albany

27

Birkenhead

Kauri Point

Herne Bay

Ponsonby

Grey Lynn

Western Springs

MOTAT/ AUCKLAND ZOO ★

18

26

SEE "DOWNTOWN AUCKLAND" MAP

To Whangarei and Bay of Islands

1

Waitemata Harbour

Hobsonville

18

West Harbour

To Waitakere Ranges Regional Parkland and Helensville

16

28

19

24

Glendene

Henderson

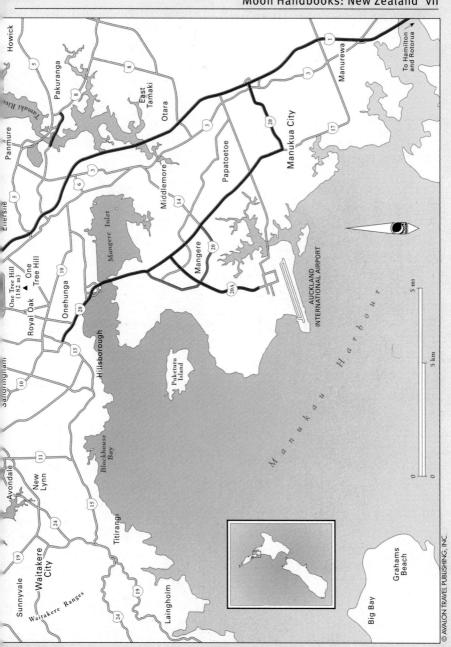

Howick

Pakuranga

East Tamaki

Otara

Manurewa

To Hamilton and Rotorua

Panmure

Tamaki River

Manukua City

Ellerslie

Middlemore

Papatoetoe

Mangere Inlet

One Tree Hill (182 m)

One Tree Hill

Mangere

AUCKLAND INTERNATIONAL AIRPORT

Royal Oak

Onehunga

Sandringham

Hillsborough

Puketutu Island

Manukau Harbour

5 mi

5 km

Blockhouse Bay

Avondale

New Lynn

Titirangi

Waitakere City

Sunnyvale

Laingholm

Waitakere Ranges

Grahams Beach

Big Bay

© AVALON TRAVEL PUBLISHING, INC.

bungee jumping

MOON HANDBOOKS®

NEW ZEALAND

SIXTH EDITION

**JANE KING &
ANDREW HEMPSTEAD**

AVALON
TRAVEL

Moon Handbooks: New Zealand
Sixth Edition

Jane King & Andrew Hempstead

Published by
Avalon Travel Publishing
1400 65th St., Suite 250
Emeryville, CA 94608, USA

Please send all comments, corrections,
additions, amendments, and critiques to:

Moon Handbooks: New Zealand
AVALON TRAVEL PUBLISHING
1400 65th St., Suite 250
EMERYVILLE, CA 94608, USA
email: atpfeedback@avalonpub.com
www.moon.com

Printing History
1st edition—1987
6th edition—November 2002
5 4 3 2 1

ISBN: 1-56691-556-2
ISSN: 1085-2662

Editor: Rebecca K. Browning
Series Manager: Erin Van Rheenen
Copy Editor: Julie Leigh
Graphics Coordinator: Susan Mira Snyder
Production Coordinators: Jacob Goolkasian, Karen Heithecker
Cover Designer: Kari Gim
Interior Designers: Amber Pirker, Alvaro Villanueva, Kelly Pendragon
Map Editor: Olivia Solís
Cartographers: Kat Kalamaras, Brian Bardwell, Bob Race, David Hurst, Mike Morgenfeld
Proofreader: Emily Lunceford
Indexer: Karen Gaynor Bleske

Front cover photo: © Claudia Dhimitri/Folio, Inc.

Distributed by Publishers Group West

Printed in China through Colorcraft Ltd., Hong Kong

ABOUT THE AUTHOR
Jane King

"Oh-h-h no-o-o-o," Jane screamed as momentum took her back up, ankles tied, arms flailing, towards the bridge again. Just as the bridge seemed within reach, she plunged down in an uncontrollable free fall to almost dip in the raging river below. Several minutes later, hanging upside down and shaking with adrenaline, she was scooped over by oar and plopped unceremoniously into a rubber raft, untied, and whizzed to shore. Triumphant, but in disbelief, she scrambled up the hill. "I did it! I actually did it!" The bungee rope that had saved her from an icy dip in New Zealand's Kawarau River slowly snaked up to disappear over the edge of the bridge far above. The crowd roared for the next jumper to go. "Five, four, three..."

Born in Scotland and brought up in Yorkshire, England, Jane King enjoyed a couple of years in a Lake District boarding school before moving at the age of 12 with her family to Sydney, Australia. She vividly remembers her first exotic impressions—hollering kookaburras sitting in rows; noisy, jewel-bright parrots and white cockatoos settling like a cloud in the gum trees; surf-kissed white-sand beaches; and a "real lemon tree in our backyard."

Travel has always been Jane's passion. Working for a few years as a registered nurse in Sydney, her first trip away from home was to New Zealand. Little did she know this would ultimately lead to marriage to a Californian, a new career as a travel guide writer for Moon Handbooks, and the publication of Moon Handbooks to New Zealand and British Columbia.

Aside from backpacking "on a shoestring" through Europe, she has explored her home state of California and 21 other U.S. states, British Columbia, New Zealand, Great Britain, and Tasmania.

Today Jane lives in "almond country" in Northern California with her husband Bruce, daughters Rachael and Stephanie, and a menagerie of family pets. They travel whenever they get the chance. The yearning for adventure, new experiences, and faraway places continues!

Andrew Hempstead

Australian Andrew Hempstead might be cheering for the Aussies when it comes to cricket and rugby, but he has developed a deep appreciation for New Zealand and its people during ten trips to and around the country. He has traveled to New Zealand on assignment for the last three editions of this book as well as to write and photograph for other publications, but he has also traveled there purely for pleasure—to kayak through the Bay of Islands and to ski the Southern Alps. To ensure this sixth edition is as up to date as humanly possible, Andrew traveled from one end of the country to the other and everywhere in between. He prefers to spend as much time as possible on the road, traveling incognito and experiencing New Zealand the way his readers do.

Andrew began travel writing in 1989, when, after leaving a career in advertising, he took off from Australia for Alaska, linking up with veteran travel writer Deke Castleman to help research and update the fourth edition of *Moon Handbooks: Alaska-Yukon*. Andrew is now the author of books on Alberta, British Columbia, the Canadian Rockies, and Vancouver. He is the co-author of *Moon Handbooks: Australia* and *Moon Handbooks: Atlantic Canada*, and has also contributed to *Road Trip USA* and other guides. Andrew's writing and photographs have appeared in *Interval World, National Geographic Traveler, Travesias*, and *Wildlife*. He has also traveled through most of the United States, Europe, the South Pacific, and India.

When not working on his books, Andrew enjoys golfing, hiking, fishing, camping, and the simple pleasures in life, such as skimming stones down on the river. He lives with his wife, Dianne, in Alberta, Canada.

CONTENTS

INTRODUCTION

THE NORTH ISLAND

THE SOUTH ISLAND

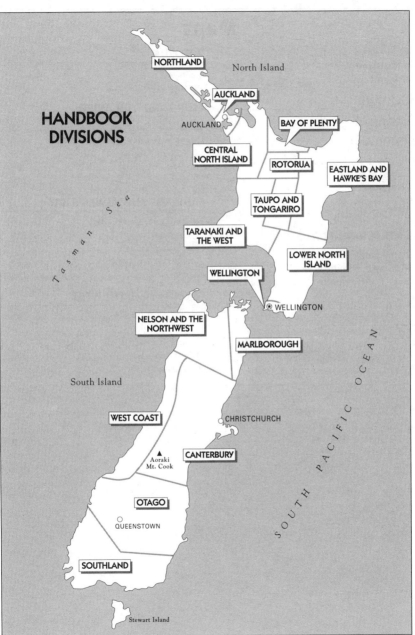

HANDBOOK
DIVISIONS

North Island

NORTHLAND

AUCKLAND

AUCKLAND

BAY OF PLENTY

CENTRAL
NORTH ISLAND

ROTORUA

EASTLAND AND
HAWKE'S BAY

Tasman Sea

TAUPO AND
TONGARIRO

TARANAKI AND
THE WEST

LOWER NORTH
ISLAND

WELLINGTON

WELLINGTON

NELSON AND THE
NORTHWEST

MARLBOROUGH

South Island

SOUTH PACIFIC OCEAN

WEST COAST

CHRISTCHURCH

▲
Aoraki
Mt. Cook

CANTERBURY

OTAGO

○
QUEENSTOWN

SOUTHLAND

Stewart Island

© AVALON TRAVEL PUBLISHING, INC.

Maps

Keeping Current

We have strived to produce the most well-researched and up-to-date travel guide to New Zealand available. But accommodations and restaurants come and go, others change hands, new attractions spring up out of nowhere, and prices rise. Your concerned travel writer loses considerable sleep over it all. You can help. You may notice discrepancies between what's written in this book and what you actually encounter in your travels. Perhaps you'd like to share some interesting information or have discovered wonderful off-the-beaten-track attractions or new accommodations. If so, please send your ideas, comments, or suggestions to:

Andrew Hempstead
Moon Handbooks: New Zealand
Avalon Travel Publishing
1400 65th St., Suite 250
Emeryville, CA 94608, USA
e-mail: atpfeedback@avalonpub.com

Introduction

Introduction

New Zealand lies between latitudes 34 and 47 degrees south and consists of two long, narrow main islands, **North Island** (114,500 square km) and **South Island** (150,700 square km). North Island, with its golden beaches, ancient kauri forests, lakes, volcanoes, thermal areas, and large cities (including Wellington, the capital), is the more densely populated. South Island, with its snowcapped mountains, glaciers, lush native bush, and fiords, is the larger of the two, proudly called "the mainland" by residents (though North Islanders are quick to disagree). Tiny **Stewart Island** (1,750 square km), an unspoiled, bird-filled bush and beach paradise at the foot of the South Island, is the closest most people ever get to the Antarctic. Also within New Zealand's territorial jurisdiction lie several small island groups, including **Chatham, Kermadec,** and **Tokelau Islands; Campbell Island; Auckland, Antipodes, Snares, Solander,** and **Bounty Islands;** and **Ross Dependency, Antarctica.**

Surrounded by the South Pacific Ocean on the east and the Tasman Sea on the west, New Zealand appears to be a mere speck on the globe, and yet it's about 1,770 km from top to bottom—similar in size to the British Isles or Japan. Australia, 2,092 km northwest, is New Zealand's closest neighbor, and because of this relative proximity the two countries are often mistakenly believed to be one. But beware! To innocently suggest this to "Kiwis" (as New Zealanders like to call themselves) is to risk running afoul of their good natures. New Zealand is an independent, self-governing nation.

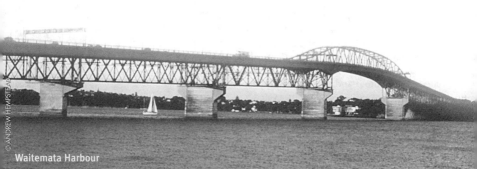

© ANDREW HEMPSTEAD

Waitemata Harbour

The Land

An Ancient Country

About 150 million years ago New Zealand was just a small part of the supercontinent called Gondwanaland, consisting of present-day Australia, Antarctica, India, Africa, and South America. About 70 million years ago, New Zealand separated from Australia and Antarctica. Geographically isolated and uninhabited by humans until A.D. 700 (at the earliest), New Zealand reveals its unique natural history in its unusual animals and plants, which have long since disappeared elsewhere.

The Pacific and Indian-Australian tectonic plates meet along a line of collision that runs through present-day New Zealand, producing the Taupo Volcanic Zone in the North Island and Alpine Fault in the South Island. A deep-sea survey has revealed that a new continent is gradually being created on New Zealand's east coast. As the Pacific Ocean crust plunges under the eastern North Island, thick slabs of sea sand and mud are scraped off in huge wedges and slowly pasted to the offshore edge, forming a series of ridges along the coast between East Cape and Kaikoura.

Volcanoes

The North Island produces enough boiling water and steam to fill all the hot tubs and saunas in the galaxy—or at least Los Angeles! Volcanic and geothermal areas smolder along the Taupo Volcanic Zone from the Bay of Plenty to the central North Island. Three volcanoes dominate this area: **Mt. Ruapehu** and **Mt. Ngauruhoe,** both active, and dormant **Mt. Tongariro.** Mount Ruapehu erupted continuously from September 1995 to late 1996, rocketing ash, steam, and car-sized rocks into the sky from the volcano's Crater Lake. About 50 km offshore from Whakatane in the Bay of Plenty lies **White Island,** an active volcano often obscured by clouds of steam. Discovered and named by Captain Cook in 1769, White Island erupts ash intermittently to this day. On the west coast the dormant cone of **Mt. Egmont/Taranaki** towers over the Taranaki Volcanic Zone, and

farther north, both Auckland and the Bay of Islands are classified as separate volcanic zones. The waters of **Lake Taupo** lie in an enormous deep crater in the center of the North Island—the area has a violent history of volcanic eruptions, though the last one was nearly 19 centuries ago. You'll find no volcanoes active within the last 2,000 years on the South Island, but you can see remains of the colossal twin volcanoes that formed Banks Peninsula, south of Christchurch.

Mountains, Glaciers, and Lakes

Although the North Island offers impressive volcanoes and mighty Lake Taupo, the South Island is really the place to go for snowcapped mountain scenery and perfect lakes set in idyllic surroundings. Most of New Zealand lies at least 200 meters above sea level, but the tallest peak, **Mt. Cook** (3,754 meters), rises among the magnificent **Southern Alps,** spine of the South Is-

Aoraki Mt. Cook

land. Spectacular glaciers are scattered throughout the landscape—the mighty **Fox** and **Franz Josef** are still easily accessible from the main route down the West Coast. In other areas of the South Island are U-shaped valleys, moraines, and deep lakes left behind by glaciers of earlier ice ages. New Zealand's numerous lakes vary greatly in size and depth, many of the largest concentrated in the South Island and fed by glaciers and snowpacks of the Southern Alps. Many fast-flowing rivers and meandering streams follow the contours of the land. Extensive flat plains of rich alluvial soil deposited by these rivers provide plenty of valuable agricultural land; vast gravel plains, such as those found in the South Canterbury region of the South Island, are predominantly used as sheep country.

The Coastline

New Zealand's coastline offers a bit of everything. Sand stretches as far as the eye can see in some areas, such as **Ninety Mile Beach** at the tip of the North Island; in other areas, such as the **Bay of Islands** in the northeast of the North Island and **Marlborough Sounds** at the South Island's northern tip, deep coves and sheltered bays dotted with tiny islands fringe the coast. The west coast of the South Island is lined with rocky cliffs, blowholes, caves, and rugged surf beaches where seals haul themselves ashore; in the far southwest corner, 14 magnificent fiords deeply indent the coastline, and along a small section of the east coast, several sandy beaches are strewn with large, perfectly circular boulders. For sandy beaches and warm, aquamarine waters, stay in the north; for rugged surf-swept beaches, intriguing rock formations, and deep, mirror-surfaced fiords, head south.

Parks

Covering more than 2.1 million hectares of the country, 14 of New Zealand's most beautiful areas have been set aside for total preservation in their natural state and designated national parks. They offer vast areas of untouched wilderness where hikers, mountaineers, anglers, hunters, and flora and fauna enthusiasts are in their element. In the North Island lie **Te Urewera, Rak-**iura, Tongariro, Egmont,** and **Whanganui National Parks;** in the South Island, **Abel Tasman, Kahurangi, Nelson Lakes, Arthur's Pass, Westland, Paparoa, Aoraki Mt. Cook, Mt. Aspiring,** and **Fiordland National Parks.** Three maritime parks, **Bay of Islands** and **Hauraki Gulf Maritime Parks** in the North Island and **Marlborough Sounds Maritime Park** in the South Island, preserve some of the most spectacular and accessible coastal scenery, and dozens of forest parks, used for conservation, recreation, and timber production, contain some of the best bush scenery in the country.

All the national parks, reserves, forest parks, and state forests are under the jurisdiction of the **Department of Conservation** (DOC), created on April 1, 1987, by the Conservation Act. The department manages the land and wildlife, promotes the conservation of natural and historic resources, protects endangered species, produces educational and promotional material, and fosters recreation and tourism in conjunction with conservation. The best way to obtain information on a particular area or park is to visit local DOC offices scattered throughout the country or check the website: www.doc.govt.nz.

CLIMATE

New Zealand has an oceanic, temperate climate; although it varies from subtropical in the north to almost subarctic in the mountainous areas of the south, overall it's relatively mild. Seasonal variations are not pronounced: summers never get uncomfortably hot; winters are mild, with snow usually confined to the high country and southern lowlands. Rainfall levels vary throughout New Zealand; winter tends to be the wettest season—but not so wet that it should be avoided. If you're coming from the Northern Hemisphere, keep in mind that the seasons are opposite—spring is September through November, summer December through February, autumn March through May, and winter June through August.

North Island

The North Island tends to be warmer and drier than the South Island, though the highest moun-

AVERAGE DAILY TEMPERATURES AND ANNUAL RAINFALL

(Tempatures are maximum, expressed in degrees Celsius; rainfall is expressed in millimeters.)

Locality	January	July	Rainfall
North Island:			
Bay of Islands	25	15	1,648
Auckland	23	14	1,268
Rotorua	23	12	1,511
Napier	24	13	780
Wellington	20	11	1,271
South Island:			
Nelson	22	12	999
Christchurch	22	12	658
Queenstown	22	8	849
Dunedin	19	10	772
Invercargill	18	9	1,042

tain peaks often have snow year-round. It has an average rainfall of 130 cm and prevailing westerly winds. **Auckland** (where most visitors enter New Zealand) averages a summer temperature of 23°C and a winter temperature of 14°C. **Wellington,** perched on the edge of Cook Strait, generally receives slightly colder weather with temperatures ranging from 26°C in summer to 2°C in winter. The capital also has a reputation for windy weather, at times making the ferry trip between the two main islands unforgettably rough.

South Island

The differences in temperature and weather in each area are more pronounced in the South Island. The pressure systems travel west to east (the Southern Alps have a noticeable "wet" and "dry" side), the lows dumping considerable rain and cold temperatures on the west side of the mountains; snow is a permanent fixture on the highest peaks. On the east side of the Southern Alps the rainfall can be as low as 30 cm and tem-

peratures are a good deal warmer. On the east coast, **Christchurch** averages temperatures in the low 20s C in summer and low teens in winter. **Dunedin,** farther south, averages 19°C in summer and 10°C in winter. **Invercargill,** New Zealand's southernmost city, experiences slightly colder temperatures. Snow is relatively common in the southern lowlands as well as the higher hills, and occasionally falls even at sea level.

Clothing to Suit the Climate

If you're traveling clear around the country you're sure to bump into most types of weather—and even if you're staying in one area, the weather still changes rapidly. The safest policy is to be equipped for everything, no matter what the season. Wear layers of clothing (shirt, sweater, and windproof jacket) to strip off and replace as needed. Wet-weather gear, a warm windproof jacket, wool sweater or cardigan, bathing suit, and comfortable footwear (hiking boots if you're venturing off the beaten track) are essentials at all times of year.

FLORA
The Bush

New Zealand's long isolation from other continents is responsible for unique developments in plant and animal life. Before humans arrived, much of the country was covered in dense tangled forests and heavy undergrowth alive with native birds, many flightless. With the introduction of grazing animals, much of the undergrowth was thinned out; early settlers felled the forests, and introduced predators chased many unique birds into extinction. Today, the remaining native forests are lush wonderlands of subtropical appearance. Ferns, mosses, and lichens carpet their floors, tree ferns grow up to 10 meters high, and twining creepers, *nikau* palms, palm lilies, tree ferns, and many species of native trees intermingle to form a dense green canopy overhead—called "the bush" by New Zealanders. For fern lovers, New Zealand is a delight. Ferns (one of the country's national emblems) seem to grow everywhere—on trees, along rivers and streams, on hillsides, and in open areas, and the more than 150 species range in size from filmy two-cm ferns to impressive 15-meter tree ferns.

Trees

Altogether 112 native tree species grow in New Zealand among the dense undergrowth and large areas of scrub (mainly *manuka* or tea-tree). A few ancient kauri pine *(Agathis australis)* forests

---

MOUNTAIN WEATHER

As the mountains generally run north-south and the pressure systems move west-east, the worst weather hits the highest barrier—the Southern Alps. Rivers and streams can flood rapidly from snowmelt and rain, avalanche risks increase dramatically, and temperatures drop quickly. Watch for an increase in wind strength and the formation of large sheets of cloud. Also watch for clouds gathering over the lee side of the ranges—and expect rain. Gale-force winds, snow, or blizzards can come with these storms at *any time of year* in the mountains. The New Zealand Mountain Safety Council, website: www.mountainsafety.org.nz, suggests three important rules to follow: be aware of approaching bad weather (expect it in the mountains); be adequately prepared with warm, wind- and waterproof clothing; and don't cross flooded rivers—wait until they' subside (generally as quickly as they flood).

For current weather forecasts, check the newspaper or tune in to local radio or TV stations. If you're in a national park, park HQ usually has the latest local weather forecast. For avalanche information, consult the website: www.avalanche .net.nz, an online advisory of backcountry conditions throughout New Zealand.

---

can still be appreciated on the North Island, growing naturally only north of latitude 39 degrees south. These magnificent trees grow up to 53 meters high, losing their lower branches to become long bare cylinders of intricate design with large bushy tops. They were the favorites of the forest for Maori war canoes—a vast canoe could be chiseled out of one tree trunk. Unfortunately, they were also the favorites of early shipbuilders and settlers, who rapidly depleted the forests without much thought to the future—the kauri takes about 800 years to mature. Nowadays, these impressive trees survive in relatively few areas, towering above the other trees in small groves or randomly in the bush. Two areas in Northland, northwest of Dargaville, are worth a special visit just to see these giants—**Waipoua Forest Park,** with two very famous trees (one is estimated to be at least 2,000 years old), and the small but beautiful **Trounson Kauri Park.**

Most of New Zealand's flowers are white or cream. However, native flowering trees and shrubs add red and yellow highlights to the evergreen flora of New Zealand. A few of the most spectacular flowering trees are the *pohutukawa, rata,* and *kowhai.* The striking *pohutukawa (Metrosideros tomentosa),* or New Zealand Christmas tree, is a mass of scarlet flowers in December. The *rata (Metrosideros robusta),* another vividly colored tree also covered in red blossoms, is initially a parasitic vine, growing up a host tree (and often strangling it) until it has grown roots and become a tree in its own right. The bright yellow hanging blossoms of the *kowhai (Sophora tetraphera)* bloom in all their glory during spring. Large beech *(Nothofagus)* forests with little undergrowth cover upland areas, and vast areas of land throughout New Zealand have been planted with exotic trees for timber, thus saving the remaining indigenous trees. The most common nonnative tree is the radiata pine. It flourishes here, growing to complete maturity within 35 years—a popular tree with the timber industry.

Flowers

At least three-quarters of New Zealand's flowering plants are endemic. Orchids are abundant, adding multihued splashes of color to the land-

native coastal bush

scape. About 60 species thrive in the lowland forests and countless beautiful parks and gardens. The alpine flowers are vastly different from those of other countries, with about 500 species of flowering plants found only in New Zealand's alpine areas. Large, white mountain daisies (genus *Celmisia*) are the most common; the beautiful Mt. Cook lily *(Ranunculus lyallii)* is the largest of the buttercups. A rather strange growth called vegetable sheep *(Raoulia eximia),* a large, low-to-the-ground, cushionlike plant covered in white hairs, grows only in the South Island and is easily mistaken for a sheep from a distance. Apart from the abundance of native wildflowers, New Zealanders also take great pride in their gardens. If you're a flower fancier, stroll through any of the suburbs (particularly of Hamilton, Cambridge, New Plymouth, Napier, and Christchurch) to see a great variety of both indigenous and exotic plantlife, tended with obvious TLC (most New Zealanders are born with green thumbs). Botanical gardens, reserves, and beautiful parks (called "domains") are found in most cities, and are highly recommended as part of any walking tour.

FAUNA

Birds

Until humans arrived these islands had no native land animals, except for two species of bat discovered by early settlers. However, the country was alive with birds, no fewer than 250 species. A perfect balance of nature existed between vegetation and birdlife, but when humans set foot on the islands they brought rats, cats, and dogs;

Kea are widespread through the higher elevations of the Southern Alps.

introduced mammals and birds; and began clearing native habitat. Many native birds, unable to adapt to the foreign predators, became extinct. Native birds in the forest today include the *tui* (with its beautiful song), bellbird (its crystal-clear call is like the ping-pong of a door bell), fantail, *kaka, kea, pukeko, morepork,* and wood pigeon. The *kaka* is a shy brown-and-green parrot. The *kea,* a dull brownish-green parrot with red underwings and a hooked beak, lives in the high country and is commonly seen in the Southern Alps as it scavenges around campsites. Cheeky and daring, it can cause a lot of damage to tents, boots, bicycle seats, or anything it can tear with its strong beak, and it has the reputation for sliding down the iron roofs of alpine huts in the wee hours of the morning.

> *Until humans arrived these islands had no native land animals, except for two species of bat discovered by early settlers. However, the country was alive with birds, no fewer than 250 species.*

The *takahe,* a rare bird unique to New Zealand, is found mainly in Southern Fiordland. Large, flightless, and blue and green with red feet and bill, it was thought to be extinct until a small colony was rediscovered in 1948. Since then, 120 *takahe* have been found and are now protected in a restricted area in the Murchison Mountains. Probably the best-known creature of New Zealand is the nocturnal kiwi, a flightless bird found nowhere else in the world—the national emblem of New Zealand. It has a round body covered in dense, stiff feathers (looks like shaggy fur from a distance), strong legs (kicks out when frightened), no tail, tiny invisible wings, a long beak, and a piercing call—"ki-wi." It's not easy to find a kiwi in the bush, but you can see them in a simulated natural environment in the many excellent nocturnal houses throughout the country.

The *weka,* another flightless bird, is as bold as the *kea* but not as common. Found in the west coast forests of the South Island and the Gisborne area of the North Island, it also helps itself to the food and property of campers.

Introduced birds include the blackbird, thrush, magpie, chaffinch, sparrow, skylark, myna, white-eye, and goldfinch.

Fishes, Insects, and Reptiles

Known for its excellent fishing (fly and lure), New Zealand draws angling enthusiasts from around the world to dangle their lines in its lakes and rivers where fish grow to a healthy size and braggable weight and put up an admirable fight. Brown and rainbow trout, salmon, and char are the best-known freshwater fish. Brown trout are widespread and common; rainbow are more common in North Island lakes, but also live in many upland lakes of the South Island. Deep-sea fishing for marlin, sharks, and tuna is a popular sport in the Bay of Islands.

Of the numerous forms of insect life found throughout the country, one of the most audible is the cicada. Twenty or so species of cicada live in New Zealand, mostly above the timberline. Often mistaken for that of crickets, their song in the summer heat is an incredibly loud, raspy, clicking noise—one that seems to intensify in the evening—a distinct part of the summer atmosphere in New Zealand. The *tuatara,* a lizardlike reptile, now inhabits only about 30 islands off the country's coast (see live ones in the Southland Museum Tuatarium in Invercargill). It is believed

© ANDREW HEMPSTEAD

One of New Zealand's few endemic reptiles is the *tuatara.*

to live at least 100 years, has a distinctly prehistoric appearance, and is often referred to as a "living fossil."

Mammals

The *wild* animals in New Zealand are descended from pigs, goats, opossums, rabbits, weasels, ferrets, and deer released by European settlers. Some of these—especially deer, rabbits, goats, and opossums—adapted to their new environment so well that they rapidly became an environmental problem and are to this day hunted to control their populations. Many domestic animals also adapted well to New Zealand, and play a large part in the success of the country's economy. Sheep (more than 45 million of which dot the countryside), cattle, and poultry are of prime importance.

Of eight species of deer, the red deer is the most common and widespread. When first released it had an abundant food supply (rapidly destroying the native forest undergrowth) and no predators, and its numbers increased rapidly. Commercial hunting from helicopters began in the 1960s, followed by profitable heli-hunting with live capture for deer farms. Hunting is still encouraged, but in recent years controlled deer farming has become a valuable part of the economy. The deer are raised for meat, breeding stock, and their antlers, which when in velvet are sold to the Asian market to be crushed and used as an aphrodisiac.

History

EARLY INHABITANTS
The Moa-Hunters

Exactly when the first Polynesians arrived in New Zealand is unknown. Maori legends claim the Polynesian navigator Kupe first sighted New Zealand in the 10th century, naming it Aotearoa, "Land of the Long White Cloud" (one of many translations), but archaeological evidence suggests that an archaic Maori population originating in Polynesia may have been established in New Zealand as early as A.D. 700. The first arrivals were hunters—stalking flightless birds, predominantly the large, emulike moa (now extinct)—gatherers, and excellent fishermen. No evidence suggests that the moa-hunters were a warrior society. Their camps were originally concentrated in the South Island, but by the 12th century they also inhabited the North Island.

Classic Maori Society

By the 13th and 14th centuries, a new kind of Polynesian culture began to replace moa-hunter society. Dwindling moa caused an increasing dependence on other fowl and fish. Legends speak of the arrival at this time of East Polynesians and the "Great Migration" of the 14th century. Crossing the Pacific in many large canoes, they came from the Society Island Group (Hawaiiki of Maori legends), where overpopulation, food shortages, and war had been a part of everyday life. Most present-day Maori claim their descent from these legendary canoe voyagers. With the new arrivals came a change in lifestyle. About 40 tribes developed, each a territorially based social unit; subtribes were based on kinship and ancestral descent. Cultivation of the fleshy *kumara* (sweet potato) became important; since the *kumara* needed warmth and sunshine to flourish, the Maori spread to the north of the North Island.

The new Polynesian culture placed great emphasis on a strict warrior code. The Maori took pride in being fierce warriors. *Pa* (fortified villages) were skillfully built on tops of hills or ridges, with at least one side blocked by a natural barrier such as a river or the sea; fences and trenches further protected the thatched cottages within from enemy attack. *Mana* (prestige) and *utu* (retribution) were important qualities. If one Maori insulted another, the offended family would demand *utu,* eventually leading to war.

The focus of community life was the *marae* (central square) in front of the large, intricately carved meeting house (today the term also covers the meeting house itself and any auxiliary buildings). Maori leaders were usually hereditary chiefs or priests. The people were governed by strong family loyalties and religious beliefs and traditions. *Tapu* (sacred) was a positive force from the gods—certain places, acts, and people were *tapu*. *Noa* was the opposing negative or evil force; together these elements regulated every area of Maori life.

To the Maori, all nature was alive and had magic or supernatural powers; the people lived in harmony with the land, respecting it as property of the gods. They had many gods; different gods looked after such things as the sea, forests, and crops. With no written language, they passed on their tribal history through song and dance, storytelling, and arts and crafts. They were (and still are) excellent craftspeople, expressing great symbolism in their intricate, decorative carvings. Rituals were another important part of life. Some, such as offering the first fish of a catch to the god Tangaroa and first bird to Tanemahuta, are still performed. Those rituals associated with traditional arts such as weaving and carving, and with Maori ceremonial gatherings, are strictly maintained and an integral part of society today.

EUROPEAN DISCOVERY AND COLONIZATION

Tasman and Cook

The Dutch navigator Abel Tasman is believed to have been the first European to discover Aotearoa in 1642. Seeking a great unknown continent in the South Pacific with which to trade, he stumbled across the west coast of the South Island. He named the new land "Staten Landt" to honor the States-General of the United Netherlands, and because he thought it might be connected with Staten Landt, an island off the tip of South America. Tasman's theory was disproved within the year, and the name was changed to "Nieuw Zeeland"—no doubt after the Dutch island province of Zeeland. In one encounter with the Maori, several of his men were killed, and Tasman sailed away disillusioned by the lack of friendly trading prospects.

In 1769 the British navigator Capt. James Cook landed on the east coast of the North Island. He was also in search of the vast unknown continent, but for scientific purposes. On arrival at Gisborne, Cook also had misunderstandings with the natives that led to bloodshed, but he persevered, circumnavigating both islands, charting the coastline in great detail, and concluding that most Maori were helpful and friendly. Cook took possession of "New Zealand" for Britain, and New Zealand became known to the world. Many French explorers followed Cook, some for scientific reasons, some for trade.

Whalers and Sealers

Within 30 years of Cook's discovery, other Europeans sailed to New Zealand shores and began a period of great exploitation. Whaling stations sprang up around the coast, sealers slaughtered the colonies along the southern shores (almost to extinction), and loggers drastically cut magnificent kauri trees for shipbuilding. Trade in whale oil, sealskins, timber, and flax began with New South Wales in Australia. In the late 1820s, Kororareka (now called Russell) in the Bay of Islands became the first European settlement—a refuge for whalers, sealers, adventurers, and escaped Australian convicts, it earned the name "Hell-hole of the Pacific." With the traders came disease, alcohol, and muskets, all of which had devastating impact on the Maori.

Intertribal Wars

The musket was of great interest to Maori warriors and quickly became a coveted weapon. The warriors welcomed the traders and their muskets, and Maori society was irrevocably changed. Hongi Hika, chief of the Northland Ngapuhi tribe, was the first to recognize the weapon's potential. With its aid he, followed by other great chiefs, slaughtered many rival tribes throughout the North Island. As the wars spread to the south, many tribes began trading for muskets, eventually equalizing the balance of power. With the realization in the 1830s that the weapon was annihilating the race, the Maori gradually ended the intertribal wars.

Colonization

Missionaries of many denominations spent the early 1800s establishing missions. Many recognized the exploitation of the Maori by the Pakeha (white people) and tried to protect them. They also taught the Maori the latest European agricultural techniques. Until 1832 there had been no law and order in New Zealand. James Busby, a New South Wales civil servant, was the first to be sent over from Australia as "British resident" to protect the Maori from further exploitation and establish some order. Busby had an impossible task and no police; he became known as "a man-of-war without guns." When he proved ineffective, Capt. William Hobson was sent from Britain in 1840 to be lieutenant-governor and to unite the Maori chiefs with Britain by extending British sovereignty to New Zealand. On February 6, 1840, Hobson, representatives of the Crown, and a number of leading Maori chiefs signed "The Treaty of Waitangi." New Zealand became a British colony. Though this made land available for European settlement, it also specified that all property belonged to the Maori and guaranteed that it could not be taken without their consent and/or payment. It gave them the "rights and privileges of British subjects." Though the treaty was meant to protect the Maori, it later became obvious that they had not fully understood the document they had signed. Colonists began flooding into the new country.

The Land Wars
The early Europeans found the concept of Maori land use and ownership hard to comprehend. The *kumara* fields and burial grounds made sense, but *tapu* areas, and land specifically designated for fishing and hunting, were considered a waste of good agricultural land. The land belonged to entire tribal groups, and consent for a change in ownership had to be agreed upon by all—new occupations had previously occurred only by conquest. At first the Maori were eager to "sell" their land (they thought they were selling the "shadow of the land" like a lease) for money and alcohol. However, the growing number of colonists demanding land put increasing pressure on the Maori, and the ideals of the Waitangi Treaty were soon overlooked. As the European population grew and the Maori became increasingly reluctant to sell land, antagonism also grew.

Fighting broke out in 1843 and continued sporadically as more settlements were established. Between 1860 and the early 1880s, war raged between the Maori tribal chiefs and government troops over land purchase (even the Maori were divided—some tribes joined the government side to even old scores with rival tribes), and the fighting spread across the central regions of the North Island.

The Maori lacked any kind of unifying nationalism, and tradition forced them to prove they were the best fighters; against artillery, they had no chance. Ancestral land was confiscated from "rebel tribes" and given as a reward to "friendly tribes," further destroying unity. Land was also given to military settlers who fought for the government, or was sold to recoup some of the cost of the wars. In 1862, Land Courts forced the Maori to name 10 owners, and then only one owner, of each block of land—this destroyed any remaining unity and made it relatively easy for crooked land agents to buy the land for less than its worth with money or alcohol. Traders deliberately let the Maori run into debt, forcing them to sell or go to jail. By 1982 only 4.5 million hectares of land remained under Maori ownership—some of it leased to settlers, the rest too rugged to be useful.

Wool and Gold
While the North was at war, the South Island forged ahead. The small Maori population was still eager to sell land. Settlement spread rapidly and farmers established many large sheep runs on the vast areas of tussockland. Thousands of sheep, predominantly merino for their fine wool, were shipped from Australia. Between 1850 and 1880, many Australian squatters came over to lease large areas of tussockland for their flocks. This became known as the "wool period." However, sheep scab came with the Australian flocks, killing thousands of sheep, and in the 1860s, a plague of rabbits forced many runholders into abandonment and bankruptcy. Some turned to rabbiting as the export in rabbit skins soared.

In 1861, gold was discovered in the South Island's Otago district. The rush lasted for less than a decade, but for those years the Shotover

River became "the richest river in the world," soon followed by the Arrow River. The discovery attracted thousands of miners from the goldfields of California and Australia, further stimulating growth and establishing the south as a commercial and industrial center. Railways and roads were built. After the rush in Otago, miners moved to the west coast, where Hokitika temporarily became a busy port.

Administration

Auckland had been chosen as the capital in 1840, and Wellington, New Plymouth, Nelson, Dunedin, and Christchurch were founded during the next 10 years. In 1852 direct rule from Britain ended, marking the beginning of "self-government." New Zealand's central government was made up of a governor appointed by London, a Legislative Council appointed by the governor, and a House of Representatives elected by the people. The country was divided into six provinces—Auckland, New Plymouth, Wellington, Nelson, Canterbury, and Otago, each with its own government. In 1865, Wellington replaced Auckland as capital of New Zealand, and by 1873, four more provinces had been added—Hawke's Bay, Marlborough, Westland, and Southland.

Trade

In 1882 the introduction of refrigeration produced a major change in farming. Many of the big wool runs were abandoned as farmers recognized new export possibilities. Many turned to meat and dairy production. The high country became the merino area for wool production, the hill country became lamb-breeding land, and fat-lamb farms were developed to breed lambs specifically for export. With the introduction of refrigerated cargo ships, Britain and Europe became eager consumers of the meat, and New Zealand entered the overseas market as a major food producer.

THE TWENTIETH CENTURY

Social Welfare

The 20th century became the era of advanced social legislation. Two major political groups, the Liberal and Labour Parties, emerged in 1890. The Liberal Party held power until 1912, introducing many changes in social policy. Its first landmark legislation was the introduction of the Old Age Pension. New Zealand was the first country in the world to give women the vote (1893). In 1894 the world's first form of compulsory state arbitration for industrial disputes was introduced. The Liberals successfully combined capitalism with socialism, and New Zealand became a country of progressive social policies. With the interruption of World War I and the following Depression, it was not until the first Labour government in 1935 that New Zealand again took up the social welfare banner. The Social Security Act was introduced, guaranteeing free health care, education, and welfare benefits for all. Sickness pensions, low-cost housing, and a 40-hour workweek were introduced over the years, and in 1972, the Accident Compensation Act was passed, insuring all people against accidental injury. These were the foundations of New Zealand's modern welfare state.

World Wars

During World War I, New Zealand sent 100,000 troops to support Britain—16,000 were killed, 45,000 wounded in action. After World War I, New Zealand became a member of the League of Nations. In World War II, 150,000 New Zealanders joined the Allied War effort; more than 11,000 were killed and 17,000 wounded. After World War II, ties with "the mother country" weakened. New Zealand claimed full independence in 1947. For most of the years between 1949 and 1978, the National Party held power. National and Labour have been the two major parties in recent years.

Modern Maori

For years New Zealand has been promoted as a country of racial harmony, though there's considerable unrest and ongoing land disputes between some Maori and Pakeha—problems that date from the Treaty of Waitangi. The Maori population grew rapidly with improved health opportunities and social education, but the adjustment to urban life further weakened Maori culture. By 1962 the Maori annual growth rate was more than twice the Pakeha rate—and one of the highest in the world. Pakeha had to adjust to an increasingly assertive, fast-growing Maori and Polynesian population. Maori language, arts and crafts, and song and dance are taught in schools all over the land, and many Maori are looking back to the ways of their ancestors, searching for their identity and regaining a culture that had been submerged in the ways of the Pakeha. Al-though many New Zealanders are showing a re-newed interest in *Maoritanga,* the Maori way of life, resentment between Maori and Pakeha con-tinues to escalate. Despite protest from present-day Pakeha landowners, an increasing number of Maori plan to reclaim land they believe was wrongfully stolen years ago. They have rejected government intervention in the form of a lump sum payment. They want only the land they be-lieve is rightfully theirs.

Government, Economy, and the People

GOVERNMENT

New Zealand is a sovereign independent state, its government based on the British parliamentary system. The head of state, Queen Elizabeth II of Britain, is represented in New Zealand by a res-ident **governor general.** Appointed for five years, he's advised by the ministers of cabinet.

Since 1950, the New Zealand Parliament has had only one chamber, the **House of Represen-tatives.** Made up of 120 members, this number includes four Maori members elected by the Maori population. The House of Representa-tives is primarily responsible for keeping the gov-ernment in check; no tax or expenditure can be made until the proposed bill has been read, de-bated, and authorized. The governor general gives final authorization, and if approved by all these channels, the bill becomes law.

Elections are held every three years, but a government may request an earlier election to vote on a topic of national importance. The party that wins the most seats becomes govern-ment; its leader automatically becomes **prime minister.** The leader of the other major party is called the leader of the opposition. The **cabi-net** is made up of the prime minister and se-lected ministers of his party; they form policy, promote legislation, and become the heads of the **Departments of State.** Cabinet ministers and other government members are together called the **Caucus.**

The 40 or so government departments are staffed by members of the **Public Service** who retain their jobs despite government changes. The departments provide services for the coun-try: mail, telephone, media, transportation, ed-ucation, finance, health, housing, and other services.

The official government website is www.govt.nz.

Local government consists of county, bor-ough, and district councils; special-purpose bod-ies; and regional government.

The **High Court** deals with major crimes,

POLITICAL PARTIES

Labour, New Zealand's oldest political party, was formed in 1916 and has had more impact on the country than any other party. It was Labour who led the world with its anti-nuclear stance in the 1980s, but it was also Labour that was in power leading up to economic turmoil in the late 1980s. The Labour Party is currently in power. Created in the 1930s, the **National Party** lead New Zealand through much of the 1990s. The Nationals created an economic blueprint that has been mimicked around the world for curtailing public spending. Along the way, ex-ports increased and the economy boomed. The **Alliance** party formed a coalition with the Labour Party to defeat the Nationals in 1999. With left-leanings, the Alliance can best be de-scribed as social democratic in their beliefs. The fourth party of note is **NZ First,** established in the 1990s by high-profile, former National Party minister Winston Peters.

© ANDREW HEMPSTEAD

The federal government is based in Wellington.

important claims, and appeals; **Lower** or **District Courts** deal with all minor offenses; and **Family Courts** deal with most family matters and divorce proceedings.

The voting age is 18. In 1893 New Zealand became the first country in the world to give women the right to vote. Registration to vote became compulsory in 1924—though not obliged to actually vote, more than 80 percent usually do. Some New Zealanders would like New Zealand to become a republic within the Commonwealth and are actively following the precedent set in Australia for a referendum on the issue.

ECONOMY

The New Zealand economy is heavily dependent on overseas trade. Traditional trading partners—Australia, the United Kingdom, and the U.S.—have been joined by many Asian countries, including Japan. Agricultural exports of dairy, meat, and wool products—worth $15 billion annually to New Zealand-dominate the economic pie, but forestry, horticulture, manufacturing, and tourism are growing in importance.

Agriculture

New Zealand's major source of income is agriculture. It has developed advanced techniques to use the country's rugged land, including specially designed aircraft to replace land machinery. Of the country's 80,000 farms, approximately 55,000 are on the North Island and 25,000 are on the South Island. Many areas are highly mechanized. About 50 percent of total export income comes from meat, dairy products, and wool; the land supports some 45 million sheep and 4.8 million beef cattle. New Zealand is one of the world's largest exporters of lamb and mutton, has a ever-expanding beef industry (about 75 percent of which is produced on the North Island), and supplies about 90 countries with meat (the major markets are the U.K., Iran, Russia, Japan, the United States, and Canada). Venison (often called cervena in New Zealand) is an important export; around 2.5 million deer are farmed. New Zealand is also one of the largest and most efficient exporters of dairy products. The combination of a good growing climate, stable rainfall, and lush grass year-round has produced an average herd of about 120 cows; most of the 3.5 million dairy cows in the country are Jerseys or Friesians (that's one cow per person!). Butter (mostly to the U.K.) and cheddar cheese (mostly to Japan and the U.K.) are the major dairy exports, but casein (mainly to the U.S.) and skim-milk powder (to a wide variety of countries, mainly in Asia) are also in demand. New Zealand's rich and creamy dairy products are among the best in the world—one taste and you'll be convinced.

Sheep are a predominant part of the landscape throughout the whole of New Zealand. New Zealand is the second-largest producer of sheep (after Australia) and largest supplier of medium to coarse crossbred wool (for carpets, upholstery, and clothing) in the world, with an average flock of about 1,800 sheep. In North Island hill country, sheep are farmed for their wool; the fertile lowland farms (up to 25 sheep per hectare) specialize in lamb and mutton production. Teams of sheepshearers travel around the country from woolshed to woolshed, many shearing more than 200 sheep each a day (don't miss any opportunity to watch shearers in action—their speed and dexterity are really something). Most of the medium-to-coarse crossbred wool used for carpet mak-

Kiwis are good-humored, relaxed, easy to get along with, and hospitable. They take the time to talk to one another—and to visitors.

ing and knitting yarn comes from Romney sheep; the fine wool used for soft fabrics and high-quality yarn comes from merino sheep. High-quality sheepskins are a popular tourist purchase.

Most of the crops—**wheat, barley, maize, oats, vegetables, berry fruit, and tobacco**—are grown for the local market. Horticultural exports are dominated by fresh fruit, worth $1 billion to the local economy. The citrus export industry has grown dramatically as kiwifruit, tamarillos, feijoas, and passionfruit have increased in popularity worldwide; apples and pears are also important exports. Orchards in the north produce apples, apricots, peaches, plums, nectarines, berryfruit, cherries, lemons, and oranges, mostly for local consumption, but increasingly for export. Other important crops include malting barley, herbage seeds, some herbs, grass seed, and clover seed. Hops and tobacco leaf (plus orchard fruit) are grown for the local market in the warm, sunny Nelson area of the South Island.

Forestry

After agriculture, forestry is New Zealand's next important industry, pumping $4 billion annually into the local economy. More than 27 percent of

Sheep are common throughout New Zealand.

© ANDREW HEMPSTEAD

the country is covered by forest—about 1.2 million hectares of production plantation forest and 6.2 million hectares of indigenous forests. As native trees are very slow growing, they are used for special purposes only. The planted forests of exotic radiata pine are the major suppliers of New Zealand's timber. Radiata grows rapidly here, producing a high amount of usable wood per tree. In addition to 20 million cubic meters of unprocessed logs (annually), forest export products consist of wood pulp and chips, paper, building boards, plywood, veneers, and various oils. Australia, the U.S., Japan, and Taiwan are New Zealand's largest customers of forest product exports.

Manufacturing

Many basic industries, such as textiles and leather goods, tobacco, rubber and plastics, fruit and vegetables, building supplies, and furniture, are flourishing in New Zealand. Light manufacturing provides an increasing range of both consumer and industrial goods. Aircraft manufacture, motor vehicle assembly, and the textiles and garment industry all provide employment. Two steel companies in New Zealand make heavy equipment from imported steel. Engineers have made many advancements in highly specialized electronic equipment for agriculture, medicine, and veterinary science.

Energy

New Zealand does not have large mineral deposits and so relies heavily on imported raw materials to manufacture chemicals. Imported petroleum supplies almost 60 percent of New Zealand's energy needs; hydroelectricity, natural coal and gas, solar energy, and geothermal steam supply the rest. New Zealand's lone oil refinery is at Marsden Point, Northland. Jointly owned by the country's five major petroleum companies, crude oil is supplied from seven offshore fields. Nuclear power is not foreseeable in New Zealand's future; the country's objective is to harness its own natural power resources. Newer ventures include oil refining, aluminum smelting, ironsand deposit mining, processing New Zealand's offshore oil and gas condensates, and processing associated with steel and glass pro-

duction. At Lake Grassmere in Marlborough, the first solar salt works in the country converts seawater from the mudflats into household and industrial salt through evaporation. Schemes to change natural gas into synthetic petrol are promoted and encouraged by the government, and solar units to heat household water are increasing in popularity as an alternative to electricity.

Tourism

Tourism is a major part of the New Zealand economy. In fact, it is the top earner of foreign exchange. **Tourism New Zealand** does an excellent job of developing facilities while maintaining the natural and cultural aspects of the country; the department also promotes New Zealand overseas through trade shows and on their website: www.purenz.com. The **Tourism Industry Association of New Zealand,** website: www.tianz .org.nz, represents over 3,500 tourism-oriented businesses across the country.

Visitor numbers are growing exponentially, with 1.8 million visitors arriving in 2001. The majority are from Australia (650,000 annually); however, more and more visitors from Great Britain (210,000), the United States (200,000), Japan (155,000), Korea (70,000), Germany (55,000), and Taiwan (41,000) are discovering New Zealand.

THE NEW ZEALANDERS

At the last national census (2001) New Zealand's population numbered 3.73 million, which equates to 14 people per square kilometer. **Kiwis** (as New Zealanders like to call themselves) are good-humored, relaxed, easy to get along with, and hospitable. They take the time to talk to one another—and to visitors. Don't be surprised if you're frequently asked to their homes for "tea" or a cold beer. Of the total population, about 280,000 are native Maori (420,000 claim Maori descent), 265,000 are Pacific Islanders, and the rest are mainly of European descent. The Maori population has increased dramatically in the last 30 years as a result of its growing awareness of the importance of good health, nutrition, and education, which lowered a previously high infant-mortality rate.

New Zealanders enjoy a high standard of living. Comprehensive health services and subsidized medicines are available to all citizens. They have high-quality housing, plentiful food, and a five-day, 40-hour workweek. Both sexes claim equal rights and opportunities. Churches of all major denominations can be found throughout New Zealand, and minor religious sects are found mainly in the larger cities. (For information regarding services, check the daily newspapers, or ask at the local Public Relations Office or Visitor Information Network office.)

Demographics

The population is unevenly distributed. Historically the South Island has always had a smaller population than the North Island (except for during the gold-rush era), but recent times have brought a *steady* drift from south to north. In the 1960s New Zealanders began to migrate in large numbers from the rural areas to cities in search of better opportunities. Today, 2.9 million New Zealanders live on the North Island while less than one million live on the South Island. And of the country's entire population of 3.73 million, more than half live in the four largest cities: Auckland, Hamilton, Wellington, and Christchurch.

Races

After a colorful history of racial resentment and resulting land wars, today the Pakeha (Caucasian people), Maori, and Pacific Islanders live in relative harmony compared to people in other parts of the world, though there's been increasing unrest over land disputes in the last few years—disputes that originated in the 1840s with the signing of the Treaty of Waitangi. Intermarriage has increased dramatically in the last three decades, leaving very few full-blooded Maori in New Zealand. It's estimated that one out of twelve New Zealanders is at least half-Maori in origin, and many more are part Maori. No longer do you find the modern Maori wearing ceremonial costume, cooking in boiling pools, and living as they are depicted on postcards. Only those involved in the tourist industry continue to give this picture of Maori life—mainly in Rotorua, where visitors enjoy authentic performances of the fierce *haka* (war dance) of Maori men, the graceful *poi* dance and beautiful singing of the women, traditional arts, crafts, and carving.

An estimated 60 percent of the Maori population live in main urban centers. The Maori had difficulties adjusting to urban life and Pakeha ways, and began to lose their culture and tradition. Recognizing these problems, the government and Maori themselves introduced programs to ease the situation. Out of these programs came a growing Maori nationalism and an eventual upsurge of Pakeha interest in *Maoritanga,* the Maori way of life. Today the Maori language, traditions, arts and crafts, music, and dance are taught in schools throughout New Zealand, and there is an increasing national interest in preserving the once fading Maori culture.

Language

The common language of New Zealand is English. The Maori also have their own melodic language, mainly heard in songs and chants and on ceremonial occasions. However, some Maori phrases, such as *Haere mai* (welcome) and *Haere ra* (farewell), have been adopted by Pakeha and integrated into general use. With the renewed interest in Maori culture, the Maori language was made an official language of New Zealand in 1974.

Beautifully descriptive Maori place-names are scattered throughout New Zealand. Places were often named after particular events, such as *Taumatawhakatangihangakoauauotamateapokaiwhenuakitanatahu*—"the place where Tamatea, the man with the big knees, who slid, climbed and swallowed mountains, known as 'landeater,' played his flute to his loved one." (There's also a longer version, claimed to be the world's longest place-name.) The Maori language was entirely oral until the early missionaries recorded it in a written form. The sounds broke down into eight consonants: h, k, m, n, p, r, t, w; five vowels: a, e, i, o, u; and two combinations: wh, and ng. "Wh" is pronounced as f, "ng" is a nasal sound, as in siNG. All words end in a vowel, and each syllable has equal stress. Many words are Maori pronunciations of English words, but they look Maori, such as *motaka* (motor car). The easiest way to say Maori words is to pronounce each syllable phonetically.

On the Road

A multitude of exciting activities awaits you in the great New Zealand outdoors. Spectacular scenery lies around every bend, and action-packed adventures are more than likely to lure you off the beaten track into some of the most beautiful countryside you're ever likely to see. Whether you want to run wild white-water rapids, ski the slopes of a smoldering volcano, skim the shallows in a high-speed jetboat, cast a fly rod in an icy stream, settle back to watch cricket or lawn bowls, or have a bet on "the trots," New Zealand offers it all.

CONSERVATION

Conservation and responsible ecotourism are recognized as extremely important issues in New Zealand. For travelers, this means self-education, an awareness of the natural environment, and a healthy respect for the land, flora and fauna, and one another.

The **Department of Conservation (DOC)**, website: www.doc.govt.nz, is the government agency whose mission is to "conserve New Zealand's natural and historic heritage for all to enjoy now and in the future." In effect, the department oversees the conservation and management of national parks, forest parks, protected indigenous forests, a wide range of conservation areas, marine reserves, and even some rivers. In conjunction with actual protection and management, the DOC operates visitor centers (called Field Centres "in the field") throughout the country; maintains hiking trails, picnic areas, and campgrounds; and issues fishing licenses.

Coastal Conservation

Pollution, garbage dumping, reclamation, and some coastal uses and developments are destroying New Zealand's spectacular coastline. You can help: support marine reserves; never dump garbage (including snagged line, holed nets, and damaged fishing gear)

HUKA JET

Jetboating is a popular adrenalin rush.

overboard; if you see trash floating at sea, try to take it back to shore for proper disposal in port bins; leave beaches cleaner than you found them; report injured or distressed marine mammals to the nearest DOC office; don't drive vehicles over estuaries and coastal dunes; be careful with fire near coastal vegetation and forest; know and observe all fishing regulations.

Worthwhile Organizations

In addition to the Department of Conservation, two publicly funded organizations are active in the fight to save New Zealand's natural wonders. **Greenpeace,** tel. 09/630-6317, website: www.greenpeace.org.nz, may have been formed in Canada, but it gained world renown after its flagship, the *Rainbow Warrior,* was blown up in Auckland Harbour by French government agents. The **Royal Forest and Bird Protection Society,** tel. 04/385-7374, website: www.forest-bird.org.nz, may keep a lower profile than

Greenpeace, but it has been instrumental in the preservation of native flora and fauna. With 40,000 members, "Forest and Bird" is New Zealand's largest conservation organization.

TRAMPING

Also known as hiking, trekking, and backpacking, tramping is one of the favorite outdoor pursuits of New Zealanders and visitors alike. The small population, vast areas of wilderness (some still unexplored), diverse landscapes, and wide variety of terrain guarantee a good walking experience. Tramping is most popular Nov.–April when the weather is best.

A great way to really see New Zealand is through the use of the National Walkway Network. The idea of a national walkway was passed as an Act of Parliament in 1975, with the aim of providing a network of tracks eventually linking the farthest point north to the farthest point south; this plan has been abandoned, however. More than 150 walkways have been created, passing through public and private property to points of scenic, historic, or cultural interest. The DOC classifies each hike as one of four types:

path—well-formed track suitable for the average family

walking track—well-defined track suitable for people of good average physical fitness

tramping track—a less well-defined trail with often steep gradients

route—lightly marked route for use only by well-equipped, experienced trampers.

Details on individual walks appear in each chapter, in brochures available at DOC offices, and on their website: www.doc.govt.nz.

Federated Mountain Clubs of New Zealand, tel. 04/233-8244, website: www.fmc.org.nz, is a national association of over 100 tramping and mountaineering clubs.

Great Walks

"Great Walks" is a designation given to nine of New Zealand's premier hiking trails. Each is famous for its own unique and outstanding scenery. They all require backcountry experience and at least one overnight camping or in trailside huts.

ENVIRONMENTAL CARE CODE

1. Protect plants and animals—they're unique, and often rare.
2. Remove rubbish—carry out what you carry in.
3. Bury toilet waste well away from waterways, tracks, campsites, and huts.
4. Keep streams and lakes clean—drain used water well away from the water source into the soil to allow it to be filtered, and boil drinking water for 10 minutes or chemically treat it.
5. Take care with fires—portable stoves are less harmful and more efficient, but if you make a fire, use only dead wood, douse it with water afterward, and check the ashes before leaving.
6. Camp carefully—leave no trace of your visit.
7. Keep to the track—avoid damaging fragile plants.
8. Consider others.
9. Respect the cultural heritage.
10. Enjoy your visit.

On the North Island, the **Lake Waikaremoana Track** wanders around Lake Waikaremoana in Te Urewera National Park; the **Tongariro Crossing** in Tongariro National Park traverses a barren volcanic landscape. The **Heaphy Track** in Kahurangi National Park and the **Abel Tasman Coastal Track** meander across the northern tip of the South Island; the **Hollyford Track, Kepler Track,** and **Milford Track** traverse rugged alpine landscapes around Queenstown and in Fiordland National Park; and the **Rakiura Track** crosses the untouched wilderness of Stewart Island. The final track isn't a track at all; the **Whanganui Journey** is a river trip through Whanganui National Park.

All tracks are extremely popular during the summer; huts are spaced at regular intervals (approximately a six-hour walk between each) but in peak periods, especially January, they can become overcrowded and you need to carry your own tent and stove (huts range $8–30 pp). The Milford Track is the most well known, and because of its popularity, booking (up to one year ahead) is required by the DOC (for independent walkers); you can also hike it as part of a guided group (expensive) Nov.–March. Get all the facts and options (most can be done independently or with a guiding company) well in advance to avoid disappointment (more details in the appropriate chapters).

Commercial Operators

Many commercially operated trekking tours cover both North and South Islands. You can book these through travel agencies, New Zealand Tourism Board offices, and Visitor Information Network offices. They offer straight hiking trips, or hiking combined with mountain climbing, canoeing, jetboating, or river rafting. Overnight or several-day trips generally include a combination of activities, camping gear or cabin accommodations, all meals, equipment, and transportation. Most are offered only during the summer; at least one experienced guide takes each tour.

Parks

In the 13 beautiful national parks and many forest parks scattered throughout New Zealand you can find everything from a short gentle stroll to a hard, adventurous, several-day hike, with huts and campsites provided along the tracks for overnight stays. DOC officers have all the information on what to see and do, including hiking track and hut information, and you can buy detailed maps for a relatively small price.

MOUNTAINEERING

Of many first-class climbing areas, the main ones are **Mount Egmont/Taranaki** (2,517 meters) and **Mount Ruapehu** (2,796 meters) on the North Island, and a multitude of climbs in the skyscraper peaks of the **Southern Alps** on the South Island. Eight out of the 13 national parks are mountainous, providing reasonably good access and well-equipped huts. All park field centers have climbing and tramping information and weather forecasts. **Mount Cook** (3,744 meters), **Mount Tasman** (3,497 meters), **La Perouse** (3,078 meters), and **Mount Sefton** (3,157 meters) in Mt. Cook and Westland National Parks are very popular with experienced climbers—but only when weather conditions are just right. Many routes are long and difficult, demanding experience and appropriate equipment, and most of the mountains have glaciers, demanding ice- and rock-climbing ability. You'll find few solid-rock climbs in New Zealand—the best is on the firm granite of the **Darran Mountains** in Fiordland National Park.

The climbing season is Nov.–April, but mountaineers attempt more and more winter climbing each year and are always discovering new routes. Several guiding companies offer climbs, walks, and various levels of instruction. Bring your own equipment to New Zealand because it's expensive to buy; however, the latest equipment is available should you need it. The Department of Survey and Lands publishes excellent topographical maps of most areas; buy them at any of its offices in all major cities, or in the larger bookshops. For more information on climbing and mountaineering, contact the New Zealand Alpine Club, headquartered in Christchurch, tel. 03/377-7595, website: www.nzalpine.org.nz; or the **Federated Moun-**

ON THE ROAD

tain Clubs of New Zealand, tel. 04/233-8244, website: www.fmc.org.nz.

RIVER RAFTING

If you seek the adrenaline high fueled by apprehension, panic, and sheer fear, look no further. Whether you're a professional rafter or a total beginner looking for instant thrills, New Zealand has a river to suit. Both islands are crisscrossed with rivers that offer the rafter everything from the peaceful pleasure of drifting with the current through spectacular scenery to wild, churning, white-water rapids where you cling on with all your strength and pray—between icy-cold dunkings. Soaking wet, feet like blocks of ice, heart pounding, poised at the top of a fearsome rapid, you may wonder for a moment why you're doing this—but when it's all over, you know you'll be back for more.

> *New Zealand rivers offer the rafter everything from the peaceful pleasure of drifting with the current through spectacular scenery to wild, churning, white-water rapids where you cling on with all your strength and pray—between icy-cold dunkings.*

OUTDOOR HEALTH

Giardia, an intestinal parasite, is present in many New Zealand lakes, rivers, and streams (even in very cold water). You can contract giardiasis by drinking water contaminated by fecal matter. Tap water throughout the country is safe.

To avoid contamination, *always* treat drinking water from outdoor sources (lakes, streams, etc.) by boiling it for at least 10 minutes, or by chemical purification with iodine solutions (available at chemist shops/pharmacies), or by filtration through *Giardia*-rated filters (pore size five micrometers or less). The signs and symptoms of giardiasis (*Giardia* contamination) are explosive foul-smelling diarrhea, stomach cramps, bloating, dehydration, nausea, and weight loss; see a doctor for simple, quick-acting, prescribed drug treatment, and avoid spreading the parasite.

The Rivers

The **Wairoa,** a rapids-filled river meandering down from the Kaimai Range to meet the ocean near Tauranga, provides both quiet water and short bursts of raging, Class III to Class V rapids. The highlights are aptly named "Waterfall" and "Roller coaster." The nearby **Rangitaiki River** (not as wild) comes down from the Ahimanawa Range to meet the ocean just north of Whakatane. The **Motu River** provides quiet-water stretches through breathtaking scenery and several exciting rapids as it winds through the Raukumara Range (East Cape) to come out at Haupoto. Hydro development has tamed much of the **Tongariro River,** but a few sections still offer exciting rafting action. The **Mohaka** (near Gisborne), **Ngaruroro** (between Napier and Hastings), and **Rangitikei** (south of Wanganui) offer combinations of quiet water and rugged scenery, and wild, heart-stopping rapids that can raise the hair on the neck of even the experienced rafter. On the South Island, the most popular rafting is on the **Kawarau** and **Shotover** Rivers near Queenstown (a large choice of companies offers Class III to Class V rapids), the **Rakaia River** near Christchurch, and the wild **Landsborough River.** Generally the best months for rafting are Oct.–Jan., though most operators run the rivers till April, depending on water levels and weather conditions. The high-water levels on all rivers are usually Oct.–Dec. and sometimes January. The low-water levels are February and March.

Equipment

Low-grade rivers (three and below) introduce you to rafting, let you employ basic rafting techniques, and at the same time, give you a few thrills. Advanced rafters head for Class IV to Class V rivers. Life jackets are mandatory, and on some trips, crash hats are also provided. Keep in mind that it's always possible to find yourself unexpectedly bodysurfing the rapids. Before you start out, you're taught basic paddling skills, how to stay afloat and ride the rapids if you're ejected, and how to get back to the raft or shore. A minimum age is often set depending on the difficulty of the river.

Wear a bathing suit, shirt, shorts, wool sweater, waterproof jacket, thick wool socks, and tennis shoes or sneakers (essential)—take a change of clothes for later. Leave your camera behind unless you're doing a float trip or one of the mildest grade rivers (or have a waterproof camera that you can firmly attach to yourself)—you generally don't have much time between rapids to take photos.

Commercial Operators

Many commercial river-rafting companies operate on both the North and South Islands (more in the south), and more spring up each rafting season. They offer trips varying from a couple of hours to 12 days, including tent or hut accommodations, meals, and transportation. Trips generally go between October and April, dependent on water levels and weather; most companies rent full- or part-length wet suits and provide the mandatory life jackets. Before you try to save pennies, remember that the rivers are icy cold. Choose a good and safe operator—avoid trips that have a reputation for fooling around, falling into the rapids for fun, etc.—they usually employ the least-experienced guides. Ask around about safety records; check with the local information center; and make sure the company is a member of the **New Zealand Rafting Association,** website: www.nz-rafting.co.nz. In addition to member listings, this website has lots of handy rafting information and an online booking form. On the **North Island** tours operate out of Rotorua rafting the Rangitaiki River, out of Taupo and Turangi rafting the Tongariro, Mohaka, and Rangitikei Rivers, and out of Tauranga rafting the Wairoa. On the **South Island** tours operate out of Christchurch rafting the Waimakariri River, out of Westport rafting the Buller, Karamea, and Mohikinui Rivers, and out of Queenstown (lots of companies) rafting the Shotover, Dart, Waiatoto, and Kawarau Rivers. The newest rage is white-water sledging—flying down the rapids on a boogie board, wearing flippers on your feet—on rivers around Queenstown and Wanaka.

JETBOATING

The world-famous Hamilton jetboats were invented in New Zealand and are very popular. Commercial jetboat companies operate tours throughout both islands, providing trips of varying lengths through spectacular scenery. Jetboating is particularly popular on the Shotover River in the Queenstown area. Experienced boat pilots operate the jetboats and provide thrilling rides ranging from a short ride skimming the shallows to combination trips including jetboating, white-water rafting, and a helicopter ride. Jetboating tends to be expensive, but if you like whizzing across rapids only centimeters deep, twisting and churning to just miss overhanging branches and the occasional bridge pylon, whirling 180 degrees on the spot at high speed, this activity is a must. The scenery is always spectacular—on the Shotover River you see abandoned gold mines and equipment along the way. Expect to get wet, particularly if you're selected to sit in the back seat. Take your camera in a waterproof container and firmly attach it to yourself. Mandatory life jackets are supplied, and some operators also provide light waterproof jackets.

CANOEING AND KAYAKING

Several tour companies offer canoe or kayak trips; you can also rent canoes without guides for a few hours or for an entire river camping trip. On the North Island, canoe tours operate out of Wanganui using the **Whanganui River.** On the South Island, you can canoe the **Kawarau River;** tours operate out of Queenstown. Because of the nature of the rivers, life jackets, crash helmets, and wet suits are essential; most equipment can be rented. For more remote areas, helicopter services are available to fly you in to the rivers. For more information, contact the **New Zealand Recreational Canoeing Association,** tel. 04/560-3590; website: www.rivers.org.nz.

ON THE ROAD

RIVER AND LAKE FISHING

Often called an angler's paradise, New Zealand fishing is world famous. Some of the friendliest New Zealanders are found congregating around rivermouths and lakeshores, fishing rods in hand, hats covered in assorted flies and lures. Originally, brown trout ova from the U.K. via Tasmania (Australia) and rainbow trout ova from the Russian River in California were introduced to New Zealand waters in the late 1860s. Streams and rivers providing both fast- and slow-flowing water, crystal-clear lakes, and an abundant supply of food all helped the fish thrive in their new environment, and modern hatcheries and good conservation methods ensure that New Zealand's good fishing continues.

Fishing Spots

In general the north is known for large rainbow trout, the south for large brown trout, and quinnat salmon run in many of the rivers of the North Island's lower west coast and the South Island's east coast.

North Island: All the lakes, particularly **Lake Taupo** (New Zealand's largest) and **Lake Tarawera,** are well stocked with rainbow trout, but the rivers seem to attract the larger rainbows and browns. The finest fishing is naturally found at off-the-beaten-track locations; boats are often necessary to get to the best stream mouths. Fly-fishing is at its best in rivers and streams that flow into lakes April–June when the fish swim upstream to spawn, and Nov.–Dec. when they return to the lake. Use a wet lure fly and fast-sinking line downstream, and a weighted nymph on floating line upstream.

South Island: Most lakes are stocked with brown trout, some with rainbow trout and landlocked salmon. The fishing is good, at times similar to prime times on the North Island lakes, but anglers use a dry fly and floating line. Spinning is popular from the shore, as is trolling with weighted lines from a boat. Dry flies (or lures) mainly snag brown trout in the rivers, and in some eastern rivers, Pacific salmon. In South Westland, brown trout come in from the sea in late summer and are caught on both wet and dry fly and spin-

ners. The rivers of the east coast are great for salmon fishing. Try the Ashburton, Rakaia, Rangitata, Waimakariri, and Waitaki Rivers Oct.–April (Jan.–March are the best months).

For fishing information, pick up a copy of the *New Zealand Fishing News* (which has the largest circulation of any New Zealand sports magazine) or check the website: www.fishing.net.nz.

Equipment

Bringing your own fishing gear into New Zealand is permitted but it may be fumigated. Renting fishing tackle and waders is difficult—it's better to bring your own. Thigh waders are suggested for South Island fishing, chest waders for North Island. For all types of trout fishing, the experts suggest you have one reel with five replaceable spools and the following lines: a floating line of 5–7 weight, A.H.D. fast-sink line of 8–10, a shooting head line (preferably number 10), a floating line with sink tip for nymphing, and a medium sinking line of 8–9. Dry flies and nymphs such as the Red Tipped Governor, Royal Wulff, Adams, Blue Dun, Hare, and Copper all work well in New Zealand. Streamer or lure flies representing smelt are best bought locally. Imported ready-made trout flies can be brought into the country without fumigation, but certain fly-tying materials, such as loose feathers, have to be fumigated.

Regulations

Most anglers flyfish or troll. Spinning or lure fishing is fairly uncommon—most of the best fishing areas are designated for fly-fishing only. Each of the 12 local regions has its own fishing rules, and fishing seasons vary area by area. **Fish and Game New Zealand,** tel. 04/499-4767, website: www.fishandgame.org.nz, is the government department responsible for managing the country's freshwater fisheries. Copies of all the regulations are available from DOC offices throughout the country and on the department website.

Licenses: One license is valid in 11 of the 12 regions (the exception is Lake Taupo and its watersheds, which require a separate license). The cost is $15 for one day, $30 for one week, $45 for the winter season (April–Oct.), and $75 for an annual pass (Oct.–Sept.). Regulations allow a 20-meter public right-of-way along the banks of fishing rivers and lakeshores; however, permission is required from the owner if you need to cross private land to reach the water.

Limits: These vary according to each district, ranging anywhere from 4–50 per day. In the Rotorua and Taupo districts on the North Island the limit is usually eight a day; on the South Island the limit ranges 4–20 per day and there are extra limitations on salmon.

Size: The sizes of New Zealand trout vary from district to district depending on environment, available food, climate, and angling pressure. In most areas the trout must be at least 356 mm long to keep, in a few districts at least 304 mm.

BIG-GAME FISHING

Big-game fishing is a very popular (and expensive) sport concentrated along 500 km of the northeast coast of the North Island from **Cape Runaway** to **North Cape.** The season is generally Jan.–April, attracting flocks of overseas visitors eager to haul in a trophy from the sea. A fishing license is not required. Broadbill, striped, black, and blue marlin; hammerhead, mako, and thresher shark; and yellowtail, kingfish, and tuna are the main gamefish species. The best months in the Bay of Islands are usually February and March. The most prolific, fighting, big-game fish is the striped marlin—the most successful months are Dec.–June; catch sharks Nov.–May and tuna Dec.–March. Big-game fishing clubs abound from Whangarei to the Bay of Islands, competition is tough, and international tournaments are held each year. To try your luck, head up to the Bay of Islands via the coastal route, comparing charter prices at the deep-sea fishing resorts as you head north. If you join the prestigious **Bay of Islands Swordfish Club** in Russell and catch something worthwhile, the fish is officially weighed in, you're issued a certificate, and you become eligible for most club trophies. Charter boats (gear provided) and experienced crews are always available, but from $500 per day, unless you have a large bud-

get, you need to find several other people willing to share costs.

SCUBA DIVING

Coral reefs, caves, multicolored sponges, various large brown kelps, friendly fish, and a large number of shipwrecks lure the scuba diver and underwater photographer to New Zealand shores. When the weather is suitable, underwater visibility is about 9–12 meters along the coast, but around the offshore islands it's usually 18–24 meters and on good days exceeds 45 meters. The **Bay of Islands, Hauraki Gulf, Coromandel Peninsula, Cook Strait,** and **Milford Sound** all offer good diving. **The Poor Knights Islands,** a small island group off the northeast coast of the North Island, are "a diver's dream," offering century-old sunken ships as an added feature. Water temperatures vary 14–22°C, lower in the far south; locals recommend wet suits. Summer usually provides the calmest weather; diving conditions are at their best Jan.–April. Some years a plankton bloom occurs in spring and early summer, clouding the coastal waters. No underwater flora or fauna are dangerous to divers apart from sharks—and they're rarely seen. Gear can be rented with at least a PADI Diver's Certificate or equivalent. Auckland-based **Dive HQ** provides an excellent introduction to diving on its website: www.divehq.co.nz.

SAILING

New Zealanders are water people—if they're not *in* the water, they're on it. Most people seem to have a yacht or boat of some sort (Auckland is "The City of Sails"), and all kinds and sizes are available for hire—however, you need a substantial budget or several people to share costs. Charter yachts are very popular Nov.–May (the yachting season), and you have the choice of hiring a crew or sailing it yourself (previous sailing experience is necessary). Some companies also offer crews that give instruction; most supply all the necessary equipment minus bedding and food. Premier sailing locations are liberally dotted around the country's coastline; the major operators on the North

Island are found in the **Bay of Islands, Hauraki Gulf** (Auckland), and **Marlborough Sounds.** Prices are not cheap, about $100–350 per day (the more expensive sleep up to six people), but special rates are offered for longer hire periods. The Tourism New Zealand website: www.purenz.com, has links to major charter companies.

SURFING

You can find surf throughout the year around the entire coastline. The best-known surfing area is around **Raglan** on west from Hamilton. Considered New Zealand's premier point break, with three left-breaking points in a row, it's rarely flat and has powerful and often large waves typical of the North Island's rugged west coast. Other popular North Island areas are **New Plymouth, Bay of Plenty,** and **Gisborne.** On the South Island, surfing beaches are most accessible on the **east coast.** A large variety of beach breaks, river bars, and reef points lie along the coastline; however, quality surf over three meters is rare. Wet suits are necessary from autumn through spring, year-round on the South Island.

CYCLING

New Zealand is an ideal place for a bicycling vacation if you're reasonably fit. Temperate climate, excellent roads, low traffic density, and a wide variety of terrain and scenery appeal to those with enough time to see the country at a slower pace. However, a beginner cyclist may find the terrain too steep and demanding to be pleasurable, particularly on the mountainous South Island, and the traffic rather frightening on narrow roads. Talk to experienced cyclists before you commit yourself to a cycling tour of the country. One way of dealing with carrying your gear is to pack up everything you don't need for a few days in cardboard boxes, then mail them to your next destination a few days down the road. This way you always have clean clothes and other basic necessities to look forward to as a reward at the end of a few days' hard work.

If you haven't cycled before, a reasonably priced tour is a good way to start. If you're taking your own bicycle over to New Zealand, buy a bike box and wash the tires well—New Zealand is

© ANDREW HEMPSTEAD

Raglan is New Zealand's premier surf break, attracting surfers from around the world.

strict on pest control and your entire bike will be washed if there's a speck of foreign dirt on the tires (same goes for tents and hiking boots). Touring maps are available from overseas Tourism New Zealand offices, and from DOC offices in all of New Zealand's large cities. When in New Zealand, be sure to pick up *Cycle Touring in New Zealand—Including both North and South Islands* by Bruce Ringer, published by The Mountaineers in 1989. *Cycle Touring in the South Island* (third edition) by Helen Crabb, published by the Canterbury Cyclists' Association, is also recommended. For more information, write: Bicycle Association of New Zealand, P.O. Box 1454, Wellington.

Rentals and Commercial Touring

Adventure Cycles, 1 Fort St., Auckland, tel. 09/309-5566, provides bikes and equipment for long-term touring. Suspension bikes cost $25 per day, $90 per week, and $190 per month, all with pumps, water bottles, locks, and helmets. Adventure Cycles also rents pannier bags ($30 per week; $65 per month) and sells a variety of touring gear, including maps.

Auckland-based **Pedaltours,** tel. 09/302-0968 or 0800/302-0968, website: www.pedaltours .co.nz, Parnell, offers a variety of bicycle adventure tours ranging 8–17 days in length; cost is $280–350 pp per day all inclusive (for example, an eight-day Bay of Islands tour is $2,700). Accommodation is in small country inns, motels or hotels, or a farmstay; three meals a day and enthusiastic tour guides are provided. All you need to bring is your bike (they can be rented). **Flying Kiwi Wilderness Expeditions,** tel. 03/573-8126 or 0800/692-396, combines bus and bike travel, allowing cyclists to ride as much or as little as they wish each day. The tours, which run four to 28 days, are well priced.

SKIING AND SNOWBOARDING

New Zealand ski fields provide some of the most spectacular skiing in the world. National teams and skiing and boarding fanatics are lured from the Northern Hemisphere for excellent skiing and boarding on uncrowded treeless slopes June–Oct. (sometimes November in the North Island). There's always plenty of good snow *somewhere* in New Zealand, even during a mild winter. Good weather, magnificent scenery, and reasonable costs (by international standards) complete the picture. In addition to 17 commercial resorts, New Zealand is home to around a dozen **Club fields.** Often facilities are fairly basic—simple rope tows with no grooming—but accommodation is provided and you will be welcomed with open arms.

Apart from numerous conventional ski fields, you can fly up to the mountaintops for an exhilarating heli-skiing, glacier skiing (ski-plane), or ski-touring adventure in virgin powder. Heli-skiing is particularly good in the Harris Mountains near Wanaka (South Island), offering more than 60 different runs (600–1,200 vertical meters) on 35 mountains.

Although New Zealand slopes never seem to get crowded, the best time to ski is still midweek; most New Zealanders are weekend skiers, but August is usually busy all month when families with school-age children take their skiing vacations.

The Ski Fields

Of the 28 recognized skiing areas in the country, most are in the Southern Alps—many are club ski fields with a friendly atmosphere making up for limited facilities. On the North Island the two major commercial ski fields, **Whakapapa** and **Turoa,** are both situated on the volcanic slopes of Mt. Ruapehu in Tongariro National Park. Other fields are operated by ski clubs in both Tongariro and Egmont National Parks. On the South Island the major commercial ski fields are **Mt. Hutt** at Methven, **Coronet Peak** and **The Remarkables** near Queenstown, and **Treble Cone** and **Cardrona** near Wanaka. Smaller commercial ski fields, with a variety of lifts, cafeterias, ski equipment rental, but limited adjacent accommodations, are found at **Rainbow Valley** near St. Arnaud; **Porter Heights** near Christchurch; **Erewhon, Mt. Dobson** and **Fox Peak** in central South Island; and **Lake Ohau** near Mt. Cook National Park. Larger fields offer varying ski packages.

March 22, 2003

BUNGEE JUMPING

This is one of the most popular ways to get an adrenaline rush in New Zealand. Imagine standing on a high bridge spanning a river-filled canyon, your ankles securely tied together with a towel and bungee cord, the river far below. And then, in front of a large audience who enthusiastically do a "countdown," you dive off for a long, long free fall. At the end of the fall, just before you hit the water or after you are momentarily submerged to your waist (you choose between a wet or dry fall), the elastic rope rebounds and you're flying upward toward the bridge again. This continues until you run out of momentum, and then you're rescued by boat and taken to shore. To experience this you have to cough up $85–130, but those who have taken the plunge proudly swagger around the countryside in a specially designed bungee-jumping T-shirt—and you have to *do* it to get the shirt. If this sounds like something you'd like to try, head for Queenstown, where the operators are the most experienced in the country—they started it all.

Arts and Entertainment

Fantastic scenery, an appreciation of beauty, and pride in their country inspire many New Zealanders to become artists. Art comes in many media—painting, pottery, sculpture, glassware, spinning, weaving, and woodcarving. Music, theater, ballet, modern dance, literature, filmmaking, and architecture are also well represented.

Performing and Visual Arts

Drama is alive and well; the two most recognized theaters for professional live drama are the **Mercury Theatre** in Auckland and the **Downstage Theatre** in Wellington. Music flourishes through the internationally known National Symphony Orchestra and Brass Band. Government-funded support for the arts is provided by the Queen Elizabeth II Arts Council, which also trains promising dancers and musicians. Regional and community arts councils provide assistance to amateur groups and individuals and promote the arts throughout New Zealand. Since 1960 the visual arts have particularly flourished. Pottery, rapidly becoming an in-demand export, is the favorite, and woolcraft is also popular—as you'd expect from a country with more than 68 million sheep.

Museums

Display museums are found throughout New Zealand—many specialize in Maori arts and crafts, history, and culture. The **Museum of New Zealand Te Papa Tongarewa** in Wellington features Maori and Pacific exhibits; the **Auckland Museum** features zoology, botany, ethnology, and Maori exhibits; the **Canterbury Museum** in Christchurch displays New Zealand birds, a diorama of a historic Christchurch setting, and a planetarium; the **Otago Museum** in Dunedin features ethnology, pottery and sculpture, marinelife and skeletons, and local history.

Architecture

New Zealand architecture generally reflects European and American influences of the appro-

Almost every town has a small museum.

© ANDREW HEMPSTEAD

priate time; however, many well-preserved pre-European Maori buildings are still extant, particularly in the north of the North Island. Some of New Zealand's most beautiful historic homes and buildings, restored and maintained by the New Zealand Historic Places Trust, are open to the public year-round; small admission charge.

MAORI ART

Sculpture

The most important and sacred Maori art was sculpture, predominantly wood but also jade, ivory, and whalebone. Trained in the art from an early age, the best carvers of early Maori society became men of high rank. Only men could become carvers—women, regarded as inferior, were not even allowed to watch the carvers at work. The canoe *(waka)*, meeting house *(whare whakairo)*, and food storehouse *(pataka)* were the main vehicles for Maori relief sculpture. Enormous pieces of indigenous timber were deeply carved into highly decorative spiritual designs, both on the interior and exterior. Well-preserved woodcarvings, decorative interior panels of woven reed, and painted rafters are best seen in *marae* or meeting grounds throughout the country, and all the major museums feature Maori art. All useful items of the Maori were covered in abstract designs, inspired by plants (a fern design is fairly common) or symbols, and inset with abalone shell. The human body, in particular the sacred head, was the major figurative element. Profiles with birdlike heads were *manaia* (evil beings).

The *tiki,* a spiritual carving of human form representing the Maori conception of the beginning of life, was worn as a good-luck pendant—it has been mass-produced in all mediums for tourists. Unfortunately, a lot of Maori art is now machine-made and you have to search for hand-carved original pieces. One of the best places to see hand-carved works is the New Zealand Maori Arts and Crafts Institute at Whakarewarewa, Rotorua, the home of Maori culture. Other areas where you can find carvers in action are the far north and the east coast of the North Island, and in the town of Hokitika on the west coast of the South Island.

© ANDREW HEMPSTEAD

Body Art

The Maori also decorated their bodies, a custom that the earliest European visitors found particularly intriguing. Apart from wearing flax cloaks and kilts decorated with woven borders, tufts of colorful feathers, or dog hair, they adorned themselves with beautiful greenstone pendants, ear pendants, and combs. The men painfully carved intricate symmetrical designs *(moku)* into their faces and thighs with tiny chisels filled with paint, and the women tattooed their lower lips and chins. Nowadays you see few authentic tattoos (only on the elderly), but they're still effectively painted on for ceremonial occasions.

Song and Dance

A cultural concert of Maori songs, chants, games, and graceful dances is a colorful spectacle that shouldn't be missed, especially when combined with a *hangi* (Maori feast). Men perform fierce war chants *(haka)* and women sing and perform graceful flowing dances, twirling *poi*. Rotorua is the best place to go to appreciate Maori culture in all its forms, past and present.

FESTIVALS AND EVENTS

New Zealand seems to have some festival or event going on somewhere almost every day of the year. Sporting events of all kinds are very popular, as is the multitude of excellent agricultural shows that draw large crowds of locals and visitors alike. Drama, ballet, and musical events are also highly recommended. Head for the nearest information center for the latest on current festivals and events. Agricultural and pastoral shows are held throughout the year. Events include animal handling, sheepdog trials, horse jumping, local crafts, and fruit and vegetable displays and competitions. These shows have a distinctly local atmosphere and typical "New Zealand feeling." Horse racing is another part of life in New Zealand. Thoroughbred horses, bred to race, compete internationally. The trots

AMERICA'S CUP

For only the third time in its 150-year history, the America's Cup, yachting's most prized trophy, will be competed for outside the United States in early 2003. In 1995, the New Zealand boat *Black Magic* beat *Young America* to take the Cup down under. Preparations for its defense commenced before the Cup had even arrived, including redevelopment of the downtown waterfront around Auckland's Viaduct Basin. In 1999, the challengers began racing for the right to compete against New Zealand for the Cup. In the end, the Italian yacht *Prada* emerged victorious, but was whitewashed by *Team New Zealand,* who won five straight races to retain the Cup and host the competition again. Qualifying races, to determine which two boats will compete for the Cup, will take place in the latter months of 2002, while actual Cup races will take place over the first two months of 2003.

A terrible footnote to New Zealand's America's Cup success was the murder of Sir Peter Blake—the popular skipper who led the charge in both successful Cup campaigns—killed by pirates off the South American coastline in late 2001.

(harness racing) is also very popular throughout the year, as is greyhound racing; meetings are generally held in the evenings under floodlights, gather an enthusiastic crowd, and are lots of fun. Following are but a few of a multitude of events held throughout the year; some large festivals are held only once every couple of years.

Summer

In Auckland, the **Annual Yachting Regatta** is a spectacular event in the harbor of a city known for its water sports. Summer in Auckland also offers both the **New Zealand Open Tennis Tournament** and the **Devonport Food & Wine Festival.** The annual **Waitangi Day** commemorates the signing of the Treaty of Waitangi on February 6, 1840. It is a national holiday, but actual celebrations are concentrated around the Bay of Islands, the signing site. Also in February, an **Art Deco Weekend** is held in Napier, and the **Marlborough Food and Wine Festival** is held in the north of the South Island.

Autumn

The **Ngaruawahia River Regatta,** the only Maori canoe regatta, is held mid-March near Hamilton. Other events include horse swimming, rowing, speedboat racing, tribal dance competitions, and much more. Check out the **Golden Shears,** a sheepshearing contest in Masterton, and up in the Bay of Islands, the exciting **International Billfish Tournament.** If you're lucky enough to meet some of the competitors, you may be invited aboard one of the deep-sea fishing boats participating in the tournament (if you suffer from seasickness, stock up on Dramamine—it can get pretty rough out there). Down on the South Island, the West Coast town of Hokitika hosts the **Wildfoods Festival,** providing a unique opportunity to taste some unusual local delicacies.

In April, Auckland offers the **New Zealand Easter Show** and **Auckland Festival;** the **Hastings Highland Games** are held during Easter. There is a real Scottish atmosphere at these games; expect haggis, hurling, caber tossing, Highland dancing, and bagpipe bands.

HOLIDAYS

National

New Year's Day: January 1

Waitangi Day: February 6

Good Friday and Easter Monday: late March/early April

Anzac Day: April 25

Queen's Birthday: first Monday of June

Labour Day: fourth Monday of October

Christmas Day: December 25

Boxing Day: December 26

Local

Wellington Day: January 22

Aukland: January 29

Northland: January 29

Nelson: February 1

Taranaki: March 8

Otago: March 23

Southland: March 23

Hawke's Bay: October 17

Marlborough: November 1

Westland: December 1

Canterbury: November 16

Winter

Ski fields throughout the country begin opening in June, with **downhill racing** held through winter at the larger South Island resorts. "Powder 8" and speed skiing events attracting international fields are another winter staple on the South Island. Queenstown and Wanaka hold **winter festivals** in July and August respectively. **New Zealand Agricultural Field Days,** at Mystery Creek near Hamilton, take place in early winter, offering everything a modern farmer would like to see. Wellington offers the **Wellington Hurdles and Steeplechase Meeting** in July.

Spring

Many towns host an annual **Agricultural and Pastoral Show,** with judging of produce and animals, arts and crafts sales, and a wide variety of exhibitions. One of the largest of these is the weeklong **Canterbury A&P Show** in the middle of November.

HOLIDAYS

On major nationwide holidays (see chart) a newcomer can quickly feel stranded as New Zealand appears to close down. Try not to travel to a new place on a holiday, don't count on attractions and restaurants being open, and stock up on necessities the day before. Also, many regions, individual cities, and towns celebrate their anniversary days by taking a holiday (see chart). If the holiday falls Tues.–Thurs., it's celebrated on the previous Monday. If it falls Fri.–Sun., it's celebrated on the following Monday. Almost all the shops close except for milk bars, usually on the outskirts of town; plan accordingly.

ON THE ROAD

Accommodations

A great thing about traveling through New Zealand is the wide range of accommodations available to suit all budgets. Free campsites, inexpensive holiday parks, budget dorm beds for backpackers, cozy bed-and-breakfasts, farmstays, holiday homes, first-class motels, hotels, and luxury lodges—New Zealand has it all. Don't be afraid to try something new while traveling through the country—traditional hostels have private rooms, campgrounds have motel rooms, and some of the fanciest hotels have rooms set aside for budget travelers.

In addition to the information provided below and individual accommodations detailed through this book, the **Automobile Association** produces the annual *Accommodation Guide* listing all hotels and motels. It can be purchased at AA offices throughout the country. Another source of pre-trip planning is the website: www.jasons.co.nz.

HOTELS AND MOTELS

Hotels

Hotels come in all shapes and sizes, and have just one thing in common—they are licensed to serve alcohol. This means that a "hotel" can be an old pub with a few basic rooms upstairs or, at the other end of the scale, a luxurious, upmarket chain hotel such as a Hyatt or Hilton.

In the old pub hotels, rooms cost from $25 s, $30 d; they often (but not always) share bathrooms and have a communal lounge area. Generally rooms lack a television or telephone. Some old hotels have been restored, offering old-style luxury from $60 s, $80 d. These establishments often are called "boutique hotels."

New Zealand has plenty of first-class hotels, including widely recognized international hotel chains. Found in all major cities and tourist areas, they cost from $180 s or d. The Tourist Hotel Corporation of New Zealand (THC) once operated a string of first-class hotels throughout the country, but all have been sold. Most of the buildings have retained their former glory and are in the most beautiful areas, have the best views,

and are often the center of activities in remote areas. Even if you're camping down the road, you'll probably visit one during your trip—to buy tour tickets, eat (some have reasonable cafes as well as first-class restaurants), be entertained, or just admire the architecture (e.g., the Grand Chateau in Tongariro National Park).

Motels

For the most part, New Zealand motels are very different from the usual motels of other countries. Each room is a complete apartment—great value for the price. For about $70–120 s or d, you get a living room with TV; a fully equipped kitchen including utensils, pots and pans, and toaster (occasionally even a blender); a bathroom with shower; and sometimes even your own washer and dryer. A "studio" is a one-room unit; one-, two-, and three-bedroom units have separate sleeping areas. Motels often also provide a swimming pool, spa, playground, and/or other facilities. Many motels belong to major chains but are privately run, and the owners are friendly and eager to suggest places to see, things to do, and good local restaurants. "Motor lodges" and "motor inns" are generally larger properties, with only some rooms having a kitchen, but with a restaurant on-site.   Major chains represented in New Zealand include **Best Western,** website: www.bestwestern.co.nz; **Golden Chain,** website: www.goldenchain.co.nz; **Mainstay,** website: www.mainstay.co.nz; **Manor Motor Inns,** website: www.manorinns.co.nz; and **Pacifica,** website: www.pacificahotels.co.nz. Other chains, such as **Accor,** website: accorhotels.com.au, manage a wide range of properties under a variety of brand names. Before you leave home, check these websites for discounted Internet rates.

Some motel chains offer a package containing both accommodation and car rental vouchers for a reasonable price. To get the savings, you must buy the package overseas. The drawback is that you have to specify a date to start the deal and use the vouchers consecutively every night. The vouchers

ON THE ROAD

© ANDREW HEMPSTEAD

Staying in an old hotel is a great way to save a few dollars while also experiencing traditional Kiwi hospitality. Pictured is the Harbour View Hotel in Raglan, where a comfortable double room costs $70 per night.

cover accommodation in motels all around New Zealand—you usually get the least fancy rooms but they're still very comfortable. A list of applicable motels comes with the vouchers, and booking is not absolutely necessary—unless you're traveling around the country during peak vacation periods.

BED-AND-BREAKFASTS

Bed-and-breakfasts, most of which are very comfortable and full of character, run about $35–180 s, $55–250 d per night, depending on the locality and facilities provided. The breakfasts usually are hearty enough to last until dinner. They're a great way to meet New Zealanders and are very popular, especially in the larger cities. If you have some idea of what area you want to stay in and if you'll be there during a vacation period, it's wise to book a room ahead of time.

The New Zealand Bed and Breakfast Book, updated annually by Moonshine Press and online at website: www.bnb.co.nz, is invaluable for those visitors who enjoy the personal feel of staying in private homes.

Farmstays

Farmstays are simply farm-based bed-and-breakfasts. Guests can either join in farm activities or just stay there and do their own thing. Many offer extras such as pool, tennis court, horseback riding, golf, hunting, and fishing. Some accommodations are in family homes with shared facilities; some may be in separate houses. A stay can range from one night with breakfast to several weeks' full board, and prices vary accordingly at about $70–150 d per night, depending on the activities offered.

HOLIDAY HOMES

Many holiday homes, or "baches," throughout New Zealand are available for rent when the owners are not occupying them. The best way to find out what's available and where is to buy a copy of *Baches and Holiday Homes to Rent* by Mark and Elizabeth Greening. Available at bookstores or online at website: www.holidayhomes.co.nz, the 2002 edition lists 700 properties and retails for $19.95.

BACKPACKER LODGES

YHA New Zealand

New Zealand has 57 YHA hostels offering inexpensive comfortable lodging and plenty of good company. Many of the hostels, ranging from cozy little farmhouses to wonders of modern architecture, are in prime locations—often not far from the center of local attractions, and they're great places to meet Kiwis and overseas travelers. Sleeping in bunk beds in single-sex dorms (most YHA properties now also have double rooms), guests share communal bathroom, kitchen, living room, and laundry; rates $12–18 pp depending on the facilities provided. You often need to supply linen or a sleeping bag, or rent it for a small nightly fee.

You don't have to be a member of the YHA/Hostelling International, but members save $3 per night on accommodation in affiliated properties. Other benefits come with membership—discount car rental; discounts on air, rail, bus, and ferry travel (up to 50 percent); discounts on some attraction admissions; special package holidays (ski packages); and discounts on some commercially operated activities (such as rafting). You can obtain your membership overseas (it's less expensive to join in your home country) or in New Zealand from any YHA office. In New Zealand, the joining fee is $10, then $30 annually for membership, or pay a $3 per night surcharge for 10 nights to gain membership. Memberships are valid internationally. Available at all hostels is the handy *YHA New Zealand Accommodation Guide;* it tells you where all the hostels are, and what each hostel is like, and lists local activities and attractions.

Hostels fill up rapidly during vacation periods and school holidays, but you can book a bed—a good idea if the hostel is in a popular tourist resort or major city. Contact the individual hostel or, at least two weeks in advance, write, call, or email the **YHA New Zealand National Reservations Centre,** P.O. Box 436, Christchurch, tel. 03/379-9808, email: book@yha.org.nz. Bookings require advance payment. YHA New Zealand maintains a detailed website at www.yha.org.nz.

Worldwide Hostelling Associations

YHA New Zealand is a member of the **International Youth Hostel Federation,** a worldwide organization that represents 4,500 hostels in 60 countries. Joining the affiliate association in your home country entitles you to reciprocal rights in New Zealand. Local contact addresses include **Hostelling International-American Youth Hostels,** Suite 840, 733 15th St. NW, Washington, DC 20005, tel. 202/783-6161, website: www.hiayh.org; **Hostelling International,** 400-205 Catherine St., Ottawa, Canada, ON K2P 1C3, tel. 613/237-7884, website: www.hostellingintl.ca; **YHA Australia,** 422 Kent St., Sydney, NSW 2000, Australia, tel. 02/9261-1111, website: www.yha.com; and **YHA England and Wales,** Trevelyan House, St. Stephen's Hill, St. Albans, Herts. AL1 2DY, England, tel. (0170) 870-8808, website: www.yha.org.uk. For other countries, click through the links on the International Youth Hostel Federation website: www.iyhf.com, to your country of residence.

Backpacker Lodges

You can find privately-run budget lodges (known in New Zealand as "backpackers") throughout the country. In no part of the world is this form of accommodation more popular, and as a consequence, budget travelers are spoiled by both choice and standard. These lodges, primarily catering to those traveling on a budget, appeal to everyone, with the choice of bunk-bed dorms, and single and double rooms; shared bathroom, kitchen, and laundry; a common room; and a laid-back atmosphere where it's usually a breeze to make new friends. Often extras are provided, such as bicycles for guest use, swimming pools, transportation, and more. Expect to pay $14–22 pp for a single bed in a dormitory that may have anywhere from three to twelve beds, $14–28 pp in a double or twin room (with shared bath), and $16–30 pp for a single room.

Pick up the latest "blue book" (officially the *BBH Accommodation Guide*) at tourist information centers; it lists almost 300 of the best lodges, rated by guests and given a percentage that is generally accurate and a great help in choosing a place to spend the night. The guide is produced by **Budget Backpacker Hostels New Zealand,** website: www.backpack.co.nz, which also offers the **Club Card.** At a price of $40, this card generates an automatic discount at all listed lodges, includes $20 worth of phone calls, and is good for a variety of other discounts—all in all an excellent investment that pays for itself quickly.

CAMPGROUNDS AND MOTOR CAMPS
Free, or Almost Free
If you enjoy camping out and have a tent and stove, New Zealand is a camper's paradise. You can put up a tent pretty much anywhere off the beaten track—but avoid camping close to tramping tracks and areas designated as "reserves." No Camping signs are only too obvious in areas where you're not permitted to camp—those who camp there anyway may be asked to move on or be fined. In remote but popular areas (such as along the road to Milford Sound), campsites with limited facilities and a source of drinking water have been provided at minimal charge ($2–8 pp per night). Serviced DOC campgrounds (flush toilets, hot showers, kitchen, laundry) are $6–8 pp. Over 900 backcountry **huts** are scattered throughout the forests of New Zealand; DOC staff have first option, but if they're not full you can stay in the huts for $2–10 pp per night. Some have stoves, others open fireplaces—some have no cooking facilities. The maximum stay is three nights and you can't book them. In peak periods they fill up rapidly—take camping and cooking gear just in case.

Holiday Parks
Holiday parks (also called motor camps) are one of New Zealand's best accommodation values, and great places to meet fellow travelers—particularly vacationing New Zealanders. They provide accommodation options ranging from tent sites to motel units (see Holiday Park Terminology for detailed descriptions). Facilities vary greatly, but generally, each park has a large communal kitchen with full cooking facilities (provide your own crockery, utensils, pots and pans), a fridge,

ON THE ROAD

HOLIDAY PARK TERMINOLOGY

With so many accommodation options at holiday parks, it can be confusing trying to work out exactly what means what. The following descriptions and accompanying price ranges should help:

Campsite: a camping site with no services ($8–10 pp)

Caravan site: a site with power and other services ($10–12 pp)

On-site caravan: a caravan (trailer) with cooking facilities. Generally bathroom facilities are shared and no linen is supplied but can be rented ($25–45 s or d)

Cabins: the most basic cabins have bunk or single beds with no linen. Cooking and bathroom facilities are shared ($25–45)

En suite cabin: a cabin with its own bathroom, but shared cooking facilities ($35–60)

Tourist cabin: a cabin with cooking facilities and hot and cold water, with a shared communal bathroom ($35–70)

Tourist flat: contains both a kitchen and bathroom. Frequently has a separate bedroom and television ($50–85)

Motel unit: bedding and towels provided in a self-contained room serviced daily ($70–120)

Backpacker lodge: many holiday parks have a self-contained building with dormitory beds, shared bathrooms, and a communal kitchen ($14–18 pp)

microwave, and dining area; a coin-operated laundry; and separate male and female bathrooms. Bed linen and blankets can be rented at most holiday parks, but it'll work out cheaper to hit a large department store and purchase your own before hitting the road. Additional facilities may include a TV and/or game room, tour booking service, bike rentals, basic groceries, public telephones, public Internet access, an outdoor swimming pool, a barbecue area, a sauna, and a playground for the kids.

Food

New Zealand is a land of plenty. Rich, creamy dairy products; lamb "fed on lush meadow grass and mother's milk"; and the brown, furry kiwifruit (brought over from central China almost a century ago, it was called a Chinese gooseberry and renamed for export) are just a few of the many delicious items New Zealand produces. Most of the food should be familiar to visitors; New Zealand boasts French, Greek, Chinese, Mexican, Japanese, Thai, Italian, East Indian, North American, Vietnamese, and vegetarian, as well as traditional New Zealand and Polynesian restaurants. A Maori *hangi* (feast), featuring Maori specialties steamed to perfection in an underground oven, is an eating experience that shouldn't be missed.

WHAT TO EAT

Meats

Lamb is naturally one of the most popular traditional dishes. Often cooked as a juicy roast with garlic and rosemary and served slightly pink with a tangy mint sauce, lamb is generally on the menu of almost every restaurant in the country. Hogget, or one-year-old lamb, is stronger tasting than younger lamb but not as strong as mutton. Beef is excellent and reasonably priced in restaurants—and nothing beats sizzling, thick juicy steaks and sausages, crisp salads, chilled wine or beer, good company, and cicadas singing from the trees at a traditional New Zealand "barby." Chicken or "chook" is another favorite. Sausages or "bangers" come in all shapes and sizes and are most frequently served at barbecues. New Zealanders are also partial to farm-raised or "homegrown" venison (expensive unless bought patty-form in a venison burger), veal, duck and pheasant (some of the sporting lodge restaurants specialize in game), and wild pork. If you like experimenting with different tastes, try muttonbird—it's a Maori delicacy that tastes like fish-flavored chicken.

Hot meat pies loaded with lamb or beef and gravy enclosed in flaky pastry, commonly served over the counter at bakeries or pub-style with mashed potatoes, peas, and gravy, are virtually a national dish. If you're a pie fancier, try the many kinds of savory pies—egg and bacon, pork, and mincemeat; they make a quick and filling, inexpensive lunch. When you're in the mood for potato chips, try salt and vinegar flavor.

Seafood

New Zealand's bountiful variety of shellfish includes *tuatua, pipi, paua,* (abalone), mussels, and oysters (several varieties), scallops (great in Marlborough, season Aug.–Feb.), and crayfish (actually spiny rock lobster, but crayfish sounds more appealing). Other seafood, such as tuna, marlin, blue nose cod, flounder, *hapuku,* kingfish, John Dory, snapper, squid, and *tarakihi,* are all good tasting and widely available. Bluff oysters (try them fresh during the winter in the south of the South Island) and marinated mussels are very popular with connoisseurs—if you can't get fresh, look for them canned in the supermarket. Freshwater-fish lovers can easily find salmon (fresh and smoked), whitebait (tiny transparent fish fried in batter or cooked in fritters—another New Zealand delicacy), and eels. To sample a rainbow or brown trout fresh from a crystal-clear stream is a real treat—both are superb. Trout are not sold commercially, but if you catch one yourself (it's not too difficult!), most restaurants will prepare it for you on request. Fish and chips, wrapped in paper and newspaper from the local take-away or

> *Vegemite and Marmite, salty spreads made from yeast extract, are usually provided for serious toast spreading —New Zealander, Australian, and British children grow up on Vegemite or Marmite sandwiches and seem to experience withdrawals if deprived for some length of time.*

HOKI OR HAKE?

New Zealand is a wonderful place to indulge in seafood, but there's more to that chalkboard of freshly caught delicacies than you might imagine. Like red wines made from different grapes, each fish species has its own distinct taste—but figuring out exactly which is which can be difficult.

Renaming foods to make them more appealing and user-friendly is a recent trend, epitomized in New Zealand by the once obscure Chinese gooseberry, which is now successfully marketed around the world as kiwifruit. For the most part, though, when we buy fruit or vegetables or meat, we all know exactly what it is and where it came from. Seafood, especially fish, is a different matter and its true origin can be very confusing, especially when it's been battered and deep-fried at a corner fish-and-chip shop.

Hoki is the most important species to the New Zealand commercial fishing industry, but you'll rarely see it sold under this name. It's the standard at fish-and-chip shops (and the fish portion of your Fillet O' Fish at McDonalds), but it's usually sold as **blue hake,** or **whiptail,** or even as **whiting,** which is a completely different species. Australia, the biggest importer of *hoki,* sells this same fish as **blue grenadier.**

The *hapuku* (or *hapuka*) you see on the menu will more often than not actually be a filet of the unimaginatively named **blue nose cod.** The more expensive **sea bass** may also be blue nose cod, or it may in fact be hapuku. **Snapper** is arguably the best-tasting saltwater fish caught in New Zealand waters. It's also among the most expensive, which leads to **sea perch** being sold as **small snapper.** Occasionally a restaurant will go to extremes, "Europeanizing" the species by calling it **schnapper** to give an exotic air to what is already a wonderfully tasting fish.

The worst-kept secret among New Zealand's fish-loving public is the way **shark** is marketed. With a reputation as man-eaters, you'd think we'd be eager to get our own back, but no, shark is generally sold as **flake** and the unattractively named **dogfish shark** is marketed as **lemonfish.**

fish-and-chips shop, are one of the best and least expensive ways to sample a wide variety of New Zealand seafood.

Fruit and Veggies

Fresh fruit and vegetables are abundant throughout the year. Try some of the more exotic ones if you have the chance. A few you may not recognize are aubergines (eggplants), beetroot (red beets), bilberries (blueberries), courgettes (small zucchinis), feijoas (an exotic-tasting fruit available April and May), Chinese gooseberries or kiwifruit (high in vitamin C, best May–Dec.), *kumara* (a root vegetable similar to a sweet potato), rock melon (cantaloupe), and tamarillos or tree tomatoes (red, jellylike fruit found May–December). Strawberries, raspberries, boysenberries, and loganberries are best in January and February, melons and avocados after Christmas, passion fruit in March and April, and asparagus in September.

Dairy Foods

New Zealand's rich dairy foods are lethal to the waistline but oh-so-good. Ice cream, especially the fruit-flavored ice creams loaded with chunks of real fruit, takes top place for any sweet tooth. Creamy milk is still delivered in glass bottles (New Zealanders generally prefer glass to cartons, though both are available), and a wide variety of tasty cheeses, including local camembert, feta, gouda, romano, gruyère, New Zealand blue vein, brie, and cheddar, are readily available.

Desserts

Every tearoom in the country offers a variety of cakes filled with fresh cream, custard- or fruit-filled tarts, and cream buns. The famous and traditional dessert, pavlova, is made of meringue, crunchy on the outside and gooey inside, filled with whipped cream and fresh fruit—traditionally strawberries and kiwifruit, dribbled with passion fruit. Both New Zealand and Australia take pride in the invention of this dessert (natives of each argue over where it was created) in honor of dancer Anna Pavlova, who visited New Zealand in the 1920s. Feeling peckish yet?

© ANDREW HEMPSTEAD

"Refreshment Rooms" are a great place to enjoy local hospitality.

MEALS

Breakfast

One of the things New Zealand lacks is chain-type restaurants serving cheap breakfasts at breakfast time and all hours. The best breakfasts are undoubtedly provided by bed-and-breakfast guesthouses, usually either continental—orange juice, rolls or croissants, and coffee—or cooked breakfasts ("a grill")—eggs, bacon or sausages, grilled tomatoes, toast, and marmalade. Usually at least one local café or hotel in each town is open for breakfast. Vegemite and Marmite, salty spreads made from yeast extract, are usually provided for serious toast spreading, as well as jam or jelly—New Zealander, Australian, and British children grow up on Vegemite or Marmite sandwiches and seem to experience withdrawals if deprived for some length of time. An alternative is to have a reasonably priced brunch (from about 10 A.M.) in one of the many tearooms scattered across the land.

Lunch

The least expensive and most delicious way to have lunch is to stop at a deli and buy a loaf of bread, butter, and a variety of cheeses, fresh fruit, and other goodies. Hot meat pies are also tasty and cheap, and numerous take-aways sell fish and chips, sausages, pies, battered and deep-fried goods, and of course hamburgers. Another alternative is the tearoom. You'll find tearooms in just about every town in New Zealand. They start with morning tea at about 10–11 A.M., progress to lunch, and follow it with afternoon tea—but eating in a tearoom can often end up costing you more because you can't resist trying something new. They sell all sorts of hot pies, sandwiches, and filled rolls (typically meat and salad, just salad, or egg salad and cheese), and other intriguing morsels such as baked beans and melted cheese on toast, and fat sausages filled with mashed potato and cheese. All sorts of desserts are available.

Dinner

Dinner is often called "tea" by New Zealanders. Cooking your own dinner is the least-expensive method, but reasonably priced take-aways are everywhere—Chinese is one of the most popular. Pubs offer good deals on dinners, and some chain restaurants (such as Cobb & Co., attached to pubs) offer substantial meals at fairly reasonable prices. Many restaurants have a special BYO (bring your own) license that lets you carry your own beer and wine in. This means they don't need a liquor or wine license so the food is generally less expensive. Some of the fanciest restaurants have a strict dress code requiring men to wear jackets and ties (almost phased out) and women to be "smartly dressed"; all restaurants require decent attire and you may not enter without a shirt and shoes. If you think you want to splurge on a meal or entertainment sometime during your stay, take a good jacket, dressy dress, and appropriate shoes, in case—old battered tennis shoes and jeans are somewhat frowned upon. Tipping is neither required nor expected, but is appreciated if extra-good service is given.

WHAT TO DRINK

New Zealand has excellent public water supplies, and tap (faucet) water is safe to drink throughout the country. All the usual fruit juices, mineral waters, and soft drinks are available—try "Lemon and Paeroa," lemon-flavored mineral water from Paeroa in the North Island. A wide range of beer and wine, both local and imported, is available from licensed hotels or pubs, bottle shops (often attached to the hotel), or discount bottle stores. For the best deals and choices, pick out something at the discount bottle store, and then take it to a BYO restaurant; a small corkage fee is generally charged for opening the bottle. Discount bottle stores offer alcohol at bargain prices but you have to buy at least two gallons.

Getting There

BY AIR

The only practical way to get to New Zealand is by air. Ticket prices vary greatly between airlines and how and where you buy your ticket (see Cutting Flight Costs), but one thing you can't control are seasonal fluctuations in prices. Low season (also called "off peak") in the Northern Hemisphere is high season in the Southern. To benefit from departing at low-season prices, you must leave the Northern Hemisphere between June and October. If you head for New Zealand in December or January, you pay high season (also called "peak") prices, generally considerably higher. However, high, shoulder, and low-season fares are not standardized throughout all airlines—call them and find out their seasons.

Before you buy your ticket, check the prices on special passes for domestic air travel within New Zealand—some passes are valid only if bought overseas or in conjunction with an international ticket (see below).

From Australia

The majority of international travelers to New Zealand are from Australia, but for visitors from other parts of the world, the close proximity of these two countries allows a stop in both for only a slightly more expensive ticket. The short flight across the Tasman Sea takes about 3.5 hours and crosses two time zones (as a Qantas pilot once announced upon arrival in New Zealand from Australia, "Please turn your watches forward two hours and back 20 years"). National carrier **Air New Zealand,** tel. 09/366-2400 or 0800/737-000, website: www.airnz.co.nz; and **Qantas,** tel. 13–13–13, website: www.qantas.com.au, offer the most flights between the two countries; from Sydney, Melbourne, and Brisbane to Auckland, Wellington, and Christchurch. Most of the airlines listed in the following two sections also fly between Australia and New Zealand.

From North America

Air New Zealand, tel. 800/227-4500, website: www.airnz.com; **United Airlines,** tel. 800/241-6522, website: www.ual.com; and **Qantas,** website: www.qantas.com.au, fly from the U.S. to Auckland via a variety of routes. The route taken by Air New Zealand is most interesting because stops are made in Pacific islands such as Fiji. From Canada, **Air Canada,** tel. 888/247-2262, website: www.aircanada.ca, has a code-sharing agreement with Air New Zealand to New

CUTTING FLIGHT COSTS

In today's topsy-turvy world of air travel, finding the cheapest fare and best-suited route can be a challenge. The **Internet** has changed the way many people shop for tickets, but even if you use this invaluable tool for preliminary research, having a travel agent that you are comfortable in dealing with—who takes the time to call around, does some research to get you the best fare, and helps you take advantage of any available special offers or promotional deals—is an invaluable asset in starting your travels off on the right foot.

In the first instance, though, to get an idea of what your agent should be able to come up with, call the airlines or check their websites and compare fares. Also look in the travel sections of major newspapers—particularly in weekend editions—where budget fares and package deals are frequently advertised. **Flight Centre,** which began as a discount airline ticket agency, has spread its wings around the world and now guarantees to match any other published fare. This company combines easy-to-navigate websites with travel agencies in towns and cities across the United States, Canada, Great Britain, Australia, and New Zealand. Contacts include www.flightcenter.com (U.S.); www.flightcentre.ca (Canada); www.flightcentre.co.uk (Great Britain); www.flightcentre.com.au (Australia); and www.flightcentre.co.nz (New Zealand).

Many cheaper tickets have strict restrictions regarding changes of flight dates, lengths of stay, and cancellations. A general rule: the cheaper the ticket, the more restrictions. Most travelers today fly on APEX (advance-purchase excursion) fares. These are usually the best value, though some (and, occasionally, many) restrictions apply. These might include minimum and maximum stays and unchangeable itineraries (or hefty penalties for changes); tickets may also be nonrefundable once purchased.

When you have found the best fare, open a **frequent flyer** membership with the airline—**Air New Zealand,** part of the Star Alliance, has a popular program that makes rewards easily obtainable.

Zealand. The prices below are the least expensive quoted for travel from the U.S. West Coast (San Francisco or Los Angeles) to Auckland. In the U.S., the farther you live from the West Coast, the more expensive the fare will be. Keep in mind that the names of promotional flights change, as do the prices—use this information only as a guide.

The less expensive the flight, the less likely you are to get a free stopover. Ask about stopovers when you first make inquiries. Also ask if taxes (domestic departure, foreign departure, surcharges, and U.S. customs fees) are included in the quote. From Los Angeles to Auckland, you can expect to pay about US $1,050 round-trip in low season, and about US $1,300 round-trip in high season, for up to a one-month stay. Advance-purchase fares are usually less expensive.

From the Rest of the World
The following is an outline of other international airlines flying into New Zealand, with local (Auckland) telephone numbers given.

From other points in the Pacific: **Air Caledonie,** tel. 09/373-2605; **Air China,** tel. 09/366-1862; **Air Nauru,** tel. 09/636-6444; **Air Niugini,** tel. 09/977-2230; **Air Pacific,** tel. 09/256-8440; **Air Vanuatu,** tel. 09/373-3435; **Garuda,** tel. 09/366-1862; **Polynesian Airlines,** tel. 09/309-5396; **Royal Tongan Airlines,** tel. 09/379-4454; and **Solomon Airlines,** tel. 09/308-9098.

From Asia: **Cathay Pacific,** tel. 09/275-0847; **EVA Airways,** tel. 09/358-8300; **Garuda,** tel. 09/366-1855; **JAL,** tel. 09/379-3202; **Korean Air,** tel. 09/914-2000; **Malaysian Airlines,** tel. 09/379-3743; **Singapore Airlines,** tel. 09/303-2129; and **Thai Airways,** tel. 09/377-3886.

British Airways, tel. 09/356-8690, is the only European airline that flies to New Zealand. From mainland Europe, the airlines of many countries have code-sharing agreements with Air New Zealand or Asian airlines. Contact your local national carrier for details.

From South America, **Aerolineas Argentinas,** tel. 09/379-3675, provides the only air link to New Zealand.

Getting Around

New Zealand is one of the easiest countries in the world to get around—good roads and an excellent public transportation system get you anywhere you want to go. Local information centers, located in nearly every town, have the latest on transportation routes, fares, and special passes; many act as booking agents for bus, domestic air, rail, and ferry transportation. These centers are listed under "Information" in each chapter.

PUBLIC TRANSPORTATION

Air

The major domestic airline is **Air New Zealand,** tel. 09/366-2400 or 0800/737-000, website: www.airnz.co.nz, with scheduled flights between all major cities, resorts, and large provincial towns. Air New Zealand offers an "Explore New Zealand Air Pass" for three ($520) to eight ($1480) domestic flight sectors, but you *must buy it overseas in conjunction with an incoming Air New Zealand ticket.*

Rail

Tranz Scenic operates all long-distance passenger trains in New Zealand. On the North Island, the main line runs between Auckland and Wellington, with a spur line dead-ending at Rotorua. On the South Island, a line follows the east coast from Picton to Christchurch and then on to Invercargill. From Christchurch, the famous *TranzAlpine* line crosses the spectacular Southern Alps to terminate at Greymouth on the west coast. The cost of rail travel is slightly higher than by bus, but a variety of discounts are available by traveling at certain times of day and by reservation. For example, the 12-hour Auckland-Wellington trip costs $70–150 depending on the time of travel, class of travel, and advance booking. Central reservations numbers are 04/498-3303 or 800/802-802, or book online at website: www.tranzscenic.co.nz. Bookings can also be made through any information center.

Bus

The bus services of the two largest coach companies—**Intercity,** tel. 09/913-6100, website: www.intercitycoach.co.nz; and **Newmans,** tel. 0800/777-707, website: www.newmanscoach.co.nz—cover every major town in New Zealand. Small towns and out-of-the-way tourist spots are generally served by smaller companies, often on demand only. Intercity is the national carrier, with a complex network of bus routes on both islands. Intercity **Travelpasses** allow great flexibility along 17 popular routes over a three-month period; the $588 pass allows travel between Auckland and Christchurch via Rotorua, Wellington, Queenstown, and Milford Sound. Both these bus companies have passes that are run in conjunction with Tranz Scenic rail services, Interisland Line ferries, and Air New Zealand. Check these companies' websites for details.

Shuttle buses run on scheduled routes and on-demand throughout the country. They range from a full-size bus to a car run by the local cab company, but most often are small minivans. The service is efficient and cheaper than the major bus companies, and you'll often get a colorful commentary thrown in for free. Shuttle bus service usually links up with Intercity's and Newmans' schedules, so when you arrive at a bus depot, these local companies will be waiting. Although we have listed the shuttle buses in the Transportation sections of the travel chapters, the best way to find out local routes and schedules is at any information center.

Backpacker buses offer another way to get around the country cheaply. Some are simply an inexpensive bus service, while others are more like a "Green Tortoise" experience. The first bus to cater exclusively to the backpacker market, the **Westcoast Express,** tel. 03/546-6703, is still going strong, and is typical of backpacker buses. It offers one route, taking six days to travel between the South Island towns of Nelson and Queenstown, stopping each night at budget accommodations, and charging just $109 each way. **Kiwi Experience,** tel. 09/366-9830, website: www.kiwiexperience.com, is a similar operation, but with a network of routes throughout the country. It allows time for activities along the way, overnights at backpacker lodges, and stops at supermarkets for food. Attracting the young "party" crowd, it offers 20 itineraries, with ticketing sold for each route or for a set period of time (up to six months costs $918).

We've heard many good things about **Magic Travellers Network,** tel. 09/358-5600, website: www.magicbus.co.nz, which operates very modern coaches along a network encompassing both islands. The "Magic Bus" offers a lot more flexibility than Kiwi Experience; travelers can get on and off as with regular scheduled buses and use whatever facilities they desire. The company also makes activity and food stops, as well as books accommodations and guarantees seats. A sample fare is Auckland to Queenstown for $345 (minimum eight days).

Ferry

The least expensive and most enjoyable way to travel between the North and South Islands is by ferry with **Interisland Line,** tel. 04/498-3302 or 0800/802-802; website: www.interisland-line.co.nz. The company offers daily services on three modern vessels. All three take passengers and vehicles, and have cafeterias and bars on board; the trip across from Wellington to Picton takes about 3.5 hours (under two hours on the *Lynx*). One-way fares are adult $52, child $31, vehicle $179. Check the Interisland Line website for discounts. If you're renting a car on either island, arrange to pick up another on the other side. If you have your own car, transporting it to the other island costs from $128. More details can be found in the special topic Crossing Cook Strait in the Wellington chapter.

DRIVING

The most important thing to remember is *you drive on the left-hand side of the road in New Zealand* (as in the U.K. and Australia). Try to get the rules of the road before you drive, espe-

cially if you're used to driving on the right side of the road (and look up the rules of "round-abouts").

The **New Zealand Automobile Association,** website: www.nzaa.co.nz, is invaluable if you're a member. With proof of any overseas AA membership, you can pick up its excellent maps covering every area of New Zealand in detail, accommodation guides covering everything from tent sites to first-class hotels, and touring information. Offices are located in all major cities and most towns. If you join the AA ($96 for six months), you get assistance with emergency breakdowns—simple problems are fixed on the spot or your vehicle is towed to the nearest service station. Use an AA card to prepay car rental and you save 12.5 percent GST.

Petrol is about $1 per liter throughout the country.

Car Rental

To rent a car you must be at least 21 years old, have a current international driver's license (or a domestic permit from Australia, Austria, Canada, Fiji, Germany, Namibia, The Netherlands, South Africa, Switzerland, the U.K., or the U.S.), and have comprehensive automobile insurance (arranged by the rental agencies).

All major international car rental agencies usually offer both car and camper-van rentals, as do many other small rental outfits throughout the country. Most agencies include unlimited mileage in the daily rate, but check before signing up. In summer, the major agencies charge from $80 a day for a compact vehicle, discounted up to 50 percent in the off-season. These agencies, along with their Auckland telephone numbers and international websites, include: **Avis,** tel. 09/526-2847, website: www.avis.com; **Budget,** tel. 09/375-2230, website: www.budget.com; **Hertz,** tel. 09/367-6350, website: www.hertz .com; **Thrifty,** 09/309-0111, website: www .thrifty.com; and **National,** tel. 09/275-0666, website: www.nationalcar.com. As the main gateway, Auckland offers most of these agencies (about 80).

The smaller, local car rental agencies offer small economy cars such as Toyotas, Hondas,

Mitsubishis, and Nissans, typically one or two years old, starting at about $40 per day for unlimited mileage or $30 per day plus about 15 cents per km. Some fly-by-night agencies have been known to rent unreliable cars and are reluctant to return your money even when you've been stranded; ask for recommendations from fellow travelers. **Scotties,** tel. 09/630-2625 or 0800/630-2625, website: www.scotties.co.nz, maintains a large fleet of vehicles with reasonable rates. Other agencies may offer cheaper deals, but for reliability (vehicles are all only a couple of years old and covered by the maximum insurance available), this agency is best. Scotties also has an outlet in Christchurch, the perfect opportunity for a one-way trip through the country (for a $50 drop-off charge). Other recommendations are **A1 Rent-A-Car,** tel. 03/349-8022, website: a1rentacar.co.nz; **About New Zealand Rental Cars,** tel. 09/256-9016 or 0800/455-565; **Dollar Save Car Hire,** tel. 09/366-0646; **Easy Car Rental,** tel. 09/275-0037 or 0800/775-775, website: www.easyrentals.co.nz; **Ideal Rentals,** tel. 09/262-0464 or 0800/736-225, website: www.ideal-cars.co.nz; **Metropolitan Rentals,** tel. 09/630-2030, website: www .metropolitan.co.nz; **Omega,** tel. 0800/525-210; **Nationwide,** tel. 09/275-4811; **New Zealand Rent-a-car,** tel. 09/308-9005, website: www .nzcars.co.nz; and **Quality,** tel. 09/275-4811.

Camper-van Rental

Cruising around New Zealand in a rented camper-van is an extremely popular way to see the country. With inexpensive and excellent camping facilities, it's only the initial rental cost that can be steep. Many companies offer camper-vans and fully-equipped motor homes, usually on an unlimited-kilometer rate only and for a minimum number of days. Most have low-season rates May–Sept., but in summer, you must reserve well in advance. **Maui,** tel. 09/275-3013 or 0800/651-080, website: www.maui-rentals.com, is a large operation based near the airport, with transfers from throughout the city to the depot and hundreds of vehicles of many configurations. Other agencies specializing in camper-van

rentals include: **Adventure Deluxe Motor homes,** tel. 09/256-0255, website: www.nzmotorhomes.co.nz; **Backpacker Camper-vans,** tel. 09/255-0620 or 0800/422-267; **Britz,** tel. 09/275-9090 or 0800/831-900, website: www.britz.com; and **Kea Campers,** tel. 09/444-4902, website: www.keacampers.com.

Buying a Vehicle

If you plan to be in New Zealand for several months, one of the cheapest ways to travel is to buy a used car as soon as you arrive, then sell it when you leave.

Used-car dealers are required by law to provide a warrant of fitness valid for six months on all cars sold. This allows you to buy something fairly cheaply that must run for at least six months. However, expect to pay at least $1,000–3,000 for a used car that still has some life in it. You hear stories of those who have bought a good used car from a dealer, traveled around New Zealand for almost six months, and then re-sold it for more than they originally paid.

You can buy registration for six months (about $150) or one year (about $300). Note: You'll be heavily fined for a vehicle without current warrant of fitness and registration papers. Insurance is also recommended—an insurance company can arrange third party, fire, and theft or full coverage. For the best deal, call the companies advertising in the Yellow Pages of the telephone directory and ask for a quote.

If you belong to an automobile association, you can have the car inspected before you buy at the **Vehicle Inspection Service Centre,** Papakura Ami Building, East St., tel. 09/296-1837—a very wise idea. Reservations are necessary. Or look in the Yellow Pages under "vehicle inspection service" and call for a pre-purchase check quote—usually about $80.

Before you arrive, use the Internet, not so much to find the actual vehicle you intend to buy, but to get an idea of prices. The websites www.autoweb.co.nz and www.carselect.co.nz are a good starting point. The Wednesday and Saturday editions of the Auckland *Herald* and the *Saturday Star* newspapers advertise a large selection of used cars. Also check out notice boards at backpacker lodges and in the Auckland Visitor Centre. While you're at the visitor center, ask for the handout on buying or selling your own car—it even lists and explains newspaper abbreviations such as warrant of fitness, registration, and insurance.

Unique to New Zealand, **car fairs** are held in various locales (shopping center car parks and parking lots) throughout Auckland each weekend. Sellers register their cars ($15–20) and wait for potential buyers, who have the opportunity to view up to 500 cars in one place. Naturally, the best-value cars are sold early in the day, but often sellers drop their prices as the day wears on. Although some buyers pay on the spot, generally a deposit secures a car and final transactions are made early in the working week.

TOURS
Guided Coach Tours
Great Sights, tel. 09/375-4700 or 0800/744-487, website: www.greatsights.co.nz, is a big flashy tour company with day and overnight tours to and from all major cities and resorts.

Several coach companies offer budget tours of New Zealand for the young and the young at heart at a reasonable price. Three of the most popular are **Kiwi Experience,** based in Auckland, tel. 09/366-9830, website: www.kiwiexperience.com; **Flying Kiwi Wilderness Expeditions,** based in Picton, tel. 03/573-8126 or 0800/692-396, website: www.flyingkiwi.com; and **Westcoast Express,** based in Nelson, tel. 03/546-6703.

New Zealand Nature Safaris
These tours are a great way to see some of New Zealand's out-of-the-way places guided by qualified naturalists who combine a love of the outdoors with a genuine desire to spread their knowledge. Tours average $100–120 pp per day, with nights spent camping or in huts and food prepared from a self-contained van. For details contact New Zealand Nature Safaris at tel. 03/547-0171 or 0800/697-232; website: www.nzsafaris.co.nz.

Information and Services

VISAS AND OFFICIALDOM
Rules and regulations come and go. The best way to find out exactly what you need is to visit a reputable travel agent; you can also visit the nearest New Zealand Embassy or New Zealand Consulate General-these are listed on their website: www.immigration.govt.nz.

Immigration
The basic entry requirements for visitors staying up to six months on nonworking visas are a fully paid onward or round-trip ticket, sufficient funds ($1,000 per month, or at least $400 per month if you're staying with a New Zealand citizen or have prepaid accommodation), and a passport (valid for at least three months beyond the date of departure from New Zealand). Australian passport holders and Australian residents with current resident return visas do not need a permit or another visa.

New Zealand has a **visa waiver agreement** with many countries. For residents of these countries, this means you do not need to apply for a visa before arriving. Upon arrival in New Zealand—and after meeting the above requirements-you will be issued a **Visitors Permit** for tourist visits of up to **six months** by British citizens, provided they hold passports that give them the right of permanent residence in the U.K.; for visits up to **three months** by citizens of Austria, Belgium, Canada, Denmark, Finland, France (if normally resident in continental France), Germany, Greece, Iceland, Indonesia, Ireland, Italy, Japan, Kiribati, Liechtenstein, Luxembourg, Malaysia, Malta, Monaco, Nauru, The Netherlands, Norway, Portugal (only if the visitor has the right to enter Portugal for permanent residence), Singapore, Spain, Sweden, Switzerland, Thailand, Tuvalu, and the U.S. (not applicable to American Samoans or any other U.S. nationals); for visits up to **30 days** by citizens of France (normally resident in Tahiti or New Caledonia).

If you wish to stay longer than the above entry permits allow (Australian citizens and citizens of Commonwealth countries and Ireland who live in Australia are exempt), you must get prior permission in the form of a visa. It is illegal to work, make financial gains, study, obtain medical treatment, overstay the period indicated on your entry permit, or settle in New Zealand without special permission before entering the country.

Visas: Citizens of all countries other than those listed above require visas to enter New Zealand. Travel agents usually arrange all necessary visas and other documentation—but allow plenty of time (at least several weeks), especially if you haven't a passport. Another source of information on vacation and work visas is your nearest New Zealand embassy or consulate; find these and all current immigration regulations on their website: www.immigration.govt.nz.

Customs

If you're over 17 years old, in addition to personal effects, you can bring duty-free items into New Zealand worth up to NZ$700, plus 200 cigarettes or 50 cigars or 250 grams of tobacco, 4.5 liters of wine or beer (six 750-milliliter bottles), and 1,125 milliliters of spirits (hard liquor). Contact your own country's customs office to find out what you may bring back duty-free. Items to be left in New Zealand (such as gifts) with a declared value over $110 attract customs charges.

New Zealand is understandably strict on agricultural requirements. Before landing in New Zealand you're required to fill in a declaration form stating whether you have been on a farm within the last 30 days, and what foods, plants, or animal products you are carrying. The "New Zealand—A Growing Land—Passenger Arrival Information" brochure is available from any New Zealand embassy or consulate. If you've been on a farm, your boots or shoes may be examined for dirt. Bicycles and camping equipment, such as tents and sleeping bags, may also be checked for soil particles, insects, and other pests. Attempting to bring in drugs (other than prescription) is ask-

ing for big trouble, as is a dishonest declaration on any official documents—don't risk it.

HEALTH

New Zealand is a healthy country. Vaccinations are not required to enter. There are no dangerous wild animals or poisonous snakes to worry about; the only poisonous spider is the *katipo,* but it's rarely seen.

It's the Water

The drinking water is good tasting and safe to drink from the tap throughout the country. However, *Giardia,* an intestinal parasite, is present in many New Zealand lakes, rivers, and streams (even in very cold water). It is spread by fecal contamination and can be passed to humans as a result of poor personal hygiene, unhygienic food handling, or contaminated drinking water. To avoid contamination, *always* treat drinking water from outdoor sources (lakes, streams, rivers) by boiling it for 10 minutes, by chemical purification with iodine solutions (available at chemist shops/pharmacies), or by filtration through *Giardia*-rated filters (pore size five micrometers or less). If you enjoy soaking in natural hot springs or thermal pools (public or private), keep your head above water at all times and don't let the water enter your nose or ears—there's always the possibility of getting amoebic meningitis (inflammation of the brain) in hot pools.

Medical Needs

Public and private hospitals and medical treatments are of high standards, but it's wise to have health insurance, as medical and hospital treatments due to illness are not free. Accident compensation (covering personal injuries occurring while in New Zealand) is free; it includes compensation for medical and hospital expenses or permanent incapacity directly due to the accident, no matter whose fault it is. (The insurance does not cover a loss of earning ability.)

If you take a prescription drug of any kind, take adequate supplies with you, and the prescription in case you run out. Chemists (pharmacies) are open normal shopping hours, and

ON THE ROAD

they usually have after-hours chemists listed on the door. Also, if you wear eyeglasses or contact lenses, take your prescription or a spare pair.

If you should need an ambulance, dial 111 in major centers; the telephone number is also listed inside public telephone booths and in the front section of all telephone directories.

Tips to Prevent Jet Lag

A long-distance flight causes your body's natural clock to go haywire, and air-conditioning causes dehydration. Try to get plenty of sleep the night before flying; wear loose, comfortable clothing and footwear during the flight; walk around the plane regularly (about once an hour) to reduce swollen feet and ankles; and drink plenty of water, fruit juices, or soft drinks (and no alcohol) throughout the flight. If you still arrive tired and grumpy with swollen feet, check into a hotel the first night and sleep as long as you can—then your vacation will get off on the right foot.

MONEY AND COMMUNICATIONS

Currency and Exchange

New Zealand has been on the decimal currency system based on dollars and cents since 1966: 5-, 10-, 20-, 50- and 100-dollar notes, and 5-, 10-, 20-, 50-cent, $1, and $2 coins are used. Banks and other financial organizations offer a variety of services. Trading banks are open Mon.–Fri. 9:30 A.M.–4:30 P.M., closed weekends and public holidays; however, automatic teller machines are widely available, and bank offices at airport terminals provide foreign exchange services for all international arrivals and departures (occasionally closed for late-night departures).

There's no restriction on the amount of foreign or New Zealand currency you bring in or out of the country, but be sure to exchange most of it before your departure to benefit from current exchange rates.

Travelers Checks

The easiest and safest way to carry your money is in the form of travelers checks—either foreign-dollar travelers checks (the best deal), which you

CURRENCY EXCHANGE

The New Zealand dollar has slowly but surely been losing value against the world's major currencies over the last decade. It steadied through the late 1990s, but slipped again in 2001.

Current exchange rates (into NZ$) for major currencies are:

AUS$1	=	$1.18
CDN$1	=	$1.35
€1	=	$1.90
HK$10	=	$2.70
UK£1	=	$2.92
US$1	=	$2.11
¥100	=	$1.62

On the Internet, the **Bank of New Zealand,** website: www.bnz.co.nz, has a handy currency converter.

need to exchange at a trading bank (or hotels, restaurants, and large stores where the exchange rate is not as good), or New Zealand dollar travelers checks which can be cashed anywhere. If you're likely to be hiking far from main tracks, it may be wise to carry checks of both currencies so that you don't have to worry about reaching a bank before weekends or holidays. Be sure to jot down the number of each check and the place where you cashed it, and keep the records separate from the actual checks. This will greatly speed up a refund if you should lose them; some companies won't refund without your transaction records.

Cash and Credit Cards

Another way to have access to money is to open a bank account on arrival in New Zealand and have your bank at home wire money over. Of course the exchange rate will be nonfluctuating (often an advantage), but you'll be making interest while you travel. Major credit cards, such as American Express, Visa, MasterCard, and Diners Club, are generally accepted throughout New Zealand.

When you first enter New Zealand, you may be asked to prove that you have enough money with you to cover your intended length of stay—$1,000 per month, or at least $400 per month if you have a guarantee of accommodation from a New Zealand resident, or evidence of pre-paid accommodation, or an American Express, Bankcard, Diners Club, MasterCard, or Visa credit card. This seems to happen with regularity to those expecting to stay in the country for at least a couple of months without a work visa (you must obtain permission to work and a work visa before entry).

Tipping

Tipping is neither required nor expected.

Telephone and Internet

Local calls from a public telephone box (or booth) are generally made using a plastic phone card—buy a $5, $10, $20, or $50 card at a dairy, service station, or Telecom Centre. You can place trunk or long-distance calls through the long-distance operator, and costs are based on the duration of the call. National and international toll calls can be dialed directly or placed through the operator (more expensive).

The Internet is well entrenched in the New Zealand way of life and you can expect the same level of service as in other parts of the world. Internet booths are located in many cafes and most major cities have at least one "cyber café." Most backpacker lodges provide computers and Internet access, as do major city hotels.

If your can't access your email account away from your home or work computer, open an email account with **Hotmail** (website: www.hotmail.com) or **Yahoo!** (website: www.yahoo.com). Although there are restrictions to the size and number of emails you can store and junk mail can be a problem, these services are handy for traveling and, best of all, free.

INFORMATION

Before you go, get on the Internet and spend some worthwhile time at the official website of **Tourism New Zealand,** www.purenz.com. The site has excellent Search and Help functions along with information on accommodations, sights, activities, transportation, general travel hints, a currency converter, and a list of travel agents around the world that will help with booking your trip. Write Tourism New Zealand at P.O. Box 95, Wellington; tel. 04/472-8860.

Once you've arrived in New Zealand, head to one of the more than 100 **tourist information centers** scattered throughout the country and at major airports. They are all part of **VIN,** the Visitor Information Network, and are the place to learn about local attractions, make accommodation bookings, and plan and book onward bus and ferry travel.

WHAT TO TAKE

Clothing

Most New Zealanders are casual dressers (by day and night), attending to comfort and suiting the occasion. However, dressing up is the norm for fine restaurants, nightclubs, and discos in the resorts and major cities—a few places still require a jacket and tie or smart attire, and restrict jeans, T-shirts, and thongs. New Zealand's weather is unpredictable, especially in mountainous areas; it's best to be prepared for everything no matter which season you arrive—and keep in mind that the seasons are opposite to those of the Northern Hemisphere. If you're an outdoor type, in summer take shorts, jeans, shirts, a good pair of slacks or a dressy dress for evenings on the town, bathing suit, warm sweater, windproof jacket, raincoat or poncho (great for covering you *and* your backpack), at least one pair of thick wool socks, hiking boots, tennis or sand shoes, and dressier sandals, plus your basic necessities. Don't forget sunscreen and a small bottle of vinegar—for dabbing on sand fly bites. In winter you'll need all of the above, but add thermal underwear, flannel shirts or lightweight sweaters, a wool sweater or two, more wool socks, an extra warm jacket (down is great) or coat, a long raincoat, and shoes instead of sandals. If you're going to hit all the resorts, take some dressier clothes and appropriate footwear to be on the safe side.

Buying clothes in New Zealand can be expensive, but wool products, in particular sweaters, bush shirts, and sheepskin coats, are of high quality and you can pick up a bargain if you're willing to shop around. Leave your electric razor or hair dryer at home, or buy an adapter—New Zealand is on 230 volts AC, 50 hertz, and sockets accept three-pin flat plugs; hotels and motels often provide 110-volt AC sockets for razors only.

One last tip: Take less than you think you'll really need—you'll invariably discard some of your "essentials." The occasional sheepskin rug, wood-carving, and other paraphernalia collected along the way soon add up. Eliminate all but the essentials—you'll be glad you did.

Photo Equipment

New Zealand is a photographer's paradise—great light, spectacular scenery, and friendly people everywhere you go. Take a 35 mm camera, several lenses, and plenty of film. Film is widely available at chemists' shops (pharmacies) and photographic dealers in New Zealand, but it's expensive to buy and develop. If you're coming from the U.S., it's cheaper to stock up on film at home and take it back with you (in your main luggage) for developing; if you're worried about the X-ray machines at the airport spoiling undeveloped film in your camera, request that the camera be hand-searched.

Special Hobby Equipment

If you're an angler, it's best to take your own fly rod, fishing pole, and waders with you—rentals are hard to come by. Flies and lures are readily available in sporting stores. Big-game fishing equipment is generally included in the cost of renting a boat and guide. Hunters can take their own guns into the country but need to get permits from New Zealand police. Scuba diving and skiing equipment are both easy to rent. If you're a mountaineer, you may want to

bring your own equipment to ensure your safety, but most of it can also be rented (bring your own rope).

WEIGHTS AND MEASURES
Time

New Zealand is the first country west of the international dateline and therefore the first to see the sun rise each day. It's 12 hours ahead of Greenwich Mean Time, making it three hours ahead of Japan, nine ahead of Moscow, 17 before Washington, D.C., and 20 hours ahead of California. Like much of the rest of the world, it does practice daylight saving time, which could throw these calculations off at certain times of year.

Shopping Hours

Most shops and stores are open Mon.–Thurs. 9 A.M.–5:30 P.M., Friday 9 A.M.–9 P.M. for "late-night shopping" (in major cities, each suburb has its own late shopping night, which is not necessarily Friday). City stores are generally open on weekends, although hours are often reduced, especially on Sunday. In smaller towns, the only shops always open on Sunday are milk bars or dairies (selling groceries, dairy products, fruit, and snacks), newsagents (usually open only for a short period to sell the Sunday paper), and tourist shops.

Electricity

New Zealand runs on 230 volts AC, 50 hertz, and most power sockets accept only three-pin flat plugs. If you're taking an electric appliance, such as a razor or hair dryer, buy a voltage transformer and suitable plug adapter from a hardware store, or an appliance that can switch to the appropriate voltage.

The North Island

T he North Island lies between latitudes 34 and 42 degrees south and has a temperate climate with rainfall levels steady throughout the year. Though more densely populated than the South Island and liberally dotted with towns and villages, it continues to boast unspoiled scenery and a diverse range of landscapes.

The far north offers kilometer after kilometer of golden sand and surf, magnificient kauri forests alive with birds and cicadas, and historic bays crowded with diving and fishing boats. Auckland, the largest city and "Gateway to New Zealand," is situated in the north. East of Auckland, on the rugged beach-fringed Coromandel Peninsula, hiking tracks wind through lush forest and logging dams that have withstood the ravages of time. In the center of the isalnd lie the exciting city of Rotorua—home of modern Maori culture, thermal activity, and geysers—and crystal-clear Lake Taupo, boasting some of the country's best brown- and rainbow-trout fishing. The bush-covered ranges of Te Urewera National Park in the east have serene lakes and sparkling waterfalls, rich birdlife, and lush greenery where Maori legends see to come alive. Tongariro and Egmont National Parks in the central and western regions claim impressive volcanos, excellent views, hiking and climbing trails, and skiing. An abundance of rivers meander through the island, providing fine fly-fishing, canoeing, kayaking, and whitewater rafter. Wellington, the exciting and picturesque capital, lies on the windswept shores of Cook Strait at the base of the island.

Whether you're in search of sun, sand, and relaxation; exciting, active, outdoor adventures; off-the-beaten-track escapades; or bustling cosmopolitan cities, the North Island has it all.

Auckland

Introduction

Note: Please see color map of Auckland on pages vi-vii

Auckland, a vibrant, exciting city, has attractions to suit both outdoor enthusiasts and those who thrive in a bustling, concrete-and-glass metropolis. Most of the country's overseas visitors arrive here first, so it's often referred to as "the Gateway to New Zealand." Largest city in the country, with almost one-quarter of the population (1.2 million) living within its sprawling urban area, Auckland is also home to one of the world's largest Polynesian populations (155,000).

Straddling a narrow piece of land between magnificent Waitemata and Manukau Harbours, Auckland is flanked by the South Pacific Ocean to the east and the Tasman Sea to the west—a sailor's paradise. All year round Waitemata Harbour is dotted with boats of all kinds, the water a sparkling backdrop to many colorful sails. It's easy to see why Auckland, home to thousands of sailing vessels, has been affectionately nicknamed the "City of Sails."

Auckland is also known for its many fine beaches, beautiful parks and gardens, and a great variety of restaurants and nightlife. The city's eastern shoreline offers calm water and protected beaches, while the western shores boast wild waves, good surfing, and desolate windswept beaches. The urban area is wrapped around a number of extinct volcanic peaks that host vantage points with great views. From these scattered lookouts, you can see how Auckland has also been developed around parks and gardens—it's packed on weekends with walkers, joggers, cricketers, kite enthusi-

Waitemata Harbour

asts, and families enjoying the year-round pleasant climate. Twenty-three degrees C is the average temperature in summer (Dec.–March), 14° C in winter (June–Aug.); you can expect rain showers any time of year (Auckland's mean annual rainfall is 1,268 mm). Take time to explore the many different features of this stimulating city, particularly from the water. A ferry ride, harbor cruise, or trip to one of the many volcanic islands that riddle the harbor are good ways to experience the true maritime aspect of Auckland.

Sights

CITY CENTER

The Edge

A few blocks up from the harbor and immediately south of Wellesley Street, "the Edge" is a bustling precinct that centers around **Aotea Square.** The square is a popular city gathering place, filled with gardens and host to markets every Friday and Saturday. The **Civic,** on the corner of Queen and Wellesley Streets, opened in 1929 as a movie palace but fell into disrepair over time. After extensive renovations it reopened in 1999, restored to its former Asian-influenced art nouveau glory. In addition to showing films, the Civic hosts touring musicals and shows.

Across Aotea Square from the Civic, **Auckland Town Hall** is an Italian Renaissance–style building that dates to 1911. Like the Civic, it has undergone extensive renovations and is now home to the New Zealand Symphony Orchestra and Auckland Philharmonic Orchestra, both companies taking advantage of the renowned acoustics of the Great Hall and Concert Chamber, respectively. Take in a performance by one of these two companies to experience the town hall in its best light, or wander through the public areas daily 9 A.M.–5 P.M.

A modern addition to the Edge, the **Aotea Centre** is a multipurpose venue that includes two major theaters and the country's largest convention center. The **Auckland Visitor Centre,** open daily 9 A.M.–5 P.M., is on Level 1 of the Aotea Centre.

Super Views

For excellent views of Auckland from New Zealand's tallest building, head to the distinctive 328-meter-high **Sky Tower** on Victoria St., tel. 09/363-6000. From the Sky City casino at street level, one of three glass-fronted elevators whisks you to four observation decks. Make the Main Observation Deck your first destination; at this level, glass floor panels allow views of the city streets directly below and live weather reports flash

QUEEN STREET

Downtown's main commercial thoroughfare, Queen Street, stretches from Waitemata Harbour as far south as suburban Newton. This busy cosmopolitan strip bustles with businesspeople, shoppers, and tourists. On weekends it's decisively quieter, with Aucklanders preferring nearby parks and beaches.

At the harbor end, the Ferry Building is the departure point for ferries to the North Shore and offshore islands. Across Quay St. (pronounced key) is the old Central Post Office, slated to be incorporated as part of a massive transportation interchange that has been on the drawing board for many years. From this point, Queen St. begins its long, uphill journey. Street level at the bottom end is lined with tourist-oriented stores, such as duty-free shopping and currency exchange outlets, as well as cafes and restaurants.

A few blocks up from the harbor, **The Edge** precinct is a combination of old and modern centered around a busy square. At the back of the square is the **Auckland Visitor Centre.**

Toward the upper end, Queen St. crosses Karangahape Rd., nicknamed "K Road." This area has a bustling Polynesian atmosphere and a variety of foreign nationalities represented in the shops, restaurants, and take-away food stands.

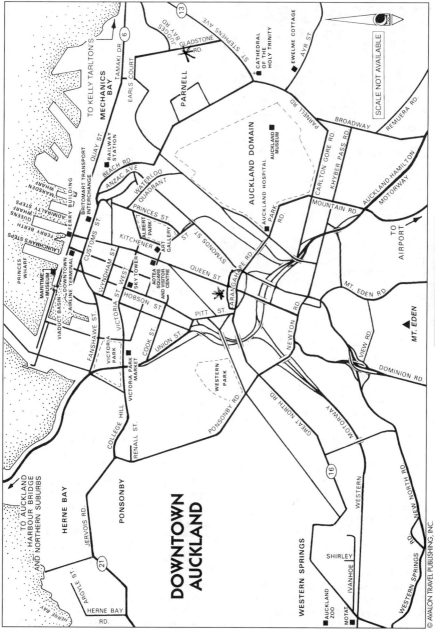

AUCKLAND

DOWNTOWN AUCKLAND

© AVALON TRAVEL PUBLISHING, INC.

© ANDREW HEMPSTEAD

AUCKLAND

Head to the top of Sky Tower for the best city views.

on a screen. The Lower Observation Deck holds a café and bar, while above the Main Observation Deck is Orbit, a revolving restaurant, and then, on the next level, the Observatory (a buffet restaurant). The highest point with public access is Skydeck, an outdoor viewing platform. Before heading up Sky Tower, you can watch a videotape that takes a look at the city's history. The ride to the Main Observation Deck costs adults $15, seniors $13.50, and children $7.50; access to Skydeck costs an additional $3 pp.

New Zealand National ✳ Maritime Museum

On Hobson Wharf at the west end of Quay St., this museum, tel. 09/373-0800, showcases New Zealand's strong maritime traditions—from the earliest craft used by Pacific islanders to the latest technology used in the America's Cup. The museum encompasses a floating boatshed where traditional Maori crafts are displayed and visitors can try their hand at rowing. Other galleries feature hands-on displays,

Take time to stroll through the Victorian-style gardens of Albert Park, admiring the groves of well-established oak trees, delightful fountains, and a historic rotunda.

an audiovisual presentation in the Pacific Discovery Theatre, a collection of canoes, boatbuilding workshops, and the Hall of Yachting, which tells the story of the America's Cup. The museum is open in summer daily 9 A.M.–6 P.M., in winter daily 9 A.M.–5 P.M.; $12 adult, $6 senior and child. A number of historic craft are tied alongside the museum, and one of them, a historic scow, the *Ted Ashby,* takes visitors around the dock area (adult $15, senior $12, child $7; discounted with museum admission).

Immediately west of the museum is **Viaduct Harbour,** developed in the 1990s for Auckland's hosting of the America's Cup. A variety of venues around Hauraki Gulf were considered for the occasion, including offshore islands, but this downtown location was the final choice for the America's Cup Village, breathing new life into a rundown commercial and industrial area that was first used as a port in the 1870s.

Auckland City Art Gallery

Two blocks from Queen St., and next to Albert Park (a pleasant green spot within the inner city area), is the Auckland City Art Gallery. The collection is housed in two buildings, the New Gallery and the Heritage Gallery, on either side of Kitchener St. at Wellesley St., tel. 09/307-4540. The gallery is the oldest and largest in New Zealand. It contains an extensive historic and contemporary New Zealand art collection, as well as British and old master paintings, and a drawing and print collection. Open daily 10 A.M.–5 P.M., with guided tours available at 2 P.M.; admission is free except to specified exhibitions. The gallery café on the first floor of the Heritage Gallery is open daily 10 A.M.–4 P.M. with reasonable prices, and there's also a small bookshop.

Albert Park

After visiting the art gallery, take time to stroll through the Victorian-style gardens of this city park, admiring the groves of well-established oak trees, delightful fountains, and a historic rotunda.

At the top end of the park is an old caretaker's cottage, which now houses a collection of clocks from around the world; open daily 10 A.M.–4 P.M.

THE DOMAIN

Auckland Domain is a large, lush, shady park within walking distance of both the city center and Parnell area. Covering more than 80 hectares, the park offers Auckland Museum, Wintergardens, Fernz Fernery, Planetarium, Herb Garden, a kiosk selling drinks and ice cream, and a restaurant that's a favorite spot for wedding receptions. On the hillsides, particularly outside the museum, kite-flying is popular—on a bright summer day the sky is alive with color and movement. Though the Domain is likely to be busy on weekends, it's still a good time to visit since many other Auckland attractions are closed.

Auckland Museum

Built on the highest point of the Domain, the museum, tel. 09/309-0443, boasts terrific views of Waitemata Harbour, Rangitoto Island, and the North Shore from the steps leading up to its impressive entrance. Inside is one of the best collections of Maori art and artifacts. Several floors feature a large variety of both permanent and changing exhibitions: the Hall of Pacific Art contains art and objects from islands throughout the Pacific; another exhibit explores Auckland's fascinating volcanic history, complete with sound effects and audiovisuals; other halls feature New Zealand's natural history, birdlife, ceramics, English furniture, military and maritime history, and Asian arts. You can lose complete track of time here—a good spot to keep in mind for a Sunday, when many attractions are closed, or for a rainy day. There's also a small coffee lounge and a good selection of Maori carvings, jewelry, books on New Zealand, and souvenirs available at average Auckland prices in the museum shop. It's a half-hour walk from downtown, open daily 10 A.M.–5 P.M.; free admission. For an introduction to Maori culture, attend one of the short tours of the Maori foyer with a traditional greeting, then a Maori Concert Party performance in the small auditorium at either 11:15 A.M. or 1:30 P.M.

Domain Wintergarden

The beautiful Wintergarden (free admission) is a short stroll from the museum. Flower gardens, several greenhouses with amazing hothouse plants, a lily pond, and shady courtyards with statue-lined footpaths make this a relaxing spot to hang out. A small lake, home to a flock of greedy ducks, makes it a popular place with small, bread-toting children. Open daily 10 A.M.–4 P.M.

Fernz Fernery

This fernery, beside the Wintergarden, reopened in 1994 after extensive reconstruction of the old layout (the site was originally a quarry). More than 150 varieties of fern thrive in three distinct zones—dry, intermediate, and wet—creating a stunning collection of species found in all parts of the country. Admission is free; open daily 10 A.M.–4 P.M.

EAST OF CITY CENTER
Parnell ✳

Parnell is another trend-setting suburb with chic shops and historic buildings; little cafés in shady arcades and Italian restaurants by the handful (often residents call it "Parnelli" with a chuckle) lure locals and visitors alike. Attractive **Ewelme Cottage** at 14 Ayr St. (off Parnell Rd.), tel. 09/379-0202, is made of kauri, New Zealand's native timber. It's one of Parnell's many buildings preserved by the New Zealand Historic Places Trust (brochures on all the city's historic buildings are available from the Visitor Centre at Aotea Square); it's open daily 10:30 A.M.–noon and 1–4:30 P.M.; $5 adult. **Kinder House,** at 2 Ayr St. (corner of Parnell Rd.), tel. 09/379-4008, built from Rangitoto Island volcanic stone and completed in 1857, contains Georgian furniture, family heirlooms, and a collection of Rev. John Kinder's pioneer photographs taken between 1860 and 1888. It's open Mon.–Sat. 11 A.M.–3 P.M.; $2 adult. Devonshire teas are available. Another local attraction is the spectacular **Parnell Rose Gardens,** containing more than 4,000 roses; admission is free. At the northeast end of the gardens there's access to Judges Bay, a popular swimming beach. Parnell is a gentle uphill hike from the city center—walk along Customs St. E (at the harbor end of Queen St.), curve left onto Beach Rd., pass the railway station, and make a left on Parnell Rise, which becomes Parnell Road.

Kelly Tarlton's Antarctic Adventure and Underwater World

New Zealander Kelly Tarlton, one of the world's premier underwater adventurers, spent most of his life traveling the world recovering lost treasures before developing this unique aquarium in underground stormwater holding tanks on Auckland's harbor, six km east from downtown along Tamaki Dr., tel. 09/528-0603. In 1994, eight years after his untimely death (he died soon after the complex opened and never saw his dream fulfilled), the second stage of the project opened—a simulation of an Antarctic environment, including penguins.

The journey begins by walking through a life-size replica of Capt. Robert Scott's hut, complete with groaning ice and fierce winds. Then it's all aboard a Snow Cat that heads through an Antarctic whiteout, under the ice, past some penguins, and into a futuristic Scott Base. The second part of the complex is the aquarium. Travel on a moving walkway through a crystal-clear acrylic tunnel and step off at any point onto the footpath running alongside. Other than the walkway beneath your feet you're surrounded by water—all sorts of indigenous New Zealand sea creatures skim past the tunnel around you, while eels and crayfish peek out of rock crevices. The lighting, dark blue carpeting, and sound effects add to the submarine atmosphere. The tunnel darkens as you enter the deep-sea area, where sharks and other exotic creatures glide above and around you. In the small theater to the left of the main entrance room, an excellent audiovisual slide show features underwater photography; it's 10 minutes long, shown every 15

The journey begins by walking through a life-size replica of Capt. Robert Scott's hut, complete with groaning ice and fierce winds. Then it's all aboard a Snow Cat that heads through an Antarctic whiteout, under the ice, past some penguins, and into a futuristic Scott Base.

minutes. Displays of shells and sea urchins and other objects of marine interest, a piranha tank (feeding time 11 A.M.) and touch tank, a souvenir shop, and lots of articles about sharks (feeding times are 10 A.M. and 2 P.M.) complete this Auckland attraction. It's open in summer, daily 9 A.M.–8 P.M.; the rest of the year, daily 9 A.M.–6 P.M. Admission is adult $24, child $10.

WEST OF CITY CENTER

Ponsonby

A fashionable suburb within walking distance from K Road, Ponsonby boasts many old homes and shops that have been beautifully restored. Entirely preserved Renall St. depicts a slice of 19th-century Auckland. Houses sit close together on the narrow and steep street, each house with a view of the harbor over the rooftops. Ponsonby is also known for its gourmet restaurants, intriguing shops, and trendy people. Buses run here from Queen Elizabeth Square past Victoria Park and College Hill. Get off at the Three Lamps stop; Renall St. is a block away.

MOTAT

On Great North Road in Western Springs, the **Museum of Transport, Technology, and Social History,** tel. 09/846-7020, is commonly referred to by its acronym, MOTAT. Next to the attractive Western Springs Park, MOTAT gives a glimpse into New Zealand's past with exhibitions of early agricultural machinery, airplanes, vintage cars, fire and steam engines, and a pioneer village. The aviation building is a flying buff's delight, with an extensive historic display featuring Richard Pearse, a South Island farmer and inventor who it's claimed made several flights in the summer of 1902, predating the Wright Brothers 1903 exploits by over a year. Nearby Sir Keith Park Memorial Airfield houses the largest vintage air-

one of Ponsonby's many historic buildings

craft collection in the Southern Hemisphere; it's connected to MOTAT by a double-decker bus and an electric tram service. MOTAT is open daily 10 A.M.–5 P.M.; $10 adult, $5 child. An electric tram runs regularly between the museum and Auckland Zoo. Take bus no. 045 (Pt. Chevalier) from Customs St. to Western Springs.

Auckland Zoo

Also in Western Springs, the zoo, tel. 09/360-3800, contains a collection of 900 exotic and indigenous animals living in a near-natural state. One of the highlights is the nocturnal house where you can see the curious kiwi (native bird and a national symbol) doing his (or her) thing during the daytime (the birds are most active in the morning—fed at 9:30 A.M.). "Keeper Encounters," using animal feeding sessions, take place throughout the day. A souvenir shop and a restaurant overlook the park. The zoo is open daily 9:30 A.M.–5:30 P.M. Admission is adult $13, senior $10, child $7. The zoo is connected to MOTAT by tram. From downtown, take bus no. 045 along Customs Street.

VOLCANIC VIEWS

Mount Eden

Head to the top of this extinct volcano, the highest point in Auckland at 196 meters, for a 360-degree view of the city. Walking tracks lead around and into the large egg-shaped depression at the top where the crater used to be. It was used as an ancient Maori fortress by the Waiohua people, and their storage pits and defense terraces remain around the outside. The inner crater area shows no signs of occupation, as it was considered sacred to Matuaho, God of Volcanoes. On the lower slopes of the hill lies **Eden Garden,** a colorful array of camellias, azaleas, and rhododendrons planted in the early 1970s; open daily 9 A.M.–4:40 P.M. From downtown you can walk to Mt. Eden in about 1.5 hours (follow the Coast to Coast Walkway signs), or catch a bus from the downtown bus terminal for Mt. Eden and Khyber Pass Roads. Mountain Road takes you to the summit. You can also drive to the top.

One Tree Hill

Situated among the 60-odd volcanic cones dominating Auckland's skyline, One Tree Hill is another prominent dormant volcano (182 meters) offering spectacular views over Auckland. Once the home of the largest prehistoric Maori settlement in the region, it was originally called Te Totara-i-ahua after the solitary *totara* tree planted on the summit in 1640. The name survived, although sadly a combination of vandalism and disease destroyed the tree in the 1990s. Nowadays a solitary pine tops the summit along with a monument dedicated to Maori-European friendship. Walk or drive to the top through the sheep-filled terraced fields and shady trees of this little inner-city oasis. One Tree Hill is the central landmark of Cornwall Park, a popular place for joggers and walkers. It's also on the Coast to Coast Walkway (see below), about a 3.5-hour walk from downtown, 1.5 hours from Mt. Eden. It takes approximately 50 minutes to walk from the base to the summit of One Tree Hill and back down.

Also in the One Tree Hill "Domain" (commonly used New Zealand word for park) near the

Manukau Road entrance is the **Stardome Observatory,** tel. 09/624-1246. Displays in the foyer area are open Mon.–Fri. 9 A.M.–5 P.M., but the real reason to visit is the multimedia presentation showcasing our solar system and beyond. It plays Tues.–Fri. hourly 7:30–9:30 P.M., Saturday 1–4 P.M. and 7:30–9:30 P.M., and Sunday 12:30–3:30 P.M.; adult $12, child $6. Weather permitting, view the Southern Cross and other Southern Hemisphere stars after the planetarium show Wednesday, Thursday, and Saturday; adult $5, child $3.

Auckland Botanic Gardens

This extensive 65-hectare garden lies 27 km south of downtown beside the Southern Motorway. As far as botanic gardens go, they are fairly recent, having been initially developed in 1973 and opened in 1982. The former farm has been transformed, now boasting more than 10,000 plants from around the world. Within the garden is a visitor center, open daily 9 A.M.–4 P.M., tel. 09/266-7158, a small library, and a café serving light snacks during the lunch hours.

Waitakere Ranges Regional Parkland

This spectacular chunk of wilderness lies on the north side of Manukau Harbour, west of Auckland (take Hwy. 16 west from downtown, then Hwy. 24 through Titirangi). It encompasses much of the Waitakere Ranges. Formed by volcanic action about 17 million years ago, the Waitakere Ranges comprise a steep eastern face, rugged valleys, rivers, streams, and waterfalls, which cascade dramatically to the Tasman Sea. A network of nearly 150 "walks" (suitable for everyone) and "tracks" (for the more experienced hiker) covers a distance of more than 200 km (many trails are impassable after high rainfall). The main road through the park traverses the main range and ends at **Piha,** a small seaside community at the protected south end of a beach continuously lashed by massive waves. North and south of Piha, the coastline is no less rugged, with trails leading to secluded beaches and rocky cliffs.

Start a park visit at **Arataki Visitor Centre,** tel. 09/817-4941, five km beyond Titirangi. Adorned by Maori carvings, this grand building is a lot more than a visitor cente—inside, the whole natural and human history of the Waitakere Ranges is laid out, and paths lead through the surrounding forest and to raised lookout platforms. Before continuing farther into the park, pick up the excellent *Recreation and Track Guide*—it gives a good overview of the various walks. The center is open daily 9 A.M.–5 P.M.

Hauraki Gulf Maritime Park

Right on Auckland's back doorstep is an archipelago of 47 islands, spread out over more than 13,600 square km of Pacific Ocean. The islands are volcanic in origin, some having erupted as recently as 600 years ago. Most of the islands are within the Hauraki Gulf Maritime Park and are administered by the DOC. Some are simply rocky islets, but many are also inhabited, with bustling little seaside villages. They all have one thing in common—the opportunity for almost unlimited recreation. They are wonderful places to hike, swim, scuba dive, sea kayak, or just visit for a picnic.

Fullers, tel. 09/367-9111, serves many of the islands with a regular and inexpensive ferry service from the piers in front of the Ferry Building, on Quay St., in downtown Auckland. Here you'll also find Fullers Cruise Centre, the place to check the ferry schedule, gather island information, and make tour and accommodations bookings. The DOC Auckland Visitor Centre is also in the Ferry Building, tel. 09/379-6476. This is a good place to pick up brochures on the islands' human and natural history, and to make campground bookings.

RANGITOTO ISLAND

This island, dominating the horizon from along the south shore of Waitemata Harbour, is easily recognized by its symmetrical and elongated shape. It last erupted only 200 years ago, spreading jagged lava flows out from the peak for a 2.5-km radius. Rangitoto has no soil or fresh running water, yet it supports an astonishing array of native and introduced plant species, small colonies of wallaby, deer, and many birds. On the island you can climb to the 259-meter summit for fabulous views by following the walking track from Rangitoto Wharf. If you're walking up (the view is worth the effort!), wear sturdy footwear and take suntan lotion and sunglasses as the glare can be intense. Several other walking tracks meander across the island. Another track follows the coast and finishes at Islington Bay, where you can catch the ferry back to downtown instead of backtracking to Rangitoto Wharf. Administered by the DOC, the island is uninhabited, so only day-trippers are permitted.

Practicalities

Fullers' Rangitoto Ferry departs the Ferry Building three times daily for the 45-minute trip to the island and costs $20 round-trip. The Harbour Cruise ($25), which gives a five-hour stopover by catching the first ferry out to the island and then jumping aboard the day's final departure, also allows a stop at Devonport. Walking around the island and to the summit of the volcanic cone is easy, but you can also take the tractor-train **Volcanic Explorer** for $49 (including ferry fare). For booking and the latest schedule, head down to the Ferry Building or call Fullers at 09/367-3111.

MOTUTAPU ISLAND

Motutapu Island is connected to Rangitoto Island by a natural causeway, yet vegetation types on the islands completely contrast with one another. Traditionally farmland, the island currently is the subject of an ambitious DOC project to transform it to its natural state. The first stage, the eradication of introduced mammals, is complete, and the introduction of endangered species has begun. The project is a long one—50 years at least. The only way to get around the island is on foot. A popular loop begins at the causeway, climbing to the island's highest point before descending to Home Bay. From this point, the trail heads north past scattered World War II gun emplacements

before returning along the shoreline to the causeway. This loop is 12 km (allow four hours).

Practicalities

The only way to stay overnight on the island is by pitching a tent at **Home Bay Campground,** a four hour hike from the Islington Bay ferry dock; $6 pp. Book through the DOC, tel. 09/379-6476. **Fullers,** tel. 09/367-9111, serves adjacent Rangitoto Island, from where it's a pleasant walk across the causeway to Motutapu.

MOTUIHE ISLAND

Motuihe, one of the most popular islands in the park, lies between downtown Auckland and Waiheke Island. Its biggest attraction is two long, white-sand beaches on either side of a narrow isthmus, separated by a band of sand dunes and tall Norfolk pines. One side or the other is always protected from the wind, making it attractive for sailing enthusiasts, beach lovers, and picnickers. Around the coastline lie extensive mudstone reefs, and at low tide the rock pools teem with life. Tracks take advantage of the numerous natural vantage points offering the most spectacular views. You can walk around the entire island in four hours when the tide is low.

Practicalities

Fullers, tel. 09/367-9111, runs out to the island twice daily three times a week (daily in January); $20 adult, $10 child. All facilities cluster around Waihaorangatahi Bay (where the ferry docks). They include a kiosk, picnic tables with barbecues, and a campground.

WAIHEKE ISLAND

Waiheke Island, second-largest of the gulf islands (92 square km), is by far the most populous, with a year-round population of 6,000. This swells fourfold in summer as city slickers swarm over to relax on the beautiful white-sand beaches or to walk through rolling farmland and native bush. The island was settled by Maori 800 years ago, at a time when its rolling inland hills were covered with kauri forests. The kauris have long

AUCKLAND

gone, to be replaced with bustling holiday villages, open farmland, and vineyards.

Sights and Recreation

The island's west end is the most built up, with an almost continuous string of villages extending eastward from the main settlement of **Oneroa** to **Onetangi.** Between the two lie a string of magnificent beaches, including picturesque **Palm Beach.** Hiking trails link all parts of the less-developed eastern end of the island (pick up a detailed description from the local information center), and a pleasant six-km (two-hour) coastal track links Oneroa with Palm Beach. Return along the same route or jump aboard a bus.

Waiheke has a reputation for excellent wine, predominantly reds, which thrive in the warm, dry climate. Over 25 wineries are spread across the island (Waiheke even has its own winegrower's association), but most are small, family-run affairs not open to the public. The most high-profile is **Stonyridge,** Onetangi Rd., tel. 09/372-8822, whose annual release of Larose-a complex Cabernet blend-is quickly scooped up by connoisseurs the world over, even at $65 a bottle. Almost all Stonyridge wine is sold by mail order; the mailing list is currently oversubscribed, so the only way to taste the wine is by visiting the vineyard. The winery is open to the public on weekends (winery tours at 11:30 A.M.; $10 pp), with lunch served at a café overlooking the vineyard and a grove of olive trees. On a high point of land near the ferry dock, the **Mudbrick Vineyard,** Church Bay Rd., tel. 09/372-9050, is best known for its restaurant (see Island Dining, below), but also offers tours ($8 pp) that are worthwhile for the wonderful views back across to Auckland alone. The only way to visit the other wineries is on the **Waiheke Island Vineyard Explorer,** which departs the Ferry Building (Auckland) daily at noon. The tour cost includes the ferry ride, wine tasting, and a tour of three vineyards; $68 pp.

Waiheke's calm waters and convoluted coastline make it ideal for sea kayaking. **Ross Adventures,** tel. 09/372-5550, charges $55 for a range of half-day trips, including one by moonlight. For horseback riding through open farmland and along unspoiled beaches, head to **Shepherds**

Point Riding Centre, Ostend Rd., tel. 09/372-8104. A one-hour ride is $25, or stay in the saddle all day for $80. **Waiheke Island Museum,** Onetangi Rd., tel. 09/372-7143, is small but provides an interesting diversion from more strenuous activities. It's open weekends only (daily during school holidays) 1–4 P.M.

Accommodations

The wide range of accommodations can be booked through the island information center, tel. 09/372-9999. Accommodations generally are more expensive than those on the mainland, but staying in one of the backpacker lodges reduces costs considerably. The best of these is **Hekerua Lodge** (also known as Waiheke Island Backpackers), 11 Hekerua Rd., Little Oneroa, tel. 09/372-8990. It's a 600-meter walk downhill to the beach from the totally private setting, surrounded by dense native bush. The modern facilities include a wide deck, deep, natural-feeling rock swimming pool, bikes, a barbecue, and cozy lounge area. Rates are $21 pp in a dorm, $32 s, $60 d, $85 s or d for an en suite, and $140 for a large self-contained cabin. All rates discounted outside of summer.

Right on the island's best beach is **Roanna-Maree Motel,** Onetangi Beach, tel. 09/372-7051, featuring 19 self-contained rooms set around a courtyard and pool; $105–145 s or d. **Palm Beach Lodge,** 23 Tiri View Rd., Palm Beach, tel. 09/372-7763, is a complex of luxurious Mediterranean-style villas, each self-contained and with a private balcony that affords stunning views. Rates of $260 s or d ($190 in winter) include breakfast provisions and use of a variety of facilities.

Island Dining

Oneroa has the biggest concentration of eateries. **Vino Vino,** 153 Ocean View Rd., Oneroa, tel. 09/372-9888, is a popular place, both for its great food and elevated ocean views from the covered deck. Favorite dishes are the Signature Platters, perfect for sharing, and seafood delights such as a filet of monkfish panfried with coconut and lime ($25). It's open daily 11 A.M.–11 P.M. Toward the ferry dock from Oneroa, the **Mudbrick Restau-**

rant, Church Bay Rd., tel. 09/372-9050, attracts the business crowd from Auckland, who catch a ferry across the bay to enjoy a relaxed lunch among the vines. Evenings are more upscale, but the food and service are equally good, with diners enjoying dishes such as grilled duck breast smothered with a red curry and plum sauce ($32).

Transportation

Many island residents commute to Auckland daily, so sailings are frequent. **Fullers,** tel. 09/367-9111, ferries depart the Ferry Building up to 20 times daily for the 35-minute trip to the island. The round-trip fare is $25 adult, $12.50 child. A number of packages can be booked through Fullers in conjunction with the ferry price.

Once on the island, getting around is easy. The ferry docks at Matiatia Bay, from where buses run along two scheduled routes to all corners of the island. The maximum fare is $5, the same cost as a day pass. Two private companies also wait at the dock for ferries, providing a door-to-door service for $3–6 pp. **Waiheke Taxi** can be reached at 09/372-8038. **Waiheke Rental Cars** has an office beside the wharf at Matiatia Bay, tel. 09/372-8386; compacts are $50 per day plus 40 cents per km, or jump aboard a motorized scooter for $35 per day.

Information

Waiheke Island Visitor Information Centre is in the Artworks Centre, 2 Korora Rd., Oneroa, tel. 09/372-9999. As well as providing information, the center makes accommodation and tour bookings, and rents bikes. Open in summer 9 A.M.–5 P.M., the rest of the year until 4 P.M.

GREAT BARRIER ISLAND

Largest of the gulf islands, Great Barrier is also the most remote, lying nearly 100 km from downtown Auckland, but conveniently linked by boat and plane. The island is mostly wilderness, with forested ranges rising more than 600 meters. Geologically, the island links to the Coromandel Ranges as part of a volcanic fault. The west coast is deeply indented, while many long sandy beaches flank the east coast. The island was first settled by Maori 800 years ago, and its nonrenewable resources, such as kauri forests, devastated by early Europeans. Today it's a peaceful place, with 1,300 residents scattered mostly over the island's southern end. Recreational opportunities abound— hiking trails crisscross the island, hot springs invite a good soaking, the road system is suited for mountain biking, and the surrounding waters are great for scuba diving and surfing.

Practicalities

Although remote, each of the island's communities offers basic services, such as ATMs and groceries. Accommodations are limited and best booked as part of a package through Fullers. The island has six basic campgrounds, some accessible only on foot. All campers must be totally self-sufficient and prepared with a campstove if a fire ban is in effect. Book campsites through the DOC at 09/379-6476; $6 pp per night.

The ferry trip from downtown Auckland with **Fullers,** tel. 09/367-9111, takes two hours each way, and once out at the island, three stops are made. The round-trip is adult $99, child $49.50, but discounts apply for same-day excursions or with advance reservations. Fullers offers a variety of packages, all reasonably priced, including island bus tours, accommodations, and flightseeing. **Great Barrier Airlines,** tel. 09/256-6500 or 0800/900-600, offers scheduled flights between the international airport and the island for $189 round-trip, or packages such as round-trip airfare, two nights' accommodation, and a fishing trip for $340.

AUCKLAND

Recreation

HARBOR CRUISES

There are so many ways to cruise Waitemata Harbour that your first stop should be the attractively renovated ferry building on Quay Street. You'll find **Fullers Cruise Centre,** tel. 09/367-9111, on the ground floor. Fullers runs scheduled transportation and tours to all the populated islands of Hauraki Gulf (see above) as well as to Devonport, on the North Shore, and around the harbor itself. One of the best ways to enjoy the harbor is to join the two-hour **Harbour Cruise,** which departs daily 10:30 A.M. and 1:30 P.M. The trip costs $30 adult, $15 child.

Watertours, tel. 09/357-0700, operate nifty little water taxis in and around the harbor. These distinctively bright yellow craft were designed and built by the same company that operates them. In addition to a taxi service, a 15-minute tour taking in Viaduct Basin, the America's Cup Village, and Princes Wharf costs $15 pp.

Sailing

Pride of Auckland, tel. 09/373-4557, operates a fleet of 45-foot charter yachts, easily recognized by their distinctive blue and white sails, from beside the Maritime Museum. Options include a 50-minute introduction to sailing departing hourly ($40 pp), a 90-minute lunchtime trip departing daily at 1 P.M. ($60), a 90-minute Coffee Cruise departing a 3 P.M. ($50), and a 2.5-hour dinner trip departing at 7 P.M. that includes a healthy seafood meal cooked on board ($85).

Another sailing option is the *Søren Larsen,* a Danish-built, square-rigged tall ship that dominates the harbor at her Princes Wharf berth during the Nov.–March sailing season. Weekdays are spent on overnight journeys through the Hauraki Gulf and to the Bay of Islands and Bay of Plenty (around $200 pp per night), then she returns to Auckland for the weekend, departing each Saturday and Sunday for three- and five-hour trips ($49 and $89 respectively) around the harbor. The rest of the year, the *Søren Larsen* takes adventurers on two-week journeys through the South Pacific (around US$130 pp per night). Call 09/411-8755 or check the website: www.sorenlarsen.co.nz for a schedule.

To Devonport

While the Harbour Cruise stops at Devonport, there's so much to do in and around this North Shore suburb that it's easy to spend a day exploring the area. It's a picturesque place-from the sandy beach beside the ferry terminal, the main street leads uphill past outdoor cafés, art galleries, and trendy boutiques. From the waterfront, a one-km (20-minute) trail leads along the harbor east to **North Head,** a historic reserve once an important base for Army operations toward the end of the 19th century. Walking tracks lead to many underground tunnels and chambers, gun emplacements and batteries, and a good viewing point. Nearby **Mount**

Waitemata Harbour is busy year-round.

Victoria, an extinct volcanic cone rising 85 meters, offers panoramic views of the harbor; a walking track leads to the top.

The least expensive way to cross the harbor is aboard the **Devonport Ferry,** operated by Fullers, tel. 09/367-9111, from the Ferry Building. Departures are every 30 minutes 7 A.M.–7 P.M., then hourly (on the hour) until 10 P.M. It costs $5 one way; $8 round-trip. From the North Shore, the **Devonport Explorer** bus ($18) takes in all the local sights, including North Head and Cheltenham Beach.

HIKES

Coast to Coast Walkway

This well-marked urban walkway crosses the nine km of land that separate the Pacific Ocean on the east from the Tasman Sea on the west. Take in tremendous views of the city and the main harbors; climb two volcanic peaks; saunter through parks, gardens, and woods; and listen to native birds on this remarkable track. It's a great way to appreciate the old and the new, the land and the water that make up Auckland today. The walk starts from the ferry building downtown, and at an easy pace takes about four hours to cover the 13-km trail through the domain, Mt. Eden, and One Tree Hill to suburban Onehunga on Manukau Harbour. A pamphlet containing a detailed map of the route, distances and average walking times, places of interest, viewing points, and parks and gardens is available from the Auckland Visitor Centre.

Point England Walk

It takes about three hours to do this 8.7-km, well-marked walk, which starts on Tamaki Drive above St. Heliers Bay and meanders through parks, paddocks, and two nature reserves. Catch tremendous views of the city from St. John's Ridge before finishing on St. John's Road. If you want to walk around the **Tahuna-Torea Nature Reserve** (Gathering Place of the Oyster-Catcher) along the way, add about 1.5 hours, including time-outs for bird-watching. A pamphlet, *Inner City Strolling,* with a map of this walk, is available from the Auckland Visitor Centre.

BEACHES

Close to Town

Beaches lie on all sides of Auckland, some surprisingly close to the city center, ranging from sheltered sandy coves on the east to pounding surf and black sand on the west. Tamaki Drive leads south out of downtown along the waterfront toward Mission Bay, Kohimaramara Beach, and St. Heliers Bay. The many sheltered beaches along the Tamaki waterfront are popular, offering good, safe swimming and calm water. The first, **Judges Bay,** is only minutes from the city center, accessible from Parnell Rose Gardens. Farther along is **Mission Bay,** known for an attractive fountain that dances at the push of a button. Here you can rent bicycles, catamarans, and windsurfers (sailboards); in summer it's usually packed. Beyond **St. Heliers Beach** is access to **Lady's** and **Gentleman's Bays,** Auckland's two nude beaches. All along Tamaki Drive are boat anchorages, boat launches, changing rooms, and cafés; buses leave from the downtown bus terminal.

On the North Shore

Over Auckland Harbour Bridge to the North Shore are many more beaches to choose from. **Takapuna Beach** is one of the best known and probably most crowded, but nine others are accessible by bus from Devonport, linked to downtown by ferry.

Along the West Coast

On the west coast lie kilometers of wind- and surf-swept beaches, many quite isolated. They're beautiful but can also be dangerous; they are known for large, unpredictable swells and strong riptides. It's safest to swim at the beaches where the local surf lifesaving club is patrolling. **Piha** is a popular surf beach, patrolled in summer, as are North Piha, Karekare, and Te Henga, all within Waitakere Ranges Regional Parkland (see above). South of Piha, the west coast meets Manakau Harbour along the sandy shores of desolate **Whatipu Beach** (accessible along Huia Rd. from Titirangi), with large sand dunes, and good surfing and bird-watching.

As well as large surf, **Muriwai Beach,** 45 km from Auckland along Hwy. 16, is known for a long black-sand (rutile) beach, extensive sand dunes, a gannet colony, and a seaside golf course. A track leads south from the beach to **Maori Bay,** where you'll see unusual geological formations known as "pillow lavas." Behind the beach lies the small community of Muriwai, with a motor camp and fish-and-chip shop.

CYCLING

For information on cycling around the city, contact the **Auckland Cycle Touring Association.** They organize rides most weekends, listed in *Southern Cyclist* magazine. A very good bike route around Auckland covers about 50 km and takes at least three hours. If you ride at a leisurely pace over a full day you'll have the opportunity to visit many city attractions along the route. A map is available from the Auckland Visitor Centre.

Rentals

Many bicycle shops rent bikes, including **Penny Farthing Cycle Shop,** on the corner of Symonds St. and Khyber Pass Rd., tel. 09/379-2524; and **Adventure Cycles,** 1 Fort St. (off Customs St.), tel. 09/309-5566. Additionally, on weekends rentals are available at many public places around town: Mission Bay, Okahu Bay, the waterfront, and Devonport, on the North Shore. Expect to pay around $25–35 per day.

In addition to hourly rentals, Adventure Cycles provides bikes and equipment for long-term touring. Suspension bikes cost $25 per day, $90 per week, and $190 per month, all with pumps, water bottles, locks, and helmets. Adventure Cycles also rents pannier bags ($30 per week; $65 per month) and sells a variety of touring gear, including maps.

ARTS AND ENTERTAINMENT

Current information and show times for music, opera, cabarets, theater, dance, and exhibitions are listed in *Alive & Happening,* a weekly Tourism Auckland publication. For musical events the *NZ Herald* gives thorough coverage of what and

where, and the Auckland Visitor Centre on Queen St. also has lots of information on Auckland entertainment. The free weekly *What's Happening* covers all the exhibitions, musical and theatrical performances, and festivals and events around town.

All major cultural and sporting events can be booked through **Ticketek,** Level 2, Aotea Centre, Queen St., tel. 09/307-5060 (information) or 09/307-5000 (reservations); website: www.ticketek.co.nz.

Music, Theater, and Movies

Auckland's main music and performing arts venues are centered around **The Edge,** on Queen Street, where the **Aotea Centre, Auckland Town Hall,** and the **Civic** provide a home for **New Zealand Opera, New Zealand Symphony Orchestra, Royal New Zealand Ballet, Auckland Philharmonic Orchestra,** and **Chamber Music New Zealand.** On the southern corner of the precinct, the restored Italian Renaissance-style **Auckland Town Hall** comprises two chambers renowned worldwide for their acoustics, the main venue for performances by the New Zealand Symphony Orchestra and the Auckland Philharmonic Orchestra. Also at The Edge is the 2,380-seat Civic, a restored movie palace that reopened in 1999 with an extravagant Eastern-themed art nouveau look, complete with a simulated night sky painted on the ceiling. The Civic hosts touring musicals and shows, occasionally reverting to its original purpose and screening movies. The modern **Aotea Centre** holds two main theater venues. The best source of information on all of the above is **Ticketek,** with a booking outlet on Level 2 of the Aotea Centre, tel. 09/307-5060 (information).

The city's newest entertainment venue is **Sky City Theatre,** in the Sky City complex, corner Victoria and Federal Streets, tel. 09/912-6000. Home to the **Auckland Theatre Company,** tel. 09/309-0390, this venue also hosts a variety of musicians.

The **Maidment Arts Centre** in the Students Union Complex, on the corner of Princes and Alfred Streets, tel. 09/308-2383, puts on films, concerts, and a large variety of musical and theatrical events throughout the year. Other live theater venues include the **Silo Theatre,** Lower Greys Ave., tel. 09/373-5151; and the **Watershed Theatre,** on the corner of Customs St. and Market Pl., tel. 09/357-0888, the place to head for alternative theater. At these smaller venues, expect to pay $20–25 for an entertaining night out.

Sky City

This large entertainment complex on the corner of Victoria and Federal Streets, tel. 09/912-6000, holds a large variety of eateries and lounges, two casinos, and one of Auckland's most luxurious accommodations. The main casino rooms feature 90 gaming tables (blackjack, stud poker, roulette, Tai-Sai, craps, and baccarat) and about 1,000 slot machines. The adjoining **Canoe Bar** is a busy drinking spot, while also on the main floor, the **New City Bar** hosts bands and karaoke nights. On Level 3, the **Alto Casino** offers the same choice of gambling opportunities but on a much smaller scale and with a quieter atmosphere. The adjacent **Alto Bar,** open daily from 4 P.M., provides soft music played by New Zealand entertainers. This section of the casino is also more upmarket, with an enforced dress code (no jeans, shorts, or sportswear). Above the main gaming rooms, the **Atrium Bar** is a quiet, intimate lounge. **Sky City Theatre** attracts touring acts and is home to the Auckland Theatre Company. Dinner/theater packages are available to many performances.

Bars and Nightclubs

The waterfront is an unbeatable location for an afternoon or evening drink. Most of the bars and restaurants in the Viaduct Basin development have wonderful outdoor seating areas that take advantage of the bustling harborfront location. One of the most popular is the **Loaded Hog,** 204 Quay St., tel. 09/366-6491, with its own in-house brewery. The **Trench Bar** in the Kermadec complex, Viaduct Quay Building, on the corner Quay and Lower Hobson Streets, tel. 09/309-0412, replicates its namesake—the deepest point of the Pacific Ocean—with dim lighting and sculptures of creatures that inhabit the ocean floor.

In the heart of downtown, the **Civic Tavern,** 1 Wellesley St., tel. 09/373-3684, is home to three bars, including the London Bar with an impressive variety of draught beer. A similar British atmosphere prevails at the **Shakespeare Tavern and Brewery,** 61 Albert St. (at Wyndham St.), tel. 09/373-5396. Backpackers gravitate to **Embargo,** under Central City Backpackers at 26 Lorne St., tel. 09/309-1850; and the **Hard Rat,** at street level of Auckland Central Backpackers, 9 Fort St., tel. 09/358-4877. Both are lively seven nights a week (unusual in Auckland) with nightly drink and food specials.

Needless to say, the bar on the Lower Observation deck of the **Sky Tower** has magnificent views across Hauraki Gulf, but a beer is $6 plus the cost of the ride up. The main levels of **Sky City,** on the corner of Victoria and Federal Streets, tel. 09/912-6000, offer a variety of other bars, most servicing gamblers, but others such as the **Atrium Bar** providing a respite from the sights and sounds of the busy casino below. The **Alto Bar,** also at Sky City, hosts New Zealand entertainers ranging from light rock to instrumentalists.

As always, the hot spots for dancing the night away to DJ music change as regularly as the patrons change their hairstyles. Downtown, the place to be for late-night drinking and dancing is Vulcan Lane, where the trendy **Equinox,** 12 Vulcan Lane, tel. 09/309-9538, plays house, techno, and trance music to an eclectic crowd until the sun comes up. **Rakinos,** upstairs at 35 High St., tel. 09/358-3535, is a quieter place open Thurs.–Sat., often with live jazz.

Up the hill from downtown, the **Temple,** 486 Queen St., tel. 09/377-4866, is a small café with pool tables and local musicians playing nightly, mostly performing their own material. At the top end of Queen Street, Karangahape Road has an inner-city, Bohemian feel, with a wide variety of ethnic bars and nightclubs. Upstairs on this busy corner, **Khuja Lounge** hosts a wide variety of musicians Tues.–Saturday. In the vicinity, **Calibre,** downstairs at 179 Karangahape Rd., tel. 09/303-1673, is an alternative dance venue with dance and house music pulsating Thurs.–Sun. until 8 A.M. Heading west along Karangahape Rd. from Queen St., the scene gets sleazy, with strip clubs and sex shops dominating. One exception is the **Dogs Bollix,** 582 Karangahape Rd., tel. 09/376-4600, a venue for Irish bands; closed Monday.

In Ponsonby proper, **Ponsonby Road** has a lively late-night scene, with trendy nightspots and cafes staying open until after midnight. **Lime Bar,** 167 Ponsonby Rd., tel. 09/360-7167; and the tropical **Hula Hut,** 212 Ponsonby Rd., tel. 09/360-6274, are two of the more popular hangouts.

Many city bars close at 10 P.M. during the week, staying open until midnight on weekends. Nightclubs close at midnight or 1 A.M. on weeknights, staying open until the early hours on Friday and Saturday morning.

Folk, Jazz, and Blues

A popular downtown jazz and blues venue is **Rakinos,** upstairs at 35 High St., tel. 09/358-3535, open Thurs.–Sat. and with a minimal cover charge. Jazz and blues are performed nightly at **Java Jive,** a small café on the corner of Ponsonby Rd. and Pompalier Terrace, Ponsonby, tel. 09/376-5870. **Poles Apart Folk, Jazz, and Blues Club,** 424 Khyber Pass Rd., Newmarket, tel. 09/524-2401, meets for music and poetry recitals. Generally, folk and blues sessions are held on Friday and Saturday nights, jazz on Wednesday and Thursday nights; small cover charge.

SHOPPING

In general, shops are open weekdays 9 A.M.–5:30 P.M., Saturday 9 A.M.–1 P.M. Most individual shops are closed on Sunday, but you can find larger shopping centers open all day. In the fashionable areas of Parnell, Ponsonby, and Herne Bay, many shops stay open all day Saturday and open on Sunday. The *Auckland Shopping Guide,* available for free from the visitor center, is a good source of information and comes complete with maps of each shopping district.

Downtown

Queen Street is lined with tourist-oriented and duty-free shops, especially the bottom end. Here you'll also find many currency exchanges. For two floors of shops, specialty stores, coffee lounges,

and lunch bars in the city center, visit the Downtown Shopping Centre at Queen Elizabeth Square and Customs Street. In the attractive building that houses the **Old Customhouse Shopping Centre,** 22 Customs St. W on the corner of Albert St., you'll find shops, a restaurant and tavern, and a movie theater. The Old Customhouse is open regular shopping hours Mon.–Sat., Friday until 9 P.M., and Sunday noon–5 P.M. Numerous other shopping arcades with regular shopping hours branch off Queen Street. Across the road is **OK Gift Shop,** tel. 09/303-1951, with a massive selection of New Zealand souvenirs.

Victoria Park Market

Markets are fun to browse at leisure-and they bring out the Aucklanders by droves on weekends, when many other places close. The biggest and most popular market is across from Victoria Park, within easy walking distance of downtown. Once Auckland's rubbish destructor, its 38-meter chimney can be seen from quite a distance. The cobbled courtyard area swarms with activity as people crowd around colorful vendor carts. The interiors of the former stable buildings have been converted into shops selling art and handcrafts, clothes and jewelry, posters, records, and all sorts of curious knickknacks. On the upper floor you can talk to local artisans and pick up bargains in woven articles, wall hangings, rugs, wool sweaters, pottery, glassware, and leatherwork. The lower floor offers a large variety of ethnic foods in the food hall; food stalls also dot the marketplace. The festive atmosphere is enhanced by daytime entertainment provided by buskers. The market is a 10-minute walk from Queen St., or on weekdays you can catch bus no. 005 from outside the Great Northern Arcade, on the corner of Queen and Customs Streets, and get off at the market entrance. The market is open daily 9 A.M.–6 P.M.

Parnell Village

Parnell is a fun place to browse and buy, but don't forget your travelers checks—it ain't cheap! The Village boasts a large variety of specialty shops, boutiques, and courtyard cafés. Cobblestone courtyards; wooden and wrought-iron lacework; steps up and down here, there, and everywhere; and intriguing alleyways leading to equally intriguing shops lure droves of shoppers.

Multicultural Karangahape Road

Locally referred to as "K Road," this is one of Auckland's oldest established shopping areas. You'll find a large variety of cosmopolitan stores and restaurants, a range of shops stocked with Polynesian and Asian foods, and many of the city's theaters in this bustling area. On Thursday nights, shop till 9 P.M. On Sunday at noon, a small but very popular market opens on the corner of K Road and Ponsonby Road. Walk from Queen St. west along K Road, crossing the motorway—the market is farther along on the right. (K Road crosses the top end of Queen St., a main bus route.)

Takapuna Village

Takapuna Village is similar to Parnell Village but lies on the North Shore in the center of Takapuna City (buses run from city center to Takapuna). Cobbled paths, covered verandas, and little alleyways separate a host of specialty shops. It's closed on Sunday.

FESTIVALS AND EVENTS

Summer

All of Auckland looks forward to the **Anniversary Day Regatta,** held on the Monday nearest to January 29, celebrating the city's birthday. The harbor is chock-a-block with sailing boats of all kinds, and people flock to the high points around the harbor for the best views.

The first Saturday in February, Mission Bay comes alive during the **Mission Bay Jazz and Blues Festival,** tel. 09/575-3184. First held in 2001, this gathering already attracts a crowd in excess of 20,000 for streetside eating, drinking, and dancing.

The **Devonport Food & Wine Festival** takes place over the 4th weekend of February on the Devonport waterfront, less than 200 meters from where ferries from downtown dock. Entry is $15, which includes a wine glass used to taste wines from throughout the country at booths set around the treed parkland. Many of Auckland's top restaurants are represented and entertain-

ment is provided from two stages. The gates are open 10:30 A.M.–6 P.M. both days.

Autumn

Head for Albert Park the first weekend of March for the **Traditional Lantern Festival,** a colorful celebration of the Chinese New Year which begins at 11 P.M.

Pasifica, tel. 09/353-9557, celebrates the culture of the Pacific with traditional island arts, entertainment, sports, and food at Western Springs Park on the second Saturday of March. It's most popular with Islanders, but visitors are more than welcome to enjoy the festivities.

The week prior to the Easter break, the country comes to the city as Auckland Showground plays host to the **Royal Easter Show,** tel. 09/638-9969. Expect displays of arts and crafts, livestock and equestrian events, and judging of the national wine awards.

Winter

The **Auckland International Film Festival** is a stop for the New Zealand Film Festival, which travels around the country showing major films from all over the world. It's held for two weeks through mid-July at venues including the Sky City Theatre and the Civic. For a schedule and ticketing details check their website: www.enzeddff.co.nz.

For the **International Music Festival,** the last two weeks of September, some of the world's great classical performers gather in Auckland to celebrate the music of Beethoven at the various venues, including the Great Hall of the Auckland Town Hall.

Spring

Celebrated on November 5 each year by real kids and grown-up kids, **Guy Fawkes Night** originated in England in 1605. It commemorates the foiling of a conspiracy by Guy Fawkes and his men to blow up London's Parliament buildings and occupants, including King James I, on opening day of Parliament. Nowadays large bonfires, bonfire feasts, spectacular fireworks, and general merriment are the order of the day. Watch the Auckland sky light up; for the best viewing position head to the top of Mt. Eden.

Accommodations

Auckland offers a full range of accommodations in all price ranges. As with large cities the world over, major hotel chains have properties in the heart of downtown, but you'll be paying well over $100 for a room. Less expensive rooms can be found in the motels that line all highways leading into the city, and you can generally find vacancies at these at any time of the year. A unique feature of Auckland's accommodation scene is the large number of backpacker lodges, especially right downtown, where you can find a bed for the night for less than $15. But be warned: You get what you pay for. The better backpacker lodges can be found in outlying suburbs, such as Parnell. As throughout the country, Auckland has many bed-and-breakfasts. We've detailed our favorites below, but a more comprehensive listing can be found in the *New Zealand Bed & Breakfast Book*. Available in bookstores throughout the city, this book will prove invaluable as you travel farther afield.

DOWNTOWN HOTELS AND MOTELS

Under $100

One of the most reasonable hotels in downtown Auckland, the **Kiwi International Hotel,** 411 Queen St., tel. 09/379-6487 or 0800/100-411, website: www.kiwihotel.co.nz, offers basic rooms with private bathrooms, TV, telephone, and tea- and coffee-making supplies for $89 s or d. If you're looking for something even more basic, ask for one of the economy rooms—there's a hand basin in each room but shared bathrooms for $39 s, $49 d. Hotel facilities include a tour booking desk, laundry, bar, and restaurant.

Through a checkered history, the **Hotel De-Brett,** 2 High St., tel. 09/377-2389, has always offered rooms. Today this art deco relic advertises rooms by the week, but they can also be rented by the night for $70 s, $80 d. Guests share a lounge area and have use of a communal kitchen.

At the top end of this price range is the **Albion Hotel,** four blocks west of busy Queen St. at the corner of Hobson and Wellesley Streets, tel. 09/379-4900; website: www.albionhotel.co.nz. Basic but comfortable rooms with renovated Victorian-style decor, private baths, tea supplies and fridge, TV, and telephone are $80 s, $90 d. Rooms immediately above the street level bar should be avoided.

$100–200

Whitaker Lodge Motel, 21 Whitaker Pl. (off Symonds St.), tel. 09/377-3623, website: www.whitakerlodge.co.nz, clings to a steep hillside near the south end of Queen Street. The rooms are nothing special, but if you are looking for self-contained motel-style rooms close to downtown, you can't beat the price—$100–170 s or d.

Park Towers Hotel, 3 Scotia Place (near the top of Queen St.), tel. 09/309-2800, website: www.parktowers-hotel.co.nz, offers simple, summery furnishings in 80 otherwise nondescript rooms. Off the lobby is a restaurant open daily for breakfast. Rates are $100 s, $115 d.

The **First Imperial Hotel,** 131 Hobson St., tel. 09/355-1503 or 0800/687-968, website: www.firstimperial.co.nz, is a midsized property within a couple of blocks of Aotea Square and Queen Street. The rooms are spacious, and each has a writing desk. Standard double rooms are $170 s or d, while self-contained units with a separate bedroom are $220.

At the waterfront end of Queen St. beside Queen Elizabeth II Square is **Mecure Hotel Auckland,** 8 Customs St., tel. 09/377-8920, website: www.accorhotels.com.au, an older hotel but with a location that affords stunning harbor views from many of the 188 rooms. The rate is $200–275 s or d.

$200–300

A historic downtown department store has been transformed into the **Heritage Auckland,** 35 Hobson St., tel. 09/379-8553, website: www.heritagehotels.co.nz, one of the city's best value, upmarket accommodations. With the addition of a "Tower Wing" in 2000, the heritage now has

467 rooms, the most of any New Zealand hotel. Public areas in the original wing have retained their 1920s art deco glory, which includes high ceilings and hardwood *jarrah* floors. In addition to well-appointed rooms (many with water views), this property features a fitness room, outdoor and indoor pools, a tennis court, and a casual dining room. Rates range $240–500, but as with all top-end Auckland accommodations, check the hotel website for rooms under $200 *with* breakfast year-round.

Sky City Hotel is part of the impressive Sky City complex on the corner of Victoria and Federal Streets, tel. 09/363-6000 or 0800/759-2487; website: www.skycity.co.nz. The hotel itself consists of 344 luxurious rooms featuring contemporary furnishings and pleasing pastel color schemes. Other facilities in this full-service hostelry include 24-hour room service, an outdoor heated pool, and a large health club. Within the Sky City complex itself are a number of eateries and lounges, a casino, and the imposing Sky Tower. Rates start at $290 s or d, but check the Sky City website for packages that include accommodation, breakfast, and Sky Tower tickets for around $200 s or d.

The newest addition to Auckland's top-end accommodation spectrum is **Sebel Suites**, on Viaduct Basin at 85–89 Customs St., tel. 09/978-4000 or 0800/937-373; website: www.mirvac.com.au. Each of the 129 units features floor-to-ceiling windows, a full kitchen, a laundry facility, and most have a private balcony. Guests also enjoy all the services of a hotel, including room service, underground parking, and a restaurant. Rack rates range $300–550 s or d.

Also close to the waterfront, and three blocks east of the Sebel, **Copthorne Harbourcity Hotel,** 196 Quay St., tel. 09/377-0349 or 0800/808-228, website: www.copthorneharbourcity.co.nz, offers 187 spacious rooms, each facing the harbor; rates from $240 s or d.

Over $300

The **Crowne Plaza Auckland,** 128 Albert St., tel. 09/302-1111, website: www.sixcontinentshotels.com, is not as fancy as other properties in this same chain, but since opening in 1991 has gained popularity with business travelers for its services and central location. Many of the rooms have great harbor views and guests enjoy use of a fitness room and the convenience of a restaurant open daily at 6:30 A.M. for breakfast, a lounge, and street-level shopping plaza. Don't be put off by the advertised rates starting at $320 s or d—book through the hotel website for savings of up to half this rate.

Closest to Aotea Square and surrounding attractions is the **Carlton Hotel,** Mayoral Dr., tel. 09/366-3000 or 0800/666-777; website: www.carlton-hotel.co.nz. All 455 guest rooms are spacious and elegantly decorated in earthy tones with luxurious granite-lined bathrooms. An impressive 12-story-high, glass-sided atrium fills the main lobby area with natural light. Other hotel facilities include a fitness room, a business center, and a variety of eateries, including Café Pacifique offering an extensive buffet breakfast. Rates start at $340 s or d, but check the hotel website for packages year-round.

HOTELS AND MOTELS IN OTHER PARTS OF THE CITY
Parnell

Easily recognized by its stylish blue and yellow exterior, the **Parnell Inn,** 320 Parnell Rd., tel. 09/358-0642, website: www.parnellinn.co.nz, is a well-priced motel in the heart of one of Auckland's trendiest suburbs. The fairly standard rooms are priced right for the location: $85 s, $90 d, $105 s, $115 d for a kitchenette. Farther up the hill is **Parnell Rise Motel,** 73 Parnell Rd., tel. 09/358-1178, which offers basic rooms for $70–90 s or d. **Barrycourt Suites,** 10 Gladstone Rd., tel. 09/303-3789 or 0800/504-466, website: www.barrycourt.co.nz, is a large motel, comprising more than 100 rooms, most with private balconies and large windows that take advantage of filtered harbor views. Standard hotel rooms are $95 s or d, while the larger one- and two-bedroom units, complete with kitchens, are $140–190. **Parnell's Village Motor Lodge,** 2 St. Stephens Ave., tel. 09/377-1463, features spacious one-bedroom units, complete with kitchens, for $135 s or d.

Ponsonby and Herne Bay

These two suburbs a few kilometers west of downtown hold a number of motels that are an inexpensive option to staying directly downtown, but they are most easily accessed if you have your own transportation. **Sea Breeze Motel,** 213 Jervois Rd., tel. 09/376-2139, website: www.seabreeze.co.nz, features 10 comfortable rooms, some with private balconies and harbor views. All have cooking facilities and breakfast is available. Rates are $109–110 s or d.

Toward downtown, **Abaco Spa Motel** lies at the north end of Ponsonby Rd. at 59 Jervois Rd., tel. 09/376-0119 or 0800/220-066; website: www.abacospamotel.com. It offers 14 simply furnished yet spacious rooms, each with a kitchen, in a sprawling three-story complex. The rate is $105–135 s or d, with the more expensive rooms including a spa bath.

North Shore (Devonport)

Along with having a large number of bed-and-breakfasts, the harborside suburb of Devonport is home to the grand old **Esplanade Hotel,** 1 Victoria Rd., tel. 09/445-1291, website: www.esplanadehotel.co.nz, built in 1903 and renovated in the mid-1990s. It stands opposite the ferry terminal, separated only by landscaped gardens, and at the end of a street chock-full of cafés and restaurants-the perfect city escape. The owners have refurnished 17 guest rooms in a simple yet stylish manner, including cane furniture; rates start at $175 s or d.

The **Emerald Inn,** 16 The Promenade, tel. 09/488-3500, website: www.emerald-inn.co.nz, is five km north of Devonport and 50 meters from Takapuna Beach. Each brightly furnished room comes with a fully equipped kitchen and opens to a courtyard filled with greenery and a small outdoor heated pool; rates $130–165 s or d.

Near the north end of Auckland Harbour Bridge is the **Green Glade Motel,** 27 Oceanview Rd., Northcote, tel. 09/480-7445, one of the North Shore's least expensive motels. It's an older style, park-at-the-door place, but each of the 13 rooms has a kitchen; rates $90–117 s or d. Take the Northcote Rd. exit from the Northern Motorway.

Mangere (Airport)

All of the following accommodations are within an eight km radius of the airport, and each provides airport transfers. **Oakwood Manor Motor Inn,** 610 Massey Rd., tel. 09/275-0539 or 0800/801-555, website: www.goldenchain.co.nz, is a large complex that surrounds an open courtyard. It has a pool and a small restaurant; rates from $100 s or d. Nearby, **Traveller's International Motor Inn,** 190 Kirkbride Rd., tel. 09/275-5082 or 0800/800-564, website: www.travellersinternational.co.nz, offers extensive landscaping around a swimming pool, complete with barbecue facility; rates $79–129 s or d. Also in the vicinity is **Airport Skyway Lodge,** 30 Kirkbride Rd., tel. 09/275-4443, website: www.skywaylodge.co.nz, with basic motel units. This place is also a backpacker lodge, but a few en suite motel rooms are available for $52 s, $64 d.

BED-AND-BREAKFASTS

Aspen Lodge

This small, friendly hotel at 62 Emily Place in the inner city, tel. 09/379-6698, has simply furnished rooms, an attractive guest lounge, a dining room with TV, and shared bathroom and laundry, but no kitchen use. Rates are a reasonable $55 s, $80 d, which includes a buffet continental breakfast. Centrally located, it's only a short walk from downtown (four blocks from Queen St.), and both airport shuttle companies stop at the front door.

Ascot Parnell

This charming B&B, 36 St. Stephens Ave., Parnell, tel. 09/309-9012, website: www.ascotparnell.com, a restored, 1910 home on a quiet street off busy Parnell Rd., is within walking distance of the city, and numerous restaurants and cafés are just a short stroll away. The friendly owners make you feel quite at home, and the elegantly furnished rooms are bright, spacious, and paneled in kauri, New Zealand's native timber. Breakfast is a filling affair with almost anything you want, continental or cooked. Rates are $95–165 s, $165–220 d, and all rooms have private baths.

© ANDREW HEMPSTEAD

Peace and Plenty Inn

Bavaria B&B Hotel

A longtime favorite with readers, this large accommodation dating to the early 1900s provides 11 comfortable guest rooms, each with private bath. In the guest TV lounge you can help yourself to tea or coffee, then enjoy the timber deck that overlooks a subtropical garden. Rates are $90 s, $130 d including a buffet-style breakfast. It's at 83 Valley Rd., Mt. Eden, tel. 09/638-9641, website: www.bavariabandbhotel.co.nz, close to a bus stop.

Aachen House

Located south of downtown in the leafy suburb of Remuera is Aachen House, 39 Market Rd., tel. 09/520-2329 or 0800/222-436, website: www.aachenhouse.co.nz, an Edwardian-era mansion converted to an upmarket bed-and-breakfast. It has been totally renovated by the latest owners, and now offers nine luxurious bedrooms, each with a private bathroom and decorated in period style. Breakfast is served in a large conservatory, complete with a marble floor, white linen, and floor-to-ceiling windows allowing garden views. Rates for six of the rooms, each named for the

dominant color scheme, range $180–215 s or d, with larger suites costing up to $345 s or d.

The Peace and Plenty Inn

Described as "a haven of hospitality," the Peace and Plenty Inn, 6 Flagstaff Terrace, tel. 09/445-2925, website: www.peaceandplenty.co.nz, is one of many upmarket bed-and-breakfasts in the harborside suburb of Devonport, a short ferry ride from downtown Auckland. It overlooks the water and is a one-minute walk from fine restaurants, trendy cafés, intriguing shops, and the ferry terminal. The house was built in 1888 and has been renovated and tastefully decorated. Each of the six guest rooms features individual character, a comfortable bed, and memorable touches such as fresh flowers and chocolates. The Garden Room, with a private entry and small courtyard surrounded by a scented garden, is a particular delight. In the lounge, guests can browse through the well-stocked library while enjoying complimentary tea, coffee, or port. Breakfast, in a dining area overlooking a tropical garden, is a memorable event featuring a delicious choice of fresh fruits and hot dishes such as Belgian waffles prepared by hosts Judith and Peter Machin. Rates are $200 s, $230 d.

Other Devonport Bed-and-Breakfasts

Set in a quiet residential area, **Badgers of Devonport,** 30 Summer St., tel. 09/445-2099, website: www.badger.co.nz, features four tastefully furnished guest rooms in a 1906 Victorian-era villa. Guests can relax in the book-filled lounge, on the shaded verandah, or in the garden. The rates of $89 s, $119–125 d include a cooked breakfast and many nice touches, such as complimentary chocolates and fresh flowers in each room.

Also in Devonport, **Villa Cambria Inn,** at 71 Vauxhall Rd. (a five-minute walk from Cheltenham Beach), tel. 09/445-7899, website: www.villacambria.co.nz, a historic house built in the early 1900s, offers bed-and-breakfast in a casual, comfortable atmosphere. The three large rooms (each with a private bathroom), wooden floors, high ceilings, and congenial hosts add to the ambience. The rates for these rooms start at $120 s, $130 d, while in the well-tended garden the self-contained "loft" is $220 s or d.

Devonport Villa Inn, 46 Tainui Rd., tel. 09/445-8397, website: www.devonportvillainn.co.nz, is a rambling Edwardian mansion that has been elegantly restored and now operates as one of the country's finest bed-and-breakfasts. No expense has been spared in ensuring guests' comfort-from four-poster beds to the claw-foot bath in the Beaconsfield Suite. Room rates range $165–180 s, $210–245 d, which includes a delicious full-cooked breakfast.

BACKPACKER LODGES

In the last decade, backpacker hostels have sprung up around the country, and Auckland is no exception. Auckland, particularly downtown, has some bad ones, but check in to any of those listed below and you can't go wrong. Make advance bookings in summer.

Hostelling International

YHA New Zealand, an arm of Hostelling International, operates two hostels in Auckland, both near the top end of Queen Street.

A five-minute walk downhill to downtown, **Auckland International YHA,** 5 Turner St., tel. 09/302-8200, website: www.yha.org.nz, is a relatively new hostel with its own travel agency, a book exchange, public Internet access, and all the usual facilities such as a communal kitchen, lounge area, TV room, and bike storage. Members pay $22 for a dorm bed (maximum four beds per room), $28 pp twin, $38 pp d.

Just one block up the hill from the International, **Auckland City YHA,** on the corner of City Rd. and Liverpool St., tel. 09/309-2802, website: www.yha.org.nz, is a renovated hotel with 153 beds in small dormitories and a large number of double rooms. It features a comfortable lounge area, large kitchen area, a food shop, an in-house restaurant (open for breakfast and dinner), luggage storage, a bike storage room, mail-forwarding service, and 24-hour accessibility; members pay $21 for a dorm bed, $26 pp in a private room.

Downtown

The only good reason for backpackers to stay right downtown is if you don't have transportation, but even then, an excellent transit system makes the journey into town from surrounding suburbs easy and reliable. Aside from the two YHAs (see above), if you do decide to stay downtown, only the following choices can be recommended.

Auckland Central Backpackers, 9 Fort St., tel. 09/358-4877, website: www.acb.co.nz, is probably the pick of the bunch. It's a large renovated hotel, only 100 meters from bustling Queen St. and 500 meters from the ferry terminals and waterfront. Facilities include a travel agency, grocery store, large kitchen, made-up beds, laundry, bike-repair room, games room, outdoor deck, two cafés, and an upstairs bar with nightly food and drink specials. Dorms are $20 pp and private rooms $42 s, $55 d.

Across the road from the ACB is the smaller **Queen Street Backpackers,** 4 Fort St., tel. 09/373-3471; website: www.qsb.co.nz. As a renovated hotel, each room has a hand basin and shares bathroom facilities; dorm bed $22, $42 s, $55 twin or d.

Away from the harbor but close to Albert Park and the Art Gallery is **Central City Backpackers,** 26 Lorne St., tel. 09/358-5685, with 160 beds and the popular travelers bar, Embargo. Prices range from $19 in a 10-bed dorm to $48 for a double room.

Continuing up Queen St. and kitty-corner to Aotea Square, part of the Kiwi International Hotel has been converted to the **Kiwiconomy Backpackers,** 427 Queen St., tel. 09/379-6487 or 0800/100-411; website: www.kiwihotel.co.nz. Rooms are small and basic, but at $15 for a dorm, this among the cheapest place to stay downtown.

Parnell

Many privately operated backpacker lodges are along Georges Bay Rd., which runs north from Parnell Rd., one of the trendiest shopping-and-dining streets in Auckland. Downtown is a 30-minute walk from all the choices below, and both airport shuttle companies will drop you at the front door.

The pick of the bunch, as well as the smallest, is **Lantana Lodge,** a restored wooden house at 60 Georges Bay Rd., tel. 09/373-4546. It features a well-equipped kitchen, a comfortable TV room and lounge, a porch, friendly management, and plenty of good tourist information on low-budget options. Dorm beds are $21 (there's one noisy room, directly below the kitchen-avoid it), twins and doubles $48 d. The only other one along Georges Bay Rd. worthy of inclusion is **City Garden Lodge,** at No. 25, tel. 09/302-0880. Surrounded by extensive gardens, it's in a grand old building that was once home to the queen of Tonga and is advertised as being of "European Standard," whatever that is. Rates range from $20 for a dorm bed to private rooms for $35 s, $48 d.

Grafton

Grafton is a business/residential suburb two km (30 minutes on foot) south of downtown along Queen Street. Here you'll find **Georgia Parkside Backpackers,** 189 Park Rd., Grafton, tel. 09/309-8999 or 0508/436-744, website: www .georgia.co.nz, in a converted old mansion across

from the Auckland Domain. You can still appreciate the original character and style in the stained-glass windows, antique fireplaces, and large spacious rooms set around a paved courtyard. There are dorms and individual rooms, shared bathroom and laundry, and a kitchen. Breakfast supplies are sold in the shop. Costs run $15–18 per night for a dorm bed, $35 s, $48 d for a private room.

Mt. Eden

Bamber Lodge (formerly Eden Lodge), 22 View Rd. (off Mt. Eden Rd.), tel. 09/623-4267, is in an old homestead with spacious grounds and a small pool in a quiet residential area. Everything is spotlessly clean, the rooms are large and bright, the kitchen is fully equipped, and there's a dining area, TV room, and plenty of space for off-street parking. Dorm beds are $20, private rooms are $35–45 s, $45–48 d.

Another excellent choice in Mt. Eden is **Oaklands Lodge,** in an older, upmarket part of town at 5 Oaklands Rd., tel. 09/638-6545 or 0800/222-725; website: www.oaklands.co.nz. This two-story Victorian-era house features large communal areas and extensive gardens; dorm $22, $42 s, $55 d.

Ponsonby

Ponsonby, a trendy suburb two km west of downtown, holds **Ponsonby Backpackers,** 2 Franklin Rd., tel. 09/360-1311 or 0800/476-676, in a historic two-story house just around the corner from lively Ponsonby Road. The facilities are all of a high standard, and the cooking and dining areas spacious. The staff will store baggage, book tours, and are keen to tell of the latest Ponsonby dining hot spots. Dorm beds are $16, private rooms $19–22 pp.

MOTOR CAMPS
North

While Auckland has no motor camps right downtown, many are located near the major arteries north and south of the city. One of the best is **North Shore Motels and Top 10 Holiday Park,** 52 Northcote Rd., Takapuna, tel. 09/418-

2578 or 0508/909-090; website: www.nsmo-tels.co.nz. There are plenty of grassy sites, with facilities catering to campers, motor-home travelers, or those who prefer their own private cabin. Campsites range $20–25, small bunkrooms (each containing two single bunk beds, heater, table and stools, sink, crockery, cutlery, and hot water jug) range $30–50 s or d, and motel-style units with private bathrooms go for $80 s or d. All guests have the use of the large communal bathroom, kitchen blocks, and laundry (large washers and dryers), but you need to provide your own sleeping bag or linen (except for the motel rooms). To get there from the city center, cross the Harbour Bridge in the Whangarei lane. Four km north, take the Northcote Rd. exit (not the Northcote-Birkenhead exit) and turn left. In less than one km, look for the sign and take the driveway on the far side of the Pizza Hut restaurant. Also in Takapuna is **Takapuna Beach Holiday Park,** 22 The Promenade, tel. 09/489-7909. As the name suggests, it's right on the beach. Tent sites are $18 s or d, serviced sites $24–30, and cabins $37.

South

The closest camping to downtown Auckland is at **Remuera Motor Lodge,** four km southeast of the city center at 16 Minto Rd. (off Remuera Rd.), Remuera, tel. 09/524-5126. It is surrounded by trees and has a large swimming pool and landscaped camping area. There are relatively few flat grassy spots for tents, but lots of space for RVs (sites $10–14 pp). Bunkroom facilities are available at $20 pp. Tourist units start at $65 d; you provide your own linen and blankets. Motel units range $70–80 s or d. **Avondale Motor Park,** 46 Bollard Ave., Avondale, tel. 09/828-7228, is nine km southwest of the city off New North Rd., close to MOTAT and the zoo. Tent sites are $10 pp, serviced sites start at $12 pp. On-site RVs are $40, with cooking facilities provided; tourist cabins are $50; and tourist flats, with a bathroom and kitchen, are $60.

Food

Auckland's hundreds of cafés and restaurants have prices from cheap to mind-boggling. Least expensive is to buy food from the markets and cook your own. However, you may be surprised to find you're able to eat out fairly often without adversely affecting your budget. Pick up a free copy of the *Aucklander Dining Guide* (put out twice a year), which contains a good number of eating and drinking choices. You can find it at the Auckland Visitor Centre.

DOWNTOWN

Breakfast

There's no better way to start a long day's sightseeing than with a hearty breakfast. A personal favorite is the **Birdcage Tavern,** right by Victoria Park Market and under the Northern Motorway flyover at 133 Franklin Rd., tel. 09/378-9104. Dating to 1884, the tavern gets its name from the restaurant, a glass-topped atrium filled with greenery. A full cooked breakfast is a bargain,

just $6.50, which includes endless coffee. The service is fast and efficient, even at the busiest times, and the food is good.

Food on the Run

Near the information center is the **Global Sandwich,** 350 Queen St., tel. 09/303-2505, where the sandwiches are premade and ready to go. They also sell soup and salads. Eat at the counter or head across to the wide-open spaces of Aotea Square. Similar fare is offered at **Feast,** just off Queen St. at Durham St., tel. 09/307-0017. Start the day with breakfast specialties such as French toast and grilled bananas. Through to closing at 6 P.M., salads and sandwiches are prepared to order using ingredients from a long glass-fronted deli.

The old Bank of New Zealand building, on Queen St., hides the modern **Tower Shopping Centre,** which has a large food hall. Head to the Robert Harris Cafe on the second floor, tel. 09/358-3891, where there are a few tables on a balcony built over the Queen St. sidewalk. Other food halls are located in the **Downtown Shopping Centre,** on the corner of Albert and Customs Streets, and **Finance Plaza,** on Queen St. at Victoria Street.

Victoria Park Market, west of downtown on Victoria St., has food stalls scattered throughout. They sell a wide range of regular and ethnic food: everything from pies and hot dogs to falafels, pasta dishes, and Chinese meals. If you're lucky, a band will be playing in the outdoor eating area, and even if it rains, you can still enjoy the food and free jazz by seeking shelter under the large table umbrellas.

Cafés and Coffeehouses

Cafés line nearly every street downtown; all generally feature a good selection of sandwiches, filled rolls, savory pastries, pies, cream cakes, and desserts. For a satisfying light lunch with coffee or a soft drink, expect to pay about $5–10 pp. High Street, one block east of Queen Street, is popular with urbanites for its profusion of happening cafes. Even if you're visiting Auckland to get away from this scene, it's the place to go for a good cup of freshly brewed coffee. **Jolt,** a small place at 47 High St.,

tel. 09/303-0066, is filled with the smell of strong coffee Mon.–Fri. 7 A.M.–5:30 P.M. and Saturday 8:30 A.M.–4 P.M. Other local favorites include **Columbus Coffee,** 43 High St., tel. 09/309-5677, with coffees from around the world; and **Paneton Cafe,** 60 High St., tel. 09/303-2515.

Pavilion, overlooking a courtyard from beside the lobby of the Royal & Sun Alliance Building at 48 Shortland St., tel. 09/359-9466, is a pleasant escape from the busy streets. It fills with workers from the law and insurance firms above. A popular breakfast dish is corn fritters with bacon, avocado, tomato, and chutney ($12.50). At lunch, choose from New Zealand favorites such as char-grilled lamb chops ($15.50) to more health-conscious selections such as chicken and pine nut salad ($14). Pavilion is open Mon.–Sat. from 7 A.M.

Waterfront Dining

Cin Cin on Quay—on the ground floor at the back of the ferry building at 99 Quay St., tel. 09/307-6966—has great water views and a classical feel with high arched doorways and elegant table settings both inside and out. Start with freshly shucked oysters (from $2.50 each) then

© ANDREW HEMPSTEAD

Head to Viaduct Basin for the best variety of waterfront dining.

tuck into the likes of ginger-crusted hapuka with Asian mushrooms and sesame vinaigrette for $29. Or try some distinctly nontraditional pizzas, such as one topped with honey cinnamon glazed ham, asparagus, and balsamic vinegar. It's open Mon.–Fri. noon–1 A.M., weekends 8 A.M.–1 A.M.

Upstairs in the Ferry Building, the elaborate **Harbourside Seafood Bar and Grill,** Quay St., tel. 09/307-0556, offers water views and an outdoor balcony lined with prime waterfront tables. The menu takes its inspiration from around the world, but local seafood dominates, with dishes like a seafood risotto smothered in a creamy Tuscan sauce ($27) and grilled kingfish combined with a milky Thai curry ($29). Crayfish, plucked live from a huge tank, are also popular; they can be steamed, grilled, or roasted-the choice is yours. New Zealand wines dominate the long wine list. Harbourside is open daily 11:30 A.M.–10:30 P.M.

From the Ferry Building, wander west along the harbor to Viaduct Basin for more excellent choices that run the gamut from bistro-style pub food to intimate upmarket dining. All Viaduct Basin eateries have outdoor, waterfront tables-providing a fabulous setting for summertime dining. **Kermadec,** in the Viaduct Quay Building, on the corner of Quay and Lower Hobson Streets, tel. 09/309-0412, stands out for its striking nautical-theme décor through five dining areas. For a casual meal, it's difficult to top the brasserie and starters such as sesame-crusted tuna with Caesar salad ($15). Then, for the main meal, simply choose a fish type, and then decide whether you'd like it steamed, char-grilled, or deep-fried. Part of the same complex is the Two Flying Fish Café & Bar, offering alfresco harborfront dining-the perfect place to sample that New Zealand classic, fish and chips.

Owned by one of New Zealand's leading chefs, Michael James, **MJs** is within Sebel Suites, 85 Customs St., tel. 09/358-2767, the only accommodation right at Viaduct Basin. This chic eatery features three dining areas-outside along the water, a casual street-level room with a bistro-style atmosphere, and a more intimate upper level. The menu is a mixture of classical and modern dishes using local game and seafood

combined with Asian spices. Serious eaters will find it hard to go past the 650-gram grilled t-bone steak ($35). Other main dishes range from $30–38, while desserts (such as a delicious banana and fudge crumble) are $12.

Jacques, 18 Tamaki Dr., tel. 09/521-3930, is a good bet after visiting Kelly Tarlton's Antarctic Adventure & Underwater World. This bright and breezy restaurant lies on the harborfront, across the road from this popular attraction east of downtown. Relax with just a coffee on the deck, or try local delicacies such as whitebait fritters ($12.50) as a starter then a whole snapper baked in sweet chili and pesto ($25.50) as a main course in the unpretentious main dining room. Jacques is open daily for lunch and Wed.–Sun. for dinner.

European

Tucked away under the Northern Motorway flyover in the corner of a historic tavern is the **Birdcage French Restaurant,** 133 Franklin Rd., tel. 09/378-9104, renowned for classically simple Continental preparations, such as salmon

LOCAL SEAFOOD

The best place to enjoy the abundance of fresh seafood in Auckland is at one of the many restaurants along the harbor. Not only do these eateries have wonderful locations for enjoying the sights, sounds, and smells of the ocean, much of the seafood comes straight from the fishing boats to the table. In the case of Kermadec, the fishing company owns the restaurant.

In this same part of the city are several fish markets, busiest before dawn, when the trawlers have docked and local restaurateurs are searching out their favorite catch. **Seamart,** on the corner of Fanshawe St. and Market Pl., tel. 09/302-8989, is open to the public. This massive seafood market offers a variety of fresh fish, live crabs and even eel, and a take-out sushi bar.

Snapper, hake, orange roughy, *hapuka* (groper), kingfish, tuna, and swordfish are all caught along the North Island's east coast. Oysters, mussels, crayfish, crabs, and prawns are also available.

in a lightly creamed champagne sauce with a selection of vegetables and gratin potatoes for under $20. In a nice touch, the potatoes are served from a cast iron pot at your table. It's open Mon.–Sat. for dinner.

A long-time Auckland favorite, the **French Café,** 210 Symonds St., tel. 09/377-1911, is beyond the south end of downtown in Newmarket. Be seated in the long narrow dining room, in the private courtyard, or at the few streetside tables to enjoy contemporary European cuisine, such as roast duckling on kumara mash accompanied by steamed bok choy for $25.50.

Mexican and South American

The **Mexican Café,** 67 Victoria St., tel. 09/373-2311, is colorfully decorated with traditional Mexican motifs and has a small outdoor patio. The food is good and inexpensive, with only a couple of dishes over $15. It's open daily for lunch and dinner.

Wildfire, Princes Wharf, Quay St., tel. 09/353-7595, is a Brazilian *churrascaria,* or barbecue restaurant, featuring favorite dishes from the south of the country. Pay $40 pp ($27 pp at lunch and 6–7 P.M.) for unlimited food, including beef, pork, chicken, and lamb, carved at the table from long skewers of meat that has been marinated then slowly char-grilled over hot coals.

Asian

Yum cha, the Chinese lunchtime tradition that allows you to choose from a trolley as it's wheeled past your table, is popular throughout Auckland. Expect bamboo baskets of steaming goodies such as dumplings, won ton, and spring rolls, as well as a huge array of sickly-sweet and savory desserts. At **Ding How Chinese Restaurant,** 55 Albert St. (enter through St. Patricks Square), tel. 09/358-4838, *yum cha* is a traditional affair and always busy with Asian families. Diagonally opposite, not much English is spoken at the **Mandarin Seafood Restaurant,** 98 Albert St., tel. 09/377-2886, but *yum cha* is ridiculously inexpensive-and besides, not knowing what you're getting is half the fun. **Ocean City Restaurant** puts a western spin on *yum cha.* All the usual choices are offered, but it's help-yourself at a buffet table that includes a build-your-own soup station. Lunch is a reasonable $10 pp.

The **New Orient Restaurant** in the Strand Arcade, 233 Queen St., tel. 09/379-7793, offers the ubiquitous Chinese buffet lunch on weekdays noon–2:30 P.M. for $18 pp, or lunch items from the à la carte menu for $6–16. On Sunday a buffet dinner costing $27 pp is available from 6 P.M. It's also open every night from 6 P.M. but the dinners can be fairly expensive.

The **Middle East Cafe,** 23A Wellesley St., tel. 09/379-4843, is a locally recommended place for cheap, tasty lunches and dinners. It serves falafels, salads, cakes, and coffee at reasonable prices. It stays open till midnight. In the same vicinity, **Mai Thai Restaurant** is upstairs in the yellow building one block from Queen St. at the corner of Victoria and Albert Streets, tel. 09/366-6258. The set lunch is $15, while the dinner menu features duck, prawns, and shrimp from $12.

Sushi is available at most downtown food halls, but for a more comfortable sit-down meal, consider **Ariake,** a quiet little place in Stamford Plaza on Swanson St., tel. 09/377-8881. At the **Sushi Factory,** 15 Vulcan Lane, tel. 09/307-3600, pluck sushi and sashimi favorites from the conveyor belt and let the wait staff add up the cost of your empty color-coded plates for a final bill.

Asian Influenced

After reaching the zenith of its popularity on North America's West Coast in the mid-1990s, "fusion" cooking—the blending of Western produce and game with Eastern spices and flair—hit the shores of New Zealand soon after. Although the buzz has passed, the style has been incorporated at many of Auckland's best restaurants, such as MJs. An innovative take on Asian-influenced cuisine is **Rice,** 10–12 Federal St., tel. 09/359-9113, at the top end of the CBD and open for lunch Mon.–Fri. and for dinner Mon.–Saturday. As the name suggests, rice features prominently. In fact, every dish and even many drinks have some association to rice, whether it is rice wine used in the salad dressing or a rice-based casserole (with calamari and quail egg-a real treat). All main dishes are under

$20, and drinks such as a sake Bloody Mary range $2.50–6. The simplicity of the food is matched by the decor, highlighted by a sleek yet harmonious color scheme.

Sky City

This massive complex on the corner of Victoria and Federal Streets, tel. 09/363-6000, features a number of eateries. **Fortuna New Zealand Buffet** is open for breakfast, lunch, and dinner. The spread is extensive, and the food is good for a buffet, but it's not cheap if you're not hungry; breakfast is $17.50 (7:30–11 A.M.), lunch is $23 (noon–2:30 P.M.; and dinner is $27.50 (5:30–8:30 P.M.). **Tamarind** is an upmarket restaurant open daily for dinner from 6 P.M. The menu is classed as "Pacific Rim," consisting of specialties from countries as diverse as New Zealand and Japan. Main meals start at $28. Immediately above the main observation decks of the Sky Tower is **Orbit,** a contemporary fine-dining revolving restaurant. It's open weekends for breakfast 10 A.M.–noon, daily for lunch 11:30 A.M.–2:30 P.M., and daily for dinner 5:30-10:30 P.M. Above Orbit is the **Observatory,** a buffet restaurant open similar hours. Other places serving food in the Sky City complex include **Rebo,** a stylish café serving up bistro-style fare; **Ming Court,** a Chinese restaurant open for a dim sum lunch and à la carte dinner; and there's a **deli** on the gaming floor.

DINING IN OTHER PARTS OF THE CITY
Parnell

You'll find many of the Aucklanders' favorite restaurants in the Parnell area.

Strawberry Alarm Clock, 119 Parnell Rd., tel. 09/377-6959, attracts an eclectic crowd ranging from students to local business owners. Exposed brick walls, a painted concrete floor, and worn timber furniture all add to the funky atmosphere. The menu features lots of healthy fare, as well as cooked breakfasts and some deliciously innovative salads. It's open Mon.–Fri. 7:30 A.M.–5 P.M., Sat.–Sun. 9 A.M.–4:30 P.M. Farther up the hill, **Verve,** 311

Parnell Rd., tel. 09/379-2860, also offers a good breakfast, as well as attractive sandwiches and interesting salads.

With a leading chef running the kitchen, stark black and white decor, and reputation as a city hot spot **Metropole,** 223 Parnell Rd., tel. 09/379-9300, had its heyday in the early 1990s. New owners have overseen a renaissance of sorts, and with exotic dishes such as filet of kangaroo accompanied by tamarind-curried potatoes ($28), Metropole is again a player in the competitive Parnell dining scene.

Continuing up the hill, **Non Solo Pizza,** 259 Parnell Rd., tel. 09/379-5358, offers gourmet pizzas, but as the name suggests, "not only pizza," with choices as varied as a modern take on moussaka ($17.50) and steaming bowls of pasta for up to four diners to share (from $12 pp).

Chutney's on Parnell, 323 Parnell Rd., tel. 09/358-2969, features contemporary East Indian cuisine in a smart setting. The menu isn't large, but it features classics like beef vindaloo in *masala* served with Basmati rice ($16). Vegetarian delicacies include *Navrattan Korma*—mixed vegetables stir-fried in a cashew and almond flavored gravy—for $14. Chutney's is open daily from 5:30 P.M.

Just south of Parnell, in Newmarket, **Bodrum Cafe,** 2 Osborne St., tel. 09/529-1931, has a wide selection of Turkish and Middle Eastern dishes starting at $15. It's open daily for lunch, and Mon.–Sat. for dinner from 5 P.M.

Ponsonby

Ponsonby Road holds dozens of hip cafés and restaurants, many of which stay open until midnight. **Thirty Nine,** 39 Ponsonby Rd., tel. 09/376-5008, attracts the trendy crowd by not being trendy. It's a down-home type of place with tables out front and in a private courtyard out back. The coffee here is good, really good, and really strong. Muffins, cakes, and cooked breakfasts are other highlights. It's open Mon.–Fri. 7 A.M.–4 P.M., weekends 8 A.M.–4 P.M.

Two popular coffeehouses are **Santos Cafe,** 114 Ponsonby Rd., tel. 09/378-8431; and **Atomic Café,** across the road at 121 Ponsonby Rd., tel. 09/376-4954. The former is a longtime favorite with families, with a wide-ranging menu and a private courtyard with toys to keep kids amused.

A strip of varied dining choices lies along Ponsonby Road between Pollen and Mackelvie Streets. The most interesting of these is the **Bronze Goat,** 108 Ponsonby Rd., tel. 09/378-4193, a rustically decorated restaurant with only a few settings of wooden furniture and bare brick walls. The menu is written up daily on a blackboard and is simple, healthy, and relatively inexpensive. **Burger Fuel,** 114 Ponsonby Rd., tel. 09/378-6466, specializes in burgers, such as the Bastard, with a bit of everything, and the extra-spicy Flame Thrower. Burgers range $7–10.

More than one U.S. reader has written us recommending **Burger Wisconsin,** 168 Ponsonby Rd., tel. 09/360-1894, for the city's best burgers. They cost from $8 each, but choices include chicken breast with cream cheese and an apricot sauce on a bun.

Thai cuisine is a popular alternative to Chinese food in New Zealand. One of the better such restaurants is **Thai House Restaurant,** a stylish place at 25 Ponsonby Rd., tel. 09/376-5912. It's open for dinner only. Dinners start at $14.

Takapuna

When you want steak and seafood, locals say go to **Oceans Buffet Restaurant** upstairs in the plaza at 159 Hurstmere Rd. (car parking in the basement), Takapuna, North Shore, tel. 09/486-2206—you get a sea and tree view from the inside or outside deck as an added bonus. Aside from the steak and fresh seafood, you'll find chicken, lamb, pasta, and other dishes on the menu. Lunch is offered Mon.–Fri., with starters costing $7–10 and light meals (seafood, pasta, and salads) $13–17. Dinner is served seven days a week. A main course is $17.50–22, but good-value specials can always be found on the menu. Oceans is open Mon.–Fri. noon–2 P.M. for lunch, and Mon.–Sun. 5:30–10 P.M. for dinner.

Transportation

GETTING THERE

Air

Auckland International Airport, New Zealand's largest airport, is 21 km south of downtown. It has three terminals—an International terminal and two domestic terminals, one for each of the major domestic airlines, Air New Zealand and Ansett New Zealand. The three terminals are connected by a free shuttle bus. Airport services include tourist information, banks, a currency exchange, post office, car rental agencies, gift shops, and luggage lockers; you'll find showers in the International Terminal building.

Air New Zealand, tel. 09/357-3000 or 0800/737-300, serves cities and towns throughout the country, with Auckland as the main hub. For information and reservations call direct, or visit one of the many Air New Zealand offices, including at the corner of Queen and Customs Streets, tel. 09/336-2424. **Great Barrier Airlines,** tel. 09/275-9120 or 0800/900-600, flies daily to major centers in the vicinity of Auckland.

Bus Service between the Airport and City Center

There are many ways to travel between the airport and downtown. The easiest way is by cab, which costs $38–42. The **Airbus,** tel. 09/275-9396 or 0508/247-287, website: www.airbus.co.nz, picks up passengers at all three terminals, and stops at major downtown hotels only, with the service ending at the Downtown Airline Terminal. It runs every 20 minutes between 6:20 A.M. and 8:20 P.M. The fare is $13 one way, $22 round-trip. Door-to-door service is provided by **Super Shuttle,** tel. 09/306-3960. This company cuts deals with the backpacker lodges, so if the trip is booked through your accommodation, the fare can be as low as $11 one way. The standard fare is $14 pp one way. For reservations call one hour in advance, or search out their minivans at the airport.

Rail

The much-anticipated Britomart Transport Interchange is slated to replace the aging redbrick **Central Railway Station** as Auckland's long-distance rail terminus sometime this decade. In the meantime, all services terminate east of downtown at the old facility. **Tranz Scenic,** tel. 0800/802-802, website: www.tranzscenic.co.nz, operates all rail services. Trains run south from Auckland to Wellington, Tauranga, and Rotorua. Fares are comparable to bus travel (Auckland-Wellington costs $95–160 depending on the class of travel), and the service reliable and frequent.

Bus

Long-distance bus travel is the most popular form of transportation for visitors, and Auckland is the main hub. **Intercity** has services to just about every point of the country. The depot is at the **Sky City Coach Terminal,** 102 Hobson St., tel. 09/639-0500. Buses arrive and depart to all destinations at least twice daily. The ticket office is open Sun.–Fri. 7:15 A.M.–6:15 P.M., Saturday 7:15 A.M.–2:30 P.M. The terminal has luggage lockers ($6 overnight) and is open daily 7 A.M.–8 P.M. **Newmans,** tel. 09/913-6200, is also based in the Sky City Coach Terminal. Their schedule is limited to the North Island, but the network of routes is extensive. **Northliner,** tel. 09/307-5873, handles bus travel north of Auckland. The depot is at 172 Quay St., opposite the Ferry Building.

GETTING AROUND

Auckland has an excellent transportation network; you can get almost anywhere by bus, rail, or ferry. These services are provided by private operators contracted by Auckland Regional Council. For all local transportation information, call the council's **Rideline,** tel. 09/366-6400 or 0800/103-080; website: www.rideline.co.nz.

The **Britomart Transport Interchange** is a grandiose scheme that has been on the drawing board for over a decade. When completed it will cover 3.5 hectares of reclaimed land between Queen Elizabeth II Square, Customs St., Quay St., and Britomart Place and incorporate the old post office building as its main entrance. This transportation hub will include a street-level bus interchange, a new terminus for local and long-distance rail services, an underground concourse linked to the Ferry Building, and, eventually, the core of a downtown light-rail transit system.

Bus

Buses cover the entire urban area, with services radiating from the Downtown Bus Terminal on Commerce St. at Quay St., and from suburban hubs in New Lynn and Otahuhu. Buses run Mon.–Sat. 6:30 A.M.–11 P.M., Sunday 6:30 A.M.–7 P.M. Fares begin at $1.20, then $1.20 additional for every stage point (zone) passed through. Senior and child discounts only apply to Auckland residents. **The Link** provides an easy way to get around downtown. This efficient service runs every 10–20 minutes daily 6 A.M.–6 P.M. (until midnight on weekends) along Quay St., up through Parnell to the museum, back past Aotea Square to Victoria Park Market and Ponsonby.

The **United Airlines Explorer Bus,** tel. 09/571-3119 or 0800/727-892, starts at the Ferry Building and makes stops at 14 of Auckland's commercial attractions (Victoria Park Market, Mission Bay Beach, MOTAT and the zoo, Kelly Tarlton's, Parnell Rose Gardens, Auckland Museum, Mt. Eden, and more). The bus leaves the Ferry Terminal daily on the hour 10 A.M.–4 P.M., and you can stop off and rejoin the bus the next time around or start from any of the attractions along the route. If you can't fit all the attractions into one day's sight-seeing ($25), a two-day pass saves a few bucks.

Rail

TranzRail operates **TranzMetro,** tel. 0800/802-802, a commuter rail service weekdays 7 A.M.–5:30 P.M.. The routes run from the city west to Waitakere via Newmarket, south to Papakura via Newmarket and Penrose, and south to Papakura via Panmure and the eastern suburbs; tickets are $1.20 per stage point.

Ferry

Fullers, based in the Ferry Building on Quay St., tel. 09/367-9111, operates a scheduled service across Waitemata Harbour to Devonport. Ferries depart every 30 minutes 7 A.M.–7 P.M., then hourly (on the hour) until 11 P.M. The fare is $8 round-trip. Fullers' Harbour Cruise stops at Kelly

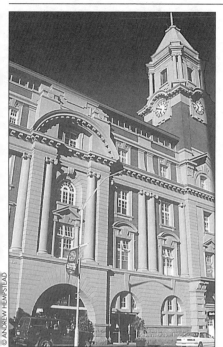

The distinctive Ferry Building, at the foot of Queen Street, is the hub for local ferries.

Tarlton's, Rangitoto Island, and Devonport. Get off at any of these places and rejoin the next cruise for $30. Fullers also operates scheduled service to Rangitoto, Waiheke, Motuihe, and Great Barrier Islands. Detailed coverage on all these routes is given under Hauraki Gulf Maritime Park.

Car Rental

Auckland has an incredible number of car rental agencies. All the major agencies are represented, but it is the small, lesser-known companies that make up the bulk (more than 80 at last count). Major agencies include **Avis,** tel. 09/379-2650; **Budget,** tel. 09/976-9100; **Hertz,** tel. 09/367-6360; **National,** tel. 09/309-3336; **New Zealand Rent-a-car,** tel. 09/444-7795; and **Thrifty,** 09/309-0111. Each of these agencies has a desk at the airport and outlets throughout the country. They charge from $80 per day,

but this usually includes unlimited mileage. **Scotties,** tel. 09/630-2625, a small agency based in Mt. Eden, has a variety of vehicles (and a few camper-vans) at good prices, and specializes in long-term rentals. The vehicles are newer models and reliable; each is covered by the maximum insurance available. Scotties also has an outlet in Christchurch, the perfect opportunity for a one-way trip through the country.

Other local agencies include **About New Zealand Rental Cars,** tel. 09/256-9016; **Dollar Save Car Hire,** tel. 09/366-0646; **Easy Rentals,** tel. 09/275-0037; **Ideal Rentals,** tel. 09/262-0464; **Metropolitan Rentals,** tel. 09/630-2030; **Omega,** tel. 0800/525-210; **Nationwide,** tel. 09/275-4811; and **Quality,** tel. 09/275-4811. These smaller agencies offer more reasonable deals, but beware of fly-by-night firms that may rent unreliable vehicles and then refuse to refund your money, or give minimum insurance coverage. Rentals can be as low as $20 per day in the off-season for a mid-1990s vehicle.

Buying a Used Car in Auckland

If you plan to be in New Zealand for any length of time, one of your cheapest travel options is to buy a used car as soon as you arrive in Auckland, and then sell it when you leave. You can find a large selection of used cars advertised in the Wednesday and Saturday editions of the *NZ Herald* and the *Saturday Star.* Car fairs are held throughout Auckland each weekend. You'll be surprised how many Aucklanders attend car fairs—they're almost a social gathering. The largest are in the Takapuna Carpark, tel. 09/480-5612, Saturday 10 A.M.–2 P.M.; at Manukau City Shopping Centre, tel. 09/358-5000, Sunday 9 A.M.–1 P.M.; and at Ellerslie Racecourse, tel. 09/529-2233, Sunday 9 A.M.–noon. If you want to buy a used car but don't have time to shop for or sell it when you leave, try **Downtown Car Rentals,** tel. 09/303-1847. After two months, this company guarantees to buy back the vehicle you bought from them for around half the price you paid.

Taxi

Flag charge for a taxi is $2.75, then $1.85 for every kilometer. Taxis wait outside all major downtown hotels, at the airport, and opposite Queen Elizabeth II Square. Companies include **Auckland Taxi Co-op,** tel. 09/300-3000; **Discount Taxis,** tel. 09/529-1000; **Dial A Cab,** tel. 09/355-3000; and **Taxi Combined,** tel. 0800/505-550.

TOURS

A bus tour is a great introduction to the city, and a good way to reach outlying sights if you don't have your own transportation. Auckland's many tour operators offer similar schedules—three-hour morning and afternoon tours that hit all the downtown sights ($45–55) and full-day tours, typically including a harbor cruise (around $100). Contact **Great Sights,** tel. 09/375-4700 or 0800/744-487; **Scenic Tours,** tel. 09/634-2266; or **Sea City Tours,** tel. 09/624-2499.

Bush & Beach, tel. 09/575-1458, offers a number of small-group nature tours to sites including Waitakere rainforest and west coast beaches, a gannet colony, east coast beaches, a sheep farm and kauri park, and an orchard. Or you can go forest trekking on horseback; trips range $60–105 pp.

Services and Information

SERVICES
Money
Trading banks are generally open weekdays 10 A.M.–4:30 P.M.—banks still serve as the best places to exchange travelers checks. Most large hotels and stores will cash checks, but the exchange rate leans considerably in their favor (particularly in the tourist shops). You can also exchange foreign money at **American Express,** 105 Queen St., tel. 09/379-8286; **Travelex,** 32 Queen St., tel. 09/358-9173; and **Singapore Exchange & Finance Ltd.,** 11 Customs St., tel. 09/302-0502.

Post and Telecommunications
The **Chief Post Office** is in the Bledisloe Building on Wellesley Street. It's open weekdays only. Over 100 other postal outlets are scattered across the city, including in all **Books and More** stores.

You can make domestic and international calls from any call box—there's a battery of phone boxes outside the main post office. Long-distance calls are made easy with phone cards.

Net Central Cybercafe, 5 Lorne St., tel. 09/373-5186, is a centrally located little café with computer access to the Internet. Computer use runs about $10 per half-hour. Food and drink is discounted for computer users. Public Internet access is also available at **Citinet Cybercafe,** 115 Queen St., tel. 09/377-3674; and **Cyber City,** 29 Victoria St., tel. 09/303-3009.

Laundromats
Look in the Yellow Pages for the one nearest you. Some are self-serve, others wash, dry, and fold your clothes for you. Central locations include **Clean Green Laundromat,** 18 Fort St., tel. 09/358-4370; and **Splish Splash,** 92 Dominion Rd., Mt. Eden, tel. 09/630-9204. Most major hotels offer same-day dry-cleaning.

Emergency Services
For all emergencies, call 111 or one of the following: **Auckland Hospital,** Park Rd., tel. 09/379-7440, has a 24-hour emergency department. For less-urgent cases, call **Auckland Metro Doctors,** Level 5, Dingwall Building, 87 Queen St., tel. 09/373-4621. Part of the same complex and on the same level, **Travelcare,** tel. 09/373-4621, provides a variety of medical services for the traveler, including routine medical examinations, dental checkups, and immunizations.

Left-Luggage Services
Many places listed in the Accommodations section will look after luggage for a limited amount of time, some for a small fee. Otherwise the main left-luggage facilities (charge per item) are the Airport Visitors Centre in the International Terminal at the airport; the Airbus ticket booth in the Air New Zealand Domestic Terminal; and the Downtown Airline Terminal on Quay St. in the city.

INFORMATION

Books and Maps

Auckland Central Library, Lorne St. at Wellesley St., tel. 09/377-0209, is open Mon.–Thurs. 9:30 A.M.–8 P.M., Friday until 9 P.M., Saturday 10 A.M.–4 P.M., and Sunday 1–5 P.M. You'll find a newspaper reading room in the basement with current papers from all over New Zealand, as well as some British, Australian, Canadian, and U.S. papers; it's generally open regular library hours.

New Zealanders are prolific readers, and this is reflected in the number of bookstores found throughout the city. **Whitcoulls,** 210 Queen St. (at Victoria St.), tel. 09/309-7725, is the largest bookshop in New Zealand, with four floors of books and magazines, and a café. The shop is a good source of information on any aspect concerning New Zealand, as well as of topographical maps. **Bennetts Bookshops,** 360 Queen St., tel. 09/377-3496; **Dymocks,** Elliott St., tel. 09/379-9919; and the smaller **Unity Books,** 19 High St., tel. 09/307-0731, all carry wide selections of New Zealand titles, both fiction and nonfiction. If you're from the U.S. and you feel patriotic, visit **Borders Books & Music,** 291-297 Queen St., tel. 09/309-3377. **Anah Dunsheath Rare Books,** 6 High St., tel. 09/379-0379, is an antiquarian bookseller specializing in New Zealand history, the Pacific, and Antarctica. They also carry historic maps and postcards.

The **Department of Lands and Survey** produces detailed topographical maps of New Zealand ($11–18). If you plan to hike, particularly in any of the national parks, get these excellent maps first—usually available at better sporting goods and tramping stores.

Auckland Map Centre, on the corner of Queen and Wyndham Streets, tel. 09/309-7725, stocks all types of maps and nautical charts, as well as a selection of travel guides.

Information Centers

After passing through immigration and then customs at Auckland International Airport, you'll be ushered down the ramp into the main airport lobby. Head *left* through the crowds to the **Visitor Information Centre,** tel. 09/275-6467. It's open seven days a week from 5 A.M. until the day's last flight clears customs and immigration. They will book accommodation for a small fee, or use the free-phone board to contact the accommodations directly.

When you leave the airport, look out for the green "I" Visitor Information Network sign on the left side of the road; **Manukau Visitor Information Centre** is just beyond the airport on George Bolt Memorial Dr., tel. 09/275-5321. Open daily 8:30 A.M.–5 P.M.

The main information center for the city is the **Auckland Visitors and Information Centre** in the Aotea Centre, 291-297 Queen St., tel. 09/979-2333. It's open year-round, daily 9 A.M.–5 P.M. The staff provides information and advice, brochures (mostly free), timetables, newspapers, maps, and a comfortable place to sit and absorb all the information or to watch the video on Auckland's highlights. The staff books accommodations and car rentals, and sells tickets for all forms of transportation. You can also buy phone cards and detailed maps, cycling guides, and pictorial guides on New Zealand. By Viaduct Basin, the **New Zealand Visitor Centre,** on the corner of Quay and Hobson Streets, tel. 09/979-7005, is open daily 9:30 A.M.–5:30 P.M. Both these centers are operated by **Tourism Auckland,** website: www.aucklandnz.com.

You'll find a combined **Department of Conservation/Auckland Regional Parks** information center in the Ferry Building on Quay St., tel. 09/379-6476. This center has all the information you need on regional parks, national parks, campgrounds, walks, and the Gulf islands; it's open weekdays 8:30 A.M.–5 P.M. In the same building is the **Fullers Cruise Centre,** tel. 09/367-9111, the best source of information on travel to the Gulf Islands.

The **Automobile Association** (AA), 99 Albert St., tel. 09/302-1825, is open Mon.–Fri. 8 A.M.–4:30 P.M. Upon proof of any worldwide AA membership, this helpful association provides free maps, information, and general travel advice. Be sure to ask for the current *Accommodation Directory* ($12), invaluable for travel throughout the country.

AUCKLAND

Northland

Introduction

North of Auckland lies a spectacular region particularly appealing to sun worshippers, island hoppers, sailors, nature enthusiasts, and history buffs. Apart from a mild climate and plenty of sunshine, the north offers great beauty and variety. The Bay of Islands, where nature and history blend in an unbeatable combination, attracts the largest number of the region's visitors. The irregular 800-km coastline is fringed with soft, sandy beaches and sheltered coves; the bay, formed by a drowned river system, is dotted with some 150 islands. Diving thrills and sensational underwater photography await you in the crystal-clear, submarine world of coral reefs and shoals of brightly colored fish, and for excitement, you can't beat a day of deep-sea fishing for the magnificent game fish that cruise the Bay of Islands in abundance. This tropical paradise also lures both overseas and New Zealand sailors, who congregate in the bay gathering supplies, getting repairs, and soaking up the atmosphere, much as the traders and whalers did at the end of the 18th century.

A great deal of New Zealand's notable early history occurred in the north, and throughout the region (particularly in the Bay of Islands) are many well-preserved, historic buildings, and remains of Maori *pa*. Magnificent Ninety Mile Beach stretches as far as you can see, and if you follow the main road to the end, you come to Cape Reinga, one of the northernmost tips of New Zealand. See the clashing waves where the Pacific Ocean and Tasman Sea merge. At the southern end of Ninety Mile Beach still

rural Northland

stand several mighty kauri forests. The north is small enough that you can cover it in a few days by car, but to spend time in its many special places deserves at least a week, especially if your interests include hiking, deep-sea fishing, or diving. Here's hoping you have the time!

Auckland to Whangarei

HIBISCUS COAST

Traveling up Hwy. 1, you quickly leave the suburbs behind and get a first taste of rural New Zealand: rich agricultural land, lush green fields, grazing sheep and cows. Greenhouses and nurseries line the roads in some areas, and roadside stalls sell fresh fruit and vegetables at good prices. The town of Silverdale, only 40 km from Auckland, marks the beginning of The Hibiscus Coast, which includes Whangaparaoa (Bay of Whales) Peninsula, and stretches as far north as Hatfields Beach.

NORTH FROM AUCKLAND

Two main highways lead north from Auckland—the fastest and most direct is Hwy. 1, which crosses Waitemata Harbour via Auckland Harbour Bridge then passes through Warkworth, Wellsford, and Whangarei and then on to the Bay of Islands and Kaitaia. The alternate route is Hwy. 16 (called the North Western Motorway within city limits) along the west coast through Muriwai Beach and Helensville. This highway rejoins Hwy. 1 at Wellsford, then branches west again as Hwy. 16 on the north side of Kaipara Harbour, closely following the west coast north via Dargaville.

By Bus

Intercity runs several coaches a day from Auckland to Kaitaia via Whangarei and Paihia, the gateway to the Bay of Islands; and from Auckland to Paihia via Dargaville. Book at least 72 hours in advance to ensure a seat. Expect to pay about $50 one way Auckland to Paihia. Buses leave from the Sky City Coach Terminal, 102 Hobson St., tel. 09/639-0500. **Northliner,** tel. 09/307-5873, runs its Express Coach Service to Paihia ($46 one way) once daily, departing 172 Quay Street.

Shakespear Regional Park

At the eastern tip of the Whangaparaoa Peninsula, the park offers good bush and farm walks, and three sandy beaches safe for swimming. If you're in the area on a windy day, head for the steep cliffs near Army Bay and check out the hang-glider action. Another popular activity is shellfishing, good at low tide; place the shellfish on a barbecue and cook them until they open.

Red Beach

If you're an early riser, head for this beach before it gets light—it's spectacular at sunrise. The wet, orange shells left by the receding tide reflect the sun rays, and the entire beach takes on a red glow. Also adding to the beauty are the native flax flowers and *pohutukawa* trees (covered in bright scarlet flowers at Christmas) at the southern end. The beach offers safe swimming, surf suitable for beginners, lifeguard patrol on weekends and holidays, and short rock walks at either end.

Orewa Beach

This beach's long stretch of white sand is popular, but beware of the strong rip where the Orewa River meets the sea; on weekends and holidays it's patrolled by local surf club members. At the northern end you can see the remains of an ancient Maori *pa* site on the hilltop above Orewa House, and at the extreme north, over Grut's Bridge and sharply to the left, lies the entrance to **Eaves Bush.** This small reserve contains some impressive kauri trees and lots of native ferns. A 15-minute walk brings you to a stream at the back of **Puriri Park Holiday Complex,** tel. 09/426-4648. Across from the beach is **Beachcomber Motel,** 246 Hibiscus Coast Hwy., tel. 09/426-5973, offering 12 modern rooms, each with a kitchen; $70–125 s or d. Continuing north, **Pillows Travellers Lodge,** 412 Hibiscus Coast Hwy., tel. 09/426-6338, website: www.pil-

NORTHLAND

NORTHLAND

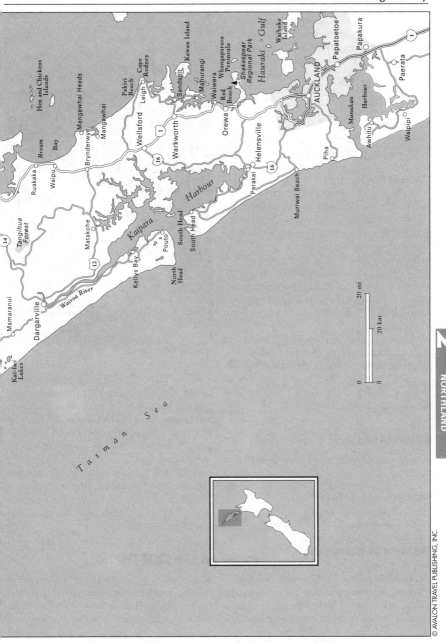

NORTHLAND

lows.co.nz, is one of the many accommodations in New Zealand built specifically to cater to backpackers. You'll find a comfortable lounge, kitchen, laundry, sundeck, inner courtyard filled with greenery, and public Internet access. Dorm beds are $18 pp, private rooms, some en suites, are $30–45 s, $38–50 d.

Waiwera

Waiwera is a thermal resort and busy tourist area. If relaxing in hot pools sounds appealing, follow the signs from the highway to **Waiwera Thermal Resort,** tel. 09/426-5369, nestled behind a beach at the mouth of a river. The 26 indoor and outdoor pools vary in temperature 28–43°C, and there are private spas, water slides, a waterfall pool, a movie pool where latest releases are shown on a big screen, picnic areas, and a food kiosk. The pools are open daily 9 A.M.–10 P.M.; admission is adult $17, senior $8, child $10. Private spas are $25 pp for 30 minutes, which includes general admission. If you don't have a bathing suit, no worries! You can rent everything you need.

Within walking distance of the resort and with gardens extending to a quiet waterway is **Waiwera Motel,** tel. 09/426-5153, with five self-contained units for $70–90 s or d. Facilities include a small pool, spa, and barbecue, and dinghies and kayaks for rent.

KOWHAI COAST

The Kowhai Coast stretches from Wenderholm Regional Park in the south to Pakiri Beach in the north. In between, the mighty Mahurangi River estuary has forged its way inland, allowing easy boat access to Warkworth, the main town on this stretch of coast.

Waiwera to Warkworth

Bush and beach trails offer good hiking in **Wenderholm Regional Park,** a beautiful reserve where a large variety of trees grow among the rolling green hills and back to the beach—a great spot for a picnic. You can launch your boat into the sheltered, beach-fringed harbor. The park is open daily 8 A.M.–6 P.M. **Pohuehue Scenic Re-**

Kowhai Coast beach

serve, off Hwy. 1, is another enjoyable place for hiking. Signposted walkways lead through a spectacular variety of native trees, ferns, and exotic plantations. **Moir Hill Walkway** also starts on Hwy. 1, six km south of Warkworth; it'll take you 3.5 hours to walk the six km (five to six hours round-trip). The path climbs through the trees, drops to a stream and waterfall, and again climbs to Moir Hill lookout, where great views of Hauraki Gulf await you. As an alternate return route, the track meanders back through Pohuehue Scenic Reserve.

WARKWORTH

Many small family orchards grow to the south of this charming fishing village (freshly picked fruit—cheaper than in town—beckons from roadside stalls) with colonial-style architecture and numerous cafés and restaurants, along the upper tidal reaches of the Mahurangi River.

Warkworth (population 2,500) is the main town between Auckland, 70 km south, and Whangarei, and well worth a side trip off the main highway before you continue north.

Warkworth District Museum and Parry Kauri Park

This beautiful half-hectare park contains some fine kauri trees—check out the two giant ones near the museum. The McKinney Kauri is 800 years old, and reaches a mere 11.89 meters at the first limb. Inside the museum you'll find stacks of information on local history, and every nook and cranny is crammed with useful objects and curios from the past. Just after entering town, take McKinney Rd. to the right, turn right on Thompson Rd., and follow signs to the museum, tel. 09/425-7093. It's open in summer daily 9 A.M.–4 P.M., in winter 9 A.M.–3:30 P.M.; admission $4.

Cement Works Ruins

Between the 1860s and the 1880s, Nathaniel Wilson and his sons began to manufacture the first "Portland Cement" made in New Zealand. The ruins are not far from Warkworth Museum, along Wilson Rd., and stay open all hours. When no one is staffing the entrance, there's an honesty box for the $3 admission fee. Before leaving the ruins, head down to the river below; several good swimming holes offer welcome relief on a hot day. Also near the old cement works you'll find the 80-year-old Wilson house, lovingly restored to an elegant home by its present occupants. It's not open to the public.

Commercial Attractions

Popular **Sheep World,** tel. 09/425-7444, lies about four km north of town along Hwy. 1. The highlight of a visit is the Dog & Sheep Show daily at 11 A.M. (plus weekends at 1 P.M.) that includes sheepshearing, dogs demonstrating their roundup skills, and the opportunity to bottle feed baby lambs; adult $10, child $5. Part of the four-hectare complex is the Sheepskin and Country Clothing Store, stocked with a huge collection of wool and sheepskin products, a small animal farmyard, and a café featuring lots of bakery items open daily 8 A.M.–5 P.M.

The **Honey Centre** on the main highway south of town at Perry Rd., tel. 09/425-8003, has the country's largest bee observatory, allowing visitors to view tens of thousands of bees hard at work making honey. There's free honey tasting and, naturally, a gift shop stocked with a wide variety of honey-related products.

Kawau Island

Sandspit Wharf, only 6.5 km from Warkworth, is the place to catch ferries and cruise boats to Kawau Island and a number of other lesser-known islands. The road to Sandspit provides a short but worthwhile scenic drive. Kawau Island was the home of Sir George Grey, governor of New Zealand 1845–53 and 1861–67. His residence, elegant **Mansion House**, has been restored to its former glory and is open to the public; admission adult $5, child $2.50. You can walk around the island—stroll across the lush farmland, discover small sheltered bays, and take in all the wildlife—or refresh yourself at the tea kiosk (lunches available in summer). Along with many bird species, four species of wallaby introduced by Sir Grey in 1870 continue to dominate the animal life.

Kawau Kat Cruises has regular ferries departing from Sandspit five times daily (more often during summer), taking 50 minutes each way; adult $24, child $14 round-trip. Daily at 10:30 A.M. the *Kawau Kat* departs Sandspit for the Royal Mail Run, stopping at many small bays and wharfs along the island's west coast to deliver mail and drop off supplies. The round-trip fare is adult $39, senior $33, child $15 ($10 extra for lunch). Another option is to simply pay for a 10:30 A.M. transfer to the Mansion House, with the option of returning at 1:30 P.M. or 4 P.M.; adult $24, senior $20, child $12. The Sandspit ticket office is open daily 7:30 A.M.–5 P.M. For more information call 09/425-8006 or (0800) 888-006.

Warkworth Practicalities

Downtown is the **Warkworth Inn,** 9 Queen St., tel. 09/425-8569, a restored 1860s hotel featuring 10 basic but comfortable rooms that open to a cobbled patio. Rates are $40 s, $65 d, which includes a light breakfast. Also within walking distance of the river is **Walton Park Motor Lodge,** 2 Walton Ave., tel. 09/425-8149, website: www.waltonpark.co.nz, where each of the 26 units has basic cooking facilities, including a microwave. Other facilities include a swimming pool, guest laundry, and restaurant offering delicious char-grilled dishes for $21–30. Rates are $80 s or d for a studio unit, $95 for a one-bedroom unit, and $110 for a two-bedroom unit. Check the Walton Park website for package deals. As an alternative to staying in motels, one great way to get to know the locals is to stay at a home providing bed-and-breakfast. In this area, take the road to Snells Beach from Warkworth and you'll eventually come to the appealing whitewashed homestead, **Mahurangi Lodge,** 416 Mahurangi East Rd. (about 11 km from Warkworth), tel. 09/425-5465—call ahead. The lodge, perched atop a small hill, has a sweeping veranda; great views of the surrounding lush countryside and distant ocean beaches (10 good ones in the area) are at your command. For $50 s or $80 d per night you get one of the four attractive guest rooms (shared bathroom), the "run of the house," and a choice of a continental or cooked breakfast. In a rural setting above Snells Beach, the **Salty Dog Inn,** tel. 09/425-5588, website: www.salty-doginn.co.nz, provides 14 spacious and modern units, each with a king-size bed and writing desk; rates from $90 s or d.

Want to camp overnight before visiting Kawau Island? Then stay at **Sandspit Motor Camp,** tel. 09/425-8610, on a great grass-and-daisy-covered bank along a pebble-and-sand beach, next to the deepwater anchorage at Sandspit. It offers kitchen and laundry, a restaurant, and a store selling basics; tent sites cost $20, sites with power $22–24, cabins from $40 d.

Park by the river in downtown Warkworth, where you'll find a number of good little cafés close by. The best of these is the **Ducks Crossing Café,** Kapanui St., tel. 09/425-9940. Lunch is a great value, with specials from $8. Out of town, at Snells Beach, consider dining at the **Salty Dog Inn** to enjoy innovative dishes, such as prawn and mushroom cheesecake ($10) for a starter, followed by lamb smothered in an apricot curry

glaze with roast potato ($20.50) for a main. It's open daily for dinner.

Warkworth Information Centre is downtown at 1 Baxter St., tel. 09/425-9081.

WARKWORTH TO WHANGAREI
Dome Forest Walkway

This track, signposted on Hwy. 1 between Warkworth and Wellsford, climbs through Dome Forest to The Dome, a flat-topped mountain, at 336 meters one of the highest peaks in the area, with great views of Hauraki Gulf. The path to the summit takes an hour; on to Waiwhiu Kauri Grove takes another 30 minutes. The path is well marked (white markings on the tree trunks). Steps have been cut in the steepest sections, but the track itself remains quite steep and gets pretty slippery when wet. Ascend to Hwy. 1 along the same route.

A Coastal Detour

As an alternative to Hwy. 1 north from Warkworth, consider taking a detour east through **Leigh** and **Pakiri Beach,** rejoining the highway at Wellsford. Eight km from the highway, Takatu Rd. spurs southeast along the **Takatu Peninsula.**

Along the way, the understated luxury of **Sandpiper Lodge,** tel. 09/422-7256, website: www.sandpiperlodge.co.nz, makes for a wonderful overnight stop. Set on a two-hectare property on an estuary, it features a pool surrounded by native gardens, a restaurant, and a bar/lounge. Rooms in the main lodge open to the pool and gardens while the larger, more private chalets lie right on the estuary. Rates for standard rooms are $202.50 s or d; chalets are $390 s or d. These rates include breakfast, but a better value is the American-plan overnight package.

Facing the open ocean, Pakiri Beach is a long, white, sandy beach, particularly known for good surfing, surf casting, and horseback riding (a Maori family owns rights to the beach; contact Pakiri Beach Horse Rides, tel. 09/422-6275; from $30 per hour). **Pakiri Beach Holiday Park,** tel. 09/422-6199, offers camping at $11–12 pp, cabins from $45 s or d, and self-contained beachside cottages from $75.

North from Wellsford

At **Mangawhai Heads,** a small resort town north of Wellsford, you'll find the head of a two-hour walk along the cliffs that provides spectacular views of the offshore islands. The local nursery, along Molesworth Dr., tel. 09/431-4374, has a great little upmarket café with a conservatory overlooking the gardens; it's open daily from 9 A.M.

From Mangawhai Heads, the road continues north to **Waipu Cove Beach,** popular for fishing and swimming, and rejoins Hwy. 1 at **Waipu.** Between the two is **Ebb & Flow Backpackers,** off Waipu Cove Rd. on Johnson Point Rd., tel. 09/432-1288, a great place to get away from the crowds. While rural, this old homestead overlooks a tidal estuary and is just 400 meters from the beach. The standard of facilities is high, and a large deck and glassed-in patio provide the perfect place to kick back and relax. Rates are $18 pp for a dorm bed or $30 s, $40 d for a private room, which includes the use of bikes, kayaks, and bodyboards.

Continuing north, not far from Ruakaka, is the turnoff to **Marsden Point Oil Refinery,** New Zealand's only oil refinery, which opened in 1964. No visitors may enter the refinery, but from the top of Pilbrow's Hill (to the south of Waipu) you can clearly see its flare. However, at the Visitors Centre adjacent to the main entrance (on Marsden Point Rd., Ruakaka, tel. 09/432-8194; eight km from the Hwy. 1 turnoff), you can view an intricate model of the refinery and videos on the half-hour 10 A.M.–4:30 P.M.; the center is open daily 10 A.M.–5 P.M., free admission. Next to the center, Cafe North serves light snacks and meals. As you approach Whangarei, the road passes through a vineyard area where quite a few places offer wine-tasting.

Whangarei and Vicinity

Whangarei (pop. 45,000), 130 km north of Warkworth and 70 km south of Paihia, stands alone as the only city in Northland. Founded on the edge of an extremely deep and sheltered harbor, it quickly became a thriving port. To the Maori, the harbor was known as Teranga Paraoa (Where the Whales Run). Today the harbor is a mecca for yachties from around the world—many of the brochures describe the city as the "International Yachting Centre of the North Island." Whangarei's mild climate boasts about 2,000 sunshine hours a year, 1,600 mm of rain, and temperatures ranging from 6° to 28°C throughout the year—the average temperature is 19°C.

SIGHTS AND RECREATION

Town Basin

A few blocks from downtown, Town Basin is the tie-up point for yachts from around the world, which sail up the Hatea River to Whangarei and one of New Zealand's best deep-water anchorages. An area on the basin's south side has been landscaped with gardens, and paved walkways wind through souvenir shops and cafés with large outdoor eating areas. An intriguing museum at the basin is **Clapham's Clocks,** tel. 09/483-3993, featuring an assortment of nearly 1,000 clocks and watches contributed by Mr. A. Clapham, who made many of them himself. Out front is Australasia's largest sundial. The museum is open daily 10 A.M.–5 P.M.; adult $5, child $3.

Whangarei Museum and Kiwi House

This excellent museum, tel. 09/438-9630, is just a small part of a large complex that comprises a kiwi house, an old homestead, and 25-hectare grounds laced with hiking trails that lead to a stream and various waterfalls. It's on Hwy. 14, four km west of Whangarei—follow signs out of town to Dargaville. The museum itself has a large number of Maori and European artifacts collected from throughout Northland, while **Clarke Homestead,** built in 1885, has been restored, with many of the rooms furnished as they would have been in that era. In the kiwi house, the natural cycle of day and night has been reversed so that visitors can watch these intriguing nocturnal creatures feeding and moving around at a decent hour. During the summer, local vol-

NORTHLAND

VICINITY OF WHANGAREI

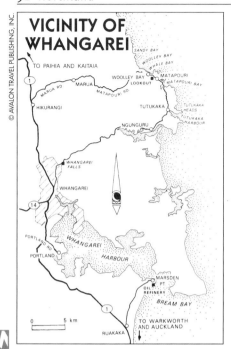

© AVALON TRAVEL PUBLISHING, INC.

unteers put on "live days" every second Sunday, operating a steam engine and antique farm equipment. The complex is open daily 10 A.M.–4 P.M.; $8 adult, $4 child, or visit just one or two of the attractions for less.

Whangarei Falls

These falls are a photographer's dream. They drop 25 meters into a deep green pool surrounded by bush, and numerous walkways allow views from above and below. On a hot summer day, the upper swimming hole, directly above the falls, is a hive of activity. Local children swing out on tree ropes, or dive from the top limbs of a tree into one of the deep holes, entertaining (or terrifying!) tourists with their audacity. With little prompting, the smaller kids enthusiastically tell tales of the local Maori boy they call "the big fella," who thrills his audience by diving off the top of the falls. Look for the falls on the outskirts of Whangarei in the suburb of Tikipun-

ga, next to Ngunguru Rd. (buses run from downtown to Tikipunga).

Tutukaka and Vicinity

Continue beyond Whangarei Falls for 30 km and the road emerges at a beautiful stretch of the northern coastline. **Ngunguru,** the first town along the route, sits on the edge of the Ngunguru River. A sandy beach, lots of swimming and boating action, and many holiday homes give Ngunguru its vacation atmosphere.

Tutukaka is the hub for deep-sea fishing and diving, claiming the title "Gateway to the Poor Knights Islands" (see the Special Topic). **Tutukaka Charters,** an arm of Whangarei Deep Sea Anglers Club, based at Tutukaka Marina, tel. 09/434-3818, provides all the information on local fishing, diving, cruising, and boat chartering. The season for catching marlin, shark, or yellowtail tuna usually runs from mid-January through April, no license required. Charter boats cost $700–1,000 per day. If you're by yourself, the club tries to hook you up with a group, lowering the cost to as little as $200 pp. Line fishing, as part of a group, costs about $70 pp per day. For spectacular views of the coastline with its irresistible bays, colorful sailing boats, and shell-studded beaches, follow Tutukaka Block Rd. up to Tutukaka Heads.

Continuing north, the holiday town of **Matapouri** has a long, white sandy beach, calm water (perfect for swimming and snorkeling), and several other small and more private beaches—reached by wading around the rocks at the northern end. At the back of the third small beach you'll find a trail (take shoes or sandals) that passes through a rock tunnel to emerge at a beautiful cove with good snorkeling potential. Sometimes in summer, the waters off Matapouri Beach become thick with plankton; local swimmers don't seem to mind, but it's a rare and unforgettable sensation to swim unexpectedly into the thick, jellylike substance when the water appears to be clear.

Around the next headland is **Sandy Bay.** Keep your eyes peeled for the lookout and great views at Whale Bay Reserve. An easily followed, cliffside

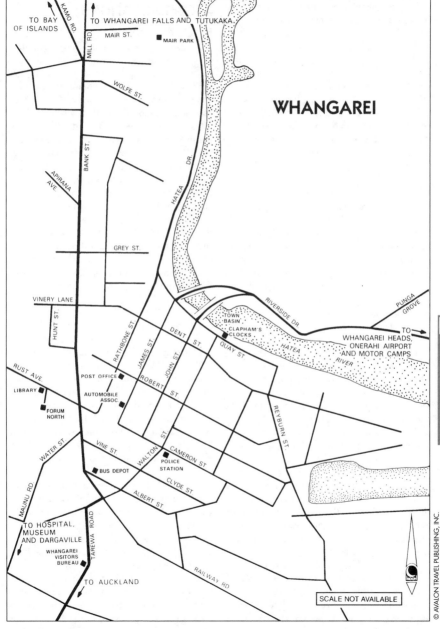

TO BAY OF ISLANDS

KAMO RD

TO WHANGAREI FALLS AND TUTUKAKA

MILL RD

MAIR ST.

MAIR PARK

WOLFE ST.

WHANGAREI

BANK ST.

HATEA DR.

APIRANA AVE.

GREY ST.

VINERY LANE

RIVERSIDE DR

PUNGA GROVE

HUNT ST.

RATHBONE ST

JAMES ST.

DENT ST.

TOWN BASIN

CLAPHAM'S CLOCKS

QUAY ST.

HATEA

TO WHANGAREI HEADS, ONERAHI AIRPORT AND MOTOR CAMPS

RUST AVE

JOHN ST.

ROBERT ST.

RIVER

POST OFFICE

LIBRARY

AUTOMOBILE ASSOC.

FORUM NORTH

REYBURN ST.

ST.

WATER ST.

VINE ST.

WALTON

CAMERON ST.

BUS DEPOT

POLICE STATION

CLYDE ST.

MAUNU RD

ALBERT ST.

TAREWA ROAD

TO HOSPITAL, MUSEUM AND DARGAVILLE

WHANGAREI VISITORS BUREAU

RAILWAY RD

TO AUCKLAND

SCALE NOT AVAILABLE

NORTHLAND

© AVALON TRAVEL PUBLISHING, INC.

trail leads from the lookout to the right. Passing through exotic natural bush and groves of *pohutukawa* trees, the trail leads down the cliffs and emerges at beautiful Whale Bay Beach. The walk from the car park to this fairly isolated beach takes about 20 minutes, but if you suffer from hay-fever allergies, this walk can be miserable in summer. After passing the road to Sandy Bay (known for good surfing—it usually boasts surfable waves when none of the other beaches do), the road swoops back inland toward Hikurangi, where it rejoins Hwy. 1, 18 km north of Whangarei.

Hiking

Several scenic reserves dot the Whangarei area. **Parahaki Scenic Reserve** contains Parahaki Mountain, with good bush walks and great views of Whangarei from its 241-meter summit. Two of the clearly marked walks originate from Mair Park, at the western foot of Parahaki, the third from Dundas Rd. at the southern foot. All converge at the summit, where the tall column of the Parahaki War Memorial stands. Ross Track features a gold mine near the summit and a waterfall near the base. About a 10-minute walk from Dundas Rd. (close to the Whangarei Hostel), the track takes about 40 minutes each way. Drummond Track takes about the same time to complete—it's pretty steep and features a giant kauri tree along a short sidetrack, one-third of the way down. Dobbie Track starts at Dobbie Park and takes about 50 minutes to the summit, featuring many varied views of Whangarei. On all the walks, Maori pits and old gum-digging workings add to the scenery. Regenerating kauri trees and a variety of ferns (from the tiny crepe and kidney ferns to the large tree ferns) abound along the tracks. Pick up the free *Whangarei Walks* pamphlet—a guide to Scenic Reserves and Walkways in the Whangarei district, available from the information center.

A. H. Reed Memorial Kauri Park, in the suburb of Tikipunga about five km from downtown next to Whareora Rd., is an appealing little park with a variety of trees and a choice of several paths; see the surviving remnant of a kauri forest, Wai Koromiko Stream, and a waterfall.

ACCOMMODATIONS

Hotels and Motels

Whangarei has about 20 hotels and motels, most of which lie along the main highway through town. The least expensive rooms run about $70 s, $75 d, but for a few extra bucks, there are several really nice places to stay. The **Continental Motel,** 67 Kamo Rd. (north of downtown), tel. 09/437-6359 or 0800/457-634, offers less expensive rates and a swimming pool to complement 16 spacious units; $70–90 s or d. Farther north along Kamo Rd., at no. 260, is Tudor-style **Kingswood Inn,** tel. 09/437-5779 or 0800/369-469; $85–110 for a room with basic cooking facilities. **Cheviot Park Motor Lodge,** on the corner of Western Hills Dr. and Cheviot St., tel. 09/438-2341 or 0508/243-846, website: www.cheviot-park.co.nz, features 15 luxury units, each with a kitchen, as well as a pool, spa, and barbecue area. And although it's on the main road, a high fence surrounds the property affording privacy. Room service includes meals and drinks. Rates are $88–106 s or d.

On the north side of Town Basin, but still within easy walking distance of downtown, is the **Quality Hotel,** 9 Riverside Dr., tel. 09/438-0284 or 0800/242-428. One of the city's larger hotels, it has 95 rooms and modern facilities, including a pool, spa, restaurant, and bar; rates from $105 s or d. Another choice just out of town is the **Settlers Hotel,** 61 Hatea Dr., tel. 09/438-2699 or 0800/666-662. Set among beautiful gardens beside the Hatea River, this hotel has a few older rooms for $95 s or d, and modern suites for $130.

If you feel like a splurge and fancy a self-contained unit with either a fantastic ocean or harbor view and use of a pool, spa, and private beach, head for **Pacific Rendezvous,** tel. 09/434-3847 or 0800/999-800, website: www.oceanresort .co.nz, spread over a high headland at Tutukaka, 29 km from Whangarei. This stretch of coast holds many accommodations, but this is by far the best. Rates range from $140 for a one-bedroom unit to $180 for a three-bedroom unit with ocean views. All are fully self-contained; other resort features include a private beach, a tennis court, and a putting green. From the south, go two km beyond Ngunguru, take the Tutukaka Block Rd., then turn onto Motel Rd. and follow it to the end.

Backpacker Lodges

The small **Whangarei YHA,** 52 Punga Grove Ave., tel. 09/438-8954, website: www.yha.org.nz, is centrally located on a hill overlooking the Hatea River and an easy five-minute walk from Town Basin. The hostel has only 27 beds, but facilities are good, including a pleasant outdoor area with a barbecue. The hosts rent bicycles and can show the way to all the local attractions. Rates are $18 for a dorm bed, $21 pp in a double room.   **Central Backpackers** (Hatea House), 67 Hatea Dr., tel. 09/437-6174, presents another option for backpackers. Formerly a private residence, the hosts are involved in the local diving industry, so it's a good place for divers to stay. They also run guided sea-kayaking trips. The house itself is fairly basic, but the price is right—$19 pp.

Motor Camps

Alpha Motel & Holiday Park, 34 Tarewa Rd., 800 meters south of the post office on the main road into town, tel. 09/438-9867, is the most central motor camp. It offers few tent sites ($18 s or d) but many serviced sites (also $18). Units start at $45, and self-contained motel rooms are $64.

Whangarei Falls Holiday Park is on the Whangarei-Tutukaka Rd., a pleasant 200-meter walk from Whangarei Falls, about five km northeast of town, tel. 09/437-0609 or 0800/227-222; website: www.whangareifalls.co.nz. Tent and caravan sites are $10 pp. Heated cabins cost from $35 s or d. There's also a bunkroom; $14 pp. Enjoy the spa or pool, and participate in the barbecues held on some summer nights.

FOOD

Cafés

You'll find many cafés offering good lunches and snacks at any time of the day throughout downtown. One of the best places for a good strong cup of coffee is **Caffeine Espresso,** 4 Water St., tel. 09/438-6925. This place is also popular for its healthy and hearty breakfasts, such as delicious Eggs Benedict served with bacon and spinach ($12.50); open daily 7 A.M.–3 P.M.

A longtime favorite, **Taste Spud,** 5 Water St. (under the railway bridge), tel. 09/438-1198, specializes in stuffed potatoes—and delicious potatoes they are! This is the place to come if you just want a quick but filling meal at a cheap price. Potatoes, filled with chili or all kinds of select-your-own combinations, start at about $5. Curries, tacos, and great-looking desserts round out the menu. It's open every day 11:30 A.M.–7 P.M. **Something Else** in the Civic Arcade specializes in croissants, quiches, and other healthy foods; it's open Mon.–Thurs. 8 A.M.–5:30 P.M., Friday till late.

Chelsea House, 83 Hatea Dr., tel. 09/437-6398, is the perfect place to relax over morning or afternoon tea. This historic home is planted with gardens in the Victorian-era style. Devonshire tea and snacks such as muffins and sandwiches are served inside or out Wed.–Sun. 10 A.M.–3:30 P.M.

Other Restaurants

A number of stylish eateries can be found at Town Basin, overlooking a harbor and surrounded by landscaped gardens. One of these, **Reva's on the Waterfront,** tel. 09/438-8969, is a Federation-style building with a narrow table-filled verandah overlooking the water. The blackboard menu features pizza (from $12), salads, and seafood dishes ($17–26). Adjacent is **Quay Café,** tel. 09/430-0467, with indoor and outdoor seating. **Moorings Cafe,** across the harbor on Riverside Dr. at Vale Rd., tel. 09/438-8105, specializes in seafood; main meals range $18–26.

Barfly, 13 Rathbone St., tel. 09/438-8761, is a big-city eatery furnished with chrome furniture. Lunchtime is the busiest, when local businesspeople flock in for wood-fired pizza. **Killer Prawn,** 28 Bank St., tel. 09/430-3333, is another trendy place. Lunch is a good value at about $12 for fish and chips. Dinner is more expensive—$24 for prawns, rice, and a salad, but if you dine before 6:30 P.M., a 50 percent discount applies. The **Cobb & Co.,** 117 Bank St., tel. 09/438-4303, is part of a chain of New Zealand restaurants usually found in old hotels. The atmosphere and menu is always family-oriented, albeit a little old-fashioned. Another thing all Cobb & Co.'s provide is excellent value. Starting at about $10 for a salad to $14–20 for a large variety of main dishes and $7 for desserts, good meals for the price are served in a relaxed atmosphere. Another casual place with a similar menu is the **Dickens Inn,** on the corner of Cameron and Quality Streets, tel. 09/430-0406, with a large open-plan restaurant and relaxing bar area. This place is open for breakfast. The side of the Inn opens to Quality Street Mall, a cobbled walkway where you'll find **Café Paparazzi,** tel. 09/438-2961, a Mediterranean-style café where the tables are covered by large umbrellas and the walls adorned by a colorful mural. For a splurge, you might want to try **Water Street Brasserie,** 24 Water St., tel. 09/438-7464, which offers a variety of dishes. Lunches range $6–18, dinners $16–25. It's open Tues.–Sun. 6–10 P.M. (lunch Tues.–Fri. noon–2 P.M.).

Kama Sutra, 74 Cameron St., tel. 09/430-0222, offers a wide range of familiar East Indian dishes. **Tai Tong,** 214 Bank St., tel. 09/438-7921, serves cheap Chinese food.

TRANSPORTATION
Getting There
Air New Zealand, tel. 0800/800-737, connects Whangarei with Auckland and points farther south. Arrange bookings at Small World Travel on Rathbone St., tel. 09/438-2939.

Intercity, tel. 09/438-2653, operates long-distance coach services leaving Whangarei several times a day for Paihia, Kaitaia, and Auckland; these link with other local services. Reservations are necessary, and your seat is guaranteed if booked 72 hours in advance. **Northliner,** tel. 09/438-3206, runs daily service to Auckland and Paihia via the main route north. Both companies operate from the Northland Coach and Travel Centre at 11 Rose St., open weekdays 8 A.M.–5 P.M.

Getting Around
Whangarei Bus Services covers local transportation; the terminal is on Rose St. by the Grand Hotel, tel. 09/432-2624.

Pay and Display Parking is available at the Forum North Car park; buy a ticket from one of the three dispensers and place the ticket on your car dashboard. The main car rental agencies in Whangarei are **Avis,** tel. 09/438-2929; **Budget,** tel. 09/438-7292; and **Hertz,** tel. 09/438-9790. The **Automobile Association,** on the corner of John and Robert Streets, tel. 09/438-4848, is open 8:30 A.M.–5 P.M. For repair and tow service call Parahaki Motors Ltd., tel. 09/438-8599.

Local taxis are operated by **Kiwi Carlton Cabs,** tel. 09/438-4444. The main taxi stand is on Rathbone Street.

SERVICES AND INFORMATION
Whangarei's main **post office** is at 16 Rathbone Street. **James St. Laundromat** is at 66 James Street.

Whangarei Area Hospital is on Hospital Rd., tel. 09/430-4100. **Primecare Medical Centre,** 12 Kensington Ave., tel. 09/437-1988, has a doctor on duty 24 hours daily. Next door is **Kensington Pharmacy,** tel. 09/437-3722. For the **police,** call 09/430-4500.

Information
As you enter town from the south on Hwy. 1, make a stop at **Whangarei Visitors Bureau,** in Tarewa Park, tel. 09/438-1079. Pick up a map (small charge) and plenty of literature on the major attractions, scenic reserves, and outdoor activities of Whangarei. The staff can provide information on both Whangarei and Northland in general, and make bookings as required; it's open Mon.–Fri. 8:30 A.M.–5 P.M., and weekends 10 A.M.–4 P.M. in summer. You can buy souvenirs and postcards, and sample a snack or light meal at the café. DOC headquarters for the **Northland Conservancy,** 149-151 Bank St., tel. 09/430-2470, is a good source of maps, charts, and books.

WHANGAREI TO THE BAY OF ISLANDS

From Whangarei, it's 70 km north to Paihia, gateway to the Bay of Islands.

To Paihia or Russell?

At Kawakawa, Hwy. 10 spurs northeast up to Paihia. If you're traveling by car, it's best to decide whether to stay in Paihia or Russell before the turnoff to Opua. It's less hassle and cheaper to leave the car in Paihia, and the passenger ferry service across to Russell is short, enjoyable, and frequent. Many of the attractions in Russell are within walking distance of the ferry. However, if you want to explore Russell by car, the only car ferry service leaves from Opua (a 15-minute drive south of Paihia), and crosses the Veronica Channel to Okiato, from where Russell is a 10-minute drive to the north. It costs $8 one way plus $1 pp. The service runs daily 7 A.M.–10 P.M. It's also possible to drive all the way from Hwy. 1 to Russell, avoiding the ferry altogether, but on the unsealed road, it takes forever.

Bay of Islands

The Bay of Islands is one of New Zealand's most beautiful and historic areas. Situated 257 km north of Auckland, its irregular coastline and 144 islands are lapped by warm, aquamarine waters and bathed in sunshine year-round. The mild climate of the "Winterless North" and the calm waters have made the area a sailor's paradise ever since its discovery by Capt. James Cook in the 18th century. Quiet coves, soft sandy beaches, sparkling waters, and island groves of *pohutukawa* trees abound. For excitement there's the challenge of deep-sea fishing for a magnificent marlin or shark, or the chance to dive into a colorful submarine habitat.

The main population center is **Paihia,** 70 km north of Whangarei and 270 km north of Auckland, the base for cruises and fishing and diving trips, as well as a large number of accommodations and restaurants. Nearby is **Waitangi,** historically important for the signing of the Treaty of Waitangi. Across the bay from Paihia is **Russell.** This delightful village is on the mainland, but road access is roundabout; most visitors arrive by ferry from Paihia. **Kerikeri,** a citrus center and home to many artists and craftspeople, is a short drive from Paihia.

HISTORY
First Contacts

Captain Cook named the Bay of Islands in 1769. At that time, it was inhabited by a large Maori population, whose *pa* (fortified dwellings) studded the bay. Captain Cook's ship, the *Endeavour,* was met by a small fleet of canoes navigated by fearless warriors who came to gaze in astonishment at the huge "winged canoe." The first meeting between European and Maori was friendly; however, this changed three years later when a series of blunders by the French explorer, Marion Du Fresne, led to his murder by the local tribe, and in retaliation some 250 Maori were slain.

Trade Center

By the end of the 18th century, the Bay of Islands had become a thriving trade center, with the whalers, timber-seekers, and traders calling in at Kororareka (present-day Russell) for supplies, as well as the proverbial wine, women, and song. The migratory path of whales, unfortunately close to the northern coastline, contributed to their plunder. The tall, straight kauri trees that fringed the bay and lowlands were quickly depleted for ship masts or export to Sydney. Traders also brought predators, disease, and massive exploitation to New Zealand. In the early 19th century many missionaries arrived, and their Christian influence helped end Maori warfare.

Treaty of Waitangi

There was considerable foreign interest in New Zealand by 1831 and, in fear of takeover, a group

NORTHLAND

BAY OF ISLANDS

BAY OF ISLANDS

PIERCY I.

CAPE BRETT

NORTH HEAD

WHANGARURU NORTH

WHANGARURU HARBOUR

OKAHU I.

WAEWAETOREA I.

URUPUKAPUKA I.

RAWHITI

RAWHITI RD

WHANGARURU NORTH RD

WHANGARURU NORTH

NGAIOTONGA

TUTAEMATAI

WHANGARURU

MOTUKIEKIE I.

MOTURUA I.

MOTUAROHIA I.

ORONGO BAY

FRENCHMANS SWAMP

RUSSELL RD

RUSSELL

RUSSELL FOREST

WAIKARE

RD

WAIKARE

MOTURUA I.

WAIROA BAY

RUSSELL

PAIHIA

OKIATO

OPUA

OKIATO RD

TE HAUMI DR

PAIHIA RD

WAITANGI NATIONAL RESERVE

MT BLEDISLOE (115 m)

HARURU RD

HARURU FALLS

PUKETONA RD

WAITANGI STATE FOREST

OPUA STATE FOREST

KAWAKAWA

TO WHANGAREI

1

10

TO KAIKOHE

KERIKERI INLET

KERIKERI INLET

RED CLIFFS RD

RAINBOW FALLS

KERIKERI BASIN

KERIKERI

KERIKERI INLET RD

KERIKERI INLET

WAIPAPA RD

TO KAITAIA

5 km

0

of local Maori chiefs asked Britain for protection. In February 1840, with the ceremonial signing of The Treaty of Waitangi, New Zealand became a British colony. Within the next year, New Zealand's "capital" was set up at Okiato and named Russell, but it was soon decided that the capital should be moved to the more desirable site of Auckland. The name Russell was then transferred to the town of Kororareka, in hopes that the new name would give the "Hellhole of the Pacific" a new image.

BAY OF ISLANDS RECREATION

The *real* Bay of Islands—a remote ocean wilderness accessible only by water-is beyond the region's main towns of Paihia, Russell, and Kerikeri.

Along with all the services you'll need for an overnight stay, these three towns do each have their own charm, and each is covered following Bay of Islands Recreation.

Commercial Cruises

Most cruise operators are based at Paihia. The two biggest companies-Fullers and Kings-have booking desks in the waterfront Maritime Building.

Operated by Fullers, the Super Cruise departs Paihia daily at 10 A.M., Russell at 10:10 A.M., and cruises leisurely around many of the beautiful islands in the bay, the captain's commentary keeping passengers informed and amused. Following a historic route known as the Cream Trip (it once delivered cream, hence the name), the

BAY OF ISLANDS MARITIME AND HISTORIC PARK

This mostly undeveloped park, comprising about 40 sites scattered throughout the Bay of Islands, protects both scenic and historic areas. The exception to this noncommercial paradise is **Urupukapuka Island,** where Fullers make a regular stop on most of its cruises. Here you'll find an undersea "submarine" ($12 adult, $6 child) and the **Zane Grey Café** (in the 1920s, American author Zane Grey made the island a base for his game-fishing expeditions). A seven-km (three-hour) hiking trail roughly circles the otherwise untainted island, passing secluded beaches, archeological sites, and several campgrounds.

Cape Brett (Rakaumangamanga) scenic reserve was named by Captain Cook. A 17.5-km track, starting at Oke Bay on Rawhiti Rd., takes seven to eight hours. Classified as a hard tramp, it's recommended only for those with above-average fitness and experience (sea access is possible in calm conditions). The old lighthouse on the point was built in 1909, and the lighthouse keeper's cottage has been converted into a hut that can sleep 12, with toilet and water.

Motukawanui (Big Cavalli Island) is a large island reserve, known for its scenic track (1.5 hours) covering the length of the island. The island hut has

eight bunks, a toilet, and fresh water.

Impressive **Ranfurly Bay Reserve,** at the entrance to Whangaroa Harbour, is known for rugged volcanic rock formations. The Ranfurly Bay hut provides 12 bunks, toilets and water, and deep-water anchorage in the bay. You can hike three well-marked tracks from the bay, each providing outstanding harbor views.

Park Practicalities

The only practical way to travel to and around the park is by boat. The cruises detailed under Bay of Island Recreation visit the more popular spots, such as Urupukapuka Island and Cape Brett, with Fullers offering the option of spending a full day on Urupukapuka.

The best source of park information is the **Russell Field Centre** on The Strand in Russell, tel. 09/403-9005, where you'll find interesting displays and an excellent audiovisual on New Zealand's early history. The staff provides hordes of information (including the brochure *Bay of Islands Walks*), issues camping and hut permits, and offers a list of charter operators. The center is open Mon.–Fri. 8:30 A.M.–4:30 P.M., Sat.–Sun. 9 A.M.–4:30 P.M.

NORTHLAND

boat makes short stops at many of the islands to deliver mail and groceries to the farmers and island-caretakers scattered around the bay. The cruise also includes Cape Brett, Motukokako Island, and Cathedral Cave, and weather permitting, the boat passes through the famous "Hole in the Rock." The cost is adult $85, child $45, including a one-hour stop for lunch at picturesque Otehei Bay on Urupukapuka Island (an optional submarine cruise is $12). Lunch itself is extra—sandwiches, filled rolls, lamb burgers, snacks, and ice cream are available—or bring your own. After lunch there's time for a quick swim or a walk up the hill for good views. This is just one of many variations offered by Fullers. If you feel like being more active (or maybe just lying on a remote beach for the day), pay for transfers to Otehei Bay (adult $35, child $18) and spend the day exploring the island. For bookings, call Fullers in Paihia at 09/402-7421.

King's Dolphin Cruises and Tours also provides similar cruises. Their Day in the Bay Cruise includes the historic Cream Trip route, local geological oddities including Hole in the Rock, as well as the opportunity to swim with dolphins, either in open water or while hanging onto a boom net. This six-hour trip departs daily from Paihia (10 A.M.) and Russell (10:10 A.M.); adult $83, child $45. Kings also operates *Mack Attack*—a 30-passenger high-speed catamaran powered by twin 600 horsepower engines—to Hole in the Rock; adult $60, child $30. For bookings on any of King's cruises, visit the company's booking center in the Maritime Building, Paihia, tel. 09/402-8288.

Take to the Water in Style

The most unusual and stylish way to tour the bay is onboard the stunning *R. Tucker Thompson,* a gaff-rigged square topsail schooner that has circumnavigated the world, taken part in Australia's Bicentenary as one of the tall ships re-enacting the Australian First Fleet voyage, and starred in the TV series *Adventurer.* Take part in the sailing or just relax; you'll stop at an island (time for swimming allowed) and savor a barbecue lunch and then afternoon tea. Departing Paihia at 9:30 A.M. (10 A.M. from Russell), the re-laxing six- to seven-hour trip is $89 adult, $49 child—take a swimsuit, towel, sunblock, warm jacket, and lunch. Make bookings at Fullers in Paihia, tel. 09/402-7421.

Charters

So many yacht outfits offer charters that it's best to stop by the information center in Paihia to pick up all the current brochures, then call around. Skippered by round-the-world sailor Vanessa McKay, the *Carino,* tel. 09/402-8040, is one of the better choices. Go day sailing (six hours) for adult $74, child $40, which includes morning and afternoon tea, fishing and snorkeling gear, swimming with dolphins, sailing tuition if required, and barbecue lunch on a deserted beach; pickups are made from both Paihia and Russell.

Pacific Promotions, tel. 09/402-8336, website: www.pacpro.net.nz, represents many local charter operators. You can take sailing lessons, island hop, swim, snorkel around the reefs, or just relax on a luxury yacht. Overnight cruises (two days, one night), all meals included, start about $300 pp. Bareboat rentals start at $500 per day for a 25-foot yacht, rising as high as $2,000 for a luxurious 60-foot vessel. For the sailing enthusiast or would-be sailing enthusiast, **Great Escape Yacht Charters,** tel. 09/402-7143, provides two- to three-berth yachts complete with outboard auxiliary, stove, and cooking equipment from only $200 per day (24 hours) or from $800 per week. It also provides a full-day **Learn To Sail** course.

Charter Pier, at Paihia Wharf, tel. 09/402-7127, rents four- to seven-seater, self-drive power-boats for $60–80 hourly, $180–240 for four hours, plus fuel used.

Fishing

The Bay of Islands is New Zealand's most popular game-fishing ground, and fishing is a year-round activity. Some say the best game fishing is in February and March, others claim June and July, but keep in mind that plenty of "big ones" are also caught in January, April, and May. Striped, blue, and black marlin; mako, thresher, blue, and hammerhead sharks; yellowfin tuna; and yellowtail (or kingfish) cruise the waters in abundance. The most prolific big-game fish is the striped marlin; the best months are Dec.–June. For sharks, the best time is Nov.–May, and for tuna, it's Dec.–March. Yellowtail are caught year-round but are mainly fished during June and July. But it's not all big-game fishing fun. Plenty of light-tackle experiences are available from smaller boats.

Paihia Wharf is a hub of deep-sea fishing activity. This town is home base to most of the local game-fishing boats, many of which can be booked through **Pacific Promotions,** tel. 09/402-8336. A solo game-fishing charter starts at $750 per day, a share charter (maximum four people) starts at $200 pp. Nonangling passengers can go along to watch the action for considerably less.

The **Bay of Islands Swordfish Club,** tel. 09/403-7857, at both the Russell and Paihia waterfronts, hosts many of the big-game fishing tournaments. Tournaments are plentiful from Tutukaka to the Bay of Islands Jan.–June. Club officials perform the weigh-ins and record the vitals whenever a game fish is brought in. You can buy day membership for $10 before going fishing, which includes an official weigh-in and certificate, and eligibility for most club trophies. Look for a crowd gathering around either Russell or Paihia wharfs as it's likely to mean they're bringing in a magnificent game fish for a weigh-in. Records of these weigh-ins are written on blackboards by 4 P.M. daily, and displayed at both wharves. There's a good licensed restaurant at the Russell club for members, affiliated and kindred members from an overseas club, or guests of members.

Swimming with Dolphins

As it has along other parts of New Zealand's east coast, swimming with dolphins in their natural habitat has quickly caught on in popularity here. Pods of dolphins are generally smaller and less active than those farther south, but the sea is warmer and generally calmer. The four-hour boat ride and swim costs $85 pp. For bookings, contact **Dolpin Discoveries,** tel. 09/402-8234; or **Dolphin Encounters,** tel. 09/402-7421. Both companies have booking desks in the Maritime Building, Paihia.

Sea Kayaking

If you've always wanted to sea kayak the bay, or learn how, give **Coastal Kayakers** a call at 09/402-8105. It offers two options: a guided day trip (instruction included) with highlights that include a paddle to a deserted island, under Haruru Falls (helmet thoughtfully provided), and through a flooded mangrove forest for $70 (backpacker discounts); or you can just rent a sea kayak for $40 per day (discount for five-day rental and longer). You can always book through any hostel in the Bay of Islands or Northland. **Kaptain Kayak,** in Russell, tel. 09/403-7252, also takes guided tours.

Diving

A diving hot spot was created on December 13, 1987, when the Greenpeace flagship, *Rainbow Warrior,* settled in 25 meters of water off the Cavalli Islands, south of the entrance to the Bay of Islands. This ship, used by Greenpeace for environmental crusades around the globe, was bombed in 1985 in Auckland Harbour by French intelligence officers trying to prevent Greenpeace from upsetting France's nuclear testing on remote atolls in the South Pacific Ocean. It was later moved north to create an artificial reef; it's now covered in brightly colored marinelife and a feeding ground for a variety of fish. **Paihia Dive and Fishing,** based in Paihia, tel. 09/402-7551, offers trips to the wreck on Monday, Wednesday, and Saturday, departing at 8:30 A.M. The cost of $145 pp includes the boat ride, all equipment, and two dives.

PAIHIA

When you enter Paihia from the south you travel past a mass of motels and hotels, many competing with one another and advertising their rates along the beachfront. Continue around the point and along the beach to the wharf and main shopping area.

Paihia Wharf

The wharf is a great place to soak up the Bay of Islands' vacation atmosphere. Whenever a shark or striped marlin is caught in local waters, the news spreads like wildfire around town, and Paihia wharf is the place to be for the official "weigh-in." If you notice a large crowd gathering at the wharf, you'll probably see at least one of the magnificent game fish close up. At the Paihia waterfront you can charter game-fishing and diving boats, go for a scenic launch ride, water-ski, take an exhilarating jetboat ride, or hop on a cruise through the Bay of Islands.

Motels

Paihia has over 40 motels. Many of those downtown are older, while in recent years a number of upmarket resorts have been developed at the town's outskirts. Rates start at about $100 for a double room in summer, with reduced rates the rest of the year, especially in the large resorts, where discounts of up to 50 percent apply in winter.

A1 Motel, 46 Davis Crescent, tel. 09/402-7684 or 0800/878-222, backs onto a wooded reserve and is only 100 meters from the waterfront; rates from $85 s or d. Also central is **Dolphin Motel,** 69 Williams Rd., tel. 09/402-8170 or 0800/101-950, website: www.dolphinmotel.co.nz, where the 10 self-contained rooms are $95 s, $115 d. On the same street is **Aarangi Tui Motel,** 16 Williams Rd., tel. 09/402-7496 or 0800/453-354, with one- and two-bedroom units facing a garden area; from $100 s or d.

A step up in quality from the above places, **Autolodge Paihia,** Marsden Rd., tel. 09/402-7416 or 0800/652-929, directly opposite the beach and 100 meters from Paihia Wharf, has a large pool, restaurant, lounge, and bikes for getting around town. Rates are from $145 s or d. One of the better downtown motels is the attractive flower-decked **Swiss Chalet Lodge Motel** at 3 Bayview Rd., tel. 09/402-7615. Amenities include appealing rooms with private balconies, a kitchen with microwave ovens, breakfast room service, parking, and all sorts of little "comforts of home." Rates start at $160 s or d in summer.

The **Nautilus Resort,** Puketona Rd., tel. 09/402-8604 or 0800/186-661, features spacious self-contained units overlooking a large pool and subtropical landscaped gardens. It's a

good value at $150 s, $165 d. **Aloha Garden Resort Hotel,** 32 Seaview Rd., tel. 09/402-7540 or 0800/425-642, website: www.aloha.co.nz, is set on a two-hectare property complete with a pool and gardens dotted with palm trees. Each of the 20 modern units has a kitchen, and most offer ocean views; from $145 s or d. **Paihia Pacific Resort Hotel,** 27 Kings Rd., tel. 09/402-8221, website: www.paihiapacific.co.nz, is another upmarket place. The pastel-themed units open to a courtyard filled with greenery and with a small pool and spa. Rates October through April range $148–178.

Across the road from the beach, **Paihia Beach Resort,** Marsden Rd., tel. 09/402-6140 or 0800/870-111, website: www.paihiabeach.co.nz, is one of New Zealand's premier accommodations. No expense has been spared in furnishing the luxurious units, each of which has cooking facilities and a large private balcony offering spectacular water views. Raised above street level for extra privacy are a large heated saltwater pool and spa surrounded by stone decking. Accommodation choices include studio units ($215 s or d), one-bedroom units ($250), and two-bedroom units ($375). Outside of January, rates are reduced (to as low as $110 in winter), making Paihia Beach Resort a fantastic value. In addition to local contacts, call 888/226-7448 for bookings from North America.

Backpacker Lodges

The **Peppertree Lodge,** downtown at 15 Kings Rd., tel. 09/402-6122, website: www.peppertree.co.nz, is the best of Paihia's many backpacker lodges. It features a large patio and barbecue area, lounge and deck, a quiet area stocked with books, modern kitchen, laundry, bike rentals, and bag storage. Every room includes a private bathroom. Dorm beds are $20, doubles and twins $29 pp. Nearby, the popular **Bay Adventurer,** 26 Kings Rd., tel. 09/402-5162, website: www.bayadventurer.co.nz, is a purpose-built facility complete with a pool and barbecue area set in a tropical garden, a spa, a lounge equipped with a DVD player, Internet access, and a large modern kitchen. Rates are $20 dorm, $32 s, $52 twin. **Mayfair Lodge,** 7

Puketona Rd., tel. 09/402-7471, offers dormitory accommodation from $20 in twins and doubles, the use of the spa, and table tennis and pool tables. The Mayfair closes for winter. Closest to the downtown waterfront, **Centabay Lodge,** behind the shops on Selwyn Rd., tel. 09/402-7466, website: www.centabay.co.nz, costs from $17 per night, hostel-style; good twins and doubles are $45 per night. **Lodge Eleven** on the corner of MacMurray and Kings Roads, tel. 09/402-7487, website: www.yha.org.nz, is another good place to go for budget accommodation. This associate of Hostelling International features dorm rooms, private facilities with each unit, TV and game room, fully equipped kitchen, covered outdoor dining, bike rentals, and off-street parking. Call for courtesy coach to and from the bus terminal. Dorm beds are $22, doubles $26 pp.

Motor Camps

Of the several motor camps in the Paihia area, none are downtown. Winning our vote as the most friendly and easygoing, **Twin Pines Tourist Park** is three km out along Puketona Rd. (the main road west out of Paihia), tel. 09/402-7322. It sits on the banks of the Waitangi River, adjacent to Haruru Falls (floodlit at night, and heard clearly throughout the camp). Many scenic walks lie close to the camp (don't miss the steep three-minute bamboo trail from the camp down to the river with its built-in loveseat, view of the falls, and water access). Tent sites are $12 pp, serviced sites $14 pp, cabins $60 s or d, and self-contained motel units $85 s or d.

Smiths Holiday Camp is 2.5 km from Paihia, on the road toward Opua (and the car ferry to Russell), tel. 09/402-7678. Set on a private cove, it offers a store, game room, boat ramp and boats for rent, and the usual communal facilities. Rates for tent and caravan sites run from $25, cabins from $60 d, and motel rooms from $90 d.

Food

The nicest place to enjoy breakfast is **Hansen's** in the Maritime Building, Marsden Rd., tel. 09/402-8526. The tables all have water views, and the atmosphere is relaxed and casual. A cooked breakfast with bottomless coffee costs $12. **Blue Mar-**

lin Diner, Marsden Rd., tel. 09/402-7590, opposite the waterfront, serves substantial cooked breakfasts all day for $10–12. **The Carvery** in the Paihia Mall, tel. 09/402-8172, is a great place to head for lunch or dinner to go. Choose from three roasted meats, carved to order, in a roll with salad for $6, or complete roast meals 5–8 P.M. for $15. It's open daily to 8 P.M.

Enjoy fresh local seafood at the **Saltwater Café,** Kings Rd., tel. 09/402-7783. I was impressed with the oysters from nearby Orongo Bay, which arrived with a tangy mango and chili salsa ($9.50 for the starter size). At 40 Marsden Rd., Paihia (next to the Stone Church on the waterfront), are **Only Seafood** (upstairs; tel. 09/402-6066) and **Bistro 40** (downstairs; tel. 09/402-7444). Only Seafood is a casual affair, simply furnished, featuring a seafood menu starting at $16 for main dishes. It's open daily from 5 P.M. More upscale Bistro 40 has a more varied menu and opens nightly at 6 P.M. **Tides,** Williams Rd., tel. 09/402-7557, has an interesting menu, mostly seafood, but it's not cheap (dinners from $21). It's open daily 11 A.M.–11 P.M.

Twin Pines Restaurant, on the upper floor of Twin Pines Brewhouse, on Puketona Rd. at Haruru Falls, tel. 09/402-7195, offers elegant dining with full à la carte menu and daily blackboard specials, but expect to fork out at least $20 for a main course, $50 pp for a meal including wine. However, downstairs in the Dewdrop Bar, you can get light lunches (a huge, yes huge, hamburger is about $6) and family-style bistro meals starting at about $15. On pleasant summer evenings, a filling barbecue meal is served in the Garden Bar for around $15, and you can enjoy it in the outside courtyard. The pub (described in a newspaper article as a "top country pub") also features Northland's first in-house brewery (beer enthusiasts swear by it), and live entertainment most nights of the week.

Transportation

Scheduled flights between Auckland and the Bay of Islands are operated by **Air New Zealand,** tel. 0800/737-000, two to four times daily. The airport is inland from Paihia near Kerikeri, but a shuttle service run by Paihia

Taxis, tel. 09/402-7506, meets all flights; $18 one way. Most visitors using public transportation arrive by bus. **Intercity** and **Northliner** provide services between Auckland and Paihia via Whangarei and Dargaville. The most direct route is via Whangarei, which takes about four hours. Both companies stop at the Maritime Building, tel. 09/402-7857.

On weekdays, local buses connect Paihia to Waitangi, Opua, and Kerikeri; fares range $1–6. For timetable information, call 09/407-7135. For a cab, call **Paihia Taxis,** tel. 09/402-7506. Rental-car companies include **Cost Busters,** tel. 09/402-8586, and **Nationwide,** tel. 09/402-8309.

Services and Information

The **post office** is on Beechy Street. **Information Bay of Islands** is beside the Maritime Building on Marsden Rd., near the main wharf, tel. 09/402-7345. This large facility has boards detailing all cruises and ferry sailings. Bookings can be made here for just about everything. It's open daily 8 A.M.–5 P.M. (in summer until 8 P.M.). In the Maritime Building are many tour operators, including **Fullers,** tel. 09/402-7421, and **Kings,** tel. 09/402-8288.

WAITANGI

From Paihia, continue north along the waterfront to the first intersection and go straight ahead toward Waitangi (if you turn left here you'll come to Haruru Falls) and one of New Zealand's most historically important sights.

Waitangi National Reserve

This is the place to absorb New Zealand history and to witness the birthplace of the nation as we know it today. In the Treaty House on February 6, 1840, the Treaty of Waitangi was signed, whereby the Maori surrendered the government of their country to Queen Victoria of Britain in return for protection and "the rights and privileges of British subjects." On first entering this historic park, don't miss the excellent audiovisual show in the Visitor Centre, then stroll through the beautifully kept grounds to the **Treaty House.** Originally designed as a home for British

resident James Busby (1832–40), drafter of the treaty, the house stands in its original condition and is open to the public. Near the Treaty House stands the intricately carved and highly decorated *Whare Runanga* (Maori Meeting House), where the local Maori discussed issues, entertained neighboring tribes, and gathered for instruction, storytelling, or games. The **Maori War Canoe,** on the other side of the reserve, known to the Maori as *Ngatokimatawhaorua* (The Adzes Which Shaped It Twice), is adorned with carvings, shells, and feathers. An amazing 35 meters in length, carved from three mighty kauri trees, it has the capacity to carry a crew of 80, plus passengers. If you're planning a visit to this area early in February, check out the annual local celebrations commemorating the signing of the treaty; the canoe is regularly launched on these occasions. Waitangi National Reserve grounds, buildings, and Visitor Centre, tel. 09/402-7437, are open daily 9 A.M.–5 P.M.; $8 adult, free to children.

For an enjoyable hike, consider the Haruru Falls-Treaty Grounds Track. Starting near the Visitor Centre, it crosses Hutia Creek via Mangrove Forest Boardwalk, and finishes at spectacular Haruru Falls. A map of the track is available in the Visitor Centre.

Mount Bledisloe

This mountain marks the northwest boundary of Waitangi National Reserve and is an excellent vantage point. The summit lookout (115 meters), a short walk from the parking lot, gives one of the best panoramic views of the Bay of Islands. Follow the road for 3.2 km beyond the reserve entrance (passing the rolling fairways of scenic Waitangi Golf Club; tel. 09/402-8207).

For an alternate route back to Paihia, turn left on Haruru Falls Rd. to Haruru Falls, and left again at the main road (Puketona Rd.), which takes you back to Paihia.

Practicalities

Copthorne Hotel and Resort, Tau Henare Dr., tel. 09/402-7411 or 0800/808-228, website: www.copthornewaitangi.co.nz, is a large waterfront hotel complex adjacent to the south end of Waitangi National Reserve and two km from downtown Paihia. The 138 rooms are spread around landscaped grounds and a large swimming pool. Rates start at $160 s, $180 d. The resort features three restaurants and two bars. **Anchorage Bistro** whips up grills, salads, and daily specials, with main courses averaging $17. It's open Mon.–Sat. noon–2 P.M. and 6–9 P.M., closed Sunday. If you're in a more dressy mood, head for the **Waitangi Room;** an average main course starts at $21. For an even bigger splurge, try the **Governor's Room.** A main course is $25–33; it's open from 6:30 P.M. Tues.–Sunday.

RUSSELL

Russell is arguably New Zealand's most picturesque town. Nestled in a west-facing bay and reached by ferry, it lacks the commercialism of Paihia; the streets are lined with historic buildings and elegant cafés and restaurants.

Russell Museum

Allow lots of time here. The museum on York St., tel. 09/403-7701, contains all sorts of relics from early Kororareka (Russell's original name), and gives insight into the people and the history of this colorful town. The highlight and pride of the museum is the seven-meter replica of Captain Cook's ship, the *Endeavour,* accurately reproduced down to the finest detail. The museum is open daily 10 A.M.–4 P.M.; admission $3 adult, $1 child.

Historic Buildings

Walk around Russell to discover many historic buildings scattered throughout. Impressive **Pompallier,** tel. 09/403-9015, is on The Strand, which runs along the waterfront. Historic relics are displayed within this stately house, named after one of its early owners, Bishop Pompallier, the South Pacific's first Catholic bishop. It's open daily 9 A.M.–5 P.M.; admission to house and grounds $5 adult, free for children. Toward the other end of The Strand stands the **police station.** Built in 1870, it has been a customs house, courthouse, and jail, and continues to serve as the

Peaceful Russell is a world away from touristy Paihia, just across the bay.

© ANDREW HEMPSTEAD

NORTHLAND

Russell police station. It's also the local policeman's home (there's only one!) and therefore is not open to the public. Check out the fantastic Morton Bay Fig Tree *(Ficus macrophyllia),* with its intricately gnarled and patterned trunk, growing between the police station and **The Duke of Marlborough Hotel.** This old hotel is the proud holder of the first liquor license issued in New Zealand and was among the many "grog shops" of Russell's rowdy past. **Christ Church,** a couple of blocks back from The Strand, was built in 1835 and is the oldest standing church in New Zealand. It still bears cannonball and musket holes from the days of the Maori Wars, and the gravestones (and the stories they tell) in the cemetery are intriguing.

Flagstaff Hill

Also known as Maiki Hill, this historic landmark offers outstanding views of Russell and the Bay of Islands—great for getting oriented and watching all the boats cruising the bay. In the early 1840s, at the top of the hill, the British raised a flagstaff. Hone Heke, chief of the Ngapuhi, saw the flagstaff as a symbol of British authority (for which he had little respect). He and his warriors spent much of their time through the years chopping it down, despite British attempts to keep the flag flying. It wasn't until 1857 that a permanent reconciliation between the Maori and the British formed. At the top of the hill is a monument to these historic events. A two-km (30-minute) track up the hill begins at the boatramp end of The Strand, follows the beach around to Watering Bay, and then heads up through native bush to the flagstaff. At high tide, take Wellington St. up instead of the track. By car, take Queen St. out of town, and follow signs to the top.

An Organized Tour
Russell Mini Tour is a one-hour tour of the local area including the main historic and scenic attractions, and it's particularly good for those on a short time schedule. The minibus departs Russell Wharf hourly 10 A.M.–4 P.M. (less often during low season); $16 adult, $8 child. For reservations book through Fullers in Russell, tel. 09/403-7866, or over in Paihia, tel. 09/402-7831.

Entertainment
There's not a lot of wild nightlife in the Bay of Islands—it's more of a wind-down-and-relax kind of place. Overlooking the beach, the **Duke of Marlborough Hotel,** tel. 09/403-7829, is a favorite watering hole, and has been since 1840 when it was issued New Zealand's very first liquor license. In the main hotel, the **Cane Lounge** is a quiet place with an oceanfront deck and an open fire inside. The adjacent tavern is the most popular local's spot-the perfect place to enjoy a drink and soak up some of the history that permeates the surroundings.

> *There's not a lot of wild nightlife in the Bay of Islands— it's more of a wind-down-and-relax kind of place.*

Hotels and Motels
Since 1827, the **Duke of Marlborough Hotel,** The Strand, tel. 09/403-7829, website: www.the-duke.co.nz, has proudly overlooked Russell Har-

bour. The rooms are medium-sized and furnished casually, in keeping with the general feel of the place. Rates range from $125 s or d to $280 for one of two suites offering fantastic water views. **Commodore's Lodge,** The Strand, tel. 09/403-7899, also sits right on the waterfront. Rates range from $105 for a basic motel room to $190 for a waterfront suite.   Behind the waterfront are a few less expensive motels, each within easy walking distance of the main wharf. **Motel Russell,** 16 Matauwhi Bay Rd., tel. 09/403-7854 or 0800/240-011, offers 15 small, self-contained units set around a landscaped pool area; from $95 s or d.

Arcadia Lodge
Dating from 1899, this elegant Tudor-style accommodation sits high above the waterfront on Florance Ave., tel. 09/403-7756. Constructed from a great variety of materials collected from around the area, including kauri and wood salvaged from shipwrecks, the lodge is surrounded by extensive gardens. The rooms lie on two levels; each has been restored in Victorian style, and some have private bathrooms. Communal areas include a large lounge, complete with a piano and library. A continental breakfast and daily newspapers come with the rates starting at $115 s or d ($150 with en suite).

Backpacker Lodges
Russell Lodge has excellent budget accommodation right in town, on the corner of Chapel and Beresford Streets (three blocks up from The Strand—walk up Cass St., opposite the wharf, which becomes Chapel); tel. 09/403-7640. Converted motel units now hold three to five dorm beds, and each unit has a private bathroom. Other facilities include a fully equipped communal kitchen, laundry, lounge room with TV, swimming pool, peaceful landscaped grounds, and free bag storage and security safe; rates are $20 pp. The lodge also has a large variety of units (family and luxury, and a self-contained flat) for $105 with shared kitchen.

The End of the Road is a small backpackers at, you guessed it, the end of Brind Rd., tel. 09/403-7632. It's a good 10-minute hike uphill from town, but the setting is magnificent, high above Matauwhi Bay. Rates in the two double rooms and six twin rooms are $22 pp.

Motor Camps

One of the best motor camps in the Bay of Islands is **Russell Top 10 Holiday Park** on Long Beach Rd., tel. 09/403-7826. Facilities include a TV, dining room, and spotless bathrooms (metered showers complete with soft piped music). Tent and caravan sites cost from $11 per adult, $6 per child. Cabins equipped with crockery and cutlery start at $45 d per night, and tourist flats range $65–125; you supply linen and blankets.

Head three km from Russell on the road from the Opua car ferry for lush, green **Orongo Bay Holiday Park,** tel. 09/403-7704. Aside from the usual shower and toilet blocks, there's a fully equipped kitchen and dining area, comfy game and TV room with fireplace, a swimming pool, and a shop in the office. Tent sites are $8 pp, caravan sites $10 pp, and cabins from $35 s or d.

Food

Many establishments along Russell's waterfront are open during the day, and they don't seem to mind if you just buy a coffee and sit there awhile soaking up the sun, the view, and the atmosphere. The best is **Verandah Cafe** (nice outside deck) on York St., tel. 09/403-7167. Breakfast is served until 10:30 A.M., and a good selection of sandwiches, snacks, and hot meals are offered the rest of the day. Continue through the café to a crafts shop and a "book swap" where you can buy or exchange reading material. **Something Fishy,** Cass St., tel. 09/403-7754, has fish and chips from $6.

Russell also boasts a large number of very good restaurants, and with ferries running back to Paihia until 10 P.M. in summer, the town is the perfect evening escape from the commercialism just across the bay. For some of the best seafood around, reasonable prices for what you get, and a casual atmosphere, head straight for laid-back

Gannets, on York St., tel. 09/403-7990. Start with the seafood chowder ($11), so thick you can stand a spoon up in it, and then peruse the blackboard for daily fish specials ($21–24). Gannets is open Mon.–Sat. for dinner.

The **Quarterdeck Restaurant** next to Fullers Cruises on The Strand, tel. 09/403-7761, serves all sorts of delectable dishes with dinners averaging $20–31, and all come with veggies or salad bar. Its seafood platter for $42 is large enough for two, and the staff doesn't mind you sharing. Desserts average $6. Savor your seafood and sea view in an appropriately nautical atmosphere, or outside amongst the real thing; it's open nightly for dinner 6–8:30 P.M. **Sally's,** The Strand, tel. 09/403-7652, is another popular local spot, but to eat here you need to be a member of the club ($10 per day), an affiliated or kindred member of an overseas club, or brought by a member. The menu features classic seafood favorites at reasonable prices. Also along the beachfront is the popular **Gables,** tel. 09/403-7618, housed in a timber building dating to 1847, complete with a sloping floor and whale bone foundations. Open through summer for lunch and year-round from 6 P.M. for dinner, Gables offers the most non-seafood choices of all Russell restaurants, including a mouthwatering herb-crusted rack of lamb, served with a port, ginger, and rosemary jus. Main dishes start at $24, but most average $30.

Other Practicalities

Passenger ferries run regularly between Paihia's main wharf and downtown Russell. They operate at least once an hour 7 A.M.–7 P.M., with later sailings most nights; $5 one way, $8 round-trip. It's also possible to reach Russell by road. From Opua, four km south of Paihia, a small vehicular ferry crosses to Okiato, from where it's a pleasant 15-km coastal drive to Russell. The ferry costs $8 per vehicle, then $1 pp. It operates daily 7 A.M.–9 P.M.

Russell has no official information center, but **Russell Field Centre,** The Strand, tel. 09/403-9005, is a good source of information; it's open Mon.–Fri. 8:30 A.M.–4:30 P.M., Sat.–Sun. 9 A.M.–4:30 P.M.

KERIKERI

This historic town, 23 km from Paihia, is well worth a visit. Once the home of Chief Hongi Hika and the Ngapuhi warriors, who conquered much of the North Island in the late 18th and early 19th centuries, it was also the site of one of the earliest missions. Kerikeri boasts impressive buildings and trees, lush agricultural land, and the attractive Kerikeri River and Rainbow Falls. It's a citrus center (the signs proclaim it "The Fruitbowl of the North"), quite obvious by the great number of orchards lining the roads between Paihia and Kerikeri, and from the delicious oranges, mandarins, and tangelos available June–January. It's also rapidly becoming an important kiwi cultivating center.

Kerikeri Basin

The historic hub of Kerikeri is this quiet waterway north of downtown, off the main highway along Kerikeri Inlet Road. Overlooking the waterway is New Zealand's oldest stone building, the **Stone Store,** tel. 09/407-9236. Built by the Church Missionary Society in 1832, the Stone Store once served as an impenetrable place of refuge in troubled times and as a storehouse. Still used as a storehouse today, it is under renovation. In recent times it has been used to display articles that belonged to early settlers and knick-knacks from the past, and as an outlet for groceries and souvenirs. It's open for inspection in summer, daily 10 A.M.–5 P.M., the rest of the year, Sat.–Wed. 10 A.M.–5 P.M.; admission is $2. **Kemp House,** beside the Stone Store, was built in 1821 and lays claim to being the oldest wooden building in the country. It has been preserved by the Historic Society in much the same state as when the early missionaries lived there, and the surrounding gardens remain beautiful despite the damage caused by severe flooding in 1981. Kemp House is open daily 10 A.M.–12:30 P.M. and 1:30–4:30 P.M.; $5 adult, $3 child. Across the road is a grassy knoll (pleasant spot for a picnic) overlooking Kerikeri Basin. The knoll is the remains of **Kororipo Pa,** a fishing base built by Hongi Hika and other Ngapuhi chiefs, where many historic meetings took place.

Rewa's Village, tel. 09/407-6454, a reconstruction of a *kainga* or unfortified Maori village, is a short stroll up the hill facing the Stone Store. To get there, cross the bridge opposite Kemp House and park on the left side of the road in the parking area. On the other side of the road is a trail that winds through the bush and up the hillside. Along the trail many of the native plants are labeled with their names and Maori uses, and at the top you'll find a variety of interesting identified structures and dwellings. It's open daily 9 A.M.–5 P.M.; $3.

Rainbow Falls Scenic Reserve

You can easily reach the top of spectacular Rainbow Falls by road, or the bottom by foot. The water plummets 27 meters over eroded soft lava columns, and there are several viewing points. To get to the falls, enter the reserve off Waipapa Rd. about two km beyond Kerikeri Basin. The road to the falls is well signposted and there's a large parking lot; a short stroll through natural bush brings you to the various lookouts. From the second lookout at the top, on a sunny day, you can see how the falls got their name.

Alternatively, a four-km (one-hour) one-way trail begins across the river from the Stone Store; it follows the Kerikeri River, passes Fairy Pools (good swimming), and comes out at the bottom of the falls. Fairy Pools is also easily reached along a walking trail just south of Kerikeri YHA.

Arts, Crafts, and Oranges

Kerikeri distinctly appeals to arts and crafts collectors and music lovers. The town supports a large community of artists; spinning and weaving, ceramics, and stained-glass art are most popular (the shopping center lies off the main road to the right just before Cobham Road). Don't miss a stop at **Origin Art & Craft Co-Op,** tel. 09/407-9065, on the main highway (Hwy. 10). Inside you'll discover pottery, knitwear, weaving, stained glass, leatherwork, woodwork, and furniture—it's a shopper's delight—and major credit cards are accepted, just to remove any last doubts you may have about buying up the entire shop. It's open daily 10 A.M.–5 P.M.

If you're interested in the area's orchard industry, the **Orange Centre,** on Hwy. 10 (as you approach Kerikeri from the south), tel. 09/407-9397, is open daily 9 A.M.–6 P.M. The center's staff provides tours on the hour (half-hourly on public and school holidays) through a commercial citrus and subtropical orchard in the Orangemobile; $6 adult, $3 child. Crafts and gifts, a fruit stall, freshly squeezed juice, and Devonshire teas are available.

Accommodations and Camping
Kerikeri offers some particularly charming bed-and-breakfasts. **The Ferns,** 4 Riverview Rd., tel. 09/407-7567, is a modern two-story house set in a delightful garden on the outskirts of town. A continental or cooked breakfast is included in the rates of $65 s, $100 d.

Kerikeri YHA is at 144 Kerikeri Rd. (between the highway and Kerikeri Basin), tel. 09/407-9391; website: www.yha.org.nz. Formerly a private residence, it has just 36 beds, but the bush setting is pleasant and the river is reached through native bush. Members pay $18, nonmembers $22, or stay in a private kitchen-equipped cabin for $70 s or d. **Kerikeri Farm Hostel,** tel. 09/407-6989, is set on a seven-hectare orchard five km from downtown off Hwy. 10. It's a small place, but the rooms are comfortable, and guests can use a relaxing lounge area and a swimming pool. Rates are $18 in three-bed dorms or a bargain at $30 s, $40 d.

If you don't mind getting a little bit off the beaten track (and have some form of wheels), drive out to **Pagoda Lodge Caravan Park,** on the upper reaches of Kerikeri Inlet, tel. 09/407-8617; website: www.pagoda.co.nz. From town, follow caravan park signs along Cobham Rd., turn left on Inlet Rd., then left on Pa Road. Grassy tent and caravan sites lie along Wairoa Stream (leads into Kerikeri Inlet), and this tranquil campground offers opportunities to row, canoe, and fish. Tent and caravan sites cost from $12 pp, self-contained units $65–85 s or d.

Food
Several cafés lie along the main street of Kerikeri. Locally recommended **Adam and Eve Café,** Kerikeri Rd., tel. 09/407-9511, features sandwiches and continental cakes at average prices for lunch. At dinner the emphasis is on French cuisine; a main course is $20–25. For good coffee as well as inexpensive pizza, pasta, and salads, try the **Fishbone Café,** 88 Kerikeri Rd., tel. 09/407-6065. For bulk natural foods and organic fruit and veggies, go to **Mother Earth Shop,** 84 Kerikeri Rd., tel. 09/407-8798.

Information
Kerikeri has no official visitor center, but **Trixi Newton's Harvey World Travel,** 65 Kerikeri Rd. (the main street downtown), tel. 09/407-9437, is a good source of local information.

BAY OF ISLANDS TO KAITAIA
The most direct route between the Bay of Islands and Kaitaia, gateway to Cape Reinga, is to backtrack from Paihia the short distance to Hwy. 1, which cuts across Northland via Mangamuka Bridge.

The following section details the longer alternative, Hwy. 10, giving the traveler-in-a-hurry the opportunity to absorb beautiful coastal scenery while driving, yet luring the hiker and nature enthusiast into frequent stops to smell the flowers. Scenic reserves intermingled with fir tree plantations line the highway, soft white-sand beaches lead you to the ocean, and in summer wildflowers border the roads. In some areas endless rows of pine trees follow the contours of the land—planted as a windbreak, these magnificent hedges separate the rolling hills and fields into giant patchworks of color.

Whangaroa
The several small towns along Hwy. 10 share a relaxed atmosphere. Fishing boats, small private beaches, cottage arts and crafts, and tempting tearooms may delay your venture north. Like being on the water? Take a sidetrack to Whangaroa, six km north of **Kaeo.** Beautiful Whangaroa Harbour has become a renowned spot for excellent fishing—some say it's much better than the famous Bay of Islands. Charter boats are always available, and in recent years

local boats have captured a large number of blue, black, and striped marlin. **Boyd Gallery & General Store,** Whangaroa Rd., tel. 09/405-0230, acts as the local information center and keeps a list of charter boats.

On the shores of Whangaroa Harbour, **Sunseeker Lodge,** Old Hospital Rd., tel. 09/405-0496, website: www.sunseekerlodge.co.nz, is known for its friendly atmosphere and magnificent harbor views from its elevated location. It's the kind of place where you plan to stay a night but end up staying a week. A dinghy and fishing gear can be rented, and big-game fishing trips and harbor cruises can be arranged. Sea kayaks are also available. Budget travelers can rent campsites (with water views) for $12 pp, dorm beds for $17, and double rooms that share the main bathroom for a reasonable $40 d. For more privacy, rent one of two self-contained units for $100 s or d.

Continuing north from Whangaroa Harbour, **Kahoe Farms Hostel,** 10 km north of Kaeo on Hwy. 10, tel. 09/405-1804, is in a beautiful setting and it's a good base from which to explore this area of Northland. Take a short walk from the farmhouse and up a small hill on the property for great views across Whangaroa Harbour. Your hosts can arrange a variety of local activities. Dorm beds are $19, doubles and twins are $24.50 pp.

Mangonui

The picturesque village of Mangonui, 30 km northwest of Whangaroa, lies on the southern edge of **Doubtless Bay,** marked as being "doubtless a bay" when Captain Cook sailed by in the late 1700s. Mangonui was originally a busy whaling base and trading station. In recent years, although the main undertaking is commercial fishing, southerners have discovered the charm of the area and the population has rapidly increased.

Ask a local for directions to the top of **Rangikapiti Pa.** The brilliant 360-degree view brings the whole area into perspective, and you can walk or drive to the top. Boats can be rented for fishing (from $20 an hour with an outboard)—though you can catch snapper, John

Dory, and kingfish from the wharf on an incoming tide.

If you're looking for somewhere to stay, try the **Old Oak Inn,** 66 Waterfront Rd., tel. 09/406-0665. You can't miss it—made of pitsawn kauri and established in 1861, the twostory whitewashed hotel stands directly across from the Magonui waterfront. The rooms are basic yet clean and comfortable, and there's a communal kitchen, lounge, and barbecue. Beds in the dormitory are $20, or enjoy the privacy of your own room for $80 s or d. Downstairs, a small café will lure you in for a delicious Devonshire tea ($7), a light lunch (up to $11), or seafood cuisine (from 6 P.M.; $18–25). Visit the crafts shop chock-a-block full of well-made kauri products, pottery, and all sorts of intriguing items. Continue along the road to the **Waterfront Cafe,** tel. 09/406-0850, a local favorite for seafood chowder, smoked fish pie (using fresh fish from local waters), huge addictive bacon rolls, pizzas, cappuccino and freshly brewed coffee; it's open daily 7 A.M.–midnight. For takeout seafood, head to the **Mangonui Fish Shop** down on the waterfront, tel. 09/406-0478.

Around Doubtless Bay to Kaitaia

West of Mangonui, Hwy. 10 hugs the southern shore of Doubtless Bay, passing **Coopers Beach, Cable Bay,** and **Taipa,** all known for their white-sand beaches and handsome groves of *pohutukawa* trees. Coopers Beach has a campground and motor camp. Though Cable Bay's small beach is attractive to campers, it's a reserve, so camping is not permitted. After crossing the Taipa River you enter the town of Taipa with another fairly large motor camp. Get great views of the Tokerau Beach peninsula and Cape Karikari from the Taipa area. Accessible on an unpaved road (turn off Hwy. 10 west of Taipa), the remote **Karikari Peninsula** offers more beaches and delightful coves, including **Matai Bay.**

After leaving Doubtless Bay, Hwy. 10 crosses a rolling rural landscape to Awanui and Kaitaia, a distance of 50 km from Taipa.

Kaitaia and Vicinity

Kaitaia (population 5,200), the main business and commercial center of the far north, lies 110 km from Paihia and 330 km from Auckland. It's a good base for exploring Aupouri Peninsula to the north and the forests and harbors to the east and west. Shopping centers, lots of motels, motor camps, and several engaging attractions within the area make it a worthwhile stop. Boosted by tourist interest in the north, the town has also become a center for bus trips up to Cape Reinga.

SIGHTS AND RECREATION

Kaitaia is a good base for surrounding attractions, but the town itself has little to hold visitors for more than a few hours. If your interests include arts and crafts, stop at the Far North Information Centre (by Jaycee Park) on South Rd. for a *Craft Trails of the Far North* brochure; there are plenty of places to visit—and shop. Primarily a learning and cultural center, **Te Wero Nui,** 237 Commerce St., tel. 09/408-0870, produces a variety of crafts, including weaving, wood-carving, and flax baskets.

Far North Regional Museum

This excellent museum, 6 South Rd., tel. 09/408-1403, is a trove of information on the historical aspects of the northern region. Displays focus on ancient Maori lifestyles, including agricultural, fishing, and hunting methods and equipment, intricate feather capes and articles of clothing, and a comprehensive display of Maori carving styles and art forms. Other highlights include a display of New Zealand birds, an ancient anchor and various shipwreck articles, and a 1909–36 photograph collection featuring kauri-gum digging activities. Don't miss the information board at the entrance where descriptions and prices of all the latest tours up the cape are advertised. The museum is open weekdays 10 A.M.–5 P.M.; $3 adult, $1 child.

Glowworms & Kiwi Nocturnal Park

Don't miss this favorite attraction. It's an excellent place to see glowworms and kiwis in their natural environment. The best time to visit is early evening (take your dinner and enjoy it in the outside picnic/barbecue area until it gets dark); however, if you have to visit during daylight you can still appreciate the glowworms in the large cave. A natural rock- and bush-filled canyon houses thousands of tiny glowworms (the farther you go, the more you see). Strolling along the path, your guide relates the fascinating life cycle of this glowing creature, and in some areas, with the aid of a flashlight, you can get close enough to the glowworms to see the threads that hang below each one to catch food. At the end of the trail is the nocturnal house, where you can get an outstanding view of kiwis in action through one-way glass, along with other indigenous creatures and plants. Admission is a worthwhile $10 adult, $5 child. The park is at Fairburn, tel. 09/408-4100, and is open daily 9 A.M.–11 P.M. (the nocturnal house is open to 10 P.M.). To get there, head southeast out of Kaitaia on Hwy. 1 for about eight km and turn left at the Fairburn sign. Continue for another nine km along a rough, semi-paved road (go slowly in the dark) and follow the signs (fluorescent at night)—the drive takes about 15 minutes from town.

Ahipara Gum Fields

Just above Ahipara sprawls a stark, barren plateau that used to be home to hundreds of Yugoslav gum diggers in the 1890s. Vast forests of kauri trees once covered the north, but most of these forests were quickly decimated by the colonial timber-cutters of the early 1800s. Sadly, they gave no thought to conserving the slow-growing giants of the forest. Kauri resin, which hardens into gum on contact with air, dribbled down the trees, collected around the bases, and petrified under forest debris. When the timber rush finished, the gum rush began. The ground where mighty trees once stood was dug up, denuded of its gum, and made barren. By the 1890s the fossilized gum, used as a base for slow-drying hard varnishes and for making linoleum, had

looking north along Ahipara Beach

become one of New Zealand's major exports. (The Maori first used the gum for fuel, tattooing, and chewing gum.) Most of the gum fields of the north have been ploughed and fertilized into agricultural land, but the Ahipara Plateau has been preserved by the Historic Places Trust as a reminder of the past, in hopes of preventing such desecration from ever happening again.

Kaitaia Track

This nine-km track, part of the New Zealand Walkway, lets you enjoy great views of the Northland Peninsula, Okahu Falls, and Diggers and Takahue Valleys. A sidetrack heads up to Puketutu summit (420 meters) for even better views. From Kaitaia, take Hwy. 1 south for about three km and turn right onto Larmers Road. Go past the quarry and continue along the metal track to the parking area where the main track starts. The track ends at Diggers Valley Rd.; classified as a walk, it takes about three hours each way. Wear sturdy footwear, particularly in wet weather.

ACCOMMODATIONS

Hotels and Motels

Dating from 1837, the **Historic Kaitaia Hotel** is downtown at 15 Commerce St., tel. 09/408-0360. The rooms are basic, but unlike most old hotels, each has a private bathroom; $50 s, $60 d. **Kauri Lodge Motel,** 15 South Rd., tel. 09/408-1190, is handily located directly opposite the information center. Each of the eight rooms has a kitchen, and there's a small pool for guest use; $65 s, $75 d. If you're taking a tour to Cape Reinga with Sand Safaris, consider staying at **Wayfarer Motel,** 231 Commerce St., tel. 09/408-2600 or 0800/118-100, because the tours leave from across the road. Each room has a kitchen; rates from $63 s, $78 d. In the vicinity is the more luxurious **Orana Motor Inn,** 238 Commerce St., tel. 09/408-1510 or 0800/267-262, where guest rooms start at $95 s or d. None have cooking facilities, but the complex includes a restaurant and bar.

Backpacker Lodges

Affiliated with the YHA, **Main Street Backpackers,** 237 Commerce St., tel. 09/408-1275, website: www.yha.org.nz, is another central budget accommodation. Hospitable owners Peter and Kerry Kitchen not only arrange horse trekking, fishing trips, glowworm and *marae* visits, and tours to the north, they also throw authentic *hangi* (Maori feast) every month (everyone is encouraged to participate and the food costs about $12 pp) and frequent lamb-on-a-spit nights or barbecues, which all guests are invited to join. It has a casual, laid-back, Kiwi-style atmosphere. They also dive for seafood, and if you want to join in on these diving trips, you're welcome. Rates run from $18 for bunkroom accommodation, $20–30 pp for family or private rooms (in summer it gets pretty busy and bunkrooms may be all that's available). Facilities include powerful hot showers, a fully equipped kitchen, a sunny dining room, a lounge, laundry, and bicycles.

Motor Camp

The only camping in town is at **Kaitaia Motor Camp,** at the southern end of town on South Rd., tel. 09/408-1212, with tent and caravan sites for $10 pp. It has a communal bathroom, kitchen, laundry, and TV and game room on-site, and a dairy (a shop selling dairy products and other essentials) and take-away next door.

Ahipara Accommodations

This oceanfront village 15 km west of Kaitaia is good alternative to staying in town. Here you'll find **Adriaan Lodge Motel,** 22 Reef View Rd., tel. 09/409-4888 or 0800/909-453, a distinctive pink and blue building overlooking the ocean. Studio units (no kitchen) are $70 s or d, or do your own cooking in a one-bedroom unit for $90 s or d. The motel also has a restaurant and bar, and guests can rent beach-fishing gear.

Views from the **Siesta Guest House,** Tasman Heights Rd., tel. 09/409-2011, and its surrounding garden are stunning—a 180-degree panorama of the south end of Ninety Mile Beach—and the beach is only a few hundred meters away. The European-style house has a separate guest wing, where the rooms feature timbered ceilings, comfortable beds, private bathrooms, writing desks, and balconies with views. On arrival, guests are treated to fresh fruit and home-baked cake. A three-course dinner is available ($40 extra pp), and a gourmet hot and cold breakfast is served each morning. Rates are $140 s, $160 d.

Pine Tree Lodge Motor Camp is on Takahe St. by the golf course, tel. 09/407-4864. Campsites are $10 pp, cabins range $28–40 s or d. Communal facilities, indoor dining, a swimming pool, and a barbecue round out the features.

FOOD

Kaitaia's several restaurants and large number of take-aways (most along Commerce St.—the main drag) offer a variety of food, but not much in the way of evening entertainment.

For lunch try one of the many take-aways along Commerce St. or one of the supermarkets (most provide salad bars and/or delis). A popular gathering spot is the **Coast to Coast Bakery,** 106 Commerce St., tel. 09/408-1350, where everything is made on the premises.

As always, local pubs provide inexpensive meals in a casual atmosphere. In the Historic Kaitaia Hotel at 15 Commerce St., tel. 09/408-0360, the **Flame Grill Restaurant** serves up cooked breakfasts daily from 7 A.M. and dinner specials for $25, including dessert. At the other end of town, the **Kauri Arms Tavern,** 195 Commerce St., tel. 09/408-1700, has a very good bistro with reasonable prices; lunches (noon–2 P.M.) are $9–14; dinners (6–9 P.M.) are slightly higher. At **Collard's Tavern,** a couple of kilometers north of Kaitaia on Whangatane Dr., tel. 09/408-3190, you can feast on generous servings of good food in the bistro; expect to pay $12–16 for a steak dinner. Dining at the **Bushman's Hut,** on the corner of Bank St. and Puckey Ave., tel. 09/408-4320, is more expensive than at the pubs around town, but the atmosphere is a little more sophisticated (it's all relative in small town New Zealand) and the steaks are cooked exactly to order.

The **Beachcomber Restaurant,** 222 Commerce St., tel. 09/408-2010, serves seafood, steak, and chicken. The decor is nothing special, but the food is good. Fish of the Day runs $20, and a small seafood basket $29. It's open for lunch 11:30 A.M.–2:30 P.M., dinner 5–8:30 P.M. The **Sea Dragon** on Commerce St., tel. 09/408-0555, is a standard New Zealand Chinese restaurant, with a huge selection of generic dishes, such as beef and broccoli in black bean sauce ($15.50). For Chinese takeout, there's another Sea Dragon across the road; no dish costs more than $14, including rice.

TRANSPORTATION

Getting There
Kaitaia Airport, nine km north of town, is served by **Air New Zealand,** tel. 0800/737-000, from Auckland. Flights from all other destinations are routed through Auckland. Cabs await all arrivals.

Kaitaia is the northernmost stop on the **Intercity** coach network. From the depot at 170 Commerce St., tel. 09/408-0540, buses arrive and depart once daily for all points south, via Paihia and Whangarei. If you plan to travel down the west coast (see below) with Intercity, you must backtrack to Paihia. From the same bus depot, **Northliner** offers the same service in a luxury air-conditioned, video-equipped coach. Book through the Kaitaia Holiday Shoppe, tel. 09/408-0540.

Getting Around
Kaitaia has no local bus service, but **Budget,** tel. 09/408-0453, has a rental agency in town. For a cab, call **Kaitaia Taxis,** tel. 09/408-1111.

Tours
The most popular tour is to Cape Reinga (see Cape Reinga Tours, below). Based in downtown Kaitaia, **Tall Tale Travel Tours,** 221 Commerce St., tel. 09/408-0870, offers an excellent variety of ways to discover the far north. Learn about Maori culture, protocol, history, and myths and legends by visiting a local *marae* for $30 pp (minimum two); take a ride in an authentic *waka* (Maori canoe) Dec.–March for $18 pp; visit the historic Ahipara Gum Fields for $24 pp (minimum four); or do the Tu Tu Bus Tour (4WD) on the sand dunes for $58 pp.

SERVICES AND INFORMATION

The main street downtown is Commerce St., on which you'll find just about everything you need. Looking for a **laundromat?** You'll find one in Kaitaia Plaza on Commerce Street. Send and receive email at **Hacker's Internet Café,** 84 Commerce St., tel. 09/408-4999. **Kaitaia Hospital,** tel. 09/408-0010, and the **police station,** tel. 09/408-6500, are both on Redan Rd., off Commerce St. heading toward Ahipara.

The **Far North Information Centre** is by Jaycee Park on South Rd., just along the road from the museum, tel. 09/408-0879; it's open seven days in summer 8:30 A.M.–5 P.M., in winter on weekdays 8:30 A.M.–5 P.M., Saturday 8:30 A.M.–noon, and Sunday 8:30 A.M.–5 P.M.

The Far North—Land of Sand and Legends

From **Awanui,** eight km north of Kaitaia at the junction of Highways 1 and 10, it's just over 100 km along the spine of the **Aupouri Peninsula** to **Cape Reinga,** with the last 21 km, from Waitiki Landing, unsealed. The alternative to the road is **Ninety Mile Beach,** along the west side of the peninsula. The beach is not recommended for regular vehicles, but this is the route taken by bus tours-either on the outward or return trip.

AWANUI TO THE CAPE— THE INLAND ROUTE

Most travelers who reach Kaitaia have one destination in mind—Cape Reinga. From the turnoff at Awanui, the landscape progressively gets drier. The colorful fields become scrubland (watch out for the odd suicidal sheep or cow on the road), and exotic pine plantations are the only evidence of human changes to this desertlike landscape. Huge sand dunes roll in all directions, and the large saltwater marshes brim with birdlife. In March, on the mighty dunes of the north, the *kuaka* or Eastern bar-tailed godwit gather in great numbers before their annual migration to breeding grounds on the Alaskan and Siberian tundra. Much of the peninsula has been made into reserve, thus protecting it from development and other intrusion.

Waipapakauri Beach, 18 km north of Kaitaia and the southern access point for Ninety Mile Beach, is home to **The Park,** tel. 09/407-7298 or 0800/367-719, website: www.ninetymile-beach.co.nz, a large and popular commercial campground. Bathroom, kitchen, and laundry facilities are communal; there's also a game room, barbecue, restaurant, and store. Tent and caravan sites are $12 pp, basic cabins with two single beds are $50 s or d, and cabins with a private bathroom and television are $65 s or d.

Houhora Harbour

This long, narrow body of water 40 km north of Kaitaia makes a good stopping point on the trip to the cape. Turn east onto Houhora Heads Rd. to reach **Houhora Heads,** at the entrance to the harbor. This little township is home to the well-known **Wagener Museum,** tel. 09/409-8850, which contains extensive natural history exhibits, Maori and whaling artifacts, a kauri gum collection, shells, firearms, and even old historic slot machines. It's open daily 9 A.M.–5 P.M.; $6. The museum is just a small part of the Wagener property, which includes a golf course, café, and campground. The 18-hole **Wagener Park Golf Club,** tel. 09/409-8850, New Zealand's northernmost golf course, has club and cart rentals. Also at Houhora Heads is **Houhora Chalets Motor Lodge,** tel. 09/409-8860, with six self-contained rooms; $70–80 s or d.

Continuing north, **Pukenui Lodge Motel,** tel. 09/409-8837, website: www.pukenuilodge .co.nz, is on the main highway north in Pukenui, overlooking Houhora Harbour. Facilities in-

JOURNEY OF THE DEAD

The main legend of the North concerns the final trip of ancient Maori spirits of the dead. After death, the spirit padded up Te-Oneroa-A-Tohe (the Maori version of Ninety Mile Beach, not a direct translation) with a token of home in hand. The spirit left the token at Te Arai Bluff, then continued to Scott Point where it climbed the highest hill and took a last look back at the land of the living. After quenching its thirst in Re-Wai-O-Raio-Po, the stream of the underworld, it trudged on to Cape Reinga. At the northern tip of this rocky promontory you can see the famed *pohutukawa* tree with its exposed root, which the spirit slid down before gently dropping into the sea. The kelp parted, and it swam to the Three Kings Island. After surfacing for a last look at New Zealand, the spirit took up the trail to Hawaiiki, its Polynesian homeland. Legend also states that the spirits of the sick sometimes got as far as Te-Oneroa-A-Tohe, but if they didn't quench their thirst at the stream the spirits returned to their bodies.

clude a game room, spa pool, and landscaped grounds. Explore the beaches, go diving or fishing; you can rent a dinghy or mountain bikes at the motel, and across the road are a restaurant and café. Dorm beds are $18–21; motel rooms $69–99 s or d.

And on to Cape Reinga

From Pukenui, it's 68 km farther north to Cape Reinga. If you're driving to the end of the road, be sure to check your gas before you leave **Te Kao,** and if you plan to camp it's a good idea to pick up food supplies, sunscreen (a must!), and stove fuel.

Take the side road west from Te Kao to the **The Bluff,** an excellent area to view Ninety Mile Beach in both directions; the surf is good, and the hard, white sand is covered with shells. Offshore lies Wakatehaua Island.

You'll find a store and tearooms farther north at the **Waitiki Landing Complex,** 21 km from the cape, tel. 09/409-7508. The Waitiki Landing Complex also has unserviced sites for $14, powered sites for $18, dorm beds for $14, and cabins for $64 s or d. Facilities for campers include a communal kitchen and coin-operated showers.

NINETY MILE BEACH

Abel Tasman called these northwestern shores "the desert coast." The etymology of "Ninety Mile Beach" remains unknown, although you could easily be forgiven for estimating this unbroken stretch of sand at 90 miles. The beach is actually 56 miles in length or almost exactly 90 km—the name-giver must have been an early advocate of the metric system. Huge white sand dunes reaching 143 meters high and six km wide fringe the beach, kept in place by mass plantings of marram grass and pine trees.

Every January, reels scream and large game fish dance in the shallows off Ninety Mile Beach as hordes of anglers compete for big-money prizes in one of the world's largest surf-fishing contests. Apart from being a shell-collector's paradise, this amazing beach is well known for good surfing conditions, particularly at Ahipara and Wreck Bay (walk around the rocks from the Ahipara

access). All beach users should beware: every now and again an unexpected roller will come way up the beach or rocks, submerging previously safe areas; keep way back from the water's edge.

Driving Ninety Mile Beach

The sand below the high-water mark along Ninety Mile Beach is concrete hard, at times solid enough to support motor vehicles. During low spring tides a belt of about 250 meters of sand is considered safe under normal conditions for motoring. The main access point is the village of Waipapakauri Beach in the south and the northern pull-off point is The Bluff. Experienced 4WD enthusiasts often continue to Te Paki stream. The Automobile Association recommends that you not drive on it for at least three hours before and after high tide. The sand is safe to *drive* on,

A RARE DELICACY

Ninety Mile Beach is famous for the shellfish that live deep within its sands. The *toheroa (Paphies ventricosum)* is like a clam, can grow up to 152 mm (six inches) long, has been a prized delicacy since ancient Maori times, and is considered New Zealand's finest seafood. Unfortunately, you'll probably never get to experience its deliciously delicate flavor.

The *toheroa* prefers to burrow deep in the sand along beaches backed by sand dunes; thus, it's most common along Ninety Mile Beach. (It can also be found on beaches near Dargaville and Levin, and along Foveaux Strait.) Traditionally, the *toheroa* is eaten raw, made into a delicious soup, minced for fritters, or baked in the shell. At one time, three canning facilities operated on the peninsula.

The great popularity has depleted supplies of *toheroa,* and digging is prohibited except on the rare occasion that the Chief Executive of the Ministry of Fisheries declares an open season, and even then limits are strictly enforced.

Another similar shellfish that lives in the sand and is often mistaken for *toheroa* is the *tuatua.* It is distinctively smaller, but lives in the same environment as the *toheroa,* and is considered less of a delicacy.

but don't leave the car standing on wet sand for even a short time: the wheels can sink very rapidly. All rental car firms specify no driving on Ninety Mile Beach. The safest way to enjoy the unique opportunity of driving along the beach is on an organized Cape Reinga bus tour.

CAPE REINGA

The road up Aupouri Peninsula ends at an elevated parking lot 108 km north of Kaitaia. From this exposed promontory you get tremendous views in all directions. Looking eastward you can see **North Cape** and the **Surville Cliffs.** To the west lies **Cape Maria Van Diemen,** and on the northern horizon, 57 km off Cape Reinga, are the **Three Kings Islands.** This nature reserve, made up of 40 islands and rocks, is clearly visible from the cape only in fine weather. Also to the north and not far offshore is **Columbia Bank,** the point at which the Tasman Sea and the Pacific Ocean converge. Look for turbulent water and large crashing waves—in stormy weather they can reach up to 10 meters high. If you walk to the very tip of the cape (see below), you'll see the famed *pohutukawa* tree, the roots of which are the legendary path for Maori spirits of the dead. Cape Reinga has no facilities, just the well-known, whitewashed **Cape Reinga Lighthouse.**

Hiking

The northern section of the New Zealand Walkway starts at Cape Reinga. Don't attempt any of the tracks without a map, and come adequately prepared for beach camping—there are no overnight huts. If you plan to hike all the tracks, start at the eastern end of Spirits Bay. A 28-km track runs from Spirits Bay to Cape Reinga, involves some steep sections toward the end, and takes about 10 hours. From Cape Reinga a 22-km cliff-and-beach track heads south to Te Paki Stream (look out for treacherous quicksands in this area), taking about seven hours. The next track starts at Te Paki Stream and follows Ninety Mile Beach all the way down to Ahipara, at the south end of the beach. It takes a good two to three days to hike the entire 83 km to Ahipara, but you can leave the track and get back onto

CAPE REINGA TOURS

Driving to the end of the road is only half of the Cape Reinga experience. Take one of the many bus tours and make the return (or visaversa, depending on the tides) journey along the hard-packed sands of **Ninety Mile Beach.**

From Kaitaia, **Sand Safaris,** 221 Commerce St., tel. 09/408-1778 or 0800/869-090, departs daily at 9 A.M. for the cape. The tour travels along the beach in one direction, while also taking in the Te Paki Sand Dunes, Cape Reinga, east coast beaches, Aupouri Forest, and the Wagener Museum. The cost of $55 adult, $30 child includes lunch and accommodation pickups in Kaitaia.

Tours also leave from Paihia, in the Bay of Islands. **King's,** tel. 09/402-8288 or toll-free 0508/888-282, departs Paihia daily at 8:15 A.M., including all of the Sand Safaris stops as well as short stop for sand tobogganing in one long day tour; $85 adult, $10 child, excluding lunch. **Fullers,** tel. 09/402-7421, offers the similar Cape Reinga Wanderer tour, as well as a Cape Reinga Heritage Tour that takes in traditional Maori heritage at a *marae.*

NORTHLAND

the main road at The Bluff (19 km), Hukatere (51 km), or Waipapakauri (69 km). Many other walking tracks in Te Paki Farm Park lead to points of historic or archaeological interest and scenic lookouts—pick and choose from a short 30-minute walk to a several-day hike.

Expect to cover beaches, sand dunes, swamps, and pastureland during the various hikes, and be sure to take plenty of water, energy food, suntan lotion, and insect repellent. A large map with lengths, times, and descriptions of the various tracks is posted in Cape Reinga's parking area. For more information and maps, see the ranger at Waitiki Landing (on the main road to the cape) or call in at the Information Centre on South Rd. in Kaitaia. For fairly detailed maps and track descriptions, pick up the free booklet "New Zealand Walkway—Walks in the Northland District" or the "New Zealand Walkway—Far North" brochure.

Cape Camping

The closest accommodation to the cape is **Wait-iki Landing Complex,** 21 km to the south. If you don't mind roughing it for a night or two, you can camp at a couple of places farther north. Most have fresh water, some have toilets, some have no facilities at all. Try the campground at **Tapotupotu Bay.** Three km from the main road and signposted, it's down the last road to the east before you reach Cape Reinga. The camping area lies at the back of a beautiful surf beach, and a park ranger supervises it during peak holiday periods from one of the resident caravans. Open all year, it operates on an honesty-box system when the ranger isn't there.

Campsites are $6 pp per night, and the camp has water, toilets, and showers. A stream (considerably warmer than the ocean) runs by the campground and out to sea, and the beach, pounded by big surf, is a long stretch of golden sand with rock formations at the south end. Be aware of the strong rip where the stream meets the sea.

The campground at **Spirits Bay,** a sacred Maori area, also has water, toilets, and showers; rates are $5 pp per night. Take Te Hapua Rd., then Spirits Bay Rd. to Hooper Point. The camping area is a long way from the main road but very handy for hikers doing the Spirits Bay to Cape Reinga Track.

Kaitaia to Auckland via the West Coast

SOUTH TO HOKIANGA HARBOUR

Mangamuka Gorge and Walkway

Mangamuka Gorge is a gorgeous drive, particularly on a sunny day, when you'll probably find yourself leaping in and out of the car at regular intervals, camera in hand, to capture giant tree ferns and assorted flora and fauna. Allow plenty of time to meander through all this lushness. Mangamuka Gorge Walkway starts 26 km southeast of Kaitaia and crosses a part of Maungataniwha Range. The route winds through the beautiful Raetea Forest and Mangamuka Gorge Scenic Reserve, emerging at Hwy. 1 north of Mangamuka township. During the hike expect to traverse open farmland, dense forest, and lush native bush with its wonderland of ferns, mosses, and lichens. Climb to the radio mast atop Raetea summit (751 meters) for spectacular panoramic views of North Cape and Karikari Peninsula to the north, Hokianga Harbour to the south, Bay of Islands

Mangamuka Gorge is a gorgeous drive, particularly on a sunny day, when you'll probably find yourself leaping in and out of the car at regular intervals, camera in hand, to capture giant tree ferns and assorted flora and fauna.

to the east, and Tauroa Point and Ahipara to the west. At the summit, the main track doubles back and continues east—don't head south along the minor track toward Broadwood unless it's familiar; this track fizzles out in places and it's easy to get lost in the dense bush. Keep on the main marked track at all times.

The 19-km (six- to seven-hour) one-way trail is steep, muddy, and hard going. It's recommended for experienced hikers only, and it's best to have transportation awaiting you at the end. Wear sturdy hiking boots, and carry raingear, a change of warm clothes (the weather can turn bad quickly), food, and water—no streams along the ridge. To get to the western entrance take Hwy. 1 south of Pamapuria, turn west onto Takahue Valley Rd., then turn left on Takahue Saddle Road.

Kaikohe

Highway 1 beyond Mangamuka Gorge runs south to Ohaeawai, where Hwy. 12 branches west to Kaikohe (population 3,500). The countryside around Kaikohe is scattered with historic buildings, and if you're traveling through the town, the local attraction is **Kaikohe Pioneer Village** on Recreation Rd., tel. 09/401-0816. A re-creation of a 19th-century Northland community, the five-acre grounds contain an indoor and outdoor museum, a bush railway, the original 1864 Waimate North Courthouse building, a kauri gum collection, and Maori and pioneer artifacts. It's open Mon.–Sat. 10 A.M.–4 P.M., Sunday 1–4 P.M. in summer; weekends only (Saturday 10 A.M.–4 P.M., Sunday 1–4 P.M.) in winter.

Nearby **Ngawha Spa Mineral Pools,** about five km off the Kaikohe-Ohaeawai section of Hwy. 12, tel. 09/401-0235, lures the aching bodies of hikers, cyclists, and those with skin ailments and rheumatism, for invigorating hot spring relief—but take off your silver jewelry or it will be black as coal when you get out.

A good option for an overnight stay is the **Mid North Motor Inn,** 158 Broadway, tel. 09/401-0149 or 0800/671-967. Each of the 17 rooms has tea- and coffee-making facilities and a small fridge. Guests also have use of a communal kitchen, barbecue, and pool, while the in-house restaurant is open daily for breakfast and dinner; rates $85 s or d. **Curly Rock Café,** 112 Broadway, tel. 09/401-1911, acts as the local information center.

HOKIANGA HARBOUR

Stretching inland for more than 50 km, Hokianga Harbour has forged a deep channel almost halfway across Northland to the Bay of Islands. In the early 19th century, this fiordlike harbor was lined with kauri forests and bustling with marine activity. Droves of ships sailed over from Sydney, defying the treacherous sandbars and large surf at the harbor mouth to keep up with demand for kauri timber. Once the shores had been stripped of their slow-growing forests, the timber mills closed and the ships left. Nowadays the harbor lies relatively undisturbed, slowly reverting to its original wildness and desolation. Few roads lead to the tangled mangrove forests, mighty sand dunes, and green valleys that line its shores. The peaceful beauty and quiet attracts

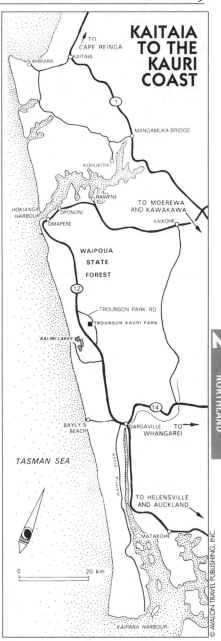

NORTHLAND

© AVALON TRAVEL PUBLISHING, INC.

quite a community of artists and people into alternative lifestyles; watch for out-of-the-ordinary houses, and for roadside arts-and-crafts stands where you can often pick up real bargains.

The best way to appreciate the harbor is by boat, and you'll find willing operators in Rawene, Opononi, and Omapere. Highway 1 detours east around this mighty harbor toward Okaihau, and the Hwy. 12 junction to Kaikohe. The shorter and more scenic route is to cross the harbor at "The Narrows" via car ferry and continue south down Hwy. 12. To get to the ferry, pass through Mangamuka Scenic Reserve, turn right at Mangamuka Bridge, and go through Kohukohu and on to The Narrows.

Kohukohu and Vicinity

For a shortcut from the north, turn south off Hwy. 1 at Mangamuka Bridge, then head south on Mohuiti Narrows Rd. to Kohukohu, a small village with many historic buildings scattered through town.

Continuing south, the Hokianga Vehicular Ferry is four km beyond Kohukohu, or follow the signs two km past the ferry landing to the **Tree House,** West Coast Rd., tel. 09/405-5855, website: www.treehouse.co.nz, one of New Zealand's finest backpackers. The wooden building, with many stained-glass windows, was built by the owners. There's plenty to do around the farm and the harbor, including hiking, mountain biking, and bone-carving. Dorm beds in the main building are $17 pp, or stay in private cabins for $29 s, $44 d.

Hokianga Vehicular Ferry

The *Kohu-Ra* operates daily between The Narrows and Rawene. In summer it departs The Narrows every hour (on the hour) 8 A.M.–6 P.M., and Rawene every hour 7:30 A.M.–5:30 P.M. In winter it departs The Narrows every hour 8:45 A.M.–5:15 P.M., Rawene 8:30 A.M.–5 P.M. Try to time it so you arrive about 10–15 minutes before the crossing—there's nothing to do while you wait (and no facilities) but you need to get in line. The crossing takes about 15 minutes and costs $13 per car and driver plus $1 per passenger each way.

Rawene

Getting off the ferry at Rawene, third oldest settlement in New Zealand, feels like taking a step back in time. On your way through don't miss **Clendon House** on the foreshore, tel. 09/405-7874. A historic building preserved by the Historic Places Trust, it was built in the late 1860s by James Clendon, ship owner, trader, and first U. S. consul in New Zealand. Admission is $2. The house, which contains many of the owner's possessions and period furnishings, is open Sat.–Mon. 10 A.M.–4 P.M. The **Masonic Hotel,** tel. 09/405-7822, built in 1875, is Rawene's local watering hole. You'll also find a small supermarket, a smattering of shops, take-aways, a gas station, and a post office.

Opononi and Omapere

After leaving Rawene, Hwy. 12 runs east to Kaikohe and Ohaeawai (where it rejoins Hwy. 1), or west to Opononi and Omapere before heading south through the kauri forests.

Situated at the mouth of Hokianga Harbour, the twin towns of Opononi and Omapere (three km apart) boast golden beaches and beautiful views up the harbor and out to sea. At Omapere you can appreciate the harbor best by cruise boat—get the details at the information center. For the best views turn off Hwy. 12 just south of Omapere and take the road out to South Head. Opononi became quite well known in the summer of 1955 when a friendly dolphin the locals named "Opo" came to play with swimmers every day—a memorial statue to the dolphin stands on the oceanfront.

Both towns have a variety of accommodations. **Opononi Resort Hotel,** Hwy. 12, tel. 09/405-8858 or 0800/116-565, is separated from the harbor by a strip of white-sand beach, and all 10 rooms have water views. Rooms with kitchens are $110 s or d, and there are a few dorm beds for backpackers that go for $18 pp per night. Affiliated with the YHA, **Okopako Lodge** on Mountain Rd. (signposted from Hwy. 12), tel. 09/405-8815, website: www.yha.org.nz, is part of a working farm. It lacks modern conveniences, but the lodge has a pleasant setting and stunning harbor views; dorm beds are $17 pp, doubles and twins $42 d. The dinner, bed, and breakfast package is $50 pp. Another backpacker lodge, this one originally recommended by readers, is **Globe Trekkers,** on Hwy. 12 in Omapere, tel. 09/405-8183. It is a modern facility with harbor views from a large deck; dorm $16 pp, $27 s, $44 d. **Opononi Beach Holiday Park,** between the two villages, tel. 09/405-8791, overlooks the harbor and sand dunes. All sites are $10 pp, on-site caravans and small cabins are $35–50, and self-contained units are $60 s or d.

Beside the BP service station in Omapere, the **Harbourside Café,** tel. 09/405-8238, serves a cooked breakfast for about $10, pizza slices for $3, and burgers starting at $5. (It's probably one of the few cafés in the country without a deep fryer).

For the rundown on the area, stop at the **Hokianga Information Centre** on the main road between the two towns, tel. 09/405-8869, open in summer daily 9 A.M.–5 P.M.

KAURI COAST

Most of splendid Kauri forests along Northland's west coast were logged in the 1800s, but the remaining stands and some wild west coast scenery make the journey between Hokianga Harbour and Dargaville the preferred, albeit longer, alternative to Hwy. 1.

Waipoua Forest

Beginning about 35 km south of Opononi, Hwy. 12 runs 16 km through the cool, lush greenery of Waipoua Forest, a place where time seems to stand still. Protected as a sanctuary since the 1950s, this remnant of New Zealand's once extensive kauri forests covers an area of more than 9,000 hectares and contains five known giant trees, each estimated to be at least 1,000 years old. Apart from these giants there are 300 other species of trees, palms, ferns, and mosses, and although it's possible to enjoy the forest from the road, the best way to appreciate the grandeur is to get on some of the tracks. The forest is crisscrossed with trails; great picnic spots abound. The well-marked tracks vary from short 10-minute walks leading to particular kauri giants, to

THE KAURI FORESTS

The forests of Northland provide the nature lover with a wide range of native plant- and birdlife and the chance to appreciate many tree varieties. These include *rimu, rata, towai, kahikatea,* and *tawa,* though all are dwarfed by the magnificent kauri. The kauri *(Agathis australis)* is a conifer, grouped botanically with pines and firs that grow north of latitude 38 degrees south. The kauri is New Zealand's native giant—similar but less majestic trees of the same family can be found in Australia, Malaysia, the Philippines, Fiji, and other Pacific islands. The kauri is easily recognized by its tall columnar trunk (it self-sheds the lower branches), massive, heavily branched crown, and thick, leathery leaves. The highly decorative bark is silvery gray in color and covered in irregular, circular patterns. Another characteristic of the older kauri trees is the large mound of *pukahu* or humus at the base of the trunk. This mound is made up of bark, shed over several hundred years, and root systems. Note that the kauri is dependent on its surface root network for essential nutrients, and survival depends to a large degree on not having its vital roots trampled—keep on the tracks to ensure these magnificent trees' future.

Some of the trees have been estimated at well over a thousand years old. Their rate of growth is very slow, taking 80–100 years to reach millable size. A young kauri is called a "ricker." The timber is straight grained, easily worked, durable, and very popular with carpenters and craftspeople. In the early 1800s the kauri dominated forest vegetation and covered about three million hectares from the North Cape to Waikato. By the end of the century only one-quarter of the kauri forests remained; the trees had been cut down for shipbuilding, leached for gum, or burned when the land was cleared for agriculture.

Nowadays the policy is to preserve these ancient forests. **Waipoua Forest** and **Trounson Kauri Park,** both on Hwy. 12 between Hokianga Harbour and Dargaville, provide excellent examples of what all this land looked like before the arrival of Europeans.

longer hikes that offer a far richer assortment of sights and sounds of the forest.

From the north, the first worthwhile stop is for a short hike to 1,200-year-old *Tane Mahuta* (Lord of the Forest). Standing nearly 52 meters high and with a girth of 13 meters, it's believed to be the largest kauri in the country.

Continuing south, a 700-meter trail leads through a particularly beautiful stretch of forest to *Te Matua Ngahere* (Father of the Forest). Although not as tall as *Tane Mahuta,* this kauri is renowned for its impressive five-meter-wide diameter. Its exact age is unknown, but it may be nearly 2,000 years old. If you have the time, sit opposite the tree for a while and soak up the surroundings. The tranquil beauty of the bush and splendor of the "Father," cheerful birdsong, and buzzing cicadas create a natural high. Nearby is the **Four Sisters,** a group of kauri nestled close together.

The **Waipoua Field Centre,** tel. 09/439-0605, is off Hwy. 12 in the southern section of the forest, to the west after crossing Waipoua River (southbound). Stop by for information on forest management, local legends, and walking tracks, and to see the cottage museum where the lifestyle of a kauri bushman is on display; it's open Mon.–Fri. 8 A.M.–4 P.M., weekends (in summer only) 8 A.M.–4:30 P.M.

Camper's Delight

If you want to stay the night somewhere along this forest-clad area of the country, keep your eyes peeled for signs advertising **Kauri Coast Top 10 Holiday Park,** three km along the road to Trounson Kauri Park, tel. 09/439-0621 or 0800/807-200, beside a river dotted with swimming holes and filled with enough rainbow and brown trout to keep any angler happy. Tent and powered sites are $22 (open fires permitted, wood provided), bunk room beds are $18 pp, a cabin for two costs $38, an on-site caravan is $40 d, a tourist cabin with kitchen and utensils is $45 d, a tourist flat is $70 d, and the comfortable motel unit is $85 s or d. A fully equipped kitchen, laundry, and shop (selling basic supplies and milk) are provided. You can rent a kayak for $7.50 an hour (choose from a white-water ride or

a quiet float), rent a fishing rod, or go for a horse-riding trek for about $40 per half-day. The owners also operate a popular evening walk up the road in Trounson Kauri Park.

Trounson Kauri Park

This small but superb stand of kauri north off Hwy. 12 was deeded to the government for protection over 100 years ago. Now totaling 570 hectares, a resolute effort has been made to eradicate nonnative species such as rats, possums, and cats. This, in turn, has dramatically increased the park's kiwi population. A walking trail through the heart of the park takes about a half-hour round-trip, and the highlight is The Four Sisters tree—actually two kauri trees, each with twin trunks that have grown together as one. At one point the track runs under a fallen kauri for a close-up view, and farther along you can appreciate the root system of a large, 600-year-old fallen kauri from a viewing platform.

To see the park's most precious residents, join the owners of nearby Kauri Coast Top 10 Holiday Park, tel. 09/439-0621 or 0800/807-200, on their hour-long guided evening walk ($15 pp). In addition to kiwis, giant *wekas* and kauri snails are often sighted.

In addition to nearby Kauri Coast Top 10 Holiday Park, you'll find an attractive campground with limited campsites near the ranger's residence; $7 pp per night includes the use of hot showers and a communal kitchen.

Kai-Iwi Lakes

Continuing south from the kauri forests, turn west (toward the coast) at Maropiu on Omamari Road to access Kai-Iwi Lakes, the collective name for three brilliantly blue, freshwater lakes (Kai-Iwi, Taharoa, and Waikere), great for swimming, fishing, sailing, and water-skiing. In addition, soft white-sand beaches, sheltered bays for swimming and snorkeling, rolling farmland, and lots of pine trees make this an even more attractive place. Lake Taharoa is stocked with trout and offers shoreside camping; on the banks of Lake Waikere is a water-ski club—a hive of activity on summer weekends. Two walks, to **Sandy Bay** (three km; one hour) and to **Maunganui**

Bluff (1.8 km to the coast), start on Kai-Iwi Lakes Road.

At the end of local Domain Rd. is **Taharoa Domain Campground,** right on Pine Beach, tel. 09/439-7059. Tent or caravan sites are $6 pp per night; drinking water, toilets, and showers are provided.

For more private swimming, follow the dirt track beyond the camping area to the next beach at Sandy Bay. The other campground is at **Promenade Point,** farther along Kai-Iwi Lakes Rd., and has drinking water and toilets only; small nightly fee. Continue along the road and you come to Lake Waikere.

Dargaville

At the northern end of Wairoa River, Dargaville (4,500) was originally a busy kauri timber and gum-trading port. When the logging industry went into decline, so did Dargaville and today it's the small commercial center for the surrounding dairy districts. The hilltop **Dargaville Maritime Museum** in Harding Park, tel. 09/439-7555, displays items of local seafaring interest, the masts from Greenpeace's flagship the *Rainbow Warrior,* Maori artifacts, pioneer relics, and an ancient Maori *pa;* it's open daily 9 A.M.–4 P.M., $5 adult, $2 child. Great views from the park. To get there follow River Rd., then turn right on Mahuta Rd. and follow the signs.

The **Commercial Hotel,** 75 River Rd., tel. 09/439-8018, has been taking in guests for more than 120 years. Built of kauri, the historic building has a number of basic rooms above the best restaurant in town. Rooms with shared bathrooms are $35 s, $45 d, while the few en suite rooms are $65 s or d. For self-contained accommodations and a swimming pool, head to the **Parkview Motel,** 36 Carrington St., tel. 09/439-8339 or 0800/324-466, website: www .parkviewdargaville.co.nz; from $95 s or d. Only a short walk from the center of town, the **Greenhouse Hostel,** 13 Portland St. (corner of Gordon St.), tel. 09/439-6342, is clean, friendly, and offers plenty of room to move around; partitioned dorm beds are $18 pp, private rooms are $27 s, $42 d. **Selwyn Park Motor Camp,** Onslow St., tel. 09/439-8296, is in a pleasant downtown lo-cation, but **Baylys Beach Motor Camp,** three km north of Dargaville then nine km west along Baylys Coast Rd., tel. 09/439-6349, is a better option, just a short walk from an unspoiled beach. All campsites are $20, or for a roof over your head, rent a cabin for $45 s or d.

Dargaville Information Centre is at 65 Normanby St., tel. 09/439-8360.

Matakohe

From Dargaville, Hwy. 12 continues south along the Wairoa River to **Ruawai,** then veers inland to rejoin Hwy. 1 30 km north of Wellsford. The highlight of this stretch of highway is the small village of Matakohe and the **Kauri Museum,** tel. 09/431-7417, which contains almost everything you'd want to know about kauri trees and gum. You'll see kauri timber, an outstanding kauri gum collection, furniture, wood flowers, old photos of lumberjacks, kauri-processing equipment, historic chain saws, and a reproduction of a colonial cottage done entirely in kauri. Volunteers Hall houses a slab of kauri from a tree milled by the landowners after it was struck by lightning in 1986. On the wall behind, this massive tree is compared to those still standing in the forest and to the largest kauri on record. Also in this section is "Transition Gateway," sculpted from kauri log that was underground for an estimated 30,000 years. Another room is paneled in all the different types of timber available in New Zealand. At the souvenir shop you can pick up beautifully crafted kauri products at reasonable prices. Don't miss it! It's open daily 9 A.M.–5 P.M.; $9 adult, $2 child.

Gumdiggers Café, tel. 09/431-7075, is farther along the road from the museum. Sample assorted baked goodies and tearoom-type snacks at reasonable prices.

CONTINUING SOUTH TO AUCKLAND VIA HWY. 16

Highways 12 and 1 intersect at Brynderwyn, where Hwy. 1 continues south to Wellsford and on down to Auckland. An alternate scenic route south, Hwy. 16 via Helensville, branches west at Wellsford, skirting Kaipara Harbour.

Helensville and Parakai

The Helensville area, less than an hour's drive north of Auckland, boasts gentle countryside, many poultry and deer farms, and orchards and vineyards; in summer, wildflowers line the highways.

If you like hot pools and masses of people, head northwest out of Helensville along South Head Rd. to the town of **Parakai,** where you'll find **Aquatic Park** at the corner of Parkhurst and Spring Roads, tel. 09/420-8998. Thermal mineral springs naturally heat the pools, so the temperatures vary a little each day—generally the outdoor pool is about 34°C, the indoor a sizzling 40°. On winter weekday evenings, you can slowly bake in the therapeutic indoor pool while taking in video movies on the giant screen. The park is open daily 10 A.M.–10 P.M.; $10 adult, $6 senior, $7 child, but free if you're staying in the adjacent campground. If you fancy whizzing down the "Hydro Slide," you have to fork out an extra $9 for all-day sliding on top of admission (concessions for campers). A private spa is an extra $5 pp per hour.

Next to Aquatic Park is the fully equipped **Aquatic Park Camping Ground,** tel. 09/420-8998. Tent and caravan sites are $15 pp; rates reduced for seven nights or more. Stay here and admission to the hot pools and use of the pools is complimentary until noon the day of departure. The motor camp has no cabins, so if you need a roof over your head, consider **Mineral Park Motel,** 3 Parakai Ave., tel. 09/420-8856, where each of the eight self-contained rooms features a private mineral pool; from $75 s or d.

Muriwai Beach

South of Helensville, the only worthwhile detour before reaching Auckland is Muriwai Beach, a sleepy village at the southern end of a

gannet colony, Muriwai Beach

© ANDREW HEMPSTEAD

windswept beach. To access Muriwai, turn off Hwy. 16 at Waimauku. Apart from the town's laid-back atmosphere, nesting **Australasian gannets** are the main draw. Offshore lies **Motutara Island,** where the gannets began nesting 20 years ago. The colony grew, spread to the mainland, and now numbers more than 1,000 nesting pairs. Barriers and two viewing platforms on the headland allow easy observation without disturbing the birds. The town has a beachside campground (tel. 09/411-9262; sites from $10 pp), a general store with hot takeout food, and a golf course.

Central North Island

Hamilton

Travelers often miss Hamilton, center of the **Waikato** region, in the rush to get down to Rotorua or back to Auckland. It's on Hwy. 1 less than 130 km south of Auckland and on all public transportation routes. The city itself offers the visitor many attractions, and is an ideal base for exploring the coast near Raglan, the famous Waitomo Caves, and the area's several forest park reserves. The Waikato River, originally the main shipping route between Hamilton and Auckland, meanders through the inner city, and along its banks are numerous parks and gardens. The east

and west banks are connected by five city bridges, and footpaths run along the river on both sides.

The lush green fields, dotted with dairy cows, that stretch away from Hamilton in all directions are part of the Waikato Plains, one of the most productive dairying and agricultural districts in New Zealand. The city started out as a fairly small Maori village, Kirikiriroa, on the west bank of the Waikato. The first European settlement was a military camp established in 1864, and

Whitianga oceanfront

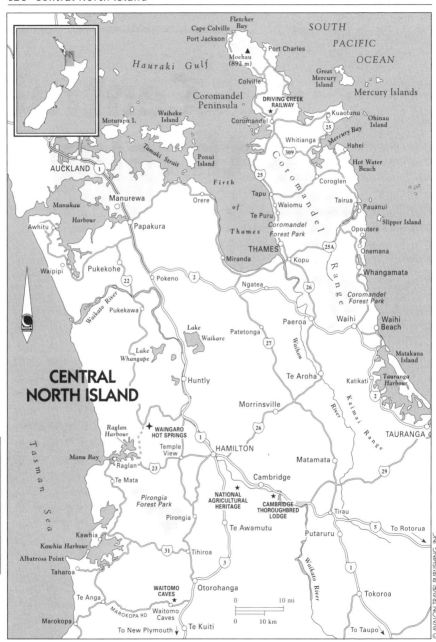

CENTRAL NORTH ISLAND

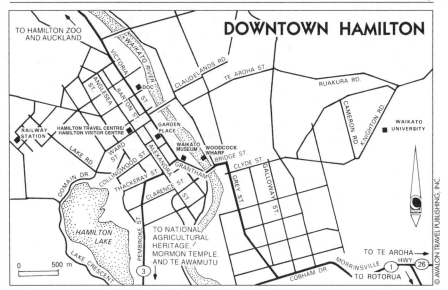

the resulting town was named after a navy officer killed in the Battle of Gate Pa at Tauranga the same year. Hamilton has grown rapidly during the years and is now New Zealand's fourth-largest population center (140,000) and the country's largest inland city.

SIGHTS

Hamilton Gardens

Masses of roses, chrysanthemums, daffodils, camellias, magnolias, and rhododendrons; vegetable gardens; a perfume garden; trees that burst into brilliant color in autumn; and display houses sheltering tropical plants, cacti, succulents, bromeliads, and insectivorous plants can all be found in the 58-hectare Hamilton Gardens. Access is from Cobham Dr. (east of the Cobham Bridge), or from the river walks, and admission is free.

Hamilton Centennial Fountain

This magnificent fountain is in Boyes Park near the Founders' Theatre. You'll find many fountains around Hamilton, but they're particularly featured among the trees, flowers, and lawns of **Garden Place.** Both the principal square and a pedestrian mall, Garden Place has become a small oasis in the heart of Hamilton's bustling commercial center.

Waikato Museum

This modern, five-level, architectural marvel, 1 Grantham St. (corner of Victoria St.), tel. 07/838-6606, sits beside the Waikato River (great water views from the upper level), and features Maori artifacts and sculptures, the fabulous 140-year-old carved war canoe *Te Winika,* contemporary Tainui carvings, Tukutuku weaving, and fine art exhibits, along with changing exhibitions. Part of the museum complex is the **Excite Centre,** a large hands-on interactive science center. Don't miss the aerial sculpture, *Ripples,* which hangs between the trees outside (best viewed from the River Gallery inside). It accurately represents a pebble dropping in water—a suspended moment in time. In the museum shop pick up some high-quality arts and crafts, posters, prints, books, and art cards. Adjoining the museum is one of Hamilton's best restaurants, the Museum Café

CENTRAL NORTH ISLAND

(see below). The museum is open daily 10 A.M.–4 P.M. General admission is adult $2, child $1. Entry to Excite costs $5 and $3 respectively.

Mormon Temple

This magnificent temple, at **Temple View** about 11 km southwest of Hamilton, offers panoramic views of the Waikato from its grounds. It was the first Mormon temple built in the Southern Hemisphere, and although only a few select people of the Mormon faith are allowed to actually enter the temple, the Visitor Centre (complete with guides) welcomes the rest of humanity with open arms. The pride and joy of the Visitor Centre is a towering statue of Christ, "the Christus." The work of Italian sculptor Aldo Rebechi, it's a replica of the original Christus created by the "famous" 19th-century Bertel Thorvaldsen of Denmark. The center is open daily 9 A.M.–9 P.M., admission free. You can trace your family tree at the Genealogy Centre, Tues.–Sat. 9 A.M.–4 P.M., and it's also free. A regular bus service links Temple View with Hamilton city; call the temple's Visitor Centre at 07/847-8601 for more information.

Animal Appeal

A place to appreciate a wide variety of animals is 20-hectare **Hamilton Zoo** on Brymer Rd., north of the city, tel. 07/838-6720. The main theme is conservation, and rare birds and animals are held here to establish breeding colonies, including many in a "free flight" sanctuary, where trails lead through a massive bird-filled aviary. Also on display are animals from around the world, including an ever-growing African collection. It's open daily 9 A.M.–5 P.M.; $8 adult, $4 child.

If you want to learn more about New Zealand's agricultural scene, **National Agricultural Heritage** will be right up your alley. It's between Highways 1 and 3 at Mystery Creek, 16 km south of Hamilton. Look for the airport—the museum is one km southeast, off Airport Rd., tel. 07/843-7990. Wander through the various farm, fire station, tree, dairy, and Clydesdale museums. Clydesdale Agricultural Museum was originally established as a tribute to New Zealand's pioneering past. Displays still focus on agricul-

tural equipment, but the main attraction is the magnificent Clydesdale horses. The horses are bred, worked, and put through their paces here. Devonshire teas or light lunches are available in the tearooms, and the crafts shop sells a variety of locally made crafts. Open Sun.–Thurs. 9 A.M.–4:30 P.M.; $8 adult, $4 child.

RECREATION

Inner-City Walks

The city has three circular walking routes: ask for a city map and "Waikato Visitors Guide" and "City Walkways" brochures at the Hamilton Visitor Centre on Anglesea Street. The **Short Historic and Scenic Walk** starts on the riverbank off Victoria St., leads along Victoria St. (Hamilton's main shopping drag), crosses Victoria Bridge, and returns along the River Walk route. The entire trip takes about 1.5 hours. The scenic three- to four-hour **River Walk,** also known as Five Bridges Walk, runs along the banks of the Waikato River. It starts from beyond Fairfield Bridge in the north and runs beyond Cobham Bridge in the south, links all five city bridges, and takes in several parks and some of the older residential streets. The **One-day Scenic Walk** covers much of the River Walk route but includes several more parks and the delightful grounds around Hamilton Lake; it takes five to eight hours to complete.

Walking Tracks

For information on local hikes in the Hamilton area and track maps, visit the Department of Conservation Field Centre on Northway St., tel. 07/838-3363.

The 15-km **Hakarimata Walkway** runs along the top of the Hakarimata Range behind Ngaruawahia (19 km north of Hamilton), with great views and two large kauris toward the end. It starts at the Ngaruawahia-Waingaro Rd., four km west of the Waipa River Bridge, and ends about 12 km north of Ngaruawahia on Parker Rd. (off Huntley West Rd.). It's classified as a track, so you need to be fit and have hiking boots, warm clothes, and water. The track takes about seven hours to complete, and it's wise to prearrange transportation at the far end. You can also join the track at Hakarimata Trig (374 meters); cross the Waipa River Bridge at Ngaruawahia and follow the Waterworks Track up Mangarata Stream (steep toward the end).

The **Karamu Walkway** is another good track for panoramic views of Hamilton, Mt. Pirongia (961 meters), Kakepuku, and Raglan. The northern end of the track starts at the eastern corner of the Four Brothers Scenic Reserve, almost at the top of the Kapamahunga Range. Take the Hamilton-Raglan Rd. (Hwy. 23) to the reserve. The track finishes 10 km south of Whatawhata on Limeworks Rd., Karamu, and takes about four hours; as a shorter alternative, you can walk the section between Four Brothers Scenic Reserve and Old Mountain Rd. in an hour. In good weather it's easy walking in sneakers, but take warm clothes for the exposed ridge sections, and carry water.

Hamilton Lake

Also known as Lake Rotoroa, this is a great place to escape the bustle of the city on weekdays. On weekends and holidays it's very popular with local residents for swimming, sailing, and sunbathing. Footpaths enable walkers, joggers, and in-line skaters to use the parklike surroundings to best advantage, and the grassy banks are perfect for a picnic. The lake is also home to a large population of swans, ducks, geese, and various other waterfowl only too willing to share your lunch. For good views of Hamilton and the surrounding countryside, walk up the path to the concrete reservoir atop the hill.

Cruising the River

Cruise the river onboard the historic paddleboat **MV *Waipa Delta,*** tel. 07/854-7813. It first transported passengers between Hamilton and Auckland in the 1870s, but now offers city visitors a pleasant river trip from the Woodcocks Wharf, across the river from downtown at Memorial Park on Memorial Drive. Options include the 90-minute Lunch Cruise (departs 12:30 P.M.; $35 pp), the one-hour Afternoon Tea Cruise (departs 3 P.M.; $20 pp), and the Dinner Cruise (departs 7 P.M.; $49 pp).

Entertainment

The most popular of several theaters offering live entertainment is the **Riverlea Theatre and Arts Centre** on Riverlea Rd. (southeast Hamilton), tel. 07/856-5450.

Many taverns and hotels around Hamilton have live music Wed.–Sat. night, with cover charges at most venues on Friday and Saturday nights. The **Bank Bar,** on the corner of Victoria and Hood Streets, tel. 07/839-4740, is a popular drinking spot that comes alive with live and DJ music after 10 P.M. Next door, the **Outback Inn,** 141 Victoria St., tel. 07/839-6354, attracts a younger crowd to its frenzied dance floor. Heading up Victoria St. at Collingwood St., **Leonardo's,** in the Le Grand Hotel, tel. 07/839-1994, is a quieter lounge bar with live music Thurs.–Saturday. At the top end of Victoria St. (no. 742), **Biddy Mulligans,** tel. 07/834-0306, has bands playing traditional Irish beer-drinking tunes every weekend.

ACCOMMODATIONS

Hotels and Motels

Parklands City Motel is a distinctive pink and white building directly across the river from downtown at 24 Bridge St., tel. 07/838-2461; website: www.parklands-motel.co.nz. It offers self-contained motel rooms for $90 s or d and a few dorm beds for $20 pp. Breakfast is available, or guests can take advantage of a communal kitchen.

Most of Hamilton's 40-odd motels are on the fringes of the city, many concentrated along Ulster St., the main route north out of the city (but bypassed by Hwy. 1). A good cheapie along this strip is **Cedar Lodge Motel,** 174 Ulster St., tel. 07/839-5569 or 0800/105-252. All the rooms have kitchens, and there's a spa pool and game room; studio $70 s or d, bedroom units $76–88 s or d. The **Ambassador Motor Inn,** 86 Ulster St., tel. 07/839-5111 or 0800/800-533, is a large five-story motel close to downtown. All rooms have a kitchen, and facilities include a swimming pool, barbecue area, and restaurant. Rates are $95–150 s or d. The **Anglesea Motel** is near the downtown end of Ulster St. on the corner of

Liverpool and Tristram Streets, tel. 07/834-0010 or 0800/426-453; website: www.angleseamotel.co.nz. All 42 units are a little plain, but are practical and spacious; rates $120–210 s or d. **Sails Motor Inn,** 272 Ulster St., tel. 07/838-2733 or 0800/252-325, website: www.sails-motorinn.co.nz, has spacious, contemporary-styled units, each with a full kitchen and a deck or verandah that opens to a garden and swimming pool. The studio units are $130 s or d, the one- and two-bedroom units range from $170–200.

In the heart of downtown, you'll find **Le Grand Hotel,** on the corner of Collingwood and Victoria Streets, tel. 07/839-1994, website: www.legrandhotel.co.nz, in a four-story building that has been elegantly restored. The rooms each have a minibar and tea- and coffee-making facilities, while downstairs is a restaurant and bar. Rates range from $100 s or d for a standard room to $190 s or d for the cavernous Honeymoon Suite.

Backpacker Lodges
Helen Heywood YHA, 1190 Victoria St. (Hwy. 1), tel. 07/838-0009, has a great location on the bank of the Waikato River. Within easy walking distance downtown, it's 300 meters from the nearest dairy, 1.5 km from the bus depot in Ward St., and two km from the train station on Queens Avenue. Because it's a converted motel, dorms are small; in fact, the whole hostel has only 23 beds, including five doubles. It has all the usual facilities, with the office open for bookings 5–11 P.M. Dorm beds are $17, and doubles are $21 pp.

J's Backpackers, 8 Grey St., tel. 07/856-8934, is across the river from downtown on the road out to Rotorua. It's small, with just 12 beds, but the atmosphere is congenial, and the river is just across the road. Dorm beds are $19 pp, doubles are $21 pp.

Motor Camps
You'll find two motor camps in Hamilton in the eastern section of town, and another camp 11 km south. **Hamilton East Motor Camp,** on Cameron Rd., Hamilton East, tel. 07/856-6220, is two km from downtown. Tent and caravan sites are $18 s or d, standard cabins are $40, and the tourist flats with kitchens are $55. To get there go to the south end of Victoria St. and cross the river via Bridge Street. Turn right on Grey St., left at the Riverina Hotel onto Clyde St., and left onto Cameron Rd. (just before the Knighton Rd. intersection). The **Hamilton City Motor Camp** is in the same area on Ruakura Rd., Hamilton East, tel. 07/855-8255. All campsites are $18, and cabins are $28 s or d. To get there, cross the central downtown bridge at Claudelands Rd., turn right on Grey St., and then turn left on Te Aroha Street. At the Peachgrove Rd. intersection, continue straight onto Ruakura Road.

Narrows Camp, next to Narrows Golf Club on Airport Rd., tel. 07/843-6862, is 11 km south of Hamilton near Hamilton Airport, and has communal facilities and a swimming pool. Tent and caravan sites are $9 pp; cabins cost $36 s or d.

FOOD
Cheap and Cheerful
Kick start your day at **Flapjacks Café,** 589 Victoria St., tel. 07/839-5969, with a stack of pancakes, U.S. style with bacon, eggs, and a dollop of maple syrup ($12). The smoothies here are also good. Café culture has hit Hamilton in a big way. One of the most popular local hangouts is **Machino Espresso,** 67 London St., tel. 07/838-9212, with seating at booths or counters and a wide range of caffeine infused drinks; open daily 7:30 A.M.–3:30 P.M.

Cobb & Co. Restaurant, in the Commercial Establishment Hotel, 287 Victoria St., tel. 07/839-1226, has the standard menu of steaks, seafood, and salads served throughout the Cobb & Co. chain—good food for the price. It's open daily 7 A.M.–10 P.M. Half a block south, **Metropolis,** 221 Victoria St., tel. 07/834-2081, is very different from its staid old neighbor. Locals gather here to enjoy a quick meal from the Express menu ($8–12) with delicious smoothies ($4) in distinctive black and white surroundings.

Gourmet Pizza
Hip **Iguana,** 203 Victoria St., tel. 07/834-2280, is a vast dining area with seating that ranges from

bar stools to couches. The menu might not be groundbreaking in Auckland, but in Hamilton, ordering pizza topped with crocodile meat and mango ($21 for two) is definitely out of the ordinary. The kitchen demonstrates its worldliness by using real bacon and anchovies in the Caesar salad ($11). Iguana is open daily from 10 A.M. until the early hours. Across and up the road a little, **Barzurk,** 250 Victoria St., tel. 07/834-2363, is another gourmet pizza joint, this one with a large outdoor dining area and an open kitchen.

Around the World

Café Centrale, 10 Alma St., tel. 07/838-1013, features slate floors, lots of polished timber, and distinctive artwork throughout. The proud Italian owner oversees a menu that combines the cuisine of his home country with New Zealand favorites and a hint of Mexico thrown in for good measure. It's open Tues.–Sun. from 6 P.M. Next door, the **Original Thai Restaurant** at 8 Alma St., tel. 07/838-3088, is original in name only. Last time around, there was an Italian restaurant at this location. For something a little more exotic, head to the **Sahara Tent,** 254 Victoria St., tel. 07/834-0409. A large restaurant, complete with belly dancers, Sahara Tent has a Middle Eastern-inspired menu featuring humus for starters ($8) and a variety of kebab main meals (from $15).

At the far northern end of town is **Bayon Cambodian Café,** 783 Victoria St., tel. 07/839-0947. With a distinctive purple and green décor, a map on the wall showing where in the world Cambodia is, and photos on the menu showing the more unusual dishes, this place stands apart from all other Hamilton restaurants. It's also well priced with the most expensive dish a spicy shrimp creation for $15. Bayon is open weekdays for lunch and daily from 5 P.M. for dinner.

Hotel and Fine Dining

Many of the motels around the city have restaurants. **Wilsons Carvery** in the Southern Cross Motor Inn, 222 Ulster St., tel. 07/838-3299, offers a four-course buffet lunch and dinner. It's open daily 7 A.M.–10 P.M. (no lunch on Saturday); lunches cost $18, dinners $32. In the vicinity, **Shakespeare's Restaurant** in the Grosvenor Motor Inn, 165 Ulster St., tel. 07/838-3399, offers more formal à la carte dining surrounded by medieval, earthy tones. Prices are good for motel dining, with dishes such as Katharina's Swine (char-grilled chops smothered in apple sauce) ranging $19–27. Choosing a dessert is easy-go with the pavlova ($8.50). It's open daily from 6:30 P.M.

The world over, dining at a museum café means lots of noisy children and cafeteria-quality food. But not in Hamilton, at the riverfront **Museum Café,** 1 Grantham St., tel. 07/839-7209, open daily for lunch and Tues.–Sat. for dinner. Through the day, the menu is highlighted by such treats as Creole-blackened ostrich and pesto bean salad ($11.50) while in the evening similarly innovative dishes range $20–25. Another choice for upmarket dining is **Seddon House Restaurant,** opposite the park of the same name at 67 Seddon Rd., tel. 07/847-8294. Dining is in rooms throughout the house (you may get an entire room to yourself on a quiet night), with lots of mirrors and antiques scattered throughout. This place has been a local favorite for over a decade. The menu is a little tired, but it's still a fine place to enjoy traditional dinners such as oven-grilled rack of lamb, covered in a minted blueberry sauce ($27.50).

TRANSPORTATION

Hamilton is a transportation hub. Air, bus, and rail services converge on the city, and in the past few years a number of charter operators have been running flights between Hamilton and Australia. For road travelers, Hamilton is easily reached in less than two hours from Auckland, from where Hwy. 1 continues southeast to Taupo and down the length of the North Island to Wellington, and Hwy. 3 branches south to Waitomo Caves and New Plymouth.

Getting There

Hamilton Airport is 13 km south of the city. Take Hwy. 3 south to Rukuhia and continue about one km. Airport Rd. branches off the highway to the east just before Mystery Creek, and eventually joins Hwy. 1. To get to the airport catch the **Airport Shuttle** bus from the Hamilton Transport Centre on the corner of Ward and Anglesea Streets or call 07/843-6286 for door-to-door service; $8 one way. The bus service departs for the airport 45 minutes before each Air New Zealand departure, and returns to the city 10 minutes after each arrival. For a few extra dollars, this company offers door-to-door service. **Air New Zealand,** tel. 07/839-9825, has direct flights from Hamilton to Auckland, Wellington, Christchurch, and Dunedin. Hamilton is also a hub for **Freedom Air,** tel. 0800/600-500, a low cost airlines with flights throughout the country and across the Tasman Sea to Australia.

Hamilton Railway Station is on Fraser St. (off Queens Ave.), west of downtown and not far from Hamilton Lake. All southbound trains from Auckland stop at Hamilton, including those heading south to Wellington and southeast to Rotorua. You can buy tickets at the station or at the Hamilton Visitor Information Centre. For all Tranz Scenic information, call 0800/802-802.

Go to the **Hamilton Transport Centre,** corner of Ward and Anglesea Streets, for all long-distance bus services. **Intercity,** tel. 07/834-3457, and **Newmans,** tel. 07/838-3114, provide regular coach service in all directions; the trip between Auckland and Hamilton takes just over two hours.

Getting Around

Local buses run weekdays only. The **City Bus Terminal** is on the corner of Ward and Anglesea Streets, the same place as the long-distance bus depot.

Car rental agencies in Hamilton include **Avis,** tel. 07/839-4915; **Budget,** tel. 07/838-3585; and **Hertz,** tel. 07/839-4824.

Cabs wait outside the Hamilton Transport Centre, or call **Combined Taxi,** tel. 07/839-9099, or **Hamilton Taxis,** tel. 07/447-7477.

SERVICES AND INFORMATION
Services

The main **post office** is at 346 Victoria St., tel. 07/838-2233; open Mon.–Fri. 8 A.M.–4:30 P.M. **Waikato Hospital** is on Pembroke St., tel. 07/839-8899. **Central Hamilton Pharmacy** is in K-Mart Plaza on Bryce St. (behind the Transport Centre), tel. 07/839-3999. The **police station** is on Bridge St., tel. 07/858-6200.

Information

The **Hamilton Visitor Information Centre** is in the Hamilton Transport Centre at the corner of Ward and Anglesea Streets, tel. 07/834-1905 or 0800/834-100. It's open Mon.–Fri. 9 A.M.–5 P.M. and Saturday and Sunday 10 A.M.–5 P.M. Two handy websites are www.hamiltoncity.co.nz and the **Tourism Waikato** site, www.waikatonz.co.nz.

The **Automobile Association,** a good source of road maps and general information for onward travel, is at 295 Barton St., tel. 07/839-1397. For general information on New Zealand and specialty maps, head for the **Map and Chart Shop,** across the river from downtown at 361 Grey St., tel. 07/856-4450. The DOC runs its **Northern Regional Office** from the Royal and Sun Alliance Building at 127 Alexandra St., tel. 07/858-0000. This is the place to go for information and maps on the parks and natural sights surrounding the city. The 200,000-book strong **Central Library** is on Garden Place, tel. 07/838-6826; open Mon.–Fri. 9:30 A.M.–8:30 P.M., Saturday 9:30 A.M.–4 P.M., and Sunday noon–3:30 P.M.

Vicinity of Hamilton

WAINGARO HOT SPRINGS

The sulphur-free bubbling waters of this thermal spring, 42 km northwest of Hamilton, have been diverted into three concrete pools and down a hot-water water slide. The temperatures range 30–42°C. It's open daily 9:30 A.M.–9:30 P.M.,

tel. 07/825-4761; $8 adult, $4 child. The resort grounds include **Waingaro Hot Springs Caravan Park,** tel. 07/825-4761, offering caravan sites for $14 pp, on-site caravans for $24 pp, cabins for $48 s or d, motel units for $85 s or d, and a camp store, petrol pump, deer park, and play area. Admission to the thermal baths is in-

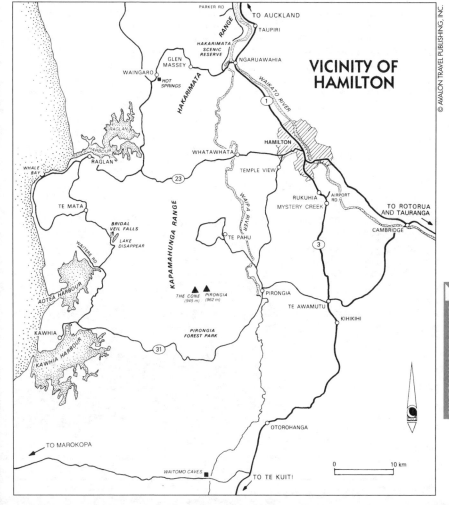

© AVALON TRAVEL PUBLISHING, INC.

CENTRAL NORTH ISLAND

cluded in the camp and motel charges. The **Waingaro Hotel,** on Waingaro Rd. adjacent to the hot pools, tel. 07/825-4827, offers rooms for $35 s, $55 d. For a good bistro meal (from $14), head for the hotel on Friday and Saturday nights 6–9 P.M., and on Sunday 4:30–8:30 P.M. The main bar overlooks the valley and has well-priced beer.

If you're coming from the north, save some time and head directly for Waingaro. This allows you to take in both the hot springs and Raglan area attractions before reaching Hamilton. Turn west off Hwy. 1 at Ngaruawahia toward Glen Massey. Before Glen Massey turn right heading for Te Akatea, continue to the Waingaro River, and turn left toward Waingaro. If you're already in Hamilton head west along Hwy. 23 toward Raglan, then take Hwy. 22 north and continue to Waingaro Hot Springs.

RAGLAN

Renowned as one of the world's greatest surfing spots, Raglan (population 2,800) lies 48 km west of Hamilton along Hwy. 23 at the mouth of Raglan Harbour. It is the nearest coastal resort to Hamilton, but is passed over by most sunseekers due to its lack of golden sandy beaches. Most of the year, it's a quiet little seaside town, but in summer it gets quite busy.

Sights and Recreation

The **surfing** takes place west of Raglan at breaks scattered along the coast. When the swell is up and the conditions are right, the breaks link up to form one of the world's longest left-hand point breaks. As Wainui Rd. winds southwest around the coast, it passes a number of spectacular lookouts before descending to **Manu Bay** and a grassy area perfect for relaxing and watching the surfing action. Continuing westward, the road passes through the small community of **Whale Bay,** another popular surfing spot with renowned breaks of Indicators, The Valley, and Outsides. As well as surfing, Raglan has good harbor and surf fishing, and whitebait fishing in the local streams.

South of Raglan along the inland roads, pass through Te Mata to reach the spectacular **Bridal Veil Falls** near Lake Disappear, 21 km southeast of Raglan off the main road to Kawhia. Walk about 10 minutes along a bush trail to emerge at a thundering torrent of water plummeting 60 meters

© ANDREW HEMPSTEAD

Raglan surfer

down a lava rock face into a deep pool, a popular swimming hole in summer. For an even more dramatic view, continue for another 10 minutes down the steep track to the base of the falls.

Practicalities

One of the best value accommodations in the whole country is **Raglan Backpackers and Waterfront Lodge,** 6 Nero St., tel. 07/825-0515, operated by friendly couple Jeremy and Lynda Watson. This purpose-built budget accommodation lies right on Raglan Harbour and just 100 meters from the main street. The rooms all open to a large courtyard, complete with outdoor furniture and hammocks, while the spotless kitchen and cozy lounge overlook the harbor. There's a large selection of recreational equipment for guest use, including surfboards and wet suits, canoes, bikes, and fishing tackle. Dorm beds are only $17, beds in the double and twin rooms are only $20, and the linen is changed daily.

The old hotel on the main street, **Harbour View Hotel,** 14 Bow St., tel. 07/825-8010, offers seven basic rooms for $50 s, $70 d. Or stay at **Raglan Palm Beach Motel,** 50 Wainui Rd., tel. 07/825-8153, where the eight spacious units, each with a kitchen and separate bedroom, are $85–105 d. Overlooking the surf break, **Whale Bay Surf Bach,** 9 Tohora Close, Whale Bay, tel. 07/825-8219, is a small beach house that sleeps four in two bedrooms. It has a wonderful oceanfront location, a kitchen, and a grassed area out front for watching the surf; $120 for the entire house. Across an arm of the harbor from downtown, but linked by a pedestrian bridge, the windswept **Raglan Kopua Holiday Park,** Marine Parade, tel. 07/825-8283, provides tent sites for $8 pp, caravan sites for $9 pp, and cabins for $50 s or d.

The Hawaiian-born owner of **Vinnies,** 7 Wainui Rd., tel. 07/825-7273, legendary in this part of the world, offers an informal atmosphere and a blackboard menu with a bit of everything—Mexican, Thai, Italian, and more. It's a great place to just hang out, and anyone who has sampled the food keeps coming back for more. On the main street, trendy little café **Tongue and Groove,** 19 Bow St., tel. 07/825-

0027, serves up a wide variety of coffee drinks, and well-prepared cooked breakfasts from $11.

At the harbor end of Bow St., **Raglan Information Centre,** tel. 07/825-0556, is open weekdays 10 A.M.–4 P.M., but generally closed for lunch.

CAMBRIDGE

If you've been through rural England, Cambridge (Town of Trees), 20 km southeast of Hamilton on Hwy. 1, will bring back memories of tree-lined avenues, immaculate flower-filled gardens, old buildings, and the traditional village green. The jade-green Waikato River runs through this scenic town, and the streets are bordered by abundant varieties of trees that meet overhead in a lush colorful archway (spectacular in late April and May when they take on brilliant autumnal colors). Between Hamilton and Cambridge you'll see field after field of racehorses intermingled with stud stables, which cater to an international yearling market. **Cambridge Thoroughbred Lodge,** six km southeast of Cambridge on Hwy. 1, tel. 07/827-8118, hosts an exhibition called New Zealand Horse Magic Tues.–Sun. at 10:30 A.M. It's an entertaining and informative show-good value at $12 pp for equestrian types. Local history is recorded at **Cambridge Museum** in the old stone courthouse on Victoria St., tel. 07/827-3319.

Practicalities

Cambridge Mews, on the north side of town at 20 Hamilton Rd., tel. 07/827-7166, website: www.cambridgemews.co.nz, is a luxurious motel with 12 spacious rooms, each with a kitchen, a writing desk, and a bathroom with separate shower and spa bath; rates $120 s, $140 d. If you're looking for country-style budget accommodation in this area, don't miss **Cambridge Country Lodge,** a backpackers' lodge on Peake Rd. (off Hwy. 1, about two km north of Cambridge), tel. 07/827-8373. An old stables building has been tastefully converted into clean, bright, budget rooms with communal fully equipped kitchen, bathroom, locker, and laundry; from $17 pp. Just across the way, on the other side of the organic vegetable garden (pick your own veggies, gather fresh eggs, and pay the owners), is the elegant old main house. Mountain bikes are available, and courtesy transportation to town can be arranged.

While you're in Cambridge, be sure to sample breakfast, morning or afternoon tea, or a light lunch at **All Saints Cafe** above **Cambridge Country Store.** You can't miss the two-story orange-red building at 92 Victoria St., tel. 07/827-7100. The café has a large variety of assorted hot dishes, sandwiches, and salads, and the dessert specialty (among many tantalizers) is delicious orange cheesecake. The store is open daily 8:30 A.M.–5 P.M., the café 8:30 A.M.–4 P.M.

The **Cambridge Information Centre** is in the town hall building on the corner of Victoria and Queen Streets, tel. 07/823-3456; open Mon.–Fri. 8 A.M.–4:30 P.M.

PIRONGIA FOREST PARK

The small town of **Pirongia,** 31 km southwest of Hamilton of Hwy. 3, sits at the foot of the impressive Pirongia mountain range where two extinct volcanic peaks, Mt. Pirongia (962 meters) and The Cone (945 meters), dominate the landscape. Nearly 1,300-hectare Pirongia Forest Park carpets the rugged slopes and offers the hiker, angler, hunter, and photographer an extensive network of trails, ranging from easy walks around the lower peaks to strenuous backcountry hikes in the high ones. On the lower northeastern slopes of Pirongia Forest Park lies a beautiful campground and picnic spot at the end of a 30-minute track. The camping area is among native bush beside Kaniwhaniwha Stream, and the immediate area offers several short tracks, delightful swimming holes, and swing bridges over numerous streams. Access to the track is from the Pirongia road to Te Pahu, 40 km from Hamilton. (It's hard to find on a map; locate Kaniwhaniwha Stream, then Te Pahu.) At Te Pahu take the Te Pahu side road (gravel) for about six km to a concrete bridge over the Kaniwhaniwha Stream; the track entrance is over a stile. To get to the camp area, follow the track over the first swing bridge. Don't cross the second swing bridge, which leads to a picnic area; continue along Track 12 to the track branch and follow the red markers to the campground.

Waitomo Caves

Waitomo, 70 km south of Hamilton off Hwy. 3, is most famous for its caves, but it has gained a reputation in recent years as the adventure capital of the North Island. Aside from touring famous Waitomo Caves and its glowworms, you can go black-water (underground) rafting, abseiling into a limestone shaft and cave system, horseback riding, you name it! All you need is time, plenty of cash, and an adventurous spirit. This entire area is part of an ancient seabed that was lifted up by enormous pressures from deep below the Earth's surface. Then erosion took over, with water action creating a complex system of caves, some with rivers flowing through them, others decorated with natural wonders such as stalactites.

To get to Waitomo take Hwy. 3 southwest out of Hamilton to Otorohanga. To the south of Otorohanga turn off to the west to Waitomo Caves.

SIGHTS

Start exploration at the intriguing **Waitomo Museum of Caves,** tel. 07/878-7640. This puts you in the mood for all the other activities and gives you as much background knowledge as you desire. Displays feature local geology, flora and fauna, spelunking, fossils, surveying know-how, skeletal remains found in nearby caves, the history of tourism in the area, preserved birds, insects, and glowworms. Don't miss the excellent 27-minute audiovisual program on spelunking. The building also houses the local information center. It's open in summer, daily 8:15 A.M.–5:30 P.M., the rest of the year, daily 8:30 A.M.–5:30 P.M.; admission to the museum and audiovisual is $4 adult, $2 child (or free with paid admission to the caves).

The Caves

Magnificent limestone caves, many still unexplored, lace the Waitomo area. Two of the most spectacular—**Waitomo** (also known as the **Glowworm Cave**) and **Aranui**—are open for guided tours.

The main attraction within Waitomo Cave is the magical glowworm grotto. Quietly glide through the water-filled grotto in a boat, gazing upward at the vast ceiling of twinkling lights. Tours through Glowworm Cave are run daily, generally every 30 minutes 9 A.M.–4 P.M., with extra tours at 4:30 P.M. and 5:30 P.M. in peak periods. Photography is not allowed in this cave.

Three km upstream, Aranui Cave is definitely the more beautiful of the two caves, but lacks water and therefore there are no glowworms. The pink and white limestone formations are exquisite. Tours leave on the hour 10 A.M.–3 P.M. from the cave entrance.

Both tours take 45 minutes and both cost adult $20, child $10. A combined ticket costs adult $30, child $15. Buy tickets from the booth at Waitomo Cave. (Plan on joining an early tour to avoid bus tours and school groups).

Marokopa Road

The narrow road west from Waitomo winds for 52 scenic km to the small coastal community of **Marokopa,** passing many natural wonders along the way. At the end of a 500-meter trail that begins 25 km from Waitomo, **Mangapohue Natural Bridge** is a massive arch spanning a small stream—it was once part of a mighty cave system. The trail passes under the bridge and leads to a bed of fossilized oysters. A few km farther west is **Piripiri Cave.** There are no cave tours, so you're on your own (bring a flashlight). Continuing west for two km, a parking lot marks the trailhead for a short (500-meter) walk to **Marokopa Falls.** Cascading 30 meters over a limestone ledge, the falls are one of the most photogenic in the country. At the end of the road lies the fishing village of Marokopa. From

GLOWWORMS

Glowworms, New Zealand's fairy lights, twinkle by the thousands in caves and other moist and shady places, much to the wonderment of humans. The larva of a luminous gnat, the glowworm is a tiny fisherman that suspends itself from a cave ceiling or other canopy with fine, silky, sticky threads 1–5 cm long. Its tail end glows bluish-green, more brightly the hungrier it gets. Its prey is bugs that breed in the mudbanks and water below the glowworm; they fly toward the light and entangle themselves in the glowworm's net. The glowworm hauls up the lines and feasts on the trapped bugs.

Proceed with caution when you enter their grottoes: they don't like loud noise; one clap and all the lights go out. They don't like bright light; shine a torch on them and the twinkles will fade. And hands off; they are fragile and a human touch will kill them.

the *very* end of the road, it's a pleasant 800-meter walk through black sand to the ocean. Early in the 1900s, when Marokopa was a bustling port town, many ships were lost attempting to negotiate the river mouth. The anchor from one such ship was salvaged and now sits in the parking lot at the end of the road.

Commercial Attractions

Billy Black's Kiwi Culture Show, at Woodlyn Park (up Waitomo Valley Rd.), tel. 07/878-6666, combines history and humor to tell the story of rural life in New Zealand. The show includes woodchopping, working dogs, a dancing pig, and sheepshearing. The fun kicks off daily at 1:30 P.M. and costs adult $13, child $7.

Otorohanga, nearest town to Waitomo, is worth a stop for **Otorohanga Kiwi House,** Alex Telfer Dr. (next to the motor camp), tel. 07/873-7391. Here you can see kiwis in the nocturnal house, walk through an enormous aviary, and see New Zealand's rare and unusual birds and reptiles in their natural habitat. It's open daily 9 A.M.–5 P.M. (4 P.M. in winter); $9 adult, $4 child.

RECREATION

In keeping with the entrepreneurial spirit evident around the country, the advertising will have you believe you can't complete the "Waitomo Experience" without parting with a pile of cash. This may be true to an extent, but there are also a number of free or inexpensive options around the village. Consider the **Waitomo Walkway,** which begins across the road from the museum. This easy trail follows Waitomo Stream through native forest and past limestone crags to **Ruakuri Scenic Reserve** and Aranui Cave. Allow three to four hours for the 10-km round-trip.

Black-Water Rafting

Black-water rafting began in New Zealand in the mid-1980s. It's offered at locations throughout the country, but the Waitomo experience is the original and still the best. It involves donning wet suits and helmets with headlamps, plunging into the Huhunui stream on an inner tube, and drifting along an underground river for around 90 minutes. In some places you need to get off and scramble, and in Ruakuri Cave, jump down a waterfall. Glowworms put on a magical display along Okohua stream. Afterward a hot shower and a snack are provided. All you need to take is a swimsuit (wear it), a towel, socks, tennis or running shoes, and a waterproof camera with flash. The tour departs up to eight times daily from the Black Water Rafting complex, tel. 07/878-6219 or 0800/ 228-464, 1.2 km east of Waitomo Village. It should be booked well in advance; $70 pp. A longer, more adventurous trip is Black Water Rafting II, a five-hour trip that begins with an abseil into Ruakuri Cave; $140 pp. For the less adventurous, consider Black Water Dry, an underground raft trip; $35 pp.

Waitomo Adventures

This company offers a number of exciting underground adventures. The most popular is the **Lost World Epic.** This involves abseiling 100 meters into a limestone cave to see gold-colored stalactites, waterfalls, and glowworms. Once at the base of the cave, lunch is served; then it's up-stream, wading, walking, swimming, and climbing, through caves, vaults, and valleys to get back out. The seven-hour trip is truly an incredible experience, one that will be a highlight of your stay in New Zealand—and anyone of a reasonable fitness level can do it; it costs $300 pp. A shorter four-hour trip, the **Lost World Abseil,** is $205. **Haggis Honking Holes** is even more adventurous, and you need to be fit to accomplish the waterfall abseil and climbing required to complete this four-hour adventure; $135. Combine these latter two trips as a **Gruesome Twosome** for $295. Book by calling 07/878-7788 or 0800/924-8666.

Horseback Riding

Horse trekking is another popular activity around here. Explore the Waitomo countryside on a one-hour ride ($30 pp), a two-hour ride ($40), a half-day ride ($70), or over a full day ($125). The operation is based at Juno Hall (see below); for details call **Waitomo Horse Trekking,** tel. 07/878-7649.

PRACTICALITIES
Accommodations and Camping

Formerly part of the government's THC chain, the elegant **Waitomo Caves Hotel,** tel. 07/878-8204, website: www.waitomocaveshotel.co.nz, dating from 1908, sits on a hill above Waitomo's main facility area. It has been completely renovated, and all the rooms now have private bathrooms. It also has a restaurant and bar. Rates are $110 s, $130 d for a standard room. The only other motel in the area is out on Hwy. 3, eight km from the caves. **Glow Worm Motel,** tel. 07/873-8882 or 0800/113-882, has nine self-contained units, a swimming pool, and an adjacent restaurant; $70 s, $75–90 d.

Juno Hall, one km east of the information center, tel. 07/878-7649, is always busy (book ahead) and offers all the usual facilities of a backpacker lodge. It's a well-run operation, with bookings made for all the local attractions. A bed in the comfortable dorms is $19 pp, while double rooms are $24 pp. If you have transportation, a quieter choice is **Oto-Kiwi Lodge,** out on the main highway in the nearby village of Otorohanga, 1 Sangro Crescent, tel. 07/873-6022, which was built specifically as a hostel. The bus depot is a handy 500 meters away, and the hosts provide transfers to Waitomo Caves. Dorms are $19 pp, $22 pp d or twin.

Campsites are limited at Waitomo, so book in advance or register early in the day. **Waitomo Top 10 Holiday Park,** opposite the hotel and information center, tel. 07/878-7639 or 0508/498-666, has a communal kitchen, barbecue area, and laundry; tent and powered sites are $22, basic cabins are $34.

Food

As well as selling groceries and souvenirs, **Waitomo General Store,** tel. 07/878-7639, has a small restaurant with good pizza from $10 and a variety of other inexpensive items to eat in or take out. On the other side of the Museum of Caves is the **Waitomo Tavern,** open daily for lunch ($6–9) and dinner ($11–15). Overlooking the valley is the grand old **Waitomo Caves Hotel,** tel. 07/878-8204, where the restaurant features a lunchtime buffet and regular à la carte dinner menu. **Black Water Café,** 1.2 km east of the village, tel. 07/878-7361, features bistro-style meals and light snacks. It's open daily 9 A.M.–5 P.M.

Transportation

The closest **Intercity** and **Newmans** bus stop to Waitomo is Otorohanga, out on Hwy. 3. The depot is at the information center at 80 Maniapoto St., tel. 07/873-8951. The **Waitomo Shuttle,** tel. 0800/808-279, runs between the depot and Waitomo, meeting all buses. The **Waitomo Wanderer,** tel. 07/873-7559, operates from Rotorua to Waitomo and also picks up passengers in Taupo.

Information

From the **Information Centre,** in the Waitomo Museum of Caves, Main St., tel. 07/878-7640, bookings can be made for cave tours and recreational activities, and the staff keeps a list of local bed-and-breakfasts. Across the hallway is a **DOC Field Centre,** the best source of information on local hiking. The DOC also sells a number of good books on the caves and caving. Both are open in summer, daily 8:15 A.M.–5:30 P.M., the rest of the year, daily 8:30 A.M.–5:30 P.M. Serious spelunkers should head up to the **Hamilton Tomo Group Lodge,** three km west of the village, tel. 07/878-7442. As headquarters for New Zealand's largest caving club, it organizes weekend caving trips and has detailed descriptions of all the mapped caves, as well as provides dorm accommodation for members and guests.

Coromandel Peninsula

Lying equidistant from both Hamilton and Auckland and less than two hour's drive from either is the Coromandel Peninsula, a place that no hiker or outdoor enthusiast should miss. This finger of land stretches northward from the gateway town of Thames, separating the Hauraki Gulf and Firth of Thames on the west from the Pacific Ocean in the east. Like vertebrae, the rugged mountains of the Coromandel Range snake down the center of the peninsula, supporting the 72,000 hectares of wilderness and bush that make up Coromandel Forest Park. The peninsula is an area of contrasts: along the western shores, steep, rocky cliffs terminate abruptly at the sea, while the eastern shores offer sandy beaches and private, sheltered coves. Wherever you go on the east coast you'll find beautiful beaches. If you also want peace and quiet, and maybe your own private bush-fringed cove, stay in the north. For lots of people and the bustle of a coastal resort, head for the large towns such as Whitianga and Whangamata at the southern end of the peninsula.

History

The Coromandel Peninsula has survived the same land exploitation as the far north. It has seen both poverty and prosperity, and a dramatically fluctuating population during the last 200 years. In the early 1800s it was ravaged for kauri timber. Vast areas were stripped, and only a few of the more inaccessible forest remnants survived. The timber seekers were followed by the gum diggers. In the mid-1800s the land was further exploited after gold was discovered in 1852 (the township of Coromandel was the first place in New Zealand to boast discovery of the precious metal) and permanently scarred with deep shafts and mines.

Today the Coromandel Peninsula is again a quiet and peaceful place, recognized for its great beauty and value as a wilderness area. The small permanent population is scattered mainly along the coastline. Although a few of the most easily reached towns (mostly along the east coast) are rapidly becoming tourist attractions, don't let the tricky gravel roads and steepness of the terrain prevent you from discovering the more beautiful, wild side of the Coromandel.

THAMES

After crossing Waihou River, Hwy. 25 swings north to Thames (population 7,000), the gateway to the Coromandel Peninsula. Sitting at the foot of the Coromandel Range, it's the ideal base for hiking in Coromandel Forest Park wilderness. In 1852 gold was first found farther north in the area of the present town of Coromandel. It wasn't till 1867 that the Thames district was officially opened up for gold prospecting. In the next three years Thames boomed. The rush continued until 1924, and many of the old-style buildings around town are reminders of this colorful past. Before a road link was built, Thames Port used to be the peninsula's link with the outside world, and was frequented by large riverboats and cutters. Today the port is very quiet, and caters to a small fishing fleet and many recreational boats. Thames is a commercial center for surrounding farmlands and is rapidly becoming more of a tourist attraction with its gold-rush history and close proximity to Coromandel Forest Park.

Before a road link was built, Thames Port used to be the peninsula's link with the outside world, and was frequented by large riverboats and cutters.

Sights

If you're into rocks, check out the **Thames School of Mines and Mineralogical Museum,** 101 Cochrane St., tel. 07/868-6227. The School of Mines was open between 1886 and 1954, teaching skills to prospective miners. It's now a museum, featuring an extensive collection of local and overseas mineral samples, and a working model of a stamper battery (used on quartz claims to pound quartz into powder). It's open in summer daily 11 A.M.–8 P.M., the rest of the year Tues.–Sun. 11 A.M.–4 P.M.; $5 adult, $2 child.

Thames Historical Museum is three blocks east of mining museum on the corner of Pollen and Cochrane Streets, tel. 07/868-8509. The building itself is more than 100 years old, and the museum features century-old printing and photographic equipment and 19th-century clothing. It's open daily in summer 1–4 P.M.; $3 adult, $1 child.

At the top end of town, where Pollen St. rejoins the highway, **Thames Gold Mine,** tel. 07/868-7448, was the site of one of the most productive gold mines on the peninsula. You can go on an underground guided tour through a mine shaft, as well as see a working stamper battery, a reconstructed mine manager's office, and a small museum. It's open in summer daily 9 A.M.–5 P.M.; tours cost $8 adult, $4 child. Other mining sites around Thames are well signposted from the main roads, but for the exact location of old gold mines, mine dumps, shafts, and abandoned mining machinery around the area, pick up the free pamphlet "The Urban Trail" from the information center.

Scenic Locales

For good views of Thames, Hauraki Plains, and Hauraki Gulf, head for **Monument Hill;** access is from Waiotahi Rd. west from the Thames Gold Mine.

For an enjoyable **scenic drive** through the native bush of Coromandel Forest Park and many opportunities to hike short tracks, head for the **Kauaeranga Valley** to the southeast of Thames. Information on all the walks is available in a brochure from the information center in Thames, or the Kauaeranga Field Centre on Kauaeranga Valley Road. See Coromandel Forest Park in the following section.

Hotels and Motels

Brian Boru Hotel, 200 Richmond St., tel. 07/868-6523 or 0800/922-622, an eye-pleas-

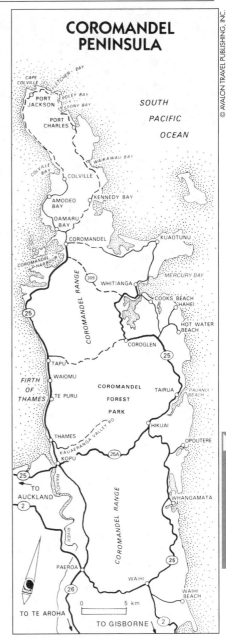

CENTRAL NORTH ISLAND

© ANDREW HEMPSTEAD

Brian Boru Hotel

ing colonial hotel built in 1868, offers a wide range of rooms. Within the hotel itself are 25 rooms, some with shared bathroom, some with private bathroom, for $75–90 s, $90–125 d, plus an attractive, old-fashioned, licensed dining room (all meals available), comfortable lounge and bar, and plenty of old-time atmosphere. Adjoining the Brian Boru Hotel's courtyard are modern motel units with queen-size beds, private bathrooms, fridge, tea- and coffee-making supplies, and TV; rates from $105 s, $135 d.

Of the many motels in and around Thames, the **Avalon Motel,** Jellicoe Cres., tel. 07/868-7755, provides the best value. At the south end of downtown and overlooking the Kauaeranga River, the Avalon features 11 kitchen-equipped units, an indoor spa pool, a barbecue area, and a laundry. Rates are from $70 s, $85. A short walk from the center of town, **Rolleston Motel,** 105 Rolleston St., tel. 07/868-8091 or 0800/776-644, is an older-style single-story motel with a pool, spa, and laundry. All rooms include a kitchen; rates $75 s, $95 d. Save a few bucks at the **Rendezvous Motel,** about five km south of Thames on the main highway at Kopu, tel. 07/868-8536. Self-contained units

sleeping two to six people run $60 s, $75 d; continental or cooked breakfast costs extra. The **Coastal Motor Lodge,** backing on the forest three km north of Thames at 608 Tararu Rd., tel. 07/868-6843, features spacious self-contained cottages and chalets in a garden setting; $90–115 s or d.

Bed-and-Breakfasts

South of town in Totara is **Cotswold Cottage,** Maramarahi Rd., tel. 07/868-6306. Right by the Kauaeranga River, a verandah offers a great view of the surrounding countryside. All three rooms include private bathrooms, and the rate includes a delicious cooked breakfast. Rates are $50 s, $80–100 d, and dinner is available for an extra $35 pp.

A few kilometers north of Thames, in the town of Te Puru, is **Te Puru Coast View Lodge,** tel. 07/868-2326. Well-signposted from the highway, it's high on a hill overlooking the town and the Firth of Thames. This Mediterranean-style accommodation has a number of rooms fronting the extensive garden, each with a private bathroom. Rates are $120–160 s or d, which includes a full breakfast, and dinner is available in the licensed restaurant on the premises.

Backpacker Lodges

Sunkist Lodge at 506 Brown St., tel. 07/868-8808, is one of Thames' appealing historic buildings left behind from gold-mining days, with a spacious upstairs verandah. Choose from dorms or single, twin, double, or triple rooms, with the use of communal bathrooms, fully equipped kitchen, dining room, TV lounge, pool table, laundry, barbecue, and garden; $18–21 pp. It's a popular place at any time of year but there's usually room—book for January and February, especially for double rooms. **Dickson Holiday Park,** three km north of Thames on Victoria St., tel. 07/868-7308, is an associate of Hostelling International. Dorm beds are $16, doubles and twins $20 pp.

Motor Camps

Three km north and closest to town is the excellent **Dickson Holiday Park,** just off the main highway on Victoria St., tel. 07/868-7308. On the grounds of a gold mine dating to the 1870s, it has a lush parklike camping area in a natural bush setting—a great spot to get away from it all and unwind—hiking local trails, gold panning in Tararu Stream, or relaxing at a nearby waterfall and wonderful swimming hole. In addition to the usual communal kitchen, there's a Pioneer Kitchen, a working re-creation of the rustic cooking facilities used by miners in days gone by. Other facilities include a laundry, swimming pool, bikes, trampolines, a half-sized tennis court, and a camp office selling basics 8:30 A.M.–7 P.M. Tent and caravan sites are $22 s or d, bunkroom accommodation $16 pp, cabins (with fridge and cooking hot plate) and on-site caravans range $35–42 s or d, tourist flats (private bathroom, kitchen, TV, and radio) are $64 s or d, and the motel unit is $84 s or d.

Food

You'll find the usual tearooms, take-aways, and cafés throughout Thames, mostly on mile-long Pollen St., the main shopping street downtown. Two casual favorites are away from this strip. In the Goldmine Shopping Centre, near the waterfront, the **Robert Harris Café,** tel. 07/868-8656, is a large modern café open daily from 7 A.M. The other local hot spot is the **Sealey Café,** 109 Sealey St., tel. 07/868-8641. In a renovated house with lots of outside table settings, the Sealey is a great place to enjoy gourmet sandwiches accompanied by a huge side of salad.

Back on busy Pollen St., the **Goldmine,** on the corner of Pollen and Mary Streets, tel. 07/868-3180, offers standard small-town fare, including cooked breakfasts (around $8) and dishes such as t-bone steak accompanied by fries and salad ($13). Two blocks south of Mary St., the **Mangrove Café,** 444 Pollen St., tel. 07/868-7784, offers the best coffee in town. **Majestic Restaurant,** 640 Pollen St., tel. 07/868-6204, serves chicken, seafood, and steak dinners for $12–19 and children's meals for $7. It's open weekdays 9 A.M.–8 P.M. and weekends 4–8 P.M. A take-away section out front offers good fish and chips, hamburgers, hot chickens, and toasted sandwiches. At the top end of town is the **Old Thames Restaurant,** 705 Pollen St., tel. 07/868-7207, serving steak and seafood in an elegant setting; open daily. For a substantial Chinese meal at a reasonable price, try the **Golden Dragon,** one block south at 648 Pollen St., tel. 07/868-8432. It's open Tues.–Sun. and has a BYO license; dinners (big enough for a very healthy appetite) will set you back only $10–18 pp. Next door you can get Chinese meals to go, hamburgers, and toasted sandwiches; open daily 11:30 A.M.–10 P.M.

Transportation

Departing Auckland, **Intercity** operates a daily service east to Thames (gateway to the peninsula), taking almost two hours. The terminus of this service is Thames Visitor Centre at 206 Pollen St., tel. 07/868-7284. Intercity also has a direct service between Thames and Rotorua. Continuing north, **Murphy Buses,** tel. 07/868-6265, runs a service Sun.–Fri. from Thames to Coromandel taking 1.5 hours and northeast to Whitianga taking 2.5 hours. Services also connect Thames with Ngatea (and on to Whitianga), Tauranga, and Rotorua.

Thames is a compact little town, and you can get just about anywhere on foot. Otherwise, call **Thames Taxis,** tel. 0800/256-652.

Services and Information

Thames Laundromat, 742 Pollen St., is open weekdays 7 A.M.–7 P.M., weekends and holidays 9 A.M.–5 P.M. The **library** is on Mackay St. (see the historic ceramic plaques), tel. 07/868-8358. The **post office** is on Pollen Street.

For medical care, call **Thames Hospital,** Mackay St., tel. 07/868-6550; or the **Thames Medical Centre,** 817 Rolleston St., tel. 07/868-9444. Call the **police station** at 07/868-6040.

Thames Information Centre, 206 Pollen St., tel. 07/868-7284, is open in summer, weekdays 8:30 A.M.–5 P.M., weekends 10 A.M.–4 P.M., shorter hours the rest of the year. The DOC operates **Kauaeranga Field Centre** on Kauaeranga Valley Rd. (about 13 km from Thames), tel. 07/868-6381; open in summer daily 8 A.M.–4 P.M. **Carson's Books,** 600 Pollen St., tel. 07/868-6301, is a great little bookstore specializing in New Zealand fiction and nonfiction.

COROMANDEL FOREST PARK

This 73,000-hectare park, extending along the spine of the Coromandel Peninsula, protects rugged bush-clad ranges with their ancient volcanic plugs and dense remnants of kauri forest. The park is laced with hiking tracks that vary from short walks to mining or kauri-logging sites, to rugged several-day hikes in the mountainous backcountry. Apart from recreation, the park is used for plant and animal conservation and as a source of domestic water supplies. The most easily accessed section of the park is from the Kauaeranga Valley, reached by following Banks St. east out of Thames and across the Kauaeranga River. This road winds through the beautiful Kauaeranga Valley, passing several good camping areas, and four short tracks, before terminating at the starting point of some of the more difficult hiking tracks.

On the way up to the park, stop at **Kauaeranga Field Centre,** 15 km from Thames, for track information, campsite and hut details, and maps, and don't miss the 25-minute audiovisual program. A detailed map of the park is available for $11, a worthwhile purchase. Be sure to check the latest weather forecasts with the staff, as flooding

and landslides can occur without warning. If you're hiking overnight in the backcountry, fill out an intention sheet. The Field Centre, tel. 07/867-9080; open daily in summer 8 A.M.–4 P.M.

Hiking

Four short walks lead off Kauaeranga Rd. beyond the Field Centre. About 30 minutes or less, each is classified as suitable for light footwear in dry weather. They wander through various types of native bush and give great views of the Kauaeranga River and Valley.

About 250 km of walking tracks crisscross the rugged Coromandel Forest Park. For details on each track pick up the "Coromandel Recreation" brochure from the Field Centre. Keep to the marked tracks on all the hikes; many deep mining shafts overgrown by bush are scattered throughout the peninsula and have claimed the lives of unwary explorers. The **Wires Walking Track,** so named because the Auckland-to-Wellington telegraph line was diverted through here during the Waikato Land Wars (you can still see some of the posts), starts 26 km southeast of Thames at the end of Maratoto Road. The track takes 2.5 hours, and joins the Whangamata vehicle track at the Wires Plateau. The **Wentworth Valley Track** is most easily reached from Whangamata by driving halfway up the Wentworth Valley. The signposted track runs up to the vehicular Loop Track, taking about two hours. Enjoy spectacular Wentworth Falls from this track.

THAMES COAST

From Thames, Hwy. 25 northbound hugs the Firth of Thames for 40 km then cuts across two low-lying peninsulas before reaching the small town of Coromandel. This coastal road, perhaps most beautiful in summer when the bordering *pohutukawa* trees are ablaze with red flowers, passes by rocky outcrops, picture-perfect bays, and small beaches. The towns and villages along the route, backed by the Coromandel Range, provide a wide choice in motor camps and stores, and activities range from bush walking and mineral fossicking to swimming and boating.

Tapu

About 18 km from Thames, Tapu lies at the junction of Hwy. 25 and an unpaved road that crosses the peninsula to Whitianga. If time is not precious and you want to see a more isolated part of the peninsula, continue north. If you're looking for action and lots of people, head across to Whitianga and down the east coast.

Tapu is known for its long stretch of sandy beach, shallow water, and safe swimming. The local commercial attraction is **Rapaura Watergardens**, six km east of Hwy. 25, tel. 07/868-4821. As the Maori name suggests, Rapaura (running water) features waterfalls, fountains, and fish-filled ponds. The highlight is Seven Steps to Heaven, a trail that winds through lush forest to a small waterfall. They're open daily 10 A.M.–5 P.M. Oct. 1—April 30; admission $6.

Tapu Motor Camp, on the beach opposite the hotel at the main road junction, tel. 07/868-4837, has a communal bathroom, a kitchen (metered), and laundry. Tent and caravan sites are $12 pp and on-site caravans are $35 s or d.

COROMANDEL

A quiet fishing and crafts village 60 km north of Thames, Coromandel is particularly appealing. Despite its small size (population 1,500), it's the business center of the far north, offering quite a variety of services—and it's the last place (other than one store at Colville) to stock up on supplies before continuing north.

Sights

Coromandel Mining Museum on Rings Rd., tel. 07/866-8825, tells the story of the town, which boomed after 1852, when a logger discovered gold-bearing quartz in nearby Driving Creek. It's open in summer daily 10 A.M.–1 P.M.; admission $2. Along Buffalo Road north of town, at **Coromandel Gold Stamper Battery,** tel. 07/866-7933, you can see ore-crushing demon-

strations for gold extraction, pan amalgamation, and plate amalgamation. The site is open in summer daily 10 A.M.–5 P.M. and admission is adult $5, child $3.

The one unique Coromandel attraction, which lures many visitors up the peninsula, is **Driving Creek Railway,** 2.5 km north of town, then 500 meters up Driving Creek Rd., tel. 07/866-8703. This unique narrow-gauge mountain railway was built by Barry Brickell, a well-known New Zealand potter, to serve his potteries with clay and pine wood for fuel for the kilns in the valley below. He carved a track through the forest, laying 2.5 km of line and even building the diesel-powered train himself. Nowadays you can take a ride on the train over a bridge, round a switchback, and through a tunnel to see the native kauri forest restoration project, displays, and views across Hauraki Gulf. The one-hour return trip departs year-round, daily at noon and 4 P.M., with additional trips in summer at 10 A.M. and 2 P.M. The cost is $12 adult, $6 child. Another reason to venture out here is to browse through Driving Creek Pottery, open daily 10 A.M.–5 P.M., where you can buy the work of the resident potters, including homegrown wool, paper, and flax products.

> *The Thames Coast Road, perhaps most beautiful in summer when the bordering pohutukawa trees are ablaze with red flowers, passes by rocky outcrops, picture-perfect bays, and small beaches.*

Accommodations and Camping

The **Coromandel Hotel,** Kapanga Rd., tel. 07/866-8760, is an old hotel up the hill from the main shopping strip but near the information center. Rooms share bathrooms, but are just $35 s, $55 d. Downstairs is a bar and dining room, with breakfast available to guests. Within easy walking distance of local restaurants, **Coromandel Court Motel,** 365 Kapanga Rd., tel. 07/866-8830 or 0800/267-626, features nine spacious units set around a pleasant garden dotted with mature trees and outdoor tables; $75 s, $100–150 d. A step up in quality but only slightly higher in price is **Colonial Cottages Motel,** 1737 Rings Rd., tel. 07/866-8857 or 0508/222-688; website: www.corocottagesmotel.co.nz. Comprising two rows of four self-contained cottages facing each other, the complex is surrounded by well-tended gardens and native bush, with a covered barbecue area and pool off to one side. Rates are $95–155 s or d.

Nestled high above the water and surrounded by native bush, **Buffalo Lodge,** north of town at 860 Buffalo Rd., tel. 07/866-8960, is arguably the peninsula's finest accommodation. Taking advantage of its elevation, the lodge features a wide wraparound deck, with native timber dominant throughout. The four well-appointed guest rooms include thoughtful touches such as heated towel rails and plush robes. Rates are $220–265 s or d, with dinner available for an additional charge. Buffalo Lodge is closed May–September.

South off Hwy. 25, **Tui Lodge,** 600 Whangapoua Rd. (Hwy. 25), tel. 07/866-8237, is surrounded by grassy paddocks and citrus and macadamia orchards; dorm beds are $15–18 pp, private rooms $21 pp. If you need a ride out from town, give the owners a call and they'll collect you.

For overnight camping with communal bathrooms (metered) and cooking and laundry facilities, try beachfront **Long Bay Motor Camp,** three km west of the village, tel. 07/866-8720. Tent and caravan sites are $20–24 s or d. Rowboats are available for rent. Closer to town, **Coromandel Holiday Park,** 636 Rings Rd., tel. 07/866-8830, has a communal bathroom, kitchen, and laundry, pool, recreation room, trampolines, and barbecue. Tent sites are $10 pp, caravan sites are $11 pp, cabins are $42 s or d, and tourist flats are $80 s or d.

Food

For delicious freshly baked bread, salad rolls, pastries (your thighs will never forgive you!), meat pies, and great pizza, check out the **Coromandel Bakehouse** on Wharf Rd., tel. 07/866-8554. It's open seven days a week 7:30 A.M.–5 P.M., in summer till 9 P.M. For inexpensive seafood take-aways, stop by **Chick's Takeaways** on Kapanga Rd., tel. 07/866-8023. There's also **Success Café** at 104 Kapanga Rd., tel. 07/866-7100, featuring lots of seafood, burgers, and sandwiches. Their advertising says to "Try our Seafood Chowder" ($7.50). I

did, and it's delicious. In the name of research I also sampled the seafood chowder at **Pepper Tree Restaurant,** 31 Kapanga Rd., tel. 07/866-8211. The Pepper Tree is Coromandel's premier dining room, with a small courtyard the preferred option on a warm summer night. Along with the chowder, dishes such as snapper with paw paw and avocado ($13) are all very well priced.

Information

For more information on the village and areas to the north, call **Coromandel Information Centre,** tel. 07/866-8598, in the Old Courthouse on the main road; open in summer, daily 9 A.M.–5 P.M., the rest of the year, weekends only 11 A.M.–3 P.M.

TO THE TOP
Colville

At the end of the sealed road, 30 km north of Coromandel, this small settlement has only one store, a restaurant, and a post office, and is the very *last* place to get supplies and petrol before heading on to the northern tip. The **Colville General Store,** tel. 07/866-6805, is open seven days a week and sells fresh fruit and veggies, dairy products, groceries, camping needs, and petrol. Within the store is the **Colville Cafe,** serving seafood, steak, and vegetarian meals from locally grown produce.

Continuing North

If heading to Port Jackson is what you have in mind, expect to ford several streams (generally not too deep except after heavy rains) along this coast-hugging gravel road. You'll pass stretches of beautiful coastline with enchanting bays and excellent camping spots, and wind up at the open white sands of Port Jackson beach—lots more perfect camping spots beside crystal-clear streams, plenty of driftwood for campfires, and relatively few fellow explorers. What more could you ask for? The rocky coastline near Port Jackson holds great appeal for anglers; the gulf water is deep and clear and abounds with large snapper. The road leads around the top of the peninsula and ends at Fletcher Bay.

On a small hilltop farm, **Fletcher Bay Backpackers,** tel. 07/866-6712, at the northern tip of the peninsula, is one of the remotest accommodations in the country. It's easy to spend a few days here—hiking the Coromandel Track, fishing, boating, swimming, or diving. Beds in the four-bed dorms are $17 pp. The alternative is to camp out. The DOC administers four camping areas in the vicinity of Fletcher Bay—at Fantail Bay, Port Jackson, Stony Bay, and Waikawau Bay. All have freshwater streams, but no toilets; sites cost $6 pp per night—give the fee to a conservation officer or leave it in the honesty box. You'll find no shops in the vicinity (except a mobile shop that operates only in summer), so be sure to take food and other supplies (don't forget matches) before heading for the campgrounds; take a stove and cooking equipment as well.

Coromandel Track

This seven-km track, part of the New Zealand Walkway network, wanders within Cape Colville Farm Park in the far northern tip of the peninsula, from Fletcher Bay to Stony Bay. It takes about 2.5 hours each way. On this rather isolated track you traverse beach, open farmland, and bush, and are rewarded with fabulous coastal scenery. The track follows an easy grade for the most part, with only one short, steep section (marked with red disks) near the center. The small, sandy beach at Poley Bay (where a stream runs out to sea) may tempt you in for a swim, but resist the urge. Many submerged rocks lie dangerously close to the surface, and you'll find safer swimming at the end of the track. Also avoid drinking from this stream—the water is bad. Farther along, the track wanders through scrub, with the Moehau Range dominating the skyline to the west. Behind Stony Bay beach, Stony Bay and Doctors Creeks merge to form a large lagoon—a good swimming hole. A separate track leads from Stony Bay to the summit of Moehau (892 m) and down the other side; allow six hours one way. The views are worth the long hard climb, and if you're lucky you may see one of the "fairies" that Maori legends claim inhabit this area. Campsites and freshwater streams are at both ends of the track, and Fletcher Bay has toilets.

ACROSS THE COROMANDEL PENINSULA

Many roads cross the Coromandel Peninsula. The main sealed road is **Hwy. 25A,** which begins south of Thames at Kopu and ends 24 km north of Whangamata. Farther north, drivers taking the winding unsealed Tapu Hill route from Tapu to Coroglen are rewarded with views of lush valleys, clear streams, giant tree ferns, and near the top of the range, the 2,500-year-old "Square Kauri."

From the north end of the peninsula, you have two choices. Hwy. 25, the route up the coast from Thames continues beyond Coromandel as a rough unpaved road, following a remote peninsula to Kuaotunu and on to Whitianga. Allow at least one hour for these 46 km.

309 Road

The most interesting route is the 32-km-long unsealed 309 Road between Coromandel and Hwy. 25 four km southwest of Whitianga (allow

© ANDREW HEMPSTEAD

Make a stop at one of the many waterfalls along the 309 Road.

at least 40 minutes to an hour depending on your familiarity with curvy gravel roads); take plenty of film to capture natural bush panoramas. The first worthwhile stop is **Waiau Water Works,** tel. 07/866-7191, where inventive owner Chris Ogilvie has created a number of interesting waterpowered machines that are dotted around his garden. Open in summer daily 9 A.M.–4 P.M.; $5 adult, $2 child. At the 7.5-km mark, a short trail leads to **Waiau Falls,** where sparkling water cascades over a rocky ledge surrounded by dense greenery. Just 500 meters farther east is a grove of kauri trees that escaped logging. They are reached by a short 10-minute (each way) trail.

Stop at **309 Honey Cottage,** tel. 07/866-5151, a retreat 12 km before Whitianga, for delicious honey, crafts, and animal petting, or to stay in an old kauri cottage in a river-and-bush setting for only $20 pp. The cottage has showers, fully equipped kitchen, lounge with log fire, and washing machine. On the farm are endless possibilities for bush walks, gem collecting in the river, and cooling off in natural swimming holes—it's a gorgeous place. Don't leave without a jar of the delicious, organic *manuka* honey.

WHITIANGA

Whitianga (population 3,500) is the largest town on magnificent **Mercury Bay.** With a sheltered harbor and long, sandy **Buffalo Beach,** Whitianga is a popular holiday resort with countless holiday homes populated by a fairly large retirement community; in summer they're inundated with families on vacation. It's also a base for big-game fishing and scuba diving, and for a short time was on the world map as the home base of the small Mercury Bay Boating Club, which Michael Fay used when he challenged the America's Cup in 1988.

Sights

From downtown, an inexpensive passenger ferry runs across "The Narrows" (7:30 A.M.–noon and 1–6:30 P.M. to tranquil **Ferry Landing** (original site of Whitianga), several scenic reserves featuring ocean views and sandy beaches, and the hamlet of Cooks Beach. Near the Whitianga side of the

ferry, **Mercury Bay Museum** features photos and relics from the days of the earliest pioneers. Highlights include relics from the HMS *Buffalo,* which was wrecked nearby in 1840, and the gigantic jaws of a white pointer shark that was estimated to weigh 1,300 kg. The museum is open in summer, daily 10 A.M.–4 P.M.; the rest of the year, Tuesday, Thursday, and Sunday 11 A.M.–2 P.M. When you're done with the museum, explore the area's historic gold mines, meander through excellent craft shops, go fishing or diving, sightsee by minibus, river raft or jetboat, experience a 4WD adventure, go pony trekking, play a round of golf, or get a bird's-eye view on a scenic flight.

Between Whitianga and Hahei, en route to Cooks Beach, is rustic **Purangi Winery,** tel. 07/866-3724, a popular venue for locals and visitors alike. Go for a fine wine-tasting from the cellars, enjoy the food in the Wine Buttery Bar, meet some of the many country critters lounging around, and leisurely explore the river on the Purangi Winery River Cruise boat that departs daily at high tide ($24 pp).

Accommodations

The many motels, backpacker lodges, and motor camps in the area provide quite a choice in accommodation. Rates given below are for January; outside of this month, expect discounted rates. Generally, it is the more expensive places that offer the larger discounts.

A great place to stay is **Buffalo Beach Resort,** on the corner of Buffalo Beach Rd. and Eyre St., tel. 07/866-5854, right on the beach and within easy walking distance of downtown. It offers a communal bathroom (metered showers), kitchen, and laundry; TV and pool room; and hot pools among four hectares of landscaped grass and trees. Camping costs $20–24 s or d; comfortable chalets, each with a kitchen, cost $50–80 s or d.

Directly opposite the beach, **Anchorage Motel,** 22 The Esplanade, tel. 07/866-5481, has standard rooms, each with a kitchen. Rates are $120 s or d for a studio unit, $150 for a one-bedroom unit. **Waters Edge Motor Lodge,** 84 Albert St., tel. 07/866-5760, enjoys a waterfront location south of downtown along Whitianga Harbour and next door to the marina. It offers a variety of rooms, ranging from studios to three-bedroom family units, a pool, and grassed gardens. Rates are $135–170 s or d in summer.

North around the bay is the modern, more luxurious **Mercury Bay Beachfront Resort,** 113 Buffalo Beach Rd., tel. 07/866-5637; website: www.beachfrontresort.co.nz. Each of the eight units has either a balcony or patio overlooking a garden-the only thing separating the resort from the beach. Summer rates range $160–220 s or d, reduced to $120–160 s or d the rest of the year.

A good choice for budget travelers is **Buffalo Peaks Lodge,** 200 meters from the beach and just around the corner from downtown at 12 Albert St., tel. 07/866-2933, website: www.buffalopeaks.co.nz, with modern facilities, Internet access, and bike rentals. Dorm beds are $20 pp, doubles are $35–55. Another good choice is **On the Beach Backpackers Lodge,** 46 Buffalo Beach Rd., tel. 07/866-5380. The Spanish-style building faces a large reserve, the beach, and the bay, and the enthusiastic owners offer guests the free use of kayaks and surf- or body boards, and have bikes for rent. Dorms are $20 pp, private rooms from $24 pp.

Food

As a seaside resort town, Whitianga has plenty of choices when it comes to casual cafés and restaurants. **Snapper Jacks,** Albert St., tel. 07/866-5482, is *the* place to get take-out fish and chips ($6–8). **Bay Bakery,** around the corner on Monk St., tel. 07/866-4840, opens early for meat pies, sausage rolls, and all the usual cakes and sweet pastries.

Stylish **On the Rocks,** across the road from the main wharf at 20 The Esplanade, tel. 07/866-4833, is the best choice for a sit-down meal. The interior features lots of polished native timber, including handmade rimu furniture and an old kauri "clinker" (dingy) cleverly incorporated into the bar. Water views from most tables complement the distinctive NZ nautical theme. As you'd expect, seafood is featured prominently; start with the seafood chowder of Mercury Bay delicacies ($9), followed by beer-battered fish smothered in a tangy tartar sauce ($22).

Information

Whitianga Information Centre, 66 Albert St., tel. 07/866-5555, is generally open weekdays 9 A.M.–5 P.M. and weekends 9 A.M.–1 P.M., but hours fluctuate according to the number of visitors in town. Ask here to see the photo album that tells the story about the friendly sea lion who fell in love with Clara, a local cow, back in the 1990s.

SOUTH TO WAIHI

Hahei

Hahei, 30 km south of Whitianga, is best known for its sheltered, soft pink beach (caused by crushed shells mixed in with the sand) and dramatic headlands with two *pa* sites at the southern end. Beyond the *pa* lie two blowholes, magnificent at high tide in stormy weather. At the northern end of Hahei Beach (signposted along Grange Rd.), a two-km (45-minute) one-way walk descends to **Cathedral Cove,** where you can walk through a huge sea cavern, and a magnificent white sandy beach. The *Hahei Explorer,* tel. 07/866-3910, is an inflatable boat that cruises around local waters to Cathedral Cove, Hot Water Beach, or snorkeling spots. Trips cost from $15 pp. The local waters are popular with divers. **Cathedral Cove Sea Kayaking,** tel. 07/866-3877, charges $55 for a three-hour paddle or $95 for a full day on the water.

The small village of Hahei has a choice of accommodations, a general store, and a small café. Behind the store is **Tatahi Lodge,** tel. 07/866-3992, which offers modern backpacker rooms and a small number of self-contained units. Bikes are available for rent, guests have free use of adjacent tennis courts, and the hosts can arrange all local activities. The backpacker section is as good as you'll find anywhere in the country; beds are $17–22 pp, with a few doubles offered. Across the courtyard are modern self-contained units, furnished in a casual yet elegant "beachy" style; from $95 s or d. On the hill above town (toward Cathedral Cove) is **Spellbound,** 77 Grange Rd., tel. 07/866-3543. Each of the four comfortable rooms in this modern bed-and-breakfast enjoys ocean views and has its own bathroom. A continental breakfast is served on an outdoor deck, and dinner is available at an extra cost. Rates are $100 s, $125 d. **The Church,** 87 Hahei Beach Rd., tel. 07/866-3533, website: www.thechurchhahei.co.nz, offers accommodation in freestanding cottages set among wonderful gardens and surrounded by native bush; $105–140 s or d. As the name suggests, a church is on the property-transformed from a small-town place of worship to an upmarket restaurant that features Swiss-influenced dishes such as grilled venison ($26), as well as an equal number of lamb, pork, and seafood choices.

Hot Water Beach

If you enjoy soaking in natural hot pools, you shouldn't miss this place, south of Hahei off Hahei Beach Road. Flooded at high tide, this area is accessible for about three hours either side of low tide, when a large number of people usually take baths in the warm spring water that seeps up through the sand. Allow around 15 minutes to dig a hole in the sand below the high-tide mark, and voilá, your own private hot pool! (The deeper you dig, the warmer the water.) Follow this with an exhilarating swim in the surf and you'll feel brand new. Stay at **Hot Water Beach Motor Camp** right beside the beach, tel. 07/866-3735; it has communal facilities, four private mineral plunge pools, and a store selling all the basics. Tent sites cost $18 s or d, powered sites $20.

On the way back from Hot Water Beach, look for a sign to the left marking **Kauri Grove Walk.** This walk leads down through exotic tree ferns and native bush to a small stream, and then parallels the stream, which descends in a series of small waterfalls. Birdsong, the buzz of cicadas, and the whistling stream add to the all-around beauty. The track eventually crosses the stream and climbs into a young kauri forest. The first loop takes about 90 minutes round-trip, the track that leads to the coast is 2.5 hours one way, and the one to the coast and on to Sailor's Bay is three hours one way.

Tairua and Pauanui

Popular with vacationers, particularly in summer, the twin towns of Tairua and Pauanui are separated by a narrow tidal waterway 28 km south of Hahei. Tairua, on Hwy. 25, is the older, more established town. Reached by ferry ($2 each way) or road (from Hwy. 25 south of Tairua), Pauanui is a modern subdivision punctuated by manmade canals. Just north of Tairua, keep your eyes peeled for **Twin Kauri Scenic Reserve**—two stunning kauri trees standing side by side right next to the road (easily missed if you're coming from the north—look for the small pullout).

Attention arts and crafts fanciers and collectors! **Easterley Gallery and Garden** on Ocean Beach Rd. (off the main road to the east at the north end of town), tel. 07/864-8677, displays and sells high-quality pottery, screen-printing, basketry, painting, leathercraft, weaving, and jewelry. And don't miss a stroll along the path through the spectacular gardens. Behind the shop are fishponds surrounded by ceramic statues, more beautiful gardens, and chicken coops filled with a fancy, fluffy hens and their baby chicks (send the children here while you shop). The shop is open daily, dawn to dusk; if no one answers the bell, look around the gardens. **Johansen Guiding Adventures,** tel. 07/864-8731, is a locally-based outfit offering hiking, surfing, and 4WD tours around the Coramandel region.

Motels in Tairua are generally expensive. **Best Western Amaroo Motel,** 156 Main Rd., tel. 07/864-8520, has a garden overlooking the harbor and spacious self-contained units for $125 s or d in January, $90 the rest of the year. For the atmosphere of a tropical island, consider spending the night at **Pacific Harbour Motor Lodge,** Hwy. 25, tel. 07/864-8581, website: www.pacificharbour.co.nz, complete with palm trees and shell-lined paths. The tastefully decorated freestanding cottages are $140 s or d. The **Flying Dutchman Backpackers,** 305 Main Rd., tel. 07/864-8448, is close to Tairua restaurants. Beds are $15–18 pp, and all the usual facilities are available, as well as a pool table.

Across the water, **Puka Park Resort,** Mount Ave., Pauánui, tel. 07/864-8088, website: www.pukapark.co.nz, is one of New Zealand's most exclusive resorts. Set among 10 hectares of native bush, the 47 freestanding chalets offer the utmost in luxury, with guests taking advantage of a large outdoor pool complex, café, restaurant, and bar. Rates start at $350 s or d for a Treehut Chalet, rising to $1450 for the Royal Puka Suite. In relation to comparable resorts in North America and Europe (where most guests are from), the rates at Puka Park are very reasonable; packages advertised on the resort website make a stay even more so.

Opoutere

Continue down Hwy. 25 south of Hikuai to the turnoff to Opoutere, at Keenan's Corner. **Opoutere YHA,** four km down Opoutere Rd., tel. 07/865-9072, website: www.yha.org.nz, is ideally situated for hiking and beachcombing. Backed by native bush and edging a tidal estuary, it has the added bonus of being within a few minutes' walk of Opoutere Beach. Rates are $16–18 pp. The nearest shop is four km away, but the hostel shop sells a wide range of supplies, including vegetarian and health foods.

Continuing south from Opoutere, as you climb up Hwy. 25, look back for spectacular views of the Coromandel Range.

Whangamata

This popular holiday resort and retirement community of 3,500 lies at the southern end of a magnificent beach 38 km south of Tairua and 60 km east of Thames. Its great surf is popular with both serious surfers and swimmers who enjoy large waves. Whangamata (Faan-ga-mata) also boasts good surf fishing. For dive and fishing charter information, continue along Port Rd. to the wharf where there's an information board. **Ocean Beach,** reached via Ocean Rd. from the highway, is a long stretch of golden sand with offshore bush-covered islands—worth a drive out there whether you're going to catch it on film, work on your tan, or plunge into the Pacific.

Brenton Lodge takes in the panorama of Whangamata and the ocean from afar, two km from the beach at 1 Brenton Pl., tel. 07/865-8400; website: www.brentonlodge.co.nz. Guests stay in the main house or two garden cottages, but all enjoy fresh flowers, fresh fruit, and muffins on arrival. The grounds hold a large pool and well-tended gardens set around mature trees. Rates of $230 s, $250 d include a choice of cooked breakfasts. **Pinefield Top 10 Holiday Park,** Port Rd., tel. 07/865-8791, is only 800 meters from the beach and close to the local golf course. It has communal facilities, a TV and recreation room, and a spa. Tent and caravan sites are $24 s or d; cabins from $45 s or d; tourist flats $70–100 s or d, and as with all accommodations along this stretch of coast, rates are reduced in the off-season.

Whangamata Information Centre is on Port Rd., tel. 07/865-8340; open daily 9 A.M.–5 P.M.

Waihi and Waihi Beach

These two towns are crowded with vacationers and tourists in summer, but Waihi, inland at the junction of Highways 2 and 25, also has a colorful gold-mining history, with the rich Martha Mine still operating. **Waihi Gold Mining Museum,** on Kenny St., tel. 07/863-9880, has a model of the mine and lots of related relics. It's open Mon.–Fri. 10 A.M.–4 P.M., Sat.–Sun. 1:30–4 P.M.; admission is $2. Tours of the operating mine can be taken Mon.–Fri.; book through the museum. Other local attractions include the **Goldfields Railway** (signposted off the highway), tel. 07/863-8251; and **Waihi Arts Centre and Museum,** 54 Kenny St., tel. 07/863-8386, which is open Mon.–Fri. 10 A.M.–4 P.M., Sat.–Sun. 1:30–4 P.M. If you're into water lilies, check out **Waihi Water Lily Gardens,** Pukekauri Rd., tel. 07/863-8267. The 2.5-hectare gardens have more than 80 varieties; open Nov.–April daily 10 A.M.–4 P.M.; $5 adult, $2 child.

Waihi Beach, 11 km east of Waihi, is considered one of the safest beaches along the coast—it's patrolled in summer and on holidays by local lifesaving club members. **Waihi Beach Holiday Park,** tel. 07/863-5504, offers communal facilities, TV and game rooms, and a camp store. Tent and caravan sites are $20–24; cabins range $42–64 s or d in the holiday season (reduced in the low season).

Continuing South to the Bay of Plenty

From Waihi, it's 35 km south to **Tauranga,** with Hwy. 2 paralleling Tauranga Harbour for much of the way. Tauranga and surrounding areas are covered in the following chapter, Bay of Plenty.

HWY. 2 WEST FROM WAIHI

From Waihi, Hwy. 2 cuts back across the southern end of the Coromandel Peninsula. The first stretch of this route, to Paeroa, is quite scenic, particularly toward the Paeroa end where the highway parallels Karangahake Gorge (part of the Ohinemuri Goldfield, opened in 1875) and River, edged by large pampas grass and luxuriant tree ferns. Stop at **Karangahake Reserve** to stroll the 4.5-km **Karangahake Gorge Historic Walkway;** do the loop track or continue to Owharo Falls. The track meanders along the river, passing old bridges, abandoned mining equipment and relics, and mining shafts (stay on the track)—a walk back in time. The walkway is signposted from the highway at each end—at the Waihi end, pull off to take a short amble down through another small, incredibly lush, scenic reserve to impressive **Owharoa Falls.** Several craft shops are signposted off the highway.

Paeroa

At the western end of Karangahake Gorge, Paeroa (population 4,000) grew as an inland port and is now a bustling rural service center at the junction of Hwys. 2 and 26, 38 km west of Waihi and 32 south of Thames. The local claim to fame is Lemon and Paeroa, a soft drink that combined local mineral water and lemon. Bottled at a plant on the main street and cherished countrywide, it's no longer produced. A seven-meter-high L&P bottle, at the southern end of town, is all that's left of the legend. Of lesser fame but more interest is **Paeroa Historical Maritime Park,** three km northwest of downtown along Hwy. 2. At the site of the original port, the park is the scene of an ongoing restoration project that includes the 1897 paddlesteamer *Kopu,* rescued from a silt-laden grave in the riverbed.

Bay of Plenty

If you're hankering for a few lazy days when the only work you do is on your tan, or if you want to try your hand at various water sports (sailing and fishing are popular), this narrow coastline has plenty to offer. However, if you're short on time and crave tourist attractions, evening action, and tons of people, you may be happier heading directly for the visitors' mecca of Rotorua.

Facing due north, the magnificent crescent-shaped Bay of Plenty stretches from the Coromandel Peninsula in the west to Cape Runaway

in the east. It includes several small islands, and is backed by the Kaimai and Raukumara Ranges to the south. Captain Cook first sailed its shores in 1769; on finding several friendly and prosperous Maori villages along the coast he was able to restock badly needed provisions, prompting him to name the area the Bay of Plenty. But the bay's history long predates Cook. According to Maori legends, nine of the original 22 emigrant canoes from Hawaiiki landed in this area, and it became home for some of the strongest and most powerful Maori tribes. You can view the remains of many *pa* along its shores.

Today this aptly named bay, with its mild climate, broad sweeps of golden sand, and crystal-clear waters, attracts thousands of vacationing New Zealanders during the summer and reverts to a quiet resort

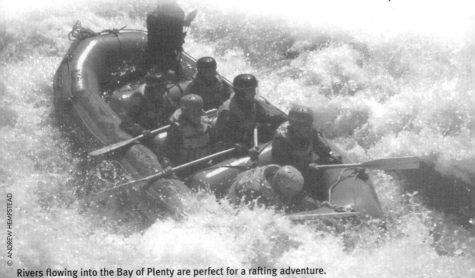

© ANDREW HEMPSTEAD

Rivers flowing into the Bay of Plenty are perfect for a rafting adventure.

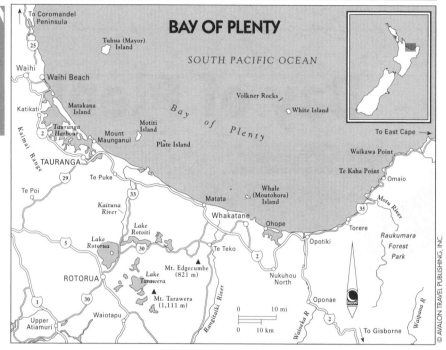

area in winter. The fertile land produces a large variety of subtropical fruit—kiwifruit, feijoas, and tamarillos—and is well known for its citrus orchards, which supply a quarter of the country's total fruit crop. You can't miss the many signs welcoming visitors to the self-proclaimed "Kiwi Coast" or "Orchard Coast." The three main towns along the coast are Tauranga, Mt. Maunganui, and Whakatane.

History

In the early 19th century, the Tauranga area was the scene of many intertribal battles between the powerful Ngapuhi tribe of Northland and the local Ngaiterangi tribe. During the 1830s the first European missionary settlement was established on the Te Papa Peninsula, and by 1839, Reverend Brown had bought the entire peninsula from the Ngaiterangi on behalf of the Church Missionary Society. A mission house, now called The Elms, was completed in 1847; this historic building, one of the oldest in New Zealand, still stands today (see below).

Many battles, both intertribal and Maori versus Pakeha (whites), were fought over land ownership. The **Battle of Gate Pa** in 1864 between British government troops and the local tribe was one of the fiercest and best-known battles in the area. Heavy fighting and great loss of life affected both sides, but the better-armed British troops eventually stamped out most resistance and confiscated the Maori land they desired. The military settlement they built on it was the beginning of modern-day Tauranga. Today, many of the local sights are memorials to these early battles, and the *pa,* redoubts, military settlements, and missions found throughout the area recall a colorful (and gory) past.

To the Bay

The three main towns—Tauranga, Mt. Maunganui, and Whakatane—are interconnected by Hwy. 2 (which continues southeast to Gisborne). Tauranga and Mt. Maunganui are also interconnected by impressive Tauranga Harbour

Bridge (toll $1). If you're driving down the coast from the Coromandel Peninsula, take Hwy. 2 south from Waihi to Tauranga. The other highways that feed the towns along the Bay are Hwy. 1, followed by Hwy. 29 from Hamilton to Tauranga, Hwy. 33 from Rotorua to Mt. Maunganui, Hwy. 30 from Rotorua to Whakatane, and Hwy. 2 from the south.

Tauranga

The city and port of Tauranga (Sheltered Anchorage) is 220 km southeast of Auckland and 88 km north of Rotorua. With a population of 60,000, it lies along a section of the large and sprawling Tauranga Harbour. Tauranga is a good place to go when you're tired of being on the road. Lots of beautiful parks and no major attractions give you the excuse to lie back and do nothing. However, if you plan to do some white-water rafting during your stay in the North Is-

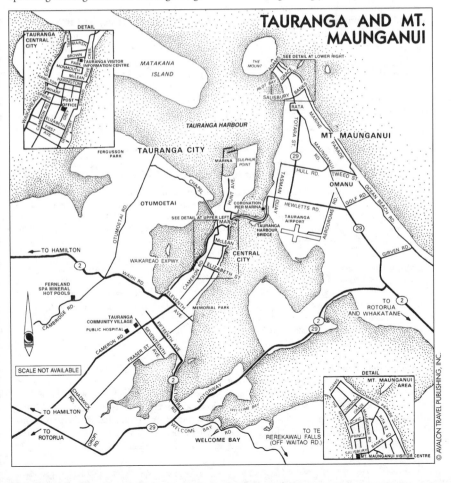

TAURANGA AND MT. MAUNGANUI

© AVALON TRAVEL PUBLISHING, INC.

land, look into the several rafting companies based in Tauranga. Unrivaled excitement on some of the North Island's most exhilarating rivers awaits the adventurous spirit, and Tauranga is a good place to investigate a variety of trips.

SIGHTS

Walking Downtown

The main shopping drag in Tauranga is **The Strand,** but you can escape the hustle and bustle of the commercial center by strolling through the **Strand Gardens** on the eastern side of the street. For an enjoyable one-hour walk back a hundred years, continue to the northern end of The Strand, where the intricately carved Maori war canoe *Te Awanui* is on display, and then follow the path up to the complex earthworks of **Monmouth Redoubt.** This area, commonly called "The Camp," was the site of the original 1864 military settlement that overlooked the bay. The oval-shaped **Robbins Park,** on the knoll between the redoubt and the cemetery, has a Be-

gonia House (open daily) and rose gardens within its grounds. For fairly graphic descriptions of Tauranga's past, check out the gravestones in the **Military Cemetery** on Cliff Road—some have quite a story to tell. **The Elms** on Mission St. (off Cliff Rd.) was the original mission house built between 1838 and 1847 by the missionary Reverend Brown. The Elms is privately owned, but the grounds are open to the public Mon.–Sat. 9 A.M.–5 P.M. Tours of the house are generally conducted daily at 2 P.M., but check with the information center on Dive Crescent, tel. 07/578-8103, for tour times.

Tauranga Community Village

This six-hectare "living" museum, on 17th Avenue W, off Cameron Rd., tel. 07/578-1302, renders a part of Tauranga's history through many working exhibits. The architecture, tools, machinery, clothing, and artifacts of previous times are displayed in an authentic, old-world village, which includes the reconstruction of a Maori meetinghouse. A visit is like stepping through a

TUHUA (MAYOR) ISLAND

If you're looking for somewhere to get away from just about everyone, 1,280-hectare Tuhua Island—40 km offshore from Tauranga—is the place for you. Privately owned but managed by a trust, Tuhua is the remnant of an ancient volcano that last erupted approximately 6,000 years ago. It's been dormant ever since, a quiet place, covered in native forest and inhabited by abundant birdlife such as bellbird, tui, kaka, and kingfisher. Surrounding crystal-clear waters are filled with marinelife and a trail leads up and over the eroded volcanic rim to two colorful lakes within the ancient crater.

Getting to the Island

The **MV** *Manutere* provides island transfers out of Tauranga and Mt. Maunganui three to four times a week late December to mid-January, departing Coronation Pier in Tauranga at 7 A.M. and Salisbury Wharf in Mt. Maunganui at 7:30 A.M. If you're

doing the round-trip in one day, the fare is $60 adult, $40 child; if you're stopping on the island overnight, the fare is $70 adult, $50 child. There's a booking office on Coronation Pier, tel. 07/578-9685, or book through the Tauranga Visitor Information Centre, tel. 07/571-3211. The rest of the year, weather permitting, you can get to the island via one of the many charter boat operators (inquire at the information center), but expect much higher prices. As the island is privately owned, all visitors are charged a landing fee of $10, payable on arrival.

Camping

You'll find a campground (the only place to stay on the island) at **Opo Bay,** in a sheltered area behind a beach. Facilities include a cooking shelter, toilets, and showers. Tent sites are $6 pp, dorm beds in small cabins are $14 pp, and two-berth self-contained units are $20 pp.

time machine to see the lifestyles of early New Zealanders. It's open daily 9 A.M.–5 P.M.; $8 adult, $4 child. It also offers vintage vehicle rides for a couple of bucks.

Winery

Wet your whistle at **Prestons Kiwifruit Winery** on Belk Rd., tel. 07/576-8800. This winery offers free tastings, kiwifruit products, winery tours, and wholesale prices (wine from $9, liqueur $24); it's open weekdays 10 A.M.–4:30 P.M. (and Saturday in summer). From Tauranga take Cameron Rd. to Hwy. 29 and turn right toward Hamilton. Continue for about 7.5 km, then turn left on Belk Rd. for another three kilometers.

RECREATION

Hot Pools

You have five hot pools to choose from in the area. The bores at Tauranga are the source of internationally known Fernland Sparkling Mineral Water, but if you'd rather immerse yourself in it than drink it, head for **Fernland Spa Mineral Hot Pools** in the Tauranga suburb of Te Reti, 250 Cambridge Rd. near the rose gardens, tel. 07/578-3081. The water (38–40°C) is pumped daily from 200 meters beneath the ground into the main public pool and eight large private pools. It's open daily 10 A.M.–10 P.M.; $6 adult, $3 child. From downtown (about six km from the postoffice) follow Cameron St. to 11th Ave. and turn right; 11th becomes Waihi Road. Continue along Waihi, then turn left onto Cambridge Road.

Te Rerekawau Falls

At the bottom of a fairly steep track through native bush you'll find three beautiful waterfalls (formerly called Kaiate Falls), the third plummeting into a very deep, bush-fringed pool and popular (icy cold!) swimming hole. It's a great place for photographers in search of slow-speed water shots. You'll need a car to get to these falls, but keep all valuables locked out of sight or with you. Take Hwy. 2 out of Tauranga toward Mt. Maunganui, but turn right toward Welcome Bay before crossing the harbor. Continue along Welcome Bay Road, and just after the bay turn right on Waitao Road—the falls are signposted from here.

Rafting

The internationally known Wairoa River is the highest graded and perhaps most popular river in the country for commercial rafting because of its two steep, grade-five rapids, 4.5-meter waterfall, and "roller coaster." **Woodrow Rafting,** tel. 07/577-0817, offers everything from a 90-minute trip on the Wairoa to a three-day trip on the Motu and provides wet suits, life jackets, and helmets. Woodrow also rafts the Mohaka, Rangitaiki, and Rangitikei Rivers—it can arrange just about anything. Call for current prices. Drop by the information center to pick up other rafting brochures and to compare prices.

Bird's-Eye View

An exhilarating way to get high in this area is to head for Tauranga Airport. It's directly across the harbor from downtown Tauranga on the Mt. Maunganui peninsula. **Tauranga Aero Club,** tel. 07/575-3210, operates scenic flights of varying lengths starting at about $50 pp, and if you're lucky, you'll have the chance to watch some great skydiving action. **Tauranga Gliding Club,** tel. 07/575-6768, will take you silently soaring on an introductory flight (lasting about 10–15 minutes, weather permitting) for $45 pp, weekends only. This worthwhile experience is a wonderful way to appreciate the beauty of the Bay of Plenty and to get oriented, but be warned: It may addict you to the sport of gliding.

Entertainment

There's not much in the way of entertainment in Tauranga other than bands playing in the local pubs on Friday and Saturday nights. The always-lively **Grumpy Mole Saloon,** 41 The Strand, tel. 07/571-1222, is a popular dance venue for the younger crowd. **Hotel St. Amand,** also on The Strand, tel. 07/579-4066, hosts live musical entertainment most nights till 1 A.M. It also has a quieter lounge bar. **Harrington's,** 10 Harrington St., tel. 07/578-5427, is a nightclub with bands on Friday and Saturday nights. Anyone with any kind of musical taste should head out to **Te Puna Tavern,** on Minden Rd., tel. 07/552-5705, for live country music every weekend. Find out what's on in the local newspaper or tourist papers, or drop by the information center.

ACCOMMODATIONS

Hotels and Motels

The **Strand Motel,** 27 The Strand, tel. 07/578-5807, website: www.strandmotel.co.nz, is an old motel, but it's centrally located and a good value at $75 s, $90 d in summer. It's within easy walking distance of everything, each unit has a kitchen, and the four upstairs rooms enjoy water views. **Harbour View Motel,** 7 Fifth Ave., tel. 07/578-8621, is right on the water in a quiet location 800 meters south of downtown. Each room has a kitchen and tea- and coffee-making facilities. Rates are $75 s, $85 d. A step up in quality, but still close to downtown and with a waterfront location, is **Tauranga Motel on Second Avenue,** 1 2nd Ave., tel. 07/578-7079 or 0800/109-007. Rates range $95–145 for the 26 rooms, each with a kitchen.

Many motels can be found on or near Cameron St., which runs the length of the peninsula upon which Tauranga lies. The least expensive of these is **Domain Motel,** 41 Monmouth St., tel. 07/578-9479, which charges $75 s or d for a small room with painted concrete walls and a kitchen. Continuing south is **Academy Motor Inn,** 734 Cameron St. (at 15th Ave.), tel. 07/578-9103 or 0800/782-9222, website: www.academymotorinn.co.nz, with 20 self-contained units featuring many nice touches, such as hairdryers. The complex includes a swimming pool, spa pool, and barbecue area. Rates are $110 s or d for a standard unit, $145 s or d with a kitchen. Farther along, five km from downtown, is **Cameron Road Motel,** 1229 Cameron Rd., tel. 07/578-2859 or 0508/500-777, featuring eight well-maintained rooms set around a thermally heated pool; $95 s, $105 d.

Backpacker Lodges

Tauranga YHA, 171 Elizabeth St., tel. 07/578-5064, provides modern budget accommodation within walking distance of downtown. It has the usual communal facilities, nearby waterside walking tracks, a variety of outside games, and a barbecue, all from $17–22 pp per night. **Bell Lodge,** 39 Bell St. (3.5 km from city center), tel. 07/578-6344, has excellent budget accommodations—heated bunkrooms with comfortable beds for $18 pp, private rooms for $38 s, $48 d—plus a fully equipped communal kitchen, a spacious dining room and TV area, a guest lounge, and a coin-op laundry. Across Waikareao Estuary from downtown is **Just the Ducks Nuts,** 6 Vale St., tel. 07/576-1366, a small backpackers with dorms for $20 pp, and doubles for $44.

Motor Camps

Waterfront **Mayfair Holiday Park,** five km south of downtown on Mayfair St. (off 15th Ave.), tel. 07/578-3323, offers tent and caravan sites and limited communal facilities; $11 pp. Cabins are $35–55 s or d and the tourist flat is $65. Almost right next door, **Silver Birch Thermal Holiday Park,** 101 Turret Rd. (extension of 15th Ave.) also enjoys a quiet waterfront location. In addition to better facilities than the Mayfair, it has a TV and game room, a boat ramp, use of mineral swimming pools, and a store stocking all the basic necessities. Tent and caravan sites are $12 pp; cabins cost from $40; tourist flats with private facilities cost from $55 s or d; motel rooms are $60 s, $75 d.

Away from the water, **Palms Holiday Park,** 162 Waihi Rd. (signposted from 11th Ave.), tel. 07/578-9337, three km west from downtown, has a park setting with modern facilities. Regular campsites are $12 pp, or enjoy the privacy of an en suite bathroom for an additional $2.50 pp. Cabins are $35 s or d, tourist flats $55.

Away from the city bustle, **Plummer's Point Caravan Park,** 19 km north of Tauranga (up Hwy. 2) on Plummer's Point Rd., Omokoroa, tel. 07/548-0669, has communal facilities, a TV and game room, a shop, a boat ramp, free use of the thermal mineral pool, and a safe swimming beach nearby. Tent and caravan sites are $12 pp, and some on-site caravans are available for $40 s or d.

FOOD

Many cafés and restaurants can be found around the corner of The Strand and Wharf St., the heart of downtown, which has been given a new look in recent years. There are cobbled sidewalks complete with flowerbeds and old-fashioned lampposts, creating the perfect atmosphere for outdoor dining. **Sunrise Natural Food Cafe,** 10 Wharf St., tel. 07/578-9302, takes advantage of this environment, with lots of outdoor tables. As the name suggests, the food is all healthy, with hot dishes and salads, combination sandwiches, healthy cakes and desserts, and a large variety of teas. It's open Mon.–Fri. 8 A.M.–4 P.M., and Saturday 10 A.M.–1:30 P.M. Just past the roundabout, the **Crowded Muffin,** 22 Devonport Rd., tel. 07/578-9285, is a good place for a quick bite to eat.

Away from the waterfront, Cameron Road also holds many eateries. The pick of the bunch is **Sirens,** 801 Cameron Rd., tel. 07/578-5857, a deli-style café serving bagels, croissants, and French bread with your choice of healthy fillings (the smoked salmon and avocado was unbeatable; $6.50). Join the crowd at the tables up front, or gravitate to the back for some peace and quiet.

Seafood

North along The Strand are a wide variety of options, but on a sunny day it's hard to go past the **Fresh Fish Market,** Dive Crescent, tel. 07/578-1789. Right on the dock, surrounded by fishing boats, the market offers all types of fresh and cooked fish. Fish and chips costs about $6. It has a couple of tables, or wander along the wharf and enjoy your meal with the seagulls. **Fish Crazee,** 87 The Strand, tel. 07/577-9375, is another great fish-and-chip joint.

For seafood without the seagulls, it's hard to beat **Harbourside,** on The Stand Extension (south along the waterfront), tel. 07/571-0520. Built

over the water as a yacht club in 1933, the original structure has been converted to a fine restaurant, losing none of its nautical charm along the way. Most tables enjoy harbor views, but the very best sit along a covered verandah. In addition to lots of seafood (including the delicious Harbourside Bouillabasse; $27.50), the menu features a variety of light pastas and salads for under $20.

Other Restaurants

In the Hotel St. Amand, The Strand, tel. 07/578-8127, there's an attractive family restaurant and bar (access from hotel lobby) with a comfortable atmosphere. Expect to pay $14–18 for a main course such as grilled rump steak with chips and salad. It's open daily for lunch and dinner. You'll find similar fare and atmosphere at the local **Cobb & Co.** in the Greerton Motor Inn, 1237 Cameron Rd., tel. 07/578-8164. This popular restaurant (entrees $10–15, good salad bar) and bar features live entertainment most nights, and even holds a children's talent quest on Sunday nights, and a jazz night (no cover charge) on Tuesday at 8 P.M. It's open seven days a week 7:30 A.M.–10 P.M.

More of a restaurant than café, **Shiraz Café,** 12 Wharf St., tel. 07/577-0059, has a great little courtyard, complete with vine-covered stone walls. Main courses from the Mediterranean-inspired menu average $18. Across the road, **Shima,** 15 Wharf St., tel. 07/571-1382, is one of the growing number of Japanese restaurants found in small-town New Zealand. **Amphora Café,** 43 The Strand, tel. 07/578-1616, is a stylish pizza place open for dinner only; from $18 for a medium pizza.

TRANSPORTATION

Getting There

If you're short on time but long on coin, **Air New Zealand** has direct flights to Tauranga from Auckland and Wellington. The airport is on the Mt. Maunganui side of the city, off Hewletts Road. **Tauranga Taxis,** tel. 07/578-6086, has a door-to-door shuttle to either town from the airport for $10 pp. Air New Zealand has an office at the corner of Devonport Rd. and Elizabeth St., tel. 07/577-7300.

Intercity coaches connect Tauranga with Auckland, Thames, Hamilton, Rotorua, Whakatane, Opotiki, Gisborne, and just about anywhere you want to go. The depot is the Tauranga Visitor Information Centre, 97 Willow St., tel. 07/578-8103.

Getting Around

Bayline, tel. 07/578-3113, runs a local bus service through all the suburbs and to Mt. Maunganui. A more pleasant way to travel between the twin towns is by ferry from the end of Wharf St. (summer only).

Car rental agencies with an office in Tauranga include Avis, tel. 07/578-4204; Budget, tel. 07/578-5156; Hertz, tel. 07/578-9143; and Rent-a-dent, tel. 07/578-1772.

For regular taxi rides or sight-seeing tours, call Tauranga Taxis, tel. 07/578-6086, or Citicabs, tel. 07/577-0999.

SERVICES AND INFORMATION

The post office is at 17 Grey Street. You can reach Tauranga Hospital on Cameron Rd. at 07/579-8000. Mainland Unichem Pharmacy is downtown at 27 Devonport Rd., tel. 07/578-9409.

The first place to head for information on Tauranga and Mt. Maunganui is the Tauranga Visitor Information, one block north of The Strand at 97 Willow St., tel. 07/571-3211. Part of the long-distance bus depot, it has brochures and tourist newspapers, and also gives out information and takes booking for the boat ride to Tuhua Island on the MV *Manutere.* It's open in summer, daily 7 A.M.–5:30 P.M., the rest of the year, Mon.–Fri. 8 A.M.–4 P.M. For information on Kaimai Mamaku Forest Park, drop by the DOC Tauranga Area Office, 253 Chadwick Rd., Greerton, tel. 07/tel. 07/578-7677. The Automobile Association has an office at the corner of Devonport Rd. and 1st Ave., tel. 07/578-2222.

Mount Maunganui

Known for its wonderful surf beach and mellow vacation atmosphere, Mount Maunganui (population 15,000) is busiest through summer when it attracts thousands of domestic vacationers to its sunny shores. It's also an important port for the growing North Island timber industry. It's just across the water from Tauranga via Tauranga Harbour Bridge (toll $1 per car). The 234-meter cone-shaped mountain (The Mount) that overshadows the town was originally an island, and the narrow sandbar that built up between the island and the mainland became the site of modern-day Mt. Maunganui. The locals often affectionately call their city "The Mount," or just "Mount."

SIGHTS AND RECREATION
The Mount

Just by looking at its classically conical shape you can see how The Mount made an impressive Maori *pa* in the 18th and 19th centuries. You can still see the old fortifications, particularly on

the southeastern side. Several tracks lead to the top of this volcanic peak, and the climb (50 minutes one way) rewards your effort with a magnificent, 360-degree, panoramic view. An easier track circles the base of the mountain; it takes about an hour to complete the circular route. A race to the top is held annually on the Saturday between Christmas and New Year's Day and the record is about 20 minutes.

Hot Saltwater Pools

Unique hot saltwater pools found at the foot of The Mount are the only ones of their kind in the Southern Hemisphere. The saltwater comes from a 40-meter-deep bore, and when the water is first brought up from underground it's a sizzling 45°C! Cooled to a still-hot 39° before being pumped into the large main pool and several (hotter) smaller pools, it's a great place to soothe aching muscles and tired feet. You can rent bathing suits and towels at the complex, open daily 6 A.M.–10 P.M. (Sunday from 8 A.M.). You'll find it off Adams Ave., tel. 07/575-0868; $4 adult, $2 child; private pools $6 adult, $4 child for 30 minutes.

Beaches

The most popular beach in this area is **Ocean Beach.** The golden sands and sparkling surf stretch for about 15 km and can be reached from Marine Parade on the eastern side of Mt. Maunganui, and from Papamoa Beach. Additionally, small, sheltered harbor beaches run along Pilot Bay, ending at Salisbury Wharf on the western side of town.

Swimming with Dolpins

Dolphin Seafaris, based at the marina near Tauranga Harbour Bridge but providing pickups from Coronation Pier, Tauranga, tel. 07/575-4620 or 0800/326-8747, departs daily at 8 A.M. in search of dolphins. Once a pod has been found, you slip off the back of the boat and spend up to an hour in the water with these magnificent creatures. The cost is $100 pp including a wet suit, mask, fins, and snorkel.

ACCOMMODATIONS

Hotels and Motels

Motel accommodation around The Mount is relatively expensive, especially in summer. One of the cheapest is the ever-popular **Blue Haven Motel,** 10 Tweed St., tel. 07/575-6508. A flat 10-minute walk from the beach, each unit features a full kitchen; rates from $85 s, $90 d for a studio unit.

Near the beachfront are a couple of luxurious accommodations. The best value of these is **Pacific Motor Inn,** 261 Maunganui Rd., tel. 07/575-7525 or 0800/556-699. It comprises 17 extra-large rooms, each with a kitchen and many with a spa bath; $125–185 s or d. Right below The Mount and 200 meters from the beach lies **Ocean Sands Motel,** 6 Maunganui Rd., tel. 07/574-9794 or 0800/726-371. With a striking blue and white interior and vaulted timber ceiling, each of its spacious units is fully self-contained. Studios are $180 s or d, while larger units with separate bedrooms range $210–260 s or d.

Backpacker Lodges

Mount Backpackers, 87 Maunganui Rd., tel. 07/575-0860, is right along the main palm-fringed shopping strip. The kitchen, lounge, and bathroom facilities are of the highest standard, and pickups from Tauranga are complimentary; dorm beds are $18, doubles $24.50 pp. A few blocks east is **Pacific Coast Lodge,** 432 Maunganui Rd., tel. 07/574-9601 or 0800/666-622, website: www.pacificcoastlodge.co.nz, featuring modern communal facilities, a game room, and a barbecue area. Dorm beds are $20 pp, doubles and twins are $23 pp, and the two single rooms are $35 each. If you're planning a trip with Dolphin Seafaris, this place offers a great package deal.

Motor Camps

Mount Maunganui Domain Motor Camp, 1 Adams Ave., tel. 07/575-4471, offers terrific sites around the hot-water pools at the base of The Mount and on both ocean and harbor beaches. They have communal facilities and free showers; tent and caravan sites cost from $22 s or d.

Cosy Corner Motor Camp, four km east of The Mount at 40 Ocean Beach Rd. (a continuation of Marine Parade), tel. 07/575-5899, offers communal facilities, a pool table, and a swimming pool, and is adjacent to the beach at Omanu. Tent and caravan sites are $11 pp; on-site caravans and cabins are $42–48 s or d. Continuing east, **Papamoa Beach Top 10 Holiday Resort,** 535 Papamoa Beach Rd., tel. 07/542-0816 or 0800/572-0816, is farther away from the tourist bustle, 13 km southeast of town, and offers communal facilities, camp store, TV and game rooms, and private spa pools (extra charge). Tent and caravans sites cost $12–13 pp, cabins are $48 s or d, and self-contained beachfront villas are $120–150 s or d.

OTHER PRACTICALITIES

Food

The usual coffee shops and lounges are scattered throughout downtown, but if you're looking for a health food shop, call in at **Harvest Health Foods,** 102 Maunganui Rd., tel. 07/575-6237— it makes great muesli (or granola) fresh daily.

For homemade baked goods to enjoy inside or outside in the sunshine, try **The Cottage Cafe,** 373 Maunganui Rd., tel. 07/575-3733. It's open every day and specializes in breakfast. **Downtown Hot Bread Shop,** 83 Maunganui Rd., tel. 07/575-3186, serves a good selection of sandwiches, meat and salad rolls, pies, pastries, and cakes to take away.

Perhaps the most enjoyable restaurants are those along Marine Parade, but be forewarned, you pay for the great beach views. **Sandrock Cafe,** 4 Marine Parade (at the base of Mt. Maunganui), tel. 07/574-7554, is a contemporary bistro featuring hardwood *rimu* floors and stylish timber and chrome furniture. The elevated deck allows for ocean views. It offers a menu featuring mostly seafood and steak; it's open for lunch weekdays noon–2 P.M. and dinner from 6 P.M.; dinners range $18–27.

> *Te Puke, nestled in the middle of a large kiwifruit growing area, claims to be "Kiwi Fruit Capital of the World."*

Transportation

Mt. Maunganui is linked to Tauranga by a toll bridge ($1) and a daily bus service, tel. 07/578-3113, but the most enjoyable way to travel between the two is by ferry. This summer-only service departs regularly from the end of Wharf Rd., Tauranga, for The Mount (15 minutes; $5 each way). For **Mount Maunganui Taxi-Cabs,** call 07/575-4054.

Services and Information

The **post office** is at the back of an arcade, one shop from the BNZ Bank on the main street before you reach The Mount. **Mount Medical Centre** is at 257 Maunganui Rd., tel. 07/575-3073.

Get more information from **Mount Maunganui Visitor Information Centre** on Salisbury Ave., near the old ferry wharf, tel. 07/575-5099; it's open weekdays 8:30 A.M.–4 P.M., Saturday and public holidays 9 A.M.–1 P.M., and daily from December 26 to the end of January.

TE PUKE

The largest town between Tauranga/Mt. Maunganui and Whakatane is Te Puke (population 6,200), 20 km from Tauranga along Hwy. 2. The town, nestled in the middle of a large kiwifruit growing area, claims to be "Kiwi Fruit Capital of the World." **Kiwifruit Country,** tel. 07/573-6340, six km through town to the east, is a horticultural theme park in a working orchard. Admission to the park (adult $10, child $5) includes a ride on a kiwifruit-shaped trailer through the orchard, a tour of the packaging plant, and fruit-tasting and wine-tasting. It's open daily 9 A.M.–5 P.M. Next door is **Te Puke Vintage Auto Barn,** tel. 07/573-6547, open Tues.–Sun. 9 A.M.–5 P.M.; 25 vintage vehicles, all in working order, are on display. Southeast of Te Puke (Hwy. 33 to Rotorua), **Longridge Park,** tel. 07/533-1515, is the starting point for an exciting 25-km jetboat trip up the Kaituna River; adult $59, child $35. The park is really a working farm; avocado, venison, and honey are its main yield. Tours cost adult $12, child $6.

Te Puke has a motor camp, tel. 07/573-9866, two motels, and a number of restaurants. **Te Puke Information Centre** is at 72 Jellicoe St., tel. 07/573-9172.

Whakatane

Go to Whakatane (fah-kah-tah-nee), around the Bay of Plenty 100 km southeast of Tauranga, to enjoy the sunshine, the beaches, and the relaxed atmosphere; raft down the Rangitaiki River, or go flightseeing over White Island, an active volcano. It's also the closest large town north of Te Urewera National Park and serves as a good quiet place in winter to rest up after strenuous hiking in the park (as an alternative to year-round crowded Rotorua). But in summer Whakatane tends to become crowded with sun-seeking vacationers.

SIGHTS AND RECREATION
Sights
When you're downtown, don't miss the impressive **Wairere Waterfall** behind the Commercial Hotel, Mataatua Street. **Whakatane District Museum,** on Boon St., tel. 07/307-9805, contains displays of Maori artifacts and the lifestyles of early Maori and European settlers, a history of the district through black-and-white photos, and a New Zealand book collection. It's open Tues.–Fri. 10 A.M.–4:30 P.M., Saturday 11 A.M.–1:30 P.M., Sunday 2–4:30 P.M.; admission $1 adult, $.50 child.

One of the most relaxing things to do around here on a sunny day is to buy some food and drink, then drive along The Strand to The Heads, where the river meets the sea. Enjoy your meal and the view (fishing boats, leisure boats, statue of a mermaid, seagulls) from the grassy banks or from more secluded sandy spots among the rocks.

Another interesting place well worth a visit is **Tauwhare Pa,** which is beside the highway from Ohope to Opotiki (just past the harbor). Interpretive boards along a short walkway explain how the reserve may have appeared and operated in A.D. 1700 (when most Bay of Plenty *pa* were built).

Hiking
Whakatane and the surrounding area have a reputation for very enjoyable local walkways, scenic

reserves, and an island wildlife sanctuary. Ask at the information bureau for the helpful (and free) handouts on **Kohi Point Walkway, Whakatane Town Centre Walk, Ohope Bush Walk** (which allows hikers to walk through beautiful bush scenery from Ohope Beach to Whakatane via Ohope and Mokorua Scenic Reserves), **Lathams Hill Track, Matata Walking Track,** and **Matata Lagoon Walk** (you can see fantastic birdlife from an observation platform). **Pine Bush Scenic Reserve** allows people with disabilities to enjoy a small remnant of *kahikatea* forest and plenty of birdlife via a wheelchair walkway.

Swimming with Dolphins
Dolphins are among the most loved of all marine mammals, and you shouldn't miss the opportunity to frolic in the open ocean with these fun-loving creatures. **Dolphins Down Under** offers a five- to six-hour trip out into the Bay of Plenty. During the trip you can swim with dolphins, possibly see whales (if you're lucky), and snorkel in the fish-filled waters around White Island. The cost is $135 pp ($100 without the White Island option), or go as a spectator for slightly less. For bookings drop by the Dolphins Down Under shop at 2 The Strand, tel. 07/308-4636 or 0800/354-773.

Other Water-based Recreation
The best-known surf beach, **Ohope Beach,** only six km from Whakatane, attracts surfers and fishermen year-round, holidaymakers by the hordes in summer, and hikers in search of great coastal views. Visit the harbor at the end of Ohope Beach for safe swimming, good windsurfing, fishing, and shell fishing. If you're looking for on-the-water action, call in at the information center to find out who offers fishing trips (usually starting at $70 pp per day). Or go for an exciting jetboat trip up the Whakatane River for $75 pp, or from Matahina Dam up the Rangitaiki River to Aniwhenua Falls for $80. Bookings are essential at tel. 07/307-0663. For a white-water rafting trip on the Wairoa, Rangitaiki, Whirinaki, or

Motu Rivers (from about $75 pp to $580 for a four-day trip), call **Whakatane Raft Tours** at 07/308-7760.

OFFSHORE ISLANDS
White Island

White Island lies about 50 km north of Whakatane, at the northern end of the Taupo-Rotorua volcanic fault line. This is an excellent active volcano to visit because of its intense thermal activity. Originally named by Capt. Cook in 1769 for the shroud of steam surrounding it, the island continues to belch steam, noxious gases, and toxic fumes into the atmosphere. Occasional eruptions send up huge clouds of ash visible from the mainland, weather permitting. Geysers, fumaroles, holes of sulfuric acid, and boiling-water pools lie within the crater, best enjoyed from a safe distance—like from the sky!

Geysers, fumaroles, holes of sulfuric acid, and boiling-water pools lie within the crater, best enjoyed from a safe distance—like from the sky!

Sulphur was mined on the island until an explosive landslide in 1914 killed all the miners and wiped out the mining settlement. Miners made several other mining attempts, but because of the unpredictable and violent nature of the island, abandoned all. Despite the lack of fresh water and the presence of toxic fumes, parts of the island are covered by *pohutukawa* trees and inhabited by quite a variety of birdlife. Gannets, red-billed gulls, and petrels seem to thrive in this strange environment and have made their breeding grounds on the island, now a private scenic reserve.

PeeJay Charters (White Island Tours) operates regular island cruises from their base at Whakatane Wharf, Quay St., tel. 07/308-9588 or 0800/733-529. Departing at 8:30 A.M., the trip out to the island takes around 80 minutes in their stable 20-meter vessel. Around two hours is spent exploring the island, time enough to walk inside the crater. Lunch is included in the tour rate of $105 pp. You can also visit the island by helicopter. **Vulcan Helicopters,** tel. 07/308-4188 or 0800/804-354, charges $375 pp (minimum four) for the return transfer and a one-hour guided walk. Departures are on demand from Whakatane Airport.

Whale Island

Smaller Whale Island (Moutohara) lies just 10 km off the coast, but is less accessible than its more famous neighbor. A wildlife sanctuary since 1965, this 143-hecatre island is also volcanic in origin. Its profile is dominated by eroded twin peaks rising 350 meters above sea level. Although there is no obvious volcanic activity, hot springs bubble up out of the ground at Sulphur Bay. Birdlife present includes a breeding colony of grey-faced petrels, sooty shearwaters, saddlebacks, little blue penguins, and the threatened New Zealand dotterel and Caspian tern.

Access is with the Department of Conservation on a guided tour. Trips depart at 8:30 A.M. from the weigh-in wharf at Whakatane Heads on four specific dates in January; $55 adult, $40 child. Tickets have to be booked and prepaid before the sailing date at the DOC office at 236 The Strand, tel. 07/308-7213.

ACCOMMODATIONS
Hotels and Motels

In a prime location across from Whakatane Wharf, **White Island Rendezvous,** 15 The Strand, tel. 07/308-9588, is an excellent choice for an overnight stay in Whakatane. Home to PeeJay Charters (see White Island, above), this accommodation comprises 24 charming units, each with a microwave and some with small kitchens. Although a little on the small side, the rooms provide good value at $80–150 s or d.

The **New Commercial Hotel,** The Strand, tel. 07/308-7399, has standard rooms with shared bathrooms for $45 s, $55 d, but it gets noisy downstairs on the weekend. Rooms at the **Whakatane Hotel,** The Strand, tel. 07/307-1670, aren't any better, but are quieter; rates $40 s, $50 d. Both have dorm beds for $20 pp. The

Bay Hotel Units, 90 McAllister St., tel. 07/308-6788, have five renovated rooms, with breakfast available for an extra cost; from $50 s, $60 d.

On the road into town from Tauranga (just east of the Whakatane River), **Camellia Court Motel,** 11 Domain Rd., tel. 07/308-6213, website: www.camelliacourt.co.nz, is a federation-style motel with 12 rooms overlooking gardens. Each room has a kitchen, and there's a barbecue area for those balmy summer evenings. Rates are $75 s, $83 d. If you're looking for a nice hotel with the convenience of in-house dining, try the nearby Tudor-style **Manor Inn,** 34 Domain Rd. (by McAllister St.), tel. 07/307-0600 or 0800/806-682. Features include a swimming pool, two spa pools (some of the units have their own spa), a sauna, and a barbecue. Rates start at $105 s, $115 d. Continuing west one km, **Pacific Coast Motor Lodge,** 41 Landing Rd., tel. 07/308-0100 or 0800/224-430, has 14 large self-contained units. Standard rooms are $115 s or d, and those with spa baths are $145.

Backpacker Lodges

On The Strand, both hotels have dorm beds, but the best option for budget travelers is to continue east from Whakatane to Opotiki, which has two good backpacker lodges.

Motor Camps

Whakatane Motor Camp and Caravan Park on McGarvey Rd., tel. 07/308-8694, offers the usual communal facilities, a TV lounge and game room, a swimming pool, and a hot spa pool (charge). Grassy tent and caravan sites are $20 s or d, cabins $35–40 s or d.

If you're going on toward Rotorua you may enjoy staying at **Awakeri Hot Springs Holiday Park.** About 16 km from Whakatane on Hwy. 30 to Rotorua (tel. 07/304-9117), it has the usual motor camp facilities but the added plus of warm mineral swim baths and hot mineral spa pools (extra charge). Tent and caravan sites are $20; cabins with kitchen are $50 s or d; tourist flats are $70 s or d.

OTHER PRACTICALITIES

Food

Kick start your day down along the waterfront at PeeJay's Coffee House, The Strand, tel. 07/308-9500. It's open daily 6:30 A.M.–6 P.M. for cooked breakfasts and light lunches. The **Bean Coffee Roastery,** 54 The Strand, tel. 07/307-0494, is another option for a light meal and good coffee. The **New Commercial Hotel,** The Strand, tel. 07/308-7399, has bar meals from $7, with roasts on Sunday. You can eat in the bar or restaurant. **Wedgewood Cafe,** 159 The Strand, tel. 07/308-8548, serves inexpensive, good-value family-style meals (lunch $5–10, dinner $12–15.50). **Barnacles Sea Food Restaurant,** 122 The Strand, tel. 07/308-7429, is a great place for fish and chips—it's surrounded by seafaring relics such as fish nets, buoys, and the like. Fish of the Day is about $16 at dinner, with many other choices, much of it from local waters.

Transportation

Whakatane Airport (intriguing architecture!) is on Aerodrome Rd. about 10 km north of town; if you don't have your own transportation, you can take a taxi (about $20 one way). **Air New Zealand,** tel. 07/308-8397, flies from Whakatane to Auckland and Wellington, with connections to other North Island centers. **Intercity** connects Whakatane with Tauranga, Rotorua, and Gisborne via Opotiki. Buses stop on Boon Street.

Hertz is at 105 Commerce St., tel. 07/308-6155. You can reach **Budget** at tel. 07/308-6399. For a cab, call **Whakatane Taxi,** tel. 07/307-0388.

Information

For more information on Whakatane, call in at the **Whakatane Information Bureau** on Boon St. (signposted off The Strand), tel. 07/308-6058; it's open Mon.–Fri. 9:30 A.M.–5 P.M., and Dec.–Feb. seven days a week. The DOC **Whakatane Field Centre** is in the Council Building at 236 The Strand, tel. 07/308-7213.

* **Rotorua**

Introduction

The resort city of Rotorua (Ro-to-roo-ah), 200 km south of Auckland, bubbles with thermal activity. All sorts of natural attractions abound throughout the region, but the best-known features are spectacular geysers, steaming cliffs, hot springs spurting from the ground, bubbling pools of boiling mud, and soothing mineral hot pools. Steam seems to waft out of every drain, crack in the pavement, and hole in the ground, and the ever-present but soon-unnoticed smell of rotten-egg gas (hydrogen sulfide) permeates the atmosphere for many kilometers in all directions. (You often hear people calling this area "Rottenrua," but this isn't wise when locals are within earshot!)

Rotorua (population 57,000) exists only because of tourism; this makes the city expensive if you plan to visit all the major attractions. However, some of the natural attractions are still free and, despite the year-round crowds, the unpredictable and volatile atmosphere seemingly seeping up

from beneath your feet sets Rotorua apart—it's one of the exceptional areas of New Zealand that shouldn't be missed. Rotorua is also an ideal base for exploring the surrounding area with its contrasting natural features: magnificent bush-fringed lakes, icy-cold springs, crystal-clear trout streams, and mighty forests. The Rotorua region is also a center of Maori culture, with a great deal of New Zealand native art, architecture, song and dance, and colorful evening entertainment to offer.

History

The Rotorua region, originally a wild and swampy wasteland dotted with steaming pools and mud holes, has been inhabited by Maori since the 14th century. The Maori had been using the healing properties of the mineral hot pools for 500 years before Europeans recognized their benefits in the late 1870s. The original Maori landowners gave 50 acres of land containing the "healing springs" as a gift to British government representatives, and the early township of Rotorua was built here. The Government Garden Reserve developed

Rotorua Bath House

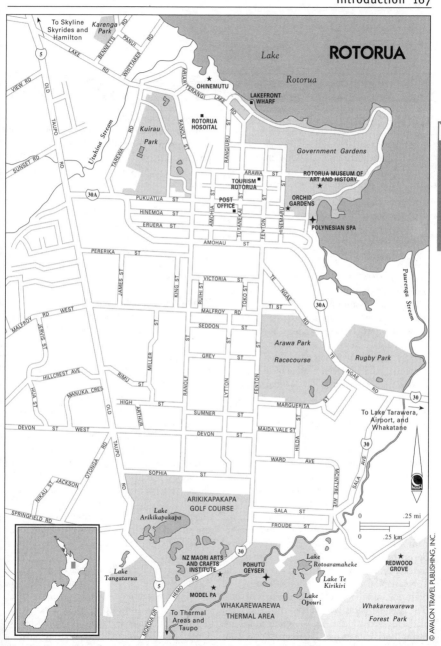

ROTORUA

© AVALON TRAVEL PUBLISHING, INC.

into a fashionable spa resort and sanitarium, where victims of the mighty Mt. Tarawera eruption of 1886 were treated. In addition to the area's healing qualities, its recreational value prompted rapid development into a tourist attraction.

Sights

GEOTHERMAL

Rotorua is situated about midway along a volcanic fault line that runs from White Island in the Bay of Plenty to Mt. Ruapehu in Tongariro National Park. The most active thermal areas have been developed in the name of tourism, and these are safe as long as you stay on the well-defined footpaths (hold onto the kids at all times). More commercial thermal areas other than those listed below lie south of Rotorua on the main road to Taupo, and north off Hwy. 30 to Whakatane. Only a couple of the less spectacular hot spots around town have not been commercialized and are still free—in Government Gardens near Polynesian Spa, and at Ohinemutu along the shores of Lake Rotorua. Some of Rotorua's natural thermal energy has been tapped through artesian-type bores and other methods for central- and hot-water heating by local hotels, motels, and some homes. The Maori continue to use it for cooking and heating as they have done for centuries, and you can see some of their methods at Whakarewarewa (see below).

Polynesian Spa

Polynesian Spa, on Hinemoa St. by Government Gardens, tel. 07/348-1328, is on the site of the first public bathhouse built in Government Gardens (see below) in the 1880s. Residents enclosed the spring Te Pupunitanga and used the soft waters of Whangapiporo Cauldron, later renamed the Rachel Pool. You can still see Rachel Spring boiling away at 100°Calong with several other steaming holes in the ground between the Polynesian Spa and the bathhouse—not walled off in any way, they offer free, fascinating viewing. The original baths were replaced by the Ward Baths in 1933 and the Aix Wing was added, offering hot air massage. The baths underwent complete renovation in 1972 and turned into the present-day Polynesian Spa. The complex continues to boast several hot mineral spring pools, private pools, an adults-only pool (live poolside jazz on Sunday nights 7:30 P.M.–9:30 P.M.), and Aix Massage. Admission is $10 adult, $4 child; a sauna is $11, massage $42 by appointment. The latest addition is the Lake Spa Retreat, comprising four manmade rock pools along the lakeshore, complete with bar service and luxurious changing rooms; $25 pp. You can rent bathing costumes and towels for $3 plus a $5 deposit; lockers are $1. The pools are open daily 6:30 A.M.–11 P.M.

Whakarewarewa

The best-known and closest thermal resort to the city is part of the **New Zealand Maori Arts and Crafts Institute,** only three km south on Hemo Rd. (follow Fenton St. south out of the city onto Hemo Rd., from which the main entrance is signposted), tel. 07/348-9047. Even the locals who can pronounce the word (fa-ka-ree-wa-ree-wa) affectionately call it "Whaka" (Whakarewarewa is a shortened version of the real name—Te Whakarewarewatangaoteopetu-aawahiao.) Unfortunately, admission costs continue to increase each year, but it's such an intriguing place that it earns a position on the "must-see-at-least-once list." The literal translation of Whakarewarewa is "to rise up," "soar," or "float." Originally the meanings referred to the uprising of a war party from Wahiao, but today it's still appropriate in reference to the area's thermal activity.

Just beyond the main entrance to the Arts and Crafts Institute are working Maori craftspeople learning the techniques of their ancestors (their works of art are on display seven days a week, but you can watch the carvers only on weekdays). Once inside the thermal area you'll see amazing geysers gushing skyward, hot-water springs, eerie

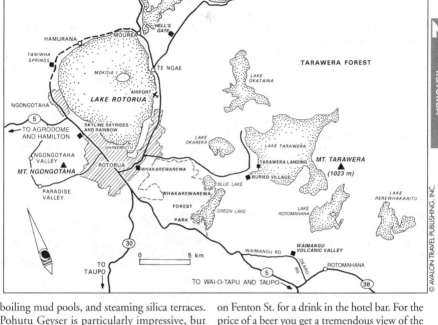

VICINITY OF ROTORUA

TO TE PUKE AND TAURANGA

TO WHAKATANE

LAKE ROTOMA

LAKE ROTOEHU

33

30

LAKE ROTOITI

ROTOITI

HELL'S GATE

HAMURANA

MOUREA

TARAWERA FOREST

TANIWHA SPRINGS

TE NGAE

LAKE OKATAINA

MOKOIA I.

LAKE ROTORUA

AIRPORT

NGONGOTAHA

5

TO AGRODOME AND HAMILTON

SKYLINE SKYRIDES AND RAINBOW

OHINEMUTU

LAKE OKAREKA

LAKE TARAWERA

NGONGOTAHA VALLEY

MT. NGONGOTAHA

ROTORUA

WHAKAREWAREWA

TARAWERA LANDING

MT. TARAWERA (1023 m)

BURIED VILLAGE

BLUE LAKE

LAKE REREWHAKAAITU

PARADISE VALLEY

WHAKAREWAREWA FOREST PARK

GREEN LAKE

LAKE ROTOMAHANA

30

0   5 km

WAIMANGU RD.

WAIMANGU VOLCANIC VALLEY

TO TAUPO

ROTOMAHANA

TO WAI-O-TAPU AND TAUPO

5

OKARO RD.

38

© AVALON TRAVEL PUBLISHING, INC.

ROTORUA

boiling mud pools, and steaming silica terraces. Pohutu Geyser is particularly impressive, but show times are unpredictable. After seeing the thermal attractions you can wander past the accurate replica of a *pa,* watch Maori women demonstrate their methods of cooking with natural steam, and take in a 45-minute lunchtime Maori Cultural Concert (daily at 12:30 P.M.). Guided tours leave every hour on the hour 10 A.M.–4 P.M., but you can cruise around the place on your own; allow about an hour.

Admission to the institute, thermal area, and model *pa* is $18 adult, $9 child, including the lunchtime Maori Cultural Concert. The entire complex is open daily 8 A.M.–6 P.M. (last tour at 4 P.M.). The local shuttle service runs past the entrance, and many of the guided tours around Rotorua include Whaka. If admission is beyond your budget, head for the Regal Geyserland Hotel

on Fenton St. for a drink in the hotel bar. For the price of a beer you get a tremendous view of the geysers from a distance—the bar and terrace overlook Whaka, and on summer evenings after the thermal area is closed to the public, you can watch Maori kids dive from Whaka's steaming white terraces into the hot pools far below. Another good (free) view of the geyser is from the viewpoint along the Yellow Trail in Whakarewarewa State Forest Park.

Waimangu Volcanic Valley

Waimangu is another large and exciting active thermal spot. It's about 26 km southeast of Rotorua at the southern end of the huge area devastated by the 1886 Mt. Tarawera eruption. Take the Valley Walk (about three km) down through beautiful bushland where thousands of deafening cicadas crowd the trees in summer while you view Southern Crater, Emerald Pools, and the steaming blue-green lake of Waimangu Cauldron. The lake occupies the crater of the 1917 explosion (the last minor eruption was in 1973), and although its temperature averages 50°C, it's claimed to be the "world's largest boiling lake." Surrounded by smoldering rocks and steaming bush, and disguised by the mysterious patterns created by surface steam, the large cauldron is both majestic and eerie.

Farther along you'll view Cathedral Rock and the colorful orange, yellow, and red decomposing cliffs, and cross Hot Water Creek where the water temperature varies 47–65°C. A worthwhile 59-step sidetrack leads up to the pale blue-gray steaming waters of Inferno Lake and Ruaumoko's Throat. Backed by tall smoldering cliffs, the water gurgles out of rock crevices around the lake, and steam cushions the surface. The main trail continues past the slimy yellow Iodine Pool with its hissing steam vents, Lake Rotomahana with the Mt. Tarawera crater in the distance, and the colorful silica formations of Warbrick Terrace. At the end of the Valley Walk, a bush trail (alive with native birds) leads down to Lake Rotomahana (1.8 km—largest of the 1886 craters) where you can catch a launch cruise (extra price) to the western shores, passing the famous Pink and White Terrace sites destroyed in the big eruption. Alternately, a minibus or truck cruises the entire track fairly regularly, giving free rides back up the hill to the tearooms. Even with average fitness it takes a couple of hours to see everything. Benches have been strategically placed at lookouts and at regular intervals, and if you get tired you can always catch the minibus back.

Admission for the Waimangu Valley Walk alone is $18 adult, $5 child; for the walk plus launch trip it's $40 adult, $10 child. Open daily 8:30 A.M.–5 P.M., Waimangu is 26 km south of Rotorua; to get there by car, take Hwy. 5 south out of Rotorua, turn left onto Waimangu Rd., and follow the signs, tel. 07/366-6137.

Hell's Gate Volcanic Park

Aside from eight hectares of ferocious and uncanny volcanic activity (which you can see in 30–45 minutes), the lure of Hell's Gate is hot Kakahi Falls, which at 38°C plummet steaming and hissing through lush natural bush—an unforgettable sight. Guide sheets are available in seven languages. It's open daily 9 A.M.–5 P.M.; $12 adult, $6 child. Hell's Gate is 16 km east of Rotorua at Tikitere, on Hwy. 30 to Whakatane, tel. 07/345-3151.

Wai-O-Tapu Thermal Wonderland

Wai-O-Tapu, tel. 07/366-6333, is perhaps the most colorful of all the thermal areas, but also the farthest away from Rotorua—30 km along Hwy. 5 toward Taupo. Follow the tracks past stunning Lady Knox geyser, which shoots water and steam up to 21 meters into the sky at 10:15 A.M. every day (with the help of good ol' soap powder); Bridal Veil Falls, where water cascades down white, red, yellow, and green silica terraces; boiling mud pools, craters, hot and cold pools, steaming fumaroles, the orange-edged Champagne

© ANDREW HEMPSTEAD

**Champagne Pool, Wai-O-Tapu
Thermal Wonderland**

Pool, and cliffs of sulphur stalactites, just to mention some of the best-known highlights. It's open daily 8:30 A.M.–5 P.M. and costs $15 adult, $5 child to wander through the park. Get your ticket at the reception, tearooms, and souvenir shop building. To get there, take Hwy. 5 south as far as the Waiotapu Hotel. Turn left opposite the hotel and continue for about one km on the loop road.

GOVERNMENT GARDENS

If you enjoy walking, head for Government Gardens on the eastern side of town, where many attractions lie within a relatively small area. Enter through the big arches along Hinemaru St. to see steaming thermal hot spots set incongruously among orderly flower gardens and lawns.

Hundreds of beautiful multicolored orchids are displayed in landscaped surroundings, and the floodlit night tour is spectacular.

Rotorua Museum of Art and History

Overlooking the gardens and a maze of croquet lawns is the impressive **Bath House,** the original Tudor Bath House building where people with joint afflictions and skin diseases came for various treatments using the soothing local volcanic mud and mineral water (the basement holds a fascinating display of equipment used in conjunction with mud bath therapy in this building between 1906 and 1966). Today the building houses the **Rotorua Museum of Art and History,** tel. 07/349-8334. If you want to know more about the Volcanic Plateau, the mighty eruption of Mt. Tarawera in 1886, and the Pink and White Terraces—a famous tourist attraction of the 19th century destroyed in the eruption-this is the place to visit. Don't miss the fascinating historical photo collection. The Maori section displays intricately carved greenstone (New Zealand jade) ornaments that "have no equal in all of Polynesia," along with beautiful feather cloaks and many other objects from the past. You can also see a large display of mounted native New Zealand birds, and upstairs, a replica of a settler's cottage furnished with colonial objects. The art gallery features

New Zealand art and sculpture and special exhibitions. All sections are open daily 10 A.M.–4:30 P.M.; $7.50 adult, $3 child.

Orchid Gardens

In the southern corners of the gardens are the Polynesian Spa and the Orchid Gardens, tel. 07/347-6699, where hundreds of beautiful multicolored orchids are displayed in landscaped surroundings (the floodlit night tour is spectacular), along with a captivating water organ (four-meter-high fountains of colored water that dance to music) and Microworld (cameras allow you to zoom in on insects and geckos for up-close and personal views), a gift shop, and the Orchid House Tearooms. The gardens are open daily 8:30 A.M.–5:30 P.M.; $10 adult, $4 child.

OHINEMUTU

The Maori village of Ohinemutu is at the northern end of town along the shores of Lake Rotorua, an easy walk from the lakefront. Here you'll find steaming holes in the ground, pipes sticking out of house foundations belching steam away from the buildings, and the awesome sound of boiling water coming from deep below (a free thermal spot!). On the shore stands the beautiful Maori Anglican **St. Faith's Church.** Completely decorated with Maori art, woven wall panels, and intricate carvings, it features a particularly effective etched-glass window at the far end. The church is open daily 8 A.M.–5 P.M.; services are held on Sunday at 10 A.M. and 7 P.M. A stone's throw from the church is the 1887 **Tamatekapua Meeting House,** another good place to admire the beauty of Maori carvings inlaid with *paua* shell. If it's open, admission is free; if it's closed, be sure to take a peek in through the windows. A Maori concert is held here nightly at 8 P.M., and you can buy tickets at the door at 7:30 P.M.; $15 adult, $7.50 child. To get there by car, take Lake Rd. north, turn right on Ariariterangi Rd. and then right at the lakefront, and follow the shoreline to the village; tel. 07/349-3949.

ROTORUA

TARAWERA ROAD

Tarawera Rd. begins southeast of downtown, branching of Hwy. 30 and leading 17 km to Lake Tarawera. Along the way are a number of attractions, but the view across the lake to famous Mt. Tarawera, which last erupted in 1886, makes the trip worthwhile in itself.

Whakarewarewa Forest Park

This 3,830-hectare park lying southeast of Rotorua can be accessed from Tarawera Rd. or from the west along Hwy. 5 (Rotorua-Taupo Rd.). Adjoining Whakarewarewa thermal area, it includes most of the older part of Whakarewarewa Forest, one of New Zealand's first exotic forests. Tree planting was begun right after the eruption of Mt. Tarewera in 1886 to renew the attractiveness of the Rotorua region and to regain tourism lost when the main local tourist attraction—the Pink and White Terraces—was destroyed. Many species of trees were planted, but the most successful species were European larch, Corsican pine, Douglas fir, and eucalyptus species, and the easiest to grow was the radiata pine from California. You'll also come across small areas of other surviving species, such as California redwoods; the two main areas of native forest are found adjoining Lake Tikitapu and north of Kakapiko. Planting was completed in 1916. Today the plantation is mainly managed for timber production, but the many tracks through lush native ferns and stately trees, the lake views, and the attractive picnic spots successfully put the forest on the map as a great recreational area. There's little thermal activity within the forest park boundaries—just one boiling mud pool on the southern side of Pohaturoa.

The best way to get around the park is on foot, but to learn more about the park and its history, head to the park's Visitor Information Centre, on Long Mile Rd. (off Tarawera Rd.), tel. 07/346-2082; open Mon.–Fri. 8:30 A.M.–5 P.M., Saturday and Sunday 10 A.M.–4 P.M. Behind the center is a flying fox (descends from a wire in a harness)—great fun for all ages—and, best of all, it's *free* (one of the few things you'll get for free in Rotorua).

Buried Village

Continue along Tarawera Rd., past the Blue and Green Lakes, to reach this historic attraction. When Mt. Tarawera erupted in 1886, it buried the Maori village of Te Wairoa in ash. At the time, Te Wairoa was one of New Zealand's premier resort towns, mainly because it was the starting point for cruises across Lake Tarawera to the Pink and White Terraces. More than 100 people were buried alive in Te Wairoa, including Tuhoto Ariki, a village elder who predicted the disaster. The village is slowly being excavated; one of the first houses completely dug out was that of Tuhoto Ariki, whose story makes interesting reading. On display are many artifacts recovered from the village, and a trail leads from the village to a spectacular 80-meter-high cascading waterfall. The Buried Village, tel. 07/362-8287, is open daily 9 A.M.–5 P.M.; $14 adult, $4 child.

Lake Tarawera

Tarawera Landing, on the western shore of Lake Tarawera, two km beyond the Buried Village, is the departure point for cruises across the lake to Rapatu Bay. From there you can walk to Lake Rotomahana, Hot Water Beach, or the summit of Mt. Tarawera. **Lake Tarawera Launch Services,** tel. 03/362-8595, depart daily at 11 A.M. and include a 45-minute stopover at the bay (enough time to walk across the narrow strip of land to Lake Rotomahana, and return). If you want to climb the mountain, you can stay overnight at a designated campground. The cruise is $27 pp. Additional, shorter cruises leave throughout the day in summer.

Just beyond the dock, **Landing Café,** tel. 03/362-8502, enjoys views across the lake to Mt. Tarawera.

NORTH OF DOWNTOWN

The following sights are north of downtown along Hwy. 5, with all but the Agrodome clustered around the base of **Mt. Ngongotaha.** Skyline Skyrides get you high up the slopes, but the only way to the actual summit of the mountain is by road. To get there from town, take Lake Rd. to the Fairy Springs Rd. intersection and continue straight ahead onto Clayton Road. Continue along Clayton Rd. (past Edmund Rd. and Thomas Crescent) and turn right into Mountain Rd., which winds slowly and steadily up the mountain toward the summit. Trees mar the view at the top. The best 180-degree views are from the lookout at Aorangi Peak Restaurant, which is on the way up, almost at the top.

Skyline Skyrides

Mt. Ngongotaha, a 760-meter-high peak four km north of Rotorua, can be reached by vehicle, but the views are best appreciated by taking the Skyline Skyrides gondola, tel. 07/347-0027, up the east-facing slopes. The gondola doesn't reach the summit, but it still offers an excellent vantage point, with views extending across Lake Rotorua. It runs daily from 8:30 A.M.; $14 adult, $6 child. Once you're at the top of the gondola, you'll find money-grabbing activities for all ages. You can ride a short chairlift, from where your downhill options are one of three luge tracks; $5 per run (or buy a book of tickets at a discounted rate). At the top of the gondola is a café and restaurant.

Rainbow

Adjacent to Skyline Skyrides, four km north of Rotorua on Hwy. 5, is this commercial attraction, tel. 07/347-9301, that combines lush gardens with salmon viewing and sheepshearing-a rather odd combination, but unique nonetheless. If you'd like to see just how large a rainbow or brown trout can grow, this is the place. Among a wide range of beautiful native ferns and natural bush, a trail leads to Rainbow Springs, a series of pools where the trout are segregated by age and size. Here you can observe fish (and duck) frenzy by throwing in "trout food." Fairy Springs Walk continues through the bush past numerous waterfalls to Fairy Springs, where 24 million liters of crystal-clear water gush out of the ground per day. Apart from all the pools teeming with trout there are underwater viewing ponds, native bird aviaries, deer, *tuatara* (a unique prehistoric reptile endemic to New Zealand that can

live 80–100 years), and wild pig enclosures, a kiwi house, tearooms, and a souvenir shop within the grounds.

Part of the same attraction, and accessed by a cobblestone walkway leading under the main highway, is **Rainbow Farm**, tel. 07/347-8104. Walk through the farm and take in a show (with plenty of audience participation) featuring past and present farming methods, animals, sheep mustering, and sheepshearing; shows are at 10:30 A.M., 11:45 A.M., 1 P.M., 2:30 P.M., and 4 P.M. See baby lambs, sheep, dogs, and goats; sit on a bull; and go on a pony-and-cart ride—the children love it.

Admission to Rainbow is adult $19.95, senior $16, child $9.50. It's open daily 8 A.M.–5 P.M. Many of the guided tours from town include Rainbow in the Rotorua itinerary.

Agrodome Leisure Park

Anyone interested in sheep, sheepshearing, or just having a good laugh should head for one of the shows at the Agrodome Leisure Park, a 160-hectare working farm. Inside the large auditorium you'll see fine woolly representatives of all the different breeds of New Zealand sheep, tied up along the sides for petting, admiring, or making funny faces at. During the Sheep Show, each well-trained sheep runs in turn up the stairs and onto the platform while its breed and characteristics are described. When they're all gathered center stage, a talented sheepdog is put through his paces. Vocal and whistle commands have the dog barking with delight as he scampers across the flock from sheep back to sheep back (much to the obvious disgust of the woolly stars of the show), and then a sheep from offstage is sheared by a professional sheepshearer. After the indoor show, the audience moves outside for a more realistic sheepdog demonstration. Daily show times are 9:30 A.M., 11 A.M., and 2:30 P.M.; $14 adult, $7 child.

One of the more unusual activities at the Agrodome is Zorbing. Another innovative Kiwi invention to relieve you of extra cash, the "Zorb" is a clear plastic sphere; for $40, you get strapped in and rolled down a hill. The Wash Cycle-a few

ROTORUA

buckets of water tossed into the Zorb-costs the same. Other Agrodome attractions include a Farm Tour that takes in everything from kiwifruit wine-tasting to emus and ostriches, trapshooting, bungee jumping, the Swoop Swing, and a driving range. A shop sells high-quality wool and sheepskin products—often with specials cheaper than city prices. Several tour companies include the Agrodome, tel. 07/354-4350, as one of the attractions. To get there, continue north along Hwy. 5 beyond the sights detailed above, and take Western Rd. to the right.

Recreation

ON THE WATER

Lake Rotorua

At the north end of downtown, the streets converge at a large lakefront park area, which is a hive of activity and the starting point for a variety of lake cruises. Each of the operators has a booth, and you simply need to choose your favorite option. For a scenic cruise over to legendary Mokoia Island in the middle of Lake Rotorua, try **Ngaroto Cruises,** tel. 07/347-9852. Its scenic cruise is offered several times a day; take your swimsuit, food, and drink. Buy the $35 pp tickets onboard or book by phone. During peak holiday times, a special lunch barbecue cruise is offered.

Cruising in old-fashioned steamer style on the *Lakeland Queen* is the most relaxing way to see the lake. Departing from the lakefront, this luxurious paddlesteamer does several cruises a day in summer (only the lunch cruise is year-round). The breakfast cruise departing at 8 A.M. costs $28 pp, the lunch cruise departing at 12:30 P.M. costs $35, the afternoon tea cruise at 2:30 P.M. costs $18, and the Evening Dine & Dance departing at 7 P.M. costs $55. Tickets are available at the on-site ticket office at the lakefront, tel. 07/348-6634 or 0800/862-784.

White-water Rafting

A big hit with the adrenaline-seeking crowd is rafting the **Kaituna River,** which crosses Hwy. 33 north of Rotorua. Along the river, a seven-meter waterfall is claimed to be the highest commercially rafted drop in the world. **Kaituna Cascades,** tel. 07/345-4199, the first operator to run the waterfall, has been joined by a whole host of other companies, including **River Rats,** tel. 07/345-6543, and **Whitewater Excitement,** tel. 07/349-2858. Rates range $70–80 pp, which includes wet suits and transportation from Rotorua. Allow three hours from Rotorua, of which 45 minutes is spent on the river. All the same companies run trips down the much tamer **Rangitaiki River** southeast of Rotorua toward Te Urewera National Park. River time is longer (up to 90 minutes), as is the trip out there, and lunch is included in the rates, which range $80–95 pp.

FLIGHTSEEING

Sight-seeing by float or land plane is always a blast. If you can afford it, it truly adds another dimension to this fascinating thermal area. **Volcanic Air Safaris,** tel. 07/348-9984 or 0800/800-848, operates a large variety of scenic flights in floatplanes from the lakefront at the foot of Tutanekai Street. The eight-minute Town and Around flight ($50 pp) looks over the city and lake, but that's about it. Thirty minutes of airtime ($165 pp) is enough to travel to and over Mt. Tarawera. The popular 80-minute excursion out to active White Island is $395 pp. Volcanic Air Safaris also operates a helicopter from the lakefront, with options ranging from a 10-minute flight ($60 pp) to a three-hour trip to White Island complete with a landing ($725 pp).

At the airport, **Volcanic Wunderflites,** operated by the Rotorua Aero Club, tel. 07/345-6077 or 0800/777-359, offers a range of flights to suit all budgets. Choose from a 15-minute flight over the lake ($70 pp), a 30-minute flight around Mt. Tarawera ($135 pp), and a 90-minute flight that takes in the entire fault line from Rotorua to White Island ($249 pp).

HIKING

Whakarewarewa Forest Park

Within this large park south of downtown are eight well-marked walks. They vary from short one- to two-km trails at rest areas and picnic spots to the 33-km "Around the Forest Park Walk," which takes about eight hours. You'll find the most people along the trail through the Redwood Grove, which begins at the visitor information center, tel. 07/346-2082. This center has brochures detailing this and the other trails, with color-coding to indicate difficulty. Another popular trail encircles Blue Lake (four km; 75 minutes), or you can reach the lake along a 5.5-km (1.5-hour) one-way trail from the information center.

Eastern Okataina Walkway

Lake Okataina (Lake of Laughter—from Maori legends) is one of the most beautiful, unspoiled lakes in the area—a paradise for outdoor enthusiasts. Deep blue and lined with sandy beaches and sheltered coves, it's backed by native bush, tropical-looking tree ferns, *pohutukawa* trees, and magnificent fuchsia flowers. The eight-km (2.5-hour) one-way Eastern Okataina Walkway weaves in and out and up and down (steep and tricky in some places) the rocky shores of the lake, allowing fairly constant access to the water. To get to the start of the track at Tauranganui Bay (toilets and picnic area) at the northern end of Lake Okataina, take Hwy. 30 toward Whakatane, and turn right at Ruato onto Okataina Road. The track is for those with average fitness; it can be done in sandshoes or tennis shoes in dry weather, hiking boots in wet weather. Take food, water (don't rely on streams), and warm clothing, and stay on the main track.

Western Okataina Walkway

This track is longer, wilder, and more remote than the Eastern Walkway. It doesn't follow the lakeshore but provides magnificent views of the Bay of Plenty, Coromandel Range to the north, and offshore islands from the 758-meter Whaka-poungakau Trig. This track climbs steadily, is steep and rugged in places, and suits the more experienced tramper. Old logging roads branch off the main track so you need to concentrate on following the markers. The 22.5-km (seven-hour) one-way track starts at Ruato on Hwy. 30 and finishes at Miller Rd. at Lake Okareka. Cut off about 4.5 km by starting at the Education and Recreation Centre off Okataina Road.

OTHER OUTDOOR RECREATION

Four-Wheel Driving

Mt. Tarawera is the destination for a number of companies operating off-road vehicles, and because access to the mountain is restricted, it's the most practical way of seeing this recently active volcano up close. The four-hour trip offered by **Mt. Tarawera 4WD Tours**, tel. 07/348-2814, is typical. After an early-morning or lunchtime pickup from Rotorua accommodations, you travel by highway through Rerewhakaaitu and climb the southern flanks of the mountain, along a narrow track that fizzles out near the summit. The lunarlike landscape above the tree line is unforgettable in itself, but then you can jump out of the 4WD and wander into a crater. The cost is $85 pp.

Graceful black swans are common in lakes around Rotorua.

Horseback Riding

At the **Farmhouse,** Sunnex Rd., tel. 07/332-3771, you can ride through open farmland or lush forests, either with a guide or by yourself, with horses available for all levels of expertise. Rates are $25 pp per hour. By arrangement, this company will bring their horses to Rotorua for guided trail rides through the Whakarewarewa Forest Park. To get to the stables, follow Hwy. 5 north out of town, continue through the lakeside village of Ngongotaha, then follow the signs.

Golfing

Playing at the 27-hole Rotorua Golf Club is a unique experience. The 18-hole course, known as Arikikapakapa, is the more difficult, with a Slope Rating of 123. Green fees are $55. The public nine-hole course is relatively easy, but take into account the hot spots, steaming vents, and bubbling pools of hot mud dotting the fairways, and you have a interesting golfing experience; $10 for nine holes. The course is south of downtown, opposite Whakarewarewa thermal area; access is from Fenton Street; tel. 07/348-4051.

Get Lost

Looking for fun and frustration? Trying to lose someone? Head for **Te Ngae Park** on Te Ngae Rd. (heading toward the Whakatane Hwy., it's several kilometers beyond the airport, about a 10-minute drive from town), tel. 07/345-5275. This carefully constructed three-dimensional maze has 1.7 km of paths to get lost on, and drinks and ice cream available—that is, if you ever get out. It's open daily from 8:30 A.M.; $5 adult, $2.50 child. Back toward the city and opposite the airport is the **Fairbank Maze,** tel. 07/345-4089, made completely from high hedges; $5 adult, $2.50 child.

ARTS AND ENTERTAINMENT

Maori Cultural Concerts

Dozens of places offer the chance to see Maori groups in traditional costume, singing and dancing, mostly in conjunction with a traditional *hangi* (feast). Very entertaining cultural concerts are presented in the **Tamatekapua Meeting House** in the Maori village of Ohinemutu, along the shores of Lake Rotorua. Concerts start at 8 P.M.; you can buy tickets at the door from 7:30 P.M. Tickets cost $15; call 07/348-4894 for details. Another concert-only venue is Whakarewarewa thermal area, where a lunchtime concert is including in the entry price ($18 adult, $9 child). The fun takes place daily at 12:15 P.M.

Drinking and Dancing

Typical of a resort town, Rotorua has many places to drink and dance the night away. The **Pig and Whistle,** in a renovated police station at the corner of Haupapa and Tutanekai Streets, tel. 07/347-3025, is one of the most popular local drinking spots. It features a wide variety of New Zealand beers, and bands play Friday and Saturday nights. This bar also has good food and an outdoor patio. **Churchill's,** 1302 Tutanekai St., tel. 07/347-1144, is an English-style pub. Most of the big hotels have lounge-style bars that welcome nonguests. South of downtown, in the **Regal Geyserland Hotel,** Fenton St., tel. 07/348-2039, the bar affords views across famous Whakarewarewa thermal area, and you needn't be a guest to enjoy the spectacle of spouting geysers. Back downtown and right on the lake, the **Mallard Bar** in the Lake Plaza Rotorua Hotel, 6 Eruera St., tel. 07/348-1174, is another good choice.

The **Lava Bar,** 1286 Arawa St., tel. 07/348-8618, features nightly drink and food specials (happy hour is 4:30–6:30 P.M.) along with video games and a pool table. It's part of Hot Rock Backpackers, so the crowd is generally young, loud, and proud. Two blocks west of Fenton St., **Monkey Jo's Jungle Bar,** 1263 Amohia St., tel. 07/346-1313, is a step up in style. **Wild Willy's,** 1240 Fenton St., tel. 07/348-7774, has a Western atmosphere and a long nightly happy hour.

Beyond the south end of downtown, **Ace of Clubs,** 8 Ti St., tel. 07/346-2204, keeps the dance tunes going until the early hours.

Accommodations

HOTELS AND MOTELS

Because Rotorua revolves around tourism, it has an incredible number of accommodations, including about 80 hotels and motels at last count. They are spread throughout the city, but most are concentrated along Fenton Street.

Under $100

The least expensive motel downtown is the three-story **Ambassador Thermal Motel,** on the corner of Whakaue and Hinemaru Streets, tel. 07/347-9581 or 0800/479-581. The rooms are nothing special, but the motel features two spring-fed mineral pools, a swimming pool, and an outdoor spa. All 19 rooms have a kitchen; $70 s, $90 d.

Cruise along Fenton St. and check the discounted rates motels post out front, or head to one of the inexpensive choices below, listed in north-south order. **Bel Aire Motel,** 257 Fenton St., tel. 07/348-6076 or 0800/423-524, is 500 meters from downtown, and each of the eight units has a kitchen. At $70 s or d, it's one of the best-value accommodations along the strip. **Gateway International Motel,** 263 Fenton St., tel. 07/347-9199 or 0800/588-988, has 15 large self-contained rooms, each with a spa bath. It's a fairly basic place, not really reflected in the rates of $75 s, $90 d. A few doors farther south, **Forest Court Motel,** 275 Fenton St., tel. 07/346-3543, has a heated swimming pool and self-contained rooms for $75 s or d.

At the south end of Fenton St., Sala St. branches east toward the airport. Here you'll find the **Birchwood Spa Motel,** Sala St., tel. 07/347-1800 or 0800/881-800, website: www.birchwoodspamotel.co.nz, a modern complex of 13 luxurious self-contained units, each with a mineral spa. Studio units ($95 s or d) have a microwave, toaster, and tea- and coffee-making facilities while one- and two-bedroom units ($115 and $155, respectively) have full kitchens.

Another bunch of inexpensive motels cluster around the junction of Ranolf and Lake Roads, two km northwest of downtown. The **South Pacific Motel,** 96 Lake Rd., tel. 07/348-0153 or 0800/223-545, features 11 self-contained units, each with a covered patio overlooking a parklike garden and heated swimming pool. Rates are $80 s, $90 d. A half-block west is **Cleveland Motel,** 113 Lake Rd., tel. 07/348-2041 or 0800/112-244, surrounded by extensive grounds and with an outdoor swimming pool and indoor thermal pools. The 30 rooms range $80–95 s or d.

$100–200

Ledwich Lodge Motel, 12 Lake Rd., tel. 07/347-0049 or 0800/803-524, enjoys an excellent location, separated from the lake by a grassed reserve and only a short walk from downtown. It's an older place, and the rates reflect the location rather than the quality of the rooms, but it does feature in-room spa baths and a swimming pool. All rooms have a kitchen; studio units are $110 s or d, one-bedroom units are $145 s or d.

Across the road from Government Gardens is the grand old **Princes Gate Hotel,** 1057 Arawa St., tel. 07/348-1179 or 0800/500-705, website: www.princesgate.co.nz. The hotel was originally located on the east coast at Waihi, but when that town was voted dry in 1917, the owner relocated the entire building to Rotorua. The hotel has been modernized, but an old-time ambience remains. Facilities include a thermally heated pool, sauna, tennis court, restaurant, and bar. The rooms have been refurnished and cost from $120 s or d.

Overlooking Whakarewarewa thermal area is **Regal Geyserland Hotel,** 424 Fenton St., tel. 07/348-2039 or book through Mainstay at 0800/624-646, with 66 fairly standard hotel rooms, many with views of the thermal area. Facilities include indoor spa pools, a sauna, an outdoor pool, a small fitness room, a restaurant, a bar, and across the road is a golf course. Rates start at $140 s or d.

Right on the lake and adjacent to the Polynesian Spa, **Lake Plaza Rotorua Hotel,** 6 Eruera St., tel. 07/348-1174 or 0800/801-440, website: lakeplazahotel.co.nz, two blocks from downtown, has 250 bright and airy rooms, many with balconies and lake views. It also features an indoor pool, a nightly *hangi,* restaurant, and bar. Standard rooms are $155 s or d, superior rooms, with a distinctly more elegant feel, are $180 s or d.

Over $200

The seven-story **Royal Lakeside Novotel,** 9 Tutanekai St., tel. 07/346-3888 or 0800/776-677, website: www.accorhotels.co.nz, is one of Rotorua's finest accommodations. This modern full-service hotel features a luxurious fitness/pool complex, indoor and outdoor dining, and a nightly *hangi.* Tasteful, earthy tones dominate the 199 rooms (request a lake view); rates from $205 s or d.

Heading south along Fenton St. are a number of other upmarket hotels. One of these is **Rydges Rotorua,** 272 Fenton St., tel. 07/349-0099 or 0800/367-793, with 135 well-appointed rooms, a thermally heated indoor pool, bike rentals, a bar, and a café. Even standard rooms have a spa bath. Rates range $210–235 s or d, discounted on weekends.

OTHER ACCOMMODATIONS

Bed-and-Breakfasts

If you want a central location, thermally heated **Eaton Hall Guest House,** 1225 Hinemaru St., tel. 07/347-0366, is the place to go. The friendly owners not only supply comfy beds and a delicious breakfast, they also make you feel right at home. Each room has a hand basin, and tea- and coffee-making supplies, and guests can use a hot tub/spa and a TV room. A three-course dinner with fresh veggies and fruit from the garden, homemade jams, and more is available for $25, if previously arranged. Bed and continental or cooked breakfast is $50 s, $75 d with a shared bathroom, $70 s, $95 d with a private bathroom.

Tresco Bed and Breakfast, 3 Toko St., tel. 07/348-9611, has a comfortable, homey atmosphere. Each of the seven thermally heated rooms has its own hand basin, but bathrooms are shared. Tea- and coffee-making supplies are available in the lounge. You'll also find a washer and thermal drying room, a TV lounge, and a hot

mineral pool. Rates are $55 s, $80 d or twin, including a continental or cooked breakfast. Sight-seeing tours can be arranged; you can also request a courtesy car from the bus depot or the airport.

North of Rotorua at Ngongotaha is **Deer Pine Lodge,** 255 Jackson Rd., tel. 07/332-3458, which has four bed-and-breakfast units for $70–75 s, $85–100 d, and two self-contained units. Dinner is available for $25 pp. The owners offer tours of their deer farm—learn all about deer farming and observe different species of deer.

Backpacker Lodges

Apart from the many motor camps, Rotorua offers many good options for travelers on a budget. One of the best of these is **Kiwi Paka YHA,** a self-contained resort set on one hectare, one km west of downtown at 60 Tarewa Rd., tel. 07/347-0931; website: www.kiwipaka-yha.org.nz. Along with the usual communal bathroom, kitchen, and laundry facilities, guests at this large complex can enjoy mineral pools, a large recreation room, and glassed-in conservatory with barbecues, restaurant, and bar. Also on-site is a small general store and bike rentals. Choose from two- or four-bed thermally heated bunkrooms in a main lodge ($20–23 pp), thermally heated chalets, each with its own deck ($54 pp), or grassy tent and power sites ($10–12 pp).

The **Funky Green Voyager,** 4 Union St., tel. 07/346-1754, is the smallest backpacker lodging within walking distance of downtown. Offering clean, bright dorm rooms with comfortable beds for $18 pp, and six double rooms at $42 per night, its well-equipped kitchen and spacious backyard add to the friendly, relaxed atmosphere. It's a short walk to city attractions, and the straightforward, environmentally-conscious owner is a good source of information on attractions and backpacker hostels throughout the country. **Hot Rock Backpackers,** 1286 Arawa St., tel. 07/347-9469, is a modern, centrally located property, with its own bar, indoor and outdoor thermal pools, a sundeck, and a barbecue area. Rates are $18 dorm, $26 s, $40 d. Also downtown is **Rotorua Central Backpackers,** 1076 Pukuatua St., tel. 07/349-3285. This rambling colonial house on a quiet street has large rooms, a modern kitchen, and a spa and barbecue for guest use.

Motor Camps

You'll find many motor camps around the shores of Lake Rotorua, but only a few are central to the city. A couple of the closest are caravan parks with a limited number of tent sites or none at all, but reasonably priced cabin accommodation is an alternative. If you definitely want to camp out, head out of Rotorua along Hwy. 30 or Hwy. 5 and follow the lake. Most of the motor camps around Lake Rotorua provide tent sites.

On the northwestern side of town, a short stroll from the lake, the excellent **Cosy Cottage International Holiday Park** on Whittaker Rd., off Lake Rd., tel. 07/348-3793 or 0800/222-424, has communal bathroom (piping hot showers!), kitchen (fully equipped) and laundry; a large TV and game room; a hot, soothing mineral pool; a steam barbecue; a heated swimming pool surrounded by ferns; a baby bath; and a camp store. Tent and powered sites are $22 (a few are thermally heated); thermally heated cabins with stove and fridge are $44–50 s or d; renovated tourist flats (two bedrooms, private bathroom, kitchen, and lounge) are $60–65 s or d.

Rotorua Thermal Holiday Park, at the south end of Old Taupo Rd. opposite the golf course, tel. 07/346-3140, is a bit of a hike from downtown (or a five-minute bus ride), but only a short walk from one of the main attractions, Whakarewarewa thermal area. It has communal facilities, a game room, a camp store, a heated swimming pool, and thermal plunge pools. Tent and caravan sites are $20–22. Bunkroom beds (supply your own sleeping bag) are $17 pp. Cabins are $34–68 s or d.

Lakeside Thermal Holiday Park two km from downtown on Whittaker Rd., tel. 07/348-1693—by the lake as the name implies—has tent and caravan sites ($22), reasonably priced cabins ($45 s or d), and tourist flats ($60–70). In addition to the usual facilities, this place has private spa pools, a barbecue area with a natural steam cooker, and canoes.

If you're into fly-fishing, or just nature for that matter, head for **Ohau Channel Lodge,** a first-class motor camp about 17.5 km from Rotorua on Hwy. 30/Hamurana Rd., tel. 07/362-4761. It's at the northern end of the lake, on the narrow strip of land separating Lake Rotorua from Lake Rotoiti. The camping area lies along the shores of both Ohau Channel and Lake Rotorua. It's a great spot for trout fishing, attracts hordes of New Zealand anglers in summer, and is the kind of place where you're likely to find entire duck and black swan families nonchalantly sunning themselves on your tent flap. It's very relaxed, and it gets some of the best views of Rotorua sparkling across the lake at sunset. Hot private spa pools cost extra. Buy your fishing license, supplies, and equipment at the camp store, and if you don't know how to angle properly, fly-fishing schools are available. Tent and caravan sites cost $10 pp; cabins range $40–60 s or d; tourist flats cost $75 s or d.

Other Practicalities

FOOD

Restaurants throughout Rotorua reflect the city's thriving tourist industry, but there's so much competition around town that dining out is not as expensive as you may expect. Many older eateries in the downtown core are seemingly oblivious to the surrounding bustle, providing a good place for an inexpensive meal. One of these is **Herb's Restaurant,** 1096 Tutanekai St., tel. 07/348-3985, which has been open since the 1950s.

Cafés and Coffeehouses

Head to **Zippy Central,** Pukuatua St., tel. 07/348-8288, for good, strong coffee and a variety of fresh pastries and cakes. Open daily from 7 A.M. **Freo's Cafe,** at 1103 Tutanekai St. (toward the lake), tel. 07/346-0976, sells pies, sausage rolls, fresh salads, seafood salad, and chocolate mousse to take away for lunch, and complete meals (such as lasagna) for $5–7 a portion or sold by the kilogram to take away for dinner. It's open Mon.–Sat. from 11 A.M. Continuing north, the **Coffee Bean,** 1149 Tutanekai St., tel. 07/348-6849, is another good spot for a coffee stop. Back toward downtown, **Fat Dog,** 1161 Arawa St., tel. 07/347-7586, offers light dishes, such as soup and salad, as well as healthy versions of lasagna, pasta, and curry ($7–11.50).

A couple of blocks from the heart of the city, **Sirocco,** 1280 Eruera St., tel. 07/347-3388, is a pleasant little café with indoor and outdoor tables surrounded by an old restored private residence. Along with coffee and light snacks, it offers a full menu of breakfast, lunch, and dinner.

Easy on the Pocket

The **Cobb & Co. Restaurant** in the Grand Establishment, 1129 Hinemoa St., tel. 07/348-2089, has satisfying main courses for about $15–27, and it's fully licensed. It's open seven days a week 7:30 A.M.–10 P.M. The bistro in the **Westbrook Tavern,** on Malfroy Rd., tel. 07/347-0687, is highly recommended for roasts and grills. An average main course costs $13–16 and

a daily chef's special three-course meal costs $14.50. Half-meals cost $10, and the children's menu lists dishes for $6.50. Open Mon.–Sat. noon–2 P.M., Mon.–Wed. 6–8:30 P.M., Thurs.–Sat. 6–9 P.M.

The menu at **Boulevard,** in the motel of same name on the corner of Fenton and Seddon Streets, tel. 07/346-1763, features something for everyone. The starters are mostly seafood, while the choice of dishes includes everything from chicken to pork. As with everywhere in New Zealand, it's hard to go past the lamb or seafood ($18–24). It's open daily from 6 P.M.

Rapscallions, 1207 Fenton St., tel. 07/349-4772, is a good bet for burgers. A couple of doors down, **Tastebuds Mexican Cantina,** 1213 Fenton St., tel. 07/349-0591, offers inexpensive food, including chili con carne from $6 and Mexican dishes from at $7. It's open daily from 10 A.M. One block north, **Kebab Diner,** 1121 Fenton St., tel. 07/349-0105, specializes in Middle Eastern cuisine; for a true experience, enjoy humus ($5) as a starter, try a kebab ($15–17) main course, and finish off with a plate of baklava ($3.50). It's open daily for lunch and dinner.

Another concentration of inexpensive places to eat is along the streets running west from Fenton St., the original part of downtown. Among the small-town style of eateries here is **Hoo Wah Restaurant,** 1266 Eruera St., tel. 07/348-5271. It offers lots of seafood dishes, ranging $14–22, as well as all the usual westernized Chinese choices (from $13). Hoo Wah is open weekdays for lunch and daily for dinner. For an excellent Indian meal, try **Mr. India Tandoori Restaurant** one block south at 1161 Amohau St., tel. 07/349-4940. Main dishes cost less than $20, including a great chicken tandoori, with vegetarian dishes considerably less. It's open Mon.–Sat. for lunch and daily for dinner.

Dining with a View

Out of town to the northwest, **Aorangi Peak Restaurant,** Mountain Rd., tel. 07/347-0046, aptly described as "Rotorua's restaurant complex n the sky," offers the bonus of fantastic views of the city and Lake Rotorua from Mt. Ngongo-aha. Seating is on two tiers, allowing views from most tables. The menu offers no real surprises. Instead, enjoy good, solid Kiwi cooking—such as the prime rib of beef for $27—in a modest setting designed to take nothing from the views. Aorangi Peak is open daily from 6 P.M.

Lower on the slopes of the same mountain, at the top of Skyline Skyrides (see North of Downtown), Hwy. 5, tel. 07/347-0027, the restaurant offers a buffet featuring seafood, a variety of meats, and delicious desserts. Lunch costs $32 pp, dinner $42 pp, and kids pay $1 per year of age up to 14.

> *"Rotorua's restaurant complex in the sky" offers the bonus of fantastic views of the city and Lake Rotorua from Mt. Ngongotaha.*

Upmarket, Downtown

At **You & Me** at 1119 Pukuatua St., tel. 07/347-6178, a Japanese-born, French-trained chef serves up dishes influenced by cooking styles from around the world in elegant pink-and-black surroundings. Try the papaya salad ($11) for starters and then order the roast lamb dish ($26.50); both were delicious.

Memories Restaurant takes pride of place in the distinctive Princes Gate Hotel, opposite Government Gardens at 1057 Arawa St., tel. 07/348-1179. The Victorian opulence of the dining room reflects the hotel's rich history, but the ambience is relatively unpretentious. Enjoy traditional dishes of lamb, duck, chicken, and pork, as

M

ROTORUA

THE MAORI *HANGI*

Rotorua is the best place in New Zealand to enjoy a traditional *hangi* (feast). Usually held in conjunction with a Maori concert, you shouldn't miss this particular Rotorua event.

In a deep hole, a fire built from native timber heats a layer of stones. Onto the hot stones go a layer of leaves, then the food, then more leaves (nowadays muslin cloth replaces this second layer). Water is thrown on just before the food, the oven is closed with a layer of soil, and the steam, flavored from the wood below, cooks the food. Local Maori villagers cook all their food in this manner using the boxes around natural steam vents in Whaka village.

Tamaki Tours, tel. 07/346-2823, puts on probably the most authentic traditional *hangi* and concert performance you're likely to encounter in New Zealand. After being collected by bus from accommodations around the city, you learn from the driver that you are now actually in a *waka* (Maori canoe) approaching a *marae*, and that the group must select a "chief" for the arrival ceremony. From then on everyone actively participates in "the challenge" (don't put your foot on that leaf!), the welcome and response, the speeches, the concert, the opening of the *hangi*, and, of course, the

eating of the traditional food. It costs $55 per person, lasts three hours, and is an excellent value.

The several large hotels in Rotorua that put on *hangi* are better able to control the steam in their ovens, so they can open them up to put delicate foods in later to cook everything to perfection. The traditional lamb and pork take about three hours to cook, seafood 30 minutes, vegetables such as *kumara* (sweet potato) 30 minutes, and traditional steamed pudding about an hour in the controlled steam ovens. The **Regal Geyserland Hotel** on Fenton St. overlooking Whaka, tel. 07/348-2039, puts on a *hangi* and Cultural Concert Party on Monday, Wednesday, and Friday nights Aug.–May, more often during the peak summer holiday period; the cost is $45 (concert alone $18). The hotel overlooks Whaka thermal reserve, so you get the added bonus of an active and steamy view while you tuck into some of the best food New Zealand has to offer. Afterward a group of talented Maori singers and dancers presents a traditional Maori concert, which includes the fierce war dances of the men, the soft fluent *poi* dances of the women, and beautiful singing. The *hangi* starts at 5:45 P.M. The concert starts at 7:15 P.M. Hangis and concerts are also put on at other major hotels.

well as more adventurous offerings such as Blackened Cajun Snapper ($28.50). Aside from the full-fledged restaurant, a more casual café opens throughout the day, with some seating outside in a pleasant courtyard.

Typical of Rotorua's better restaurants, dining at **Poppy's Villa,** a colorfully decorated villa at 4 Marguerita St., tel. 07/347-1700, is not as expensive as you might imagine. The dishes are distinctly New Zealand, and the kitchen does them well. Italian-style breads are warmed to perfection and the Lamb Racks Canterbury ($26) is coated in a honey, mustard, and rosemary glaze and served with minted kiwifruit. For something lighter, consider the Princess Scallops, combing scallops, ginger, basil, and lemongrass on a bed of rice ($27).

TRANSPORTATION

Getting There

Rotorua Airport is nine km northeast of town along Hwy. 30. At the airport you'll find car rental offices, a souvenir shop, and a phone for free local calls. **Super Shuttle,** tel. 07/349-3444, provides a door-to-door shuttle service; it's $10 for the first passenger, then $2 per extra person. A taxi between the airport and downtown costs about $20. **Air New Zealand** flies from Rotorua direct to Auckland and Wellington in the North Island, and to Christchurch in the South Island. Book flights at the Air New Zealand Travel Centre on the corner of Fenton and Hinemoa Streets, tel. 07/343-1100 or 0800/800-737.

Rotorua is at the end of a rail line that spurs from the main Auckland-Wellington line. **Tranz Scenic,** tel. 0800/802-802, runs the Geyserland service twice daily along this route; traveling time between Auckland and Rotorua is just over four hours. The railway station is along Dingsdale Rd., one km northwest of downtown. It only opens for train arrivals and departures. Buy tickets from Tourism Rotorua.

Traveling by bus to Rotorua is possible with a number of companies, and arriving is convenient because the main depot is the Tourism Rotorua complex right downtown on the corner of Fenton and Arawa Streets. The main carrier

into Rotorua is **Intercity,** tel. 07/348-0366, with services from Auckland, Hamilton, Tauranga and Whakatane in the north. From the south services from Napier, New Plymouth, Wanganui, and Wellington are all routed through Taupo. **Newmans,** tel. 07/343-1730, follows the same routes.

Getting Around

If you don't have your own transportation, the best way to travel to all the sights is with **Magic of the Maori,** tel. 07/349-3949, who operate a shuttle to all major attractions from the Tourism Rotorua complex on Fenton St. hourly 8:45 A.M.–4:45 P.M.; $10 pp. **Ritchies Coachlines,** tel. 07/345-5694, serves the suburbs (including south to Whakarewarewa and north to Ngongotaha).

Car rental agencies in Rotorua include **Avis** tel. 07/345-6055; **Budget,** tel. 07/348-8127 **Hertz,** tel. 07/348-4081; and **Rent-a-dent,** tel. 07/349-3993.

Rotorua is very flat, which makes it an ideal place to get around by pedal power. Many backpacker lodges rent bikes, as do **Lady Jane's Ice Cream Parlour** at the lake end of Tutanekai St. tel. 07/347-9340, and **Rotorua Cycle Centre,** 1120 Hinemoa St., tel. 07/348-6588.

For a cab, call **Rotorua Taxis,** tel. 07/348-1111

Tours

If you don't have your own transportation, no worries! You can see many of Rotorua's main attractions, and some of the lesser-known sights, on one of the many tours available. Call in at Tourism Rotorua, peruse all the current brochures, and compare prices.

The most popular trips are run by **Carey's Rotorua Tours,** 1108 Haupapa St. (one block south of the visitor center), tel. 07/347-1197 The tours were originally designed for backpackers, but have gained popularity with all age groups for their enjoyable and entertaining nature. The classic tour is Carey's Capers, which includes three major geothermal attractions combined with a swim in an off-the-beaten-path thermally heated swimming hole, lunch, and a gondola ride up Mt. Ngongotaha. This full-day tour starts at 8 A.M., returns at 5:15 P.M.; adult

$110, child $55 includes admissions. The same company offers a 4.5-hour City Sights Tour (adult $80, child $40) that includes visits to Whakarewarewa, the Agrodome, and the Rainbow attraction, and a variety of other excursions.

The best way to get insight into Maori culture is to enjoy some time with **Tamaki Tours,** 1220 Hinemaru St., tel. 07/346-2823, who take guests by coach to the Tamaki Maori Village. At this re-creation of a pre-European Maori village, visitors use Tamaki currency to barter for arts and crafts in the marketplace, listen to traditional music, learn Maori fishing techniques, and dine on time-honored delicacies. Admission is adult $10, child $5, or is included on all Tamaki Tours (from $35 pp).

SERVICES

All major banking institutions, represented on Hinemoa St., are open Mon.–Fri. 10:30 A.M.–4:30 P.M. Foreign currency services are available at the banks, or at **Travelex,** in the Tourism Rotorua complex at 1167 Fenton Street. **Rotorua Post Office** is on the corner of Hinemoa and Tutanekai Streets; it's open weekdays 8:30 A.M.–5 P.M. A self-service **laundry** is at 1231 Pukuatua Street.

Emergency

For a **police, fire,** or **ambulance emergency** phone the operator, tel. 111. For a **doctor** or **dentist** call St. John Ambulance, which keeps a roster of doctors and dentists available to visitors, tel. 07/348-6286. The **Lakes Care Pharmacy** is on Tutanekai St. (at Arawa St.), tel. 07/348-4385; open Saturday and holidays 11 A.M.–1 P.M., 3–5 P.M., and 6:30–9 P.M. The **police station** is at 1215 Hinemoa St., tel. 07/349-9554.

INFORMATION

Tourism Rotorua, 1167 Fenton St. (at Arawa St.), tel. 07/348-5179, website: www.rotorua .co.nz, is the best place in town for information on commercial attractions—in Rotorua and the entire country. The hardworking staff can advise you on everything and make bookings for tours, transportation, and accommodations; it's open in summer, daily 8 A.M.–6 P.M., the rest of the year, daily 8 A.M.–5:30 P.M. The information center is just a small part of a large complex that includes luggage storage, a currency exchange (open 8 A.M.–6 P.M.), map shop, souvenir shop, and café. Rotorua is headquarters for the DOC **Bay of Plenty Conservancy,** 1144 Pukaki St., tel. 07/349-7400. The **Automobile Association,** 1191 Amohau St., tel. 07/348-3069, is another good place for general travel information and maps (free for members). Hours are Mon.–Fri. 8:30 A.M.–5 P.M. **Rotorua Public Library** is at the north end of Haupapa St., tel. 07/348-4177.

ROTORUA

[handwritten note] lovely resort town, could plan to stay 1-2 nights + shop and do activities. Beautiful gift + art shops

Taupo and Tongariro

Introduction

Lying along the same fault line as Rotorua, the Taupo region and Tongariro National Park to the south are also geothermally active. **Lake Taupo,** also known as Taupo Moana (Sea of Taupo), is New Zealand's largest lake. Located exactly in the middle of the North Island, the crystal-clear, bright blue waters of this inland sea cover a 616-square-km area—about 42 km long and 30 km wide. White pumice beaches and sheltered rocky coves line its shores, vast pine forests cover much of the surrounding plains and ranges. At the northeastern end of the lake **Taupo** is a relaxed resort town best known as a base for lake and

river trout fishing. Highway 1 follows the eastern shore of Lake Taupo, connecting Taupo and **Turangi,** another angler's paradise. It is possible to circumnavigate the lake by taking Hwy. 41 from Turangi northwest to Kuratau Junction, then Hwy. 32 north up the western side, but most travelers continue south to **Tongariro National Park.** The park's three impressive peaks—Tongariro, Ngauruhoe, and Ruapehu-can be seen from as far away as Taupo, but you'll want to get closer to appreciate these mountains, and the barren lava fields that surround them.

Tongariro National Park

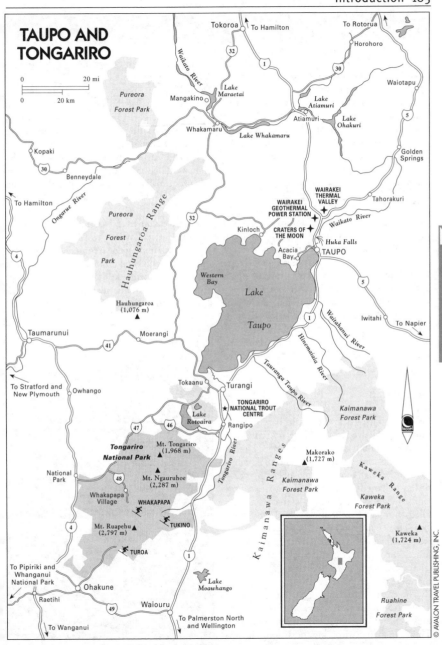

TAUPO AND TONGARIRO

0 20 mi
0 20 km

To Hamilton
Tokoroa
To Rotorua
Horohoro

32
1
30

Waikato River
Lake Maraetai
Mangakino
Lake Atiamuri
Atiamuri
Lake Ohakuri
Waiotapu

Pureora Forest Park

Whakamaru
Lake Whakamaru

5

Kopaki
Golden Springs

30
Benneydale

To Hamilton

Ongarue River

Pureora Forest Park

Hauhungaroa Range

WAIRAKEI THERMAL VALLEY
WAIRAKEI GEOTHERMAL POWER STATION
Tahorakuri

32
Kinloch
Waikato River
CRATERS OF THE MOON
Huka Falls

4

Acacia Bay
TAUPO

Western Bay
Lake Taupo

5

Hauhungaroa (1,076 m) ▲
Moerangi

1

Iwitahi
To Napier

Taumarunui
41

Waitahanui River

Tokaanu
Turangi

To Stratford and New Plymouth
Owhango

Lake Rotoaira
TONGARIRO NATIONAL TROUT CENTRE ★
Rangipo

Tauranga Taupo River

Hinemaiaia River

Kaimanawa Forest Park

47 **46**

Tongariro River

Mt. Tongariro (1,968 m) ▲
Tongariro National Park

Makorako (1,727 m) ▲

Kaimanawa Forest Park

Kaweka Range

National Park
48
Mt. Ngauruhoe (2,287 m) ▲

Kaimanawa Ranges

Kaweka Forest Park

Whakapapa Village
WHAKAPAPA

4
Mt. Ruapehu (2,797 m) ▲
TUKINO

Kaweka (1,724 m) ▲

TUROA

To Pipiriki and Whanganui National Park

1
Lake Moawhango

Raetihi
Ohakune

49
Waiouru

To Wanganui

To Palmerston North and Wellington

Ruahine Forest Park

© AVALON TRAVEL PUBLISHING, INC.

N
TAUPO AND TONGARIRO

Taupo

Taupo (population 21,000) lies at the head of Lake Taupo, 80 km south of Rotorua. Though not as touristy as Rotorua, Taupo still attracts large numbers of vacationers year-round to take advantage of its excellent lake fishing for rainbow and brown trout, sailing and water sports, spectacular lake views, and local geothermal attractions.

SIGHTS AND RECREATION THAT DON'T COST A CENT

After the commercialism of Rotorua, Taupo is a pleasant reprieve for your pocketbook. Although it lacks the famous large-scale thermal activity of Rotorua, there are still thermal areas around Taupo to explore, along with a whole range of sights and activities, many of which are free.

Stretching north from Taupo along the Waikato River is **Wairakei Park,** in which many of the thermal sights lie—don't miss them. Highway 5 from Rotorua and Hwy. 1 from Hamilton merge just north of the geothermally active Wairakei area, eight km north of Taupo.

Lake Taupo

Like other bodies of water on the Central Plateau, Lake Taupo itself is a volcano, its base and surroundings involved in several gigantic eruptions 330,000, 20,000, and 1,850 years ago. During those explosions, pumice, ash, and rock debris were hurled high into the atmosphere, pyroclastic flows charred and devastated vast areas of the landscape, and the resulting crater eventually filled with water to become Lake Taupo. It's a great chance to swim or sail in a volcano! You'll see the remains of volcanic activity in the pumice beaches, coves of "floating rocks" around the lake, and colorful steep cliffs along Western Bay that were part of the ancient volcano.

The clear, refreshingly cold water of Lake Taupo is a joy for swimming, boating, or catching an elusive rainbow or brown trout for dinner. There are many swimming spots along the waterfront beaches, especially at the lake's edge

about two km from town along Lake Terrace (almost opposite Taharepa Road.). Here Waipahihi Hot Springs bubble up into the lake, noticeably warming the water when the lake is at a suitable height. One of the best places for swimming, boating, or fishing is six km west of Taupo at **Acacia Bay.** Lie on the sandy public beach and befriend the large local duck population, swim leisurely out to the pontoon, or hire one of the rowboats, canoes, or motorboats from the friendly owners of Acacia Bay Lodge across the road.

For a pleasant several-kilometer walk, continue along Acacia Bay Rd.; you'll eventually reach a good track leading down through the bush to a rocky point and good fishing. Keep in mind that the road eventually dead-ends at private property—not much traffic apart from the occasional angling enthusiast or land developer.

Craters of the Moon

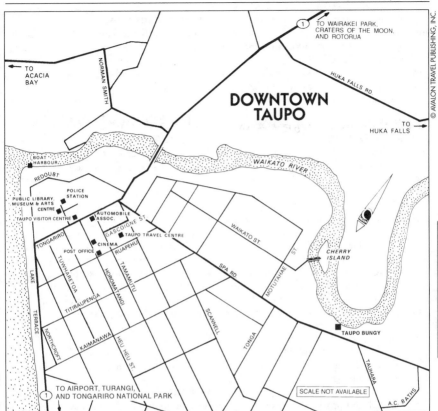

DOWNTOWN TAUPO

TO WAIRAKEI PARK, CRATERS OF THE MOON, AND ROTORUA

HUKA FALLS RD

TO HUKA FALLS

TO ACACIA BAY

NORMAN SMITH

WAIKATO RIVER

BOAT HARBOUR

REDOUBT

PUBLIC LIBRARY, MUSEUM & ARTS CENTRE

POLICE STATION

TAUPO VISITOR CENTRE

AUTOMOBILE ASSOC.

GASCOIGNE ST

TAUPO TRAVEL CENTRE

WAIKATO ST

CHERRY ISLAND

TONGARIRO

POST OFFICE

CINEMA

RUAPEHU

MOTUTAHAE ST

TUWHARETOA

HOROMATANGI

TAMAMUTU

SPA RD

TITIRAUPENGA

SCANNELL

TAUPO BUNGY

LAKE TERRACE

NORTHCROFT

KAIMANAWA

HEU HEU ST

TONGA

TAUHARA

TO AIRPORT, TURANGI, AND TONGARIRO NATIONAL PARK

SCALE NOT AVAILABLE

A.C. BATHS

Hot Spots

One natural thermal area that shouldn't be missed is **Craters of the Moon,** in Wairakei Park, just three km north of Taupo off Hwy. 1. Apart from man-made paths through the thermal area and lookouts, everything has been left untouched. Steaming, bubbling areas lie among bush-covered hills and valleys, steam-filled craters give brief glimpses of boiling mud below, and small holes on the hillsides forcefully belch out torrents of steam. Follow the trail up the steps to the top of the hill for a great view of the thermal valley and Taupo in the distance, and continue down through the bush back to the car park. Allow about an hour to see the whole thermal area. Look out for the paved road leading to Crater of the Moon Lookout and car park. Place

all valuables in the locked trunk of your car or out of sight, as there has been a problem with theft here in the past. If the area is particularly active, thermally speaking, you may find the gate closed for safety; otherwise it's generally open dawn to dusk, and admission is free.

A little farther north you'll find the huge and highly developed **Wairakei Geothermal Power Station,** the world's first commercially viable operation to produce power from naturally occurring steam. It taps a vast underground water system, heated by very hot, perhaps molten, rocks. Bores release the high pressure of the water far below, causing it to reach boiling point and produce the desired steam. At present, over 50 bores supply enough steam to generate 150 megawatts of power, or around five percent of

New Zealand's total consumption. For heaps of information and a good 15-minute audiovisual, drop by the **Geothermal Visitor Centre** on Wairakei Rd., tel. 07/378-0254, at the turnoff beside the BP petrol station. It's open daily 9 A.M.–4 P.M.; someone is always on hand to answer questions, and admission is free.

The Waikato River and Taupo Walkway

TOE- PAW

The magnificent Waikato, longest river in New Zealand, runs northward 425 km from its source on the slopes of Mt. Ruapehu in Tongariro National Park (this first stretch is called the Tongariro River), through Lake Taupo, to finally meet the Tasman Sea southwest of Auckland. The river pours out of the lake at Taupo, and about four km downstream hurtles with tremendous force through a narrow rock chasm and down the well-known **Huka Falls.** This massive volume of water falls in a raging torrent to a frothy, churning pool below. A footbridge and path provide access to various viewpoints overlooking the falls (this is another spot where valuables have been stolen from vehicles—keep them out of sight, locked in the trunk, or with you). You can walk to Huka Falls from town by taking the one-hour (one way) Taupo Walkway along the eastern banks of the river, starting at Spa Thermal Park (off Spa Rd.) in Taupo. If you have wheels, take Hwy. 1 out of town to Huka Falls Rd. and turn right. Pass Huka Village (see below) and continue along this scenic road to the various lookouts; the road eventually rejoins the main highway.

Taupo Walkway continues from Huka Falls along the eastern bank to the impressive **Aratiatia Rapids,** 11 km north of town. The Aratiatia Powerhouse control gates (part of the hydroelectric scheme) are released at 10 A.M., noon, 2 P.M., and 4 P.M. daily (check these times with the information center), which causes spectacular flooding of the river valley below within a matter of minutes. (If you don't take photos, no one will believe you!) The trail takes about two hours each way. You can also reach the rapids by car; take Hwy. 1 out of Taupo, then Hwy. 5, and turn right onto Aratiatia Road.

Botanical Reserve

At the end of Shepherd Rd. is a 28-hectare garden boasting a wide variety of native and alpine plants. It is particularly well known for a large collection of rhododendrons. It's open daily from dawn to dusk.

COMMERCIAL ATTRACTIONS

Volcanic Activity Centre

From this research center, scientists from the Institute of Geological & Nuclear Sciences (website: www.gns.cri.nz) monitor the Taupo Volcanic Zone, which extends from the volcanoes of Tongariro National Park in the south to White Island in the north. A large area of the center is devoted to visitors, with a massive three-dimensional map showing all volcanic features in the area; wall displays of volcanoes, geothermal activity, and the earth's makeup; an earthquake simulator; an audiovisual of the eruption of Mt. Ruapehu; working models; and a seismograph linked to Mt. Ruapehu. It's open Mon.–Fri. 9 A.M.–5 P.M., Sat.–Sun. 10 A.M.–4 P.M.; $5 adult, $2.50 child. The center is on the Huka Falls loop road, north of the Craters of the Moon turnoff; tel. 07/374-8375.

Wairakei Thermal Valley

Adjacent to the Geothermal Power Project, the entrance is 50 meters from the Wairakei Steam Pipe Bridge (on the right if you're heading south). Drive to the end of the road, passing all sorts of tame birds, a tame pig, and a large caged area of guinea pigs, and enter through the Barn Tearoom and ticket office. The main features of this natural thermal spot are the steaming pools of boiling pink, gray, and brown mud, colorful rock formations, and the surprisingly cold Wairakei Stream that flows through this hot, steamy area. The best time for viewing this area is after rain. Allow at least an hour to see everything; $7 adult, $2 child. The friendly owners also operate the tearoom, serving reasonably priced sandwiches, cakes, coffee, and tea daily 9 A.M.–5 P.M. in winter, 9 A.M.–7 P.M. in summer, plus a small motor camp on attractive grounds, tel. 07/374-8004.

© ANDREW HEMPSTEAD

Wairakei Geothermal Power Station

Hot Pools

Taupo Hot Springs, off Hwy. 5 South (to Napier), tel. 07/377-6502, is a good place to relax and enjoy the soothing qualities of clean hot water in attractive landscaped surroundings; $8 adult, $5 senior, $2.50 child. In addition to the main inside and outside pools, a number of private rock pools are scattered through the native bush ($9 pp, including general admission) and cooler pools are set aside for the younger ones. If you're staying in adjacent campground, admission is discounted. It's open daily 7:30 A.M.–9:30 P.M.

Wildlife

If you've always wondered what goes on at a prawn farm, and in particular, the world's first geothermally heated freshwater prawn farm, you can take an informative guided tour for $6 pp. **Prawn Park** is beside the Waikato River, off Hwy. 1, nine km north of town, tel. 07/374-8474. The tours depart daily on the hour 11 A.M.–4 P.M.

If you're interested in deer farming, ask at the information center if any of the local farmers are willing to show you around. Otherwise, take a guided tour that includes one of the large farms where the deer run free in large paddocks (arrange through Information Taupo; expect to pay an admission fee).

Cherry Island Tourist Park, which lies in the middle of the Waikato River and is link to the end of Waikato St. by a footbridge, is the place to watch trout cruise by the underwater viewing windows, take a walk around the parklike island grounds to view all kinds of birds and baby animals, or check out the upstairs gallery, which features New Zealand artists. You can sit inside, or outside on the sundeck, while you enjoy food and drinks from the island tearoom. It's open daily 9 A.M.–5 P.M., tel. 07/378-9028; admission is a little on the steep side—$10 adult, $5 child. To get there take Spa Rd., turn left on Motutahae St., then turn right on Waikato Street.

RECREATION
Lake Cruises

Taupo's marina, **Boat Harbour,** lies at the mouth of the Waikato River, easily reached on foot from downtown or by road along Redoubt St. through the domain. Here you can hop on a boat for lake sight-seeing, assist in sailing a fabulous yacht, or charter one of many fishing boats and/or trout

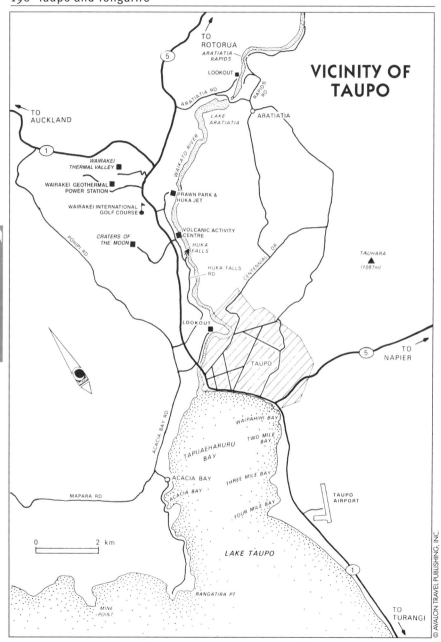

FISHING LAKE TAUPO

Lake Taupo is generally regarded as one of the world's great trout-fishing destinations. It is not the lake itself, but surrounding rivers and streams where dry-fly aficionados delight in challenges of casting for **rainbow** and **brown trout.** Introduced to the lake in the late 1800s, the fish consider the lake an inland sea, swimming up surrounding rivers and streams to spawn through winter months. But trout fishing with a dry fly is a definite art form, and certainly not for everyone. Without a knowledgeable guide it can be a fruitless endeavor; with a guide it can be expensive.

In Lake Taupo itself, trout feed in shallower waters during the cooler months, moving into the lake's deeper reaches through summer. To catch these fish a technique known as "downrigging" is employed. It's popular because anyone can do it, catching a pan-sized trout is almost guaranteed, and using the services of a local guide and his boat is relatively inexpensive.

When it comes to local guides, the name Richard Staines and his boat *Whitestriker* inevitably come up. He has been taking visitors out onto

guides. If you only want a boat to tootle around the lake for a joyride, **Punch's Place,** tel. 07/378-5596, rents self-drive runabouts. Punch also offers charter launch fishing, scenic cruises, water-skiing rides, and parasailing at $40 a flight. The other waterfront booking agent is **Launch Charters Booking Office,** tel. 07/378-3444. Use these numbers to book the following lake cruises.

One of the best ways to get to know the lake, past and present, is to take a cruise onboard the

the lake for longer than anyone else and has an excellent reputation for ensuring that quotas are filled (three fish) within a couple of hours. On your return to the marina, you have the option of keeping and cooking the fish yourself, or Richard can recommend a local restaurant and will deliver the fish there. Then you just need to turn up at dinnertime and your fish will be cooked to your liking. The charter rate is $70 per hour for the entire boat; allow about three hours to find and fish the best spots. Richard also will take you over to Maori rock carvings at Mine Bay, which can only be accessed by boat. Book through the information center or call him direct at 07/378-2736.

You also can rent a boat and head out onto the lake by yourself, but the costs add up, and you're really better off with a guide. **Waitahanui Lodge,** eight km south of Taupo, tel. 07/378-7183, rents motorboats for $30 per hour, as well as rods, lures, and all the gear you'll need. Successful anglers can take advantage of the lodge's smoking service; $50 per fish.

MV *Ernest Kemp,* an attractive replica of a paddlesteamer. The captain offers a fascinating historical commentary while you enjoy the lakefront; Hot Water Beach; Two, Three, and Four Mile Bays; Mine Bay and the intricate Maori rock carvings; and the serene beauty of Acacia Bay. A variety of trips are offered, including a one-hour cruise ($15), a two-hour cruise ($28), and a dinner cruise ($48), which includes an all-you-can-eat buffet barbecue.

a successful catch

TAUPO AND TONGARIRO

Another great way to take to water is onboard a chartered yacht. On the 13-meter ketch *The Barbary,* built in California in 1926 and once owned by Errol Flynn, you're encouraged to take part in the sailing activities, or you can just sit back, relax, and work on a Taupo tan. A fantastic three hours of sailing bliss costs only $25 per adult, $12.50 per child, and the yacht leaves from Taupo Wharf, Taupo Boat Harbour (bookings advisable) at 10:30 A.M. and 2 P.M. On Wednesday nights (summer only) *The Barbary* joins the local yacht club race at 5:30 P.M. ($15 pp).

At the opposite end of the speed spectrum to the two vessels detailed above is the *Superjet,* tel. 07/377-4855 or 0800/ 278-737. Reaching speeds over 40 knots, this twin-jetted catamaran zooms out to and beyond the Maori carvings to **Motutaiko Island,** a volcanic plug that has survived the ravishes of erosion, on a two-hour cruise; $59 adult, $29 child.

Jetboating

For speed demons, an exciting, 25-minute jetboat trip upriver to Huka Falls costs $55 adult, $35 child. The boat departs half-hourly, on demand, from the end of Huka Falls Rd. in Wairakei Park. If requested, free coach transfers can be arranged from Taupo. Take cameras and video cameras onboard at your own risk. Bookings are essential at **Huka Jet,** tel. 07/374-8572.

Taupo Bungee

Queenstown, on the South Island, is the New Zealand home of bungee jumping, but Taupo is the most popular place on the North Island to jump. If you want to plunge off a specially designed, cantilevered platform 47 meters above the clear, cold, blue-green water of Waikato River, head out to Taupo Bungee off Spa Rd., tel. 07/377-1135 or 0800/888-408. The jump costs $95. This is also a good spectator sport; viewing platforms allow access to all performances.

Golfing

North of Taupo, **Wairakei International Golf Course,** tel. 07/374-8152, is regarded as one of the best 50 courses in the world. Designed by Peter Thompson, the rolling fairways traverse wooded countryside dotted with thermally active areas. The par 72 course is a challenging 7,000 yards in length. Green fees are $60 for 18 holes.

Flightseeing

A great way to see the Taupo area is by air, especially if you don't have a lot of spare cash to fritter away on commercial attractions. **Taupo Floatplane,** tel. 07/378-7500, down at the lakefront, gives several short and exciting scenic flights, ranging from a 10-minute Taste of Taupo flight over the geothermal power station, Huka Falls, Taupo, and the Boat Harbour for $60, to a one-hour flight beyond Lake Taupo over the snowcapped volcanoes of Tongariro National Park for $185. If you want to do the latter, book as soon as possible so that weather conditions can be evaluated and a suitable time arranged. The calmest flights, particularly in summer, are those early in the day when it's still cool; overcast skies are generally the best weather conditions for smooth flightseeing.

Several aviation services based out at Taupo Airport, on Hwy. 1 six km south of town, operate scenic flights and fly-in services to remote locations such as the Kaimanawa Mountains (southeast of Taupo) for tramping and trout fishing in wild and beautiful backcountry. For details call **Taupo Air Services,** tel. 07/378-5325, or **Air Charter Taupo,** tel. 07/378-5467.

> *A great way to see the Taupo area is by air, especially if you don't have a lot of spare cash to fritter away on commercial attractions.*

Tandem skydiving is heavily promoted in the area. If you plan on jumping somewhere in New Zealand, expect to pay more at more popular destinations, such as Queenstown. **Taupo Tandem Skydiving,** tel. 07/377-0428, and the **Great Lake Skydive Centre,** tel. 0800/373-335, both charge from $170 per jump.

Entertainment

Ploughmans Restaurant is south of Taupo on Rainbow Point, tel. 07/377-3422. This Tudor-

We went up to the mountain but the motels looked nice

style pub has a large outdoor area dotted with umbrella-covered tables, or drink inside at the typically English bar (lots of British beers on tap). The food here is also good. In the vicinity, **Mad Dogs and Englishmen,** 80 Lake Terrace, tel. 07/378-0457, has a similar atmosphere. For live music, check out the main drag downtown (Tongariro St.) on Friday and Saturday nights and follow your ears—expect a minimal cover charge at the hotels on weekends. **Holy Cow!,** 11 Tongariro St., tel. 07/378-0040, is a popular backpackers' hangout offering drink and food specials nightly. Locals head for the **Red Barrel,** opposite the lake at 4 Roberts St., tel. 07/378-0555—it's busy every night, and bands play on the weekend.

The local **cinema** is on Horomatangi St., off Tongariro, tel. 07/378-7515. The two local papers list current entertainment in the back pages.

ACCOMMODATIONS

Hotels and Motels

Taupo has an ever-expanding number of motels—more spring up along the lakeshore every year, along with timeshare after timeshare. Expect to pay from $65 d at the least expensive end, up to $160 for a luxurious villa with lake views.

The least expensive motels are scattered around town away from the lakefront. The **Continental Motel** is close to downtown at 9 Scannell St., tel. 07/378-5836. Each of the nine rooms is self-contained; $75 s or d. A little farther out is the **Dunrovin Motel,** 140 Heu Heu St., tel. 07/378-7384 0508/386-768, which charges $65 s, $85 d for a small self-contained room.

One of the cheapest lakeside accommodations is the **Motel Taupo,** but it's seven km south of town at 50 Wharewaka Rd., Four Mile Bay, tel. 07/378-5115; rates from $65 s, $75 d.

Most of the best motel accommodations can be found along Lake Terrace. Highly recommended by readers is **Colonial Lodge Motel,** 134 Lake Terrace, tel. 07/378-9846 or 0800/353-636, a pleasant 10-minute walk from downtown and across the road from a beach. Each of the 12 units is well appointed and features a large spa bath, full kitchen, writing desk, and laundry facility. Rates are $110 s or d for a studio

unit and $145 for a one-bedroom unit. Next door is **Gables Motor Lodge,** 130 Lake Terrace, tel. 07/378-8030 or 0508/378-888, with a similar number of unitsand the same facilities; $120–140 s or d.

Continuing around the lake, **Oasis Beach Resort** enjoys awaterfront location three km from downtown at 241 Lake Terrace, tel. 07/378-9339 or 0800/555-378. The spacious rooms come in a variety of configurations, but each is decorated with a stylish yet casual pastel decor and enjoys water views; from $100 s or d. The resort has a large pool, restaurant, and bar. Also right on the lake, **Boulevard Waters Motor Lodge,** 215 Lake Terrace, tel. 07/377-3395 or 0800/541-541, website: www.boulevardwaters.co.nz, is fronted by an imposing colonnaded façade. Each of the 10 units features a spa bath, king-size bed, and modern kitchen in each room. Rates are $145 s, $165 d. Farther south is the **Anchorage Resort Motel,** Lake Terrace, Two Mile Bay, tel. 07/378-5442 or 0800/991-995, website: www.taupomotel.co.nz, featuring a large pool complex, spa pools, sauna, and fitness room. Each room has a kitchen and private balcony overlooking the garden. Rates are $150 s, $165 d.

Dating to the 1920s and long regarded as one of the world's great sporting lodges, **Huka Lodge,** tel. 07/378-5791, website: www.hukalodge.com, lies on the Waikato River between Taupo and Huka Falls. The 20 rooms each enjoy private entrances that open to views extending across well-tended gardens to the river. Formal dinners are served in the main lodge or, if requested, in more private settings, such as the terrace or wine cellar. A travel writer's budget doesn't extend to this sort of luxury, but apparently it's very nice, and if you want to hobnob with the rich and famous, this is the place to do it. Rates are US$660 s, US$440 pp d, which includes meals. Fishing guides cost extra, with guests whisked away to fish by 4WD, boat, or helicopter.

Bed-and-Breakfasts

One of the closest bed-and-breakfasts to downtown is **Bramham B&B,** 7 Waipahihi Ave., tel. 07/378-0064, a two-minute walk from the lake. The hosts are well traveled, having lived in North

TAUPO AND TONGARIRO

America for a number of years, and include a cooked breakfast and airport transfers in the room rate of $70 s, $100 d.

Backpacker Lodges

Hospitable and enthusiastic Mark and Susan Dumble own and operate **Rainbow Lodge,** at 99 Titiraupenga St., tel. 07/378-5754; website: www.rainbowlodge.co.nz, providing Taupo with excellent budget accommodation in a central location 500 meters from town and the bus station. The atmosphere is comfortable and relaxed, and it's a great place to stay. Facilities include heated dorms and individual double and twin rooms, a single room, communal facilities, a large fully equipped kitchen and living area with a pool table and a woodstove, a sauna, off-street parking, and luggage storage. Guests can rent all sorts of recreational gear at a minimal rate: mountain bikes, bicycle gear and panniers, a canoe, tennis rackets, and fishing equipment. Wilderness horse treks, white-water rafting, fishing trips, skiing, hunting, sight-seeing tours—anything can be arranged. Check out the excellent information board to find out more. Dorm beds are $18 pp, single rooms are $32, doubles or twins are $42 ($48 en suite). To get there from the bus depot, head east along Tamamutu for two blocks to Titiraupenga and turn left, then continue north for another two blocks.

A similar distance from the center of town and the bus depot is **Action Down Under Hostel,** 56 Kaimanawa St., tel. 07/378-3311, an associate of Hostelling International; website: www.yha.org.nz. Originally a motel, the hostel features a large lounge area, raised patio, modern kitchen, game room, and mountain bike rentals. Dorm beds are $18 pp, private rooms start at $20 pp.

Sunset Lodge, 5 Tremain Ave., tel. 07/378-5962, is another budget accommodation, close to the lake and beach, but a good hike (two km) south from downtown. It has a fully equipped kitchen, a comfortable TV lounge, laundry, a gas barbecue and a nice deck. It offers free transfers to local sights and free use of mountain bikes-a bonus for those without their own transportation. Dorm beds are $17 per night, doubles and twins are $21 pp.

Motor Camps

The most central is the tree-shaded **Taupo Motor Camp** on Redoubt St., tel. 07/378-3080, website: www.taupomotorcamp.co.nz, along the banks of the Waikato River and only a short walk from town. It has communal facilities, a TV lounge, and a shop. Tent sites and caravan sites cost from $22, cabins are $40–45. It's very busy during holiday periods—book well in advance.

De Bretts Thermal Resort, off the Taupo-Napier Hwy., tel. 07/378-8559, is a great place to stay. It has clean communal bathrooms, a bright airy kitchen and dining area with TV, play equipment for the kids, a restaurant serving buffet breakfast, and an office/store where friendly efficient staff do bookings and sell all the basics. When you have spare time to kick back and relax, enjoy the adjacent hot pools (concession on admission if you're staying here). Tent and powered sites are $12 pp, cabins range $25–35 pp, and motel rooms are $100 s or d.

To get to **Great Lake Holiday Park** three km from town on Acacia Bay Rd., tel. 07/378-5159, website: www.greatlake.net.nz, you need your own transportation, or call ahead and the friendly staff will come and get you from town. The campground offers lots of grassy, well-kept grounds for tent and caravan sites from $11 pp; standard cabins are $38 s or d, on-site vans are $42 s or d, and self-contained units are $64 s or d. The park has a spotlessly clean bathroom, kitchen, and laundry, and a TV/dining room.

FOOD

Two Favorites

When it comes to dining in Taupo, two places stand out. For breakfast, it's hard to recommend anywhere but **Replete,** 45 Heu Heu St., tel. 07/378-0606, and the Complete Replete-honey-cured bacon, poached eggs, grilled mushrooms, and focaccia for $11.50. The rest of the day, this fashionable, ambitious café features an Asian-influenced menu and healthy delights such as panini bread stuffed with artichoke, brie, and sweet Indian salsa ($8). Replete is open Mon.–Fri. 8:45 A.M.–5 P.M., Sat.–Sun. 8:45 A.M.–3:30 P.M.

Villino, 45 Horomatangi Rd., tel. 07/377-4478, is Taupo's premier dining room. Owned and operated by a German guy and a Kiwi gal, lunch is an elegantly casual affair while at night the setting is more intimate, with muted lighting and candles on each table. Even though this is the trout-fishing capital of country, you won't find trout on the menu here or at any other restaurant (it's not fished commercially). But stick with the seafood theme and start with oysters, slightly warmed and splashed with sesame oil, ginger, and soy sauce ($16) then get serious with a thick slab of salmon poached in a saffron jus ($31). Open daily for lunch and dinner, reservations are recommended.

Cheap Eats

Maxi's 24-Hour Diner, 38 Roberts St., tel. 07/378-8444, serves light meals, hamburgers and hot dogs. Sit there or order food to go. For excellent take-out Chinese (and hamburgers, fish and chips, curry dishes, and grills), try **Grasshopper Chip Bar** in the Hilltop Shopping Centre, tel. 07/378-7533. Most Chinese dishes are in the $9–12 range. Add a container of steamed rice for $3 and you have a meal for two and a snack for one for the next day. However, expect a wait if you haven't pre-ordered—business is always booming. Taupo also has a **McDonald's** with a difference—some of the tables are in the body of a DC3. It's on Ruapehu Street.

Out at **Wairakei Valley Tearooms** (next to Wairakei Geothermal Power Station, a few km north of town), tel. 07/374-8004, you can choose from a good selection of morning and afternoon teas and lunch fare at reasonable prices. It's open seven days a week. In the same vicinity, and another good place for lunch, particularly if you're out doing a bit of thermal sight-seeing, is the grand **Wairakei Resort,** on Hwy. 1 at Wairakei, tel. 07/374-8021. Part of the resort is the casual **Fairways** complex, which includes a café with a huge verandah.

Other Restaurants

The most central of Taupo's family restaurants is the **Cobb & Co.** at the Lake Establishment Hotel on Tuwharetoa St., tel. 07/378-6165. It serves the usual good meals, with main courses including a deliciously thick Beef Hot Pot ($13), as well as daily specials around $16. It's open seven days a week 7:30 A.M.–10 P.M. South of town you'll find **Ploughmans Restaurant** at 43 Charles Crescent, Rainbow Point; tel. 07/377-3422. The blackboard menu changes daily but generally includes a ploughmans platter, fish and chips, and steak and kidney hot pot, each for about $10. A selection of English beers is on tap. It's open daily 11 A.M.–1 A.M.

Nonni's, at the lake end of Tongariro St., tel. 07/378-6894, serves up rich coffee and a good breakfast, but it's not particularly cheap. The rest of the day, the specialty is Mediterranean (from $15.50 at dinner). It's open daily from 7 A.M. The **Brantry Restaurant,** 45 Rifle Range Rd., tel. 07/378-0484, is a stylish Irish dining room offering lunch Fri.–Sun. and dinner nightly. Expect to pay about $27–31 for a main meal.

Looking for more interesting spicy meals? The **Cajun-Kiwi Restaurant,** 92 Roberts St., tel. 07/378-5276, is one of the few restaurants in New Zealand specializing in the cuisine of the deep south of the United States. Smoked, cured, and blackened dishes include fish and other seafood, lamb, chicken, and vegetarian, as well as specialties such as jambalaya and gumbos. Most dishes are $13–19. The restaurant opens daily at 5:30 P.M. and, for the first hour, offers special deals on the main menu. **Mr. India Tandoori Restaurant,** 30 Tuwharetoa St., tel. 07/377-1969, features starters from $5.50 and dinners ranging $16–21. The chefs will spice the food to your desired level. Open Mon.–Sat. for lunch and daily for dinner.

TRANSPORTATION

Getting There

Taupo Airport is about six km south of town, off Hwy. 1 to Turangi. The **Airporter,** tel. 07/378-5713, is a door-to-door shuttle between the airport and downtown; $8 pp. **Air New Zealand,** tel. 0800/737-000, connects Taupo with Auckland and Wellington. Flights to all other destinations (including nearby Rotorua) are routed through these two cities.

Intercity, tel. 07/378-9032, and **Newmans,** tel. 07/378-9030, bus services arrive at and depart from **Taupo Travel Centre,** downtown at 16 Gascoigne Street. The depot is open Mon.–Fri. 8:30 A.M.–5:30 P.M. Both companies run several services a day from Taupo to Auckland, Rotorua, Hastings, Napier, Hamilton, and Wellington. A local company, **Alpine Scenic Tours,** tel. 07/378-7412, has a daily shuttle service from Taupo to Turangi, continuing south to Tongariro National Park on weekdays.

Getting Around
There's no local bus service around Taupo; instead, take a tour (see below) or use pedal power. Riding along the lakeshore is enjoyable, as is the ride through Wairakei Park (check first at the information center—some trails are closed to bikes). Because the city is relatively flat, biking is easy. Most backpacker lodges, including Rainbow Lodge, rent bikes to guests. Otherwise, head to **Cycle World,** 30 Spa Rd., tel. 07/378-6117, which rents mountain bikes for $5 per hour or $24 per day.

Car rental agencies include **Avis,** tel. 07/378-6305; **Budget,** tel. 07/378-9764; and **Hertz,** tel. 07/378-8056. Taxi companies include **Taupo Taxi,** tel. 07/378-5100, and **Top Cabs,** tel. 07/378-9250. The taxi stand is outside the bus station.

Tours
One of Taupo's best-loved characters is Walter, of **Walter's Tours;** book through the Taupo Information Centre, tel. 07/378-9000, or after hours 07/378-5924. His popular tours are tailored to suit the folks on his tour that day. Generally, they last three to five hours and take in all the area's attractions, but this can be extended to include the Waitomo or Tongariro areas. Tours start at $25 pp for three hours, $30 for five hours, or $75 for a full-day tour to Waitomo Caves or Tongariro National Park.

SERVICES AND INFORMATION
Services
Taupo's main shopping area lies east of Tongariro Street. The main **post office** is on Horomatangi Street. **Taupo Library** is on Storey Place (off Tongariro), tel. 07/376-0070.

Taupo Hospital is on Kotare St., tel. 07/378-8100. For less urgent cases, head to **Taupo Medical Centre,** on the corner of Kaimanawa and Heu Heu Streets, tel. 07/378-4080. **Main Street Pharmacy** is on Tongariro St., tel. 07/378-2636; open nightly till 9 P.M. **Taupo Police Station** is at the lake end of Tongariro St. on Storey Place, tel. 07/378-6060.

Information
For information and maps of Taupo, the lake, and the surrounding area, and for souvenirs and postage stamps, visit the amiable people at the **Taupo Visitor Centre,** 13 Tongariro St. (next to the traffic lights), tel. 07/376-0027; open daily 8:30 A.M.–5 P.M. The town and lake are promoted by **Destination Lake Taupo;** website: www.laketauponz.com. The **Automobile Association** office at 93 Tongariro St., tel. 07/378-6000, is a good source of road information and maps. It's open Mon.–Fri. 8:30 A.M.–5 P.M. Taupo's local newspaper, the *Taupo Times,* is printed four times a week, and the free *Friday* comes out once a week on Friday—a good source of local happenings and current entertainment.

Turangi and Vicinity

The town of Turangi (population 4,000), at the southern end of Lake Taupo on the banks of the Tongariro River, used to be a small village famous for its fishing before the opening of the Tongariro Development Project. It was developed into a town in 1964 to accommodate hydroelectric construction workers, but since then, it's been recognized (though little publicized) as an excellent resort area for anglers, hikers, whitewater rafters, skiers and boarders, and lovers of the great outdoors. The locals, proud of their self-proclaimed title "Heart of the Great New Zealand Outdoors," are eager to assist you in discovering their neck of the woods.

SIGHTS

The first place to go is the **Turangi Visitor Centre,** Ngawaka Pl. (opposite the shopping center), tel. 07/386-8999. The amicable people running the center offer information on the town and surrounding area. An audiovisual program on the local area is screened on request, and displays focus on fishing and forestry. Models of the Tongariro Power Development, the major contributing factor in the town's development, fill the museum area, and if you're suddenly overwhelmed by an urge to see it in person, the center does free guided tours. You can also view and buy local arts and crafts, postcards, phone cards, and more.

Trout Hatchery

A place that no angling enthusiast should miss is the **Tongariro National Trout Centre,** one of three government-operated trout hatcheries. It's five km south of town on Hwy. 1—the entrance is hard to see; look out for a dip in the road and a small sign. The attractive building houses a small museum full of assorted fishing tackle used during the last hundred years, mounted trophy trout, and displays depicting the life cycle of a trout stream. Downstairs is a fascinating underwater viewing chamber looking into the hatchery stream, where in winter you can watch the spawning process, and the rest of the year watch

trout of all sizes observing *you* through the window. It's open 9 A.M.–4 P.M.; admission is free. Trout eggs are hatched and young fish reared in the other hatchery buildings—feeding times are 10 A.M. and 3 P.M. daily, and there's also an outdoor fishing pool full of tiny trout (open six days a year so children can try the art of fly-fishing). The grounds around the hatchery are quite superb, especially in the summer when the *kowhai* trees are in bloom. A short walk brings you out on the sandy beach along Birch Pool, a popular fishing hole in the Tongariro River.

Tokaanu

If you're driving around Lake Taupo, don't miss the small, historic settlement of Tokaanu (five km west of Turangi) with its thermal area of boiling mud pools and hot water cauldrons (free), and adjacent **Tokaanu Thermal Pools,** Mangaroa St., tel. 07/386-8575, which lie along the same volcanic fault as the volcanoes of Tongariro National Park. Soak away the aches and pains of a hard day's hiking or skiing in your own private thermal pool or the main heated swimming pool. The pools are open daily 10 A.M.–9 P.M.; $4 adult, $2 child; private pool for 20 minutes $5 adult, $2.50 child.

RECREATION
Fishing

Turangi is the self-proclaimed "Trout Capital of the World," where you can expect to catch four-pound-plus trout (up to 10 pounds) year-round. Trout are caught in local rivers and streams, as well as out on the lake. The best months for brown trout are March and April, and the best for rainbow trout are May to September. Find out about the hottest fishing spots by talking to the locals (everyone is into fishing, or knows someone who is), and check out the sporting stores and fishing tackle shops in downtown Turangi. They have the latest information on what's biting what and where, and will sell you an appropriate license and all the gear you need.

Naturally, many local fishing guides are ready and willing to give you a blissful day of angling on some of New Zealand's best trout rivers, with all tackle supplied and instruction if necessary. Mark Aspinall, tel. 07/378-4453, is based in Taupo but is knowledgeable on rivers around the Turangi area and has an excellent reputation for his guiding skills. A full day's fly-fishing, complete with equipment, lessons, lunch, and light snacks, runs $350 for one or two people.

Rafting and Eco Tours

Rafting the Class III Tongariro River at the foot of the Kaimanawa Ranges is one of the most exhilarating, heart-pumping activities around, and if you're looking for this kind of action the Turangi area is a good place to try it out. Some of the Tongariro has been harnessed for hydroelectric power generation, but the most scenic and untouched stretches still provide plenty of white-water thrills. Several rafting operators run the river. **Tongariro River Rafting** offers gentle family trips on the river's lower reaches for $120 (first four people), plus $15 each additional person, and an exciting 4.5-hour trip (two hours on the river) for $80 pp. The company supplies excellent quality, *full-length* wet suits (an unusual bonus and one you'll appreciate), helmet, and life jacket; you supply your own sand or tennis shoes (a necessity), wool socks, wool sweater, and waterproof windbreaker (and wear a swimsuit). After you arrive at the river, a thorough safety talk covers mastering the paddle, paddling techniques, how to stay in the raft, and what to do if you fall out. The company supplies paddles and expects you to use them. A few quick practice strokes in the calm water and you're off with no turning back. Tongariro rapids with horrifying names are interspersed with short, beautiful, calm stretches. Fat trout cruise the water, birdlife tweets from the trees, and you quickly become a mere speck on the river between the tall cliffs. By the time you've survived (and mastered) Snooker Hole, Devil's Elbow, and other appropriately named rapids, you'll be feeling a little more confident, maybe even ready for "your next white-water river." Tongariro River Rafting is based at the Rafting Centre on Atirau Rd., tel. 07/386-6409 or 0800/101-024.

Tongariro Eco Tours, tel. 07/386-6445, is also based in the Rafting Centre on Atirau Road. This company operates a flat-bottomed boat through bird-filled wetlands at the southern end of Lake Taupo. The two-hour cruise departs daily at 8 A.M. and 6 P.M. and binoculars are supplied.

ACCOMMODATIONS
Motels and Fishing Lodges
Most of Turangi's accommodations cater to anglers. Some offer all-inclusive fishing packages, while others may have nothing more than fish-cleaning facilities. The least expensive place is **Sportsman's Lodge,** 15 Taupehi Rd., tel. 07/386-8150 or 0800/366-208. Its rooms are basic, and kitchen facilities are shared, but it has a pleasant outdoor deck and a lounge with a log fire. Rates are $55 s, $70 d. Along the same street is **Creel Lodge Motel,** 183 Taupehi Rd., tel. 07/386-8081, featuring an excellent bushland location on the banks of the Tongariro River (with some fishing holes in sight of the lodge). It has spacious private grounds, a tepid swimming pool, and a smokehouse; you can rent fishing tackle and buy licenses. The 14 self-contained units are simply furnished and priced at $75–85 s or d.

A step up from the two places detailed above is the **Bridge Tongariro Fishing Resort,** beside the Tongariro River on the north side of Turangi (on the right as you enter town from the north), tel. 07/386-8804 or 0800/887-688. Dating to the 1930s, this resort was completely rebuilt in the mid 1980s and now features 32 comfortable units, many with kitchens. Enter the main lodge, and there's no doubt you're in a fishing lodge-the walls are decorated with an interesting collection of trophy fish and antique fishing rods and tackle. The Rod & Gun Restaurant serves hearty breakfasts and will cook your catch for a small charge. Rooms are a reasonable $105–115 s or d.

At the top of the heap is **Tongariro Lodge,** upstream of Hwy. 1 along Grace Rd., tel. 07/386-7946, website: www.tongarirolodge.co.nz, a luxurious fishing lodge of world renown. Set on a nine-hectare riverfront property, it features a magnificent lounge/bar area, dining room, resident fishing guides, spa pool, tennis court, and lavish chalets. The lodge is open year-round, but is busiest May through October for the dry fly fishing season. Rates are $426 s, $371 pp d inclusive of all meals. River and lake guided fishing is $530 per day for two anglers.

Backpacker Lodges

Bellbird Lodge, 3 Rangipoia Pl., tel. 07/386-8281, website: www.bellbird.co.nz, lies beyond the information center and mall off Tautahanga Road. A little off the beaten path, it's a friendly place popular for its comfortable atmosphere and accommodating owners, who drop guests off at local trailheads and help out with fishing tips (and trips). Dorm beds are $18, doubles and twins are $20 pp. **Extreme Backpackers,** 26 Ngawaka Place, tel. 07/386-8949, is a modern, custom-built accommodation with a large communal lounge area and a private courtyard out back-both the perfect place to plan hiking and skiing trips. Dorm beds are $19, private rooms are $32 s, $44 d or twin. Both lodges provide transportation for the Tongariro Crossing (see below).

Motor Camps

Originally built to house construction workers, **Club Habitat Holiday Park,** 25 Ohuanga Rd., opposite the fire station, within easy walking distance of downtown, tel. 07/386-7492, now provides a wide range of accommodations. The setup is mainly aimed at skiers looking for a cheap holiday, with transfers to Whakapapa provided during the winter. The rest of the year the place is fairly quiet and functions as a base for a variety of adventure activities, making it especially popular with groups. Camping is $20–22, dorm beds are just $15 pp, basic cabins start at $42, and motel rooms are $85. If it's quiet you'll have free run of all the facilities, including a sauna, spa, game room, bar, and inexpensive bistro-style restaurant.

Turangi Cabins and Holiday Park on Ohuanga Rd. off Hwy. 41 south, tel. 07/386-8754, with the usual communal facilities and a TV/recreation room, is within walking distance of the downtown shops. Tent and caravan sites are $10–11 pp, cabins are $38 s or d, and on-site vans are $42 s or d.

OTHER PRACTICALITIES

Food

There's not much in the way of restaurants or entertainment; ask cooperative locals for their recommendations. The main shopping center has a number of good tearooms/coffee lounges, including **Mountain Café,** tel. 07/386-8758, open daily for breakfast and lunch. The restaurant at **Club Habitat,** 25 Ohuanga Rd., tel. 07/386-7492, has a sterile atmosphere, but the food is cheap. A small cooked breakfast costs just $5, and the rest of the day it's a blackboard menu of basic hearty food. There's a good takeout, with great oyster burgers (when in season), next to the Shell gas station on the main road into town, just before the turnoff to the information center. It's open six days a week, closed Mondays.

Many of the fishing lodges have restaurants, and these are the best places to head for a full meal. Because trout aren't caught commercially in New Zealand, you'll need to catch your own (all the restaurants below will cook up your catch-just drop it off upon returning from your fishing trip). The **Rod & Gun Restaurant** at the Bridge Tongariro Fishing Resort, tel. 07/386-8804, oozes rustic appeal. It serves a wide selection of steak and seafood dishes from around $20. If you catch your own trout, the kitchen will cook it to order.

In the shopping center along Tautahanga Rd., **Valentino's,** tel. 07/386-8821, is a stylish Italian restaurant open Wed.–Mon. for dinner. Main courses range $20–27.50.

Transportation

Turangi Bus and Travel Centre is just past the shopping center on the corner of Ohuanga Rd. and Ngawaka Pl., tel. 07/386-8918. **Intercity** and **Newmans** operate regular services north to Taupo and Rotorua and all points south via National Park. **Alpine Scenic Tours,** tel. 07/386-8918, runs a local shuttle service from Turangi to Taupo, Tongariro National Park, and all points in between. Both the backpacker lodges detailed above also operate park shuttles.

Services and Information

In the shopping center along Tautahanga Rd.

you'll find the **post office** and a number of banks. **Turangi Public Library,** tel. 07/386-8908, is also in the shopping center; open Mon.–Fri. 10:30 A.M.–5 P.M. and Saturday 10 A.M.–noon.

The main source of information is **Turangi Visitor Centre,** in the center of town on Ngawa-ka Pl., tel. 07/386-8999; it's open daily 9 A.M.–5 P.M. For information on Tongariro National Park, Kaimanawa Forest Park, hunting permits, and hut tickets, check in at headquarters of the DOC **Tongariro/Taupo Conservancy** on Turanga Place, Turangi, tel. 07/386-8607.

Tongariro National Park

New Zealand's original national park is dramatic, spectacular, and beautiful—a restless land of contrasting elements and continuous change: rolling hills carpeted in purple heather, and green and yellow tussocklands dotted with *toetoe;* dense *rimu* forest sheltering an abundance of birdlife; a desolate desert area and a lunar landscape scattered with sharp chunks of black volcanic rock; icy cold waterfalls and bubbling hot springs; and three magnificent volcanoes that dominate the surrounding landscape—these are the images of Tongariro in summer. In winter a thick blanket of snow turns the park into a white wonderland. Backcountry explorers and ice-climbers joyfully head out into the frigid elements, skiers ride gravity down the steep volcanic slopes. Any lover of the great outdoors shouldn't miss this ancient land.

The only facilities within the park are in the west, at **Whakapapa Village.** Nearby is the town of **National Park,** and on the park's southern outskirts is **Ohakune.** All three places offer a variety of accommodations and restaurants, coming alive with hikers in summer and skiers in winter.

THE LAND

The geological features and volcanic activity of the park, lying at the southern end of the Volcanic Plateau, are direct results of the Indian-Australian Plate's overriding the Pacific Plate. Three major volcanoes tower above the surrounding landscape, dominating the horizon from all directions. Snowcapped **Mount Ruapehu,** the highest mountain on the North Island (2,797 meters), consists of vents, lava flows, and many mudflows that have occurred over thousands of years. Erup-tions (the last in 1996) have repeatedly ejected sulphurous water and ash from the 17-hectare crater onto the upper slopes of the mountain. In the past, this caused mudflows *(lahars)* to run far out onto the surrounding land, creating a distinct ring plain around the mountains, valleys, and ash-covered desertscapes. The seemingly calm but suspiciously warm and highly acidic water of **Crater Lake** continues to hide the violent nature of this volcano that smolders not far below the surface—but this doesn't deter the thousands who ski Ruapehu in winter or hike up it throughout the year.

The composite andesite volcano of **Mount Ngauruhoe** is the most easily recognized with its perfectly symmetrical cone and 32-degree slopes. It's 2,287 meters high, rises 650 meters above the southern slopes of Tongariro, and is still active. Steam wafts eerily from its crater. **Mount Tongariro,** a truncated multiple volcano, stands 1,968 meters high and contains a number of small craters. **Red Crater** and **Te Maari Craters**—the most recently active—emit steam, gas, and hot air. You can watch the volcanic activity at **Ketetahi Hot Springs** on the north side of Mt. Tongariro.

On the eastern side of the volcanic peaks lies the **Rangipo Desert,** a desolate windswept landscape where few living things survive the temperature extremes. On the contrasting western side of the park the hills and valleys are covered in dense bush and beech forest, home to myriad insects, birds, and small animals. Two areas of Tongariro National Park are designated as "wilderness areas" (meaning totally undeveloped)—**Hauhungatahi,** which stretches from the western slopes of Mt. Ruapehu to Erua on Hwy. 4, and **Te Tatau-Pounamu,** which lies northeast of Mt. Tongariro between Central Crater and the Desert Road.

Climate

Wind, which assaults the volcanic peaks from all directions, is the main climatic factor affecting Tongariro National Park. The prevailing moist westerlies drop almost all of their moisture on the west side of the mountains—by the time they reach the east side they're pretty dry. Although the winds from the west to northwest bring most of the rain, they carry only light snowfalls; southerly winds are generally colder and can bring snow at any time of year. The rainfall around Whakapapa Visitor Centre is about 2,200 mm and evenly distributed throughout the year. At Ohakune, on the south side, about 1,250 mm of rain falls per year. No particular month is considered "the wettest"—most months are wet.

The rainfall around Whakapapa Visitor Centre is about 2,200 mm and evenly distributed throughout the year.

Frosts can occur year-round, and snow heavily blankets the peaks most winters. Average daily temperature is 13°C with a maximum of 25 and a minimum of 1°C (in midwinter the average is down to a frosty 3°C). Daily mountain forecasts are available at Whakapapa Visitor Centre and ranger stations.

If you're backcountry hiking, keep in mind that the air temperature drops at the rate of about 6°C per 1,000-meter gain in altitude; be adequately prepared at any time of year for all kinds of weather—conditions can change rapidly.

Flora and Fauna

Five distinct vegetation types—mixed rainforest, beech forest, tussock grasslands, wetlands, and alpine desert—live within the park, which ranges in altitude. In the lower areas you find the large podocarp trees, broadleafs, vines, orchids, and

WHY THE MOUNTAINS MOVED

Maori mythology explains the location of the major North Island mountains in a vividly romantic and imaginative way. All the mightiest mountains once huddled together in the center of the North Island—Tongariro reigned as chief. They were all males, except for the beautiful forest-clad Pihanga, who stood (and still stands) at the eastern end of the Kakaramea Range between Lakes Taupo and Rotoaira. All were in love with Pihanga but she took a fancy only to the great Tongariro, who had fiercely battled the others and won. Pihanga gladly gave herself to him and the losers were forced to retreat, fleeing in anger and sorrow during the cover of darkness (mountains can move only at night) to many parts of the North Island. Putauaki traveled northeast to the Bay of Plenty, where he stopped at the northern end of the Kaingaroa Plain overlooking the Rangitaiki valley. Tauhara traveled only as far as the shores of Lake Taupo so that he could forever (masochistically) gaze back at the lovely Pihanga. Taranaki (also known as Mt. Egmont) angrily fled with great speed to the west coast, where he stopped when he reached the sea.

Many centuries passed before the mountains "came alive with fire." A great priest, Ngatoro-i-rangi, climbed Ngauruhoe to view the surrounding terrain. On reaching the top he was suddenly trapped in a terrible snowstorm, and in his fear (snow was a new and unpleasant experience) he called out for help to his priestess sisters in the north, begging them to send him fire so that he wouldn't freeze to death. Hearing his pleas, they got the fire-demons to send volcanic heat via White Island and Rotorua, the fire bursting up through the ground in many places before finally reaching the summit of Ngauruhoe. The priest sacrificed a female slave, Auruhoe, to add impact to his pleas, and when the fire burst forth he ceremoniously hurled her body into the bubbling crater. The volcano became known as "Ngauruhoe" after this gruesome incident. Tongariro was also named during this event from *tonga* (south wind—mentioned in the priest's prayers) and *rio* (seized).

ferns that make up the mixed rainforest—a lush and tropical home for an abundance of native birds. Birds such as the **native pigeon** (which literally stuffs itself on berry fruits), the nectar-sipping *tui* and **bellbird,** and the insect-eating **robin, fantail,** and **tomtit** are the most easily seen birds in the rainforest, along with the **whitehead** and nocturnal **kiwi.** A large variety of insects lives in the trees and among the debris on the forest floor, and the noisy **cicadas** can be quite deafening in summer. A good place to experience this kind of exotic greenery is the Ohakune area in the southwest sector of the park.

Climb to the 1,000-meter level and the rainforest gives way to mountain beech and cedar forest, where you'll see the tiny green **rifleman** (one of New Zealand's smallest birds), **silvereye,** and occasional **parakeet.** Continuing upward, the forest opens out into attractive tussock shrublands, where alpine plants, tussock, and heather are dominant. Here the **native falcon** searches for small birds and animals, the sounds of the **pipit** and secretive **fernbird** can be heard, and mice and hares scurry in the dense shrubbery.

You'll find the wetlands environment along the bogs, pond edges, stream banks, and waterfalls within the park. **Ourisia** (a delicate plant with white flowers), buttercups, daisies, and sundews live along the water's edge with freshwater crayfish and a large variety of aquatic insects. Check out the extensive bogs and intriguing plantlife on the western slopes of Mt. Ruapehu, near Mt. Hauhungatahi. You can still see the endangered **blue duck** (or *whio* to the Maori) in park areas around fast-flowing streams.

The deserts on the park's east side are mainly barren, an amazing contrast to the western side of the park. This is due not only to a lack of rain but also to the harsh dry winds blowing from the northwest over Mt. Ruapehu. The soil is sandy gravel, the wind and temperature extremes attract little in the way of flora or fauna, and fairly frequent flash floods further desecrate the surface. The highest level of the park is an alpine environment where low-to-the-ground plants suited to harsh winds, snow, frost, and dust storms survive in their extreme but natural habitat. The **woolly mountain daisy, mountain snowberry,** and **whipcord hebe** are several of the most recognizable alpine flora. Most of the park flowers are white, apart from an occasional purple or mauve orchid, and the region is quite spectacular in December and January when everything begins to bloom. You'll also see tussockland birds in this area, along with the odd rabbit or hare.

The boundaries of each vegetation type aren't really obvious when you're hiking leisurely along—they gently merge into one another. The best way to appreciate the changes in both landscape and flora is from Mt. Ruapehu. Hike to the top, or drive up the northwest side via Bruce Rd. to Top O' The Bruce, or up the southwest side via Ohakune Mountain Rd. to Turoa Skifield.

RUAPEHU BLOWS ITS TOP

Beginning in late September 1995, Mt. Ruapehu started belching ash, steam, and the occasional rock as big as a car from Crater Lake. The mountain erupted every two to three minutes in its most sustained activity since 1945, with continued activity well into 1996. Scientists feared that it was building up to a major blast. Authorities warned residents to expect falling ash and potential water pollution from the ash and steam that shot as much as 19 km into the air; though they forced no one to evacuate, they closed airspace, highways, railways, and ski fields, the area's major attraction. But New Zealand tourism officials seized their chance to promote a natural wonder and encouraged tourists to take a look at the volcano, from a safe distance, of course.

Ruapehu continues to be a major attraction. You can still walk up to the crater rim, either by yourself or on a guided hike from Whakapapa Ski Area. But be aware that Ruapehu is an *active* volcano and an alpine area. The main hazard now is gas in the crater basin—continually assess the wind direction and position of any gas clouds. And the possibility of eruptions large enough to throw blocks and lake water out into the crater basin remains.

An Area Saved

The original 6,518-acre block of Tongariro land was given as a gift to the government from Chief Te Heu Heu Tukino IV of the Tuwharetoa tribe in 1887. The wise chief wanted to ensure that the volcanic center of the North Island would never be divided and sold in sections to the Pakeha by future Maori landowners. He believed that this area, rich in beauty and legends, should be forever enjoyed by all New Zealanders. This generous gift was gladly received by the government, which promised that the area would be left undivided and in its natural state. It officially became Tongariro National Park in 1894—one of the first national parks in the world. With the addition of much land over the years, the park has since expanded into a spectacular 188,000-acre area of New Zealand wilderness.

ex cellent experience but

MOUNTAIN SCENERY *difficult*
Viewpoints   *all day*

The best and quickest way to get oriented to this magnificent volcanic area is by taking one of two roads up Mt. Ruapehu as far as you can go. Each gives a different aspect of the park and is worth checking out if you can afford the time.

The busiest park road is Hwy. 48 off Hwy. 47, which takes you up to **Whakapapa Village,** past the Visitor Centre, and eight km up the steep Bruce Rd. to Whakapapa Ski Area—from here you get spectacular views of the volcanoes and northern sector of the park. In summer two chair-lifts at **Whakapapa Ski Area,** tel. 07/892-3738, operate from Top O' the Bruce (the base village) to 2,000 meters above sea level, where you can enjoy panoramic views and lunch from the verandah of the Knoll Ridge Chalet. The lifts operate mid-Dec. to late April, daily 9 A.M.–4 P.M.; $15 adult, $8 child. The safest way to continue higher is on a guided walk. Departing daily at 9:30 A.M., the walk climbs to the rim of a crater formed during the 1996 eruption. Cost (including lift) is $45 adult, $20 child. Hiking boots and poles can be rented at the day lodge. An interpretive trail from the top of the chairlift back down to the day lodge (90 minutes) is a more interesting alternative to taking the chair—and it's downhill all the way.

If you're approaching the park from the south, take Hwy. 49 (or Hwy. 4 and then 49 from Wanganui) to the town of Ohakune, then follow Ohakune Mountain Rd. past the Ohakune Field Centre up through the subalpine forest that carpets the western side of Mt. Ruapehu. This road lends great views of Mt. Ruapehu and its glaciers above as you climb, passes a couple of tracks to magnificent waterfalls, and terminates at Turoa Ski Field, where you get equally fabulous views of the park stretched out far below (this road requires chains in winter).

Circling the Park

The third way to admire the contrasting and varied scenery of this area is to circumnavigate the park via Highways 1, 49, 49A, 4, and 47. Highway 1, the Desert Rd., is the most direct route south. If you don't have time to get into Tongariro, this is the route to take. It passes through the amazingly desolate landscape (great for dramatic photographs) on the dry, windswept, eastern side of the volcanoes, and presents some craggy mountain views. To reach the most popular park attractions, head for the western side of the park. Drive clear around (just over three hours without stops, or one day to include stops at the main attractions) and you can see it all. A hiker worth his or her salt won't be able to resist staying at least a few days.

HIKING

The many tracks provide a wide variety of scenery and terrain and vary from short 15-minute walks suitable for anyone to a strenuous six-day hike around the mountains recommended only for very fit people. If your route involves leaving the marked track, you need to be an expert map reader and compass navigator; the park experiences "whiteout" conditions every now and again that can be both frightening and hazardous if you're not adequately prepared. If you're hiking across snow, take sunglasses, sunscreen, and something to drink.

The park offers an extensive network of well-graded tracks that suit everyone from the first-timer to the serious and experienced hiker. The park has so many hiking opportunities that the best thing to do is to drop in at the DOC Whakapapa Visitor Centre or Ohakune Visitor and describe the kind of terrain you'd like to see—you'll get plenty of suggestions and can load up with relevant brochures and maps.

Tramping huts are situated along the walking tracks at regular intervals—five or six hours between huts. They accommodate up to 22 people (bunk-bed style) and are supplied with firewood—carry your own stove, fuel, and utensils or you may have to settle for dried fruit and nuts for dinner. The hut fee is $12 pp, $6 child—buy tickets in advance at the Whakapapa Visitor Centre or the Ohakune Field Centre.

Short Walks

Some of the most easily accessible shorter walks are around Whakapapa Village and Ohakune. The shortest walk (20 minutes one way) in the Whakapapa Village area is along **Ridge Track,** starting 100 meters above the Visitor Centre and leading to a lookout point above the tree line. The six-km (two-hour round-trip) **Whakapapanui Walk** starts 300 meters above the Visitor Centre at the Whakapapa Motor Camp, follows the Whakapapanui Stream through beautiful beech forest and native bush, and ends on Hwy. 48, three km below the center. The enjoyable seven-km (2.5-hour round-trip) track to colorful **Silica Springs and Rapids** starts just above the motor camp, follows the Waikare Stream to the white rapids and on to the spring source, and returns back to Bruce Road. The 15-minute (round-trip) **Mounds Nature Walk** starts on Hwy. 48, five km below Whakapapa Visitor Centre. **Tawhai Falls** splashes down over the lip of a lava flow near the Whakapapanui Stream and is worth the short walk (30 minutes round-trip); the track starts on Hwy. 48, 3.5 km below the Visitor Centre. You can reach beautiful Taranaki Falls plummeting 20 meters down a major lava flow, by a track starting from Grand Chateau Tongariro or Skotel in Whakapapa Village. It takes about one hour to get to the falls, up to 2.5 hours round-trip, and the return route follows the banks of the Wairere Stream. 2 people did this one in 2 hrs

Take Ohakune Mountain Rd. up the southwest side of Mt. Ruapehu for several more short hiking trails. **Waitonga Falls Walk** takes about 30 minutes one way, and the spectacular **Mangawhero Falls** lookout, to the right farther up the road, is only a couple of minutes' walk from the main road—well worth a stop and click of the camera. **Mangawhero Forest Walk** starts opposite the Ohakune Field Centre and takes you for a one-hour (round-trip) walk through podocarp forest. The 20-meter **Rimu Track** also starts opposite the Ohakune Field Centre.

Another short walk, but in the northern sector, winds along the track to the small and serene **Lake Rotopounamu** that lies sheltered in a forested crater on the northwest side of Mt. Pihanga. Access is from Te Ponanga Saddle Rd. (Hwy. 47) between Turangi and Lake Rotoaira; the walk takes about 20 minutes one way to the lake, or 1.5 hours around the lake.

Tongariro Crossing

Often described as the "finest one-day walk in New Zealand," the Tongariro Crossing is the park's most popular track. It is 20 km long, but takes seven to eight hours one way due to the strenuous going. A shuttle service links each end of the trail, making a day trip possible. The track passes through a variety of vegetation zones, and crosses an active part of the volcano at **Ketetahi Hot Springs** on the northern side of north crater (where the legendary fire sent by the fire demons spurted from the ground on its way to Mt. Ngauruhoe). Here you'll see boiling mud, blowholes, fumaroles, small geysers, and hot springs. Ketetahi Hot Springs is on private land, and at present there is no public access to the warm "health-giving" stream below the thermal area. You can see the springs from the lower end where the track passes by.

The Tongariro Crossing track begins from the end of Manatepopo Rd. and climbs through lava flows of varying ages, each with a different stage of regenerated vegetation. The trail then climbs steeply to a saddle between Mt. Tongariro and Mt. Ngauruhoe before descending to Blue Lake and the thermal area, 2.5 hours from the trail's end at the Ketetahi car park on Hwy. 47A. These routes cross open and exposed terrain subject to severe weather conditions—ensure you have adequate clothing and equipment. Wear sturdy boots and don't forget your swimming gear (have it on underneath if you're shy). Keep on the marked track at all times when you're in the thermal area—if the steam gets too concentrated to see, wait until it clears before you progress along the track—or you may find out firsthand how a lobster feels when it's plunged into boiling water!

Tongariro Track Transport, tel. 07/892-3716, drops hikers at the southern trailhead at 8:30 A.M. and makes pickups at the other end at 4:30 P.M. and 6 P.M. The cost, which includes transportation to and from Whakapapa and National Park accommodations, is $18 pp. Call for exact pickup times, or check at your accommodation.

Round the Mountain Track

This track is also popular, but you need to be in pretty good shape and able to carry five days' worth of food, supplies, and warm clothing on your back. Huts lie five or six hours apart along the track, which links to form a roughly circular trail around the three main volcanoes. Other tracks lead off to various attractions, such as hot springs and splendid waterfalls, or cross the rugged and eerily desolate tops of the volcanoes. Before you set off on any of the longer hikes, leave your itinerary with the rangers in case you get stranded or lost in bad weather. A "Round The Mountain—Mount Ruapehu" track guide is available from local information centers for $1.

SKIING AND SNOWBOARDING

Thousands flock to the three beautiful ski fields of Mt. Ruapehu each year. Apart from the excellent snow conditions, variety of trails, and long ski season—from late June to early November—you can't beat the views of snow-covered mountains and steaming craters. The best time for skiing and boarding the volcanic slopes of Tongariro National Park is September when the snow is deep and the weather fair. As far as skiing conditions go, Turoa on the southern slopes generally receives drier snow and colder temperatures than Whakapapa on the western slopes.

The two largest fields—Whakapapa and Turoa—are owned by the same company, Ruapehu Alpine Lifts, but are separated by a one-hour drive. The company markets them as a single entity, **Mt. Ruapehu.**

Whakapapa Ski Area

New Zealand's largest ski field, Whakapapa, is served by 25 chairlifts, T-bars, rope tows, and platter lifts. Encompassing 400 hectares and 44 named runs, it has a base elevation of 1,625 meters and an impressive vertical rise of 675 meters. While first-timers try their skill on gentle beginners' slopes of Happy Valley, experts can play on slopes that test even the most experienced skiers. Snowboarders enjoy a terrain park and half pipe. Food service is available at Top O' The Bruce, at the Schusshaus on Hut Flat, at the top of the Waterfall Express chairlift, and at the top of the West Ridge chairlift. You'll find public shelters at the top of the Waterfall chairlift and Top O' The Bruce—the many private lodges on the field are for members only. You can rent skies, snowboards, and clothing on the field, and take advantage of ski repairs and a ski shop at Top O' The Bruce. The season runs from mid-June with lifts operating into November. Lift tickets are $54 adult, $27 child, or buy a five-day pass interchangeable with Turoa for $189 and $95 respectively.

The road to Top O' The Bruce parking lot is paved, but often chains are required. Inexpensive shuttle buses run several times a day from beside the Whakapapa Tavern to the ski field—get your ticket at the car park kiosk. For ski field information, call 07/892-3738.

Turoa

Also on Mt. Ruapehu, but accessed from Ohakune, south of Whakapapa, Turoa's four chairlifts and seven surface lifts provide access to diverse terrain interspersed with small valleys and wide-open, unobstructed slopes. The base of the ski field is 1,600 meters, the top is at 2,320 meters, the vertical rise is 720 meters (New Zealand's greatest vertical rise), and there are runs to suit all levels of experience. Turoa provides a terrain park, a half pipe, various food outlets, a ski school, and rentals. The season runs mid-June to mid-October. Tickets are $54 adult, $27 child; a five-day pass interchangeable with Whakapapa is $189 and $95. If you don't have transportation, catch a ride on the regular 4WD bus that runs up the 17 km from Ohakune to the ski field each day. For general information, call 06/385-8456.

Tukino Ski Field

Tukino, on the eastern slopes of Mt. Ruapehu, typifies noncommercialized skiing at its New Zealand best. The lifts lie at the end of a rough nine-km road, which branches off Hwy. 1 (the Desert Road) 20 km north of Waiouru. Access in winter for the last six km is possible only with 4WD vehicles. Once at the top, you'll find three rope tows, no grooming, no rentals, and no food. Just a bunch of locals enjoying skiing and snowboarding in its rawest form. The ski field is operated by three ski clubs, with lifts open weekends only ($20 adult, $10 child). Call 07/387-6294 or 09/817-8987 for accommodation and transportation options.

OTHER PARK RECREATION

Climbing

The three volcanoes afford exciting climbing over a variety of terrain, and are good practice climbs if you plan to attempt the difficult peaks of the South Island's Southern Alps. Within the park you'll find intriguing peaks, walls, towers, buttresses, and couloirs, and you can expect hard snow and icy rocks on all exposed ridges. Both ice- and rock-climbing are popular activities throughout the year.

Climb up to the mysterious, steel-gray **Crater Lake** at the top of Mt. Ruapehu, or to Tahuran-gi, at 2,797 meters the park's highest peak. The steep slopes of **Mount Ngauruhoe** offer quite a challenge in summer, when loose stones frequently threaten from upper slopes, and the knowledge that the volcano could erupt at any time provides quite an adrenaline rush. Winter conditions require more specialized equipment—ice axes, ropes, and crampons—and a competent knowledge of ice climbing. Many other peaks in the park provide a wide range of climbs that satisfy the beginner right through to the most experienced.

Check at Whakapapa Visitor Centre or Ohakune Visitor Centre and find out if you're properly equipped for the Tongariro climbing experience and local weather conditions. If possible, climb in a group. If you want to learn how to snow-and-ice-climb or to improve your skills, **Plateau Outdoor Adventure Guides,** tel. 07/892-2740, gives one- to five-day courses—the cost of each includes equipment, food, and transportation.

Flightseeing

One of the best ways to appreciate the abundance of natural beauty in this area is to take a scenic flight with **Mountain Air,** at the airport (known as Chateau Airport) on Hwy. 47, eight km from the park boundary, tel. 07/892-2812 or 0800/922-812. Choose from one of three regular trips—over the Grand Chateau and Tama lakes for $70 pp, over the Grand Chateau, Kete-tahi Springs, Mt. Tongariro, and Mt. Ngauruhoe for $110 pp, or over the entire park for breathtaking views of Mt. Ruapehu during a 35-minute flight for $145 pp.

WHAKAPAPA VILLAGE

Everything lies within walking distance from this compact little village nestled along the western slopes of Mt. Ruapehu, and it's a five-minute drive from New Zealand's largest ski field. Whakapapa Village Rd. branches off Hwy. 47, which links to Hwy. 4 and the town of National Park. The village boasts a nine-hole golf course. While not particularly challenging, its alpine environment and the trio of snowcapped volcanoes as a backdrop prove both interesting and unique. Call 07/892-3809 for details.

Staying in the nearby town of National Park is a lot cheaper than staying in the village, but the surroundings and position farther up the road can't be beat. All room rates quoted below are for summer. In winter the rates almost double, but ski packages are offered at a considerable discount.

we had a wonderful dinner

Room 203 + view
Need reservations

Grand Chateau   *here - highly recommend staying*

If you feel like a splurge, French chateau-style Grand Chateau, tel. 07/892-3809 or 0800/733-944, website: www.chateau.co.nz, is probably one of the best places in New Zealand to do it. The large and magnificent blue-roofed brick building on the lower slopes of Mt. Ruapehu (you can't miss it heading up the road to Whakapapa) is a luxury hotel and local landmark. Guests enjoy fantastic mountain views, comfortable lounges, upmarket dining, a heated indoor pool, and a small fitness room. Nonguests aren't supposed to go farther than the lobby unless they pay for morning coffee or afternoon tea, or are heading for the restaurant (see below). However, nonguests can play tennis ($8 per hour; $4 racquet rental), or play a round of golf ($15 for nine holes; $12 club rental) at New Zealand's highest golf course—pay in the hotel lobby. Through summer, economy rooms are $125 s or d, standard rooms are $155, and premier rooms are $195.

Skotel Alpine Resort   *Very Nice*

The only other rooms in the village can be found at the Skotel Alpine Resort, tel. 07/892-3719. Its excellent location (behind the chateau) offers outstanding mountain and valley views from the verandah. Aptly described as the place "for all seasons," the Skotel has a fitness room, a TV room, indoor and outdoor saunas and spas, communal cooking facilities, and a restaurant and bar. There's nothing quite like soaking in the hot bubbling water of the spa at the end of a hard day's hiking or skiing—outside and separate from the main building but glass enclosed, it's a very appealing spot to kick back and gaze at mountains or stars while the swirling water brings your body back to life. In summer, dorm beds are $25 pp, with each room containing three beds, a hand basin, and heater, but sharing bathroom and kitchen facilities. Standard but spacious hotel-style rooms, each with a private balcony, are $105–125 s or d, discounted to $70–90 s or d in spring and fall.

Campground

Excluding the backcountry, the only place to camp is **Whakapapa Holiday Park,** in a forest of enchanting beech trees 100 meters beyond the information center, tel. 07/892-3897. It has the usual communal facilities and a store stocked with foods and essential items—open every day 8 A.M.–6 P.M. Rates are $10 pp for tent sites (lim-

Grand Chateau

ited number of sites), $12 pp for powered sites, and $45 s or d for the five small cabins, or $55 for the lone tourist flat. Several short hiking trails lead out from the campground.

Food

The least expensive way to eat in Whakapapa Village is to stock up on food supplies before heading up the mountain road, and to cook your own meals in the communal kitchen at the motor camp or Skotel. You can buy basic foodstuffs, some canned and frozen foods, and snacks at **Whakapapa Holiday Park Store**—open daily 8:30 A.M.–5:30 P.M. The restaurant in the **Skotel Alpine Resort,** tel. 07/892-3719, is open year-round for breakfast 7:30–10 A.M. and for dinner 6:30–10 P.M. Enjoy one of the bistro and salad meals in summer (entrees average $18, and there's always a daily special), salad bar and hot veggies with all meals in winter.

The Grand Chateau, tel. 07/892-3809, offers a variety of dining choices, all open to guests and nonguests alike. For morning coffee or afternoon tea in luxurious surroundings, head for the main lobby; it's free for hotel guests, but $7 for nonguests and worth every cent just to sink into the supremely comfortable chairs and take in magnificent mountain views. The **Ruapehu Restaurant,** the resort's premier dining room, is open for breakfast 7:30–10 A.M.; $6–16 continental or $24 for a cooked meal. On Sunday, it serves a delicious buffet-style lunch 12:30–2 P.M.; $32 pp. Dinner, served from 6:30–9 P.M., is a more formal affair—expect to pay from $28 for a main course alone, and note that a "high standard of dress" is required (no jeans, tennis or sandshoes, or shorts)—reservations are essential.

Transportation

The closest that long-distance buses and trains come to Whakapapa Village is the town of National Park, on Hwy. 4, 16 km to the west (see below). **Alpine Scenic Tours,** tel. 07/386-8918, provides a shuttle service between the village and National Park, as well as from the larger center of Turangi in the north. **Tongariro Track Transport,** tel. 07/892-3716, links all the major trail-

heads. In winter, the same company operates as **Whakapapa Shuttle,** transporting skiers and boarders between the village and ski field.

Information

The main source of park information is **Whakapapa Visitor Centre,** 100 meters up the hill from The Grand Chateau, tel. 07/892-3729. Open daily 8 A.M.–5 P.M., the center features many interesting displays describing local geology, volcanism (including an interesting look at the latest explosions), earthquakes, and flora and fauna, as well as a small skiing museum, track descriptions (brochures detailing each track are $1 each), hut information, and a summer interpretive program. If you'd like to see the technicolor spectacle of a volcanic eruption complete with awesome stereo effects, check out *The Ring of Fire* audiovisual in the theater. Equally spectacular is another audiovisual, *Sacred Gift of Tongariro*.

NATIONAL PARK

This small town (population 500) at the junction of Highways 4 and 47 is the gateway to Tongariro's western slopes and Whakapapa Village 16 km to the east. It holds numerous accommodations and is a stop for both Tranz Scenic and Intercity. **Mountain Air,** tel. 07/892-2812, offers flightseeing from the local airport, but apart from that the town offers little else.

Accommodations

Howard's Lodge on Carroll St., tel. 07/892-2827, website: www.howardslodge.co.nz, is the best-value accommodation in National Park. The newer wing features comfortable rooms with private bathrooms for $70 s or d. Guests staying in these rooms have use of a great lounge area and a modern kitchen. Across the parking lot and completely self-contained are rooms and facilities designed for backpackers, who enjoy the use of a private lounge and two kitchens. Dorm beds here are $19, a double room with shared facilities is $24 pp. But what makes this place really great are the hosts. Last time I stayed here, they somehow managed to remember everyone by name, arrange track transportation, and serve

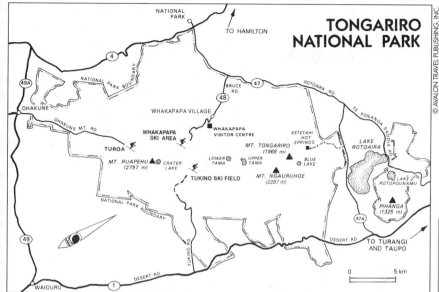

© AVALON TRAVEL PUBLISHING, INC.

TONGARIRO NATIONAL PARK

TAUPO AND TONGARIRO

up breakfast each morning (from $7) and complimentary coffee and cake each evening.

Like Howard's Lodge, the other places to stay in town provide beds for all budgets. **Pukenui Lodge,** Millar St., tel. 07/892-2882, website: www.tongariro.co.nz, has full view of the mountains from the large lounge area. Dorm beds are $22 pp, or pay just $35–50 s, $45–65 d for a private room. The restaurant on-site serves up reasonably priced meals, which can be bought separately or as part of a package ($55 for a dorm bed, breakfast, and dinner). The **Ski Haus,** Carroll St., tel. 07/892-2854, website: www.skihaus.co.nz, offers backpacker accommodations for $20 pp, self-catering rooms for $28 pp, and powered sites for $10 pp. Like all the other places in town, it is designed for the winter crowd with a spa, drying room, cozy lounge with an open fire (open from 6 P.M. year-round), and ski field transfers.

Transportation

If you're visiting Tongariro National Park and arriving by bus or train, you'll end up in town. National Park is a stop on the **Tranz Scenic,** tel. 0800/802-802, Auckland to Wellington route. Ticket prices vary considerably, but start at $65 for a one-way ticket between Auckland and National Park. **Intercity** has no depot in town, but buses arrive and depart once daily in each direction for Auckland ($61 one way) and Wellington ($65 one way), stopping outside the Ski Haus on Carroll Street. All Intercity buses from Auckland travel via Taumarunui, so if you are coming from the Lake Taupo area, hook up with the **Alpine Scenic Tours** shuttle; tel. 07/386-8918. **Tongariro Track Transport,** tel. 07/892-3716, links National Park with both ends of the Tongariro Crossing with a stop at Whakapaka Village.

OHAKUNE ✓

The small town of Ohakune, 32 km south of National Park on Hwy 49, provides the main access to the southern reaches of Tongariro National Park and is the jumping-off point for the Turoa ski field. Ohakune really only comes alive in winter, when the population rises from 1,500 to well over 5,000. Many businesses don't even open the rest of the year, but inquire at the information center about white-water rafting and horseback riding. The main summer draw is the hikes that radiate from Ohakune Mountain Road.

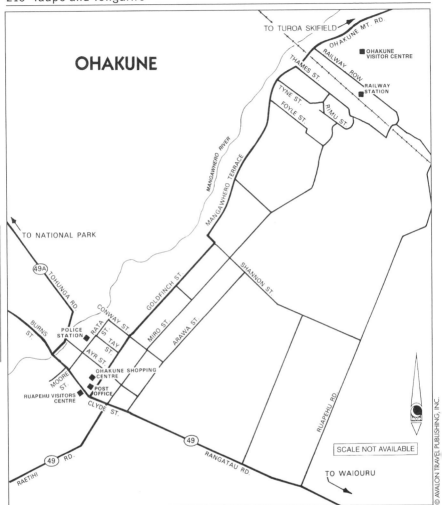

In nearby Waiouru, 27 km east of Ohakune, the **Army Museum,** tel. 06/387-6911, is dedicated to New Zealand's military history, from the great Maori Land Wars through to the country's involvement in Vietnam. It's open daily 9 A.M.–4:30 P.M.; $8 adult, $5 senior and child.

Hotels and Motels

Ohakune has more than 20 places to stay, ranging from standard roadside motels to upmarket lodges. Most rely on the busy ski season, when prices skyrocket and rooms need to be booked well in advance. Outside of winter, some places don't bother opening. The least expensive beds can be found at the **Ohakune Country Hotel,** a modern low-rise complex at 72 Clyde St., tel. 06/385-8268, where single rooms with shared bath are $55 and doubles are $65 d; en suite rooms are $90 s or d. Also on the south side of the highway, **Mountain View Motel,** 2 Moore

St., tel. 06/385-8675, has basic cabins from $60 s or d and more luxurious chalets from $100. All units include a private bathroom and kitchen.

Alpine Motel, 7 Miro St., tel. 06/385-8758, website: www.alpinemotel.co.nz, has medium-sized rooms with small kitchens for $80 s or d and larger freestanding chalets for $109 s or d. Dorm beds out back are $17 pp. One step up is the **White House Inn,** 22 Rimu St., tel. 06/385-8413, where a double room with a private spa goes for $90, breakfast included.

The finest place in town is the **Powderhorn Chateau,** on the corner of Mangawhero Terrace and Thames St., tel. 06/385-8888. It caters primarily to wintertime clientele, with an après-ski bar, the Matterhorn Restaurant, equipment rentals, drying rooms, and a heated pool. In summer, when rooms are $145 s or d, the place is dead; in winter, rates start at $180 and you should book well in advance. Around the corner, **Turoa Ski Lodge,** 10 Thames St., tel. 06/385-8274, is a historic hotel opposite the railway station. It has been thoughtfully restored and renovated, with charming rooms for $110 s, $120 d. It's open in winter only.

Backpacker Lodges

Ohakune YHA, 300 meters west of information center at 15 Clyde St., tel. 06/385-8724, website: www.yha.org.nz, is in a perfect spot for the outdoor enthusiast, but be sure to book way in advance if you plan on staying here during the busy winter season (July–October). It's close to public transportation; a shuttle bus leaves daily from across the road for the ski fields in winter. If the weather is bad the common room is left open during the day. Twin or family rooms are available (own key); rates $19–27 pp.

Rimu Park Lodge, 27 Rimu St., tel. 06/385-9023, is a charming 1914 residence offering a variety of accommodation choices. Dorm beds in the main house are $16–18 pp, while adjacent are basic cabins ($40 s or d) and self-contained chalets ($90 s or d). These are summer rates, when it's very quiet. During the ski season, rates start at $32 pp for a dorm bed, which includes breakfast.

Motor Camps

Ohakune Top 10 Holiday Park, 5 Moore St., Ohakune, tel. 06/385-8561, provides communal facilities (the showers and electric cooking rings are coin-operated), a limited number of tent sites, and plenty of caravan sites. Centrally located, the motor camp is next to an attractive scenic reserve, and Turoa Skifield, only 18 km away, is easily reached by bus in season. Tent sites are $16; some are usually available any time of year. Campsites are $15, but usually are fully booked way in advance through winter. Cabins are $45–60 s or d.

Mangawhero, a camping area with tent and caravan sites, toilets, and fireplaces, lies above Ohakune on Ohakune Mountain Rd., which leads up to Turoa Ski field; $4 pp per night.

Food and Entertainment

Utopia, 47 Clyde St., tel. 06/385-9120, features lots of light, healthy choices to eat in or take out. A few doors down the road, **Mountain Kebabs,** 29 Clyde St., tel. 06/385-9047, has take-out kebabs from $5. Also on Clyde St., the restaurant in the **Ohakune Country Hotel,** tel. 06/385-8268, serves inexpensive meals year-round. The specialty is pizza ($18–24 feeds two).

Sassi's Bistro, in the Alpine Motel at 7 Miro St., tel. 06/385-8758, has a warm, inviting alpine atmosphere with lots of exposed timber and thick wooden tables and chairs. Befitting the needs of hungry skiers and boarders, the menu is filled with hearty, straightforward choices such as an oven-baked filet of pork served with mint and mango salsa for $20. Sassi's is open year-round, daily for dinner.

Ohakune's winter-only lodges and restaurants are clustered together at the top end of town in an area known as "the Junction." **Margarita's,** 5 Rimu St., tel. 06/385-9222, is a Mexican restaurant that comes alive in winter. Several of the ski lodges open their restaurants to drop-in guests, but most recommend calling to make reservations. **Kings Court Ski Lodge** on Tyne St., tel. 06/385-8648, has a restaurant (wide range in meal prices), cocktail bar, and après-ski bar. **Powderhorn Chateau,** on the corner of Mangawhero

Terrace and Thames St., tel. 06/385-8888, has upmarket dining year-round.

Transportation

The main Auckland-Wellington rail line runs through Ohakune. The railway station is at the top end of town, within walking distance of a number of accommodations, including the Powderhorn Chateau. Two trains stop daily; for further information call **Tranz Scenic,** tel. 0800/802-802. The first **Intercity** stop south of National Park is Ohakune, making connections between these two towns easy. From these two towns, bus travelers continue south to Wellington and north to Auckland. There is one service in each direction daily. Buses stop at the **Ruapehu Information Centre,** 54 Clyde St., tel. 06/385-8427.

Services and Information

The **post office** is in the Broadbent Bookshop at 5 Goldfinch St., tel. 06/385-8645. **Ruapehu Information Centre** is at 54 Clyde St., tel. 06/385-8427; it's open weekdays 9 A.M.–4:30 P.M., Sat.–Sun. 10 A.M.–2 P.M. Another good source for local information, especially if you're heading into the park, is the DOC **Ohakune Visitor Centre,** at the bottom of Ohakune Mountain Rd., tel. 06/385-0010.

Eastland and Hawke's Bay

Te Urewera National Park

As the largest park on the North Island (212,000 hectares), Te Urewera National Park protects a remote and mountainous landscape between the Bay of Plenty to the north and Hawke Bay to the south. The only road through the park is unpaved Hwy. 38, which winds its way southwest from Rotorua, climbing into the park and to **Lake Waikaremoana** before exiting the park and joining the coastal highway at Wairoa.

Te Urewera boasts rugged ranges, almost continuous green forest, serene lakes, rivers, and dazzling waterfalls—a vast, untamed wilderness where the sounds of running water and melodic birds are ever present. In the early morning and late evening dense fog blankets the high forest peaks, and mist creeps across the lakes to swirl upward through the trees. Flapping wings and sharp notes pierce the silence, giving away the presence of a variety of birds, hard to spot among the dense greenery. You can feel the silence, and lose yourself in the beauty.

The park preserves the hauntingly beautiful land of the Tuhoe Tribe or "Children of the Mist," where legendary fairies and goblins play deep in the forest, where every tree has its own spirit, and where every rock, lake, and waterfall has a symbolic "presence." For hikers and photographers, Te Urewera abounds with mysterious and unspoiled splendor, freeing your imagination while you get back to nature.

East Cape coastline

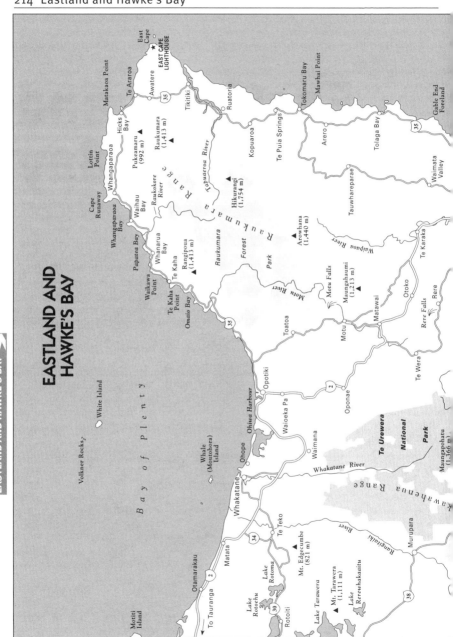

EASTLAND AND HAWKE'S BAY

East Cape

★ EAST CAPE
LIGHTHOUSE

Matakaoa Point

Te Araroa

Awatere

35

Tikitiki

Ruatoria

Tokomaru Bay

Mawhai Point

Gable End
Foreland

Hicks
Bay

Whangaparaoa

Pukeamaru
(992 m)

Raukumara
(1,413 m)

35

Lottin
Point

Te Puia Springs

Kopuaroa

Arero

Tolaga Bay

Cape
Runaway

Whangaparaoa
Bay

Waihau
Bay

Raukokore
River

Tapuaeroa River

Raukumara Range

Hikurangi
(1,754 m)

Tauwhareparae

Waimata
Valley

Papatea Bay

Whanarua
Bay

Te Kaha

Raukumara

Forest

Park

Arowhana
(1,440 m)

Waipaoa River

Te Karaka

Waikawa
Point

Te Kaha
Point

Rangitukia
(1,413 m)

Motu River

Motu Falls

Maungahaumi
(1,213 m)

Matawai

Oto ko

Rere

Omaio Bay

35

Toatoa

Motu

Rere Falls

Te Wera

B a y   o f   P l e n t y

White Island

Volkner Rocks

Whale
(Moutohora)
Island

Ohope

Ohiwa Harbour

Opotiki

Waioeka Pa

2

Oponae

Te Urewera

National

Park

Maungapohatu
(1,366 m)

Waimana

Whakatane River

Whakatane

Te Teko

34

Te Teko

Rangitaiki River

Kawhenua Range

Murupara

Otamarakau

Matata

2

To Tauranga

Lake
Rotoehu

30

Lake
Rotoma

Rotoiti

Lake Tarawera

Mt. Edgecumbe
(821 m)

Mt. Tarawera
(1,111 m)

Lake
Rerewhakaaitu

38

Motiti
Island

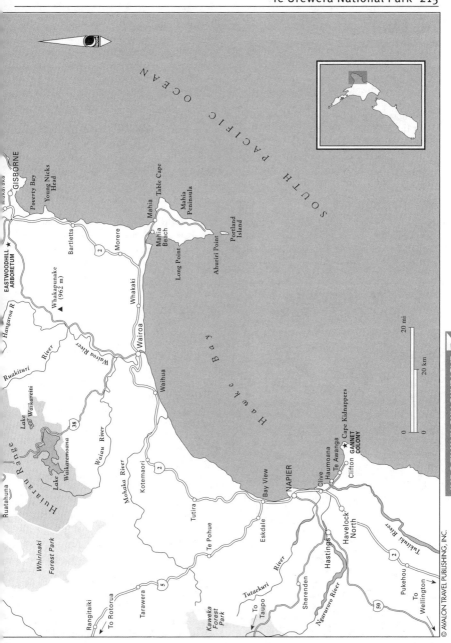

EASTLAND AND HAWKE'S BAY

THE LAND

The Huiarau Range runs across the middle of the park dividing the north from the south. In the northern sector the Waimana and Whakatane Rivers run northward and empty into the Bay of Plenty, and the Whirinaki River passes through the western edge of the park; in the southern sector the catchment waters of Lakes Waikaremoana and Waikareiti run southeast through several hydroelectric power stations and out to sea at Hawke's Bay. Most of the other forest-clad ranges run north-south, all cut by many faults—a main structural feature evident from a high viewpoint (such as Huiarau Summit) or from the air. The 54-square-km Lake Waikaremoana (Sea of Rippling Waters; 585 meters deep), one of the park's focal points, offers good swimming, boating, fishing, and walks. The impressive

Panekiri Bluff, regularly obscured by a dense blanket of fog that appears to pour off the end and down to the water below, rises 600 meters above lake level to dominate the southern shores. The other, much smaller, lake, almost 300 meters higher than Lake Waikaremoana, is the secluded Lake Waikareiti (Little Rippling Waters), reached only by track. Both lakes can be very cold even in midsummer—take adequate clothing. Waterfalls are dominant features throughout the park. Some of the most magnificent are close to the main road, or at the ends of short tracks through lush forest (see below).

Highway 38, between Rotorua in the west and Wairoa in the southeast, is the main route through the park. The last town before you enter the park from Rotorua is Murupara, where you'll find a Field Centre (two km south of town, close to the park boundary). The main visitor center is in Aniwaniwa, on the eastern arm of Lake Waikaremoana.

Climate

The ubiquitous lush greenery, wide rivers, and cascading waterfalls are evidence of Te Urewera's high precipitation—daily rainfall of more than 100 mm is not uncommon. The lake area receives the most rain (the average rainfall is 2,500–3,000 mm per year); the western area is generally much drier. In February, the warmest month, daily temperatures range about 12–21°C. The coldest month is July, when the temperatures range 3–9°C, and snow covers the upper forest peaks. Fog and mist, integral parts of the Te Urewera landscape, form throughout the year but are most common in winter and spring, and high winds blow at any time of year. If you want to be comfortable when hiking in the park, be adequately prepared for all kinds of weather in any season.

Flora and Fauna

Te Urewera National Park is the largest remaining area of native forest on the North Island, and because of the range in altitude (about 150–1,400 meters) contains quite an astonishing array of vegetation. The lower altitudes grow *rimu, north-*

TE UREWERA NATIONAL PARK

BAY OF PLENTY

TO TE PUKE AND
MT. MAUNGANUI

WHAKATANE

OPOTIKI

TO
ROTORUA

MURUPARA

TE WHAITI

RUATAHUNA

TE UREWERA
NATIONAL PARK

LAKE WAIKAREITI
VISITOR CENTRE
LAKE WAIKAREMOANA

GISBORNE

TUAI

WAIROA

TO
NAPIER

HAWKE BAY

0   20 km

© AVALON TRAVEL PUBLISHING, INC.

WHERE THE MOUNTAIN MARRIES THE MIST

Te Urewera's past is an intriguing mixture of mysterious legends and historic facts. The original people of Te Urewera, the Tuhoe, claim descent from the symbolic union of Te Maunga, the Mountain, and Hine-Pukohu-Rangi, the Mist-Maiden. This seems quite appropriate once you've spent any time in this legendary "Land of Mist." The Maori named Urewera (burnt penis), from the time an old helpless man, Mura-kareke, was lying by a fire and accidentally roasted his privates. Urewera became the designated name of the area after this incident, and Mura-kareke's descendants traditionally acquired the tribal name "Te Urewera." The sound of the Maori word is definitely more appealing than its translation as a name for this beautiful park!

Lake Waikaremoana was formed more than 2,000 years ago by a giant landslip that blocked off a narrow river gorge, but local legend explains its formation with much more magic and imagination. The great chief Maahu was angered by his daughter, Hau-mapuhia, and in his rage he tried to drown her. To help her escape, the gods turned her into a *taniwha* (monster) so that she could free herself from her father and burrow through to the sea before daylight (rays of the sun turn a *taniwha* to stone). In her frantic struggle she gouged out a deep area that became the "Sea of Dashing Waters." The sun came up and the *taniwha* was captured in stone to lie forever at the mouth of the Waikaretaheke River, just below Kaitawa. Sometimes jets of water shot high into the air above the rock of Hau-mapuhia and the sounds of wailing rose above it—a signal to the ancient Maori that a great storm was on its way. In recent times the waters of the Waikaretaheke River were diverted for hydroelectric power, and the hillside slip that resulted completely buried the rock that was Hau-mapuhia.

ern *rata,* and *tawa* forest, and *toe toe* grass (largest endemic grass in New Zealand, similar to pampas grass) is rampant (if you suffer from allergies, come to Te Urewera prepared!). Beech and *rimu* forest starts at about 800 meters, and at 900 meters the *rimu* disappears and beech dominates the higher ranges, along with *Hall's totara* and *tawari*. To the northwest of Lake Waikareiti lie the open tundra regions where woody scrub, mosses, and subalpine plants have adapted to the very wet conditions.

Bats, lizards, and introduced animals such as deer, pigs, cats, hares, weasels, and opossums live in the park, but the bush is so dense you're unlikely to spot them unless particularly hunting them down. The large variety of birds is also hard to see, yet you hear them all around you. The most easily seen (and heard) bird is the plump, white-breasted *kereru,* New Zealand's only native pigeon, which makes a loud and heavy flapping noise when it flies. Other birds you're more likely to hear than see are the nocturnal kiwi with its shrill whistle "keee-weee," and three species of parrot—*kaka, morepork,* and red-crowned and yellow-crowned parakeet.

DRIVING HIGHWAY 38

You can find lookout points, waterfalls, rivers, and other scenic stops along the length of Hwy. 38, which dissects this magnificent park. Here are some of the most accessible, from north to south.

Murupara to Lake Waikaremoana

Near the northwest entrance to Te Urewera, Hwy. 38 passes 20-meter-high **Totarapapa Stream and Falls** before entering typically rugged Te Urewera scenery—look on the right side of the road. You can see the beautiful **Hopuruahine Cascades and Falls** only by going down Hopuruahine Landing road and walking back up and in the river. A huge waterfall that even the least adventurous will be able to view without getting out of the car is the fabulous 34-meter **Mokau Falls**—the highway runs in a loop toward, over, and away from it, 11 km north of the visitor center.

Te Maraateatua Point (Garden of the Gods) is not marked—the signpost on the main road, between Mokau Landing and the visitor center, reads Access to Lake 5 Minutes. After travers-

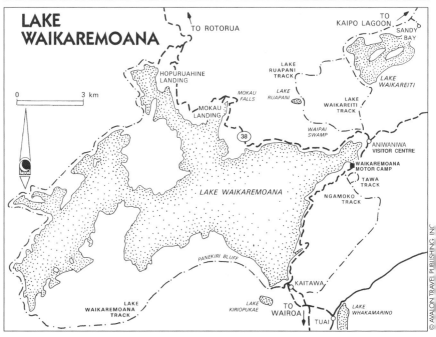

LAKE WAIKAREMOANA

TO ROTORUA

TO KAIPO LAGOON

SANDY BAY

HOPURUAHINE LANDING

LAKE RUAPANI TRACK

MOKAU FALLS

LAKE RUAPANI

LAKE WAIKAREITI

0   3 km

MOKAU LANDING

38

LAKE WAIKAREITI TRACK

WAIPAI SWAMP

ANIWANIWA VISITOR CENTRE

WAIKAREMOANA MOTOR CAMP

LAKE WAIKAREMOANA

TAWA TRACK

NGAMOKO TRACK

PANEKIRI BLUFF

KAITAWA

LAKE WAIKAREMOANA TRACK

LAKE KIRIOPUKAE

TO WAIROA

TUAI

LAKE WHAKAMARINO

© AVALON TRAVEL PUBLISHING INC

ing the very steep five-minute bush trail, you emerge at a rock- and boulder-strewn beach and a good fishing point. Walk around to the right (facing the lake) over the boulders for another 10 minutes and you'll find a beautiful sheltered cove. Small sandy areas among the rocks are suitable (and more comfortable than they look) for a picnic lunch or camping.

Lake Waikaremoana

Continue along the highway to the visitor center at Aniwaniwa, where a wide variety of hikes leads to waterfalls, to lakes, and deep into the bush. **Hinerau's Track** starts and finishes at the visitor center, is only a half-hour walk, and gives great views of the three spectacular **Aniwaniwa (Rainbow) Waterfalls**—Momahaki and Bridal Veil Falls (15 meters), and Te Tangi O Te Hinerau (11 meters). **Aniwaniwa Valley Walk** also starts at the visitor center, follows Old Gisborne Rd. for two km (a track continues to Ward's Hut), and turns down a two-minute bush track to emerge at the bottom of dazzling 20-meter **Papakorito**

Falls. Another small track allows access to the top of these falls, but at the bottom a great swimming hole (pleasant temperature in summer) is surrounded by enormous boulders, tree ferns, and heaps of *toe toe*—a super-secluded spot for soaking up some sun.

From the lakeside motor camp, a **cruise boat,** tel. 06/837-3729, makes a loop around the lake, stopping a couple of times to let off campers and picnickers; $25 pp. Inquire at the small store about renting a fishing boat or going on a guided kayak tour.

HIKES
Short Walks

Apart from short walks to the most accessible waterfalls, literally hundreds of kilometers of track riddle the park. Call in at the visitor center at Aniwaniwa for brochures, track guides, and maps, or refer to the park handbook *Land of the Mist,* which contains all the short walks and a fairly detailed map.

The enjoyable **Lake Waikareiti Track** leads about 3.5 km through dense beech forest, exotic fuchsia gullies, and sunny fern-filled glades alive with songbirds, up to a small sheltered lake (878 meters) popular with hikers, anglers (an average rainbow trout is one kg), and swimmers who enjoy an icy dunking. It takes about an hour to hike up to Lake Waikareiti, less coming down, and you'll find toilets and a day shelter (no overnight stays) at the lake. The lake is dotted with six small islands, one of which, Rahui, contains a small lake of its own called Tamaiti-O-Waikaremoana—unique because of its total isolation from humans or browsing animals. Rowboats for rent on Lake Waikareiti must be paid for at the visitor center, where you can get your key, oarlocks, and directions before you set off. You can hike farther around the west shore to the sandy beach at Tawari Bay (20 minutes one way) or continue to the northern end and stay at the Sandy Bay Hut (another three hours one way). To get to the start of the Lake Waikareiti Track, cross the bridge from the visitor center and follow the highway for about 200 meters to the signpost.

Another good one-hour track starts at the same place as the Waikareiti Track and leads past a series of small silted lakes to **Waipai Swamp,** known for its swamp plants, sundews, and orchids. The **Lake Ruapani Track** passes through red and silver beech forests with mixed stands of *rimu, miro, kahikatea, kamahi,* and *tawari* on the way to the swamp, and the mysterious quiet of these green and serene groves is disturbed only by birdsong and fluttering wings. You can continue past the swamp for another hour and come out at the grassy verges and groves of beech trees that edge small Lake Ruapani, or continue another three hours to join the Waikareiti Track.

Long Hikes

Many extensive tracks lead to fabulous waterfalls, rapids, spectacular scenic views, or good fishing and hunting areas. Get a complete rundown at the visitor center. Before starting out on any trip, get the latest information on river conditions and weather forecasts, track descriptions, maps, and hut availability. The rangers suggest you leave details of your plans—you'll be venturing out into rugged ranges and wild backcountry, days away from help should you need it. Be equipped for all kinds of weather, and take a tent, cooking equipment, and energy food. Water is reportedly drinkable throughout the park, but boil it for several minutes to be safe.

Perhaps the most popular is the well-defined 46-km **Lake Waikaremoana Track,** which starts at Onepoto off Hwy. 38 at the southern end of the lake, crosses the spectacular Panekiri Range (great views), and then closely skirts the western shores all the way north to Hopuruahine Landing on the main highway. It takes about three days to cover, with five huts along the route. Most hikers leave their vehicles at the motor camp and take an inexpensive water taxi (tel. 06/837-3729) to and from the trailheads.

FISHING

Anglers can expect excellent fishing for rainbow trout (and some brown trout) in the lakes and rivers throughout the park. The lake fishing season runs all year; river fishing season is Dec.1–June 30.

Regulations

A license is required for fishing anywhere in the park—on sale at Waikaremoana Motor Camp, in the store at Ruatahuna, and at sporting goods stores in the towns closest to the park. Don't bring homemade trout flies made from bird feathers or skins into the park unless they, and all fly-tying equipment, have been fumigated: at present the park is free of some of the worst bird diseases—and everyone wants it to stay that way. Ready-made imported trout flies are okay, and you can buy appropriate locally made flies in any of the sporting goods stores near the park.

Lakes

Lakes Waikaremoana and Waikareiti provide the easiest access for anglers, with both fly- and spoon-fishing permitted. The average rainbow trout is 1.3 kg, the average brown trout 2.3 kg in Lake Waikaremoana; in Lake Waikareiti you'll catch only rainbows that average one kg. The main trout spawning streams for Lake Waikaremoana are the Waiotukupuna, Hopuruahine, and Mokau. If you want to get out on Lake Waikaremoana, hire a rowboat from the motor camp or charter a fishing trip on a motor camp launch. If you prefer fishing Lake Waikareiti from on top, the visitor center hires rowboats and dinghies.

Rivers

The lakes may have easier access, but the back-country rivers often provide better fishing. The Waimana, Whakatane, Waiau, Whirinaki, and Ruakituri Rivers offer kilometer after kilometer of angling heaven. The upper reaches of the Ruakituri and Waiau Rivers and tributaries have produced some monsters in recent years—up to six-kg rainbow trout (no browns) have been reported by gleeful anglers. The Whakatane, Waimana, and Whirinaki Rivers and tributaries (except for Horomanga and Wheao) are also fished with fly or spoon, but many of the other rivers permit fly only, under strict seasonal regulations. Check with the visitor center or field stations before you set out.

ACCOMMODATIONS
Camping

Campers have plenty of options in and around the park. The only accommodation within the park is **Waikaremoana Motor Camp,** tel. 06/837-3826, on the southeastern arm of Lake Waikaremoana one km south of the visitor center. Surrounded by tree-covered hills and right on the lakeshore, it's run by the DOC, but don't count on staying here in summer or during Easter vacation if you haven't booked up to six months ahead. From the motor camp many well-marked trails lead off in all directions, ranging from 15-minute walks to two-hour hikes. The motor camp shop (open 8 A.M.–noon and 1–5 P.M.) sells basic grocery supplies, fishing gear and licenses, and petrol, and has rowboats for hire; community kitchen and hot showers are available. Tent sites are $10 pp, caravan sites are $20, cabins are $40 s or d, and motel units are $65.

Mokau Landing, down a two-km road from

Hwy. 38, is a great place to camp—put your tent wherever you like on the large grassy area backed by tree-covered hills, right on the edge of the lake. A small beach, crystal-clear water, and boat ramp attract a relaxed crowd of anglers and boaters in summer. **Te Waiiti,** north of the park boundary, offers primitive riverside camping.

Hotels and Motels

Apart from the cabins at Waikaremoana Motor Camp, there are no indoor accommodations within the park boundary. Immediately south of Lake Waikaremoana, but just outside the park, **Lake Whakamarino Lodge,** tel. 06/837-3876, features lake views and a restaurant. Standard rooms are $50 s, $80 d, while larger units start at $95 s or d.

The **Ruatahuna Motel,** on Hwy. 38 35 km northwest of Lake Waikaremoana, tel. 07/366-3393, has four units (with kitchens) from $56 s, $64 d. Adjoining are tearooms, a store, and a petrol station. Continuing west, in the small village of Murupara, are more choices. The **Murupara Hotel** on Pine Dr., tel. 07/355-5871, has a TV lounge and rooms with shared bathrooms for $30 s, $45 d, meals available. The **Murupara Motel,** tel. 07/366-5583, has four units with cooking facilities for $55 s, $65 d.

OTHER PRACTICALITIES
Food

There's not much in the way of stores (and no restaurants) once you enter Te Urewera National Park—take as much food and supplies as you can carry. As you come from the northwest, Murupara is the last town where you can buy produce and basics at an average price. You'll find a small store and tearooms at Ruatahuna on Hwy. 38, but the only places you can really restock once you're in the park (the higher prices reflect the cost of transporting goods to this remote location) are the Waikaremoana Motor Camp Store or the store at Tuai. You can buy fishing gear, licenses, and petrol, and can rent boats here. If you enter the park from the southeast, get all your supplies in Wairoa, the last town of any size, 54 km south of the park.

Transportation

Neither of the major bus companies runs along the remote road that passes through the park, but there may be a shuttle service between Rotorua and Gisborne (inquire at any information center). Otherwise you're on your own. Bicycle touring through the park is only recommended for confirmed masochists because the 100 km of Hwy. 38 through the park is often steep and unpaved.

Information

Aniwaniwa Visitor Centre, the main source of information, is in the heart of the park one km north of Waikaremoana Motor Camp, tel. 06/838-3803. The center has vivid displays, plentiful reading on Te Urewera legends and local history, and detailed information on the park's natural history. Ask a staff member to put on the excellent audiovisual—it really gets you in the mood for further exploration. The friendly staff can assist you in planning hiking trips and fishing and hunting expeditions, and will let you in on the fine, lesser-known camping spots and the hottest fishing areas if you ask; it's open seven days a week 8 A.M.–noon and 1–5 P.M. all year.

Before undertaking any of the longer tracks, check out the local weather forecast and river conditions (many of the tracks ford or run along rivers), and leave details of your plans with the visitor center or field stations. A detailed map of the park, with an equally detailed map of Lake Waikaremoana on the reverse side, is available for $11.

East Cape

Well off the main tourist route, the East Cape is rich in Maori history and easy on the eyes. From **Opotiki,** 45 km east of Whakatane (see Bay of Plenty chapter), Hwy. 35 winds past exotic bush, past golden sandy beaches, and through groves of ancient, gnarled *pohutukawa* trees that in summer become a magnificent mass of red flowers. This route gives plenty of opportunities for swimming and tanning, snorkeling and scuba diving, good land and sea fishing (large yellowfish tuna are often caught), and gratifying, time-absorbing, colorful coastal views. Captain Cook took his first steps on New Zealand soil along the cape in 1769, naming many of the points and coves. Numerous historic landmarks commemorating his visit are interspersed with scenic lookouts all along the coastal highway. No enormous foreign-owned hotels will be lining this coastline in the near future, and if you expect to find touristy towns, you'll be disappointed. The inland side of Hwy. 35 is an inaccessible, rugged land dominated by the **Raukumara Range.** Hwy. 2 from Opotiki cuts south across the interior to Gisborne, but unless time is an issue, the longer oceanfront route is recommended.

OPOTIKI

Situated on a harbor inlet formed by the junction of the Waioeka and Otara Rivers 45 km east of Whakatane, Opotiki (population) is the first and largest town around the East Cape.

Opotiki Museum, 123 Church St., tel. 07/315-5193, open Mon.–Sat. 10 A.M.–3:30 P.M., Sunday 1:30–4 P.M., displays locally collected items that give insight into the town's past; $1 adult, $.50 child.

Accommodations and Food

At Waiotahi Beach, five km west of Opotiki, is **Opotiki Beach House,** Appleton Rd., tel. 07/315-5117. Right on the beach, this great budget accommodation has a relaxed atmosphere, a friendly host, and surfing equipment for guest use. The beach house is open plan, with a kitchen and lounge area downstairs and dorm beds in the loft. Dorms are $15 pp, while an adjacent unit holds two double rooms for $19.50 pp-a great value. Downtown, **Central Oasis Backpackers,** 30 King St., tel. 07/315-5165, offers an appealing garden, clean spacious dorm rooms, a kitchen, and a living room; rates $14–16 pp. An inexpensive motel is **Ranui Motel,** 36 Bridge St., tel. 07/315-6669 or 0800/828-128, with 10 kitchen-equipped units. Studios are $65 s or d, one- and two-bedroom units are $75 and $80 respectively. Breakfast and dinner are available for a modest extra charge. **Opotiki Holiday Park** along Potts Ave., 200 meters from downtown, tel. 07/315-6050, has tent and caravan sites for $20, on-site caravans and cabins from $36 s or d, tourist flats from $58 s or d, and motel units from $70 s or d.

The old-fashioned **Masonic Hotel** on Church St. is open daily for lunch noon–2 P.M., dinner 6–8 P.M. (good pub meals at reasonable prices), and it offers a special children's menu. A meaty steak sandwich with chips and salad is $9. Head to the **Flying Pig Café,** 95 Church St., tel. 07/315-7618, for filled pita bread, salads, and kebabs.

> *Waioeka Scenic Highway, part of Hwy. 2 at the Opotiki end, is a particularly magical stretch for lovers of ferns and native forest.*

Information

Opotiki Information Centre, on the corner of Elliot and St. John Streets, tel. 07/315-8484 (24-hour number), is open weekdays 9 A.M.–4:30 P.M. and weekends 8:30 A.M.–4:30 P.M. The staff can suggest and arrange all sorts of things to do from Opotiki—white-water rafting, jetboating on the Motu, horse trekking, fishing, hunting, local walking routes, long-distance tramping tracks, and scuba diving.

INLAND ROUTE TO GISBORNE

Highway 2 is the 148-km route (about two to three hours nonstop) that connects Opotiki and Gisborne, to the south. The winding road passes through fern-lined gorges with riverbank rest areas and waterfall views, and by dairy farms, orchards, and vineyards that neatly patchwork the land as you approach Gisborne. The 30-km **Waioeka Scenic Highway,** part of Hwy. 2 at the Opotiki end, is a particularly magical stretch for lovers of ferns and native forest. The **Motu Gorge,** a sidetrack that runs from Matawai to Toatoa, offers wild and rugged scenery. To get in there take Motu Rd., which closely follows

the untamed Motu River, but take note: although it looks like an hour's drive on the map, it really takes about a half-day—pretty hairy driving at that, not recommended for the fainthearted. If you take this sidetrack, don't miss splendid **Motu Falls,** five km downstream from Motu.

Another waterfall, a large variety of nonnative trees, and an abundance of flowers will enhance on your trip to Gisborne if you don't mind a 48-km sidetrack (35 km from Gisborne). At the town of Makaraka turn right onto the main highway south (instead of going into Gisborne) and continue through Makaraka to the Waipaoa River Bridge. Don't go into Patutahi township, but keep on the road to Ngatapa. As you near Ngatapa follow the AA signs to Eastwoodhill, continuing past Ngatapa village and onto Wharekopai Rd. toward Rere. At the junction of Rere and Hihiroroa Roads the **Eastwoodhill Arboretum,** tel. 07/863-9800, is well worth a stop. It's a huge collection of trees, shrubs, and climbers not native to New Zealand—most of them are from the Northern Hemisphere. If you're there in spring and bulbs turn you (or your camera) on, the daffodil patch is a flower spectacular that you shouldn't miss. The gardens are open year-round (except June and July), on weekends and holidays 10 A.M.–4 P.M.; admission $5. After visiting the arboretum, continue along Wharekopai Rd. to **Rere Falls.** The falls and picnic area are within a two-hectare reserve along the banks of the Wharekopai River. The 24-meter-high, 45-meter-wide falls are perhaps most impressive in winter, but in summer the deep pool at the foot is a great swimming hole and the river itself has a reputation for good trout fishing. You can cross the waterfall along a ledge at the base, which takes you behind the thundering wall of water, or at the top when it's not in flood, but look out for slippery rocks.

OPOTIKI TO THE CAPE

Between Opotiki and **Omaio** (free campground near the Motu River; no facilities), Hwy. 35 is stunningly colorful, particularly in December when the *pohutukawa* trees clinging to the cliffs are covered in scarlet blossoms and the ocean alternates between deep turquoise and a brilliant blue. All along the road are places to stop for breathtaking coastal views, sandy shell- or driftwood-covered beaches, bird colonies, picturesque farmland, and rocks where you can try your luck fishing. *Pohutukawa* trees continuously splash the landscape with red and green as you continue along the coast.

Te Kaha

At Te Kaha, 25 km beyond the Motu River bridge, don't miss **Tukaki,** the triangular-shaped, intricately carved, Maori Meeting House. Visits or tours can be arranged; however, no cameras are allowed inside.

Te Kaha Hotel & Motel, tel. 07/325-2830, has rooms for $70 s or d. Beautifully landscaped **Te Kaha Holiday Park,** five km north of Te Kaha on Hwy. 35, tel. 07/325-2894, has a great location, just across the road from a gray sandy beach with driftwood, rocks to climb on, and, of course, *pohutukawa* trees. The park has good

---

MOTU RIVER

The Motu River flows from high in the Raukumara Range, through dense remote forests, draining into the Bay of Plenty between Hawai and Omaio. This waterway creates the perfect destination for a rafting trip through unadulterated New Zealand wilderness.

Wet 'n' Wild Rafting, tel. 07/348-3191 or 0800/348-3191, website: www.wetnwildrafting.co.nz, offers a variety of trips down the river, with around five hours per day spent on the water and nights spent camping out. On the overnight trip you fly to the area by helicopter from Opotiki, with a trip highlight the traverse through the Lower Motu Gorge; $690 pp. The four-day trip begins farther upstream; access to the starting point is by 4WD off Hwy. 2; $635 pp.

Opotiki-based **Motu River Jet Boat Tours,** tel. 07/315-8107, offer jetboat tours on the river's lower reaches.

---

communal facilities, a camp store, a well-stocked shop with hot take-away foods available certain hours, a swimming pool, a barbecue, a trampoline, a game and TV room, and a playground. Tent and caravan sites (made more private with clever positioning of trees and shrubs) are $20; a bed in the bunkhouse with a kitchen and TV room is $17 pp; tourist cabins are $50–60 s or d; tourist flats (large and comfy with private facilities and color TVs) are $80 s or d.

The road continues through **Whanarua Bay** and passes the turquoise **Raukokore River,** known for its good fishing at the rivermouth. As you continue along the highway, you'll see plenty of cows, sheep, and horses, and native paradise ducks (black and white) and pheasants.

Waihau Bay

As you approach Waihau Bay from the south, don't miss a stop at the small, pleasing-to-the-eye, whitewashed **Raukokore Anglican Church** and the graveyard behind. The family graves are marked with photo-adorned stones giving all sorts of fascinating details. The **Catholic church** is almost opposite. For good fishing, head for the sandy beach near the school. The village, half a kilometer off the main road, is made up of a post office, a general store with hot take-away foods and small information booth, a petrol station, and public toilets.

You'll pass black and gray jagged rocks with occasional patches of sand before reaching the next sandy swimming beach at **Mangatoto Bridge,** just after the sign to **Waihau Bay Holiday Park** (tent and caravan sites, on-site caravans, and tourist cabins), tel. 07/325-3844. The main road then meanders inland, running parallel with stunning **Whangaparaoa Bay** and beach.

Whangaparaoa

Two famous canoes from Hawaiiki, the *Tainui* and the *Arawa,* landed at Whangaparaoa about A.D. 1350. **Te Kura O Whangaparaoa,** the *pa* and meetinghouse, is here—you can't miss the ornately carved, bright red archway marking the entrance. Just along the road is the Cape Runaway post office. The highway then wanders up to the top of the cape through relatively uninteresting farmland. About 25 km from Whanga-paraoa, keep your eyes peeled for gravel Lottin Point Rd. to the left, which, after about a 10- to 15-minute drive through grassy rolling hills, planted forests, and *pohutukawa* trees, ends at the rocky coastline, where you can clamber down to volcanic lava platforms, rock pools, and al-ways-turquoise water. These are great spots for picnics, fishing, and diving, but remember this is private land, and camping is not allowed without first obtaining permission from the landowner.

Hicks Bay

Peaceful Hicks Bay has a general store, a motor lodge with restaurant, and **Hicks Bay Back-packers Lodge** (just keep following the signs for another 1.5 km along Onepoto Beach Road), tel. 06/864-4731. The lodge offers light airy dorm rooms, communal bathrooms and a fully equipped kitchen, ocean views and sounds, and barbecues in summer—all this a stone's throw from a large swimming beach. The owners know several good bush walks in the local area, can take you diving (without tanks), offer a tour to the East Cape Lighthouse (well-worth seeing) and transportation from Opotiki by arrange-ment. A stay here costs $16–24 pp per night.

Te Araroa

The village of Te Araroa snuggles at the base of impressive towering cliffs 10 km southeast of Hicks Bay. It comprises a couple of stores, a bot-tle shop, a gas station, a post office, and take-aways. The best reason to stop here is to see and photograph the oldest and largest *pohutukawa* tree in the country (along the beachfront at the north end of town). It's a truly amazing and awe-inspiring sight—more than 600 years old with 22 trunks spreading out 37.2 meters and a girth of 19.9 meters.

Attractive **Te Araroa Holiday Park,** 6.5 km northwest of Te Araroa on Hwy. 35, midway between Hicks Bay and Te Araroa, tel. 06/864-4873, has campsites and a variety of accommo-dations, a cinema with a giant screen (the latest movies are shown during school holidays, pub-lic holidays, and in peak season; $7 adult, $4 child), a well-stocked general store (open seven

days 7 A.M.–7 P.M.), a game room, TV rooms, a playground, a fish smokehouse, barbecue, pet ducks, and a card phone, as well as all the usual holiday park communal facilities. Cabins sit be-side the landscaped grassy camping area, which has plenty of large shade trees and a freshwater stream running through the grounds, and is only a four-minute walk from a safe, sandy beach. Tent sites are $16; powered sites are $18; cabins are $38 d; and tourist flats are $64 d.

East Cape Lighthouse

New Zealand's easternmost lighthouse stands at the end of a 22-km drive along a gravel road from Te Araroa (south end of town). This scenic road is at first sandwiched between tall cliffs and a sheer rock ledge that drops straight into the sea. It passes white-sand beaches edged by *po-hutukawa* trees, then meanders inland through rolling grassy meadows filled with sheep, cows, and many horses, and a few inland sand dunes. The hike up the hill to the lighthouse is quite a workout—25 minutes of steep climbing up about 500 uneven steps—even more of a work-out if you're carrying a two-year-old! However, once you've reached the top, the 360-degree view of **Hautai Beach, Whangaokeno Island** (East Is-land), and inland makes the effort worthwhile.

CONTINUING SOUTH TOWARD GISBORNE

Tikitiki

The next definite stop is Tikitiki to see the in-credibly ornate **Anglican Church.** Although the whitewashed exterior is fairly plain, the interior is a masterpiece of Maori design—woven panels, carved faces with *paua* shell eyes, beams covered with fern and other nature-inspired designs, benches with ends intricately carved, and stained-glass windows. Don't miss it! Tikitiki also has a store and gas station.

Ruatoria and Te Puia Springs

From Ruatoria, the **Mount Hikurangi Track** climbs to to the summit of the 1,752-meter mountain, starting at Pakihiroa Station at the end of Tapuaeroa Valley Rd., about 20 km inland from Ruatoria. The road to the trailhead is gravel and takes about 30 minutes by car, though it crosses two creeks and may be unpassable after heavy rain. Allow six hours each way for the 15-km trail.

To the south of Ruatoria many gravel roads lead to beautiful bays—if you have the time, explore! Te Puia Springs is a small town with its own golf course, motel, store, hospital, and **Te Puia Hot Springs Hotel,** tel. 06/864-6755, providing rooms ($35 s, $55 d), meals, and the use of hot pools.

Tokomaru Bay

This coastal town, a stronghold of Maori culture, lies along a sandy beach and, if you follow the beachfront road north, passing old houses in various states of beauty or disrepair, you come to a scenic rocky bay backed by hills, old brick buildings (one now containing a pottery store), and a very long pier (good fishing). The town has a couple of stores, good take-aways, a motel, a card phone, and a relaxed vacation atmosphere.

Backpackers all head for New Zealand's easternmost hostel, the **House of the Rising Sun** (follow the signs from the main road), tel. 06/864-

5858. This colorful house, adorned with a tattered flag and permanent resident on the front verandah, has bright dorms, a good kitchen with help-yourself spice rack, a comfortable living area, and an unusual reading room supplied with magazines and books in the backyard. It's only a one-minute walk from a beautiful sandy beach. Dorm beds are $17 pp, private rooms are $27 s, $38 d.

Anaura Bay

This quiet spot seven km off Hwy. 35 is renowned by surfers for clean waves that peel off the adjacent headland. Before you descend to the bay, the top of the hill affords great views of an offshore island, a yellow sandy beach, green hills, and tree-covered mountains.

Anaura Bay Walkway is an easy 3.5-km walk through Anaura Bay Scenic Reserve. The track starts at the north end of Anaura Bay on Anaura Rd., takes about 1–1.5 hours each way and brings you back out on Anaura Rd. about one km south of the starting point.

Tolaga Bay

Stores, tearooms, an inn, a motel, a nine-hole golf course, and a gas station are all located here.

EASTLAND AND HAWKE'S BAY

© JANE KING

the House of the Rising Sun, New Zealand's easternmost backpacker lodge

© JANE KING

This wharf, longest on the Southern Hemisphere, stretches spectacularly into Tolaga Bay.

A few kilometers south of town, turn left at the road marked Motorcamp, Cooks Cove Walkway and Historic Wharf. Continue to the end of the road, where you'll find the longest wharf in the Southern Hemisphere. This wharf used to serve the area in the days of coastal shipping. If you walk to the end (worthwhile), take a jacket. It may be sunny and warm when you start out, but by the time you reach the far end, it can be windy and quite cool. Locals jog and sunbathe along the wharf, which is popular with fishermen (watch crayfish being brought up). It's a regular hive of activity, and there's always a local to talk to or something to see.

Cooks Cove Walkway

For the most spectacular ocean views and a bit of history, head for Cooks Cove Walkway at the southern end of Tolaga Bay. This five-km walkway (closed during lambing) climbs a ridge to a lookout point (90 meters) at the top of Tolaga Bay's southern cliffs, then follows a farm track just below the cliff tops to another lookout point (120 meters) over tranquil Cooks Cove. Stay on the main track for the best viewing points. From here the track leads down onto Cooks Cove flats, passing the "Hole in the Wall" and the monument commemorating Captain Cook's visit to Tolaga Bay in 1769. The *Endeavour* anchored at Cooks Cove for six days to take on water, firewood, and supplies, hence the name. This easy track takes just over an hour each way. Take a windbreaker and something to drink—there's no fresh water—and wear sturdy shoes. You'll find toilets at the wharf near the beginning of the track, and there's a motor camp nearby.

Gisborne

A CITY WITH A TALE TO TELL

Gisborne (population 38,000), 340 km east of Taupo and 500 km southeast of Auckland, is one of New Zealand's most historic cities. The hills behind Gisborne were the first New Zealand promontories sighted by Captain Cook and his crew on October 6, 1769. Nicholas Young, *Endeavour* cabin boy, was the first to see land— **Young Nick's Head** at the southern end of **Poverty Bay** was named in his honor. The crew landed at **Kaiti Beach,** where Captain Cook took formal possession of the new country in the name of His Majesty King George III. On attempting to make friends with the local Maori and restock supplies, Cook found the natives more than a little hostile, and the crew lifted anchor and left with nothing but a small amount of firewood. During the next five months they circumnavigated the new land that became known as New Zealand. As they had not been welcomed with open arms, Cook named the bay on which Gisborne now stands Poverty Bay—a name that the locals have humorously retained despite the obvious agricultural wealth of the fertile alluvial Poverty Bay flats, busy fishing fleet, and abundant natural attractions that the area presents to the explorers of today.

SIGHTS

Historic Sights on Foot

The first place to go is the Gisborne Information Centre off the main shopping street downtown. The staff gladly hands out brochures and maps, and can suggest more things to see and do than you can possibly handle. Next to the center is small **Alfred Cox Park,** dominated by the unusual sight of a large totem pole, a gift from Canada to celebrate the bicentenary of Captain Cook's first landing in 1769.

From Grey St. turn right onto Gladstone Rd. and continue over the bridge. Veer right under the railway embankment and follow the harbor past the freezing works and wharf on The Esplanade.

This road leads to Kaiti Beach and **Cook Landing Site National Historic Reserve.** The impressive **Capt. James Cook Monument** marks the spot where Captain Cook first landed. From this point, a short track leads up Kaiti Hill to a lookout. Take in a fantastic 180-degree view of the city, harbor, meeting of the Taruheru, Waimata, and Turanganui Rivers, and magnificent Poverty Bay. Check out the amazingly clear blue water that appears to surround Gisborne. The white cliff headland to the south is **Young Nick's Head.**

At the foot of Kaiti Hill where Queens Dr. and Ranfurly St. meet, the road passes the **Te Poho-o-Rawiri Maori Meeting House,** tel. 06/867-2835, one of the largest decorative meeting halls in New Zealand. A small Maori church lies above. The hall is usually open to the public (enter via the side door); the intricate Maori carving and *tukutuku* reedwork (done in Rotorua) are worth seeing. If it's closed, ask the caretaker who lives next door for permission to enter.

Gisborne Museum and Arts Centre

This fascinating complex, standing on the other side of the Taruheru River from downtown at 18 Stout St., tel. 06/867-3832, features east coast, Maori, and colonial artifacts; natural history; and a huge photographic collection. Wyllie Cottage, originally built in 1872 and the oldest house in Gisborne, stands within the museum grounds. The art gallery (open seven days) has changing exhibitions, and local art and crafts on display are for sale.

The *Star of Canada* was shipwrecked on Kaiti Reef in 1912. The ship's bridge, deck, captain's cabin, and chartroom were salvaged and turned into a house, and were then moved to their present location overlooking the river and opened as a maritime museum adjacent to the main museum. Inside you can follow the mariners' impressive contributions to the development of Gisborne through a number of whaling, shipping, and water transportation displays, and can view hundreds of photographs with a decidedly maritime theme.

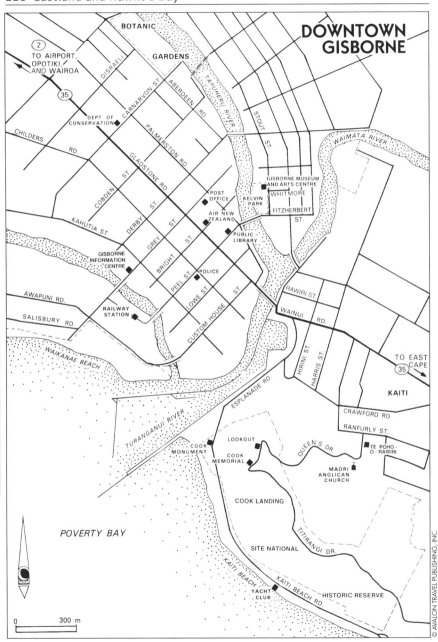

Both museums are open Mon.–Fri. 10 A.M.–4 P.M., weekends and public holidays 1:30–4 P.M. (hours changeable); $4 adult, $2 student or child, which covers the museum, the art gallery, the *Star of Canada,* and Wyllie Cottage.

Botanic Garden

This tranquil garden, sandwiched between Aberdeen Rd. and the banks of the Taruheru River, features a free-flight aviary among the flowers, trees, and lawns. It's a peaceful green place to take your lunch and catch up on postcard writing. Walk along Gladstone Rd. away from downtown, turn right on Carnarvon St., and turn left on Aberdeen Road.

RECREATION

Town Beaches

Kaiti Beach is the only one unsuitable for swimming or surfing (but is popular with sailboarders and yachters)—the bottom is a reef and the beach is not patrolled. The closest good beach to town is **Waikanae Beach.** A short walk from the main shopping area, it has a sandy bottom, safe swimming, and small surf, and is crowded in summer. Popular with sailboarders, it's patrolled by the surf club during summer. Walk along Grey St. (same street as the information center) until you hit the sand. If you continue along beachfront Salisbury Rd., Waikanae becomes **Midway Beach.** Also patrolled in summer, Midway's generally safe if you stay between the flags. "The Pipeline" at the west end attracts lots of surfers. Behind Midway you'll find a large motor camp, and farther along the **Olympic Pool Complex** (Centennial Marine Dr., tel. 06/867-6220), which has swimming and diving pools and a water slide, open in summer 10 A.M.–6 P.M.; $2 adult, $1.50 child.

Northern Surf Beaches

Sponge Bay, just north of the city around the point from Kaiti Beach, is for experienced (or foolhardy) surfers who enjoy rocks, seaweed, rips, and sharks. Not recommended for swimming. For the best surfing, head north along Hwy. 35 to

Wainui Beach (six km from town) or **Okitu Beach** (another six km), where local surfers pray for bad weather and subsequent mean waves. Wainui has a sandy bottom, beach break with good conditions, and offshore northwest wind. It's generally safe, but rips can be prevalent in adverse surf conditions. Okitu has good beach break conditions and offshore northwest winds, is generally safe in calm conditions with only occasional rips, and is patrolled in summer. **Makorori Beach,** about 10 km from town, has a very appealing setting. Backed by green rolling hills, this golden beach has both a reef and sandy bottom. It's not patrolled but still attracts lots of swimmers and surfers in summer; beware of rips.

Thermal Pools

One of the best places to enjoy a relaxing soak in thermal pools surrounded by lush vegetation and abundant birdlife is **Morere Hot Springs** on Hwy. 2, about 58 km south of Gisborne, tel. 06/837-8856. Soak in the Nikau Pools (two hot pools, cold plunge pool, hot foot pool, changing rooms, showers, and toilets), in the private hot pools, in the hot indoor pool, or in the cold freshwater outdoor pool—with choices like that, how can you go wrong? Everything is beautifully landscaped to blend in with the forest environment. Or go for a woodland walk through the 360-hectare property (the tracks range from 20 minutes to 2.5 hours) to appreciate all the tweeting from the trees, have a picnic, or take advantage of the next-door tavern and restaurant. Open weekdays 10 A.M.–5 P.M., extended hours until 8 P.M. on summer weekends; $5 adult, $2.50 child; private pools $7 adult, $3.50 child.

Drinking and Dancing

One of New Zealand's most interesting bars, the **Smash Palace Wine Bar** is on the wrong side the tracks at 24 Banks St. (east from downtown off Awapuni Rd.), tel. 06/867-7769. In the heart of an industrial subdivision, it's easily recognized by the dinosaur standing guard at the front door. And by the body of a DC3 on the roof. Once inside, the eclectic surroundings continue, with junk from around the world decorating the walls and floor. Even without method to this madness, it's a popular spot with locals and out-of-towners in the know. Out back is a small winery that specializes in Methode Champenoise, which along with many other local wines is available by the glass. The knowledgeable wait staff will help recommend a glass to suit your taste. Food is also available and there's often live music on weekends.

Even as the birthplace of opera diva Dame Kiri Te Kanawa, about the best music you'll find around Gisborne is from bands playing cover songs in local hotels. The **Gisborne Hotel,** corner Huxley and Tindall Roads, tel. 06/868-4109, attracts out-of-town acts, while the **Albion Hotel,** 13 Gladstone Rd., tel. 06/867-9997, features more local groups. Nearby, **Scotty's Bar and Grill,** 35 Gladstone Rd., has a little more class.

ACCOMMODATIONS

Hotels and Motels

Separated from Waikanae Beach by only a strip of grassy reserve is **Blue Pacific Beachfront Motel,** 90 Salisbury Rd., tel. 06/868-6099 or 0800/732-376; website: www.seafront.co.nz. Just over two km from downtown, the rooms are basic, but each has a kitchen and breakfast is available for a small charge. Rates range $95–135 s or d. With the same outlook but halfway back to town is **Whispering Sands Beachfront Motel,** 18–22 Salisbury Rd., tel. 06/867-1319 or 0800/405-030. Each of the 14 rooms has a private balcony, ocean view, and a small kitchen; $100–150 s or d.

Gladstone Rd., west of downtown, is Gisborne's "motel strip." One of the city's cheapest, **Endeavour Lodge Motel,** 525 Gladstone Rd., tel. 06/868-6075, with a swimming pool and nine self-contained rooms, charges $70 s, $75 d. **White Heron Motor Lodge,** 470-474 Gladstone Rd., tel. 06/867-1108 or 0800/997-766, features spacious, comfortable rooms, many with a spa bath. Rates are $100–140 s or d. Across the road is **Teal Motor Lodge,** 479 Gladstone Rd., tel. 06/868-4019 or 0800/838-325. This property has a large saltwater pool surrounded by gardens and outdoor furniture. Rooms are

$100–150 s or d. Continuing west, **Champers Motor Lodge,** 811 Gladstone Rd., tel. 06/863-1515 or 0800/702-000, is directly opposite the golf course, and the standard of the rooms is high; $90–140 s or d.

Backpacker Lodges

Gisborne YHA, 32 Harris St. on the east side of town, tel. 07/867-3269, is in a rambling house with a rambling atmosphere, $16–19 pp. The staff actively organizes frequent hikes and outings—a good source of information on what to see and do in the great local outdoors, including hints for traveling the East Cape. From Gladstone Rd. (the main street), cross the bridge and turn right at the traffic light. The hostel is in the second block beyond the bridge, about 500 meters from downtown.

On the other side of downtown, along the busy main road, an old orphanage has been converted to **Gisborne Backpackers,** 690 Gladstone Rd., tel. 06/868-1000. Dorm beds are $16–18 pp, twin and double rooms are $22 pp.

Motor Camps

Waikanae Beach Holiday Park on Grey St., tel. 06/867-5634, is adjacent to sandy Waikanae Beach, only 800 meters from downtown—a great spot for walking and swimming. Along with the usual community facilities (spotlessly clean), the camp has a cool room with lockers and tennis courts (racket hire $5 per hour), and at the office you can rent bicycles, surfboards, boogie boards, and other equipment. Rates for tent sites are $10 pp, power sites $22 d, ranch-house cabins $35–40 s or d, tourist cabins (with private bathroom and cooking facilities, but you supply bedding) $60–70 s or d.

Showgrounds Park Motor Camp in Showgrounds Park, tel. 06/867-5299, is a long walk from the center of town on the west side, and not available as a motor camp when it's used as a showground (October). However, if you're into golf you'll probably enjoy staying here—it's next to the nine-hole Park Golf Course. Sites are $10 s, $12.50 d, and cabins are a reasonable $20 s, $24 d. From downtown, follow Gladstone Rd. to the west end—it becomes Hwy. 35. When you see the golf course to the left, start looking for the motor camp—it's just down the road, also on the left.

If you want to camp out of town, you'll find several motor camps scattered around the East Cape.

FOOD

Robert Harris Cafe, like those found throughout the country, serves up a good selection of coffees and light pastries. The Gisborne franchise is in Treble Court on Peel St., tel. 06/867-0661. Around the corner, the **Lyric Cafe,** 124 Gladstone Rd. between Peel and Bright Streets, tel. 06/867-4134, specializes in seafood (from $12) and tasty grills ($10–15), and is one of the relatively few places open for breakfast (from 9 A.M.). A couple of locals recommended **Dago's Famous Pizza** at 50 Gladstone Rd., tel. 06/867-0543. The pizza looked okay, but I tried a Thai curry dish ($12) and it was fine. For a good selection of tasty salads try **Captain Morgan's** at 285 Grey St., tel. 06/867-7821, across from the motor camp—a stroll from the beachfront. Aside from the salad bar (small $5, large $7), a variety of tearoom fare, and specialty ice creams, it also serves light lunches, and steak and seafood dinners (entrees $18–22, desserts $4) until 8 P.M. Eat inside, or out on the sunny deck. At dinner it pays to book a table.

On the waterfront across the Taruheru River from downtown, an old row of dock buildings have been converted to restaurants. The most casual of these is **Oasis Bar & Cafe,** Shed One, tel. 06/867-1103, where lunches average $10 and dinners range $18–24. The decor is nothing special, but the food is fine and the outlook great. In the vicinity, the **Wharf Café,** 60 The Esplanade, tel. 06/868-4876, features a chic interior and the same great water views. Open for daily for breakfast (from 9 A.M.), lunch, and dinner, try the seared salmon with poached eggs on an English muffin ($12.50) if it's early, or the beef tenderloin with blue cheese and peppercorn sauce ($27) for dinner. Another waterfront eatery is the **Marina Restaurant** at River Junction, Marina Park, tel. 06/868-5919; dishes start at $20. It's open for lunch and dinner.

C View, opposite the Olympic Pool at Midway Beach, tel. 06/867-5861, is another of Gisborne's better restaurants.

TRANSPORTATION

Getting There

Gisborne **airport** is on the west side of the city. Get there via taxi (about $10 one way) or the **Link Shuttle,** tel. 06/868-8385, for $7 pp. The easiest route by car is to take Gladstone Rd. west out of town, and just before the golf course make a left on Chalmers Road. Continue almost to the end and turn right on Aerodrome Road. **Air New Zealand** flies regularly to Auckland and Wellington. Flights to all other points, including nearby Napier, are routed through these two cities. The local ticket office is at 37 Bright St., tel. 06/868-2700.

All buses arrive and depart from Gisborne Information Centre at 209 Grey Street. **Intercity,** tel. 06/868-6139, runs to Gisborne from Rotorua and Auckland via Opotiki and from Taupo via Napier and Wairoa. **Coachrite Connections,** tel. 06/868-9969, runs daily between Gisborne and Napier, with some services continuing south to Hastings.

Getting Around

Gisborne District Buses, tel. 06/867-9900, runs a suburban transport network, while **Red Bus Service,** tel. 06/867-7423, covers the rural areas of Bartletts, Whatatutu, Te Karaka, and Muriwai.

Local cab companies are **Eastland Taxis,** tel. 06/868-1133; **Gisborne Taxis,** tel. 06/867-2222; and **Sun City Taxis,** tel. 06/867-6767.

Car rental agencies with offices in Gisborne include **Avis,** tel. 06/868-9084; **Budget,** tel. 06/867-9794; **Hertz,** tel. 06/867-9348; and **Scotties,** tel. 06/867-7947.

SERVICES AND INFORMATION

The central **post office** is at 74 Grey St. between Gladstone and Palmerston Roads. **H. B. Williams Memorial Library** is on Peel St., tel. 06/867-6709; open Mon.–Fri. 9:30 A.M.–5:30 P.M., Saturday 9:30 A.M.–1 P.M.

For **emergency** help (ambulance, police, fire, pharmacy) dial 111. The **police station** is on the corner of Peel St. and Childers Rd., tel. 06/869-0200. **St. John Ambulance** on the corner of Palmerston Rd. and Bright St., tel. 06/868-7715, is the place to find a local on-duty emergency doctor, dentist, or urgent pharmacist. **Gisborne Hospital** is on Ormond Rd., tel. 06/869-0500. **Kaiti Medical Centre** is on De Lautour Rd., tel. 06/867-7411; open daily 8 A.M.–8 P.M.

Information
Tourism Eastland, website: www.eastland .tourism.co.nz, promotes Gisborne and the surrounding area to the world. Once in town, head to the **Gisborne Information Centre,** 209 Grey St., tel. 06/868-6139; open Mon.–Fri. 9 A.M.–5 P.M., weekends 10 A.M.–4 P.M. In summer it's open seven days a week at 9 A.M. and closes late.

For information on New Zealand Walkway tracks, call in at the **East Coast/Hawke's Bay Conservancy** headquarters at 63 Carnarvon St., tel. 06/867-8531; open weekdays 8 A.M.–4:30 P.M. The **Automobile Association,** 363 Gladstone Rd., tel. 06/868-1424, is a great place for road maps and travel information.

Napier and Vicinity

One of the world's best examples of the distinctive art deco style, Napier (population 55,000) is perched on the edge of the Pacific Ocean 210 km southwest of Gisborne and 150 km southeast of Taupo. It's another great place to enjoy sea breezes whipping through your hair and bright sun on your face, but its distinct seaside-town atmosphere and earthquake history set it apart from the other towns along the east coast.

Napier boasts a climate that is quite Mediterranean, with lots of sunshine, cool sea breezes, and an average temperature of 21°C in summer and 10°C in winter. Though large crowds of holidaymakers descend in summer, it manages to retain a small-town feeling. Napier offers plenty of local attractions, but the relaxed by-the-sea atmosphere may tempt you to spend an extra day lounging on the beach.

History
Sauntering along stately, Norfolk pine-lined Marine Parade, you will find it hard to believe that this elegant city was completely rebuilt after total destruction in the Hawke's Bay earthquake of 1931. During the earthquake the city, at that time a busy trading post, was lifted six to eight feet, and the salt marshes, swamps, and inner harbor were completely drained. Although there was great loss of life and almost all the brick buildings of the city collapsed, the earthquake gave the survivors an extra 10,000 acres of land, and now the airport and a large section of Napier stand on what used to be the sea floor. A few years before the earthquake, a world away in Paris at the International Exposition of Modern Decorative and Industrial Arts, a new bold, geometrical architectural style now known as art deco was unveiled to the world. The 1931 earthquake coincided with the peak of this style's popularity, which is reflected in Napier's rebuilt commercial core.

SIGHTS AND RECREATION
Marine Parade
You can spend an entire day soaking up the Napier feeling by taking a leisurely walk along the attractive, four-km, oceanfront Marine Parade, the main drag for visitors. View interesting 1930s architecture on the west side of the street, nothing but ocean to the east (there's no land between Napier and Chile), or visit the many commercial attractions. Before continuing elsewhere, stop at the **Visitor Information Centre** (at the bottom of Emerson St. on Marine Parade). Pick up the Napier street map and information guide or a scenic drive folder if you have wheels, and you'll be set for the rest of your stay.

To the north of the information center is the **Sound Shell and Colonnade,** where you can collect fine pottery and handicrafts in a market setting on weekends.

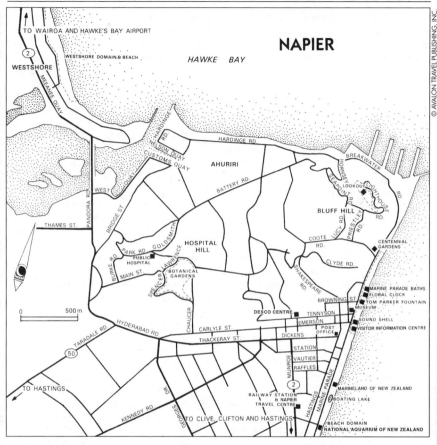

Marineland of New Zealand, tel. 06/834-4027, south of the information center, is one of Napier's best-known attractions and worth a visit, but take a warm sweater even in midsummer—the wind howls through the stands where you sit facing the ocean, completely in the shade by late afternoon. Dolphins, sea lions, penguins, seals, and otters strut their stuff to a lively commentary and put on an entertaining show with the lure of tasty morsels from their trainers. You can view pens of recuperating gannets and other seabirds injured in the wild, and a well-stocked shop sells tourist paraphernalia. It's open daily 10 A.M.–5:30 P.M., with regular shows at 10:30 A.M. and 2 P.M., extra shows in summer; $9 adult,

$4 child. If swimming with dolphins in the open ocean doesn't appeal to you, it's possible to do it here without getting seasick (daily at noon; $40). Another "Behind the Scenes Tour" is Touch the Dolphins (daily 9 A.M.; adult $20, child $10).

To the south of Marineland is the grandly named **National Aquarium of New Zealand,** tel. 06/834-1404. Built soon after the earthquake, it underwent massive renovations in 2002 and is now one of the largest in the Southern Hemisphere. The main aquarium—30 meters long by 24 meters wide and filled with local species including sharks—has a clear-walled walkway winding through it for close-up viewing. On the upper floor, the continents of the world are showcased with a wide variety of exhibits, including an Australian outback diorama, the re-creation of an African fishing village, and a Japanese garden. A diver hand-feeds many of the residents of the main aquarium daily at 10 A.M. and 2 P.M. It's open in January, daily 9 A.M.–9 P.M., December and February, daily 9 A.M.–7 P.M., and the rest of the year, daily 9 A.M.–5 P.M. Admission is $12 adult, $6 child.

At the aquarium's northern end is the **Lilliput Model Railway.** Local Bill Napp built the railway over 50 years ago, transporting it around the country until it found a permanent home here in Napier. The train ride is $2.50 adult, $1 child, or free with entry to the National Aquarium.

Art Deco Napier

To appreciate all the intriguing art deco and Spanish mission styles of architecture (built at lightning speed during the depression after the earthquake in 1931), pick up the Art Deco Walk brochure ($2) from the **Desco Centre,** 163 Tennyson St., tel. 06/835-0022. The center is home to the **Art Deco Trust,** which manages and promotes the city's unique architecture. Knowledgeable locals lead guided walks from the center Oct.–June daily at 2 P.M., and July–Sept., Wednesday, Saturday, and Sunday at 2 P.M., that start with a short slide presentation explaining the art deco style. Then you walk around Napier, watch another film, and finish things off with a cup of tea or coffee; $15 pp. In the same building, the trust runs a shop selling maps, prints, books, and other art deco material. It's open daily 9 A.M.–5 P.M.

The trust runs its annual **Art Deco Weekend** on the third weekend of February, featuring guided walks, an antique show and auction, theater, and lots of jazz. Contact the trust for all the details.

Scenic Lookouts

Just past the wildlife center at the northern end of Marine Parade, Coote Rd. branches off to the left, passing attractive **Centennial Gardens,** where an artificial waterfall splashes down a 100-meter cliff face into ponds and rock pools among flowerbeds and lawns. Coote Rd. continues up Bluff Hill to the **Bluff Hill Lookout** for great

ocean views. (Turn right off Coote Rd. onto Thompson Rd., then right on Lighthouse Rd. and follow it to the end.) If you don't have a city map it's quite easy to get lost up here, even when you're trying your best to follow the blue-and-yellow scenic drive signs. If you don't mind stumbling around in a maze of one-way streets and fascinating architecture, fancy homes, and the odd glimpse of city or sea, try finding your way to **City View Outlook** while you're in the mood. It's a great spot at night to view the city lights. Take Coote Rd. (off Marine Parade) to the top, turn left, then turn immediately left again onto Clyde Rd. passing the Girls High School, and you *should* end up at the viewing point. (Temporarily ignore the scenic drive arrows if you're following the above directions.)

Hawke's Bay Museum

For an excellent collection of Maori art, historic presentations of early Hawke's Bay, 18th- and 19th-century European antiques, and an extensive art collection, stop by Hawke's Bay Museum for a few hours. Art and film presentations are regularly shown in the Century Theatre. Perhaps the most remarkable feature is the audiovisual presentation of the 1931 earthquake—if you get there and find it already playing, explore the rest of the museum and come back to get the full impact of the film from the beginning. The museum and shop are open weekdays 10 A.M.–4:30 P.M., weekends and public holidays noon–4:30 P.M.; $5 adult, free to children. The adjoining museum of natural history is open only on weekends and public holidays 2–4 P.M. The museum is on Herschell St., off the Marine Parade end of Tennyson St., tel. 06/835-7781.

Botanical Gardens

Napier residents are understandably proud of their Botanical Gardens. Perfect lawns give way to beds of flowers and blooming shrubs, and paths lead through shady groves of assorted trees in this small, inner-city oasis. A stream flows through the gardens and trickles down in tiny waterfalls; here and there miniature ornamental bridges or stepping-stones allow passage back and forth. The main feature is a spacious aviary. You'll find the Botanical Gardens in the Hospital Hill area, a couple of kilometers west of downtown between Napier Terrace, Spencer Road, and Chaucer Road S. To get there from the information center, cross Marine Parade and take Emerson St. past Clive Square (it becomes Carlyle St.). Continue down Carlyle, turn right on Chaucer Rd., turn left on Napier Terrace. Next to the gardens is an old, tree-shaded graveyard where some of the older gravestones date from the 19th century and lie abandoned or broken among grass and wildflowers.

Industry Tour

If you've ever wondered what goes on in a sheepskin factory, head for **Classic Sheepskins Tannery,** 22 Thames St., tel. 06/835-9662. It offers free tours daily at 11 A.M. and 2 P.M. describing the entire tanning and manufacturing process, but the tour naturally ends in the factory shop where suckers for sheepskin products can kiss their money goodbye. The shop is open Mon.–Fri. 7:30 A.M.–5 P.M., and weekends 9 A.M.–4 P.M. From the city center take Emerson St. (away from the ocean), which becomes Carlyle St., and continue onto Hyderabad Road. Continue around the corner (following Hwy. 2 north signs) and branch off over the railway line onto Pandora Road. The first street to the left is Thames Street.

Vineyards

If you enjoy a bit of wine-tasting, you can get more than your fill of the drink of the gods in the Hawke's Bay Wine Region—there are more than 30 small wineries from which to choose. Before heading out, collect the free "A Guide to Hawke's Bay Wineries" brochure from the information center. It features all of the wineries in the region, and gives good road directions so you can easily find them on your map (important after a few stops). Most of the vineyards are open for tasting and buying Mon.–Sat. 9 A.M.–5 P.M. (some longer). The best-known (and all open for lunch) include **Brookfield Winery,** Brookfields Rd., Meeanee, tel. 06/834-4615; **Crab Farm Winery,** 511 Main Rd., Bay View, tel.

06/836-6678; and New Zealand's oldest winery, **Mission Estate Winery,** Church Rd., Taradale, tel. 06/844-2259.

Contact **Bay Tours,** tel. 06/843-6953, for wine tours. Departing from the information center at 1 P.M., the basic tour visits three wineries and costs $40 pp.

Beaches

The long stretch of shingle beach directly in front of **Marine Parade** is better for walking than for swimming. It's safe when calm, but easterly winds quickly whip up coastal breakers and rough conditions. It's patrolled on weekends until March—during the week look out for red-flag warnings on the lifesaving clubhouse. The closest sandy beach with safe swimming and light surf is **Westshore** (about two km north of city center) on the northern side of Bluff Hill. Unpatrolled **Waipatiki Beach,** about 40 km north of Napier, also has good swimming, but the currents can be dangerous, particularly in easterly winds. **Waimarama Beach,** 48 km south of Napier, has a long stretch of sand and rolling surf but is subject to rips on the incoming tide. The safest place to swim is the area directly in front of the lifesaving club, which is patrolled on weekends until March.

Hiking Trails

You'll find several walkways in the Hawke's Bay region. **Tangoio Walkway,** 25 km north of Napier on the main highway to Wairoa, is the closest to the city. It winds for six km through the native forest and pine plantations of scenic Tangoio Valley, providing a panoramic view of the bay and many waterfalls along the route. The nine-km **Tutira Walkway,** 45 km north of Napier, runs to and along the eastern shore of Lake Tutira, providing rugged hill-country views and (on a fine day) a view of Hawke's Bay from the Ruahine Range all the way to Te Urewera National Park. You need sturdy boots for this track, and it's wise to take along a windproof jacket, food, and drink. **Boundary Stream Walkway,** 60 km north of Napier, passes through Boundary Stream Scenic Reserve; the highlight of this 12-km hike is the spectacular **Shine's Falls.** Starting on Po-

EASTLAND AND HAWKE'S BAY

CAPE KIDNAPPERS

Cape Kidnappers, a dramatic bluff that forms the southern extremity of Hawke's Bay, 21 km southeast of Napier, is worth visiting for its natural beauty alone, but its main attraction is the four **gannet colonies,** perched precariously around its farthest tip. More than 20,000 of the birds call this site home, making it the world's largest mainland nesting place of Australasian gannets. They are members of the Sulid family (often called booby), with pale gold crowns and striking black eye markings. They arrive in July to nest and breed in several gannetries atop the high cliff plateau. Gannets lay their eggs in October and November; about six weeks later the chicks hatch. The birds start leaving in February, and by April almost all the gannets have gone; the colony is closed to the public from July 1 to mid-October so that the birds aren't disturbed in their early nesting phase. The best time to visit the gannet colony is between November and late February.

The Napier information center has a blackboard detailing tours, times, and costs, and its staff makes bookings. The cape can be reached in the following ways:

On Foot

From Clifton, south of Napier through Te Awanga, it's eight km along a beautiful sandy beach to Cape Kidnappers. The walk is relatively easy, so only about two hours each way is required to reach the cape. The track follows the beach past Black Reef gannet colony and climbs the cliff. About one km beyond the reef is a rest area with water and toilets. The formed track continues up to the plateau, where you can see the gannets close up (but keep your distance so as not to disturb them). Don't forget your camera, plenty of film, suntan lotion, a hat if you burn easily, and a windbreaker.

The tide is the most important consideration for those taking the beach route; it can only be walked at low tide. The safest time to leave Clifton is no sooner than three hours after high tide and to leave the cape no later than 1.5 hours after low

hokura Rd., it takes up to four hours to reach Heays Access Rd., then another hour to the falls. (You can also start on Heays Access Rd. if you just want to do the four-km walk to the falls.) This track demands strong boots, a windproof jacket, warm sweater (the weather can be quite unpredictable), food, and drink.

Entertainment

Most hotels and taverns are open for serious drinking Mon.–Sat. 11 A.M.–8 P.M. (some open earlier). You'll find a band playing or music videos Thurs.–Sat. nights at the **Masonic Hotel** on Tennyson St., tel. 06/835-8689, and **Westshore Hotel** on Main Rd. in Westshore, tel. 06/835-9879. For a quieter drink in stylish surroundings, head to **Mango Jacks Café,** 18 Hastings St., tel. 06/834-0405, or one of two bars in the **Masonic Hotel,** corner of Tennyson St. and Marine Parade, tel. 06/835-8689. In a renovated theater, **Mossy's Art Deco Café,** 88 Dickens St., tel. 06/835-6696, is a café first and bar second, but often has acoustic jams.

ACCOMMODATIONS

Hotels and Motels

Napier's least expensive motels are in suburban Westshore, on the northern outskirts of town. One of the best value of these is the **Cedar Court Motel,** 100 meters from the water at 50 Meeanee Quay, tel. 06/835-9477 or 0508/233-272; rates $60 s, $75 d.

The centrally located **Masonic Hotel,** on the corner of Tennyson St. and Marine Parade, tel. 06/835-8689 or 0800/627-664, website: www.masonic.co.nz, features an art deco style exterior and lobby, modern rooms, and a variety of eateries; rates from $80 s or d.

A few blocks back from the beach, **City Close Motel,** 50 Munroe St., tel. 06/835-3568, is close to everything. It's a small place, with just eight rooms, but each has a kitchen; rates from $78 s, $88 d. A similar distance from downtown but directly opposite the beach, **Edgewater Motor Lodge,** 359 Marine Parade, tel. 06/835-1148, is an older place with a saltwater tide. For current tide times, call in to the Napier Visitor Information Centre, Marine Parade, tel. 06/834-1911. Note that the farmland between the domain and the cape is privately owned, and the high cliffs between Clifton and Black Reef are unstable—look out for rock slides and avoid walking directly under the cliffs.

By Tractor-Trailer

The unusual, fun tractor-trailer ride is the most popular way to reach the cape. **Gannet Beach Adventures,** tel. 06/875-0898 or 0800/426-638, consists of an entourage of tractors pulling trailers along the beach at the base of the cliffs, passing the Black Reef gannet colony on the way to Cape Kidnappers. Once at the cape, you face a short but steep 20-minute climb from the end of the beach to the colony. The trip departs Charlton Rd. at Te Awanga daily during the season, about 2.5 hours before low tide. It takes about four hours for the round-trip, with about 90 minutes of that time spent at the cape. Extra time is set aside for swimming or enjoying a picnic lunch (bring your own). The cost is a reasonable $24 adult, $15 child. Tours operate Oct.–May but departure times are entirely dependant on the tides, so call ahead.

By Four-Wheel Drive

The easiest way to get to the cape is overland, crossing the privately owned Summerlee Station in a four-wheel drive bus with **Gannet Safaris,** tel. 06/875-0888 or 0800/427-232. The 18-km trip takes about an hour each way, with an hour at the gannet sanctuary, providing spectacular views of Hawke's Bay; $55 adult, $27.50 child. To get to the starting point you'll need your own vehicle. Leave Napier on the main road south to Clive and take Mill Rd. to the left, following the signs to the cape along the coast road. Drive through Te Awanga and cross the Maraetotara Stream; not far after the bridge, a large sign to the right says Summerlee Station.

plunge pool, a game room, laundry, and 20 smallish but comfortable units starting at $95 s or d. A few doors to the south is the modern **Beach Front Motel,** 373 Marine Parade, tel. 06/835-5220 or 0800/778-888, a three-story place featuring 28 luxurious rooms, each with a private balcony, king-size bed, spa bath, and modern kitchen. At $120–160 s or d, this motel is a great value.

The **County Hotel,** 12 Browning St., tel. 06/835-7800 or 0800/483-468, website: www .countyhotel.co.nz, is a restored Edwardian-era building downtown and across from the beach. Originally a council building (and one of the few buildings to survive the earthquake), it has been transformed into a boutique hotel, with a fine-dining restaurant and English-style cocktail lounge downstairs and a magnificent *rimi* stairway leading up to 12 guest rooms. Each named for a native bird, the rooms feature a high ceiling, timber paneling, a tiled bathroom, and an art deco-influenced décor. Rates start at $195 s or d, and go up over $300 for a suite.

Bed-and-Breakfasts

Just down the street from the information center, **Waterfront Lodge,** 217 Marine Parade, tel. 06/835-3429, has excellent accommodation at budget prices, and it's often full no matter what the season. From outside appearances you'd never guess that there are 14 attractively furnished rooms, community bathrooms, a TV lounge, a communal kitchen, and a laundry beyond the front entrance. Single rooms are $35 s, $55 d, which includes breakfast, and you can make your own dinner at night. Call and reserve a room as far ahead as possible. Continuing south, **Pinehaven Travel Hotel,** 259 Marine Parade, tel. 06/835-5575, has a hostess who makes you feel right at home, a comfy TV lounge, tea- and coffee-making supplies, and a nonsmoking policy; six guest rooms, all with hand basins and some with great waterfront views, are $48 s, $78 d, with continental breakfast. **Sea Breeze Bed and Breakfast,** 281 Marine Parade, tel. 06/835-8067, is located in a tastefully decorated two-story building on busy Marine Parade, a short walk from all seaside attractions and restaurants. The guest rooms have a decidedly exotic Asian ambience and guests have access to a covered lounge overlooking the ocean. Rooms are $55 s, $75 d, which includes a continental breakfast.

As well as the old-style guesthouses along the waterfront, more luxurious bed-and-breakfasts are scattered around the city. One of these is **Mon Logis** ("my dwelling" in French). This 1860s terrace house, at 415 Marine Parade, tel. 06/835-2125, has fantastic ocean views and four splendid rooms for $120 s, $160 d, which includes a breakfast basket delivered to the room. A five-course evening meal served in the downstairs dining room is $55 pp.

Backpacker Lodges

Criterion Art Deco Backpackers is above an attractive mall downtown at 48 Emerson St., tel. 06/835-2059. Located in the old, rather grand, and spacious Criterion Hotel, this budget accommodation provides large dorms at $17 pp, twin or doubles for $22 pp, plus a roomy living room with a TV and pool table, and a fully equipped kitchen. Downstairs the bar serves excellent bistro meals during the day from $6 and evening meals every night from $9.50.

In a renovated beachfront house **Napier YHA,** 277 Marine Parade, tel. 06/835-7039, website: www.yha.org.nz, is spacious, and quite luxurious as hostels go, with small dorms giving more privacy than the norm, twin or family rooms, and large kitchen, dining room, and common rooms. It also has an excellent central location on oceanfront Marine Parade across from Marineland; $18–21 pp.

A little farther south along the waterfront, but still in an excellent location, is purpose-built **Stables Lodge Backpackers,** 370 Hastings St. (enter from Marine Parade), tel. 06/835-6242, with 10 rooms set around a pleasant brick courtyard. All facilities are modern, and there's a television lounge, free barbecue, and bike rentals and lockers available. Rates are $16 pp in a four-bed dorm, $18 pp double or twin.

If you're heading north, consider staying at **Glenview Farm Hostel,** 32 km north of town on Aropaoaunui Rd., two km off State Hwy. 2 (look for the AA sign on the main road at the top of the hill), tel. 06/826-6232. Here you can join in on hill country sheep station activities, go horseback riding (from $20 half-day) or on scenic walks, or just relax; beds from $15.

Motor Camps

The most central motor camp is in the Napier suburb of Marewa, about 2.5 km from downtown. The attractive grounds of **Kennedy Park Top 10 Accommodation,** Kennedy Rd., tel. 06/843-9126, website: www.kennedypark.co.nz, are adjacent to beautiful Kennedy Rose Gardens. Communal facilities, a TV lounge, a pool table, trampolines, a general store, breakfast, and dinner are available. Tent sites are $18, caravan sites $20, bunk-bed huts $30 d, cabins $45 d, tourist flats $82 d. The next closest camp is **Westshore Holiday Camp,** Main Rd., Westshore, tel. 06/835-9456, four km from downtown but with a great location 150 meters from Westshore Beach (safe swimming and good surf). It has communal facilities, an indoor spa pool (extra charge), a TV room, and an adjacent store. Tent sites are $18, powered sites are $20, cabins start at $40, tourist flats start at $65.

Sullivan's Te Awanga Motor Camp, on the beach at Te Awanga, tel. 06/875-0334, is 17 km southeast of Hastings but only 12 km from Cape Kidnappers—the perfect base for visiting the gannet colonies. The camp is on a sandy beach next to a boating stream—good swimming, surfing, and fishing—and has communal facilities, spa pool, and store. Campsites are $18–20 and cabins start at $36 s or d.

Free Camping

At Tutira, about 35 km north of Napier off Hwy. 2, there's a great camping area by **Tutira Bird Reserve.** Camping spots are on grass, under shady trees, and along the southern edge of a serene lake where many ducks and black swans live; several walkways of various lengths start here. Water (boil it for at least 20 minutes to be on the safe side) and toilets are provided (no showers), and it's free! If you go there during a public holiday, expect the campground to be full; otherwise there's plenty of room and privacy.

FOOD

Cafés

The café scene around Napier has improved markedly since the last edition of this book. For good, strong coffee and a variety of other caffeine-infused drinks, head to the **Brazilian Coffee Shop,** 68 Emerson St., tel. 06/835-6069, or **Sappho & Heath,** 68 Emerson St., tel. 06/834-3933. Emerson Street runs inland from Marine Parade one block north of Dickens Street. To the south of these two places off Hastings St., **Café Graaz,** 82 Dalton St., tel. 06/835-6118, is another good choice for coffee, as well as a huge array of cakes. Breakfast here is also good. Open Mon.–Sat. 8:30 A.M.–4:30 P.M. The phrase "gourmet pie" is considered an oxymoron by many, but at **Campbell's Gormet Pies,** 50 Dickens St., tel. 06/835-8359, the meat pies are about as good as they come.

Restaurants

Along with guest rooms, the oceanfront Masonic Hotel, corner of Tennyson St. and Marine Parade, tel. 06/835-8689, has undergone major changes in its many eateries. At the **Breakers Café & Bar,** you can order pancakes with maple syrup ($7.50), or have a full cooked breakfast ($12) from 8 A.M. daily. The rest of the day, regular North American-style bar food is all under $12, while steak and seafood dishes, such as a whitebait omelet, range $14–18. Also in the hotel is **Acqua,** a modern brasserie with lots of seafood and an extensive wine list featuring local bottles. The mussel chowder ($9.50) is a great appetizer, while cedar-plank salmon in a caramelized crust with baby potatoes and a generous serving of greens ($24) is my recommendation for dinner.

Also right downtown is **Mango Jack's Café,** 18 Hastings St., tel. 06/834-0405. This casual eatery has a great range of dishes and award-winning art deco decor, and is one of Napier's most popular watering holes. It's open daily from 11 A.M. Dinners cost about $20, while desserts are $8. **Alfresco's,** upstairs at 65 Emerson St., tel. 06/835-1181, is a café/restaurant/bar with a predominantly Italian menu starting at $14 for main dishes. The food is good, but the cavernous dining area can seem very empty on a quiet night. **Ujazi,** 28 Tennyson St., tel. 06/835-1490, is open for breakfast and lunch, but it is for dinner that this restaurant really shines. The menu is small but varied, offered everything from an Indonesian curry to locally caught seafood, with a couple of vegetarian dishes thrown in for good measure. Dinners are less than $24.

If you're more in the mood for a splurge, dressing up, and sea views, try **Bayswater Bistro,** a small unassuming restaurant on Hardinge Rd. (a continuation of Marine Parade northbound), tel. 06/835-8517. Enjoy a seafood-oriented menu, cooked and presented with a European leaning, in the main dining room or out on the terrace. Salmon grilled in a coriander crust is a New Zealand favorite, and the Bayswater does it beautifully for $25.50. It's open daily for lunch and dinner. In the vicinity, **Shed 2,** West Quay, tel. 06/835-2202, is exactly that-an old shed used for storing wool bales before they were exported. The basic structure remains intact, including exposed framework throughout the ceiling and worn timber floorboards. A little more casual than the Bayswater, the food is still good, with lots of simple favorites ranging from a pile of wedges with sour cream and sweet chili ($8.50) to grilled salmon ($19). It's open for lunch, Fri.–Sun. noon–2 P.M. and for dinner, Mon.–Sat. from 6:30 P.M.

Many of the local wineries offer delicious lunches in pleasant surroundings. If you're heading for Hastings, stop in at **St. George Estate Winery** on St. George Rd. between Hastings and Havelock, tel. 06/877-5356, which serves lunch (and other meals) in the gardens in summer; expect to pay about $25 pp.

TRANSPORTATION

Getting There

Hawke's Bay Airport is a couple of km north of Napier. Take main Hwy. 2 north to Westshore and turn left onto Watchman Road. The **Super Shuttle,** tel. 06/844-7333, offers door-to-door drop-offs from the airport for $8 pp one way to Napier and $16 pp to Hastings. **Air New Zealand** has direct flights from Napier to Auckland, Wellington, and Christchurch and a booking office on the corner of Hastings and Station Streets, tel. 06/835-1171.

Intercity and **Newmans** are based at the **Napier Travel Centre** at the railway station on Munroe St., tel. 06/834-2720. It's open Mon.–Fri. 8 A.M.–6 P.M., and weekends 12:30–4 P.M. The companies operate daily coach services from Napier and Hastings to Auckland, Hamilton, Rotorua, Taupo, Tauranga, Gisborne, Palmerston North, New Plymouth, Wanganui, and Wellington.

Getting Around

For car rental information, call **Avis,** tel. 06/835-1828; **Budget,** tel. 06/835-5166; **Hertz,** tel. 06/835-6169; or **Thrifty,** tel. 06/835-8818.

A taxi stand is on Lower Emerson St. near Clive Square. Local cab companies include **Napier Taxis,** tel. 06/835-7777, and **Star Taxis,** tel. 06/835-5511.

SERVICES AND INFORMATION

Services

The **post office** is in Books & More at 57 Dickens Street. **Napier Public Library** is on Station St., tel. 06/834-4180; open Mon.–Fri. 9 A.M.–5 P.M., Saturday 10 A.M.–1 P.M., Sunday 2–4 P.M. Send and receive email while enjoying a coffee at **Cyber's Internet Café,** 98 Dickens St., tel. 06/835-0125.

Napier Public Hospital is on Hospital Terrace, west of the Botanical Gardens, tel. 06/834-1800. **City Medical,** for less urgent cases, is on Wellesley Rd., tel. 06/835-4999. **Unichem Pharmacy** is at 288 Gloucester St., tel. 06/844-2673. The **police station** is on Station St., tel. 06/831-0700.

Information

Napier Visitor Information Centre on Marine Parade, tel. 06/834-1911, website: www.hawkesbaytourism.co.nz, is the first place to go for general and accommodation information, brochures, a city map, and to book all tours (including to the gannet colony) and onward transportation. It's open Mon.–Fri. 8:30 A.M.–5 P.M., weekends

and public holidays 9 A.M.–5 P.M., and till 8:30 P.M. in summer.

HASTINGS

This large agricultural center of 50,000, 18 km southwest of Napier, is known as "The Fruit Bowl of New Zealand" and is Napier's twin city in the center of the vineyard region. It is known for its Mediterranean climate, fertile soil, and artesian water, and is particularly worth a visit in spring when all the colorful magnolia trees are in bloom.

Sights

The highlight of a visit to Hastings includes the many parks and gardens dotting the city, especially Te Mata. The most central is **Cornwall Park,** well-established with 100-year-old English trees, a lake, and a begonia display; open daily 10 A.M.–4 P.M. Also of interest is Oak Avenue, a stately row of trees planted along a driveway in the 1860s and now a public road. To get there from downtown, take Heretaunga Street W out of the city.

Splash Planet, on Grove Rd. (off Karamu Rd. N or Hwy. 2), tel. 06/876-9856, is the biggest commercial attraction in Hastings. It features lots of water slides, hot pools, go carts, mini-train rides, a skating rink, and a huge children's playground with all sorts of activities and rides. It's open in summer, daily 9 A.M.–9 P.M. Admission is $15 adult, $8 child.

Hiking

The 2.2-km **Te Mata Peak Walkway** starts 14 km south of Hastings, climbing to the 399-meter high point of Te Mata Trust Park. The trail is pretty steep (allow one hour for the uphill slog), but the summit provides magnificent views of Hawke's Bay, the Ruahine Range, and the volcanic peaks of Tongariro National Park.

Two-km **Monckton Walkway,** 12 km northwest of Takapau, passes through a steep gorge in Monckton Scenic Reserve and crosses the beautiful Tanarewai Stream with its good swimming holes. It takes about 1.5 hours round-trip; wear strong shoes. For more detailed information on any of the above tracks, pick up the individual track brochures from the information center.

Accommodations

Hastings has the usual array of standard motels, but head five km east of town to escape the ordinary at **Weldon Boutique B&B,** 98 Te Mata Rd., tel. 06/877-7551 or 0800/206-499; website: www.weldon.co.nz. Dating to the early 1900s, the house has undergone a tasteful restoration with period furnishings and a distinct French Provincial style. Each of the five guest rooms has its own bathroom, tea- and coffee-making facilities, and a television. Rates are $90 s, $120–140 d, which includes breakfast in the main dining room or outside overlooking the extensive gardens. Dinner is available for $30 pp.

Information

Hastings Visitor Information Centre on Russell St., tel. 06/873-5526, is open Mon.–Fri. 8:30 A.M.–5 P.M., Sat.–Sun. 10 A.M.–3 P.M.

Taranaki and the West

On the northwest coast of Cape Egmont, 375 km south of Auckland, this city of 50,000 is the metropolitan and cultural center for the lush agricultural Taranaki region. The tourist brochures have aptly named it "The Garden City" for its beautiful parks and reserves (one-fifth of the urban area is green). Sandwiched between popular surf beaches along North Taranaki Bight and dominated by majestic snowcapped Mt. Egmont/Taranaki to the south, the city is also recognized for its scenic beauty. Rich on- and offshore oil and natural gas fields have led to increasing affluence and development and the title "Energy Centre of New Zealand." Apart from local city attractions, New Plymouth is an ideal base for exploring Egmont National Park, the "Round-the-Mountain" route, and the gently rolling hedge-divided countryside of the surrounding Taranaki dairylands.

The ocean and beaches are New Plymouth's main attraction, but on the waterfront right downtown is another impressive water-based sight—**Port Taranaki,** the largest port on New Zealand's west coast. The three main wharves, which are protected by a massive breakwater, handle five million tons of freight (everything from natural gas to timber) annually. The best views of the port are from Breakwater Rd. as it climbs westward from the city toward the old power station.

SIGHTS AND RECREATION

Head directly for New Plymouth Information Centre, in Puke Ariki on Ariki St., and collect the "City Walks" brochure. The brochure covers inner-city parks, historic sites, Maori *pa,* fine swimming beaches, and general

Mt. Egmont/Taranaki

places of interest. Many attractions (too many to list here) await discovery in the Taranaki region: inland to the dairylands, up volcanic Mt. Egmont/Taranaki, and along the attractive coastal section of the "Round-the-Mountain" route.

Puke Ariki

One of the most comprehensive collections of Maori art and Maori, colonial, and natural history exhibits are at **Puke Ariki,** New Zealand's newest museum. Scheduled to open in early 2003, this world-class facility takes pride of place along the waterfront on Ariki St., tel. 06/759-6080. It incorporates the historic War Memorial Building, which is linked by a glass-walled "airway" across Ariki St. to a new ultramodern building. The North Wing holds the main lobby, the New Plymouth Information Centre, a café, and a lounge area affording magnificent ocean views. In addition to showcasing Taranaki's Maori and European history, there are a large number of interactive science displays and a Discovery Centre for children. Puke Ariki is open Mon.–Fri. 9:30 A.M.–4:30 P.M., Sat.–Sun. 1–5 P.M.

Other Downtown Sights

Two blocks west, at Brougham St., is **Richmond Cottage,** dating to 1854 and occupied through the years by three prominent Taranaki families. The cottage is built of stone, unusual for a private residence from this era. It's open Friday 2–4 P.M., Sat.–Sun, 1–4 P.M. Admission is $1 pp.

Continuing another two blocks west, the modern **Govett-Brewster Art Gallery** on Queen St. (between King and Devon Streets), tel. 06/758-5149, has many fine art collections and changing contemporary art exhibitions; it's open daily 10:30 A.M.–5 P.M. New Zealand's oldest stone church, the Anglican **St. Mary's Church** on Vivian St. between Robe and Brougham Streets, is another historic site in the downtown area worth a visit. Built in 1846, the church features intricate stained-glass windows and is surrounded by pleasant gardens, dotted with gravestones and memorials that tell a vivid story of the city's early days.

Parks and Gardens

If you enjoy beautiful parks, take a 10-minute walk from the city center to the 20-hectare **Pukekura Park**—a lush urban oasis that shouldn't be missed. Paths lead through native bush and flowers, an abundance of tree ferns and exotic flowers, and along streams and lakes that provide the photographer with good scenery shots and Mt. Egmont/Taranaki reflections. An illuminated fountain (very colorful at night) plays at the drop of a 50-cent coin, and for another coin you can enjoy an 11-meter-high illuminated waterfall bordered by lush ferns. The park is open daily; the fabulous Fernery and Begonia display houses, interconnected by moss-festooned tunnels, are open daily 10 A.M.–noon and 1–4 P.M. The Tea House is open daily except Tuesdays. The main entrance to the park is past the sportsground on Liardet St., a couple of blocks south of the downtown information center; admission is free. The south end of Pukekura Park is accessed from Victoria Road. Here you'll find **Gables Gallery,** tel. 06/758-9311, housed in New Zealand's oldest remaining hospital building (as a hospital, it was totally unsatisfactory-even its surgeon died after he contracted pneumonia from its draughty rooms) and is now open as an art gallery each Saturday and Sunday 1–4 P.M.

Beyond the old hospital is **Brooklands Park,** quite a contrast with its sweeping perfect lawns and formal plantations of both introduced and native trees. Beside the main path through the center of the reserve stands an enormous *puriri* tree, thought to be more than 2,000 years old. Also within the park are the largest *karaka* and *kohekohe* trees on record, and the largest *Magnolia soulangeana* in the country. The main park entrance is on Brooklands St. (off Victoria Road). The **Bowl of Brooklands Soundshell,** a large outdoor amphitheater surrounded by native bush, lies to one side of the main gates; on the other side is the entrance to a small zoo, best known for its comprehensive collection of colorful birds; open daily.

If viewing wildlife is your cup of tea, take a leisurely walk through 36-hectare **Barrett Domain** on the western side of New Plymouth (ask at the information center for the "Barrett Domain" brochure). Open space, native tree plantations, natural forest, and the wetland area of

Barrett Lagoon make up this domain and wildlife refuge that attracts a large range of waterfowl, especially paradise and grey ducks, black swans, *pukeko,* pied stilt shags, Canada geese, and white-faced herons. The main entrance is on Roto St. (at least five km from downtown as the crow flies).

New Plymouth Observatory

On Marsland Hill (along Robe St. south from downtown) is New Plymouth Observatory, tel. 06/758-7886. Along with stargazing, it features planetarium displays and a short slide show. It's open to the public every Tuesday night from 8 P.M.; admission $2. It's also worth driving up to the observatory at any time for the views, which extend over the entire city and to the Sugar Loaf Islands beyond.

West of Downtown

If you have transportation, head out to the west side of the city to the **Rangimarie Maori Art and Craft Centre** to see a working display of traditional arts and crafts. It's open Mon.–Fri. 9 A.M.–3 P.M., tel. 06/751-2880. It's on Centennial Dr. beyond the thriving, man-made **Port Taranaki.** While you're in this neck of the woods, don't miss the **Moturoa Lookout,** which provides good views of Mt. Egmont/Taranaki to the south and, on a clear day, Mt. Ruapehu to the east of Mt. Egmont/Taranaki.

Out Carrington Road: Fauna and Flora

If you have your own transportation, a trip along Carrington Rd. is a worthwhile jaunt from downtown New Plymouth to view two local attractions, and if you're continuing south, the road rejoins the main coastal highway without the need for any backtracking. From New Plymouth Information Centre take Liardet St. south, turn right on Gilbert St., and left on Victoria Road. Turn left on Brooklands Rd. and continue to the end, where it becomes Carrington Road.

   Pouaki Zoo Park, 1296 Carrington Rd., tel. 06/753-3788, offers bush walks past lakes where you can view waterfowl, foreign birds, ornamental ducks (not of the garden gnome variety),

TARANAKI AND
THE WEST

Tasman

Sea

North Taranaki Bight

Waitara

New Plymouth

3A

Oakura   45

Egmont
Village

PUKEITI
RHODODENDRON
GARDENS ★

Inglewoo

Okato

*Egmont
National
Park*

Inglewoo

3

Cape Egmont

Pungarehu

MANGANUI
SKIFIELD

CAPE EGMONT
LIGHTHOUSE ★

Taranaki/
Mt. Egmont
(2,518 m)

Stratford

Rahotu

Oaonui

Te Kiri

Eltham

Kaponga

Opunake

45

Oeo

Normanby

Manaia

South Taranaki Bight

Hawera

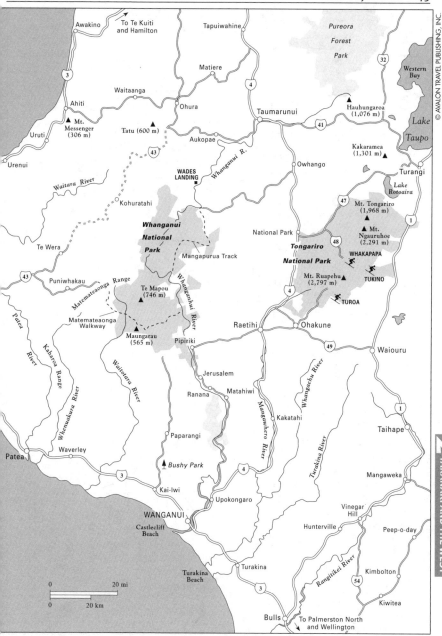

Awakino

To Te Kuiti
and Hamilton

Tapuiwahine

Matiere

Pureora
Forest
Park

32

Western
Bay

3

Ahiti

Waitaanga

Ohura

Taumarunui

Hauhungaroa
(1,076 m)

Lake
Taupo

Uruti

▲ Mt.
Messenger
(306 m)

Tatu (600 m) ▲

Aukopae

41

Kakaramea
(1,301 m) ▲

Urenui

43

Owhango

Turangi

Waitara River

WADES
LANDING

Whanganui R.

47

Lake
Rotoaira

Mt. Tongariro
(1,968 m)

1

Kohuratahi

Whanganui

National

National Park

Mt.
Ngauruhoe
(2,291 m)

Te Wera

Park

48

Tongariro

WHAKAPAPA

43

Puniwhakau

Mangapurua Track

National Park

TUKINO

Patea River

Matemateaonga Range

Te Mapou
(746 m) ▲

Whanganui River

Mt. Ruapehu
(2,797 m) ▲

🎿 TUROA

Kahatoa Range

Matemateaonga
Walkway

Maungarau
(565 m) ▲

Pipiriki

Raetihi

Ohakune

Waiouru

49

Whenuakura River

Waiotara River

Jerusalem

Whangaehu River

1

Patea

Ranana

Matahiwi

Kakatahi

Mangawhero River

Turakina River

Taihape

Waverley

Paparangi

↑ *Bushy Park*

4

Mangaweka

Patea

Kai-Iwi

3

Upokongaro

Vinegar
Hill

Peep-o-day

WANGANUI

Hunterville

Castlecliff
Beach

0   20 mi

0   20 km

Turakina
Beach

Turakina

Rangitikei River

Kimbolton

54

Kiwitea

3

Bulls

To Palmerston North
and Wellington

NEW PLYMOUTH

BEACH ST

FITZROY

DEVON ST EAST

NOBS LINE

TO WAITARA AND HAMILTON

WAIWAKA TERRACE

3

FITZROY ROAD

EAST END BEACH

TIDEPOOLS

BEACH ST

LEACH ST

LEMON ST

EAST END

ELIOT ST

COURTENAY ST

LEACH ST

CORONATION AVE.

3

BROOKLANDS PARK DR.

MOTORWAY

TO HAWERA AND WANGANUI

LIARDET ST

GILBERT ST

PUKEKURA PARK

GABLES COLONIAL HOSPITAL

BROOKLANDS PARK

ZOO

UPJOHN ST.

JUNCTION RD.

DEVON ST

BROUGHAM

VICTORIA RD.

BROOKLANDS ST.

HORI ST.

CARRINGTON RD.

SEE DETAIL

POWDERHAM ST

VIVIAN ST.

MILL RD.

NEW PLYMOUTH OBSERVATORY

FRANKLEY RD.

GLENPARK AVE.

HUATOKI ST.

HUATOKI DOMAIN

WEYMOUTH ST.

WALLACE PL.

CLAWTON ST.

BROIS ST.

YOUNG ST.

MORLEY ST.

BELT RD.

WAIMEA ST.

TUKAPA ST.

ST AUBYN ST.

DEVON ST. WEST

TARANAKI BASE HOSPITAL

OCEAN VIEW PARADE

BREAKWATER RD.

MOTUROA

ROTO ST.

PARK ENTRANCE

PORT TARANAKI

TIDEPOOLS

NGAMOTU BEACH

CENTENNIAL DR.

SOUTH RD.

OMATA RD.

45

TO HAWERA AND OPUNAKE (ROUND THE MTN. ROUTE)

N P POWER STATION

PARITUTU ROCK

MOTUROA LOOKOUT

BARRETT DOMAIN

BARRETT LAGOON

0

1 km

DETAIL

PUKE ARIKI

LIARDET ST

POST OFFICE

RICHMOND COTTAGE

QUEEN ST.

POWDERHAM ST

LEACH ST

BROUGHAM

TRAVEL CENTRE

ART GALLERY

POLICE

AUTOMOBILE ASSOC

VIVIAN

ST. MARY'S CHURCH

DAWSON ST.

and peacocks; saunter through the interior of a large aviary; and view deer, cattle, several kinds of goats, "uncommon" sheep, ponies, and opossums. A souvenir shop sells local handcrafts, pottery, and light refreshments. The park is open daily; $4 adult, $2 child.

Perhaps one of the best-known regional attractions is the fantastic **Pukeiti Rhododendron Gardens,** a garden of international repute farther along Carrington Rd. (20 km from New Plymouth) on the border of Egmont National Park. This 360-hectare garden, featuring New Zealand's largest collection of rhododendrons and azaleas—trees, shrubs, and perennials—is colorful at all times of the year, but the peak flowering of rhododendrons is generally Sept.–November. Bush walks lead through spectacular gardens dominated by native forest, all kinds of birds twitter in the trees (particularly *tui* and bellbirds in the early morning and evening), and you can get outstanding views of the surrounding countryside from the summit of **Pukeiti Hill.** The gardens are open daily 9 A.M.–5 P.M.; admission $8. Refreshments, maps, brochures, postcards, slides, and plants are for sale at the gatehouse.

Sugar Loaf Islands

Continue along Breakwater Rd., around the headland from the port, to Paritutu Centennial Park, and the city's most magnificent natural feature is laid out in front of you. The Sugar Loaf Islands are the remains of ancient volcanic activity. The actual volcano has long since eroded, leaving solid cores of lava that were thrust upward more than one million years ago. One of these remaining cores, Paritutu Rock, is on the mainland. A (very) steep track leads to its summit, where the views are stunning. The islands themselves are mostly vegetated, and some show evidence of early Maori settlement. Free from mainland predators, they are a haven for birdlife,

OIL AND GAS IN THE TARANAKI REGION

The economic boom of the Taranaki region is mainly due to the discovery of oil and natural gas, both on shore and off shore. Since the first well was drilled at the Kapuni Field in 1959, the Taranaki has become the energy capital of New Zealand, with most of the drilling now done off shore. The **Maui A Field,** where gas was first discovered in 1969, is about 35 km off shore from Oaonui, 55 km southwest of New Plymouth. The platform can be seen from the coastal road, while at the Maui Production Station at Oaonui, tel. 06/758-7609, a 1:25 scale model of the platform is open for public viewing. Combined with the nearby Maui B Field, discovered in 1993, the two fields are New Zealand's largest energy resource, supplying 85 percent of New Zealand's natural gas and 85 percent of the country's liquid petroleum gas (LPG). The gas is transported from the two platforms by pipeline to the production station at Oaonui, where it is used to produce electricity.

Continuing around the cape on Hwy. 45, you'll find Kapuni, the site of the first producing well. At nearby Okaiawa is the **Gas Treatment Plant,** the first large-scale natural gas plant. Opposite it is the **Ammonia Urea Plant.** No tours are available at these sites, but you can drive past them via Palmer Road.

On the east side of New Plymouth at Motunui (20 km northeast), **Methanex New Zealand** operates a synthetic fuel plant; its information center, tel. 06/754-8009, is open daily 8 A.M.–5 P.M. A **Chemical Methanol Plant** in the Waitara Valley (15 km northeast) offers visitors a view of the plant from the "lookout" on Matarikoriko Rd., just off Mamaku Rd. at the rear of the plant. **Petrocorps Exploration's McKee No. 2 Well,** on Otaraoa Rd., Waitara (13 km southeast of Waitara), has an observation platform only.

The energy site closest to the city is the gas-operated **New Plymouth Power Station;** to get there take St. Aubyn St. (at the west end of town), which leads directly to Port Taranaki on Breakwater Road. If you're interested, take a two-hour tour that departs Sunday at 2 P.M. from the security gates on Breakwater Road. Call ahead at 06/751-0680 to confirm.

including penguins, and New Zealand fur seals breed on two of the islands.

Chaddy's Charters, tel. 06/758-9133, offers scheduled tours through the islands in summer; from $25 pp.

Beaches

New Plymouth's city beaches stretch along the curved sandy seafront in both directions, but the best surfing beaches are at the eastern end of town. The most popular, **Fitzroy Beach,** is known for its excellent surf. It forms a continuous 1.6-km sweep of luxurious sand; you can reach it from Beach St., about three km from the city center. Farther east, about seven km from downtown (as you head for the airport), is **Bell Block Beach,** on Mangati Rd., Bell Block. **East End Reserve and Beach** is west of Fitzroy Beach, at the end of Nobs Line. If you're continuing north, stop at beautiful, soft, black-sand **Awakino Beach.** Fed by small, clear streams, the beach is decorated with perfect shells, and the surf is just right. On the west side of the city lie the protected harbor beach **Ngamotu** on Ocean View Parade—a good place to watch yachting and boating activities—and **Back Beach** on Centennial Drive.

About 14 km west of New Plymouth is the premier beach resort, **Oakura.** Head here if you just want to lie on a beautiful beach all day and soak up a great tan (convenient campgrounds nearby—see below). If you're heading northeast, plop down on one of the sandy beaches at **Waitara** (16 km east of New Plymouth) for more tanning and swimming.

ENTERTAINMENT AND EVENTS

The **Bowl of Brooklands,** a magnificent outdoor theater surrounded by native bush, seats hundreds; it's beside the entrance gates to Brooklands Park—call the information center for performance information and current ticket prices.

Pubs and Clubs

Many of the local pubs and hotels provide good entertainment a few nights a week—bands, discos, talented local groups, and more. Look in the daily newspaper. **Peggy Gordon's Celtic Bar,** on the corner of Devon and Egmont Streets, tel. 06/758-8561, has a lively, welcoming atmosphere and bands on weekends. The bar at the **Westown Motor Hotel** on Maratahu St. is open for entertainment on Thurs.–Sat. nights. At the time of writing, **Crowded House,** 93–99 Devon St., tel. 06/759-4921, was the most popular nightclub in town.

Races and Rhododendrons

If you're in the New Plymouth area in March, check out the exact date of the annual running race, **The Mountain To The Surf Marathon,** which finishes at Waitara Beach, about 17 km northeast of the city—all those sweaty bodies staggering over the finish line are quite a spectacle.

If you're lucky enough to be in New Plymouth in November, your eyes are in for one heck of a flowery spectacle. The annual **Rhododendron Festival,** usually starting at the end of October/beginning of November, features flowers, flowers, and more flowers. Attend all sorts of flower-oriented events, competitions, and horticultural lectures, and visit many of the area's private homes that have spectacular rhododendron gardens. For more information call 06/757-9909.

ACCOMMODATIONS
Hotels and Motels

The best-value rooms downtown (two blocks from Queen St.) can be found at **Braemar Motor Inn,** 152 Powderham St., tel. 06/758-0859. Each room has a kitchen, with the older rooms costing $65 s, $70 d and the newer and larger rooms starting at $95. In the same vicinity is **Mid City Motel,** 22 Weymouth St., tel. 06/758-6109; rates $75 s or d. On a quiet street one block from Hwy. 3 is **Cottage Mews Motel,** 50 Lemon St., tel. 06/758-0403. Each of the five self-contained units has basic furnishings, but because it's one of the city's newest motels, they are a good value at $70 s, $75 d.

Amber Court Motel, 500 meters east of downtown at 61 Eliot St., tel. 06/758-0922 or 0800/654-800, website: www.ambercourtmotel.co.nz, features a large indoor pool, game room, barbecue area, and playground. Rates for the 34 kitchen-equipped units start at $85 s, $95 d. In the vicinity, the **Devon Hotel,** 390 Devon St. E, tel. 06/759-9099 or 0800/800-930, website: www.devonhotel.co.nz, is a large complex with 100 rooms, a stylish indoor pool and spa complex, popular Marbles restaurant, and 24-hour room service. Smallish economy rooms are $80 s or d, regular rooms are $125 s or d, and suites are $175 s or d.

Set on sprawling parklike grounds one km west of downtown is the **Flamingo Motel,** 355 Devon St. W, tel. 06/758-8149 or 0508/352-646; website: www.flamingomotel.co.nz. Guests enjoy an indoor and an outdoor pool, shaded barbecue area, laundry, and charge-back (bill your room) from local restaurants. All the units are self-contained, many with a sliding door that opens to the garden. Studios are $84 s, $99 d, one-bedroom units are $105 s or d.

Brougham Heights Motel, 54 Brougham St., tel. 06/757-9954 or 0800/107-008, website: www.broughamheights.co.nz, is right downtown. The 34 units are modern and the kitchens compact. Choose from large studios ($105 s or d), one-bedroom units ($115 s or d), or two-bedroom units ($130 s or d).

Bed-and-Breakfast

Balconies, 161 Powderham St., tel. 06/757-8866, is a very central bed-and-breakfast offering three rooms (shared bathroom) in a rambling house dating to the 1880s. The comfortable lounge area has tea- and coffee-making facilities, and a cooked breakfast is included in the rates of $60 s, $75 d.

Backpacker Lodges

Egmont Lodge, 12 Clawton St., tel. 06/753-5720, an associate of Hostelling International, is a modern suburban hostel a couple of km south of the city center. Overlooking an extensive garden and small stream, it is usually pretty quiet, and with a well-equipped kitchen, comfortable rooms, and a large lounge area, it is a good choice for budget travelers. The hosts are enthusiastic about promoting the region, so ask them for ideas and you'll never be bored. Dorm beds are $17, doubles and twins are $22 pp.

Motor Camps

A 10-km drive south from New Plymouth **Hookner Holiday Park,** 885 Carrington Rd., tel. 06/753-6945, provides a unique New Zealand camping experience. Set on a 100-hectare working dairy farm, guests are offered the opportunity to help with the milking each morning (4–5 A.M.). It is small, but spotlessly clean and ultra-modern. All sites are $18, on-site vans are $32 s or d, and cabins range $32–44 s or d.

Belt Road Seaside Holiday Park, 2 Belt Rd., tel. 06/758-0228, is only 1.5 km from the city center and has sheltered sites on the coast overlooking Port Taranaki (west side of town). It offers communal facilities, a TV lounge, and sea views. It's close to boating, yachting, and fishing activities, and only a 10-minute walk from a municipal swimming pool. Campsites are $20, and the wide variety of cabins range $30–55 s or d.

Fitzroy Beach Holiday Park, Beach St., tel. 06/758-2870, the closest motor camp to the city center (about three km), boasts an excellent surf beach, a recreation and TV hall, and the usual facilities. Tent and caravan sites are $9 pp, and cabins range $35–45 s or d. In the same vicinity, one km from the beach and 3.5 km from the city center, is **New Plymouth Top Ten Holiday Park,** 29 Princes St., tel. 06/758-2566 or 0800/758-256. It has communal facilities, a tepid swimming pool and hot spa, and a TV and recreation room. All campsites are $20, cabins start at $38, tourist flats start at $65, and motel rooms are $75.

If you're looking for a beach resort atmosphere, head for Oakura, 14 km southwest of New Plymouth. **Oakura Beach Camp,** Oakura Beach, tel. 06/752-7861, has hedge-sheltered sites on or near the beach, and you can rent kayaks. Tent sites are $18, caravan sites are $20 d.

FOOD

Casual Fare

If you like healthy natural food, head straight for **Steps Restaurant** at 37 Gover St., tel. 06/758-3393. Away from touristy spots, the enthusiastic staff serve good cheap lunches made on the premises (a huge slab of broccoli and feta pie with two types of salad starts at a meager $6.50).

Dinner is a little more formal but no less enjoyable. Mediterranean-influenced dinners range $14–25. It's very popular with locals—get there early for the best selection and a table in the courtyard. It's open Mon.–Thurs. 7:30 A.M.–4 P.M., Friday 7:30 A.M.–9 P.M., Saturday 10 A.M.–2 P.M. and 5–9 P.M., and Sunday 11 A.M.–2 P.M. for brunch. For a light lunch (noon–2 P.M. daily, except Tuesday) or morning or afternoon tea (daily 10 A.M.–4 P.M., except Tuesday) in beautiful park surroundings, head for **Pukekura Park Kiosk** on Liardet St. in Pukekura Park. At the **City Shopping Centre** on Gill St. is **Tastings Foodcourt,** with six over-the-counter boutiques featuring Chinese, Italian, and seafood meals; natural foods; sandwiches; and desserts.

Restaurants

The Devon Hotel, 390 Devon St. E, tel. 06/759-9099, is home to the popular **Marbles Buffet.** The setting is a Caribbean island, complete with costumed waitpersons, island dancing, and even a wrecked Spanish galleon, and the food comes mostly from the sea. Open daily from 6:30 P.M. for dinner, Buccaneers (adults) pay $30, Old Salts (those aged 60 and over) pay $19.95, Pirates (ages 11–15) pay $15, Stowaways (ages 6–10) pay $10, and Deckhands (under five years) pay $5. **Chino's Cafe,** 146 Devon St. E, tel. 06/758-6843, specializes in healthy meals with lots of choices for vegetarians, and is open long hours every day. **Golden Phoenix Chinese Restaurant** offers lunches Tues.–Fri. noon–2 P.M., dinners Mon.–Sun. from 6 P.M., and a good Sunday night smorgasbord recommended by locals.

At the City Shopping Centre on Gill St. is local hot spot **Portofino,** opposite the main entrance to Centre City, tel. 06/757-8686, a very popular, casual, BYO Italian restaurant. At dinner expect to pay $13–24 for a main course, from $10 for a tasty pizza. More expensive is **Andre L'Escargot Restaurant,** 37 Gover St., tel. 06/758-4812, in a historic downtown building and featuring the classic dishes from the south of France.

> *The setting at the Marbles Buffet is a Caribbean island, complete with costumed waitpersons, island dancing, and even a wrecked Spanish galleon.*

TRANSPORTATION

Getting There

New Plymouth Airport, 12 km north of town (take Hwy. 3 north and it's signposted off to the left before you reach Waitara), is linked to downtown by an airport shuttle run by **Withers Coachlines,** tel. 06/751-1777; $12 one way. Scheduled flights operated by **Air New Zealand** depart daily for Auckland and Wellington. Its downtown office is in the Norwich Union Building at 12–14 Devon St., tel. 06/757-3300. **Air New Plymouth,** tel. 06/755-0500, offers charters and sight-seeing, including the short "City Roundabout Flight," to flights over the north coast, Mt. Egmont/Taranaki's summit, and the Taranaki energy projects.

For long-distance coach service out of New Plymouth, go to the **Travel Centre** at 32 Queen St. (corner King St.). From this depot, **Intercity,** tel. 06/759-9039, and **Newmans,** tel. 06/759-9039, run regular services south to Wanganui and Wellington, and north to Hamilton and Auckland. Both companies make stops at smaller towns along the way such as Te Kuiti and Waitomo (to the north) and Stratford and Hawera (to the south).

Getting Around

All the regular car rental agencies have offices in New Plymouth, including **Avis,** tel. 06/755-9600; **Budget,** tel. 06/758-8039; **Hertz,** tel. 06/758-8189; **NZ Rent-a-car,** tel. 06/758-7923; **Rent-a-dent,** tel. 06/757-5362; and **Thrifty,** tel. 06/757-4500.

For a cab call **Energy City Cabs,** tel. 06/757-5580, or **New Plymouth Taxis,** tel. 06/757-3000.

Tours

Neuman's Tours, 80 Gill St., tel. 06/758-4622, provides a range of excursions from half-day to full-day trips from New Plymouth, including a scenic city tour ($55 pp), tours to and around Mt. Egmont/Taranaki ($50–75), and to the Taranaki energy complexes. Pick up one of their pamphlets at the information center or visit the tour office.

SERVICES AND INFORMATION
Services
The main shopping precinct is the **City Shopping Centre** on Gill Street. The **central post office** is on Currie Street. **New Plymouth Library** is in Puke Ariki on Ariki St., tel. 06/758-4544; open Mon.–Fri. 9 A.M.–5:30 P.M., Saturday 10 A.M.–3 P.M. **Devon Laundrette,** 282 Devon St. E, is open Mon.–Fri. 8 A.M.–5:30 P.M.

Taranaki Base Hospital is on David St., tel. 06/753-6139. **Pharmacy 97** is at 283 Devon St. W, tel. 06/759-2380. The **police station** is on Powderham St., tel. 06/759-5500.

Information
New Plymouth Information Centre is in the lobby of Puke Ariki, New Plymouth's magnificent new museum complex on Ariki St., tel. 06/759-6080; website: www.newplymouthnz.co.nz. It's open Mon.–Fri. 8:30 A.M.–5 P.M., weekends and public holidays 10 A.M.–3 P.M. Ask the helpful personnel for their dining guide, recommended sight-seeing tours, and free tourist newspapers. Also look out for the brochures detailing contingency plans in the event that Mt. Egmont/Taranaki erupts. Chances are the volcano will remain dormant while you're visiting New Plymouth, but the information makes interesting reading. For local road information, head to the **Automobile Association** office at 49–55 Powderham St., tel. 06/759-4010.

Egmont National Park

Snowcapped Mt. Egmont/Taranaki, a solitary 2,518-meter peak that seemingly rises from the ocean, is the kind of mountain that begs to be climbed or hiked just because it's there. This dormant volcano stands loftily on Cape Egmont where the western coastline juts into the Tasman Sea, its remote location, height, and harsh climate producing interesting flora and fauna; 145 km of hiking trails; and skiing and boarding have made it one of the most visited mountains in New Zealand. The mountain is surrounded by a circular 33,534-hectare national park that protects a 9.6-km radius from the mountain summit.

To and Around the Park
Access to the upper slopes is easy if you have your own transportation, and the energetic are amply rewarded with fabulous views from the summit—Tongariro National Park to the east, New Plymouth to the north, the Tasman Sea to the west, and to the south (on a clear day) the faint outline of the South Island mountains. Three main roads lead into the park, all branching off Hwy. 3 between New Plymouth and Hawera. They lead to the **North Egmont Visitor Centre,** 26 km south of New Plymouth, **East Egmont,** 68 km south of New Plymouth via

Stratford, and **South Egmont** (Dawson Falls), east of Eltham.

Completely encircling the park, but at a distance, is a paved 180-km "Round-The-Mountain" route dotted with small towns that cater to park visitors. Highway 3 runs down the east side from New Plymouth (the main city in the area) to Hawera, and coastal Hwy. 45 completes the circle on the west side.

If you plan to explore the park on foot, drive straight up the access roads. If you're not so much into outdoor activities but enjoy scenic views, take the slightly longer coastal route on your way north or south (about two hours nonstop) for great views of Mt. Egmont/Taranaki from various angles. If you can time it, travel the coastal road on a clear evening—the snowcapped peak tinged in pink and regularly wreathed in wispy clouds makes a striking picture you won't quickly forget.

THE LAND
Egmont National Park's dominant features are the volcanic cone of dormant **Mt. Egmont/Taranaki** and the two older volcanoes, **Kaitake,** 15 km southwest of New Plymouth, and **Pouakai,** 10 km southwest of Kaitake, in the

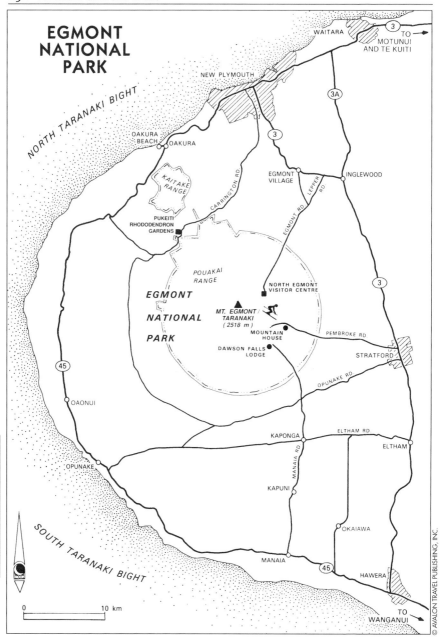

EGMONT
NATIONAL
PARK

NORTH TARANAKI BIGHT

WAITARA

TO MOTUNUI AND TE KUITI

3

NEW PLYMOUTH

3A

OAKURA BEACH

OAKURA

EGMONT VILLAGE

INGLEWOOD

3

KAITAKE RANGE

CARRINGTON RD

PUKEITI RHODODENDRON GARDENS

EGMONT RD

LEPPER RD

POUAKAI RANGE

NORTH EGMONT VISITOR CENTRE

EGMONT

NATIONAL

PARK

MT. EGMONT / TARANAKI (2518 m)

MOUNTAIN HOUSE

DAWSON FALLS LODGE

PEMBROKE RD

STRATFORD

3

45

OPUNAKE RD

OAONUI

KAPONGA

ELTHAM RD.

ELTHAM

MANAIA RD

OPUNAKE

KAPUNI

OKAIAWA

SOUTH TARANAKI BIGHT

MANAIA

45

HAWERA

TO WANGANUI

0   10 km

Kaitake Range. Mount Egmont/Taranaki is believed to have formed more than 70,000 years ago, becoming active as the other two volcanoes became extinct. It formed two peaks (the northern peak collapsed 23,000 years ago) and, through repeated *lahars* or mudflows, thousands of small rounded hills on the mountain's west side (the Pungarehu *lahar* mounds). Elsewhere on the ring plain the *lahars* progressed as a flood and created no mounds. More recently, geologically speaking, lava regularly spilled down the mountainsides to form a series of lava cliffs and gorges; volcanic ash, the basis of Taranaki's rich topsoil, repeatedly blanketed the surrounding land, giving rise to the agriculturally affluent Taranaki region. The last volcanic eruption was in 1755 (a minor affair), when ash alone was ejected onto the upper slopes. In the last 400 years, most damage to the park has been caused by "debris flows" due to severe storms—the torrential rain runs down the bare, unstable upper slopes, causing destructive landslides.

All that remains of the extinct Kaitake volcano, active about 500,000 years ago, is the eroded 683-meter-high Kaitake Range; extinct Pouakai, active 250,000 years ago, has also been eroded from its original height of possibly 2,000 meters to its present height of 1,399 meters. Water is another powerful and artistic element seen in all its forms throughout Egmont National Park. Ice and snow permanently cover the upper slopes and peak, splendid waterfalls roar over jagged lava flows to drop into deep, dark pools far below, and rivers sing over the smooth, polished rocks and dance down to the lower altitudes in a series of waterfalls.

Climate

Ask the locals in any of the towns around the base of Mt. Egmont/Taranaki for a recent weather forecast and you're likely to hear something like, "If you can't see the mountain, it's raining up there. If you can see the mountain, it's going to rain!" Coastal position, a wide range in elevation (100–2,500 meters), continually changing winds, and frequent alternation between fine and stormy weather are the main climatic features affecting

Egmont National Park. Long periods of fine, settled weather are common in summer; winter brings the intense, long-lasting lows that result in nasty storms. The coldest month is usually July, the warmest February, with most of the high annual rainfall May–Oct.—the northwestern slopes of the mountains generally receive the most rain. Expect wet weather when a low-pressure system is forecast and there are northerly winds and mild temperatures.

You should seriously consider the weather affecting Egmont National Park before venturing up the mountain—detailed weather forecasts are available at all the field centers. The park is notorious for rapidly changing weather (usually for the worse) and although it's generally okay in summer, it can cause hazardous situations in winter. Freezing temperatures have been recorded in all months of the year (except January). Low clouds or fog can disorient even the most experienced outdoorsperson, and the frequent combination of rain, rapid drop in temperature, and strong wind can quickly turn a pleasurable hike into a life-threatening situation of exposure and hypothermia. The conservation officers strongly suggest that you leave your intinerary and estimated time of return at the field centers or with someone reliable if you're climbing or hiking in the park, and turn back at the first sign of bad weather. Be adequately prepared, get a weather forecast, take warm clothing, carry food and drink, observe cloud and temperature changes—particularly when venturing up to the higher altitudes—and resist trying to make the summit when the weather is obviously deteriorating.

Flora

The combination of a wet mountain climate and periods of dry hot weather promotes a luxurious growth of vegetation, and the variations in altitude on Mt. Egmont/Taranaki give rise to several distinct vegetation zones—large forest trees, small shrubs, tussocks and herbs, mosses and lichens—easily seen from any of the three main access roads. The lower slopes (about 500–900 meters) are covered by the broadleaf-podocarp rainforest where many varieties of native trees grow—*rimu,* northern *rata, kamahi, mahoe,* broadleaf and tree fuchsia. Beneath the tree canopy the undergrowth is prolific—creepers grow in profusion garlanding the smaller trees, and lush ferns, mosses, and lichens carpet the forest floor. The Kaitake Range, the oldest and most eroded, has forest to the top, and semicoastal forest on the lower slopes dominated by *puriri, karaka, kohekohe, pukatea,* and *nikau* palm trees. The higher Pouakai Range has several zones: forest (dominated by *montane kamahi*), shrub, tussock, and herbfield. On Mt. Egmont/Taranaki at the 900–1,100-meter level, the *totara* and *kaikawaka* (mountain cedar) trees become dominant, and above lies a dense belt of leatherwood scrub followed by a broad tussock grass zone.

> *Above 1,400 meters you find many plants unique to Mt. Egmont/Taranaki—the long history of volcanic disturbance and relative isolation from seed sources caused this mountain region to evolve differently from other alpine habitats.*

Above 1,400 meters you find many plants unique to Mt. Egmont/Taranaki, and other alpine species that you'd expect to find (such as mountain beech) are conspicuously absent—the long history of volcanic disturbance and relative isolation from seed sources caused this mountain region to evolve differently from other alpine habitats. A variety of small (some unique) herbaceous plants, ferns (the rare *Polystichum cystostegia* flourishes only on Mt. Egmont/Taranaki), and mountain daisies (two species are slightly different from those found elsewhere in New Zealand) cover the slopes just below the permanent snow line (for more detailed info. refer to the *Park Handbook*). Other Mt. Egmont/Taranaki plants that are slightly different from their relatives elsewhere are the large-leaved *ourisia,* tussock grass, harebell, broom, and *koromiko.*

Fauna

Many of the birds you'd expect to find in Egmont National Park have made their homes elsewhere, or else there aren't very many left. The most common birds are the native pigeon, rifleman, whitehead, and kingfisher on lower slopes, and *tui,* bellbird, fantail, and tomtit up to about 1,300

meters. You can hear shining and long-tailed cuckoos in forested areas, and see the New Zealand *pipit* on higher open slopes. Grey warblers and silvereye are widespread. If you want to hear the beautiful liquid birdsong of *tui* and bellbirds, head for the point where Egmont National Park meets the entrance to Pukeiti Rhododendron Gardens on Carrington Rd.—the birds tune up their voices early in the morning, so grab a cup of coffee and a filled roll to go, and start your day with a magnificent after-dawn chorus.

The park boasts a great number and variety of insects, some endemic to Mt. Egmont/Taranaki. Several moths are found only on the mountain—*Tortrix antichroa, Graphania averilla, Leucania harti,* and *Leucania paraxysta,* but Egmont is poor in butterfly species. Because of its isolation and volcanic activity, the mountain also missed out on some alpine insects found commonly elsewhere at similar altitudes, such as certain grasshoppers, cicadas, and common butterflies.

The park is free of deer—they were never liberated in the Egmont/Taranaki region (except for one male red deer deliberately introduced in the late 1800s), but goats, stoats, opossums, rats, mice, hares, and rabbits are all common wildlife (considered pests). Goats and opossums do the most damage to the vegetation and are actively hunted, trapped, or poisoned.

PARK RECREATION
Hiking and Climbing

Besides its wintertime skiers and boarders, Mt. Egmont/Taranaki lures hikers and climbers year-round. Walking and climbing routes crisscross the park's mountains, ranging from short easy walks to difficult several-day hikes to poled climbing routes. Tracks lead up to the summit, around Mt. Egmont/Taranaki via the popular **Round-The-Mountain Track,** through all the various vegetation zones, to dramatic waterfalls or quiet streams, and to scenic lookouts. When the snow melts off the main slopes in summer, the scoria slopes are fairly easy to negotiate in fine weather and many hikers reach the summit. Above the tree line (1,500 meters) from Nov.–Jan. the alpine flowers in bloom make the climb worth the effort. In bad weather the scoria slopes can become treacherous as they are entirely unmarked—it's easy to get lost if thick clouds or fog suddenly descend on you, and some of the slopes and gullies end in sheer bluffs. To reach the summit of Mt. Egmont/Taranaki in winter, climbers need crampons, ice axes, rope, companions, and experience.

On the longer marked tracks, huts with facilities are available for overnight stays—take your own sleeping bag, cooking equipment, and sup-

THE VOLCANO THAT BECAME A GOD

According to legend, Taranaki (or Mt. Egmont) was forced to flee from his original location in the center of the North Island when he lost a battle to Mt. Tongariro over his love, Mt. Pihanga. As he angrily fled through the cover of darkness toward the west coast he gouged out the bed of the mighty Whanganui River, and on reaching the sea he traveled north to the Pouakai ranges on Cape Egmont. A spur was thrown out to anchor him and Taranaki was forced to settle there forever. The Maori originally called the mountain "Taranaki" (many New Zealanders believe it should still be called Taranaki—you may see it written as Egmont/Taranaki). They had great respect for the impressive volcano, worshipping the mountain as a god and recognizing its great influence on the weather of the local region. The upper slopes were *tapu* and they believed that the stones were part of the skull of the mountain and the shrubs were its hair. So strong was this belief that when some early European climbers brought stones and shrubs down to study, the Maori quickly replaced them on the mountain so as not to anger the spirits. The only times the Maori climbed the mountain were when they needed red ochre or to ceremoniously bury their chiefs in secret places.

plies. Before you venture off the beaten track, head for the field centers, accommodation houses on the mountain, or for visitor information centers in New Plymouth, Stratford, or Hawera. Pick up a detailed Department of Survey and Lands Information topographical map ($11) and the "Walks in the Egmont National Park" brochure with individual track maps and descriptions. If you're heading for the higher altitudes or one of the long hikes, get a detailed weather forecast from the DOC offices and ask if you're properly equipped—more than 60 hikers have died since 1891 after suffering disorientation, exposure, and hypothermia in rapidly deteriorating weather.

NORTH EGMONT

To get into the northern area of the park take Hwy. 3 to Egmont Village (5.5 km west of Inglewood), then the 16-km Egmont Rd., following signs to Kaimiro and the park. The alternate route is via Lepper Rd. off Hwy. 3 just west of Inglewood, which joins Egmont Rd. at Kaimiro. Along the road within the park are picnic areas, lookouts, the start of several tracks, and, toward the end, the **North Egmont Visitor Centre** (26 km south of New Plymouth), a cafeteria, public shelter, and toilets. The visitor center, open daily 9 A.M.–5:30 P.M. most of the year (to save yourself a trip, call ahead to check if it's open in the off-season, from Egmont Village tel. 06/756-0990), offers exhibits, comprehensive displays on its natural history, a track orientation map, displays of local walks, and regular films and talks. It also offers guided walks with park staff in summer and by arrangement. Four local walks of varying difficulty, suitable for most people, start from both the upper parking lot and visitor center parking lot—they're marked with color-coded tags so you can't get lost.

Short Walks

The easy **Nature Walk** (color-coded red) takes only 15 minutes. It starts at the southern end of the visitor center parking lot, passes through a *totara* and *kamahi* forest, gives great views over the Ngatoro Valley, and leads up to a ridge overlooking the Ngatoro Stream. The walk comes out on Translator Road—turn right, and you'll end up at the upper parking lot. The **Ngatoro Walk** (blue) takes approximately 45 minutes, and starts at the bottom eastern corner of the visitor center parking lot below the Camphouse. After taking the first turnoff to the right, you descend and cross the Ngatoro Streambed, then climb up through beautiful mountain cedar trees to Translator Road. Follow the road to the right for five minutes to the upper parking lot. The **Connett Walk** (orange, 30 minutes) starts on the same track as the Ngatoro Walk, but you descend farther down the ridge before branching off at the first turn to the left. The track crosses the slope of the mountain and joins the Ngatoro Track before you turn right and climb gradually uphill to the parking lot.

The longest of the short walks in this area is the **Veronica Walk** (yellow, 1.5 hours-plus). The track starts at the western corner of the upper parking lot, crosses the slope of the mountain through *totara* and *kamahi* forest (don't take the Veronica Track on the right—continue straight ahead), passes an old reservoir, and takes you up the mountain for great views of the Ram Stream and Pouakai Range. Near the highest point the track joins an old track to the summit; turn left and head down the well-beaten track to the Ambury Memorial, and finish at the upper parking lot below the Camphouse.

Several of the long hiking tracks also start from Egmont Rd. and the two main parking lots. For details, track descriptions, maps, and weather forecasts, call in at the North Egmont Visitor Centre and leave your intended route and time of return in the trampers' book.

Egmont Village

Egmont Village is a small hamlet at the northern gateway to Egmont National Park, 16 km from the end of the road and 12 km from New Plymouth. Right downtown is **The Missing Leg,** 1082 Junction Rd., tel. 06/752-2570, a great little backpackers where you can get a comfortable bed for the night—in a dorm or private room—for just $16–18 pp. The lodge is set on a two-hectare property, and there are farm animals, a barbecue area, and a lounge with a log fire. The hosts also provide shuttles up into the park.

EAST EGMONT

To get into the eastern area of the park, take Hwy. 3 to Stratford, then turn onto Pembroke Road. This 15-km road takes you past the **Stratford Area Office,** tel. 06/765-5144, soon after leaving Stratford (just past Barclay Rd.), goes by picnic areas and the start of several walking tracks, and leads up to **Mountain House,** where you'll find a public shelter, toilets, motel, restaurant, tearooms, and souvenir shop; ski and tramping gear are available for rent. Pembroke Rd. continues past Mountain House Motor Lodge for another three km, passing lookouts to end up at the **Plateau.** From the lookout at the Plateau, the highest point on the mountain you can reach by car, begin many tracks of varying difficulty. Above the Plateau, within walking distance of the parking lot, lies **Manganui Ski field.**

Short Walks

The intriguing 15-minute **Kamahi Walk** starts at the right end of the Mountain House at the direction sign (red), and winds through a magical moss-clad forest of *kamahi* trees and dense undergrowth—just the kind of place where you'd expect to find elves and goblins frolicking in the greenery. The one-hour **Patea Walk** (yellow) takes you through more lush forest. It starts at Mountain House, follows the Waingongoro Track for a distance, then turns sharply right to parallel the Patea River. It crosses Pembroke Rd. and continues down the other side.

A bit longer is the two-hour **Enchanted Walk** just below Mountain House. It crosses the Patea River and its tributaries and the Waingongoro River tributaries, passes the junction with the lower track to Dawson Falls, and climbs a long ridge to the Trig at Jackson's Lookout for fabulous views. Connecting with the Round-The-Mountain track, it's then only a short walk to the Plateau. The longer and more difficult **Curtis Falls Track** (1.5 hours one-way) starts near Mountain House and crosses typically rugged volcanic land to descend into the Manganui

© ANDREW HEMPSTEAD

The mountain's lower slopes are covered in a lush forest.

Gorge to two spectacular waterfalls plunging over ancient lava flows. From the Plateau you can take various tracks to **Twin Falls, Wilkies Pools, Bubbling Springs,** and **Dawson Falls.** For more detailed information on the longer walks and track maps, call in at the Stratford Field Centre on Pembroke Road.

Skiing and Snowboarding

Mount Egmont/Taranaki offers exciting volcano skiing with its club-operated **Manganui Ski field,** tel. 06/759-1119, a small but challenging ski area. The main feature is the 30-degree (average) gradient slope of the entire upper field, served by the Top Tow. Due to the incline, skiers and boarders attach themselves to the tow by a belt. The lower reaches are more suitable for beginners and intermediates, and are served by three rope tows. Manganui has a vertical rise of 420 meters and covers around 60 hectares. One unusual feature of the ski field is that it can open with a very light snow cover—the entire field is covered in a layer of moss. A normal season runs June–September and lift tickets are $30.

Manganui Ski field is a 1.5-km walk through Manganui Gorge from the end of the sealed road at the Plateau. A lift transports equipment between the parking lot and the base area, but it's still a 20-minute walk to the slopes. Radio Taranaki, the local radio station, gives ski reports and snow conditions 8–8:30 A.M. during ski season. You can rent ski equipment from Mountain House, which offers the closest accommodation (expensive) and facilities to the ski fields. For cheaper accommodations head back down to the town of Stratford.

Practicalities

The privately owned **Mountain House Motor Lodge** lies high up the slopes of Mt. Egmont/Taranaki 15 km from Stratford on Pembroke Rd., tel. 06/765-6100 or 0800/668-682; website: www.mountainhouse.co.nz. It features a restaurant, bar, café, souvenir shop, and ski and tramping gear for rent (you needn't be a guest to take advantage of these services), and it's the trailhead for a couple of interesting tracks. Accommodation is either in hotel rooms ($105 s or

d) or off to one side in self-contained chalets ($145 s or d). The restaurant presents simple but surprisingly good fare. Choose from the usual New Zealand favorites, such as venison or lamb, or something a little more unusual, such as a grilled filet of kangaroo covered in a red currant sauce ($25.50). For dessert, look no further than the pavlova ($8).

The DOC **Stratford Area Office,** along the access road, tel. 06/765-5144, is open Mon.–Fri. 8 A.M.–4:30 P.M.

SOUTH EGMONT

To get to the Dawson Falls resort on the southern slopes of the park, take Hwy. 3 to the town of Eltham, then 15-km Eltham Rd. to Kaponga. At Kaponga, turn north up Manaia Road. This 15-km stretch of sealed road winds steeply up the mountainside through fantastic lush greenery and shady green tunnels where the trees meet overhead; passes lookouts, track starting points, and magnificent waterfalls (at the end of short walks); and terminates at **Dawson Falls Display Centre** and **Dawson Falls Lodge.** The Display Centre (open daily 9 A.M.–5 P.M.) features park flora and fauna, and volcanic and human history displays. A large model highlights all the volcanic features. In the immediate vicinity you'll find picnic areas, a public shelter, toilets, a lookout, and starting points of numerous tracks leading to crystal-clear streams, bubbling springs, and waterfalls.

If you're in Stratford and want to take a shortcut over to Dawson Falls, take Opunake Rd. west out of Stratford toward the villages of Cardiff and Mahoe, and continue straight until you meet Manaia Rd. (not far after crossing Kapuni Stream). Turn right toward the mountain.

Short Walks

Before setting off anywhere, call in at the **Dawson Falls Display Centre** and check out a detailed display showing the comprehensive track system that radiates from Dawson Falls. **Kapuni Walk** is probably one of the easiest walks and leads to a "must-see" local attraction. Start-

On a clear day, you'll get stunning views of Mt. Egmont/Taranaki from Dawson Falls Display Centre.

ing at the sign on the road just below Dawson Falls Lodge, the track (pink, one hour) follows the forested banks of Kapuni Stream to a view of magnificent **Dawson Falls** dropping an impressive 18 meters down a 1,000-year-old lava flow—you can also get down to the base by taking the steep track farther along. For great mountain views, take the short sidetrack before the falls that crosses the stream and leads to a lookout; the main track returns to the road and parking lot through mature rainforest. The circular **Konini Dell Walk** (blue, one hour) starts above Dawson Falls Tourist Lodge, and runs along a ridge top and through a *totara* and *kamahi* forest (a favorite spot in spring for the melodic bellbirds and *tui*) to a lookout. The nearby popular **Wilkies Pool Walk** (red, one hour) starts at the Display Centre. It's an easy walk upriver along Kapuni Stream to Kapuni Gorge, where the water has carved an intricate channel through an old lava flow to form a series of spectacularly polished rock pools. A sidetrack leads to **Victoria Falls,** and you can easily reach many other interesting tracks from this walk.

Hasties Walk is longer and more difficult (orange, at least 2.5 hours round-trip), but the unobstructed views of Mt. Egmont/Taranaki, plains, and Tourist Lodge are worth the climb. It starts above the Display Centre and follows a section of the Summit Track. At the second junction turn left onto the track leading to the Round Trip and Hasties Hill. At the next junction turn right onto Hasties Hill Track. It goes down to cross the middle branch of Kaupokonui Stream, then climbs to the top of 996-meter Hasties Hill for fabulous views of South Taranaki and ancient lava domes called the Beehives. The return route backtracks to the stream and the junction of the Round Trip Track—for an alternate return route, turn right toward Lower Kaupokonui Falls on the east branch of Kaupokonui Stream.

Practicalities

Comfortable **Dawson Falls Mountain Lodge,** 23 km from Stratford, tel. 06/765-5457 or 0800/651-800, website: www.dawson-falls.co.nz, has 11 Swiss chalet-style rooms for $90 s, $110 d, and a few basic rooms that share baths for $40 s or d. The Alpine Inn Coffee Lounge in the lodge serves morning and afternoon tea and lunch. Packed lunches are available for guests on request. Breakfast is $8–12. The more formal Chalet Restaurant offers a four-course dinner for about $45. Also on this side of the mountain, near the visitor center, is **Konini Lodge,** offering basic bunk-bed accommodations, a large common room, electric heating, kitchen, and showers; $16 pp. Take your own sleeping bag, cooking equipment, and food. Accommodating up to 38 people, it attracts large school groups, so if you plan to stay here, call 06/758-6710 first to see if it's fully booked before heading up the mountain.

Egmont National Park to Wanganui

STRATFORD

Named after William Shakespeare's birthplace, Stratford, 41 km southeast of New Plymouth, is the principal gateway to Egmont National Park, as well as being a worthwhile stop in itself. Many private gardens lie around the village, with most opening for the **Rhododendron Festival** each November. One that's open year-round is **Ngaere Gardens,** five km south of town, which has been established for more than 100 years.

Practicalities

Regan Lodge Motel, 16 Regan St., tel. 06/765-7379 or 0800/112-027, offers eight one- and two-bedroom units a short 10-minute walk from the main street; rates from $68 s, $82 d. A less-expensive option is **Stratford Top 10 Holiday Park** on Page St., 800 meters from Broadway, tel. 06/765-6440, adjacent to a quiet park with native bush walks, river swimming, and municipal swimming baths nearby. Tent and powered

sites cost $10 pp, backpacker dorm beds are $16 pp, cabins $32–47 s or d, and motel rooms $80 s or d.

For quick tearoom treats, walk down bustling Broadway (everything you need is on the main street) and try the **Backstage Cafe,** tel. 06/765-7003.

Stratford Information Centre is also on Broadway, tel. 06/765-6708.

ELTHAM

Eltham lies 10 km south of Stratford toward Hawera. Along this stretch of highway, the distinctive peak of Mt. Egmont/Taranaki is always visible to the west and a number of small villages dot the route. The first of these is Eltham, known throughout the land for its cheese. Take Upper Manaia Rd. west from town to **Hollard Gardens,** tel. 06/764-6544, best-appreciated in late fall, when the extensive collection of rhododendrons is in full bloom. Open daily between 9 A.M. and dusk.; $6 adult, $3 child.

TARANAKI AND THE WEST

© ANDREW HEMPSTEAD

Dairyland

HAWERA AND VICINITY

Hawera, a historic dairying town at the junction of Highways 3 and 45, has a number of interesting sights. The **Tawhiti Museum,** Ohangai Rd., tel. 06/278-6837, is an eclectic collection of artifacts and displays detailing the history of the Taranaki region. In summer, a narrow-gauge railway operates around the property each Sunday. This private museum is open Fri.–Mon. 10 A.M.–4 P.M. On the road out of town to the north is the site of Turuturu-mokai Pa.

Dairyland

A combination of lots of sunshine and rich volcanic soil makes south Taranaki one of the world's premier dairying areas. In this environment, two km east of Hawera, **Kiwi Co-operative Dairies,** one of New Zealand's top 12 companies, has built the world's largest dairy products manufacturing plant with a large visitor center. The numbers are staggering: the company collects milk from 4,000 farms and 750,000 cows in 100 tankers, for an annual volume of 2,500 million liters. Once at the plant, the milk is mostly processed into powder for export and use in such specialty products as Egmont Cheese, specifically developed for the U.S. market. Mozzarella cheese (the one on pizza) and protein products derived from milk are also produced. Annually, the plant manufactures 190,000 tons of milk powder alone.

At the entrance to the plant is **Dairyland Visitor Centre,** Hwy. 3, tel. 06/278-4537, featuring dairy displays, an audiovisual on the industry and plant, and a simulated tanker ride. Part of the center is a café that features delicious banana milkshakes. It's open daily 9 A.M.–5 P.M.

Practicalities

Furlong Motor Inn, 256 Waihi Rd., tel. 06/278-5136, is the best place in the area to stay. It features 23 modern and comfortable rooms, and a café and restaurant. Rates are $78 s, $98 d. **Avon Lodge Motel,** 215 South Rd., tel. 06/278-7144 or 0800/288-048, is a typical roadside motel. All units have a kitchen, or have breakfast delivered to your door; rates $85–98 s or d. **Ohangai Farm Backpackers** on a dairy farm 10 km east of Hawera on Urupa Rd., tel. 06/272-2878, is a great place to experience life on a farm, hike in the surrounding bushland, swim in the pool, play tennis, or just kick back and relax. Dorm beds are $16 pp, double rooms are $18 pp. Call ahead for pickups from Hawera. **King Edward Park** on Waihi Rd., tel. 06/278-8544, a domain with attractive gardens and a lake, has tent and powered sites for $18, and cabins from $32.

Information South Takanaki, 55 High St., tel. 06/278-8599, is beside a water tower that dominates the horizon.

West from Hawera toward New Plymouth

From Hawera, Hwy. 45 heads west, hugging the coast all the way back to New Plymouth. This 110-km stretch of highway is spectacular, passing through dairyland flanked by the ocean on one side and by the imposing peak of Mt. Egmont/Taranaki on the other. The only major settlement along the way is **Opunake,** 43 km from Hawera. Nestled behind a crescent-shaped beach and flanked by two high headlands, Opunake has good swimming. Its coastal walkway leads east to the mouth of the Waiaua River and west past an old wharf dating to the 1890s to a great lookout point. **Opunake Beach Holiday Park,** tel. 06/278-8010, has campsites right on the beach for $10 pp.

One of the few accommodations along this stretch of coast is the **Opunake Motel,** 36 Heaphy Rd., tel. 06/761-8330. All rooms are $65 s, $75 d; out back is a cottage with dorm beds and double rooms for $19 pp.

Continuing around the cape, turn off at Pungarehu to **Cape Egmont Lighthouse** and a coastal lookout. At Oakura, 15 km from New Plymouth, the hedge-sheltered grounds of **Oaku-ra Beach Camp** are right on the beach, tel. 06/752-7861. Communal facilities include metered showers. Tent sites are $17, caravan sites are $18, and cabins are $42.

Wanganui

If you don't have much time and are doing the old one-day-here one-day-there routine, the west coast city of Wanganui (population 45,000) is a great base for exploring the river and bush scenery of Whanganui National Park to the north, the volcanic wonders of Tongariro National Park to the northeast, and Egmont National Park to the northwest. Situated on the shores of South Taranaki Bight at the mouth of the Whanganui River,

163 km southeast of New Plymouth, and 195 km north of Wellington, Wanganui offers river attractions, good surfing beaches, beautiful parks, and many hospitable locals eager to show you their hometown. If you're looking for the bustle, comforts, and attractions of a city, or want to explore the inland beauty of the wild upper stretches of the Whanganui River, take a few days to appreciate life in Wanganui, "The River City."

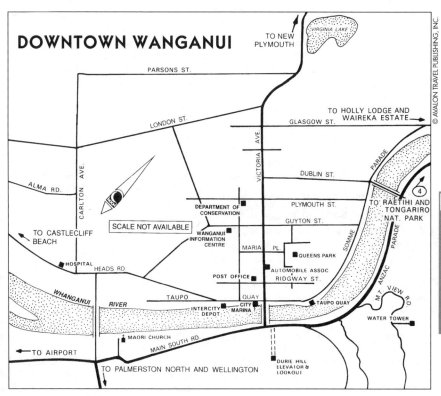

Wanganui or Whanganui?

The city of Wanganui has retained the Maori spelling of what was historically Whanganui (great wait) while in all other references the "h" has been restored, including the river, the national park, and the region. To confuse matters further, both are pronounced the same. The correct pronunciation (Wan-ga-nue) is unlike elsewhere on the North Island where "wa" is pronounced "fa."

THE WHANGANUI RIVER

From Tongariro to the Tasman

The magnificent Whanganui River, often called "the Rhine of New Zealand," is the second-longest river and the longest navigable waterway in the country. Starting on the slopes of Mt. Tongariro, the river runs a 315-km course north to Taumarunui and then south toward Wanganui, the last 32 km as a wide tidal estuary before flowing into the Tasman Sea. It's navigable as far as Taumarunui (only by jetboat above Pipiriki) and contains 239 rapids; the upper and middle stretches are exhilarating. The quieter but equally scenic lower stretch near the city treats boaters to romantic reflection shots, native bush-covered

> *Today most of the original Whanganui villages lie abandoned, but priceless Maori artifacts found along the banks have been preserved and are on display at various riverside settlements.*

banks, and a different aspect of Wanganui's bridges and city sights. The river also offers a large range of outdoor recreation activities, including hiking and hunting along its banks and scenic reserves, and canoeing and jetboating the many rapids. Several areas already have been preserved as Whanganui National Park.

History

For centuries Maori people lived in villages along the shores of the Whanganui; before the arrival of the first white settlers (1830s), today's modern city was a thriving Maori center (see special topic Birth of the Whanganui). The river was an important Maori canoe route to the center of the North Island; with the Europeans came the first steamboats to puff upriver. Today most of the original villages lie abandoned, but priceless Maori artifacts found along the banks have been preserved and are on display at various riverside settlements. You can still see the remains of many Maori *pa* from the river. In 1870, Town Bridge was erected over the river, which considerably opened up the district and began a connection with Wellington in the south. The original bridge stood for almost 100 years before it was replaced with the modern Wanganui City Bridge. Today three city bridges and a railway bridge span the mighty river.

SIGHTS

The best way to get the feel of the city is on foot, and the **Wanganui Information Centre** office at 101 Guyton St. is a good place to start. Collect a Wanganui city map and the various "Heritage Trail" brochures.

Whanganui Regional Museum

This, the largest regional museum in New Zealand, is also one of the best in the country. A vast display room features Maori architecture, carving, art, greenstone weapons, feather cloaks, ceremonial portraits, intriguing displays on tattooing, and the incredible 25-meter Te Mata-O-

BIRTH OF THE WHANGANUI

When the majestic mountains Tongariro and Taranaki fought over the beautiful mountain Pihanga, Taranaki lost. In his anger and grief he fled north through bush and forest, tearing a deep wound in the earth as he traveled to his permanent resting place, where he stands today as Mt. Taranaki/Egmont. Soon a clear spring spurted from Tongariro's side and the water filled and healed the wound in the earth. Lush green forests filled with birds sprang up along the newly formed river. Today that river is called the Whanganui.

Hotoroa War Canoe that carried a crew of 70. Throughout the rest of the museum there's a reconstruction of a colonial cottage and an entire Wanganui street from times gone by; a spectacular and comprehensive collection of mounted birds (see the display of moa—a huge flightless bird native to New Zealand, extinct for centuries), parrots of the world, mounted fish, whales, and animals; a shell collection; and a room full of fluorescent butterflies and moths. The museum is open Mon.–Sat. 10 A.M.–4:30 P.M., Sunday 1–4:30 P.M., and is well worth the small admission cost of $3 adult, $1 child. The museum is in Queens Park, downtown on the corner of Wicksteed and Watt Streets, tel. 06/345-7443.

Sarjeant Gallery

Also in Queens Park, this gallery is contained in an imposing domed building. It holds an impressive permanent collection, but the special exhibitions attract crowds. It's open Mon.–Fri. 10:30 A.M.–4:30 P.M., Sat.–Sun. 1–4:30 P.M.

Durie Hill Elevator and Vicinity

Head to Durie Hill for great views of the city, its three major bridges, and the Whanganui River winding out to the coast. A unique way to reach the summit is on a 66-meter elevator that goes through the hill. The entrance to this unique attraction lies across the river from downtown near the end of Victoria Avenue. To get there on foot from downtown, cross the river via Wanganui City Bridge (the main bridge). Admission to the elevator is free; it's open till 6 P.M. every night. It's also possible to reach the top of the hill by road; to get there, cross the Whanganui River, turn left, and follow the signs to "Scenic Drive View Point." At the summit you'll find a 34-meter Memorial Tower built entirely out of fossilized seashell rock (indicating that the river must have been a large inlet at one time for the builders to find seashells so far up the banks).

For another aspect and views of the rolling hills behind the city, head for the **water tower** on the same side of the river as the Memorial Tower but a couple of km north. To get there, go back down to the river (but don't cross it), and turn right on the main road, Anzac Parade. Just after the start of

Kowhai Park (a child's paradise) on the left, turn right on Mountain View Rd., which twists and turns up Bastia Hill. Turn left on Bastia Ave. and you'll end up at the tower—climb it for great views.

Virginia Lake

Tranquil Virginia Lake nestles between woods, lawns, and beds of bright flowers. Although it's only one km from the top end of Victoria Ave. (about three km from downtown), the lake and grounds have a parklike atmosphere; apart from birdsong and wind whistling through the trees, the odd dog barking in the distance, and running feet (it's popular with joggers), everything is quiet. Some features include the large walk-through aviary at the northwest end, colorful **Higginbottom Fountain** (startling at night), and the tropical flower- and fern-filled **Winter Gardens** (open Mon.–Sat. 10 A.M.–4 P.M., Sunday 10 A.M.–5 P.M.; admission free). Some delightful tracks weave through the trees and around the lake—if you have time, follow the trail around the left side of the lake (from the road) to the small statue of *Tainui*—the romantic legend of the lake is inscribed below. To get to the lake from downtown follow Victoria Ave. away from the river. At the top end turn right onto Great North Rd.; follow its curves until you reach the lake on your right. If you're driving, park on Babbage Place just beyond the park at the aviary end.

Bason Botanical Reserve

This botanic garden lies in the rolling countryside west of Wanganui. It features a conservatory bursting with the color of begonias and various tropical plants, and gardens devoted to ferns, irises, and camellias. It's open daily from 9:30 A.M. To get there, head northwest out of town on Hwy. 3, turn south onto Rapanui Rd. after five km, and follow the signs.

Holly Lodge Estate

Originally a winery, this historic property, tel. 06/343-9344, is now open to the public as an outdoor museum. See the wine-making process, or visit the memorabilia museum from World War II days. Saunter through the grounds and you'll discover an aviary and a croquet lawn and swimming pool available to guests. In the delightful old-style house you can sample morning or afternoon tea, or a light lunch. It's open daily 8 A.M.–8 P.M. The best way to get there is to ride the *Otunui* paddleboat from Wanganui, or if you have a car, drive north out of the city along Somme Parade, which follows the river. Continue onto Papaiti Rd. (Upper Aramaho).

RIVER ADVENTURES

Stop by the Wanganui Information Centre, where you'll be inundated with brochures on exploring the scenic beauty of the Whanganui River and its historic places by jetboat, raft, historic paddlesteamer, or foot—the great variety allows you to pick the best one to suit your budget and fancy.

Canoeing and jetboating on the Whanganui are both popular. Details of local operators are covered in the Whanganui National Park section of this chapter.

Waimarie

In January 1993, the *Waimarie* was raised from the water after 40 years at the bottom of the Whanganui River. This 34-meter coal-fired paddlesteamer plied the river for 50 years before sinking at its moorings in 1952. A painstaking restoration project has been completed and now the *Waimarie* takes visitors on a 13-km round-trip cruise from her berth at Taupo Quay, one block east of Queens Park, tel. 06/347-1863. Departures are weekdays at 1 P.M. and weekends at 4 P.M. The cost of the two-hour trip is $25 adult, $20 senior, $10 child. At the departure point, a small museum cataloging the *Waimarie's* life story is open Mon.–Sat. 9 A.M.–4 P.M., Sunday 1–4 P.M.

Whanganui River Road

If you have a car and plenty of time, you won't want to miss the 79-km scenic drive north along the east bank of the Whanganui River to the picturesque village of Pipiriki. The river road begins 14 km north of Wanganui along Hwy. 4. At the junction of the two roads, interpretive boards describe the river's history and give general information about it. From Hwy. 4, the road climbs quickly to Aramoana summit, below which the

river is laid out in all its glory. Aside from the magnificent wilderness scenery en route, a number of historic Maori villages are worth a stop. The first of these is **Atene,** and then the road passes **Koriniti,** 47 km from Wanganui. This village features a number of historic buildings transported from the original village site across the river. Visitors are welcome. One km farther north is the remains of a *pa,* then another eight km north is a restored flour mill. At km 66 is **Hiruharama** (the Maori word for Jerusalem, the name given to the village by an early missionary), home to a church and convent.

At the end of the road, Pipiriki is the gateway to the "wilderness" reaches of the Whanganui River (only jetboats can continue upriver) and Whanganui National Park, and a meeting place for hikers, campers, canoeists, rafters, and jetboaters. A large Maori population used to live across the river from the present-day village. Then, in the early 1900s, steamboats that could cruise the river only as far upstream as Pipiriki brought great numbers of tourists to what quickly became a booming resort. Today it's again a quiet little village attracting those who wish to explore the river and surrounding national park. The days of Pipiriki as a tourist resort ended abruptly in 1959, when the grand Pipiriki Hotel burned to the ground; all that marks the site today are some foundations, but next door, in the restored **Colonial House,** the story is told through photographs and an assortment of relics. Head to the DOC **Pipiriki Field Centre,** tel. 06/377-5022, for local information.

Rivercity Tours, tel. 06/344-2554, has the contract for mail delivery to residents along Whanganui River Rd. They always have room for a few passengers to come along for an interesting tour to Pipiriki and back. The bus departs from the post office Mon.–Fri. at 7:15 A.M. The fare is $25 pp, with the added option of a jetboat trip for $30–65 pp extra.

OTHER RECREATION
Beaches and Bush

The most popular city beach is **Castlecliff,** immediately west of where the Whanganui River drains into South Taranaki Bight. Eight km west of the city center, it has a Marine Parade, and is known for good beach-break surf (dangerous currents at the rivermouth). To get there from downtown, follow Taupo Quay along the riverfront onto Heads Road, turn down Bryce St., and at the end, turn right onto Cornfoot St., then left on Manuka St.—you'll end up at Castlecliff Beach Domain.

Kai Iwi Beach is another good place for surfing and swimming, eight km farther north—take Hwy. 3 north, then turn off just south of the town of Kai Iwi onto Kai Iwi Valley Rd., which ends at the beach. Another great spot and a nature-lover's paradise in the Kai Iwi area is **Bushy Park,** tel. 06/342-9879, where you can visit an interpretive center and then walk through 95 hectares of native bush and see and hear plenty of birds in this natural sanctuary; it's open daily 10 A.M.–5 P.M. (in summer until 8 P.M.). You can stay in the old colonial homestead. Entry is $5 adult, $2 child. It's along Rangitatau East Rd. off Hwy. 3 north, just north of Kai Iwi.

Thirty km southeast of Wanganui is the popular **Turakina Beach**—take Hwy. 3 south and turn off just north of Turakina onto Turakina Beach Road.

Entertainment

The hotels and public bars do a booming business—just follow your ears to the most popular watering spots in town. A classic old pub that has been extensively restored, the **Rutland Arms,** on the corner of Ridgeway St. and Victoria Ave., tel. 06/347-7677, is a great place for a quiet beer. The **Grand Hotel,** on the corner of St. Hill and Guyton Streets, tel. 06/345-0955, is a popular local drinking hole, with three stylish bars. One of the most popular nightclubs, the **Fuel Shed,** 2 Victoria Ave., tel. 06/345-7278, often has live music.

ACCOMMODATIONS
Hotels and Motels

The old **Grand Hotel,** on the corner of St. Hill and Guyton Streets, tel. 06/345-0955, website: www.thegrandhotel.co.nz, has been tastefully renovated. Rooms, each with a private bathroom,

start at $65 s, $77 d, with suites for $110–125 s or d. Another restored hotel is the **Rutland Arms,** on the corner of Victoria Ave. and Ridgway St., tel. 06/347-7677 or 0800/788-526; website: www.rutland-arms.co.nz. Each of the eight upstairs guest rooms has a traditional English feel, reproduction period furnishings, and extra-comfortable beds; Rates of $130–160 s or d include a light breakfast.

Along Somme Parade, which follows the Whanganui River through town, are a string of motels within walking distance of downtown (they are easily confused—five start with "River"—so double-check your booking before checking in). The closest of these is **Riverview Motel,** 14 Somme Parade, tel. 06/345-2888 or 0800/102-001, where the self-contained rooms start at a reasonable $70–90 s or d (the more expensive rooms enjoy river views). Rooms at **Riverside Motel,** 30 Somme Parade, tel. 06/345-2448 or 0800/853-333, are similarly priced but larger; $80 s, $90 d. Continuing north one block is **Astral Motel,** 45 Somme Parade, tel. 06/347-9063 or 0800/509-063, a 15-minute walk from downtown along the river. It features a pool, barbecue area, and laundry. The 15 rooms each have a kitchen; rates $80–100 s or d.

A little farther out, **Halswell Court Motel,** 59 Halswell St., tel. 06/343-9848 or 0800/809-107, has 20 well-appointed rooms, each with kitchen facilities and set around parklike grounds. Rates range $99–109 s or d. Continuing north, beyond Virginia Lake, is **Oasis Motor Lodge,** 181 Great North Rd., tel. 06/345-4636. Rooms overlook a pleasant garden area, and it has indoor and outdoor pools; rates from $85 for a self-contained room.

Bed-and-Breakfast

If you have your own transportation and don't mind the 24-km drive northwest to Kai Iwi, consider staying at the beautiful **Bushy Park Homestead,** an Edwardian-era home dating to 1906 surrounded by forests and walking trails. The rooms share bathrooms, but there's plenty of space for guests to relax—a long verandah, comfortable lounge, and extensive gardens that surround the homestead. Rooms in the main house range $85–130 s or d including breakfast, while a freestanding chalet costs $40 s or d plus $20 for every extra person. Campers pay $25 for a powered site. It's on Rangitatau East Rd., off Hwy. 3 eight km north of Kai Iwi, tel. 06/342-9879; website: www.bushypark-homestead.co.nz.

Backpacker Lodge

Tamara Backpackers, north of downtown at 24 Somme Parade, tel. 06/347-6300, website: www.tamaralodge.com, features good, clean accommodations in an Edwardian house across the road from the river. The friendly hosts make you feel at home while you get a house tour, a map of the town, and information on what to see and do in Wanganui. Facilities include a lounge, a game room with a piano, a garden filled with palm trees and hammocks, Internet access, a barbecue area, bikes, and bus depot pickups. Dorm rates are $18 pp, doubles or twins are $19 pp. Rooms with a private bathroom are $27 s, $48 d.

Motor Camps

The area offers quite a few choices. **Aramoho Holiday Park** at 460 Somme Parade in Upper Aramoho on the city-side bank of the Whanganui River (five km from Dublin St. Bridge), tel. 06/343-8402 or 0800/272-664, is a great place to stay if you want to surround yourself with greenery and get a bit of rest, if you don't mind sharing your food with numerous noisy families of waterfowl. The park is situated in lush parklike surroundings with lots of trees, and the river is a just few steps away. It has all the usual facilities (as good as any on the North Island). Tent and caravan sites are $20, basic cabins start at $30 s or d, tourist flats are $55, and motel units are $75. A little closer to downtown, the **Avro Motel,** 36 Alma Rd., tel. 06/345-5279, offers a limited number of powered sites, each with a private bathroom, for $22. Campers have use of the motel facilities, including a large swimming pool, private spa pools, a playground, and a guest laundry.

On the oceanfront, **Castlecliff Holiday Park,** 1 Rangiora St., Castlecliff, tel. 06/344-2227, is adjacent to a rugged black-sand and driftwood-covered beach and eight km from downtown Wanganui; it offers communal facilities, a TV and game room, and an adjacent store. Tent sites are $17, powered sites $18, on-site caravans $34, and cabins from $35. To get out to Castlecliff Beach, follow Taupo Quay west onto Heads Rd., continue onto Bryce St., at the end turn right on Cornfoot St., then turn left on Rangiora Street.

FOOD

Light Meals

The **Red Eye Café,** 96 Guyton St., tel. 06/345-5646, serves up good strong coffee and a range of cakes and pastries. With a great riverfront setting, **Amadeus,** 69 Quay St., tel. 06/345-1538, is a good choice for a casual lunch. Expect to pay $10–15 for lunch and from $17 at dinner. The **Shangri-La Restaurant,** 113 Great North Rd., tel. 06/345-3654, a tearoom overlooking beautiful Virginia Lake, serves morning and afternoon tea, and lunch seven days a week. The best fish-and-chips joint in town is **George's Fisheries** at 40 Victoria Ave., tel. 06/345-7937. Fresh fish starts at $4.50 per piece; it's open daily till 7 P.M.

Restaurants

Clareburt's, at street level of the Grand Hotel on the corner of St. Hill and Guyton Streets, tel. 06/345-0955, offers upmarket pub dining in a well-lit room. All starters are under $11, the Roast of the Day is $16, and dinners, such as a T-bone steak with mashed potatoes and vegetables, range $17–23. Dining at the **Rutland Arms,** on the corner of Victoria Ave. and Ridgway St., tel. 06/347-7677, is like taking a step back in time. Although a distinctive small-town England atmosphere prevails-complete with agricultural implements on the walls-the menu is anything but bangers and mash. Modern New Zealand cooking is the best way to describe dishes such as Lord Nelson's Anguish, a rack of lamb roasted in a rum and juniper berry marinade and served with mango relish and red wine jus ($22). Other dinners are priced at $16–25, with a separate selection of appealing light meals ($10–13).

Wanganui has a number of Chinese restaurants; the best of these are **Wing Wah,** a cheap place at 330 Victoria Ave., tel. 06/345-6096; and **Beijing Restaurant,** 30 Maria Pl., tel. 06/345-4889.

TRANSPORTATION
Getting There
Wanganui Airport is four km west of the city center on the south side of the river. Providing two northbound and two southbound flights a day, **Air New Zealand,** downtown at 133 Victoria Ave., tel. 06/348-3500, offers direct flights from Wanganui to Auckland and Wellington. Traveling between the airport and downtown is made easy by **Ash's Coach Lines,** tel. 06/347-7444, which provides door-to-door service for $10 pp.

Wanganui is on a number of **Intercity** and **Newmans** routes, which makes traveling to the city by bus easy. Regular services arrive and depart from Auckland, Taupo, New Plymouth, Palmerston North, and Wellington. For travel between National Park (Tongariro National Park) and Wanganui, a transfer must be made at Bulls. The depot used by both companies is the **Wanganui Travel Centre,** 156 Ridgeway St., tel. 06/345-4433. The ticket office is open Mon.–Fri. 8:45 A.M.–5:15 P.M.

Getting Around
Local buses are operated by **Wanganui Taxis,** tel. 06/345-5555, departing from Maria Place in the town center, near Victoria Ave. (weekdays only).

Cabs also depart from Maria Place, or call **Wanganui Taxis,** tel. 06/345-5555.

Car rental agencies in Wanganui include **Budget,** tel. 06/345-5122; **Hertz,** tel. 06/345-7357; and **Rent-a-dent,** tel. 06/345-1505.

SERVICES AND INFORMATION
Services
The main **post office** is at 60 Ridgway Street. The **Automobile Association** office is at 78 Victoria Ave. between Maria Place and Ridgway St., tel. 06/348-9160. **Wanganui Laundrette** is at 43 Hatrick St., tel. 06/349-0600.

Wanganui Hospital, Heads Rd., tel. 06/348-1234, has a doctor on duty 24 hours daily. **Wicksteed Pharmacy,** 214 Wicksteed St., tel. 06/345-6166, is open daily 8:30 A.M.–8:30 P.M. For the **police** call 06/345-0600.

Information
Wanganui Information Centre, 101 Guyton St. (at St. Hill St.), tel. 06/349-0508, is open Mon.–Fri. 8:30 A.M.–5 P.M., weekends 10 A.M.–2 P.M. The people running it ensure a most enjoyable experience in Wanganui. They have heaps of information on the city, as well as the Whanganui River, its reserves, and its many boat operators, and will make bookings for any trip or accommodation you desire. These folks love their city and it shows—don't go anywhere else first! For the complete rundown on Whanganui National Park, visit the **DOC** office at 74 Ingestre St. (at St. Hill St.), tel. 06/345-2402, where you can get all sorts of brochures covering basic information, short nature walks, many hiking tracks, and a map. It's open Mon.–Fri. 8 A.M.–4:30 P.M.

Whanganui National Park

Established in 1987, 74,231-hectare, remote, and relatively isolated Whanganui National Park is one of the three newest national parks in the country. Divided into three major sections, most of the park lies within the catchment of the mighty Whanganui River, the longest navigable river in New Zealand. However, although the river is without a doubt a major feature and the main accessway into and through the park, the riverbed itself is not included in parkland.

The Maori have lived in villages along the Whanganui for many centuries, evidenced by the many archaeological sites found in the park, and the river and adjoining forests still have important spiritual and traditional values to the Whanganui Maori people. Starting in the 1840s, European pioneers, explorers, missionaries, traders, and farmers also set up homes along the river. The worst hazards they faced (and modern-day explorers still face) were landslides and flooding—the entire park lies within the most active seismic zone in New Zealand.

Today, visitors to the park can choose from a variety of energetic recreational activities—hiking, canoeing, jetboating, hunting, and fishing. But if sight-seeing is more what you have in mind, drive the scenic Whanganui River Rd. from Wanganui to Pipiriki to see picturesque villages, a colonial house and museum, several historic sites, a swing bridge, and captivating waterfalls, and perhaps stroll along some of the short trails. You'll get a taste of the park without wandering too far off the beaten track.

THE LAND

Whanganui National Park covers several separate areas of land, linked to one another by the Whanganui River. At the north end, starting 17 km downstream from Taumarunui at Te Maire, a series of small riverside blocks of land extend south to Whakahoro. The large, rugged, central core of the park begins at Whakahoro, and extends 92 km south—downstream from Pipiriki. Farther

south, the third main section lies between Ranana and Atene. Much of the park is dense lowland forest lying along the Whanganui River—the park's focal point. Third longest in the country, this magnificent 290-km river meanders for 170 km through the park. The Whakapapa, Ongarue, Ohura, Tangarakau, Retaruke, Whangamomona, and Manganui o te ao are major tributaries. With its gentle gradient, large volume of water, and 234 km of navigable water, the Whanganui has always been a major transport route. Today it's extensively used by canoeists, to a lesser extent by jet-boaters, and is the main accessway into the wilderness sections of the park.

The Whanganui basin is an uplifted mass of young Tertiary marine sediments—soft sandstone and mudstone deposit—deeply incised by erosion. The main geological features you're likely to see as you explore the park are steep sharp ridges, *papa* cliffs (some bare, some covered in vegetation), deep, narrow, winding gorges, and river valleys with small areas of flat terraced land. Add to this a dense blanket of broadleaf-podocarp forest, grasslands, regenerating native bush, river tributaries, and inspirational waterfalls, and you can understand why the park attracts people in search of a scenic wilderness experience. Almost half of this lowland park is less than 300 meters above sea level, the rest 300–600 meters, with a few higher peaks. The most dominant feature northwest of Pipiriki is the Matemateaonga Range.

Climate

The park has a mild climate. Rainfall varies from 1,000 mm at the coast to 1,250 mm at Taumarunui to more than 1,700 mm on the inland high country. Frosts are rare, snow even rarer, but mist occurs frequently in sheltered pockets of the park—usually lasting until late morning and heralding a fine day. However, explorers should be prepared and equipped for all kinds of weather—it's wilderness out there, and transportation is unavailable unless previously arranged. Warm

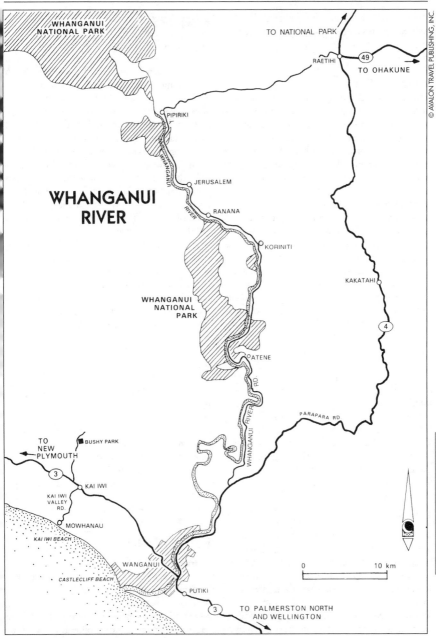

© AVALON TRAVEL PUBLISHING, INC.

WHANGANUI
NATIONAL PARK

TO NATIONAL PARK

RAETIHI

49

TO OHAKUNE

PIPIRIKI

WHANGANUI
RIVER

WHANGANUI
RIVER

JERUSALEM

RANANA

KORINITI

KAKATAHI

WHANGANUI
NATIONAL
PARK

4

ATENE

WHANGANUI RIVER RD.

PARAPARA RD.

TO
NEW
PLYMOUTH

BUSHY PARK

3

KAI IWI

KAI IWI
VALLEY
RD.

MOWHANAU

KAI IWI BEACH

WANGANUI

CASTLECLIFF BEACH

PUTIKI

3

TO PALMERSTON NORTH
AND WELLINGTON

0   10 km

TARANAKI AND THE WEST

(preferably wool) waterproof gear and sturdy footwear are necessities when taking off on any of the longer tracks. Also don't forget your sunblock and insect repellent.

Flora and Fauna

Heavily forested Whanganui National Park protects one of the largest remaining tracts of unmodified lowland forest on the North Island, and provides a habitat for a wide variety of native wildlife. It's a predominantly green and brown environment, with colorful tree species dotting the forest with red, yellow, and white, and impressive towering tree ferns that always make great photographic subjects. *Kamahi, tawa, miro, rimu, totara, kahikatea, matai,* northern *rata,* and black, silver, and hard beech are all represented in the park's central core. Native vegetation, *totara, nikau, akeake, ngaio,* and *karaka,* blanket the areas closest to the coast. You'll also find grasslands (about 6,000 hectares altogether) and areas of regenerating bush within park boundaries, and pastureland (now regenerating) and introduced plants (some of which are considered a problem and will be controlled) along the riverbanks and in areas where the land used to be farmed.

Birds abound in this forested habitat, particularly in the more isolated central areas of the river valley. Brown kiwi (one of the largest populations in the country), fantails, grey warblers, silvereyes, tits, and North Island robins (very common) are easily spotted, as are native bellbirds, New Zealand pigeons, *tui,* and yellow-crowned parakeets. Even *kokako* sightings have been reported. Along the Matemateaonga Range you'll find *kaka,* whiteheads, riflemen, and New Zealand falcons. Along the waterways live paradise shelducks, grey ducks, black shags, and rare blue ducks. In the Whanganui River system you can find (that's if you're trying!) 18 species of native fish, plenty of eels, lamprey, and freshwater crayfish and flounder.

Native bat colonies, introduced animals—opossums, rats, goats, wild cattle and sheep, deer, pigs (pig hunting is actively encouraged, but a permit is required)—and, of course, myriad insects, share this small, lush, and very green piece of the planet.

HISTORY

Because of the Whanganui River's easy navigability, the area has a long and varied Maori and European history. The river has always been an access to the North Island interior, and the Maori, finding an abundance of fish, birds, and berries along the river and in the forest, lived in villages along its banks. You can still see the evidence of earthworks and regenerating stands of native forest where villages once stood. Today's Maori generally live along the lower reaches of the river.

In the 1840s the first European missionaries arrived. Settlers built villages on land suitable for farming, and planted wheat along the river. They established flour mills in the 1850s, and in the 1860s, when the river's scenic attractions were recognized, tourism began in a big way. The Hatrick & Co. Riverboat Service introduced a steamer service that, by the turn of the 20th century, had a fleet of 12 vessels carrying passengers to the Pipiriki House Hotel and the Houseboat—a fancy, floating hotel moored in the upper reaches of the river. The boats also served villagers and farmers right up to the Depression years of the 1930s.

In the early 1930s, development in the form of roads and farming settlements was planned, but the densely forested countryside, the isolation, erosion, and decreasing soil fertility collectively proved just too big a barrier to overcome. Today you can stumble across signs of previous settlement—clearings in the bush, regenerating forest, homestead ruins, fences, old roads and bridges—now reclaimed by the forest. In 1934 Whanganui River Rd., which took 30 years to build because of the rugged terrain and regular floods and slips, was finally opened to traffic. It remains to this day one of the most scenic roads in the area.

RECREATION

Canoeing and Kayaking

Often proclaimed "the most canoed river in New Zealand," the Whanganui River is a mecca for river lovers from around the world. Despite the 239 rapids that lie between Taumarunui and the sea, it's still considered suitable for novice canoeists. An estimated 6,000 canoeists and kayakers use the river each year. The most popular section is between Taumarunui and Pipiriki, a 144-km trip that takes up to five days. An easy overnight trip (and therefore popular on weekends with the locals) is the 50-km stretch of river between Taumarunui and Wades Landing. Usage is greatest between December and Easter, but the river is especially busy in January.

Yeti Tours, tel. 06/385-8197 or 0800/322-388, website: www.canoe.co.nz, has been guiding on the river for over 20 years. The company also rents gear for independent travelers. Canoes and single kayaks cost $125 for three days, then $20 for every extra day. These rates include transportation, life jackets, and waterproof barrels for food. Yeti also rents camping equipment. Guided trips begin from the Hobbit Motor Lodge in Ohakune, and include transportation to and from the river, equipment rentals, and all meals. The six-day trip begins just downstream of Taumarunui, while four-, three-, and two-day trips begin at Wades Landing. The pull-out point on all trips is Pipiriki. The trips are no mad dash down the river-only a few hours a day are spent in the canoes, with plenty of time for hiking and exploring the wilderness. Prices start at $295 for a two-day trip.

Bridge to Nowhere Jets at Pipiriki, tel. 06/385-4128, rents canoes and kayaks. The company provides transfers upstream as far as you desire; then you can simply paddle back down to the Pipiriki dock at your leisure. Based at Wades Landing, **Whanganui River Jets,** tel. 07/895-5995, provides canoe and kayak rentals, as well as jetboat transfers to all points along the river. From Taumarunui, **Pioneer Jet Boat Tours,** tel. 07/895-8528, also rents canoes and kayaks, and provides river transportation.

Jetboat Tours

Several jetboat operators cruise the river, offering fun trips ranging from an hour or two (about $30 pp) to several-day trips costing hundreds of dollars depending on time, distance, and numbers. Based in Wanganui, Pipiriki, and Taumarunui, they also provide a necessary transportation service to hikers trekking the popular hiking tracks. From Wanganui, drive Whanganui River Rd. and take a jetboat trip from Pipiriki or surrounds for a full day's adventure. **Bridge to Nowhere Jets** at Pipiriki, tel. 06/385-4128, offers a choice of two tours: the 20-minute Drop Scene tour for $35 pp, and the particularly popular four-hour Bridge To Nowhere tour (includes a 40-minute guided walk to the bridge and tea and coffee) for $70 pp (bring your own lunch, warm clothes, and sturdy footwear). It also provides track drop-off and pickup service for hikers doing either the Matemateaonga or Mangapurua Tracks. Bookings are required for all tours. Other jetboats are based at Wades Landing and Taumarunui in the north.

Hiking

While a float trip down the Whanganui River is the most popular park activity, hikers are attracted by two main tracks, both beginning and ending deep in the wilderness and taking three to four days each way. Both tracks provide a total wilderness experience, and hikers should be experienced and totally self-sufficient. As well as waterproof clothing and sturdy boots, hikers should take a tent and stove (in case the huts are full), and a topographical map. The DOC has maps, hut passes, and all the relevant information.

Running east to west through the south-central section of the park, the **Matemateaonga Walkway** is a wild 42-km bush walk along the top of the Matemateaonga Range and through Mt. Humphries State Forest. It follows a route first used by Maoris, and then by settlers traveling to the Taranaki region, but what was once a road has been partly reclaimed by nature and is now a narrow track through dense forest. Five huts along the track have woodstoves and rainwater tanks; $8 pp per night. The track's eastern terminus is the Whanganui River. **Bridge to Nowhere Jets,** tel. 06/385-4128, provides transfers from Pipiriki. Many hikers beginning or ending the trip at this point stay at the nearby Ramanui Lodge. The western end of the track is Mangaehu Rd. (unsealed), inland from Makahu (48 km east of Stratford).

The 40-km **Mangapurua Track** is no more remote than the Matemateaonga Walkway, but it's less traveled. It runs north-south through the park's north-central section, beginning and ending along the Whanganui River. The track traverses two watersheds, with a high point at 663-meter-high Mangapurua Trig, where the view extends west to Mt. Egmont/Taranaki and east to the volcanic peaks of Tongariro National Park.

PRACTICALITIES

Accommodations

Ramanui Lodge, tel. 06/385-4995 or 025/480-308, is the only accommodation actually in the park. It lies in a remote location, 21 km upstream from Pipiriki. There's plenty to do around the 500-hectare property, with canoes for guest use and hiking on the nearby Matemateaonga Walkway. Accommodation is in an old woolshed converted to dorms ($18 pp) or in the main lodge, in one of four rooms ($85 pp includes breakfast and dinner). You can also camp. The only access is by jetboat, with Bridge to Nowhere Jets, tel. 06/385-4128, providing transfers for $40 pp round-trip.

Huts and Campgrounds

Within the park are nine huts and numerous campgrounds, many of which lie along the section of river between Taumarunui and Pipiriki, perfect for a wilderness canoe or raft trip. The huts are of a varying standard; all have bunk beds, a water supply, and a toilet, and some have cooking facilities. In summer, a Great Walks pass is required for travelers overnighting on the river, whether you're staying in a hut or campground. Valid for six nights, the pass costs $25 if bought in advance from a DOC office. The rest of the year, and for huts and campgrounds in other parts of the park, the fee costs $8 pp per night in a hut and $4 in a campground.

At **Pipiriki,** the main jumping-off point for park visitors, the DOC maintains a campground with toilets and a water supply. The DOC has a similar facility along Whanganui River Rd., north of Atene.

If you are planning to overnight at Taumarunui before heading down the river, **Taumarunui Holiday Park** is handily located on the river four km east of town, tel. 07/895-9345 (campsites and cabins). In town itself, you'll find comfortable, self-contained rooms at **Central Park Motor Inn,** Maata St., tel. 07/895-7132; rates from $80 s or d.

Getting to the Park

The most pleasant way to get to Pipiriki is along Whanganui River Rd. from Wanganui. **Rivercity Tours,** tel. 06/344-2554 or 0800/377-311, provides a shuttle service along this route Mon.–Fri. for $25 round-trip. Taumarunui, the park's northern gateway, is a stop on **Intercity's** Auckland-Wanganui route. The buses stop downtown in front of the information center.

River Tours and Transportation

The main way into and through the park is along the river. A number of companies run jetboats into the park. The boats run both as scheduled tours and as a transportation service for hikers and campers. The most popular tours leave from Pipiriki, 79 km north of Wanganui. **Bridge to Nowhere Jets** at Pipiriki, tel. 06/385-4128, offers a four-hour tour to the Bridge to Nowhere. This famous Mangapurua Valley landmark was constructed in 1936 as part of a road that was meant to open up the area to settlers. That never happened, and today the bridge is slowly being reclaimed by the forest. The tour includes a jetboat ride, an easy 40-minute guided hike to the bridge, and tea or coffee for $70 pp. The company also provides a drop-off and pickup service for hikers, or can drop canoeists upstream for a float trip back to Pipiriki. **Pioneer Jet Boat Tours** is based on the upper reaches of the river at Taumarunui, tel. 07/895-8528. They offer everything from a 15-minute spin downstream to overnight trips within the park, as well as rent canoes and kayaks.

Information

The headquarters of the **Wanganui Conservancy,** 74 Ingestre St. in Wanganui, tel. 06/345-2402, is the main administration center for the park; it's open Mon.–Fri. 8 A.M.–4:30 P.M. See displays and information boards, collect resource material, and buy maps and accommodation passes here. The best source of information regarding tour operators within the park is the **Wanganui Information Centre,** 101 Guyton St., tel. 06/345-3286. The DOC also operates the **Pipiriki Field Centre,** tel. 06/385-5022. In Taumarunui, there's a large **Information Centre** in the railway station on Hakiaha St., tel. 07/895-7494.

Lower North Island

Introduction

Three main roads funnel traffic from the north into the **Manawatu** district, converging near Palmerston North, the area's major city. Highway 3 on the west coast is the main route south from New Plymouth, Egmont National Park, and Wanganui (about a 3.5-hour drive to Wellington); central Hwy. 1 connects Taupo and Tongariro National Park (5.5 hours to Wellington) with the south; and Hwy. 2 connects the east coast cities of Gisborne and Napier (about six hours to Wellington) with the south. The at-

Mount Bruce National Wildlife Centre

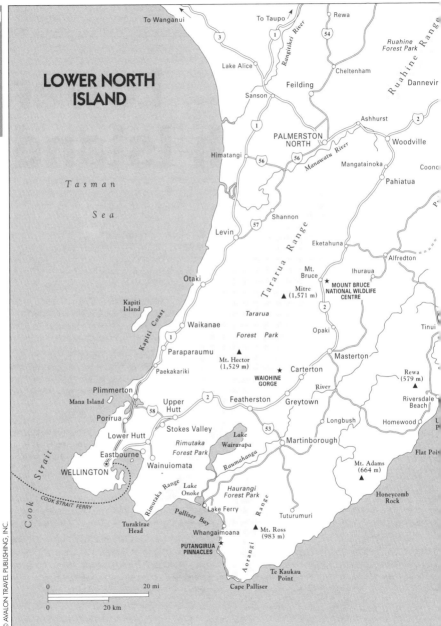

LOWER NORTH ISLAND

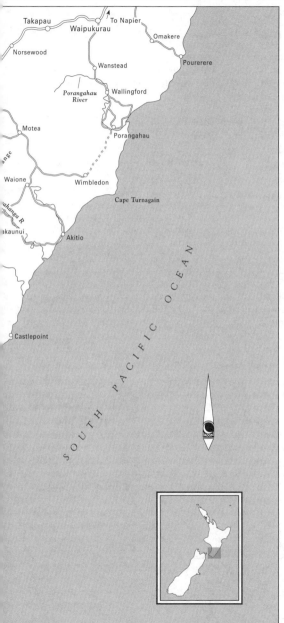

tractive city of Palmerston North is a good place to break up a long day's drive or relieve the numb bum bus syndrome on your way to Wellington. Two main routes continue south from Palmerston North toward the capital: Hwy. 1 (the most direct route) runs down the attractive Kapiti Coast; and Hwy. 2 meanders inland to Masterton, then passes Lake Wairarapa and the "dormitory" cities of Upper Hutt and Lower Hutt before entering Wellington.

Whichever route you choose has things to see and do—but keep in mind there's a lot *more* to do in the elegant capital of New Zealand before you catch the ferry to the South Island. If time is relatively precious, head straight down the coast to Wellington, and content yourself with good beach stops along the way. If time is relatively unimportant and you want to get off the beaten track, take the inland route south that passes through scenic hilly countryside scattered with sheep, trout-filled streams, lakes, and little villages where excitement is a new face in town. The southeast area of the North Island is wild, remote, untouched (in direct contrast with the highly populated urban southwest), and well worth checking out if transportation and time are your own.

Palmerston North

The geographical and regional center of the Manawatu region is Palmerston North, a city of 65,000 on the banks of the Manawatu River 60 km southeast of Wanganui. As home of Massey University, New Zealand's second largest university, the population rises and falls with seasons, but it's a pleasant place to visit at any time of the year and well worth a stop before continuing south to Wellington.

SIGHTS AND RECREATION
Around Town

To see what New Zealand artists are doing in the worlds of painting, ceramics, and sculpture, head for **Manawatu Art Gallery,** beside the Convention Centre at 398 Main St. W (opposite Andrew Young St.), tel. 06/358-8188, open Mon.–Fri. 10 A.M.–4:30 P.M., weekends 11:30 A.M.–4:30 P.M. The interesting **Science Centre and Manawatu Museum,** 396 Main St. (access is easiest from Church St.), tel. 06/355-5000, is also worth a visit, featuring the history of the district from Maori to European settlements,

and the beginning of the local dairy industry. Open daily 10 A.M.–5 P.M.; museum admission is free, while the science gallery costs $6 adult, $4 child. For an excellent view of The Square, the city, and surrounding hills, whiz up to the **Lookout** at the top of the Civic Centre building, open 10 A.M.–3 P.M.

If you're still in a museum mood, the **New Zealand Rugby Museum,** 87 Cuba St. at the Showground complex, tel. 06/358-6947, is a must for anyone interested in New Zealand's national sport. Photographs, badges, jerseys, caps, and all sorts of rugby paraphernalia from around the world occupy this *different* museum. It's open Mon.–Sat. 10 A.M.–noon and everyday 1:30–4:30 P.M. Admission is $3 adult, $1.50 child.

For more cultural and scenic suggestions, pick up the excellent *Heartland Manawatu* map and "Tour Guide Heartland Manawatu" pamphlet (they contain everything you need to know about Palmerston North), and a variety of other brochures from the Information Centre in The Square.

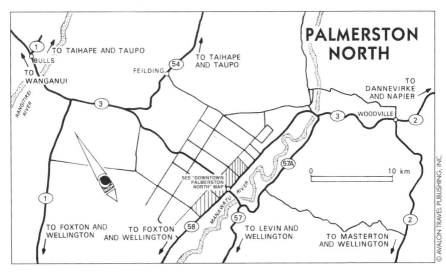

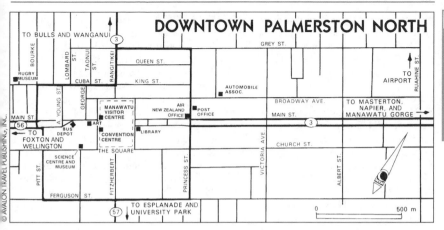

© AVALON TRAVEL PUBLISHING, INC.

Parks

Palmerston North is an attractively laid-out city where the emphasis has been given to shady parks and flower-filled gardens. **The Square,** a six-hectare park in the middle of the city, provides welcome green relief to the busy commercial center. Saunter past perfect lawns, beds of shrubs and flowers, and all sorts of trees, and don't miss the sunken gardens, floral clock, ornamental ponds and fountains, and chiming clock tower. In summer, large numbers of Palmerstonians head for The Square for lunch or afternoon tea, and throughout the year **The Soundshell** and **Open-Air Amphitheatre** host musical performances and public speaking events. (**Palmerston North Information Centre** is on the western side of The Square.)

One of the most popular city parks, **The Esplanade** (a couple of blocks south of The Square—walk down Fitzherbert Ave.) covers 25 hectares of bush and gardens along the banks of the Manawatu River and will appeal to all your senses. It features the **Lido Aquatic Centre** (indoor pool open daily 6 A.M.–9 P.M. Easter through October, outdoor pool open Oct.–April), tel. 06/357-2684, an aviary of native and exotic birds, rose gardens, a tropical plant conservatory, riverside nature trails, and (give your nose a treat) special scented gardens. Drive through the park by entering at Park Road. Within a short walk of The Esplanade (heading east, cross Fitzherbert Ave. onto Centennial Dr.) is **Centennial Lake,** home to a large percentage of the Palmerston duck population, and a good place for a few hours' suntanning in a canoe or paddleboat (available for hire on weekends). For more park, reserve, walkway, beach, and river suggestions, ask at the information center.

> *Massey University is a 35-hectare campus consisting of an intriguing blend of historic homesteads and ultramodern architecture set in superb surroundings.*

South of the River

For terrific views of Palmerston North, the surrounding countryside, and (on a clear day) Mt. Ruapehu to the north and Mt. Egmont/Taranaki to the northwest, take a short drive to **Anzac Park** (about four km south of the city along the southern banks of the river) where there's a lookout and observatory; cross the river at Fitzherbert Bridge and turn left on Cliff Rd. just before the university turnoff. **Massey University,** five km south, is a 35-hectare campus consisting of an intriguing blend of historic homesteads and ultramodern architecture set in superb surroundings; from city center take Fitzherbert St. south, cross the river, and turn right on Tennent Drive. **Bledisloe Park,** on the northern campus boundary, is a quiet place for a bit of reading or a swim in a small woodland stream; it's off Tennent Dr. just before the university entrance.

Entertainment

For dining and live professional theater entertainment, call **Centrepoint Theatre** on the corner of Pitt and Church Streets, tel. 06/354-5740, to see what's playing. A show and coffee costs $28 pp, show and a meal from $42 pp. Go to **Abbey Theatre,** 369-373 Church St., tel. 06/355-4165, for more live theater and the licensed dining area. The **Globe Theatre,** on the corner of Pitt and Main Streets, tel. 06/358-9663, houses a local amateur theater group.

ACCOMMODATIONS

Hotels and Motels

As a transportation hub and major convention city, Palmerston North has a great many hotels and motels, with most lining the main highways into the city. Fitzherbert Ave., south from downtown, holds the most choices.

Many of Palmerston North's old hotels offer convenient, affordable accommodations. The renovated **Shamrock Inn** lies three blocks west of The Square at 267 Main St. W, tel. 06/355-2130, with a restaurant (open for breakfast; $8) and in-house brewery. Each of the 20 rooms is en suite; rates $45 s, $70 d. A couple of doors farther west, the **Masonic Hotel,** 249 Main St. W, tel. 06/358-3480, is similarly priced. On the other side of downtown, the **Empire Establishment,** on the corner of Princess and Main Streets, tel. 06/357-8002, has a handful of rooms, each with a small bathroom; rates $70 s, $75 d.

One block north from The Square, **Consolidated Mid City Motel,** 129 Broadway Ave., tel. 06/357-2184 or 0800/666-400, is a good value. Facilities include a swimming pool, spa, fitness room, and laundry. Rooms are spacious, and each has a kitchen; rates $75 s, $85 d. Farther north lies another of the city's least expensive motels. **Pioneer Motel,** 632 Pioneer Hwy., tel. 06/357-7165 or 0800/274-663, charges

$70 s, $85 d, and has an outdoor swimming pool. The following motels are all on Fitzherbert Avenue: **Kauri Court Motor Lodge,** 248 Fitzherbert Ave., tel. 06/356-6040, has standard rooms, each with a well-equipped kitchen; rates $85 s, $105 d. **Motel Tokyo,** 167 Fitzherbert Ave., tel. 06/356-7074 or 0800/486-596, lies close to The Square; each of the 14 rooms has a kitchen with microwave, and a video player. There's also a pool and garden courtyard. Rates are $95 s, $115 d.

Shadzz Motel and Conference Centre, 145 Fitzherbert Ave., tel. 06/357-9145 or 0800/505-252, website: wwwshadzz.co.nz, is a futuristic-looking, black-and-white motel featuring well-equipped rooms, each with a spa bath, kitchen, and large TV; rates $100–125 s or d.

Backpacker Lodge

For $17–20 pp per night, backpackers can stay in a homey setting at **Peppertree Hostel** (an associate of Hostelling International), 121 Grey St., tel. 06/355-4054. Bright, uncrowded dorm rooms, a well-equipped kitchen, a comfy TV lounge with piano, an outside barbecue area, and off-street parking are all provided in this lodge five blocks north of the The Square.

FOOD

Right by the information center and with a few outdoor tables, **Café Express,** 47 The Square, tel. 06/358-8829, offers good coffee, cakes, and pastries.

Broadway Ave., which runs northeast from The Square, has a number of good casual eateries. One of these, **Bathhouse,** 161 Broadway Ave., tel. 06/355-0051, features a wonderful courtyard filled with ferns and palms and with a retractable roof for sunny days. Most meals are under $15, but no one seems to mind if you just stop by for a snack, such as the corn and kumara chowder ($8). In the vicinity, **Aqaba,** 186 Broadway Ave., tel. 06/357-8922, is easily recognized by its colorful façade. The bold colors continue inside, along with a subtle Egyptian theme. The Aqaba Fry Up ($11) is a good way to start the day. Throughout lunch and dinner, meals are all around $20. It's open Mon.–Fri. from 7:30 A.M. and Sat.–Sun. from 9 A.M.

Sherwood on Featherson, 250 Featherston St., tel. 06/357-0909, has a licensed restaurant open for lunch weekdays, when it offers an all-you-can-eat buffet for only $14 pp. On Sundays, its buffet carvery lunch costs $25, dinner $28; or choose from a variety of à la carte main dishes for $14–24. **Mr. India,** 79 George St., tel. 06/354-5075, has typical Indian decor and softly piped music, and a menu featuring tandoori dishes and several vindaloos. It's open for dinner only. The Irish-style **Celtic Inn,** in the Regent Arcade on Broadway, tel. 06/357-5571, serves pub lunches and dinners starting at just $5, and offers a wide variety of British beers, as well as Guinness; it's open daily 11 A.M.–11:30 P.M., with live music on weekends. **Ambrosia Restaurant** at 149 Rangitikei St., tel. 06/357-5777, is another good place to enjoy dinner (from $12) or a late-night dessert ($10).

The **Cobb & Co.,** in the Empire Establishment at 526 Main St. (corner of Princess St.), tel. 06/357-8002, is always a safe bet ($14–22 average main course at dinner). It's open seven days a week 7:30 A.M.–10 P.M.

Fishermen's Table Restaurant, on the corner of Church St. and Fitzherbert Ave., tel. 06/357-2157, offers a good brunch menu for about $12 pp and dinners $18–27. It's open daily 11:30 A.M.–2 P.M. for lunch, Sun.–Thurs. for dinner 5–9 P.M., Friday and Saturday for dinner 5–10 P.M.

TRANSPORTATION
Getting There
Palmerston North's **Milson Airport** is about five km north of the city center—the only way to get out there other than by car is by taxi; it's about $12 each way. **Air New Zealand** has direct flights from Palmerston North to Auckland, Wellington, and Christchurch. Air New Zealand's Travelcentre is at 30 Broadway, tel. 06/351-8800.

Palmerston North is on the main north-south railway line (Auckland to Wellington), and on the eastern Wellington to Napier/Gisborne line. The **railway station** is off Tremaine Ave.; take Rangitikei St. north from The Square, turn left on Tremaine Ave., pass Coronation Park on the right, and turn right at the next street. The Northerner and Overlander run north to Auckland and south to Wellington daily. On weekdays only, a direct rail service connects Palmerston North with Woodville, Masterton, and Wellington. Book rail travel through the information center, or call Tranz Scenic at 0800/802-802.

Both **Intercity,** tel. 06/354-6155, and **Newmans,** tel. 06/357-7079, provide the city with regular service from all over the North Island, with many runs requiring a bus change in nearby Bulls for a connection into the city. The main depot is the Palmerston North Travel Centre, on the corner of Pitt and Main Streets.

Getting Around
Local **buses** depart from Postbank on Main St. on the corner of The Square.

Car-rental companies in Palmerston North include **Avis,** tel. 06/358-4284; **Budget,** tel. 06/358-1575; **Hertz,** tel. 06/357-0921; and **NZ Rent-a-car,** tel. 06/358-9586.

For a cab, call **Manawatu Taxi Services,** tel. 06/355-5111, or **Palmerston North Taxi Society,** tel. 06/351-0800.

SERVICES AND INFORMATION
Services
The main **city shopping areas** are **The Plaza** in The Square (opposite McDonald's) and the **Downtown Shopping Complex** on Broadway. You'll find suburban shopping centers at Hokowhitu, Highbury, Terrace End, Awapuni, and Milson. **New Zealand Post** is at 338 Church Street. **Palmerston North City Library** is on The Square and Main St., tel. 06/351-4100. **Sunshine Super Laundry** at 392 Ferguson St., tel. 06/358-6719, is open seven days a week; do your own or have it done for you. A same-day dry-cleaning service is also available.

Palmerston North Hospital is on Ruahine St., tel. 06/356-9169. **Victoria Medical Centre** is at 482 Church St., tel. 06/952-5560. An **urgent pharmacy** is on the corner of Main and Ruahine Streets, tel. 06/358-8287; it's open until at least 9 P.M. The main **police station** is at 351 Church St., tel. 06/351-3600.

Information

The source of all the Palmerston North information you need is the excellent **Manawatu Visitor Centre** in The Square, opposite the main entrance of the Civic Centre, tel. 06/354-6593; it's open Mon.–Fri. 8:30 A.M.–5 P.M., Sat.–Sun. 9 A.M.–5 P.M. Pick up a city map, tourist pamphlets and papers, Telecom phonecards, and the handy *Palmerston North: Your Personal Guide,* which has lots of handy information and a good city map. Other main sources of maps are the DOC **Palmerston North Area Office,** 717

Tremaine Ave., tel. 06/358-9004; and the **Automobile Association,** 185 Broadway Ave., tel. 06/357-7039.

TWO ROUTES TO WELLINGTON

Two main routes south connect Palmerston North to Wellington, with public transportation on both. If you have your own wheels, many spots along each route await further exploration. The most direct route is via Hwy. 1 through Levin and along the scenic Kapiti Coast. However, if you have time and want to get off the main road to explore the relatively undeveloped Wairarapa area, take the inland route via Hwy. 2.

The Wairarapa

PALMERSTON NORTH TO MASTERTON

From Palmerston North, Hwy. 3 makes a wide loop to the northeast through a low area of land between the Ruahine and Tararua Ranges before linking up with Hwy. 2, which continues south from Napier to Masterton and Wellington.

Tui Brewery

This historic brewery lies in the small village of Mangatainoka, 36 km from Palmerston North. Established in 1889, Tui grew to become one of New Zealand's most successful small-town breweries. Brewing giant DB Breweries bought it in 1969, but the beer remains the same, with its distinctive taste (East Indian Pale Ale is the best known) and packaging. Tours are offered Mon.–Fri. by appointment, tel. 06/376-7549. The brewery is hard to miss; it's beside a seven-story brick tower that was once part of the brewery.

Continuing south, in Eketahuna, the **Hotel Eketahuna,** tel. 06/375-8126, has Tui on tap and serves inexpensive bar meals.

Mount Bruce National Wildlife Centre

About 85 km south of Palmerston North and 35 km north of Masterton is an excellent native bird reserve, tel. 06/375-8004, on the outskirts of beauti-

ful **Mount Bruce State Forest.** Walk through the forest past gigantic cages cleverly constructed around trees and shrubs, and if you look hard and long enough, you'll spot all kinds of native birds, including some of New Zealand's rare and endangered birds (each cage has identifying pictures and characteristics of the birds inside). If you enjoy birdsong your ears will be in seventh heaven. The purpose of the sanctuary is to protect the rare, study and breed the endangered, and liberate the successfully bred into appropriate habitats in the wild. The complex features a large visitor center with many outstanding displays on New Zealand wildlife; also a theater showing videos, a nocturnal house, a crafts shop, and tearooms. Admission is $8 adult, $3 child, $16 family. It's open daily 9 A.M.–4:30 P.M.

MASTERTON

Masterton (population 20,000) is the largest town along the inland route between Palmerston North and Wellington. It's best known for its sheepshearing competition, but also makes a good place for an overnight stop or as a base for exploring the east coast.

Sights

The highlight of Masterton is beautiful **Queen Elizabeth II Park** on Dixon Street. Take the time to explore all the nooks and crannies of this well-established park. There's a pond and stream where you can rent large tricycle boats and duel with ducks for water space, an aviary, a sunken garden, an aquarium, miniature train rides, and a long, bouncy suspension bridge that leads over the river to a large deer park—pick long, dark-green grass on the outside of the pen and you'll soon have quite a (deer) following. If you enjoy browsing for arts and crafts, children's wooden toys, pottery, willow baskets, jewelry, wood carvings, or dried flowers, or just enjoy chatting with friendly locals, wander along Queen St., which is lined with arty shops open seven days a week.

Golden Shears

What began back in the 1950s as a small exhibition at the Masterton Agricultural and Pastoral Show has grown into one of world's premier sheepshearing competitions, known as the Golden Shears. Competitors from around the world compete in various events over fours days in early March, strutting their stuff on a massive stage. The best seats are sold a year in advance, with latecomers watching the action on a big-screen TV. For information, call 06/378-8008.

Accommodations

South Park Motel, 55 High St., tel. 06/378-2340, features 12 spacious rooms, each with a kitchen; rates range $85–120 s or d. **Solway Park Hotel,** High St., tel. 06/370-0500 or 0800/765-929, has more than 100 rooms and a huge range of sporting facilities, including indoor and outdoor pools, squash courts, tennis, a driving range, a game room, and even a jogging track. Part of the complex is a Cobb & Co Restaurant, a casual café, and a bar. Rates start at $107 s or d, or pay $120 s or d for a much larger room in the new wing.

Stay at the attractive, sheltered **Mawley Park Motor Camp,** Oxford St., tel. 06/378-6454, on the bank of Waipoua River (good river swimming)—it's a very friendly camp where you're bound to meet many vacationing New Zealanders, especially if you're traveling as a family. Features include communal facilities, and game and TV room. Tent sites are $16 s or d, caravan sites are $18, and cabins start at $38.

Food

For good bistro meals ($8–14) seven days a week from 5 P.M., head for **Burridge's Cafe,** in the Golden Shears Tavern on Queen St., tel. 06/377-1107. A popular watering spot with the locals (Burridge's Beer is brewed here), the pub's outdoor verandah (upstairs) is the perfect spot in summer to relax with a cold beer. For above-average motel dining, head to the **Lodge Restaurant** in the Masterton Motor Lodge, High St., tel. 06/378-2800, and enjoy dishes such as seared venison with pumpkin and nutmeg risotto for $26. It's open daily from 6:30 P.M. for dinner.

Information

Tourism Wairarapa Visitor Information Centre, 5 Dixon St., tel. 06/378-7373, is along the main road through town. If you plan to head out to the remote east coast or tour the Martinborough vineyards, this is the place to stock up on information. It's open Mon.–Fri. 9 A.M.–5 P.M., Sat.–Sun. 10 A.M.–4 P.M.

SOUTH FROM MASTERTON

Waiohine Gorge

If you've plenty of time to explore scenic countryside, want good bush hiking, or are looking for your own special swimming hole or trout-fishing spot, the Waiohine Valley and Gorge just southwest of Carterton is a little piece of heaven on earth—in summer that is; in winter or during a bad storm the upper section of the road may be flooded in several places. South of Carterton, turn right on Dalefield Rd. (also signposted to Tararua Forest Park)—if you cross the Waiohine River by the highway, you've missed your turnoff. From Dalefield Rd. turn right on Moffats Rd., then left on Josephs Rd., which becomes Waiohine Gorge Road.

The scenery all through the valley is glorious—lush green fields, good-looking sheep, crystal-clear wide Waiohine River and, farther along, the densely forested mountains of the Tararua Range on each side of the gorge. Along the road are several steep access tracks down to the deeper swimming holes in the river (and the water is *cold!*), a campground, the Waiohine Shelter, and another shelter complete with rainwater tank and raised sleeping platform. Trails lead off into the bush in all directions. A parking lot surrounded by beautiful forest lies at the end of the road, and the natural swimming holes in the river attract a lot of local kids lucky enough to own cars that can make it that far.

Continuing South to Martinborough

On passing through **Greytown,** once the center of the Wairarapa region, don't miss **Cobblestones Museum,** 169 Main St., tel. 06/304-9687. This early settlers' museum, once the site where Cobb & Co. coaches used to wait, has all sorts of antique agricultural machinery and coach equipment outside, and a well-deserved reputation as the most interesting museum in "these 'ere parts"; it's open daily 9 A.M.–4:30 P.M., admission $2 adult, $.50 child, $5 family. For another scenic ramble off the main highway, take the road just south of Greytown to Morrisons Bush, then follow the signs to the quaint town of Martinborough (but don't try this detour without a detailed map). The scenery all along the route is flat farmland (a rainbow of color in the late afternoon and early evening), and the road crosses the meandering Ruamahanga River just before entering the wide verandah-lined street of Martinborough.

Martinborough

This small town lies in the heart of a region that has seen enormous growth in the wine-making industry in recent years. Most of the 16 local wineries are small operations, and the wines are difficult to obtain outside the area. Head to the information center and grab a wine trail map to plan a great day out. The town of Martinborough itself is interesting, with eight streets converging on the town square, laid out as a Union Jack. Downtown, the **Colonial Museum** is open weekends and public holidays 2–4 P.M.; admission is by donation. **Hau Nui Wind Farm,** 21 km southeast of Martinborough toward Whiterock, comprises seven wind turbines strung along a high

ridge. Prevailing westerly winds averaging 35 km per hour help generate enough electricity to power about 2,000 local houses.

Martinborough Hotel, The Square, tel. 06/306-9350, website: www.martinborough-hotel.co.nz, has been extensively restored since its glory days of the late 1890s, with 16 rooms set around a flower-filled courtyard. Each is decorated in colonial style and opens to either a balcony or the courtyard. Downstairs you'll find a bar and a bistro. Rates range $240–260 s or d.

Martinborough Visitor Information Centre, 18 Kitchener St., tel. 06/306-9043, is open daily 10 A.M.–4 P.M.

To Cape Palliser

Cape Palliser, the southernmost tip of the North Island, is accessible by road from Martinborough, with many interesting stops along the way. The first is **Lake Onoke,** where the waters of the Tauherenikau River and shallow **Lake Wairarapa** (known for good fishing and boating) run out into **Palliser Bay.** On the lake's eastern shore is the seaside resort of **Lake Ferry** (about 60 km south of Martinborough), which attracts quite a crowd in summer. **Lake Ferry Holiday Park** is situated on the shores of Lake Onoke, tel. 06/307-7873. The ocean beach drops off steeply, and dangerous rips make the rugged shores of Palliser Bay an unappealing place to swim, but the swampy shores and mudflats of Lake Onoke are a bird-watcher's paradise, and good surf casting from the beach keeps anglers happy.

Inland from Palliser Bay on the way to Lake Ferry, Cape Palliser Rd. branches east. The first settlement along the road is Whangaimoana, which is made up of a cluster of colorful seaside baches (holiday cottages). About 12 km farther along this road lie the fantastic gray vertical rock pillars and intriguingly shaped cliffs of **Putangirua Pinnacles.** The 1,000-year-old eroded rock hoodoos are 30 minutes' walk from the head of the Putangirua Stream. After returning to the road, continue the drive around

> *Most of the 16 local wineries are small operations, and the wines are difficult to obtain outside the area. Head to the information center and grab a wine trail map to plan a great day out.*

the bay to **Te Kopi** and **Ngawihi,** where beaches cling to the rugged oceanfront, and tractors and boats litter the beaches. At the latter village there's a small café, and four km beyond, a massive slab of sandstone is filled with fossilized seashells. At the end of Cape Palliser Rd. is a **lighthouse** and a fairly large **seal colony.** The seals drag themselves out of the ocean on stormy days and rest in the long grass. An **underwater wreck** also attracts divers to these waters.

Kaitoke

After rejoining Hwy. 2 at Featherston and before continuing south, stop at the **Fell Engine Museum,** tel. 06/308-9379 (if it's between 10 A.M. and 4 P.M. on a weekend). It houses the last remaining Fell steam engine in the world, beautifully restored by a group of enthusiasts—the engines were used to haul passenger trains over the rugged and steep Rimutaka Range to Wellington. You'll also find the last place for a bit of bush hiking in **Kaitoke Regional Park** or **Tararua Forest Park** around the small town of Kaitoke, before becoming submerged in the sprawl of suburbia.

THE HUTT VALLEY AND VICINITY

The Hutt River valley lies hemmed in by the **Kapiti** and **Porirua** coasts to the west, the impressive **Rimutaka Range** to the east, the **Tararua Range** to the north, and the bay of **Port Nicholson** (Wellington Harbour) to the south. Although often referred to as the dormitory suburbs of Wellington, **Upper Hutt,** 32 km north of Wellington, and **Lower Hutt,** 14 km north, are cities in their own right, with a large percentage of the population engaged in either in-town manufacturing industries (biscuits, leather goods, motor vehicles, glass, plastics, electronics, to name but a few) or research work (large units of the Department of Scientific and Industrial Research are based here, along with a soil bureau and a nuclear reactor). They *were* originally spillover residential areas for Wellington, but have now grown into important industrial and commercial cities of their own.

The residents obviously take pride in the appearance of their inner cities, attractively laid out and abloom with summer flowers and flowering trees and shrubs. If you're passing through Lower Hutt, feed your soul at the beautiful **Tutukiwi Orchid and Fern House** downtown (corner of Laings Rd. and Myrtle St., by the fountain). It's open weekdays 10 A.M.–4 P.M., weekends and public holidays 1–4 P.M.; admission is free. Another place to browse is the **Dowse Art Museum** at 45 Laings Rd., tel. 04/570-6500; it's open daily 10 A.M.–4 P.M., Sat.–Sun. 11 A.M.–5 P.M., and admission is free. It also has a cafe.

If you'd rather stay in the Hutt Valley than battle your way into Wellington, the excellent **Hutt Park Holiday Village** at 95 Hutt Park Rd., Lower Hutt, tel. 04/568-5913 or 0800/488-872, website: www.huttpark.co.nz, is the last motor camp before you enter the capital city (it's 13 km from downtown Wellington). The office is open daily 8 A.M.–8 P.M.—pick up all the handy free information on Lower and Upper Hutt, including the several-page Lower Hutt restaurant guide and a guide to recreation. The camp offers all the usual facilities (everything spotlessly clean), in immaculate grounds—and ducks to feed in the morning. Tent sites are $20 d, caravan sites $22 d; cabins start at $36 d, tourist cabins $40–44 d, tourist flats $66, motel rooms $85.

The main north-south railway line runs through both Upper and Lower Hutt, and both are well served by bus companies. Pick up the *Cityline Hutt Valley Times & Routes* guide, map, and timetables from the information center or from Hutt Park Holiday Village.

Rimutaka Forest Park

If you're not quite ready to enter Wellington, take a sidetrack from Lower Hutt up over the hill (great views of the Hutt Valley, Wellington, and the harbor) to **Wainuiomata,** a suburb of Lower Hutt. Continue along Coast Rd. to scenic **Catchpool Valley,** part of Rimutaka Forest Park, where many short walks range from 30 minutes to two hours. There's safe swimming in the surrounding streams, and a campground. Stop at the information center on Catchpool Rd. (off Coast Rd.) about nine km from Wainuiomata, and pick up park brochures. Longer hikes go to **Mount Matthews** (940 meters) and along the **Orongorongo River** (about two hours one way)—track brochures and maps are available at the information center.

Turakirae Head

Got to see what's at the end of the road? Continue toward Turakirae Head and the **Turakirae Head Scientific Reserve**—the road ends at a parking lot. From here it's a three-km walk along a private road that crosses the Orongorongo River bridge and runs along the shores of Cook Strait to the reserve. Earthquakes during the last 7,000 years (the last in 1855) raised a sequence of five beaches; platforms of large boulders separate the ridges. Amongst the dense scrub and swamp vegetation and along the beaches grow all sorts of unusual flora (for the region) such as wild spaniards, a native viola, eyebright, and bamboo orchids. On the beach terraces one km farther along the cape lies a remnant of the *karaka* forest that once covered the area. The cape is particularly interesting in winter; up to 500 New Zealand fur seals colonize the point, getting into shape for the summer breeding season, when they leave for the south of the South Island. You'll also see various kinds of lizards, black-backed gulls, gannets, spur-winged plovers, swallows, yellowhammers, chaffinches, and starlings in the reserve.

The Coastal Route to Wellington

The most direct route south from Palmerston North is Hwy. 57 west to Levin, then Hwy. 1 down the gently curved sandy beaches of the Kapiti Coast to the harbourside suburb of Porirua and on into Wellington.

Levin ✓

This town sits on the fertile Horowhenua Plain, which stretches from the foothills of the rugged Tararua Range to the Tasman Sea. The lush scenic area is the second-largest vegetable producer in the country, but is best known for its kiwifruit, berries, apples, and cut flowers. The roads at the south end of town are lined with stands selling fruit and veggies in season; quite a few of the gardens and orchards have pick-your-own specials—fun, delicious, and economical.

✱ Otaki   *Brown Sugar Cafe (lunch)*

A well-populated Maori area before European settlement in 1840, Otaki has a Maori church that shouldn't be missed. The **Rangiatea Maori Church** on Te Rauparaha St. was built in 1849. Plainer than most on the outside, its interior is beautifully decorated with red *totara* slabs and intricately designed *tukutuku* panels representing the stars in heaven; it's open daily 8 A.M.–sunset. Farther along the street is **Otaki Maori Mission** with a church and buildings from the early 19th century, and memorials and graves of early missionaries. The **Otaki Museum,** containing Maori artifacts and relics from the pioneering days, is at Hyde Park Craft Village, about five km south of Otaki on Hwy. 1. Get information on the Otaki area and Kapiti Coast at the **Kapiti Coast Visitor Information Centre** at the railway station on Hwy. 1, tel. 06/364-7620; it's open seven days, weekdays 7 A.M.–7 P.M. and weekends 10 A.M.–4:30 P.M. Access to marked **hiking trails** in the Tararua Range is easy from Otaki if you have your own transportation. Head south out of town, cross the Otaki River, and turn left onto Otaki Gorge Rd., following it to the end. The seaside resort of **Otaki Beach,** patrolled in summer, has several motor camps adjacent to the beach.

THE KAPITI COAST

The Kapiti Coast stretches from Waikanae in the north (about 58 km from Wellington) to Paekakariki in the south, and includes the offshore islands of Kapiti (a wildlife sanctuary), Tokomapua, Motungarara, and Tohoramaurea. The largest town and administrative center along this stretch is Paraparaumu. Lying between the mountains of the Tararua Range and endless kilometers of golden sandy beaches littered with shells (within an hour's drive of Wellington and easily reached by train from the capital), the coastal towns naturally attract large numbers of vacationing Wellingtonians, backcountry hikers, beach bums, and a large retirement community.

Waikanae Beach

This long, flat beach is backed by sand dunes and sheltered by offshore Kapiti Island. At the northern end of Waikanae Beach lies the wreck of the fishing trawler *Phyllis,* and if you continue north you'll come to **Peka Peka Beach** with good surf casting and a refreshing lack of commercial development. The **Waikanae River Estuary** (a reserve attracting more bird species than anywhere else on the Wellington coast), **Waimanu Marina,** and **Waimanu Lagoon** lie at the southern end of Waikanae Beach.

In the old post office is **Kapiti Coast Museum,** 7 Elizabeth St., tel. 06/293-2359, chockfull of local memorabilia telling the story of the coast's colorful past.

Wildlife Reserves and Bush Walks

Nga Manu Nature Reserve, tel. 04/293-4131, hosts more than 50 species of native birds in 10 hectares of native bush and swamp, but the main interest is breeding the once-common redcrowned parakeet. Take a short bird-spotting walk through the bush, past the aviaries and ponds and through the fernery, arboretum, and gardens. It's open daily 10 A.M.–5 P.M.; you'll pay a small admission charge. From the main highway at Waikanae, turn right on Te Moana Rd. just past the shopping center, then right on Ngarara Rd. (passing Waikanae Pool, cemetery, and riding school), then right again on the access road to the sanctuary. For a longer bush walk or hike through a beautiful bird-filled *kohekohe* forest with great views of Kapiti and the west coast, head east of Waikanae (a short walk from Waikanae shopping center) to the **Hemi Matenga Memorial Park Scenic Reserve** in the foothills of the Tararuas. The "walk" takes 30 minutes round-trip and the "track" takes three hours round-trip.

Mangaone Track

Part of the New Zealand Walkway network, the Mangaone Track is a fern-lover's delight (more than 50 species have been identified along the route). It runs along the western foothills of the Tararua Range east of Waikanae, fords several streams along the way (expect to get wet feet), and runs through **Kaitawa Scenic Reserve.** Start at either the end of Mangaone South Rd. (eight km east of Waikanae via Reikorangi, signposted from the main road) or at the end of Mangaone North Rd. (six km east of Te Horo); it's eight km and three hours one way—arrange transportation at the far end or retrace the track.

Paraparaumu

Paraparaumu is the main center on the Kapiti Coast: several motor camps; plenty of coffee lounges, take-aways, and restaurants; and a main shopping center. If you plan to stay any length of time, your first stop should be the **Paraparaumu Information Centre** in the Coastlands Shopping Centre parking lot (watch out for "trundlers"—a.k.a. shopping carts), tel. 04/298-8195; it's open Mon.–Sat. 9:30 A.M.–3:30 P.M. Pick up maps of all the coastal towns, brochures on what to see and do, walking track brochures and maps, and restaurant and entertainment guides. Anyone interested in vintage cars should stop at the **Southward Car Museum** on Otaihanga Rd. (off Hwy. 1), tel. 04/297-1221, and check out the 250-car collection which includes Bugattis, a de Lorean, and Cadillacs with famous past owners; it's open daily 9 A.M.–5:30 P.M., admission $5 adult, and $2.50 child.

Kapiti Island

One of the pleasurable things to do here is take a day visit to Kapiti Island, which lies just offshore. Originally a stronghold of Maori Chief Te Rauparaha, the island became a whaling base, then an official bird sanctuary. Permits for landing on the island are issued by the DOC in Wellington: 2nd Floor, Bowen State Building, Bowen St., tel. 06/472-5821. The permit costs $30 per group, but you can also head down to Paraparaumu Beach in the morning and hope there's a no-show. The island is closed Monday and Tuesday. The DOC also has a list of operators running out to the island, as does the Paraparaumu Information Centre, tel. 04/298-8195.

Paekakariki

Paekakariki (Hill of the Parakeet), affectionately shortened to Paekak (sounds like Piecok) by the locals, has a good sandy beach patrolled in summer—a treasure strip for avid shell collectors—and safe swimming. The other main attractions are the attractive 638-hectare **Queen Elizabeth II Park** (yes, *another* QE Park) which runs along the coast; two Maori *pa;* a **Tramway Museum,** tel. 06/292-8561, providing vintage tram rides ($5 adult, $2 child) from the Memorial Gates at McKays Crossing to the beach on weekends and public holidays 11 A.M.–5 P.M.; and some old campsites of American Marine camps from World War II. For extensive views of the Kapiti Coast, Kapiti Island, and the South Island on a clear day, head up Paekakariki Hill Rd. (left off Hwy. 1 heading south) to **Summit Viewpoint.** Traveling between Wellington and Paekakariki is a snap by train—a main line ends at Paekakariki and a ticket costs only a few dollars.

Paekakariki Backpackers, 11 Wellington Rd., tel. 06/292-8749, sits atop a high ridge, with the small village of Paekakariki on one side and the Tasman Sea on the other. It's one of the better lodges you'll come across in your New Zealand travels, and its proximity to the capi-

tal, 40 km south, makes it an ideal base. Guests are greeted with a hot drink upon arrival, with the hosts explaining everything the area has to offer. The dining/lounge area overlooks the ocean, and no room has more than four beds. Dorms are $19 pp, doubles are $21 pp.

If you're not in the mood to cook, try **Fisherman's Table,** overlooking the Tasman Sea two km south of Paekakariki, tel. 06/292-8125. The menu is extensive, but most diners are attracted to the $14 two-course special. **Paekakariki Cafe** on Wellington Rd., tel. 06/292-8860, and **Paekakariki Hotel** on Beach Rd., tel. 06/292-8123, are other local choices.

Colonial Knob Walk

Another New Zealand Walkway, Colonial Knob Walk climbs the bush- and farmland-covered hills along the coast west of Porirua and Tawa, passes through two scenic reserves containing some of the last remaining native forest in this area, and reaches the summit of Colonial Knob (468 meters) for one of the most spectacular views of the offshore islands, Wellington peninsula, Cook Strait, and the South Island. The 7.5-km track is pretty steep in places and the upper section is exposed to the wind; it takes five to six hours round-trip. Start at either the Broken Hill entrance to Colonial Knob Scenic Reserve, or at Elsdon Youth Camp, Raiha St., Porirua. Porirua town is mainly a suburb of Wellington—continue on down to the big city!

Wellington

Introduction

Wonderful, windy Wellington, scenic capital of New Zealand and "City of a Thousand Views," perches on the edge of Cook Strait in the southwest corner of the North Island. Hemmed in by the Tararua Range to the north and the Rimutaka Range to the east, the city spills up and down bush-covered hills around the large sparkling bay of Port Nicholson. Colorful, cosmopolitan, exciting—Wellington is fun to explore whether you thrive in the great outdoors or in little seaside cafés. Sandy beaches, sheltered coves, rocky outcrops, and boat-filled marinas line Wellington Harbour, where the water is always a bright, bright blue dotted with multicolored sails. Imposing Parliament buildings, old and new,

and modern skyscrapers dominate Wellington's center, in contrast to historic pioneer homes and elegant mansions that line the steep and narrow streets of the older suburbs. Scattered throughout the city are flower-filled gardens and shady parks that provide a quiet escape from the continuous hum and bustle of the busy commercial center.

History

According to the Maori, Wellington Harbour was first discovered in ancient times by the Polynesian navigators, Kupe and Ngahue, and it wasn't until the early 19th century that Europeans first sailed all the way into the magnificent harbor (Captain Cook missed the harbor entrance on his 1770 expedition but sailed through the heads in1773). In 1826 Capt. James Herd entered in

Wellington Harbour

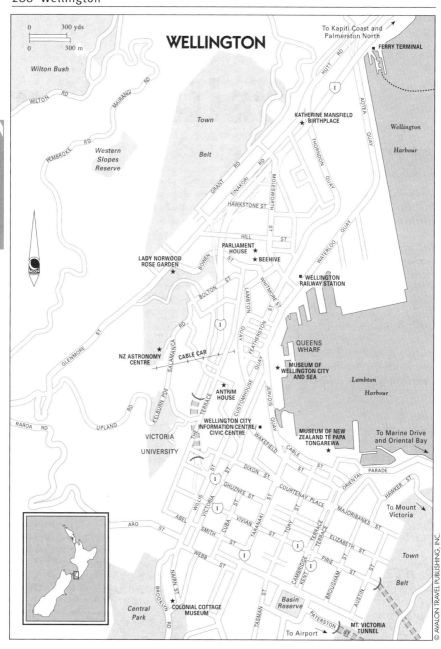

WELLINGTON

Wellington sprawls around a magnificent natural harbor.

arrived on January 22, 1840, nowadays celebrated as a holiday throughout the region. In 1865, after much argument from Aucklanders, Wellington was chosen as New Zealand's official capital because of its central location, natural harbor, and population growth—the city became the seat of government, the harbor flourished, and banks, insurance companies, traders, and stock and land agents moved to the capital. Today, Wellington is New Zealand's second-largest city, with an urban area population of 335,000.

Climate

Tell anyone you're going to Wellington and you're more than likely to hear horror stories about the weather—non-Wellingtonians seem to enjoy the capital city's bad reputation, rubbing it in any chance they get. Wellington's weather could best be described as . . . changeable. On just about any day of the year you can get bright sunshine, a sudden downpour, fog, and almost always wind. The wind, which howls in through Cook Strait, batters the city with everything from sea breezes (most days) to Antarctic gales (not too often), but no matter what the weather, there's always a scenic viewpoint, sandy beach, exotic restaurant, or snug reading nook to be found. Take a windbreaker, raincoat, and umbrella (*everyone* in Wellington has an umbrella) and you'll be ready to tackle Wellington's sights *and* elements!

his barque *Rosanna,* landed, and officially named the harbor Port Nicholson—the name by which it's still known today. The New Zealand Company bought the land that was to become Wellington City from the Maori in 1839, and the first settlers

Sights and Recreation

DOWNTOWN SIGHTS

Civic Centre

The first place to visit in the Civic Centre is the **Wellington City Information Centre.** It's on the corner of Wakefield and Victoria Streets (enter from the square), tel. 04/801-4000 and is open seven days a week 8:30 A.M.–5:30 P.M. Get all your questions answered by the excellent staff, and load up with free brochures, a tourist newspaper, and a city map before you start exploration of the city.

The Civic Centre is a good spot to wander on the weekend when it's fairly quiet. **City Art Gallery** has a distinct character of its own, regularly featuring all sorts of fascinating modern art exhibitions; it's open daily 11 A.M.–3 P.M., Thursday to 8 P.M. Also visit the impressive **Central Library, Capital E** (a hands-on museum for kids, open daily 10 A.M.–5 P.M. during summer; $8 adult, $6 child), and the modern **Wellington**

© ANDREW HEMPSTEAD

Museum of Wellington City and Sea

Convention Centre (tours daily at 11 A.M. and 2 P.M.; tel. 04/801-4242). Continue toward the waterfront, cross Jervois Quay, and head for **Frank Kitts Park**—a peaceful retreat with good harbor views and an excellent children's playground with ball-bearing-fast slides (if you're traveling with children, don't miss this one). On some Sundays in summer it's the site of an outdoor artists' market.

Museum of Wellington City and Sea

While Te Papa (see below) gets all the attention, this small museum on Queens Wharf, tel. 04/472-8904, is also well worth a visit. Housed in renovated bond store-where goods were held until duty was paid-it tells the story of Wellington's maritime and social history through three levels of well-planned displays. The relics from shipwrecks, ancient maps, sea journals, and old diving gear are particularly interesting. It's open Mon.–Fri. 10 A.M.–5 P.M., weekends 10 A.M.–5:30 P.M.; $5 adult, $2.50 child.

Museum of New Zealand Te Papa Tongarewa

Continuing around the harbourfront from Queens Wharf, you can't miss New Zealand's five-story national museum on Cable St., tel. 04/381-7051. Opened in February 1998, it rates as one of the world's finest national museums, and best of all, admission is free. It's impossible to get around the museum's 36,000 square meters of gallery in less than three hours, and a full day can easily be spent inside. It's open daily 9 A.M.–6 P.M. (Thursday until 9 P.M.).

The complete history of New Zealand comes alive through a massive Maori exhibit, which tells the story of this intriguing race who arrived in New Zealand from Polynesia at least 1,000 years ago. Other exhibits include relics and engravings from Captain Cook's voyage; New Zealand's natural history, which includes interactive displays that explain the volcanic nature of the land; European settlement; a number of art galleries showcasing all media; and a

© ANDREW HEMPSTEAD

WELLINGTON

The Parliamentary Library is housed in a distinctive neo-gothic building.

simulator that takes visitors on a stunning historic journey through to the thrills of today's adventure sports. The museum is bordered on two sides by Bush City, which contains thousands of New Zealand native plants, with paths leading past ponds over a swing bridge above a stream, past a waterfall, and around a lagoon. A lava flow, limestone cave, and rock-embedded fossils have also been re-created in this outdoor section of the museum.

Parliament House and the Beehive

Three totally different styles of architecture add interest to the Parliament buildings on Molesworth St. (north of the Civic Centre). The oldest of the three is a Gothic-style stone building housing the General Assembly Library; the middle building—brick, granite, and marble—houses the House of Representatives; the most modern, an 11-story circular building aptly called The Beehive, houses the ministers, their staff, and the cabinet room. Free tours are conducted Mon.–Fri. on the hour (except when Parliament is in session) from the main reception desk between 10 A.M. and 4 P.M. If you're visiting in the afternoon and a session is on (generally Tues.–Thurs.), go up to the Gallery of the Debating Chamber and see what's happening. Tours are also offered on weekends, but the times change according to what's on the agenda—double-check session and tour times at 04/471-9999.

Historic Houses

Antrim House, 63 Boulcott St., west of the Civic Centre, tel. 04/472-4341, is the headquarters of the New Zealand Historic Places Trust; go there for information if you'd like to visit any of the many historic homes and buildings scattered around Wellington. The mansion itself is one of the best preserved large townhouses of the Edwardian period, with its elegant exterior and kauri-paneled interior; the grounds and a section of the house are open to the public on weekdays 8 A.M.–5 P.M.

Katherine Mansfield, New Zealand's best-known author, was born in a house built by her father in the historic suburb of Thorndon. The house has been lovingly restored and the garden replanted, as described by Mansfield in her book *Prelude.* Exhibits include an audiovisual program and photos from the era. **Katherine Mansfield Birthplace** is at 25 Tinakori Rd., tel. 04/473-7268. It's open daily 10 A.M.–4 P.M.; $5 adult, $2 child.

BOTANIC GARDEN AND VICINITY

On a high ridge above downtown is a sprawling botanic garden and university campus. It's possible to drive or take a bus to the garden, but catching the cable car from downtown is the most popular way to get there.

Wellington Cable Car

An excellent way to get acquainted with (and fall for) the city is to take the cable car from Cable Car Lane (off Lambton Quay) up the super-steep track to Kelburn Terminal. Three stops (a six-minute journey) along the way allow you to discover Clifton Terrace, Talavera Terrace, and Salamanca Rd., but the view from the top is by far the most spectacular. Also at the top, allow time to stop at the **Wellington Cable Car Museum,** tel. 04/475-3578, to view one of the original cars and lots of old winding gear. It's open daily 9:30 A.M.–5:30 P.M. and admission is free. The cable car operates Mon.–Fri. 7 A.M.–10 P.M. (every 10 minutes), Sat.–Sun. 9 A.M.–10 P.M.; $3 round-trip. For details call 04/472-2199.

Wellington Botanic Garden

This garden stretches for more than 26 hectares over several ridges just west above the city center. Formal rose gardens contrast with wild indigenous areas and exotic tree, flower, and shrub plantations—it's a colorful tiptoe through the tulips while enjoying city views.

At the highest point of the garden is **NZ Astronomy Centre,** tel. 04/472-5053, featuring astronomical displays, videos, and a planetarium. The observatory is open daily 10 A.M.–5 P.M.; $3 adult, $1.50 child. On Tuesday and Saturday evenings it's open from 7:30 P.M. for stargazing (weather permitting); $6 adult, $3 child. Behind the observatory

Wellington Cable Car

try the Sundial of Human Involvement—it is amazingly accurate.

The fabulous **Lady Norwood Rose Garden** (open daily 10 A.M.–5 P.M.) is at the northern end, where thousands of perfumed roses bloom from early November through April (quite intoxicating on a warm summer evening), and where, in spring, masses of bulbs burst into a spectacular floral display. Wander through the garden and discover a waterfall, Begonia House (open 10 A.M.–4 P.M.), Tea House (open 10 A.M.–4 P.M.), Camellia Garden, Sunken Gardens, Interpretive Centre in The Dell (open Mon.–Fri. 9 A.M.–4 P.M., weekends 10 A.M.–4 P.M.), and many lookouts over the city. Get there from downtown by cable car (to Kelburn Terminal), or by a no. 12 bus to the main gates on Glenmore Street. Once you're at the Rose Garden, the easiest way to get back to the city center is down Bolton Street.

Victoria University

Situated high on a hill above the city, not far south of the Botanic Garden, Victoria University's campus commands great city views. Stroll around the well-kept grounds past attractive old ivy-covered buildings, and if you're a rock hound, check out the **Alexander McKay Geological Museum** in the Cotton Building (the lecture block at the top of Kelburn Parade), tel. 04/472-1000, with its comprehensive New Zealand rock, mineral, and fossil display. It's open weekdays 9 A.M.–5 P.M., but closed Dec. 23–Jan. 5. The university's a heavy-breather hike uphill from downtown (attempt it only with a map) but is easily reached by cable car. Get off at the Salamanca Rd. stop and walk south toward Kelburn Parade and the main entrance. By bus, take no. 20 from the railway station.

SIGHTS IN OTHER PARTS OF THE CITY

National Cricket Museum

Fans of cricket, New Zealand's most popular summer team sport, won't want to miss this museum, beneath the Old Stand at the Basin Reserve, tel. 04/385-6602. Displays are mainly centered around cricketing memorabilia related to New Zealand. There's also a cricket bat from 1743—one of the three oldest cricket bats in the world. It's open through the cricket season only (Oct.–April), daily 10:30 A.M.–3:30 P.M. Admission is $3 adult, $1 child.

Colonial Cottage Museum

This attractive two-story house on a steep hill is quite a hike south from city center. Built in 1858 and slowly restored, the typically small rooms, steep staircase, and fine handcraftsmanship throughout this Victorian-era pioneer cottage give insight into life in Wellington's colonial days. The cottage is open in summer, daily noon–4 P.M., the rest of the year, Wed.–Sun. noon–4 P.M.; $4 adult, $2.50 senior, $1.50 child. The address is 68 Nairn St., tel. 04/384-9122. From the Basin Reserve, walk west along Buckle St. to Taranaki St. and turn left. Turn right on Webb St., left on Thompson, right on Hankey, and immediately right on Nairn. The cottage is on the left side. Notice the mixture of assorted architectural styles in this hilly area.

Mount Victoria

The best place for orienting yourself to the layout of Wellington is from the top of Mt. Victoria (194 meters), southeast of the city center. The summit lookout provides a 360-degree panorama and one of the best cityscapes of Wellington (unreal at night), and it's easy to get there by bus (a 15-minute ride from downtown, weekdays only) or car (get a map first). Catch a no. 20 bus at the railway station (every hour Mon.–Fri.), or on Lambton Quay, Willis St., Cuba St., Manners St., or Courtenay Place. If you'd rather walk back down, several paths take at least 20 minutes through the forested town belt and suburb of Mt. Victoria, one of the oldest city suburbs (many colonial-style homes), to Courtenay Place where you can catch the bus back. If you're driving or cycling (guaranteed to get your old heart a-pumpin') from city center, take Jervois Quay south to Wakefield St. and turn left, then right on Kent Terrace and left on Majoribanks Street.

Turn left on Hawker St. and follow the signs to the lookout.

Wellington Zoo

While small, Wellington's zoo, in Newtown Park, four km south of downtown off Adelaide Rd., tel. 04/381-6750, is worth a visit for its nocturnal kiwi house and collection of tuataras. It also holds all the regular zoo animals-from monkeys to tigers. It's open daily 9:30 A.M.–5 P.M.; $9 adult, $4.50 child.

Marine Drive

Thirty-km Marine Drive, "one of the world's best coastal drives" and a route anyone with wheels and a camera shouldn't miss, runs from **Oriental Bay** (southeast of the city center) along the inner harbor and outer shoreline to **Owhiro Bay.** The route takes you past at least 20 small bays and most of Wellington's sheltered sandy **beaches,** past built-up areas where striking homes perch on precarious sites high above the road (cable car systems lead up to some), and through surprisingly wild areas that seem quite uninhab-

ited. The views along the route are stunning on a bright sunny day, but the locals claim that the drive is most spectacular during a southerly storm (preferably a gale). Start at Oriental Bay, an area of coffee shops, fashionable restaurants, and a strip of sandy beach where the younger set, and people-watchers in general, gather in large numbers (particularly in summer) to check each other out—it's a good place to find out the current Wellington trends in fashion, hairstyles, music, and flirting.

From Oriental Bay, Marine Drive is signposted here and there, but it really helps if you have a good, detailed map of the city center and outer suburbs to Cook Strait (and a compass, tent, two days' food ration, water, and flare. . . !). The return route to the city sounds simple enough, but has the potential to become a nightmare without a map—from Owhiro Bay take the road through Happy Valley to the suburb of Brooklyn (about 28 km), turn right on Brooklyn Rd., go down the hill and straight ahead onto Upper Willis St., and continue straight into the city center.

© ANDREW HEMPSTEAD

Marine Drive winds its way through suburban Wellington to the coast.

WELLINGTON WALKS

City

Several city walkway routes, devised by the Parks and Recreation Department, encourage walking through some of the most attractive areas of the "Harbour City." Pick up a city street map, the various brochures ("Northern Walkway," "Southern Walkway," and more) containing route descriptions and maps, a "Walking Around Wellington" pamphlet, and a "Discover Wellington" brochure, which contains scenic driving and walking routes; all are usually available at the Information Centre.

The **Otari Native Botanical Garden** is a must-walk attraction, less than 20 minutes by bus west of the city center. Several walkways, graded and color-coded according to length and difficulty, run through this unique sanctuary "devoted solely to the cultivation and preservation of indigenous New Zealand plants." Eighty hectares of native bush and five hectares of cultivated garden contain more than 1,200 plant species, and the area is alive with native birds. Natural forest and cultivated gardens, rock garden and fishpond, fernery, alpine garden, and numerous picnic spots are just some of the features along the various trails. You'll often spot native wood pigeons, fantails, silvereyes, and kingfishers, along with introduced magpies, thrushes, goldfinches, and starlings; the beautiful native songbird, the *tui,* is often heard but rarely seen. To get there take a no. 14 Wilton bus from the city to the main entrance at the junction of Wilton Rd. and Gloucester St.; it's open daily from dawn to dusk—to get the best out of your visit, take a picnic lunch.

Red Rocks Coastal Walk and Sinclair Head Seal Colony

Red Rocks Walk begins south of the city center at Owhiro Bay. Although an enjoyable walk year-round, it is perhaps the most rewarding from April to early October when a colony of up to 100 New Zealand fur seals makes a rocky headland along the route its home. The seals migrate north from sub-Antarctic rookeries in April and then spend up to six months here recovering from their frantic southern breeding season. Only the bulls come north (the pregnant females stay behind) to feed and sleep (and give off a very distinct odor). They stay until October, when they return south to establish their territories in the rookeries before the pups are born. The walk to the colony and beyond begins from a quarry at Owhiro Bay (take the no. 1 bus to Island Bay and walk along the Esplanade). It is just over four km along a rough gravel road to Sinclair Head, but it's possible to drive (4WD not necessary) the first three km (except on Sunday when the quarry gate is locked). Just before Sinclair Head is an outcrop of red rock formed about 200 million years ago when lava spewed from a volcano and then cooled on contact with water.

Regional

The six-km **Makara Track,** part of the New Zealand Walkways network, starts and finishes at Makara Beach (16 km northwest of Wellington). This popular walk lets hikers experience remote and rugged coastal scenery, fabulous views, hilly farmland, and good swimming at sheltered beaches. The "track" requires good fitness and takes about four hours round-trip; note that the inner section is closed during August and September for lambing. Wear good boots, take warm clothing (you'll be exposed to the wind, and quite possibly blown along the track in places), and carry water—there's nothing drinkable along the route. It's another good place to take a picnic. To get there from Wellington you need your own transportation and a detailed map (the information center provides a free brochure); head for Karori Rd. in the western suburb of Karori West. Take Makara Rd. west and continue to Makara Beach, where the walkway is clearly signposted.

ENTERTAINMENT

Schedules and Information

If you're in the mood for some action, pick up the free tourist paper *Capital Times* or the entertainment weekly *City Voice.* The daily newspapers list all the current movies, and Wellington Visitor Information Centre puts out a very handy "What's on in Wellington, the Harbour Capital" leaflet, which is updated every month; ask the staff what it suggests in the way of entertainment—it's the most reliable and up-to-date source of information around. To find out what annual events and public holiday happenings are going on, pick up the free *Greater Wellington Region Calendar of Events.* It also lists museums and galleries (and their hours), and suggests sightseeing trips by bus, boat, and airplane.

Theater and Dance

The **Circa Theatre** at 1 Taranaki St., tel. 04/801-7992, puts on performances Tuesday and Wednesday nights at 6:30 P.M. and Thurs.–Sun. at 4 P.M. Book through the State Opera House Agency at tel. 04/385-0832, or buy your ticket at the door Tues.–Sat. nights 6:30–8 P.M. or on Sunday afternoon 2:30–4 P.M. Other performance venues to check out are the **Downstage Theatre** on the corner of Cambridge Terrace and Courtenay Place, tel. 04/801-6946; **Taki Rua Productions** at 85 Victoria St., tel. 04/472-7377; **Bats Theatre,** 6 Majoribanks St., tel. 04/802-4175; **Capital E,** Jervois Quay, tel. 04/384-8502, a kids' theater; and the **Wellington Convention Centre** on Wakefield St. in the Civic Centre (there's a ticketing office inside where you can book for all sorts of venues throughout Wellington and the entire country), tel. 04/471-1573. Expect to pay $5–20 for a theater ticket.

Bars and Nightclubs

Bands come and go, as do venues, but some places have live music on a regular basis (good bands fetch a small cover charge). **Chicago Sports Café,** enjoys an excellent location on Queens Wharf, tel. 04/473-4900. Themed as a U.S. sports bar, in addition to screenings of major overseas sporting events, bands play on weekends, and there's a quieter upstairs bar and pleasant courtyard. Around the harbor, the **Backbencher Pub,** 34 Molesworth St., tel. 04/472-3065, is in the heart of the politicians' territory and is especially busy at lunch and early evening.

Bodega, 286 Willis St., tel. 04/384-8212, is a longtime favorite for local bands playing their own music to an alternative crowd. Monday features jazz and there's lots of New Zealand beers on tap. **Tatou,** 22 Cambridge Terrace, tel. 04/384-3112, holds a number of different bars, each appealing to different musical tastes.

Courtenay Place, the entertainment center of the city, has a wide variety of music venues and dance clubs. Check out **Molly Malone's** on the corner of Taranaki St. and Courtenay Place, tel. 04/384-2896. Aside from the decidedly Irish atmosphere, bands play every Thursday, Friday, and Saturday nights, and on Monday and Wednesday nights it's "Irish night," with real Irish bands and no cover charge. The bar is open daily from 11 A.M. and really hops till 1 or 2 A.M. on the weekends. The cavernous **Wellington Sports Café,** 58 Courtenay Place, tel. 04/801-5115, has five huge TV screens showing sports from around the world. The **Big Easy,** 74 Courtenay Place, tel. 04/801-5060, and **Coyote Street Bar,** Courtenay Place, tel. 04/385-6665, both fill with serious dancers strutting their stuff to dance, hip-hop, techno, and progressive music.

Movies

For the latest in film, check out **Embassy Theatre,** 10 Kent Terrace, tel. 04/384-7657; **Hoyts Mid-City Cinemas,** Manners St., tel. 04/384-3567; **Paramount,** 25 Courtenay Place, tel. 04/384-4080; **Penthouse Cinema,** 205 Ohiro Rd., Brooklyn, tel. 04/384-3157; and the Memorial Theatre at **Victoria University,** tel. 04/473-8566.

FESTIVALS AND EVENTS

Every other March (2004, 2006, etc.) Wellington celebrates the **New Zealand Festival,** which is launched with a spectacular harbourfront fireworks display and continues through the month. It features Maori dancing, opera, ballet, theater, comedy, and jazz at open-air and indoor venues throughout the city. A dragonboat festival is also held in conjunction. For information, call 04/384-3840.

Summer City

December through February, Wellington comes alive with its annual festival, Summer City. To find out what's happening where, pick up a brochure from the information center, check out the ads in the local newspapers, listen to the local radio stations, or call Summer City at 04/801-3500. Lunchtime activities take place in the inner-city parks and malls, special day and evening entertainment (live concerts, jazz bands, dancing, country hoedowns, crazy competitions, entertainment for the kids, and much, much more) happens at The Dell (next to the Rose Gardens) in the Botanic Garden. Just before Christmas, Carols by Candlelight sessions spontaneously combust at several locations around town—an enjoyable event on a warm summer's eve.

> *December through February, Wellington comes alive with its annual festival, Summer City. Just before Christmas, Carols by Candlelight sessions spontaneously combust at several locations around town—an enjoyable event on a warm summer's eve.*

Local Holiday

January 22 is the provincial anniversary and annual holiday for the entire Wellington area, including Lower and Upper Hutt. On this day you'll be hard pressed to find *anything* open, so stock up on food, drinks, and essentials beforehand. (When the holiday falls Fri.–Sun. it's usually observed on the following Monday—if it falls Tues.–Thurs. it's observed on the preceding Monday.) No particular events take place—everyone just takes the day off! If you don't need a shop or service, it's a good time to explore Wellington's non-commercial attractions—all the locals seem to take this opportunity to leave town, but you're likely to find fellow travelers wandering vacantly around the inner-city area (hungry and thirsty) trying to figure out why it's closed.

Accommodations

DOWNTOWN HOTELS AND MOTELS

Under $100

The least expensive downtown accommodation is **Trekkers Hotel** on Dunlop Terrace (off Vivian St. or Upper Cuba St.), tel. 04/385-2153, website: www.trekkers.co.nz, with plenty of budget rooms, each with its own hand basin. There's a TV lounge on the ground floor, a spa and sauna, and a house bar. All meals are available in the café or licensed vegetarian restaurant. Rooms with shared bathrooms are $50 s, $58 d, those with private bathrooms are $65 s, $79 d, and motel-style rooms (no cooking facilities) start at $99 s or d.

$100–200

If you plan to do your own cooking and want to be within walking distance of downtown, **Halswell Lodge Motel,** 21 Kent Terrace, tel. 04/385-0196, website: www.halswell.co.nz, offers a number of choices. Fully self-contained motel-style rooms are $120–130 s or d. Behind the main complex, a 1920s villa has been restored and contains eight spacious guest rooms; $145 s or d includes use of a modern kitchen. Halswell also has budget hotel rooms that although small are good value at $75 s, $85 d.

The centrally located **Quality Hotel,** 355 Willis St., tel. 04/385-9819 or 0800/808-228, website: www.qualitywillis.co.nz, has 82 standard hotel rooms for $129.50 s or d. Facilities include an indoor heated pool, a small fitness room, a brasserie open from 6:30 A.M., and a bar open from 5 P.M.

Abel Tasman Hotel, 169 Willis St., tel. 04/385-1304 or 0800/843-827, is an eight-story property right in the heart of the city. The 76 rooms are nothing special, but each has a writing desk, and downstairs is a restaurant; $145–240 s or d (rates are greatly reduced on weekends).

WELLINGTON

Above downtown at 285 Tinakori Rd. is **Shepherds Arms Hotel,** tel. 04/472-1320 or 0800/393-782, website: www.shepherds.co.nz, which has been taking in guests since 1870. Restored by the original owners' descendants, it has 14 guest rooms, some with four-poster beds. It also has a bar and restaurant. Rates start at $75 for a single room with shared bathroom, but the deluxe queen rooms at $140 s, $150 d are the best value. These rooms feature modern timber furnishings, hardwood flooring, and comfortable leather couches.

Mercure Hotel Wellington, 345 The Terrace, tel. 04/385-9829 or 0800/288-880, website: www.accorhotel.co.nz, features 108 refurbished rooms, each with modern decor and some with harbor views. Facilities include an indoor heated pool, business center, fitness room, restaurant, and bar. Rates are $145–280 s or d, which makes the $120 weekend package deal (including breakfast) a great deal.

Central City Apartment Hotel, 130 Victoria St., tel. 04/385-4166 or 0800/804-255, website: www.centralcityhotels.co.nz, is exactly that—very central. Half the rooms have tea- and coffee-making facilities, while the other half have a full kitchen. The rooms all configured differently, with some studios, some one-bedroom suites, and some two-bedroom suites. Rates range $160–200, and start at $110 on weekends.

✸ **Museum Hotel,** 90 Cable St., tel. 04/385-2809, is a low-rise hostelry with harbor views from the top couple of stories. The hotel was originally built where the Te Papa museum now stands. Rather than demolish it to make room for the new museum, a decision was made to move it to a new site, 120 meters away. The move—one of the largest of an entire building ever attempted anywhere in the world—was a success. Along with a new location, the rooms underwent a major refurbishment and now start at $160 s or d. If it's in your budget, consider paying from $200 for a harbor view room.

Over $200

Around the harbor is **Hotel Raffaele,** 360 Oriental Parade, tel. 04/384-3450 or 0800/739-333, website: www.raffaele.co.nz, one of the city's finest accommodations. Luxuriously furnished in a classical Italian style, all 61 rooms have a private balcony with views across the harbor to downtown. The hotel also features a restaurant and bar. It offers a variety of rates. Through the week, a standard room costs $240 s or d. There are also standby rates and a weekend rate of about $140.

HOTELS AND MOTELS IN OTHER PARTS OF THE CITY

Johnsonville

Immediately north of downtown, in suburban Johnsonville, is **Glen Alton Motel,** 5 Glen Alton Ave., tel. 04/478-8146 or 0800/424-222. The 16 rooms are basic but huge, and each has a kitchen; $80–130 s or d. Nearby is **Manor Inn Wellington,** Newlands Rd., tel. 04/478-7812 or 0800/806-688; website: www.manorinns.co.nz. This Tudor-style accommodation features spacious, well-decorated rooms for $110–150 s or d. A restaurant and guest laundry are also on-site.

Porirua

Farther north along Hwy. 1 are a number of hotels and motels within a 15-minute drive or train trip of downtown. **Aotea Lodge,** Whitford Brown Ave., Porirua, tel. 04/237-4257, website: www.aotealodge.co.nz, has older rooms, but they are large and each has a fully equipped kitchen. The lodge also has a large pool complex and a restaurant with alfresco dining. Standard rooms are $99 s or d, $105 s or d with a kitchen, $115 s or d with a kitchen and spa bath.

Hutt Valley

From downtown, Hwy. 2 branches northeast to the Hutt Valley, which has many more motels. Close to the city is **Du Pont Motel,** 95 Hutt Rd., Petone, tel. 04/569-3799 or 0508/387-668, with self-contained units for $79 s, $89 d. **Settlers Motor Lodge,** 83–85 Hutt Rd., Petone, tel. 04/569-4088 or 0800/838-583, website: www.settlersmotel.co.nz, is a modern facility, built in a colonial style and with an on-site restaurant and bar; $108–180 s or d.

Continuing north through the valley, **Abbeycourt Motel,** 7 Pharazyn St., Lower Hutt, tel. 04/569-3967, offers seven basic rooms for $85 s or d. On the same street is **Camellia Court,** 3 Pharazyn St., Lower Hutt, tel. 04/569-4700 or 0800/500-004, website: www.camelliacourtmotel.co.nz, where the 15 modern units each have a kitchen. Rates start at $108 s or d.

BED-AND-BREAKFASTS

Tinakori Lodge, 182 Tinakori St., tel. 04/939-3478, website: www.tinakorilodge.co.nz, has delightful owners. The eight rooms all have plenty of character, tea- and coffee-making supplies, and TVs, and guests are provided a key to the lodge. A laundry is available. With continental breakfast, a room with shared bath is $70 s, $95 d, private bath $95 s, $130 d.

Eight Parliament Street, 8 Parliament St., tel. 04/479-6705, website: www.boutique-bb.co.nz, is an upmarket bed-and-breakfast in a beautifully renovated timber house high above the downtown core. Even though the house is almost 100 years old, the décor throughout is decidedly contemporary, including modern furnishings in the lounge area and private courtyard. Rates of $120–185 s or d include a gourmet breakfast.

BACKPACKER LODGES

Although Wellington lacks Auckland's choice of hostels and backpacker lodgings, the quality is of a similar standard and, best of all, each lodging lies within walking distance of the city center.

YHA Hostel

Wellington City YHA is at the corner of Wakefield St. and Cambridge Terrace, tel. 04/801-7280; website: www.yha.org.nz. The building used to be a hotel, and there's lots of space and facilities. Although it's quite a walk from the railway station and bus depot, the hostel is in an area undergoing an extensive facelift. Across the road are a large supermarket and the Museum of New Zealand, and you'll find some of the city's most

popular cafés and nightspots in this area. The hostel has single, double, four-bed, and five-bed rooms, and each room has an *en suite* toilet and shower (and the top two floors have harbor views). Facilities include a kitchen, laundry, a hostel shop, a travel service doing bookings for all kinds of transportation (with discounts for members), and a notice board. Dorm beds are $22 pp, doubles are from $28 pp.

Downtown Backpackers

This hostel, on Waterloo Quay opposite the railway station, tel. 04/473-8482, website: www.vip.co.nz, is a five-minute walk from Queens Wharf, the information center, and the main concentration of restaurants. Located in what used to be the grand old Waterloo Hotel (the queen stayed here on her 1953 Coronation Tour), all rooms have *en suite* bathrooms. Facilities include a huge lounge area, a giant TV room, an equally massive kitchen, a game room, a bar (open nightly 4 P.M.–late), a laundry, an information service and booking office, notice boards, a shop, and free luggage storage. Three- to four-bed dorms are $18 pp, single rooms are $30, doubles and twins are $22 pp.

Beethoven House

Beethoven House, on the southern side of the city at 89 Brougham St., Mt. Victoria, tel. 04/939-4678, is usually crammed with bodies spilling out into the overflow building during peak visitor periods; it's well known because it's been there a long time, and it's also one of the places that will accept late arrivals from the South Island ferry. Smokers are not made welcome (signs on the door make this quite clear) but drinkers are, and you can expect to be woken promptly at 8 A.M. every morning with classical music (hangover or not). Beethoven House offers dormitory rooms (provide your own sleeping bag), communal bathrooms (readers have complained about the plumbing), a kitchen, a guest lounge, and a music room. It has no laundry. You'll find a courtyard and a teahouse out back, a "beer garden" in front. Dorms cost $19 pp, doubles and twins $21 pp.

Maple Lodge

This laid-back accommodation, in the southeast suburb of Mt. Victoria at 52 Ellice St. (a 15-minute walk from downtown), tel. 04/385-3771, is not on the backpacker bus route so it's generally quieter. Dorm beds are $19 pp, a single room is $27 pp, a double or twin room is $23 pp, and facilities include communal bathrooms, a kitchen and dining room, a TV lounge, a washer and dryer, and private parking at the back. The hotel's locked annex is a real bonus—store your excess luggage and/or bicycle for free until you return (very handy if you're going down to the South Island and don't know how long you'll be gone). A small store up the street sells all the basics; take-away places and several bars are within walking distance. The easiest approach is by bus from the railway station bus terminal to Basin Reserve (many bus routes pass Basin Reserve—ask at the terminal), then walk up Ellice St. (one of the main streets off the square). By car from the city center, head east along Cable St. and continue to the end. At the traffic lights, turn right onto Kent Terrace. At the square (notorious for rowdy cricket matches in summer), turn left onto Ellice Street.

MOTOR CAMPS

The closest motor camp, **Hutt Park Holiday Village,** tel. 04/568-5913 or 0800/488-872, website: www.huttpark.co.nz, is about 13 km north of Wellington in Lower Hutt—well worth the 15-minute drive; take the Petone exit off the motorway along The Esplanade and Waione St., following signs to Wainuiomata (not Petone). Cross the river, at the roundabout turn right on Seaview Rd. toward Eastbourne, then turn left on Parkside Rd. to the motor camp. It's a good idea to phone ahead to reserve a cabin/tourist flat (plenty of campsites) if you're arriving late. The camp includes spotlessly clean bathroom blocks, a kitchen, coin-operated commercial-size washers and dryers, a TV room, and a playground that would keep any energetic rug-rat happy. Tent sites cost $10 pp, powered sites are $11 pp, cabins $36 s or d, tourist flats $66 s or d, and motel rooms $85 s or d.

If you're heading north via the coastal route to Palmerston North or Wanganui, you'll find many motor camps beside the attractive sandy beaches of the Kapiti Coast.

Food

You'll find good cafés and restaurants almost everywhere you look in Wellington; at last count the city had more than 100 cafés alone. The tourist paper *Capital Times* is a good source of dining-out and entertainment information.

CASUAL DINING

Market

On Friday, Saturday, and Sunday you can choose from a wide assortment of take-away foods at **Wakefield Market,** the brightly painted, several-story building on the corner of Jervois Quay and Taranaki St., tel. 04/801-8812. Many of Wellington's young and trendy folk hang out here on weekends, particularly on Sunday afternoon—shopping for clothes, jewelry, the latest haircuts, and knickknacks—along with hamburgers, hot dogs, sandwiches, ice cream, you name it.

Cafés and Coffeehouses

Right downtown, around the corner from a park with an impressively large and ever-trickling water sculpture, **Midland Park Cafe,** 32 Waring Taylor St. (between Lambton and Customhouse Quays), tel. 04/472-6815, offers breakfast, lunch (average $6–9), and take-aways in attractive woodsy surroundings. The house specialties are soups, salads, and sandwiches; it's open Mon.–Sat. 8 A.M.–5 P.M. **City Limits Cafe,** near the information center at 122 Wakefield St., tel. 04/472-6468, is a small locals place, complete with an old pinball machine. Choose from an assortment of light savories, pies, and cakes, or try a homemade feta cheese, tomato, and onion pie ($4.50) with a good cup of coffee ($2). Across from Civic Square, **Nui Espresso,** 101 Wakefield St. (at Victoria St.), tel. 04/801-4188, has much of the same, including delicious filled rolls.

Canadians may want to stop by for a Nanaimo Bar (but someone should point out the correct spelling of this chocolate layered delight). In the vicinity, **Lido Café,** on the corner of Victoria and Wakefield Streets, tel. 04/499-6666, is another busy café central to the information center.

Along Cuba St. are a number of small cafés attracting loyal local clientele. **Krazy Lounge,** 117 Cuba St., tel. 04/385-2567, is popular, as is the more upbeat **Midnight Espresso Bar,** 178 Cuba St., tel. 04/384-7014, with a good range of coffee from around the world. A few doors down the hill is **Olive Café,** 170 Cuba St., tel. 04/802-5266, spanning two old shopfronts. The decor is very plain-the walls are whitewashed, and that's about it. Head here for a caffeine fix. Across the road, a cheap place for breakfast (open daily) is **Steinburg Café,** 181 Cuba St., tel. 04/801-5333. For a funky, off-beat atmosphere, drop by **Fidel's,** 234 Cuba St., tel. 04/801-6868, and sample cooked breakfasts under $10 and dishes such as citrus scallop and bacon fettuccine for $15.

South along Cambridge Terrace from Courtenay Place is another concentration of cafes. **Café L'Affare,** just off Cambridge Terrace at 27 College St., tel. 04/385-9748, is the best of these (and among the best in the city) for coffee. The epicenter of the action is the coffee-roaster-in plain view through the open kitchen. Café L'Affare imports the coffee beans, along with upmarket espresso machines, and distributes them both throughout the country, so you can be assured of a good, fresh, strong cup of coffee from these guys. The food is also good, with breakfast served all day, and lunch specialties highlighted by a great Caesar salad ($8.50). Back toward the city and off Courtenay Place, the **Dixon Street Delicatessen,** 45 Dixon St., tel. 04/384-2436, is stocked daily with gourmet breads, bagels, meats, pickles, preserves, and seafood delicacies, such as smoked salmon and mussels. Eat in the adjacent café or have lunch packed to go.

Pub Meals

Pub meals are usually filling and a good value, with the added bonus of a bar and entertainment of some sort (usually big-screen movies or rock videos weeknights, disco or live music Friday and Saturday nights). **Chicago Sports Café,** Queens Wharf, tel. 04/473-4900, has indoor and outdoor seating on busy waterfront pedestrian-only thoroughfare. Pizza is all under $15, a BLT is $13.50, or chose from the flexible fingerfoods menu for $8–20 pp. The weekend brunch menu includes pancakes with bacon, banana, and maple syrup for $10.

The **Southern Cross Tavern** on Abel Smith St. (southeast of city center), tel. 04/384-9085, serves lunches 11 A.M.–3 P.M. and dinners 5–9 P.M.—and the food is great! Try one of its pepper, garlic, or barbecue steaks with french fries and salad bar, lamb chops, ham steaks, or various seafood specials for $10–18. From downtown take Willis St. south to Abel Smith Street.

Above Molly Malone's, a lively bar featuring live Irish music every Monday and Wednesday night, is the **Dubliner Restaurant** on the corner of Taranaki St. and Courtenay Place, tel. 04/384-2896. It has lots of picture windows for streetscene appreciation and a variety of tasty main courses for $12–18 at lunch, $15–22 at dinner.

The historic **Shepherds Arms Hotel,** 285 Tinakori Rd., Thorndon, tel. 04/472-1320, has a cozy little dining room open daily for lunch and dinner. Traditional New Zealand dishes with a global twist (lamb pie with peach chutney and red wine jus; $13.50) are a step up from regular pub dining, while on weekends the Brunch menu includes a stack of pancakes doused with Canadian maple syrup, eggs Benedict, and a smoked salmon omelet.

RESTAURANTS
Seafood on the Harbourfront

On a sunny day, *the* place to have lunch is the waterfront—with your legs dangling off Queens Wharf—and the necessary food item is takeaway fish and chips. Before locating your perfect waterfront spot, head straight for the fish markets at the north end of Shed 5, a redeveloped waterfront warehouse, where you can buy freshly battered fish, chips, and coleslaw for $8. Avoid going noon–1 P.M. weekdays when there's always a long line. In the same building is **Shed 5 Restaurant & Bar,** tel. 04/499-9069, offering reasonably priced lunchtime specials and outdoor seating on the wharf. Try mussels steamed in a mild curry broth ($14.50). Dinner is a more elaborate (and expensive affair), but seafood dominates the menu; dinners range $27–33. In nearby Shed 3, **Dockside,** tel. 04/499-9900, attracts a business crowd for lunch weekdays but is also open for dinner.

Vegetarian

If you're looking for good vegetarian food, try **The Globe** at 213 Cuba St. (downstairs from Trekkers Hotel), tel. 04/385-2566. Aside from a self-serve salad bar, there's typical and not-so-typical spicy vegetarian fare, and desserts and fruit-or cream-filled pastries. The owner also likes to cater to those on special diets (specific food allergies). Enjoy your dish (main dishes run $8.50-12 on average) in the mod, black-and-white, artsy surroundings; open at 11 A.M.

> *On a sunny day, the place to have lunch is the waterfront—with your legs dangling off Queens Wharf. Before locating your perfect waterfront spot, head straight for the fish markets at the north end of Shed 5, a redeveloped waterfront warehouse.*

North American

Chevys, 97 Dixon St., tel. 04/384-2724, open daily 11:30 A.M.–10:30 P.M. or later, is a little bit of Americana, with a menu featuring everything from Tex-Mex to BLTs to apple pie. It's not cheap, but is extremely popular. Look for the gigantic neon cowboy marking the entrance. Following a similar theme is the **Arizona Bar & Grill,** on the on the corner of Grey and Featherston Streets, tel. 04/495-7867. It's open all day, every day, with a full American breakfast costing $15 and a full meal of tacos, nachos, or burritos starting at $15.

The brick, wood, and poster-decorated **Armadillo Cafe,** 129 Willis St., tel. 04/384-1444, is a popular spot with locals (good music). Try its oyster entrees or deliver some pizzazz to your mouth with its spicy Mexican dishes; dinners are $18–34.

Asian

Istana Malaysia, 5 Allen St., tel. 04/471-2909, is a large place, with an inexpensive Southeast Asian menu. Lunches all run less than $10, while dinners range $10–18. I enjoyed the lamb curry ($13.50). Around the corner, **Angkor,** 43 Dixon St., tel. 04/384-9423, is another place for budget-minded and adventurous diners. Cambodian cuisine has a distinctive style that follows its geographical location between India and Southeast Asia. Try *Mahope Kari,* a chicken curry dish with coconut cream, lemon grass, curry paste, and coriander ($17.50). Angkor is open Mon.–Fri. for lunch and Mon.–Sat. for dinner.

King Wah, 27 Courtenay Pl., tel. 04/801-5657, is open daily for Chinese lunches and dinners. Weekend yum-cha lunches are particularly popular, and there's usually a wait for tables. Off Courtenay Place, **Little India,** 18 Blair St., tel. 04/384-9989, is open weekdays for lunch and daily for dinner from 5 P.M. You'll find a menu filled with curries and vindaloos ($14–18), as well as unfamiliar choices such as *Murg Mumtaz* ($16), a chicken-based dish which combines classic tandoori cooking with curry. And don't forget to order delicious side dishes such as papadoms, coconut-dipped banana slices, and mint chutney ($1–3.50 each).

The **Bengal Tiger,** 94 Victoria St., tel. 04/472-8706, is the place to go if you're hankering for a spicy Indian meal. The cooks can make their dishes mild or spicy to suit your fancy; prices range $12–25 for a main course. It's open Mon.–Fri. for lunch, seven days for dinner. **Great India Restaurant,** 141 Manners St., tel. 04/384-5755, looks simple from the outside, but don't let first impressions deceive you. This stylish restaurant features upmarket furnishings and well-prepared dishes, of which the tandooris ($17–20) are excellent.

Middle Eastern

Sahara Café, 39 Courtenay Pl., tel. 04/385-6362, is another Middle Eastern restaurant, this one with kebabs, tabouli, and kosha for $12–20. Next door is **Sahara Takeaway,** tel. 04/384-6589, where kebabs to go are $8.

Along busy Courtenay Pl., at No. 48, is **Firat Café,** tel. 04/384-6589, a small, inexpensive Turkish restaurant offering a relaxed atmosphere.

Theater District

In the theater district at the eastern end of Courtenay Place are a number of cafés and restaurants that attract arty types. Blair St., which runs north from Courtenay Place to Wakefield St., is a cobbled road lined with warehouses that have been converted to restaurants and bars. The **Opera Restaurant and Bar** at the corner of Blair St. and Courtenay Place, tel. 04/382-8654, is an upmarket place, with prices to match and dress regulations indicative of the customers it attracts. The food and ambience generate much praise from the locals. **Brava,** 2 Courtenay Pl., tel. 04/384-1159, is crowded for weekend brunch, which combines the best of the breakfast and lunch menus for $8–16.

Other Upmarket Restaurants

In more of the splurge category, **Logan Brown,** 192 Cuba St., tel. 04/801-5114, is open Mon.–Fri. noon–2 P.M., daily for dinner. Housed in an opulently restored 1920s bank building, this restaurant has reputation as one of Wellington's finest. The three-course table d'hote Bistro menu, offered at lunch and before 7:30 P.M., takes from the regular menu, but at the reduced price of $30. Main courses alone range $23–35 and include innovative seafood dishes, the very best cuts of beef and venison, and local delicacies such as *paua* (abalone) ravioli. The wine list includes hard-to-get New Zealand wines, as well as premium labels from around the world.

In over a decade of traveling and writing I'd never recommended a museum restaurant as a dining option, but now I'm suggesting two in the same book. As with Hamilton's Museum Café, you can't go wrong dining at **Icon** in the Museum of New Zealand Te Papa Tongarewa, Cable St., tel. 04/801-5500. At this bustling, contemporary bistro enjoy a basket of steamed seafood for $20 and sensibly innovative takes on monkfish, *hapuka,* and *terakihi* for $26–32. Icon is open daily 11 A.M.–10 P.M.

Transportation

GETTING THERE

Wellington is, not surprisingly, one of the easiest places in New Zealand to get to by public transportation. It has an international airport, local bus and long-distance coach depots, a railway station, an overseas cruise-liner terminal, a ferry terminal, a fast motorway leading in and out of the city, all the major car rental companies, and taxis.

Air

Super Shuttle, tel. 04/387-8787, and **Airport Shuttles,** tel. 04/939-9590 or 0800/959-595, make **Wellington International Airport,** on the south side of the city, easy to reach. Both companies offer a door-to-door shuttle between the airport and city hotels or wherever you nominate. Inner-city hotel-to-airport fare is $10 pp. The services run "on-demand" from the first to last flights. On weekdays, Super Shuttle also runs a scheduled service between the airport and downtown every hour; $6 pp. The **Stagecoach Flyer,** tel. 04/801-7000, is a city-operated scheduled service that runs between the airport and downtown every 30 minutes for $4.50 adult, $2.50 child. A cab runs around $18 for up to four passengers.

The **International Terminal** is quite dead unless a flight is arriving or departing. The duty-free store is open for all international departures, the bank is open for all incoming and departing flights, and there are shops for gifts, books, and coffee, an observation deck and bar, and a covered walkway through to the Domestic Terminal.

The **Domestic Terminal** teems with life at all times of the day and night-and offers all the regular airport services. The **information center** is open Mon.–Fri. 7:30 A.M.–8 P.M., shorter hours on weekends. The friendly staff will book all long-distance rail, ferry, and coach travel and

CROSSING COOK STRAIT

From Wellington, onward southbound travel necessitates a crossing of Cook Strait to the **South Island.** Whether you get your first glimpse of landfall from aboard the ferry as it enters Marlborough Sound or through the window of a plane bound for Picton or Christchurch, the wild untamed landscape makes it obvious that new and very different experiences await.

Ferry

The most popular way to cross Cook Strait is by ferry. The **Interisland Line,** tel. 04/498-3302 or 0800/802-802, website: www.interislandline.co.nz, operates a modern fleet of vessels that cross year-round between downtown Wellington and Picton.

The *Arahura* and newer (1999) *Aratere,* cross up to five times a day, departing from Wellington's Aotea Quay Terminal. These large ferries carry passengers, vehicles, and box-cars; each has an information center, cafeteria, restaurant, gift shop, newsstand, cinema ($8 per movie), bar, cafeteria, desk area for working, play room, and Club Class ($25 extra) for added comfort. The 83-km crossing usually takes about 3.5 hours. Standard fares are $52 adult, $31 child, $179 vehicle, $10 bicycle. The Interisland Line's third vessel is the *Lynx,* a high-speed catamaran that makes the crossing in less than two hours. It's smaller than the two regular ferries, and travel is slightly more expensive ($68 adult, $40 child, $199 vehicle). It operates twice daily mid-December through mid-April only.

All fares quoted above are for tickets booked from overseas or close to the time of booking; the pricing structure is a lot more complicated, but you can save by planning ahead. Although it is important to book as far ahead as possible, you will save money by waiting until you arrive in New Zealand, and then book at information centers across the country, at many travel agencies, or by calling 0800/802-802. A percentage of vehicle and passenger spots for Saver (30 percent discount), and Super Saver (50 percent discount) discounts are designated for each sailing, with the more inconvenient times (i.e., late night-early morning) having more spots designated at the more steeply discounted fares. Other discounted fares include day excursion and overnight packages. Check the Interisland website before leaving home to get a feeling for the various options.

If you're driving a rental car, arrange to drop it off at Wellington and pick up another in Picton to save the ferry fare. Be sure to make reservations well in advance if you're taking a vehicle over, or be prepared to go standby and expect a wait in summer (standbys need to line up by 6 A.M. to have a chance of getting on).

To get to the terminal, catch the free Picton Ferry bus from Platform 9 at the railway station, departing 35 minutes before each sailing. Check in your luggage up to one hour before sailing (the earlier the better if you want to avoid long lines). Ticket check-in is 30 minutes ahead of sailing, an hour if you have a vehicle.

Air

Flying is the quicker option, and preferred if the ocean is rough, as it often is in winter. **Soundsair,** tel. 04/801-0111 or 0800/505-005, flies between Wellington International airport and Picton several times a day. The fare of $75 pp one-way includes transfers into downtown Picton from the local airfield. **Air New Zealand,** tel. 04/474-8950 or 0800/737-300, has scheduled flights from Wellington to Nelson, Christchurch, Dunedin, Nelson, Queenstown, Invercargill.

local accommodations. For short-term **luggage storage,** get one of the lockers near baggage pick-up (from $1 for up to eight hours). Also in the Domestic Terminal is a bank branch (open weekdays, regular hours) and ATM machines; a lounge bar and a café open 11 A.M.–8:30 P.M. each day; **book and souvenir shops;** and Avis, Budget, and Hertz **car rental** branches.

Air New Zealand, tel. 04/388-9737, the primary domestic carrier, has direct flights from Wellington to Auckland, Hamilton, Rotorua, Gisborne, Nelson, Christchurch, Dunedin, and many smaller towns. Flights to Queenstown are routed through Christchurch. The **Air New Zealand Travelcentre** is on the corner of Lambton Quay and Grey St., tel. 04/474-8950. Other airlines flying into Wellington include **Air Pacific,** tel. 0800/800-178; **Origin Pacific,** tel. 0800/302-302; **Polynesian Airlines,** tel. 0800/800-993; **Qantas,** tel. 0800/808-767; and **Soundsair,** tel. 04/801-0111 or 0800/505-005.

Train

Wellington Railway Station's main entrance is off Bunny St. (between Featherston and Waterloo Quay), north of the Civic Centre. Inside the station is the **Tranz Scenic Travel Centre,** which has long-distance train, bus, and ferry information. The center is open Mon.–Fri. 7:30 A.M.–5:30 P.M., Saturday and Sunday 7:30-11:30 A.M. You'll find luggage lockers beside Platform 9; they're open daily 6 A.M.–10 P.M. and cost 50 cents for 24 hours.

The long-distance trains run north to Auckland via Palmerston North, National Park, and Hamilton (the *Overlander* leaves daily at 8:45 A.M. and the *Northerner* leaves Sun.–Fri. at 7:50 P.M.). For all **Tranz Scenic** information, call 0800/802-802; website: www.transcenic.co.nz.

Bus

You'll find the **Intercity Terminal** at Platform 9 at the railway station, on the Bunny St. side. Intercity runs from Wellington to Auckland, Hamilton, Rotorua, Tauranga, Palmerston North, New Plymouth, Wanganui—in fact, just about everywhere you want to go—with connections

everywhere else. Make bookings in the railway station at the **Tranz Scenic Travel Centre** or call 04/472-5111.

Newmans Coach Lines also depart from Platform 9, but the booking office is in the ferry terminal, tel. 04/499-3261 after hours; it's open weekdays 8 A.M.–5 P.M. and Sat. 8:30–10:30 A.M. Coaches run to Auckland, Rotorua, Taupo, Napier, Hastings, Levin, Palmerston North, Wanganui, and New Plymouth.

GETTING AROUND
Bus and Train

Once you're in Wellington, it's easy to get around by local transportation—bus service is excellent and numerous special fares encourage further exploration by bus. The best bonus of all is how easily you can get all the transportation information you need. Each *Wellington City Bus Route Guide* map (available at the information center and at the railway station) has a detailed timetable, along with all the things to see and do along the way. Bus timetables and route diagrams are posted outside Rutherford House, where buses depart. For more information, call the Ridewell Service Centre, tel. 04/801-7000 or 0800/801-700.

Wellington Regional Council has come up with special deals to encourage you to use local public transportation, run by a variety of private companies. Each time you get on a bus, you pay for one section—about $1 in the city, $1.30–2.50 out of the city—but **The Downtowner** ticket costs only $3 for five trips within the city section (between the railway station and the other end of the city). It's valid weekdays 9 A.M.–3 P.M.; buy it from any bus driver and hold on to it until you've had your five rides. The **STARpass** ticket allows you to travel anywhere in Wellington by bus (best value) for $7 per day but it can be used only after 9 A.M. on weekdays, all day (till midnight) on weekends.

Tranz Metro suburban trains depart from Wellington Railway Station for the northern suburbs of Ngaio, Khandallah, and Johnsonville; the western coastal towns as far north as Paraparaumu; and the northern cities of Lower and Upper Hutt.

Taxi

You'll find taxi stands at Wellington Railway Station, on Whitmore St. (between Lambton Quay and Featherston St.), outside the James Smith Hotel on Lambton Quay, on the Bond St. corner (off Willis St.), outside the Woolworth's Store on Dixon St., and at the Willis and Aro Streets intersection. Taxi companies include **Capital City Cabs,** tel. 04/388-4884; **Central City Cabs,** tel. 04/499-4949; **Gold and Black Taxis,** tel. 04/388-8888; **Harbour City Taxis,** tel. 04/388-8111; and **Wellington Combined Taxis,** tel. 04/384-4444.

Car Rental

All the major car rental agencies (and many minor ones—check the phone book) have offices in Wellington, and a couple have outlets at the ferry terminal. The major companies don't allow their vehicles on the ferry. Instead, you must leave the car in Wellington, catch the ferry across to the south island, and pick up another. The major agencies include **Avis,** tel. 04/802-1088; **Budget,** tel. 04/802-4548; **Hertz,** tel. 04/384-3809; **Rent-a-dent,** tel. 04/387-9931; and **NZ Rent-a-car,** tel. 04/384-2745. As throughout the country, smaller companies offer the best rates. Those in the capital include **Darn Cheap Rentals,** tel. 04/568-2777 or 0800/800-327; **Embassy Rentals,** tel. 04/385-3401 or 0800/807-040; and **Wellington Carhire,** tel. 04/389-2983 or 0800/746-378.

Tours

A fun and inexpensive way to appreciate Wellington's harbor aspect is to catch the **East by**

Wellington Marina

West Ferry, tel. 04/499-1282, between Queens Wharf and Days Bay ($8 one-way, $6 senior, $4 child). At Days Bay visit Williams Park and the beach (favorite summertime hangouts for Wellingtonians toting barbecues and picnic lunches), look through local shops and galleries, eat at the restaurants, go for nearby bush walks, or hike along the Pencarrow Coast where New Zealand's first permanent lighthouse still stands. Some sailings stop at Somes Island, formerly a quarantine station, and now a pleasant place for a short hike.

Services and Information

SERVICES

Regular shopping hours are Mon.–Thurs. 9 A.M.–5 P.M., Friday till 9 P.M., and Saturday 9 A.M.–1 P.M. Tourist shops, milk bars, and take-aways stay open longer hours and are generally open throughout the weekend. The **Duty-Free Shop,** next to the Air New Zealand building on Grey St., sells the usual jewelry, watches, perfume, cameras, radios, clothing, and typical New Zealand products, but the prices aren't particularly cheap—if you shop around you may find better. It's open Mon.–Fri. 8:30–5:30 P.M.

New Zealand Post has outlets at 27 Waterloo Quay and at 153 Lambton Quay.

Emergency

Wellington Hospital is on Riddiford St., Newtown, tel. 04/385-5999. For emergency **dental** services, call 04/472-7072. **City Medical Centre** is at 142 Featherston St., tel. 04/471-2161, while the **After Hours Medical Centre** is at 17 Adelaide Rd., tel. 04/384-4944.

INFORMATION

Libraries

You'll find the impressive three-story building that houses **Wellington Central Library** at 65 Victoria St., tel. 04/801-4040. The first floor is devoted to fiction, the second floor contains magazines, and the third floor holds newspapers from around the world. The library also features a large travel section (third floor), a reference room, computer terminals, a café, and a bookshop. It's open Mon.–Thurs. 9:30 A.M.–8:30 P.M., Friday till 9 P.M., and Saturday till 5 P.M. The **National Library of New Zealand,** on the corner of Molesworth and Aitken Streets, tel. 04/474-3000, holds a large number of literature collections. Particularly impressive is the number of New Zealand and South Pacific books, which are held along with newspapers, magazines, and maps from throughout the region. This library also has large archives and a good website

(www.natlib.govt.nz/). It's open Mon.–Fri. 9 A.M.–5 P.M., Saturday 9 A.M.–1 P.M., and Sunday 1–4 P.M.

Wellington City Archives, 28 Barker St. (off Cambridge Terrace), tel. 04/801-2096, contains the history of the capital, from 1842 when it first became a borough, in print and audio. It's open Mon.–Wed. and Friday 9 A.M.–4 P.M.

Bookstores

Wellington has a large number of bookstores, most centered in the downtown core along Lambton Quay. These include **Bennetts Bookshop,** on the corner of Lambton Quay and Bowen Streets, tel. 04/499-3433; **Dymocks Booksellers,** 366 Lambton Quay, tel. 04/472-2080; and **Whitcoulls,** 312 Lambton Quay, tel. 04/472-1921, and 91 Cuba St., tel. 04/384-

entrance to Wellington Central Library

2065. **Unity Books,** 57 Willis St., tel. 04/499-4245, is an independent bookseller with a wide range of New Zealand and travel titles. **Parson's Books & Music,** 126 Lambton Quay, tel. 04/472-4587, has a similar selection, as well as homegrown music and an upstairs café.

Looking for out-of-print or secondhand books? Then head uptown to **Arty Bee's Books,** 17 Courtenay Pl., tel. 04/385-1819; or **Bellamy's Bookshop,** 105 Cuba St., tel. 04/384-7770.

The **Map Shop** on the corner of Victoria and Vivian Streets, tel. 04/385-1462, has the city's best selection of maps, including topographical maps and marine charts.

Information Centers

The main source of city and regional information is **Wellington Visitor Centre** in the Civic Centre, entrance on the corner of Wakefield and Victoria Streets, tel. 04/802-4860; website: www.wellingtonnz.com. It's open every day 8:30 A.M.–5:30 P.M., including public holidays, and the knowledgeable staff dispenses free brochures and pamphlets on attractions, walks, accommodations, and restaurants; all the latest entertainment and transportation information; and a city street map ($1). The staff also sells stamps, phonecards, and souvenir T-shirts, and makes bus and ferry bookings.

There's also an information center in each terminal out at the airport. They are open Mon.–Fri. 7:30 A.M.–8 P.M., shorter hours on weekends. The exuberant staff will load you up with information on everything you need to know (and more!) and will do bookings for coach, rail, and ferry travel, and for city accommodations. You can also buy stamps and phonecards here. If the office is closed when you arrive, check out the useful notice boards nearby.

The **DOC** maintains an information center in the old Government Building at 15 Lambton Quay, tel. 04/472-7356, while the head office of the **Wellington Conservancy** is in the Bowen State Building, Bowen St., tel. 04/472-5821.

The South Island

The South Island, like the North, is a landscape of great contrast. Spectacular scenery appears to change form, shape, or color around every bend in the road, and the variable weather and play of light and shade make it a photographer's dream. You'll find a maze of waterways separated by bush-covered peninsulas and islands edged with gold-flecked sand in the north; mighty forest-fringed glaciers inching down almost to the sea, unusual cliff formations, and gray sandy beaches pounded by the surf on the west coast; the towering snowcapped mountains of the Southern Alps; isolated glassy fiords that cut deep into remote and untouched native bush in the southwest corner; and richly colored farmland and hilly pastureland throughout. Lakes are scattered across the South Island and, along with the trout- and salmon-laden rivers, provide excellent fishing, canoeing, swimming, and white-water rafting.

City action and nightlife are available in abundance in the "Garden City" of Christchurch, the "Scottish City" of Dunedin, Invercargill at the base of the island, and the two bustling resorts of Queenstown and Aoraki/Mt. Cook. At the foot of the South Island lies Stewart Island, carpeted in dense bush, home to all kinds of native birds and wildlife. Hike through virgin wilderness without seeing a soul for five days, cruise remote inlets, or bask on your own perfect South Pacific beach on this island where time stands still and the hum and bustle of the rat race are easily forgotten.

The main difference between the North and South Islands is weather. Temperatures are distinctly cooler in the south and the annual rainfall is much higher; the climate ranges from sunny, dry weather in the northern region to rain almost every day of the year in the southwest fiords (7.5 meters or more per year is the norm). Unpredictable Stewart Island can experience the weather of four seasons in a single day!

Marlborough

Introduction

After a spectacular ride across Cook Strait (especially beautiful on a bright day), the interisland ferry cruises up colorful Queen Charlotte Sound, one of the two major inlets of Marlborough Sounds Maritime Park. If you've become addicted to sunshine, beach life, and outstanding water views, you might want to stay a little while in this area, making Picton your base.

From Picton, you have a major decision to make: either head southwest to Nelson or south-east to Blenheim, known for its wineries, then south along the coast toward Christchurch on Hwy. 1. This beautiful stretch of road winds along sandy beaches, rocky shores, and aquamarine waters of the scenic east coast. On the way down, stop for fresh crayfish at one of the many roadside stands, and pull off at **Kaikoura.** Sandwiched between the rugged Kaikoura Range and the sea, this attractive coastal town is known for whale-watching, but also offers other wildlife viewing opportunities, empty beaches, and good surf fishing.

Outer Sounds, Marlborough Sounds Maritime Park

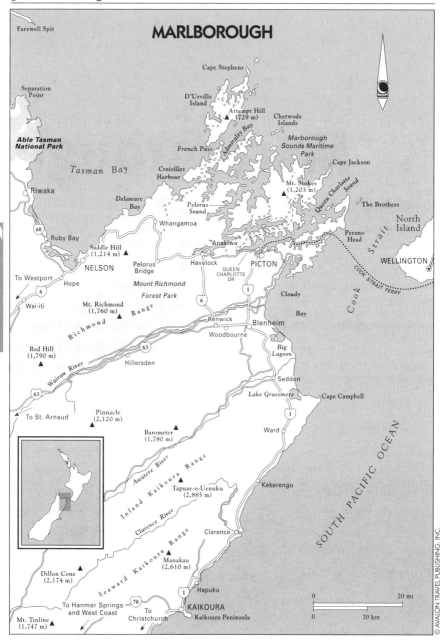

MARLBOROUGH

Farewell Spit

Separation Point

Able Tasman National Park

Cape Stephens

D'Urville Island

Attempt Hill (729 m)

Chetwode Islands

Marborough Sounds Maritime Park

French Pass

Admiralty Bay

Cape Jackson

Tasman Bay

Croisilles Harbour

Riwaka

Delaware Bay

Pelorus Sound

Mt. Stokes (1,203 m)

Queen Charlotte Sound

The Brothers

North Island

Whangamoa

Ruby Bay

60

Saddle Hill (1,214 m)

Anakiwa

Perano Head

Cook Strait

WELLINGTON

NELSON

Pelorus Bridge

Havelock

PICTON

QUEEN CHARLOTTE DR

To Westport

6

Hope

Mount Richmond Forest Park

1

Cloudy

COOK STRAIT FERRY

Wai-iti

Mt. Richmond (1,760 m)

Richmond Range

Renwick

Blenheim

Bay

Woodbourne

Red Hill (1,790 m)

63

Wairau River

Hillersden

Big Lagoon

Seddon

Lake Grassmere

Cape Campbell

To St. Arnaud

Pinnacle (2,120 m)

Barometer (1,780 m)

Ward

63

Awatere River

Inland Kaikoura Range

Tapuae-o-Uenuku (2,885 m)

Kekerengu

SOUTH PACIFIC OCEAN

Clarence River

Seaward Kaikoura Range

Clarence

Dillon Cone (2,174 m)

Manakau (2,610 m)

To Hanmer Springs and West Coast

70

To Christchurch

1

Hapuku

Mt. Tinline (1,747 m)

KAIKOURA

Kaikoura Peninsula

0   20 mi

0   20 km

Picton

The gateway to the South Island, Picton (population 3,600), is a popular seaside resort in the heart of the Marlborough Sounds. If you enjoy magnificent seascapes, cruising up sounds, island hopping, hiking, fishing, sea kayaking, diving, beach camping, or wine-tasting, the Picton area has a lot to offer.

History

When Captain Cook sailed up Queen Charlotte Sound in 1770, he found about 400 Maori living in huts along the shores—the remains of their pits and middens are clearly visible today. Ship Cove at the northwest side of Queen Charlotte Sound was the first anchorage spot in Marlborough Sounds for the crew of the HMS *Endeavour*. After European discovery, Marlborough Sounds became famous for productive whaling stations (the last closed in 1964), gold mining in the 1860s, timber milling from the 1860s to 1915, farming in the 1920s, and from then on for exotic tree plantations—check them out from the ferry.

On Arrival

If you're trying to decide whether to push on south or stay in Picton a few days, leave your backpack, luggage, and gear in lockers at the terminal building in the **left-luggage area** while you look around town. A ride to town, only a short walk away, will cost a couple of dollars by taxi. It's also easy to rent a car—the major car rental company offices beside the terminal open for all ferry arrivals and departures. When you arrive, the first place to go is the **Picton Visitor Information Centre** along the foreshore on Auckland St., tel. 03/573-7477; it's open seven days 9 A.M.–5 P.M.

SIGHTS

All the action happens in and around the harbor, with the most popular local activities taking place on the water. Picton Harbour is a hive of activity year-round, but it's busiest during summer, when a constant stream of water taxis, cruise boats, and privately owned watercraft heads into

© ANDREW HEMPSTEAD

Picton Waterfront

and out of the marina. This form of transportation is covered comprehensively in the section, "Marlborough Sounds." Briefly, the two main tour companies are **Beachcomber Fun Cruises,** tel. 03/573-6175, and **Cougar Line,** tel. 03/573-7925. As well as tours, both offer drop-offs throughout Queen Charlotte Sound, along with many small water taxis, including **Arrow Water Taxi,** tel. 03/573-8229, and **Endeavour Express,** tel. 03/579-8465. **Buzzy Bikes and Boats,** tel. 03/573-7853, rents canoes, paddleboats, and motorboats.

Picton Museum

Walk down the Memorial Steps at the harbor end of High St. into the attractive flower-filled park that lines the harbor, and turn left. Just past the public restrooms you'll find the museum on London Quay, tel. 03/573-8283. It features the town's colorful colonial past and contains all sorts of intriguing objects, Maori clothing, carvings, ancient clocks, a fantastic shell collection, old photographs, even the 1902 Picton doctor's bicycle. Learn about local whaling history and the lifestyle of early Maori. Picton Museum is open seven days 10 A.M.–4 P.M.; admission $3.

Along the Waterfront

Go to Picton Marina to soak up some of the nautical vacation atmosphere for which Picton is famous. Of historical interest is **Casey's Boatyard,** where you can watch the building of wooden boats using traditional methods from a specially constructed viewing platform. The marina is also a departure point for commercial launch rides, fishing charters, and water taxis to the outer islands.

Beyond the museum and information center is the floating teak hull of the ***Edwin Fox.*** Launched in 1853 and used to carry convicts from England to Australia, it is one of the world's oldest vessels that is still afloat (albeit, just). It is slowly being restored, and, in the meantime, is open to the public daily 8:45 A.M.–5 P.M.; admission $4 adult, $1 child.

In the opposite direction, cross the "coat hanger" bridge to the north side of the marina and turn left to the ***Echo,*** a 1905 cargo boat with kauri-frame timbers. The boat played an important part in Marlborough's transport industry between Blenheim and Wellington for more than 50 years. Tied up on Picton harbor, she's now an art gallery with a distinctive maritime theme. Open daily 10 A.M.–6 P.M.; tel. 03/573-7498. Admission is $3.

SCENIC DRIVES AND RECREATION

Scenic Overlooks

If you have your own transportation, cruise out to **Waikawa Bay Marina** (a 10-minute drive east of town along Beach Rd.) to see hundreds of boats clinking and twinkling in the sun. **Waikawa Bay** also warrants a visit—sit in the sun and take in the bay view, watch local children taking sailing lessons, and have a snack on the deck of the Waikawa Bay Food Market and Tearooms.

Victoria Domain, an area of unspoiled bush along the headlands east of the harbor, offers spectacular views of the Picton Ferry Terminal, the sound, and Waikawa Bay—take your camera.

© ANDREW HEMPSTEAD

Picton Marina

MARLBOROUGH

© ANDREW HEMPSTEAD

Picton from Queen Charlotte Drive

To get there from town take Dublin St. east, continue past Picton Hospital onto Waikawa Rd., and go about 800 meters. Turn left at Sussex St. and follow the steep road to the lookout.

You'll also find a lookout and picnic spot up on **Queen Charlotte Drive** (which leads west out of Picton toward Havelock and Nelson). You can reach it by car (take Dublin St. west and turn right at Queen Charlotte Dr.), or on foot via **Beatty's Track,** which starts near the base of Waitohi Wharf and leads up to the lookout. If you have wheels, continue along the twisty bush-clad Queen Charlotte Dr. for some of the best waterscapes in the South Island—the views of the next couple of sounds are well worth the drive. However, the road is steep and tortuous, and is not recommended for unreliable cars (or unreliable drivers) or for cars towing long caravans.

Short Walks Close to Town

From town, a track follows the harbor edge east for one km and comes out at sheltered **Bob's**

Bay—enjoy its pleasant picnic sites and safe swimming. From here you can climb up the bush track to the headland, Victoria Domain, and a lookout for spectacular views of Queen Charlotte Sound and Picton. **Essons Valley Reservoir** is another enjoyable short walk (45 minutes one way)—particularly good in the dark when glowworms sparkle along the track. It starts at Garden Terrace at the south end of Picton and leads to **Humphries Dam. Tirohanga Walkway** gives you a great view of Picton and the sounds. The walk, which takes 45 minutes one way, also starts at Garden Terrace, ending at Newgate St. near the Blue Anchor Holiday Park.

Exploring Marlborough Sounds ✳

If you have a tent, cooking equipment, food, and cash for a boat or floatplane ride, this maze of bright blue waterways, 900 km of foreshore reserves separated by high peninsulas, islands with soft, sandy beaches, and fine camping spots is a place that you should seriously explore for at least a couple of days. Load all your supplies, suntan lotion, sunglasses, hat, fishing rod, and a friend onto a boat, and head out for the wilds of Marlborough Sounds—it's guaranteed to drop your blood pressure and give you one heck of a suntan.

ACCOMMODATIONS

As a transportation hub, Picton has a wide range of accommodations in all price brackets. If you're looking to spend a night at either end of the Cook Strait ferry trip, Picton is by far the preferred choice. If you haven't made reservations in advance (recommended, especially in summer), stop at the information center to see what's available.   *Marahaua lodge*

Hotels and Motels

Overlooking the harbor is the **Federal Hotel,** 12 London Quay, tel. 03/573-6077, one of Picton's original hotels. Its position is perfect, and many of the rooms open to a balcony with water views. But, like most older hotels, the rooms are fairly sparse. Rates are $30 s, $55 d for a room with shared facilities, or $75 d for a room with its own

DECISIONS, DECISIONS

If you're relatively short of time to spend on the South Island, take an invaluable moment to decide what kind of scenery and activities you're looking for. If you're not in a hurry, Nelson and the northwest are definitely worth exploring, but those with limited schedules shouldn't miss the glaciers and mountains of the west coast; city lovers will appreciate Christchurch, the most picturesque city in the South Island; and adventure-lovers will want to make a bee-line for Queenstown. If you find the decision a tough one to make, don't worry—wherever you go something special awaits.

bathroom. Of the many motels in downtown Picton, one of the more reasonably priced, the **Tourist Court Motel,** 45 High St., tel. 03/573-6331 or 0800/366-555, website: www.tourist-court.co.nz, is a small, single-story place right on the main street charging just $65–75 for one of the 10 basic self-contained units.

Ancient Mariner Hotel, on the corner of Waikawa Rd. and Wellington St., tel. 03/573-7002 or 0800/991-188, website: www.ancient-mariner.co.nz, is a modern accommodation that was last refurbished in 1996. Many rooms have water views from their private balconies, and there's a large swimming pool and the Edwin Fox Restaurant. Rates start at $75 s, $85 d, rising $160 for a suite with a king-size circular bed.

Part of the Golden Chain, the downtown **Americano Motor Inn,** 32 High St., tel. 03/573-6398 or 0800/104-104, website: www.americano.co.nz, has 26 spacious, self-contained units with TV and radio, as well as a private spa pool, licensed restaurant and bar, laundry facilities, a children's play area, and off-street parking; rates are a reasonable $90 s, $100 d.

Two blocks up from the harbor, **Jasmine Court,** 78 Wellington St., tel. 03/573-7110 or 0800/421-999, doesn't look anything special from the outside, but each room is well-decorated, and has a comfortable bed and a modern kitchen. Rates are $95 s, $135 d.

Bed-and-Breakfast

The Gables at 20 Waikawa Rd., tel. 03/573-6772, provides comfortable rooms (private or shared facilities) and a large lounge area on the upper floor of a two-story 1924 home, only a short walk from town and the marina. Breakfast is huge, and fresh fish is served when available. Rates are $75 s, $95 d. Also available are two small cottages at the back of the property.

Backpacker Lodges

Picton has many backpacker lodges, most of which are of an excellent standard; many have bike rentals and all have Internet access. Right in the center of town, within walking distance of the ferry terminal, is **The Villa,** 34 Auckland St., tel. 03/573-6598, website: www.thevilla.co.nz, an excellent backpacker lodge with all the usual facilities, as well as free tea and coffee, free breakfast, free use of bikes, and a large backyard with a barbecue and spa pool; dorm $20, double or twin $23.50 per person.

Near the ferry terminal and associated with Diver's World, **Atlantis Backpackers,** London Quay, tel. 03/573-7390, website: www.atlantishostel.co.nz, features an indoor pool. Dorm beds are a reasonable $14, while private rooms are $27 s, $44 d. Rates include breakfast.

Two km south of downtown, **Juggler's Rest,** 8 Canterbury St., tel. 03/573-5570, is a friendly place, with plenty of free food (including fruit fresh from the garden), free use of bikes, and juggling lessons each evening. Most beds are in dorms ($15 per person), but there are also two double rooms ($18 per person).

Bayview Backpackers at Waikawa Bay Beach, 318 Waikawa Rd., tel. 03/573-7668, is bright and modern: amenities include bunk, twin, and double rooms, a well-equipped kitchen with a microwave, a living area with a stereo, a log fire, a barbecue, free use of bicycles, and kayaks, dinghies, and catamarans for rent. It also offers free pickup and drop-off at the ferry terminal, downtown, and hitching points; rates are from $18 per night.

Get Away From it All

Picton is the jumping-off point for one of New Zealand's more unusual accommodations, and one that is consistently rated by travelers as the best backpacker lodge in the country. Located on a private bay 12 km from Picton, the **Lazy Fish,** tel. 03/579-9049, website: www.lazy-fish.co.nz, is accessed by boat only, and you must call to reserve a bed. This waterside farm homestead with its own stream and lots of native bush provides the usual facilities, plus a hot outdoor spa and barbecue, volleyball equipment, and free use of a sailboard, a canoe, a rowboat, and fishing and snorkeling gear. Dorm beds are $22 pp, cabins that share bathroom facilities are $55 s or d, private cabins are $125 s or d (minimum two-night stay), all in all, a great value. Several boat operators can take you to the lodge for about $15 pp each way; book through the Lazy Fish.

Motor Camps

Blue Anchor Holiday Park on Waikawa Rd. at the eastern end of town, tel. 03/573-7212 or 0800/277-666, website: www.blueanchor.co.nz,

Look for this eye-catching sight as you head out to Waikawa Bay from downtown Picton.

provides the usual facilities, a TV and recreation room, and a swimming pool. Rates for tent and caravan sites start at $20 s or d; cabins range $34–44; and fully self-contained tourist flats range $60–80. **Alexander's Holiday Park** on Canterbury St., tel. 03/573-6378, is one km from the post office (an easy 10-minute walk), in the quiet southern area of town. Waitohi Stream rushes through the attractive grounds. Alexander's has communal facilities, a TV lounge, kitchens where travelers mingle, and an office where you can pick up information on the local area, and buy basic foodstuffs, postcards, and supplies. Tent and caravan sites are $19; cabins are $32–42 d. From town, cross the railway tracks, follow Wairau Rd. (the sign says Hwy. 1 south) to Devon St., and turn left. At Canterbury St. turn left, following the motor camp signs.

The next closest motor camp to Picton, **Parklands Marina Holiday Park,** is three km east at Waikawa Bay on the corner of Beach Rd. and Mara Place, tel. 03/573-6343 or 0800/111-104. There are communal facilities, a TV and game room, and a boat park and wash. Tent and caravan sites are $18–22 d; on-site caravans and cabins cost from $33 d; a tourist flat is $48 d. **Waikawa Bay Holiday Park,** 302 Waikawa Rd., tel. 03/573-7434, has a grassy camping area and on-site caravans and cabins; it's a short drive from a food market and the bay beach. Tent sites start at $12 d; cabins at $29 d; and on-site caravans are $24–27.

Momorangi Bay Campground has an excellent spot on the shores of Queen Charlotte Sound; it's on Queen Charlotte Dr., tel. 03/573-7865. The camp has communal facilities, a store (open seven days), dinghies for rent (great for fishing in the protected offshore waters), and a restaurant. Tent sites are $14 s, $16 d, powered sites are $18 s, $20 d. Take Queen Charlotte Dr. out of Picton toward Havelock; it's about 15 km to Momorangi Bay.

FOOD

Picton offers a good choice of cafés and restaurants, most within a couple of blocks of the harbourfront. For a cheap quick breakfast or

MARLBOROUGH

lunch, try one of the many tearooms and cafés, or **Picton Bakery,** 46 Auckland St., tel. 03/573-7082, which features delicious European-style breads and pastries (great fudge slices). I enjoyed a good cooked breakfast at the **Sea Spray Café,** 6 London Quay, tel. 03/573-6633; it was under $10 and came with delicious plunger coffee. **Espresso House,** 86 Auckland St., tel. 03/573-7112, is a big city-style coffeehouse, which also offers a variety of good salads and open sandwiches.

For a substantial meal, try the **Federal Hotel,** 12 London Quay, tel. 03/573-6077, open daily noon–2 P.M. for lunch, 5:30–8 P.M. for dinner. A main course (meat, chips, and salad) at dinner runs $8–10. **Oxley's Tavern,** 1 Wellington St., tel. 03/573-6401, serves bistro meals—local seafood, steaks, chicken dishes, and roast—for $10–14, and daily specials for about $9; it's open Mon.–Sat. noon–2 P.M. and 5–8 P.M.

At **Marlborough Terranean,** 31 High St., tel. 03/573-7122, enjoy dishes such as a creamy seafood chowder ($11), a wide-ranging menu of seasonal seafood dinners ($22–31), and finish your meal with the chocolate mousse ($6). It's open Thurs.–Sun. from 10 A.M., and daily from 5 P.M. Candlelit **Americano,** 32 High St., tel. 03/573-7040, is another locally recommended restaurant, serving lunches from $8 and dinner for $15–29. It also offers sizzling "Hot Rocks" cuisine (meat and/or seafood on a hot granite slab served with Cajun or Asian condiments, salad, and veggies) for $24–30, and a children's menu for $8.50. For gourmet local seafood, steaks, and vegetarian fare, head to the **5th Bank Restaurant** in a renovated BNZ building at 33 Wellington St., tel. 03/573-6102. Tables are in private rooms or spread around a pleasant verandah. It's open daily from 6 P.M.; dinners start at $22.

GETTING THERE

Getting to Picton is easy by ferry from Wellington on the North Island, from where train and bus services depart regularly for all points on the South Island. Make sure to check which ferry crossing to catch to make the onward connection.

The **Wellington Travel Centre,** in Wellington's railway station, is the best place to begin planning onward transportation before arriving on the South Island.

Air

The ferry crossing of Cook Strait is sometimes rough, and occasionally very rough, so flying between Wellington and Picton can be a welcome option. **Soundsair,** tel. 03/573-6184, flies over the strait up to six times daily for $75 one way (discounts apply). These flights land at Koromiko Airfield, seven km south of town, from where free shuttle buses run into Picton. The closest airport served by **Air New Zealand** is Blenheim (28 km south of Picton), with regular flights from Wellington.

Train

The **railway station** is just around the corner from London Quay on the way to the ferry terminal. The *Coastal Pacific* train departs from Picton daily for Blenheim, Kaikoura, and Christchurch, arriving at Christchurch about 5.5 hours later. Get your timetable and book tickets at the railway station, tel. 03/573-8857, or call **Tranz Scenic** at 0800/802-802.

Bus

Picton is a hub for bus travel, with many companies based in town. **Intercity,** tel. 03/573-7025, buses arrive and depart from the Picton Travel Centre at the ferry terminal, and head west to Nelson and south along the east coast to Christchurch via Kaikoura. At least one departure daily links up with the arrival of a ferry from Wellington. Other companies operating between Picton and Christchurch (via Kaikoura) are **Compass Coachlines,** tel. 03/578-7102; **Ko-op Shuttles,** tel. 03/366-6633; and **Atomic Shuttles,** tel. 03/573-6855. Expect to pay about $35 one way for the five-hour bus trip to Christchurch. As well as Intercity, **Kiwilink Shuttles,** tel. 03/577-8332, and **Knightline,** tel. 03/528-7798, make the 2.5-hour run to Nelson; $22 one-way. Head to the information center for shuttle bus timetables.

Ferry ✱ 3 ✓.

Picton's ferry terminal, 500 meters from downtown, is the main port of entry and exit from the South Island. Two **Interislander** ferries make up to five crossings daily from Wellington to Picton. *The Lynx,* a 74-meter catamaran, is also part of the Interislander fleet. It crosses Cook Strait in just under two hours, is more luxurious than the other boats, but is slightly more expensive. Check the current schedule and make bookings at any visitor information center, most travel agencies, by calling 0800/802-802, or at website: www.interislandline.co.nz. If you're taking a vehicle across, you need to book a space, particularly during holidays. Otherwise expect to end up in a long standby line and miss several ferries before you get on. Booking in advance is also cheaper.

The pricing structure for ferry travel is complicated, but book in advance for the cheapest tickets. The regular one-way fare is $52 adult, $31 child, and from $179 for a vehicle. Various discount levels apply, including Saver (30 percent discount) and Super Saver (50 percent discount). On each sailing, a percentage of spots are reserved at each fare level, with the more inconvenient times (late night-early morning) having more spots designated at the more steeply discounted fares. Travel on the *Lynx* is $68 adult, $39 child, and $199 vehicle, and all the same discounts apply. Other discounts apply to seniors or those traveling over to the South Island for just the weekend.

GETTING AROUND

If you've rented a car from one of the major car rental agencies on the North Island, you'll be asked to leave it at the ferry terminal in Wellington and pick up another once you've crossed Cook Strait and arrived in Picton. The agencies with cars in Picton include **Avis,** tel. 03/573-6363; **Budget,** tel. 03/573-6081; **Hertz,** tel. 03/573-7224; **Pegasus,** tel. 03/573-7733; and **Thrifty,** tel. 03/573-7387.

Sounds Connection, 10 London Quay, tel. 03/573-8843, has motor scooters for rent, and most of the backpacker lodges offer guests complimentary use of bikes. In both cases, take care on the narrow winding roads throughout the area.

For a taxi, call **Picton Taxis,** tel. 03/573-6207; they also offer one- to three-hour scenic tours (up to five adults per vehicle).

SERVICES

General

Picton Post Office is on High St., next to Mariners Mall. **Bank of New Zealand** is on High Street. **Picton Laundry** is at 14 Auckland Street. You'll find **public toilets** on the harbourfront—go down Memorial Steps and turn left. There's also a ladies' restroom in the Plunket Rooms on Lower Wellington St., and toilets in the Red Cross Rooms on Auckland Street.

Emergency

For an **ambulance,** call 111 or 03/578-4099; for a non-life-threatening emergency, call 03/573-6405 or 03/573-6092 (local GP). **Rob Roy Pharmacy** is at 6 High St., tel. 03/573-6420. **Queen Charlotte Pharmacy** is in Mariners Mall, also on High St., tel. 03/573-7927. One or the other of these is open until 9 P.M. weeknights and all weekend. The **police station** is at 36 Broadway, tel. 03/520-3120.

INFORMATION

The two main sources of local information are in the same building at 14 Auckland St., between the ferry terminal and downtown. **Picton Visitor Information Centre,** tel. 03/573-7477, is open in summer daily 8:30 A.M.–7:30 P.M., shorter hours the rest of the year. It holds information on the entire South Island and makes bookings for all transportation. Local tours can also be booked from here. In the same building is the DOC's **Sounds Area Office,** tel. 03/520-3002. Its comfortable lounges, friendly staff, and lots of information on Marlborough Sounds make it a worthwhile stop. The **Automobile Association** agent has an office at Marlin Motel, 33 Devon St., tel. 03/573-6784.

Marlborough Sounds

Most of the sounds is protected as **Marlborough Sounds Maritime Park.** The park is a maze of waterways, islands with sandy beaches, and high peninsulas. Within the park boundary lie innumerable reserves, the two major inlets of Queen Charlotte and Pelorus Sounds, D'Urville Island, and Croisilles Harbour, altogether covering about 2,914 square km of coastline and islands. If your vehicle is reliable, you can reach many areas of the middle and outer sounds by road (some of it paved, some gravel); you can reach the more remote areas by boat only, but commercial cruises and the mail boat make regular trips everywhere. All the commercial operators (in Picton or Havelock) are willing to drop you off and pick you up at prearranged points and times, allowing one-day island exploration or a several-day hike. For information and maps of the park, head to the DOC Sounds Area Office in Picton. It's on Auckland St., between downtown and the ferry terminal, tel. 03/520-3002.

Picton to Havelock

While Picton is the park's main gateway, Havelock, to the west, is the jumping-off point for Pelorus Sound. **Queen Charlotte Drive,** linking the two towns, is a winding, tortuous road along the edge of the sounds offering some of the South Island's best waterscapes. To access this road, take Dublin St. west from High Street. Beyond the quiet settlement of **Momorangi Bay,** a side road provides access to Anakiwa and the southern end of the Queen Charlotte Track. Continuing west, another secondary road at **Linkwater** winds for almost 100 km into the heart of Marlborough Sounds.

At **Havelock,** where many outdoor activities await discovery—walking and hiking, cruising the sounds, mail boat adventuring, fishing, and glowworm viewing, to name but a few—stay at the excellent **Havelock YHA,** 46 Main Rd., tel. 03/574-2104, a converted, classic country school-

house (Lord Rutherford, the first person to split an atom, went to school here). A large comfy living room, a well-equipped kitchen, spotlessly clean bathrooms, a notice board packed with useful information on the area and surroundings, and bike rentals are just some of the reasons to stay here. Rates are $16–20 per night.

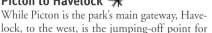

WALKING TRACKS

A track network, from 15-minute walks to several-day hikes, winds throughout Marlborough Sounds Maritime Park, but access for many trails is by boat. In many cases, you can walk just a short section of the trails, returning to Picton that same day, or stay in one of the many lodges out on the sounds. For information and maps of the park, head to the DOC Sounds Area Office in Picton.

Queen Charlotte Track

The most popular and well-defined hiking trail, the 71-km Queen Charlotte Track runs along Queen Charlotte and Kenepuru Sounds from **Ship Cove** to **Anakiwa.** A hiker of average fitness takes about four days to cover it comfortably. You'll find road access at Anakiwa, Te Mahia, Portage, and Kenepuru Saddle. Sea access at Anakiwa, Mistletoe Bay, Torea Bay, Camp Bay, Endeavour Inlet, Resolution Bay, and Ship Cove allows hikers to cover as much or as little of the track as they want. The first 11 km (four hours) of this track, from Ship Cove around Endeavour Inlet to the Kenepuru Saddle, are the most spectacular. They can be completed easily as a day trip from Picton or as an overnight excursion, staying at one of the lodges along the way. Accommodations are spaced at short intervals along the track (no more than a seven-hour walk separates them), and all should be reserved. **Cougar Line,** tel. 03/573-7925, departs Picton as many as four times daily for Ship

> *A track network, from 15-minute walks to several-day hikes, winds throughout Marlborough Sounds Maritime Park.*

Cove and does bus pickups at the end of the trail for $48 per person round-trip. This same company offers a track package for $412 pp, including track transfers, lodge accommodations, packed lunches, and transportation of your pack between overnight stops.

Anakiwa Walk ~~Dea Kyatea~~

Anakiwa Walk (19 km) takes about 6.5 hours to walk from the starting point just beyond the Outward Bound School at Anakiwa (at the head of Queen Charlotte Sound) to the finish at Portage. The track follows the coastline to Davies Bay (safe swimming and campsites), climbs through dense native bush with great views, and emerges at Mistletoe Bay (3.5 hours). You'll find a camping area and guesthouse at Te Mahia and encounter several steep climbs between Mistletoe Bay and the finish at Portage (three hours). Accommodations here include the Portage Hotel and a public camping area at Cowshed Bay, half a km west of the hotel. Either end of the track can be reached by car.

Nydia Track

This track starts at Kaiuma Bay, 1.5 km east of Havelock. On this 22-km hike you pass through farmland, climb through lush native forest to the Kaiuma Saddle, and drop back down into beautiful Nydia Bay (four hours), where you'll find good places to camp. The walk then follows the western shore of the bay, climbs through beech forest to a great lookout, drops down to Ngawhakawhiti Bay (four hours), and finishes at Duncan Bay (one hour) on the shores of Tennyson Inlet. Total track time is at least eight hours, with road access to both ends—prearrange transportation.

Archer Track

Another walk in this area, about three hours each way, is the Archer Track, which starts at Penzance Bay (follow the road around from Duncan Bay). This easy walk (minimal elevation gain) follows the coastline through forest and along a pine plantation, and finishes at Elaine Bay where there are campsites. You can reach Elaine Bay by road—prearrange transportation.

ON THE WATER
Cruising

Many commercial launch operators cruise Queen Charlotte Sound (from Picton) and Pelorus Sound (from Havelock). The easiest way to find out what's available is to head down to the Picton harbourfront, where most operators are based. **Beachcomber Fun Cruises,** tel. 03/573-6175, offer a variety of options. The Portage Luncheon Cruise departs daily at 10:15 A.M. For just $38, it includes a scenic trip to Torea Bay, a bus trip across to Kenepuru Sound to the Portage Resort, and the return trip to Picton. The shorter Round the Bays cruise lasts two hours and costs $34. The Pelorus Mail Boat cruise takes passengers on several different routes depending on the day of the week (Tuesday, Thursday, and Friday), departing from Havelock (9:30 A.M.) or Picton (10:15 A.M.). You'll cover an extensive area of Queen Charlotte Sound, appreciating beautiful secluded bays, isolated homesteads, old whaling stations, historic landmarks, perfect beaches, and lots of birdlife. Take a picnic lunch—tea-making supplies are on board. The cost is $90 adult, children free.

Kayaking

Adventurers shouldn't miss a chat with the owners of the **Marlborough Sounds Adventure Company,** next to the main wharf in Picton, tel. 03/573-6078 or 0800/283-283. They offer a variety of sea kayaking trips to suit all standards and most budgets. Rent one of the kayaks and set off on your own ($35–40 pp per day for a single or double kayak), or take a guided trip. These range from a three-hour evening paddle ($40) to a three-day adventure ($425), which begins with a water taxi ride to the outer sounds. According to kayakers, *this* is the only way to really appreciate the beauty of the sounds.

Fishing

Snapper is the best fighting and perhaps most delicious local fish, averaging 4.5 kg. The most popular places for snapper fishing are Pelorus and Kenepuru Sounds; for blue cod try Queen Charlotte Sound, the head of the sounds, and

Tory Channel. Surf fishing is best anywhere along the east coast from the sounds to Kaikoura (particularly well known), and you're likely to catch snapper, *moki, kahawai* (an exciting fighter but not so good in the taste department), red cod, and dogfish. Any of the local fishermen, launch operators, and sports dealers can provide helpful information on what's biting, how, and where. Expect to pay from $75 pp for a half-day trip with all the necessary equipment supplied.

Diving

Scuba divers will find an abundance of natural underwater wonders throughout Marlborough Sounds, but the most popular dive site is *very* unnatural. In 1986, a Russian cruise ship, the 175-meter-long **Mikhail Lermontov** sank near the entrance to the sounds, coming to rest on its side in around 25 meters of water. Today it's the world's largest diveable cruise ship, with divers able to explore its entire length and even enter the dining room.

The local dive operation, **Diver's World,** at the corner of London Quay and Auckland St., Picton, tel. 03/373-7323, fills tanks, rents equipment, and has a charter boat stocked for divers to take you out to the best spots. Expect to pay from $110 pp for a two-dive trip, and around $200 pp to dive the *Mikhail Lermontov,* which lies a long 60-km boat ride from Picton.

PRACTICALITIES
Accommodations

Lodges are spread throughout the Marlborough Sounds, and because access is generally only by boat, they provide a great way to get away from it all. Each accommodation usually has a restaurant, or meals can be provided, and most offer guests the use of watercraft and fishing gear. The best way to reach them is by water taxi or on a scheduled cruise; the lodges themselves will advise you of transportation options when booking. Expect to pay $60 for the return trip to Endeavour Inlet.

Many varied accommodation options lie along the Queen Charlotte Track. As well as numerous campgrounds, lodges are evenly spaced along

the route, allowing hikers the "luxury" of a roof over their heads. Most hikers spend their first night on Endeavour Inlet, where three lodges provide comfortable accommodations. The closest of these to the start of the track, **Furneaux Lodge,** tel. 03/579-8103, website: www.furneaux .co.nz, has dorm beds, self-contained cabins, and camping. Spread over one hectare of gardens sloping to a sandy beach, this large complex also features a rental shop with kayaks and fishing tackle, boat charters, a restaurant, a bar, and a laundry. Campers pay $10 pp, dorm beds are $18–25, and two-bedroom self-contained cabins are $110 s or d. Continuing around the bay, **Endeavour Resort,** tel. 03/579-8381, has nine cabins and a wide range of facilities, including a small restaurant, general store, library, TV and game room, and a comfortable boat for fishing charters. Rates range $75–110 s or d.

Punga Cove Resort, 11 km beyond the above two resorts but still on Endeavour Inlet, tel. 03/579-8561, website: www.pungacove.co.nz, is an ideal destination in itself, or at the end of the second day on the Queen Charlotte Track. It's set at the head of secluded Punga Cove. Backpackers can stay in the inexpensive dormitories ($20 pp), and there are also A-frame chalets, each with a private balcony ($155 s or d), and more luxurious self-contained cabins (from $200 s or d). The resort's restaurant features imaginative dishes featuring lots of local seafood.

In 2002, new owners began a major upgrade to rooms and facilities of the **Gem Resort** in the Bay of Many Coves, tel. 03/579-9771; website: www.gemresort.co.nz. The lodge is easily reached in one day's walk from Endeavour Inlet, or by water taxi from Picton. Surrounded by native bush, and with boats to rent, a restaurant, and a relaxing spa bath, this is naturally a popular spot; rates from $70 s or d.

Gem Resort is off the main Queen Charlotte Track, but from its access point, the main hiking route descends to Kenepuru Sound (accessed by water taxi from Havelock) and the **Portage Resort Hotel,** tel. 03/573-4309; website: www.portage.co.nz. Accommodations are in bunk rooms ($24 pp) that share a communal kitchen or colorful, contemporary rooms ranging

$145–235 s or d. Join in a wide range of activities, including fishing, diving, tennis, and hiking, or just relax in the swimming pool or delightful rock pool spa. Dining options include a restaurant and a casual waterfront café.

Lying on narrow French Pass, which separates the mainland from D'Urville Island, is **French Pass Motel,** at the end of French Pass Rd., tel. 03/576-5204. The emphasis here is on water activities, with sea kayaking, fishing, scuba diving, and nature tours available. The three self-contained waterfront units are $90 s or d.

Camping

Within Marlborough Sounds Maritime Park lie a large number of coastal reserve campgrounds. The following "campsites" in Queen Charlotte Sound have no facilities and are accessible by boat only: Bottle Bay, Wharehunga Bay, Ngaruru Bay (Arapawa Island), Blumine Island, and Cannibal Cove. Torea Bay can be reached by road. You'll find "camping areas" with toilets and access by sea or road in Queen Charlotte Sound at Whatamongo Bay, Aussie Bay, Davies Bay, Kaipakirikiri Bay, Ratimera Bay, and Camp Bay (Endeavour Inlet, access by sea only).

Lodges are spread throughout the Marlborough Sounds, and because access is generally only by boat, they provide a great way to get away from it all. The best way to reach them is by water taxi or on a scheduled cruise.

The only campgrounds in Queen Charlotte Sound are at Momorangi Bay (accessible by sea or road) and at Resolution Bay (cabins also available), with showers, toilets, a caretaker, and a shop, for a small charge. For a full list of camping possibilities in Pelorus Sound, Tennyson Inlet, Kenepuru Sound, and outer sounds, contact the DOC in Picton or Havelock.

Transportation

Unpaved roads lead throughout the sounds, including to many of the lodges listed above, but you'll need a reliable vehicle and a good map. Most travel through the sounds is by cruise boat (see above) or water taxi, with fares averaging $30 pp one way to most destinations. Departing from Picton is **Endeavour Express,** tel. 03/579-8465, while **Beachcomber Fun Cruises,** tel. 03/573-6175, offers transfers from Havelock.

Information

For Marlborough Sounds Maritime Park information, head to the DOC's **Sounds Area Office,** on Auckland St. in Picton, tel. 03/573-7582 (open Mon.–Fri. 8:30 A.M.–4:30 P.M., Saturday and Sunday 10 A.M.–4:30 P.M.).

MARLBOROUGH

Picton to Christchurch

If you plan to whiz down Hwy. 1 between Picton and Christchurch at a frantic pace because it looks as if there's not much to see and do, you're in for a surprise. Around **Blenheim,** numerous vineyards offer wine-tasting and garden settings for light meals, and galleries and pottery outlets display and sell expressive arts and crafts. Pick up brochures at the information center in Picton before you head out. As you continue south, the highway meanders along a spectacular section of coastline with ocean, beach, and mountain views. Must-see **Kaikoura** is a place where it's only too easy to spend at least several days exploring coastal walkways and reserves, relaxing on the beach, savoring fresh seafood, and experiencing delightful, up-close wildlife adventures with assorted marine mammals—by foot, boat, or plane.

BLENHEIM

Blenheim (population 26,000), 30 km south of Picton, is the capital of the Marlborough region and the center of a large grape-growing area. The first place to go is the **Blenheim Information Centre,** right in the center of town in the Forum Building on Queen St., tel. 03/578-9904, where you can pick up all the brochures on the various wine and crafts trails that radiate from town. **Deluxe Travel Line,** tel. 03/578-5467 or 0800/500-511, takes in four of the best wineries, as well as other local sights and the spectacular Queen Charlotte Drive, for $50 pp, with pickups in either Blenheim or Picton. **Marlborough Wine Tours,** tel. 03/578-9515, is a smaller company, which allows for a flexible itinerary and charges $70 for a full day touring local wineries.

Aside from the wineries, another local attraction is five-hectare **Brayshaw Park,** just off New Renwick Rd., tel. 03/578-6042. The park features a reconstructed colonial village, a boating pond, and a miniature railway, and admission is free. If you like to hike, ask at the information center for a map of **Wither Hills Walkway.** From the high

Seymour Square, Blenheim

points along the trail you can see the entire Marlborough region, and even the North Island.

If you're looking for adventure, call **Action in Marlborough,** tel. 03/578-4531. An adventure outfitter, it offers small, personalized walking and white-water rafting trips in the Marlborough Sounds and Nelson Lakes National Park.

Accommodations

The Grapevine (formerly Blenheim Backpackers), 29 Park Terrace, tel. 03/578-6062, is in a building that used to be a maternity hospital more than 100 years ago. It's within walking distance of town, the bus depot, and the train station. The hosts offer a variety of day trips, or you can just cruise around town on their tandem bike. Shared dorms are $15 pp, doubles are $18 pp. Just north of town is **Blenheim Motor**

Camp, 27 Budge St., tel. 03/578-7419. Campsites are $20, basic cabins are $35–60, and dorm beds are $16 pp.

Alpine Motel, 148 Middle Renwick Rd., tel. 03/578-1604 or 0800/101-931, provides good value in its seven self-contained rooms for $65 s, $70 d, which includes pickups from anywhere in town. It's west of downtown on the main road (Hwy. 6) to Nelson.

For a real splurge, consider a stay at **Hotel d'Urville,** 52 Queen St., tel. 03/577-9945; website: www.durville.co.nz. This boutique hotel is housed in a government building that has been extensively renovated but still holds its historic charm, right down to a distinctive colonnaded façade. The nine guest rooms are each very different but equally chic-request the Colour Room for bold, contrasting colors or the D'Urville Suite for a stylish nautical theme in keeping with the hotel's namesake, an 1820s explorer. Rates are $235 s, $240 d.

Food

Many of the wineries around Blenheim serve meals, and these are the places to really tuck in and splurge. **Hunter's** on Rapaura Rd., tel. 03/572-8803, has an excellent reputation for its Sauvignon Blanc and Chardonnay wines, but also for its restaurant. Morning and afternoon teas are available in an outdoor dining area, but more substantial meals-such as local green mussels steamed in the winery's own Riesling-make a meal at Hunter's memorable. The restaurant is open for lunch daily noon–3 P.M. and for dinner Thurs.–Sun. from 6 P.M. Back in town, the **d'Urville Wine Bar and Brasserie,** 52 Queen St., tel. 03/577-9945, is a narrow dining room with tables paralleling a long wooden bar shaped like ship's bow and walls decorated with old maps and nautical charts. The menu features dishes such as a mouthwatering pepper-crusted rack of Canterbury lamb, as well as seasonal seafood dishes such as mussels steamed in white wine, with a hint of chili and garlic. It's open Mon.–Fri. for lunch and daily for dinner. **Peppercorns** at 73 Queen St., tel. 03/577-8886, is the spot for light and healthy inexpensive dining.

Services and Information

Blenheim Station Travel Centre in the railway station on Sinclair St., tel. 03/577-2890, is an agent for **Tranz Scenic,** and **Intercity.** These transportation services use the station as a base, as do a number of shuttle buses that connect Blenheim to Picton and Kaikoura.

KAIKOURA

Kaikoura (a Maori word: to eat crayfish) has grown rapidly in recent years from a sleepy little fishing village to one of the country's premier wildlife-watching destinations. The highlight is the proximity of sperm whales, which feed within one km of the coast, but there's plenty of other opportunities to interact with nature if you have the time (and cash). Sandwiched between the steep mountains of the Kaikoura Range and the deep blue South Pacific Ocean midway between Picton and

Kaikoura Beach

MARLBOROUGH

Christchurch, the town is a natural overnight stop between the two major centers.

Start your discovery at the excellent **Kaikoura Visitor Information Centre,** The Esplanade, tel. 03/319-5641; it's open daily 9 A.M.–5 P.M. in summer; the rest of the year Mon.–Fri. 9:30 A.M.–4 P.M.

Sights

The many exhibits, argillite and greenstone artifacts, photographs, records, implements, and utensils on display at the **Kaikoura Museum** on Ludstone Rd., tel. 03/319-5831, trace the life and history of the Maori and European people and the district of Kaikoura. It's open daily 2–4 P.M.; admission $2. Continuing on the historic trail, visit **Fyffe House,** 62 Avoca St. (south of town), tel. 03/319-5835, a colonial cottage from the 1860s when Kaikoura, then known as "Fyffe's Village," was a whaling station. It's on the way to the seal colony, and open daily 10 A.M.–4 P.M.; admission $3.50.

Two km south of Kaikoura on Hwy.1, a guided tour of **Maori Leap Cave,** a sea-formed limestone cave more than two million years old, is worth the admission of $8.50 adult, $3 child. The 40-minute tours are conducted six times daily; book at the adjacent restaurant, tel. 03/319-5023.

Quite a number of potters and craftspeople live around Kaikoura. Pick up a "Kaikoura Potters Trail" brochure at the information center. It briefly describes six pottery outlets with their locations and business hours.

Whales, Dolphins, and Seals

The Kaikoura coast is the only place in New Zealand where sperm whales lives year-round (Kaikoura used to be a whaling station). Therefore, visitors can usually see these impressive mammals, subject to conditions and seasonal fluctuations, whenever they visit Kaikoura—though locals say the winter months are best for viewing. The local Ngai Tahu, who have lived in the area for over 3,000 years, are the only ones permitted to operate tours. Their operation, **Whale Watch Kaikoura** is based in a beachside railway station that has been converted to the Whaleway Station, tel. 03/319-6767 or 0800/

unique coastal geology south of Kaikoura

655-121. They operate three-hour whale-watching trips up to six times daily in search of sperm whales, orcas (summer only), humpback whales (winter only), Hector's and dusky dolphins, seals, and albatross; $100 adult, $60 child. Wear warm clothing and long pants in summer, plus a warm jacket, hat, and gloves in winter (and consider restricting your fluid intake a little before you go—there's a toilet only on the large boat). Naturally, whale sightings cannot be guaranteed. Book two weeks ahead to be sure of a spot—in summer the tours are filled at least a week ahead. The alternate way to see the whales is from above—by plane. **Wings Over Whales,** tel. 03/319-6580 or 0800/226-269, provides a 30-minute flight for a bird's-eye view of the whales for $95 pp. A courtesy van will collect you from town, if needed, for the eight-km trip to the airfield.

The best way to get close to the pods of dusky dolphins in the bay is by swimming with them. **Dolphin Encounter,** 58 West End (the main street), tel. 03/319-6777 or 0800/733-365, offers this experience (the first in New Zealand to do so—operators are now everywhere) that you won't forget in a hurry. The boat trip and swim (Oct.–April) are $95 pp (wet suit, mask, and snorkel provided); nonswimmers pay $48.

Want to swim with seals? Then give Graeme or Bev Chambers of **Seal Swim Kaikoura** a call at 03/319-6182. In summer, Graeme takes small groups equipped with full wet suits, snorkels, and gear for a two-hour South Pacific adventure and close encounter with maybe a dozen or more fur seals; $45 pp.

Tours and Treks

Kaikoura Experience, booked through the information center, offers a six- to seven-hour trip rafting down the scenic Clarence River with a stop for a barbecue and a short bush walk to a waterfall for $65 pp, and abseiling (if there's demand) for $35 pp. For two-hour horseback rides through farmland, riverbed, and bush scenery with great views, give **Fyffe View Horse Treks** a call at 03/319-5069; $40 pp. It also offers all-day adventure rides up Mt. Fyffe (on request).

Walks

Hikers can pick from a large variety of local short walks and longer hikes in the surrounding area. At the information center collect the pamphlet "On The Right Track" (50 cents) with a map and short description of seven walks ranging from 10 minutes to three hours. The "Kaikoura Peninsula Walks" brochure covers four walking tracks (part of the New Zealand Walkway network) and takes you to cliffs where you can view the seal colony. For scenic reserve discoveries farther afield, pick up the "Southern Marlborough Recreation Areas" brochure. Two walking tracks lead into **Mount Fyffe Forest,** a forest walk and a track climbing to the 1,602-meter summit of Mt. Fyffe (eight hours round-trip). The mountain dominates the western skyline of Kaikoura Plain and Kaikoura. A brochure on the forest is available.

Accommodations

Most motels are spread out along The Esplanade, immediately south and within walking distance of the information center. Least expensive of these is the **Sierra Beachfront Motel,** 160 The Esplanade, tel. 03/319-5622 or 0800/474-377, charging from $75 s or d for a small room with a kitchen. **Blue Seas Motels,** 222 Esplanade, tel. 03/319-5441 or 0800/507-077, offers a variety of units on the Kaikoura seafront. Prices range $85–135 s or d for self-contained units.

A step up in quality is the **White Morph Motor Inn,** on the edge of downtown and directly opposite the beach at 94 The Esplanade, tel. 03/319-5014 or 0800/803-666; website: www.whitemorph.co.nz. It features modern, spacious rooms and a seafood restaurant. Standard rooms are $115 s or d, two-room suites are $136, and units with a king-size bed and whirlpool bath are $175.

Kaikoura has a large choice of excellent backpacker lodges. **Cray Cottage,** 190 The Esplanade, tel. 03/319-5152, is a 10-minute walk east from the information center (free pickups), but the waterfront location and modern facilities are outstanding. Rates are $18 pp in a dorm, $22 pp in

© ANDREW HEMPSTEAD

deserted beach, south of Kaikoura

one of two twin rooms. Continuing east, the modern **Maui YHA,** 270 The Esplanade, tel. 03/319-5931, website: www.yha.org.nz, has a great location with excellent views—and its homemade bread rolls and chocolate cake are house specialties. Rates are $17 for a dorm bed, $20 d or twin.

On the hill behind downtown is the **Dolphin Lodge,** 15 Deal St., tel. 03/319-5842. The friendly owners can advise on local activities and make the place feel quite homely. A huge balcony overlooking the bay tops this off as a great place to stay. Dorm beds are $17 pp, doubles $20 pp. Diagonally opposite, **Topspot,** 22 Deal St. (off Churchill St.), tel. 03/319-5540, is an old character house with a renovated modern interior—a large bright kitchen, a comfy living area (good music), a garden with deck, a barbecue, great views, and a friendly manager who offers free use of bikes. Rates are $18–30 pp.

Kaikoura Searidge Top 10 Holiday Park along Beach Rd., tel. 03/319-5362, has a large grassy area for tents and vans ($8 pp), a number of great little cabins ($28), and a modern kitchen. **A1 Kaikoura Motels & Holiday Park,** 11 Beach Rd. (main highway), tel. 03/319-5999, provides grassy tent sites among the trees (can get crowded in summer) for $20, caravan sites for $22, cabins from $34 d, tourist flats for $60 d, and motel rooms from $75 d. Communal facilities include a kitchen and dining area, a laundry, a small above-ground pool, and a trampoline.

Food

On The Esplanade, near the information center, **Why Not Café,** tel. 03/319-6486, is a good place for a big, filling cooked breakfast U.S. diner-style; expect to pay about $10. It's open daily from 5 A.M.

In season, the one delicacy you must try in Kaikoura is locally caught crayfish (lobster). You can get it with all the trimmings in restaurants throughout town, as well as enjoy it as a take-out meal. At **Continental Seafoods,** 47 Beach Rd. (across the road from Kaikoura Searidge Top 10 Holiday Park), tel. 03/319-5509, a half crayfish, chips, and salad cost $20. Or choose from several

fish of the day, mussels, smoked fish patties, and take it away fresh or have it cooked on the spot. **Flukes Café,** in the Whaleway Station, tel. 03/319-7733, features a contemporary Maori-influenced interior and an outdoor eating area overlooking the beach. The menu offers no surprises, but the setting can't be beat. Another place to try fresh seafood (crayfish in season Aug.–May, weather permitting, for $28, great seafood soup for $6, fish and salad sandwiches) is **Caves Restaurant** on the main highway heading south, tel. 03/319-5023. Eat inside or use the outdoor courtyard at the back, then work it off with a walk on the beach just across the road. It's open daily 7 A.M.–6 P.M. For informal yet elegant surroundings (and great marinelife-inspired art on the walls), try **White Morph Restaurant** in the old Bank of New Zealand building at 94 The Esplanade, tel. 03/319-5676. It's open daily from 6 P.M. Main dishes are "from the land" or "from the sea" and range $20–32, or splurge on the seafood platter for two, piled with local seafood, including crayfish, for $68.

Transportation

Kaikoura has scheduled flights, but **Wings Over Whales,** tel. 03/319-6580, flies into the small airfield eight km south of town on demand from Christchurch. The rail line runs right through town, making Kaikoura a popular stop for those traveling on the daily *Coastal Pacific* service between Picton and Christchurch. For all the details, call **Tranz Scenic** at 0800/802-802. The main bus stop is the parking lot for the information center on The Esplanade. Look for the board out front advertising arrival and departure times. In addition to **Intercity,** tel. 03/319-5641, many shuttle services have buses stopping here on the run between Picton and Christchurch, including **Atomic Shuttles,** tel. 03/319-5641; **Compass Coachlines,** tel. 03/578-7102; and **South Island Connections,** tel. 03/319-5641.

It's easy to get around Kaikoura on foot or bike. **Kaikoura Taxi,** tel. 03/319-6214, charges around $6 pp to get out to the seal colony or airfield and $15 pp per hour for a guided tour.

Services and Information

Banks are on West End (Trust Bank Canterbury has a 24-hour Cashflow machine). For an **ambulance** call 111 or 03/319-5040. A **doctor's office** is on Deal St., tel. 03/319-5040 or 03/319-5027. **Kaikoura Pharmacy** is at 37 West End, tel. 03/319-5035. The **police station** is at 12 Hastings St., tel. 03/319-5038.

For all information and bookings, go to **Kaikoura Visitor Information Centre** on The Esplanade in the town center, tel. 03/319-5641, website: www.kaikoura.co.nz; it's open daily 9 A.M.–5 P.M. in summer, weekdays 9:30 A.M.–4 P.M. plus Saturday mornings (if there's a demand) in winter. An excellent staff assists visitors, screens a stunning 20-minute audiovisual on the whales on the hour (admission $2 adult, $1 child), and provides plenty of literature.

HANMER SPRINGS

Most people zoom down the east coast from Kaikoura on Hwy. 1, but while the alternate inland route (Hwy. 70) is longer, it provides a very different glimpse of the South Island. Around 120 km south of Kaikoura (allow at least 2.5 hours), Hwy. 70 ends at Hwy. 7, a major cross-island highway. From this point, it's 90 km south to Christchurch, but a worthwhile detour is Hanmer Springs, 43 km west off Hwy. 7. This alpine town of 700 is a popular getaway for those who enjoy soaking in thermal pools, hiking in exotic forests, fishing, or skiing. It attracts large numbers of New Zealanders and tourists year-round.

Sights and Recreation

The hot springs that feed **Hanmer Springs Thermal Reserve** on Amuri Rd., tel. 03/315-7511, are saline and alkaline, and the 10 indoor and outdoor pools vary in temperature 32–40°C. For some soaking privacy, rent a private thermal pool for $15 per 30 minutes. The complex is open daily 10 A.M.–9 P.M.; $8 adult, $4 child; swimsuit, towel, and safe deposit rental available.

Hanmer Forest Park, one of New Zealand's oldest government-owned exotic forests, covers 16,844 hectares of land near the town; the most

widely grown tree is the *Pinus radiata*. Many good tracks allow you to amble through the different types of forest to panoramic lookouts. For trail maps, stop by the **Forest Park Information Centre** on Jollies Pass Rd., about one km from Hanmer Springs Post Office; it's open most days 9 A.M.–5 P.M.

At **Hanmer Springs Ski Area,** 24 km beyond the town, tel. 03/315-7201, you'll find one long platter lift and two rope tows. Spread over 52 hectares, the terrain is mostly beginner and intermediate. Lift tickets are $35 and rentals are available at the day lodge.

Practicalities

It's not too difficult to find a place to stay in Hanmer Springs—take your choice of a number of hotels and motels, tourist flats and cabins, and several good motor camps. The town also has restaurants, coffee shops, and take-aways.

West of downtown and adjacent to the golf course, the **Willowbank Motel,** 121 Argelins Rd., tel. 03/315-7211 or 0800/258-246, offers the cheapest self-contained rooms in town; $55–85 s or d.

Alpine Lodge Motel lies across the road from the thermal pools at 1 Harrogate St., tel. 03/315-7311 or 0800/993-377; website: www.alpinelodgemotel.co.nz. Its standard rooms are comfortable and self-contained ($105 s or d), but the Tower Suites provide Hanmer's finest lodging. These massive units feature circular beds, large spa baths, and a private balcony ($195 s or d).

Heritage Hanmer Springs, 1 Conical Hill Rd., tel. 03/315-7021 or 0800/368-888, website: www.heritagehotels.co.nz, one of Hanmer's original accommodations, has undergone extensive renovations in recent years. It features landscaped gardens, a tennis court, a heated outdoor pool, and guests enjoy 24-hour room service. It also holds the village's premier restaurant. Rates start at $145 s, $160 d, but check the website for discounted package deals.

Braemar Lodge is a luxurious accommodation overlooking the Hanmer River, tel. 03/315-7049; website: www.braemarlodge.co.nz. It's signposted off Hwy. 7A south of Hanmer. Each of the spacious rooms has panoramic mountain views and guest enjoy tennis, a swimming pool, and a spa, but the highlight is the food. Rates of $320 s, 270 pp d include a gourmet breakfast and lunch and a four-course dinner in the formal dining room. The menu changes with the seasons, but also includes multiple choices of seafood and game.

AA Tourist Park, three km from the township at Jacks Pass, on Jacks Pass Rd., tel. 03/315-7112, has communal facilities and a TV and game room. Tent and caravan sites start at $18, cabins $42 d, and tourist flats $62 d. **Mountain View Top 10 Holiday Park** on the southern outskirts of Hanmer, tel. 03/315-7113 or 0800/904-545, has communal facilities, a squash court, a TV and recreation room, and milk available daily. Tent and caravan sites are $18–20 d, cabins from $58, and tourist flats $72 d.

Hanmer Springs is served by **Hanmer Connection,** tel. 03/315-7575 or 0800/377-378, a daily service between Christchurch, Kaikoura, and Hanmer Springs.

For information on the town and surrounding area, call in at the **Hurunui Visitor Information Centre** on Amuri Ave. (at Jacks Pass Rd.), tel. 03/315-7128 or 0800/733-426, website: www.hurunui.com; it's open daily 10 A.M.–5 P.M.

HANMER SPRINGS TO THE WEST COAST

From the Hanmer Springs intersection, Hwy. 7 climbs to 907-meter **Lewis Pass** (this route is often called the Lewis Pass Highway), then descends to the west coast. Allow six hours for the crossing, but expect to take longer if you want to stop and explore the wild, rugged, South Island interior with its high mountain peaks, fast-flowing rivers, forests, and tranquil lakes.

Lewis Pass National Reserve

Rediscovered by Europeans in 1861, the pass was used by generations of Maori to cross the mountains from the Canterbury coast to west coast greenstone country—the Ngaitahu tribe

used to hike over the pass, gather greenstone, then take prisoners to carry the precious rock back. As food supplies ran low around **Cannibal Gorge** (the original Maori name means good feed of human flesh), the slaves became more useful as fresh meat. Let your imagination run wild at this gorge by taking the short 25-minute one-way track starting at the Lewis Pass picnic area, which runs along the first section of the Ada Pass-St. James Walkway to Cannibal Gorge Bridge. Other tracks range from the short 10-minute **Waterfall Nature Walk** to the three- to five-day hike along the **St. James Walkway** (pamphlets available), and during the summer the rangers lead walks through the reserve. If you're doing any of the longer hikes, be prepared for sudden rain or snowstorms and take extra food.

Maruia Springs

This tiny settlement, a few km west of the pass itself, is a great place to stop for a hike, then a soak in the mineral pools of **Maruia Springs Thermal Resort,** tel. 03/523-8840; website: www.maruia.co.nz. Choices include a covered Japanese-style bathhouse, private spa pools, and outdoor pools surrounded by bird-filled native bush. Entry is $7 ($20 per hour for a private spa) and it's open to the public daily 11 A.M.–5 P.M. Hotel rooms, all with spa baths, are $95–145 s or d, with free entry to the mineral pools. Backpacker rooms are available for $26.50 pp or camp for $10 pp. Another good reason to stop is to eat in the resort café—healthy meals and casual surroundings. Breakfast is available 8 A.M.–9:30 A.M., lunch noon–2 P.M., and dinner 6–8 P.M. Shoot some nine-ball while you wait. The complex also holds a Japanese restaurant.

Continuing West Toward the Coast

From Maruia Springs, it's 17 km to **Springs Junction,** a small hamlet with one motel, a café, a service station and a post office. At this point, the highway divides. Hwy. 7 continues west to **Reefton** and Hwy. 65 spurs north to **Murchison,** on Hwy. 6. In the heart of a historic gold-mining area, Reefton offers varied opportunities for hiking, to relics of the mining era and through the surrounding wilderness, much of it protected by Victoria Forest Park. From Reefton, Hwy. 7 turns south, reaching the Tasman Sea at Greymouth. If you take this route, you miss one of the highlights of the west coast, Paparoa National Park, which can be reached by taking Hwy. 69 north from Reefton to meet Hwy. 6, then following the Buller River to the coast.

Nelson and the Northwest

For those of you with plenty of time, the deliciously laid-back atmosphere of **Nelson,** home to many of New Zealand's best potters, weavers, and arts and craftspeople, is well worth a visit, and it's the kind of place where you're likely to meet other relaxed travelers.

Continue farthernorthwest around Tasman Bay to the isolated and ruggedly beautiful **Abel Tasman National Park** for outstanding hiking and scenery, and on to **Golden Bay,** which stretches round to the far northern tip of the South Island and has secluded sandy beaches, not many people, lots of birdlife, and scenery ranging from water panoramas to rugged mountains.

Nelson's Trafalgar Street

© ANDREW HEMPSTEAD

Nelson

Nelson (population 53,000), according to proud residents, is no less than the center of, well, everything. Not only is it recognized as the geographical center of New Zealand, it's also the center of apple-, hops-, and tobacco-growing areas. In addition, locals claim that Nelson is the "sunshine" center, the "arts and crafts" center, and even the "conference" center of the country. Hyperbole notwithstanding, the city of Nelson *is* a lively base from which to head out for hiking trips in Abel Tasman National Park in the northwest, Nelson Lakes National Park in the south, or the well-known Heaphy Track on the northwest coast. Add plenty of sunshine, sea, and sand, and you have the local equation for perfection. The people are creative and relaxed, and make you feel right at home. Partly because of this atmosphere the town attracts a mellow crowd—even in midsummer when New Zealanders flock to the region for R & R, a deep suntan, and bargain hunting from a wide array of locally produced crafts. Finally, Nelson is also the main commercial center for the northwest (Motueka to the west is busy but smaller—less variety), and it's a good idea to stock up on camping equipment and hiking supplies here before continuing to the national parks or walking tracks.

SIGHTS

Trafalgar St., which runs south from Hwy. 6 as it enters town from the north, is the main shopping strip, ending below an impressive cathedral that towers over downtown. The large **Visitor Information Centre,** on the corner of Trafalgar and Halifax Streets, is the first place to go; if you're exploring Nelson on foot, pick up the handy *Nelson: The City of Walks* pamphlet. Ask if there's anything going on in the local parks—regular "park days" with bright carnival atmosphere and various festivities are put on to promote the use of the many parks. Another brochure worth finding is *Nelson Potters.* Before you leave the information center, be sure to check the outside notice boards: there's useful information on local tours, launch trips, guided walks, arts-and-crafts outlets, and

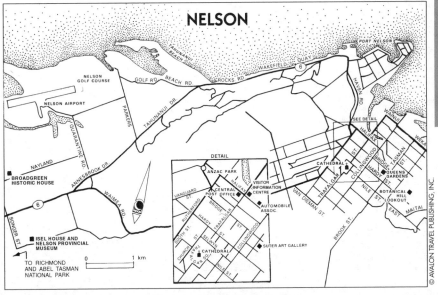

NELSON AND THE NORTHWEST

© AVALON TRAVEL PUBLISHING, INC.

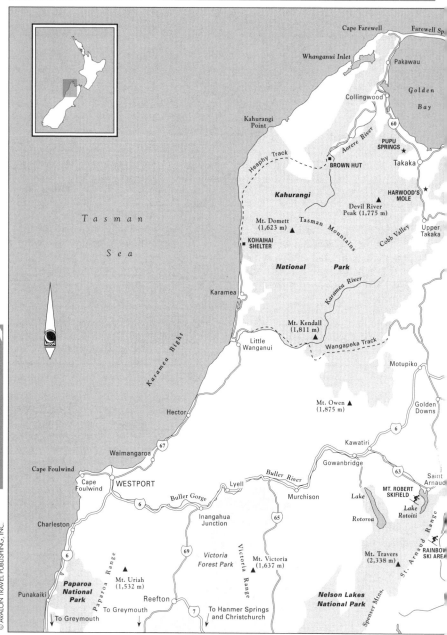

transportation to and from the two main hiking tracks (Heaphy and Wangapeka) in the Nelson region.

Nelson Cathedral

Walk south from the information center along Trafalgar St. to Nelson's impressive cathedral, on Church Hill at the south end of the main shopping street. Much of this Anglican cathedral, completed in 1925, is made of Takaka marble (from Takaka Hill, about 70 km west of Nelson), and its landmark 35-meter tower dominates the inner-city area. It's open daily 7 A.M.–7 P.M., and during church services, and volunteer guides (on hand during the busy summer) point out the many memorials and historic links with early Nelson housed inside the cathedral.

Suter Art Gallery

Described as "the most lively and central art gallery in New Zealand," this one shouldn't be missed by any art lover. Along with the large permanent art collection are varied exhibitions, films, performances, and recitals; at the excellent crafts shop you can buy top-quality pieces of local pottery, weaving, and prints. A restaurant overlooks adjacent **Queen's Gardens,** one of Nelson's most attractive reserves containing many rare tree specimens (all named), a fernery, flowering bushes, and an ornamental pond swarming with ducks—don't miss it! The gallery and restaurant (if it's near lunchtime, you'll smell the aroma from the kitchen as soon as you walk into the gallery) are open daily 10:30 A.M.–4:30 P.M.; $2 adult, $.20 child. It's on Bridge St., tel. 03/548-4699; from Collingwood St. turn east onto Bridge Street.

Historic Houses

Broadgreen Historic House, on Nayland Rd., Stoke, tel. 03/546-0283, is a magnificent, two-story, mid-Victorian "cob" house made from mud and clay mixed with straw, horsehair, and other reinforcing materials. The house, built around 1855, is set among perfect lawns and rambling rose gardens, and the interior period furnishings are an antique buff's delight; it's open daily 10:30 A.M.–4:30 P.M.; small admission.

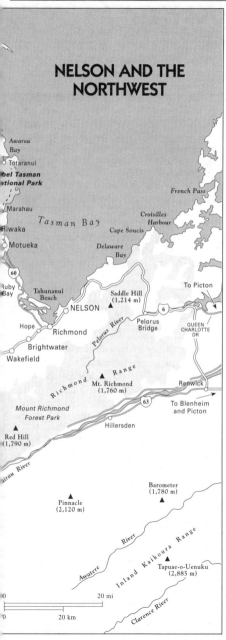

NELSON AND THE NORTHWEST

NELSON ARTS AND CRAFTS

Nelson is known throughout New Zealand for its fine, varied clays; excellent raw materials; a large community of talented, creative potters; and a vast number of outlets. Many of the clay and glaze materials (ground from naturally occurring minerals) used by potters throughout New Zealand come from around the Nelson region. You can spend days visiting all the pottery shops throughout the area. For directions, pick up the free brochure "Nelson Potters" from the information center, along with other brochures on spinning, weaving, jewelry making, and other local crafts. Following are some favorites.

Nile Street, lined with some of Nelson's attractive older cottages—some dating from the 1800s, is home to many galleries. **South Street Gallery,** 10 Nile St., tel. 03/548-8117, is definitely worth a stop to view its rustic interior while appreciating the works of more than 20 local artists, and maybe

picking out a superb piece of the local pottery for which the gallery is renowned. It's open Mon.–Fri. 10 A.M.–5 P.M. (later on Friday), weekends 10 A.M.–4 P.M.

Out of Nelson to the southwest, **Craft Habitat,** on the corner of Main and Champion Roads (near the Stoke Bypass), tel. 03/544-2981, features an excellent selection of pottery, weaving, wood and metal products, carved bone, handcrafted baskets, fabric art, and handblown glass. You can watch many of the craftspeople actually creating their works of art; open daily. Save a few dollars for a refreshing Devonshire tea or light lunch in the **Habitat Café,** tel. 03/544-5657.

On the north side of Nelson, you'll be continually tempted to part with your money at the small roadside stalls, snazzy shops, and isolated potters' retreats among the many arts and crafts outlets.

Isel House, on Main Rd., Stoke, tel. 03/547-7529, is an impressive two-story wood and stone house built around 1886. Chockablock with priceless antiques and surrounded by 12 acres of woods, it's open weekends 2–4 P.M.; admission $2.

Nelson Provincial Museum

While you're visiting Isel House, don't miss Nelson's fascinating Provincial Museum (at the rear), which features early Nelson history: displays of Maori carvings and artifacts found in the district, and objects and curios originally brought over by English settlers. The attractive gardens and grounds of **Isel Park,** where many of the trees have stood for more than a century, surround the museum, set in the western Nelson suburb of Stoke. It's open Tues.–Fri. 10 A.M.–4 P.M., and Saturday, Sunday, and public holidays noon–4 P.M.; $2 adult, $1 child, and varying admission fees for special exhibitions.

RECREATION
Short Walks

The many pleasant walks of varying distances around the city and throughout the suburbs are

described in a series of pamphlets put out by the Nelson City Council at the information center. One of the best-known and most scenic is the one-km **Centre of New Zealand** track, which gradually zigzags up Botanical Hill (148 meters) to a lookout and monument marking the first trig station (a survey marker atop a hill) in Nelson. Start at the Botanical Reserve on Milton St. (east of downtown). **The Grampians,** another popular hike to a lookout, provides excellent views of the city and surrounding area, but note that the steep climb takes about 1.5 hours each way. If you're still in an energetic mood once you've reached the top, continue south over the hilltops for about two km to Flaxmoor (390 meters), which you can also reach by footpath from Waimea Road. The first section of the Grampian foot track starts at the top (south) end of Collingwood St. in the city—take something refreshing to drink. The **Maitai River Walkway** starts at the bridge near the information center and meanders along the river (past some good swimming holes), taking about four hours round-trip—take a picnic lunch and enjoy.

For an easy walk following the historic line of New Zealand's first railway, try the 9.5-km

Dun Mountain Walkway. It starts on Tantragee Rd. (left off Brook St. in the suburb of The Brook, five km south of city center), finishes one km from the starting point on Brook St., and takes about three hours round-trip. One of the most scenic walks in the Nelson region is the **Dun Mountain Track,** which passes through native bush to Third House and the summit. The track starts at Brook Street Motor Camp (contact the caretaker before setting out), or from the Maitai Valley.

Beaches

The closest, **Tahunanui Beach** (also called Tahuna Beach), is five km west of the city center, and is one of the safest, most popular beaches in the region. To get there from the city center take Haven Rd. west to Port Nelson and follow Rocks Rd. (Hwy. 6 south) along the waterfront, or catch the suburban bus (it runs every hour) from Bridge Street. This pleasant route is especially colorful in early summer, when striking *pohutukawa* trees bloom in a mass of scarlet flowers. Don't miss the incredible Aotearoa (Land of the Long White Cloud) wall mural (a Nelson Provincial Arts Council Mural Project) on the right side of Rocks Rd. as you follow the waterfront toward the beach. The enormous Tahuna Beach Holiday Park is within walking distance of the beach (see below).

If you don't mind a 27-km drive west toward Motueka, you'll be rewarded with about 12 km of soft golden sand, dunes, pine trees, safe swimming, and good surf casting at **Rabbit Island.** Take Hwy. 6 south out of Nelson, go through Richmond following signs to Motueka (Hwy. 60), and turn right at Pea Viner Corner. For more beautiful sandy beaches and fewer and fewer people, continue north to Golden Bay.

Entertainment

For entertainment listings, see the local newspaper and tourist papers, and call in at the information center. For a quiet afternoon or evening drink overlooking the water, head out toward Port Nelson and the **Quayside Restaurant,** 309 Wakefield Quay, tel. 03/548-3319. Downtown, bars and nightclubs are concentrated at the east end of Bridge Street. The most popular backpacker hangout is **Shark Club,** 136 Bridge St., tel. 03/546-6630, with an outdoor beer garden, a large pool room, and live entertainment on weekends. **Little Rock Café,** 165 Bridge St., tel. 03/546-8800, is busiest on weekends after 10 P.M., when a DJ spins dance tracks until the early hours of the morning.

Festivals and Events

Nelson holds enough attraction to warrant a visit at any time of year, but also look out for the following annual events. The **Sealord Summer Festival,** tel. 03/546-0254, extends over six weeks from the Christmas holiday break. Check at the information center for a schedule of lunchtime music concerts, street entertainment, outdoor movie screenings, and local businesses that open for behind-the-scenes tours. In the middle of these festivities, on the third Sunday in January, Neale Park is host to the **Nelson Summer Kite Festival.** On the middle Saturday of February, **Sealord Opera in the Park,** tel. 03/546-0212, attracts a crowd of up to 10,000 to Saxton Field, Stoke. It's a casual affair, with admission just $5 and buses transporting the masses from Nelson.

Hooked on Seafood, the 4th Saturday in March, features Nelson chefs showcasing their cooking skills at booths set up along Vickerman St., Port Nelson; expect lots of local seafood complemented by New Zealand wines.

Arts Council Nelson promotes a wide variety of events through the year, including the **Nelson Arts Festival,** through the last two weeks of September. Details can be found on the website: www.nelsonart.co.nz.

ACCOMMODATIONS
Hotels and Motels

Most motels are southwest of downtown along Hwy. 6 as it passes through Tahunanui Beach. A good-value motel within walking distance of downtown is **Trafalgar Lodge Motel,** opposite Trafalgar Park at 46 Trafalgar St., tel. 03/548-3980. The six self-contained units go for $68 s, $88 d. Even more central, **Mid City Motor Lodge,** 218 Trafalgar St., tel. 03/546-9063 or

NELSON AND THE NORTHWEST

0800/643-2489, offers spacious self-contained studio units on three levels above the main shopping strip; $85 s, $95 d. **Trailways Motor Inn,** 66 Trafalgar St., tel. 03/548-7049 or 0800/872-459, website: www.trailways.co.nz, boasts a peaceful location right on the Maitai River, but still within walking distance of downtown. The rooms are spacious and well furnished. They lack kitchens, but the inn has a good restaurant and a lounge bar. Rates are $105 s or d.   Nelson's most luxurious accommodation is the **Rutherford Hotel,** Trafalgar Square, tel. 03/548-2299 or 0800/437-227; website: www.rutherfordhotel.co.nz. It features 115 elegantly decorated rooms, a pool, spas, sauna, and fitness room, as well as a restaurant, café, and bar. Rates range $175–200 s or d.

Aloha Lodge, 19 Beach Rd., tel. 03/546-4000 or 0800/462-5642, is separated from Tahuna Beach by only a park, and many of the rooms offer water views. Standard rooms are $99 s or d, but the suites provide the best value. Set in towers with wraparound windows, the views are stunning; rates $130 s or d. Another option in this same area is **Riviera Motel,** 62 Golf Rd., tel. 03/548-6020, which charges $75 s, $95 d s or d for one of six self-contained units.

Bed-and-Breakfasts

Where do we start? Nelson boasts the highest concentration of bed-and-breakfasts of any New Zealand region.

If you feel like being pampered while staying in a beautifully restored old home, head directly for **California House Inn** at 29 Collingwood St., tel. 03/548-4173; website: www.california-house.co.nz. Built in 1893, this elegant colonial home features five spacious guest rooms, each with a private bathroom, English oak furnishings, high ceilings, stained-glass windows, and fireplaces throughout. The cozy parlor is well stocked with reading material on Nelson and New Zealand, and you can help yourself to tea and coffee throughout the day. The breakfast menu features fresh fruit and cream, baked goodies, pancakes, blintzes, or omelets—sumptuous and different each morning (forget all notions of a diet). Rates are $130–160 s, $160–210 d.

Palm Grove Guest House at 15 Tasman St., tel. 03/548-4645, is an attractive old house with six sunny guest rooms, a TV room, a garden, coffee- and tea-making supplies, but no guest use of the kitchen or laundry; $50 s, $80 d or twin includes a hearty breakfast with homemade goodies.

At **Cambria House,** 7 Cambria St., tel. 03/548-4681 or 0800/548-4681, website: www.cambria.co.nz, the welcoming owners happily share their home, offering guests bright spacious rooms with private facilities, a comfortable living room with TV, and a sumptuous cooked breakfast in the attractive country-style dining room for $145 s, $185 d, discounted to $115 s, $145 d outside of summer.

Richmond, just to the south of Nelson, has a number of excellent bed-and-breakfasts but you need your own transportation. The pick of the bunch is **Mapledurham** at 8 Edward St., tel. 03/544-4210. This century-old house has been immaculately restored and provides three huge rooms—each with its own character and very comfortable beds—a lounge area with a log fire, and a tree-shaded garden for sunny afternoons. Rates of $145–180 s, $185–215 d include a gourmet breakfast, and dinner is optional at $45 pp.

Backpacker Lodges

There's no lack of choice when it comes to budget accommodations in Nelson (more than a dozen at last count). Check the latest ratings in the BBH Blue Book to see what's hot and what's not, because things change quickly on the Nelson backpacker scene. Representatives of some backpacker lodges meet bus arrivals down at the information center, and they have been known to undercut each other to fill beds during quiet periods. Book a bed in advance at one of the places below and you can't go wrong.

One of the best choices is **Paradiso,** 42 Weka St., tel. 03/546-6703, a 500-meter walk to downtown. Formerly a YHA property, it has been renovated and is surrounded by extensive gardens. It offers all the usual facilities, including a spacious kitchen, as well as a pool, spa, sauna, and mountain bike rentals. Dorms are $18 pp, doubles are $20 pp, and a single room goes for $28.

Another excellent choice is the **Tramper's Rest,** 400 meters east of downtown at 31 Alton St., tel. 03/545-7477. In a renovated house, this friendly lodge is small, but the facilities are of the very highest standard. Dorms are $20 pp, doubles are $22 pp. A little farther out and a relative newcomer to the backpacker scene is the **Green Monkey,** 129 Milton St., tel. 03/545-7421, also in a renovated house. With just 16 beds, the atmosphere is congenial, with guests gravitating to the courtyard each evening for a barbeque.

Out at Tahunanui Beach, four km southwest of downtown, is the **Beach Hostel,** 25 Muritai St., tel. 03/548-6817. The atmosphere here is less hurried than at the downtown lodges, and the beach is a five-minute walk away. Breakfast is included in the rates of $17–20 pp. Transportation isn't a problem because the hostel offers town pickups and bikes for guest use (free), and buses heading down the west coast or out to Abel Tasman National Park stop out front.

Nelson Central YHA Hostel, 59 Rutherford St., tel. 03/545-9988, website: www.yha.org.nz, is just that-very central, one block from busy Trafalgar St. and two blocks from the information center. It's a purpose-built facility, with areas set aside for reading, relaxing, and watching TV. The two kitchens are spacious, modern, and well equipped. Most of the 90 beds are in comfortable four-bed dorms ($21 pp), with a few doubles and twins ($25 pp).

Motor Camps

The center of town has no motor camps, and if you arrive during holiday periods (especially Christmas), finding a spot may be a problem. Nelson's largest motor camp is **Tahuna Beach Holiday Park** at Tahunanui Beach, tel. 03/548-5159 or 0800/500-501, five km from the city center—but if literally hundreds of people in close proximity to one another cause you any degree of claustrophobia, you may find the 400 tent sites and 600 caravan sites, plus cabins, a problem. It's adjacent to a sandy beach, has a shop (open daily 8 A.M.–7 P.M.) and the usual facilities. Tent and caravan sites are $20 d; cabins range $32–50, and motel units (equipped for wheelchairs) are $65–70 d. Follow the road west along the waterfront (Hwy. 6) to Tahunanui, and turn off Rocks Rd. onto Beach Road.

You'll find the closest caravan sites and cabins to the city center at **Nelson Cabins and Caravan Park,** 230 Vanguard St., tel. 03/548-1445. It has communal facilities and a TV lounge, but no tent sites. Caravan sites are $20 d, cabins start at $45 d, and tourist flats are from $58 d.

Peaceful **Maitai Valley Motor Camp** on Maitai Valley Rd. (a 5.5-km scenic drive from downtown) lies along the Maitai River, tel. 03/548-7729. There's a swimming hole across from the picnic ground, good brown trout fishing, a golf course nearby, and bathrooms, kitchen, and laundry. Plenty of grassy tent sites ($18) and caravan sites ($20) lie among trees (complete with opossums!).

FOOD

Nelson brims with cafés and restaurants—take a short stroll around town and you're bound to see plenty of places likely to lure you back later for a snack or meal. If you have a particular fancy, drop by the information center and ask for a recommendation.

Coffee and Light Meals

The always busy **Rooftop Coffee Shop,** City Centre Arcade (219 Trafalgar St.), tel. 03/548-0797, has a huge selection of sandwiches, hot and cold foods, a salad bar, and desserts, all reasonably priced; it's open Mon.–Thurs. 8:30 A.M.–3:30 P.M., Friday, 8:30 A.M.–7 P.M. Nelson's **Robert Harris Cafe** is at 193 Trafalgar St., tel. 03/548-1183. For healthy delicious snacks, light meals (from $3.50–9.50), and good music in electric blue, red, and yellow surroundings, try **Zippy's,** 276 Hardy St., tel. 03/546-6348. It's open daily 9 A.M.–late.

Nelson Feasteries

Chez Eelco, 296 Trafalgar St., tel. 03/548-7595, draws a good local crowd and offers all kinds of salads for $15, a variety of omelets for about $11.50, and various steaks with salad from $17. Try the house specialty—a plate of tasty Marlborough mussels with salad. Desserts start at $6. It's open every day 8 A.M.–11 P.M., Sunday to 9 P.M., and you can sit outside at the sidewalk tables and watch the world go by. The local **Cobb & Co.** is at 83 Collingwood St., tel. 03/548-4299. It serves filling main courses ($14–18.50) with french fries and vegetables; desserts are $5. It's open daily 7:30 A.M.–10 P.M. Across the road, the obviously Italian **Ciao,** 94 Collingwood St., tel. 03/548-9874, is open Mon.–Sat. from 6:30; expect to pay about $16–23.50. According to one reader, the desserts here are scrumptious.

Flinders on Hardy, 90 Hardy St., tel. 03/545-7174, is a large dining room filled with bright contemporary furnishings and opening to a popular outdoor patio that catches the afternoon sun. Wood-fired pizza, pasta, and bistro-style steak and seafood dishes range $15–24.50. The menu at **Broccoli Row,** 5 Buxton Square (just off Trafalgar St.), tel. 03/548-9621, is small, but the vegetarian and seafood dishes, such as grilled scallops with rosemary, are inexpensive; closed Sunday.

Appelman's, 294 Queen St., Richmond, tel. 03/544-0610, features venison, salmon, and lamb, as well as pasta, omelets, and salads, for $7.50–15 at lunch, $19–29.50 at dinner; open Mon.–Fri. 11 A.M.–2 P.M. and daily from 6 P.M.

Heading out of town on Hwy. 6, you'll pass **Quayside Restaurant,** 309 Wakefield Quay, Port Nelson, tel. 03/548-3319, across the road from the bay and with great water views from tables inside and out. Farther along the harbourfront, the **Boatshed Café,** 350 Wakefield Quay, tel. 03/546-9783, is true to its name, housed in a renovated boatshed built on piers over the water. Local seafood is the specialty, including crabs and crayfish from a holding tank prepared in a variety of ways, some with an Asian twist. The Boatshed is open daily for breakfast, lunch, and dinner. Also at Port Nelson, the **Anchor Bar & Grill,** 62 Vickerman St., tel. 03/546-6614, features steak and seafood in a nautical atmosphere.

Winery Restaurants

Many of the wineries in the Nelson region have restaurants, generally open for lunch only. **Seifried Estate,** Redwood Rd., Richmond, tel. 03/544-1555, offers a simple country-style menu of local produce daily at lunch and dinner. The **Grape Escape Cafe** sits aside McShane Rd., Richmond, tel. 03/544-4341, in a 130-year-old cottage that also contains a wine-tasting room and a craft shop; open daily 10 A.M.–4:30 P.M.

If you don't mind a short drive to Stoke (about 16 km south of Nelson), and it's January or February, enjoy lunch or dinner in an outdoor orchard setting at **Robinson Brothers** on Main Rd., tel. 03/547-5259; it's open daily. Savor barbecued steak or lamb ($18–29), and a variety of salads, fruit, and wines (imported and local wines are available for tasting).

TRANSPORTATION
Getting There

Nelson Airport is right on Tasman Bay, eight km southwest of downtown. **Super Shuttle Nelson,** tel. 03/547-5782, meets all arrivals. This door-to-door services costs $7 pp. A taxi to the airport is about $15 one way. **Air New Zealand,** tel. 0800/737-000, has direct flights from Nelson to Auckland, Wellington, and Christchurch. For the short (and scenic) hop across Cook Strait from Wellington, consider **Flight Corp.,** tel. 03/547-8175, to save a few bucks.

It's easy to reach Nelson by bus from Picton with either **Intercity,** tel. 03/548-1538, or with one of the shuttle services such as **Kiwilink Shuttles,** tel. 03/577-8332, or **Knightline,** tel. 03/528-7798. Intercity services arrive and depart from the Nelson Travel Centre, 27 Bridge St., open Mon.–Fri. 7 A.M.–6 P.M., Sat.–Sun. 7 A.M.–4 P.M. From Nelson, Intercity continues northwest as far as Takaka, to Westport and down the west coast, and back across the island to Blenheim via Hwy. 6. All other bus services use the information center, on the corner of Trafalgar and Halifax Streets, as an arrival/departure point. **White Star,** tel. 03/546-8687, connects Nelson with Christchurch via Lewis Pass. If you're heading out to Golden Bay, **Abel Tasman National Park Enterprises,** tel. 03/528-7801 or 0800/223-582, provides transportation as far as Takaka, as well as day trips to destinations along the route. **West Coast Express,** New Zealand's original backpacker bus line, departs Nelson twice weekly for Queenstown, via the west coast. The trip takes a leisurely six days and costs just $99 (transportation only). Call 03/546-6703 for all the details.

Getting Around

Nelson Suburban Bus Co., tel. 03/548-3290, provides local service covering the city center, Port Nelson, Tahunanui, Bishopdale, Stoke, Richmond, and Wakefield, and a variety of local bus tours. For schedules and bus stops, call the office.

Quite a few car rental agencies are scattered around town. Call ahead for price comparisons—the smaller companies are often cheaper but have more restrictions on drop-off points, etc. The main agencies are **Avis,** tel. 03/547-2727; **Budget,** tel. 03/546-9255; **Hardy Cars,** tel. 03/548-1681; **Hertz,** tel. 03/547-2299; **NZ Rent-a-car,** tel. 03/548-5888; **Rent-a-dent,** tel. 03/546-9890; and **Thrifty,** tel. 03/547-5563. Rent bikes from **Natural High,** 52 Rutherford St., tel. 03/546-6936.

The friendly drivers from **Nelson City Cabs,** tel. 03/548-8225 or 0800/108-855, will gladly take you on a tour of Nelson and the surrounding country, or just home from the pub.

SERVICES
General

The **central post office** is at 86 Trafalgar St.; the postal section is open Mon.–Fri. 8:30 A.M.–5 P.M. Nelson's main **public library** is at 27 Halifax St., tel. 03/546-0410 (branches at Stoke, Tahunanui, and Richmond); it's open Mon.–Fri. 10 A.M.–6 P.M. (till 8 P.M. on Monday, Wednesday, and Friday), and Saturday 10 A.M.–noon. The main local newspaper is the *Nelson Evening Mail.* For arts and crafts, fruit and veggies, flowers, clothes, trash and treasures, visit the **Nelson Market** in Montgomery Square (between Bridge and Harvey Streets) on Saturday 8 A.M.–1 P.M. and Sunday 9 A.M.–12:30 P.M. For camping gear

and supplies before heading into the surrounding wilderness, **Rollo's,** 12 Bridge St., tel. 03/548-1975, probably has what you need.

Bubbles Laundrette is at 635 Rocks Rd. (across from Tahuna Beach). You'll find **restrooms** at the cathedral steps on Trafalgar Square, and at Buxton car park, Millers Acre car park, Montgomery car park, and the Tahunanui playground.

Emergency

For emergency **ambulance, police,** or **fire brigade,** call 111. **Nelson Hospital** is on Waimea Rd. (main entrance on Kawai St.), tel. 03/546-1800. For the name of a local **doctor,** call the hospital at the above number or call 03/548-2304, Mon.–Friday. If you need a doctor or pharmacy on weekends, refer to the back page of the Friday newspaper. **Prices Pharmacy,** on the corner of Hardy and Collingwood Streets, tel. 03/548-3897, is open Mon.–Fri. 8:30 A.M.–8 P.M., Saturday 9 A.M.–8 P.M., and Sunday 9 A.M.–8 P.M. If you need the **police,** call 03/546-3840.

INFORMATION

The main source of information is the **Nelson Visitor Information Centre** on the corner of Trafalgar and Halifax Streets, tel. 03/548-2304, website: www.nelson.net.nz; it's open daily 7:30 A.M.–6 P.M. in summer, Mon.–Sat. 7:30 A.M.–5:30 P.M. the rest of the year. It's also a booking and transportation center, so you can get everything you need in the one location. Collect a city map, a "Welcome to Nelson" pamphlet, and various tourist newspapers before you hit the pavement, and check out the outside notice boards. There's also a DOC officer on duty in the visitor center (limited hours), the best source of information on Abel Tasman National Park. The DOC **Nelson/Marlborough Conservancy** is headquartered in the Munro Building at 186 Bridge St., tel. 03/546-9335; it's open Mon.–Fri. 8 A.M.–4:30 P.M.

Abel Tasman National Park and the Remote Northwest

Traveling from Nelson to the South Island's remote northwest is a worthwhile adventure if you enjoy the great outdoors and have plenty of time. Abel Tasman National Park, 80 km northwest of Nelson, is one of the area's major attractions. There's all kinds of scenery to appreciate—undulating valleys where hops, tobacco, apples, nectarines, and kiwifruit grow in abundance, a "marble mountain" riddled with underground caves and sinkholes, rugged ranges, crystal-clear springs, golden-sand beaches, and spectacular coastal views. Waterfowl, such as black swans, ducks, and Canada geese, flock in great numbers to the more isolated areas along **Golden Bay,** and oystercatchers and godwits to the sandy shores of remote **Farewell Spit** in the far north. The farther north you go, the fewer people and the more wildlife you see.

It's best to see the region at a leisurely pace by car or bicycle, but you can also use public transportation. Golden Bay Connection runs daily from Nelson and Motueka as far north as Takaka, and a connecting bus runs on demand to Collingwood and the well-known 77-km Heaphy Track.

TO THE PARK

Abel Tasman National Park (80 km northwest of Nelson) lures people of all ages and fitness levels to its meandering hiking tracks. In summer **Totaranui,** the only coastal spot accessible by road in the far northern section of the park, rapidly fills with sunseeking campers who grab their section of the beach and stake their territory. If you plan to visit Abel Tasman National Park, pick up as much information as you can from the information center and DOC in Nelson before you head northwest—you pass the south and west park entrances before you reach the town of Takaka, where you'll find the Abel Tasman National Park Visitor Centre. Otherwise stop at the DOC **Motueka Area Office,** on the corner of King Edward and High Streets, Motueka, tel. 03/528-1810; it's open weekdays 8:30 A.M.–5 P.M.

Leaving Nelson

Take Hwy. 6 southwest out of Nelson and, after going through Richmond, swing west on Hwy. 60. This scenic road along Tasman Bay passes pottery shops, weaving sheds, deer farms, and apple orchards (excellent apples in March). If staying at a dress-optional holiday resort sounds appealing, look for the sign to **Mapua Leisure Park** on Toru St., Mapua, tel. 03/540-2666; website: www.nelsonholiday.co.nz. It's about a half-hour drive from Nelson, 15 minutes to Motueka. Aside from swimming, fishing, tennis, golf, and many other recreational activities, the camp has tent and caravan sites from $11

ABEL TASMAN NATIONAL PARK

© AVALON TRAVEL PUBLISHING, INC.

per night, on-site caravans and chalets from $44 d, and motel units starting at $80 s, $90 d. If nudity offends you, keep driving.

Motueka

About eight km south of Motueka you can see the **Moutere tame eels** being fed at 10 A.M.–noon and 1–4 P.M., on Wilsons Rd., Moutere Valley (look for the AA sign on the highway); admission $3.

Motueka itself is a small relaxed town nestled between the peaks of Kahurangi National Park and the white sands of Tasman Bay. It's also the last place of any size where you can pick up camping supplies before you continue north. Make your first stop **Motueka Information Centre,** 236 High St., tel. 03/528-6543. The staff provides brochures, books accommodations, orders tickets, arranges horticultural tours in the local area, sells fishing licenses, and offers the latest park transportation information; it's open weekdays 8:30 A.M.–7 P.M., weekends 9:30 A.M.–5 P.M., with shorter hours in winter. **Motueka Museum,** housed in the 1913 redbrick building on High St. (the main road), tel. 03/528-7660, is open weekdays 10 A.M.–3 P.M.

Motueka has a range of accommodations to suit all budgets. The **Equestrian Lodge Motel,** Tudor St., tel. 03/528-9369 or 0800/668-782, website: www.equestrianlodge.co.nz, features 15 large units, each with a modern kitchen, set around extensive gardens and a swimming pool; $90 s, $105 d. At the top end of High St., **Bakers Lodge,** 2 Poole St., tel. 03/528-1012 or 0800/800-102, website: www.bakerslodge.co.nz, is an excellent choice for budget travelers. A historic bakery building has been transformed for the purpose. The dorm beds are $22 pp, while doubles, some with private bathrooms, are $25 pp. Also at the northern end of town, **Fearon's Bush Camp** on Fearon St., tel. 03/528-7189, provides communal facilities and tent and caravan sites for $10 pp, cabins for $36 s or d, and motel rooms for $80 s or d.

For a quick snack, try one of the mouthwateringly good bakeries on the main street, such as the **Rolling Pin** at 100 High St., tel. 03/528-9578. In the museum complex at 136 High St.,

Annabelle's Café, tel. 03/528-8696, is open all day; it serves breakfast (from $5), lunch ($6–10), and dinner ($12.50–18) inside, or outside in the courtyard. For a sit-down lunch or dinner, **Gothic Gourmet Restaurant** in the pink church at 208 High St., tel. 03/528-6699, serves tasty fare at reasonable prices ($8–17.50).

Continuing North

After running through **Riwaka,** Hwy. 60 passes the turnoff east to the beach resort town of **Kaiteriteri,** one of the best swimming beaches in the Nelson region. Here you'll find **Kaiteriteri Motor Camp,** tel. 03/527-8010. Features include a store, tearooms, an 18-hole mini-golf course, and trampolines, along with the usual facilities. Tent and caravan sites are $20 s or d, and cabins start at $35. You'll also pass the road that runs northeast to **Sandy Bay,** another good swimming beach, and **Marahau,** the southern entrance to Abel Tasman National Park and the start of both the Coastal and Inland Tracks.

From the turnoff to Marahau, Hwy. 60 continues north around the back of Abel Tasman National Park to the park's northern gateway, Totaranui. The road first ascends **Takaka Hill** (made of marble with four major caves—the locals call this speleologist's delight "Marble Mountain") You can take a tour of the **Ngarua Caves,** tel. 03/528-8093, Sept.–June for $10 adult, $5 child. The western entrance to the park is the 12-km gravel Canaan Rd. that leads to **Canaan.** It turns right off Hwy. 60 before the summit of Takaka Hill, but if you don't already know where you're headed, venture to the summit for splendid views of Kahurangi National Park, and continue down to Upper Takaka, passing the "Rat Trap" Hotel.

Takaka

At Takaka, Hwy. 60 continues north to Golden Bay, while a side road leads east to Totaranui, the northern gateway to Abel Tasman National Park. The main local attraction is **Pupu Springs,** New Zealand's largest freshwater springs. The springs can be found in a scenic reserve seven km northwest of town beyond the Waitapu Bridge.

The **Junction Hotel,** 15 Commercial St., tel. 03/525-9207, has basic rooms with shared bathrooms for $55 s or d. **Anatoki Lodge Motel,** 87 Commercial St., tel. 03/525-8047 or 0800/262-333, is right downtown. It features 10 spacious first floor units, each with a kitchen. Rates range $90–120 s or d.

Closer to the northern section of Abel Tasman you'll find **Pohara Beach Top 10 Holiday Park,** Pohara (10 km northeast of Takaka on the way to the park), tel. 03/525-9500. On yet another beautiful beach (along Golden Bay, not Tasman Bay), it offers sheltered swimming and sunbathing along with the usual facilities. Tent sites are $9 pp, caravan sites $10 pp, and cabins $35–52 s or d.

The best place for a meal in Takaka is one of the two hotels. The **Telegraph Hotel,** 2 Motupipi St., tel. 03/525-9308, presents quick bistro meals in the lounge bar 11:30 A.M.–1:30 P.M. and 6–7:30 P.M. The hotel restaurant (pricier and dressier) is open for dinner 6:30–8 P.M. only. **Junction Hotel,** 15 Commercial St., tel. 03/525-9207, offers similar fare. At the other end of the health scale, the **Whole Meal Cafe,** up a small alleyway at 60 Commercial St. (look for flowerpots hanging outside the street entrance), tel. 03/525-9426, dishes up delicious home-baked goodies and main courses (more expensive than those at the pubs).

Golden Bay Visitor Information Centre is easy to find on Willow St. as you enter Takaka from the south, tel. 03/525-9136; pick up complete information on Golden Bay farther north, and maps of park tracks. The center is open daily 9 A.M.–5 P.M. in summer and is staffed by friendly volunteers.

THE LAND

Abel Tasman National Park (22,139 hectares) is the smallest national park in New Zealand. Its highest point, **Mount Evans,** is only 1,134 meters. The northernmost part of this steep and rugged coastal park extends from **Separation Point** (which separates Tasman and Golden Bays) in the north to **Sandy Bay** in the south, and includes all the islands and reefs up to 2.5 km out to sea. Its western boundary includes Mt. Evans and Murray's Peak (1,101 meters), both in the **Pikikiruna Range.** No roads run through the park, but three main access roads lead to **Marahau** in the south, **Canaan** in the west, and **Wainui Inlet, Totaranui,** and **Awaroa Inlet** in the north. The only way to get into the interior and to most of the main attractions is on foot via the many tracks that lead off the main access roads.

Despite its small size and remote location, the park attracts outdoor enthusiasts by the masses—in summer the tracks are often overcrowded and there is the danger that this park may be spoiled by its great popularity. Dense beech forest, golden sand, and azure waters are its obvious attractions, but adventurous hikers can also enjoy sculptured granite gorges and marble outcrops, icy waterfalls and polished swimming holes, impressive cave systems and an enormous vertical shaft, pockets of rainforest, isolated beaches, and lush native bush alive with birds. Many seabirds nest in the park—shags, gannets, blue penguins, terns, oystercatchers, herons, and stilts—and you can often catch sight of seals or the occasional dolphin frolicking not far offshore. The park is not known for its great hunting (or fishing), though if you do plan to hunt the few deer, pigs, goats, and opossums present, a permit is required. No hunting is allowed from mid-December to the end of January because of the high number of hikers in the backcountry.

Adventurous hikers enjoy sculptured granite gorges and marble outcrops, icy waterfalls and polished swimming holes, impressive cave systems and an enormous vertical shaft, pockets of rainforest, isolated beaches, and lush native bush alive with birds.

History

The stretch of coastline along Abel Tasman National Park has quite a history. Maori may have been living along the shores of Tasman Bay as early as the 13th century (the earliest carbon-dated site shows occupation about A.D. 1540)—

you can still see sites of their ancient settlements. In 1642 Dutch explorer Abel Tasman first spotted the shoreline that officially became the eastern boundary of the park exactly 300 years later. In 1827 the French explorer D'Urville sailed along the western shores of Tasman Bay naming many of the landmarks, and after his detailed exploration, European settlement began in earnest.

Farmers moved into the Totaranui area, successfully clearing the bush, farming the land, and becoming self-sufficient. Shipbuilding from local timber began in the Awaroa Inlet area, and hordes of farmers, loggers, shipbuilders, fishermen, and quarry workers flooded many of the bays and inlets. The entire coastal area was modified and settled, and a few small areas (Totaranui, some of Awaroa, and Bark Bay) took on an almost English-countryside appearance. However, during the Depression in the early 1900s even the most prosperous farmers eventually found they could no longer afford to run their properties. Logging and shipbuilding also ceased, and the residents sadly abandoned their homes and farms. Today the coast shows little sign of past occupation and activities, and the bush grows down to water's edge in most places. Evidence of one of the most flourishing settlements of the recent past can best be seen in the Totaranui area.

RECREATION
Cruises

For a good introduction to Abel Tasman National Park without hiking the tracks or driving all the way to Totaranui, take a cruise with **Abel Tasman National Park Enterprises.** This company, run by the Wilson family, who have been associated with the park for well over 100 years, is based in a converted residence at 265 High St., Motueka, tel. 03/528-7801 or 0800/223-582; website: www.abeltasman.co.nz. They run buses out from Nelson that link up with their cruises. Their boats leave Kaiteriteri daily at 9 A.M. and noon, making stops at many secluded spots en route, including the family's lodge at Awaroa, to Totaranui, the turnaround point. The round-trip cruise takes five to six

hours and costs $50 pp, which includes a running commentary, tea, and coffee. Take your own lunch or order ahead for $14. Most people don't make the full trip, instead opting to disembark along the way, and either walk a section of the coastal hiking track or just relax on the beach. A popular combination is to cruise as far as Tonga Bay, then walk back to Bark Bay (three km) to pick up the cruise on its return to Kaiteriteri; adult $49, child $22.

Abel Tasman Coastal Track

The spectacular coastal scenery and accessibility of the Abel Tasman Coastal Track makes it one of New Zealand's most popular (and busiest) tramps. The trailheads are at Marahau and Totaranui, which are separated by 51 km of native bush, secluded bays, and long stretches of golden sand. The track takes three to four days, with huts and camping areas at regular intervals. Before you set out, check tide times for crossing the Awaroa and Wainui Bay inlets—posted at the ends of main roads to the park, at Totaranui, and at all coastal huts. You can cross Awaroa and Wainui Bay inlets on foot two hours each side of low tide only; Torrent and Bark Bay inlets have high-tide as well as low-tide tracks.

Abel Tasman National Park Enterprises, tel. 03/528-7801, runs daily water-taxi services to Totaranui, dropping hikers off at Tonga and at Bark, Torrent, and Tinline Bays; rates are $22 for a drop-off anywhere along their cruise route. The flexible schedule allows you to spend a couple of hours hiking the coastal track and be picked up again on the same day. A two-, three- or five-day guided walk in the park includes accommodation in private lodges and all meals; call Abel Tasman National Park Enterprises for more details and prices.

Before you set out on the coastal track, you also must buy a **Great Walks** hut or campsite pass, which must be attached to your backpack and clearly visible—you get useful track information with the pass. The pass costs $8 pp per night, whether you stay in the huts or camp. The huts fill quickly in summer, so bring a tent. Buy the pass at any DOC office (Nelson, Motueka, and Takaka).

NELSON AND THE NORTHWEST

Short Walks

Take any of the access roads to park boundaries for a variety of short walks to scenic spots or lookouts. Coming from the south, turn northeast off Hwy. 60 to Sandy Bay and continue along Sandy Bay Rd. to Marahau. **Tinline Walk** starts from the coastal track, about two km from Marahau car park, and loops through groves of beech, *kahikatea, pukatea, rimu,* and other native trees; it takes about 30 minutes round-trip. If you're feeling a little more energetic, follow the tracks to beautiful **Coquille Bay** (about 45 minutes from Marahau car park) or to **Apple Tree Bay** (1.5 hours); or take the Coastal Track to **Torrent Bay** (about four hours one way), one of the most scenic bays in the park. From Torrent Bay, two other short walks lead to **Cleopatra's Pool** and **Cascade Falls,** and you can return by water taxi.

From Totaranui, at the northern end, a short 45-minute walk north takes you to golden **Anapai Beach,** or if you want to make it an overnighter, continue for another two to three spectacular hours to **Whariwharangi Bay** and hut. Another popular short walk is the **Waiharakeke Track.** It starts on Awaroa Rd. about one km south of the Totaranui turnoff and runs down to Waiharakeke Beach, taking about 1.5 hours to pass through valleys, fern-filled gullies, and crystal-clear streams to end at yet another beautiful beach.

A geologically fascinating area to explore on foot is **Canaan,** a haven for cavers. Take Hwy. 60 to Takaka Hill, turn off on Canaan Rd., and continue almost to the end. The winding road passes amazing granite and marble rock outcrops and ends at rocky Canaan basin. Look out for the track marker to the left leading to **Harwood's Hole,** an incredible marble-walled vertical shaft 50 meters wide and 200 meters deep that leads to one of the most impressive cave systems in the area. The track to Harwood's Hole is an easy 45 minutes through beech forest, but be careful around the edge of the shaft as the ground is very unstable—a fall into this hole would definitely end your vacation. From the car park at the end of Canaan Rd. are several other short walks, or you can join the inland track system to either Wainui or Marahau.

Sea Kayaking

An extremely popular way to discover the beauty of the Abel Tasman coastline is by sea kayak. **Abel Tasman Kayaks,** based at the end of the road in Marahau, tel. 03/527-8022, offers kayaking options for all levels of expertise. Day trips ($99 pp) are the most popular; you begin from the beach and paddle up the coastline to a remote spot for lunch, then out to a number of islands where seals are often spotted. Then, if the wind is right, a sail is hoisted for the return trip. The guided two-day trip ($160) involves paddling up the coast, hiking part of the Coastal Track, and returning to Marahau by water taxi. Other options include a three-day trip ($320) taking in the seal colony on Tonga Island, and a four-day trip ($590) that includes all meals and a final night's lodging at Awaroa Lodge. Experienced kayakers wanting to explore the park with-

Sea kayaking is popular in Abel Tasman National Park.

NELSON AND THE NORTHWEST

out a guide can rent single and double kayaks for $45–50 pp per day. For those not wanting to hike the tracks, sea kayaking is the way to go. **Ocean River Adventure Co.,** based in Marahau, tel. 03/527-8266, also specializes in sea kayaking, with rentals (from $45 per day and $35 per kayak, with pickup anywhere along the coastline), kayak tours of the Abel Tasman National Park coastline, and **white-water rafting trips** down the Gowan and Buller Rivers (from $75 pp for a half-day trip).

There is a boat shotel also!

PRACTICALITIES

Marahau

At the southern end of the park, the small community of Marahau has a variety of accommodations. **Ocean View Chalets,** tel. 03/527-8232, are scattered along a ridge overlooking Tasman Bay at Marahau. Each handcrafted cedar chalet has a kitchen, lounge area, and balcony. The chalets are priced at $115 s or d in summer, with up to a 40 percent discount the rest of the year. Breakfast is an additional $12 pp. **The Barn,** on Hervey Rd., tel. 03/527-8043, is right by the starting point of all the best hiking trails and just down the road from Abel Tasman Kayaks. Dorm beds are $16 pp, doubles are $20 pp, and a few campsites scattered around the property are $10 pp. **Marahau Beach Camp,** tel. 03/527-8176, offers communal facilities, tent and caravan sites for $18 d, cabins from $40 d, and a self-contained flat for $65 d.

Park Café, tel. 03/527-8270, offers ocean views and a casual atmosphere right in the heart of the village. It's open Oct.–April daily 8 A.M.–8 P.M.

Accommodations within the Park

Aside from backcountry huts and campsites, three privately owned lodges lie within the park boundaries, all on beautiful beaches. The Wilson family, operators of Abel Tasman National Park Enterprises, rebuilt the original family homestead on its original site in Awaroa Bay. **Homestead Lodge** offers all the expected comforts in a setting accessible only by boat or on foot. The Wilson family also operates a modern, 13-room lodge at Torrent Bay, tel. 03/528-7801; website: www.abeltas-

man.co.nz. You can stay in both on their overnight, guided walks. Also at Awaroa Bay is **Awaroa Lodge and Cafe,** tel. 03/528-8758, website: www.awaroalodge.co.nz, tucked behind the sand dunes. It's a popular stopover for hikers, but a worthwhile destination in itself, with kayaks, good fishing, and a delightfully rustic sauna. Rates are $85 s or d shared bath, $155 with en suite.

Totaranui

At the north end of the park is the beachside **Totaranui Beach Camp,** with plenty of grassy tent and caravan sites (no powered sites), toilets, and fresh water; rates are $8 adult, $4 child, payable to DOC officers at Totaranui or Takaka. It's very popular and usually booked solid Dec. 20–Jan. 31 (the only period when bookings are accepted). If you're there then but haven't already booked, check at the DOC Golden Bay Area Office, 62 Commercial St., Takaka, tel. 03/525-8026, before you head out. Also look out for Camp Full signs placed along the main public access roads.

Transportation

There are a number of ways to get to the park by public transportation, but the easiest way is with **Abel Tasman National Park Enterprises,** tel. 03/528-7801 or 0800/223-582. As well as running cruises along the park's coastline, this company provides a scheduled bus service from Nelson. Departing Nelson daily at 7:20 A.M., it arrives in Kaiteriteri to coincide with the 9 A.M. cruise departure. By itself the bus fare is $25 round-trip, but this is discounted when bought in conjunction with a cruise.

In conjunction with a variety of cruise options, Abel Tasman National Park Enterprises, tel. 03/528-7801 or 0800/223-582, can make drops at designated points along the park's coastline on their twice-daily cruise schedule. They depart Kaiteriteri daily at 9 a.m. and noon, and make a pickup at Marahau before entering the park. The 9 a.m. sailing links up with the daily bus service from Nelson. Sample fares from Kaiteriteri or Marahau are $20 to Bark Bay (an easy six-hour walk back to Marahau), $27 to Awaroa, and $28 to Totaranui. **Abel Tasman Water Taxi,** tel. 03/528-7497 or 0800/423-397, operates a smaller and faster craft that departs Kaiteriteri up to four times daily; the round-trip fare to Awaroa Bay is $45.

Information

The best sources of park information are DOC offices. These include the **Nelson/Marlborough Conservancy** headquarters at 186 Bridge St., Nelson, tel. 03/546-9335; **Motueka Area Office,** on the corner of King Edward and High Streets, Motueka, tel. 03/528-1810; and **Golden Bay Area Office,** 62 Commercial St., Takaka, tel. 03/525-8026. For information on the park's commercial operators and local transportation, try the information centers in these same three towns.

TO FAREWELL SPIT

Pupu Springs

Continue along Hwy. 60 north of Takaka and look for a sign on the left at Waitapu Bridge to Pupu (also known as Waikoropupu) Springs. This natural jumbo-sized freshwater spring pumps out an incredible 1.197 million liters of icy-cold, crystal-clear water a day—the largest freshwater spring in Australasia (if not the world). It's really worth the time to drive the three-km gravel road and take the short track (about 15 minutes) through this amazing scenic reserve. Take either the Fish Creek Springs route or the one that passes the remains of gold-working claims from the 1800s. At the end of the track is a large multicolored pool, calm around the edge but turbulent in the middle, where water (about 11°C) gushes and bubbles to the surface at a rate of 14 cubic meters a second. Local old-timers claim the vent is so deep that divers have been unable to find the bottom of the pool, but divers regularly visit the main vent, actually only eight meters down. In summer a few enthusiastic swimmers brave the cold waters, not seeming to mind the "unknown depth" or turbulence in the middle. A fascinating diagram and display near the pool gives you the rundown on the what, where, and why of the springs—don't miss the striking underwater photographs taken by adventurous divers.

If you'd like to do a short, very interesting, three-km bush walk, continue to the end of the road (beyond the springs) to the beginning of **Pupu Walk.** About 90 minutes round-trip, the track follows an old gold-mining water race, part of which has been reused for power generation, and finishes at a weir (good picnic spot). It's steep in the beginning (wear rugged shoes), and you need to be careful on the boardwalks on the concrete fluming—not a good walk for small children.

Collingwood

Twenty-nine km from Takaka and the northernmost town of any size (Pakawau and Port Puponga farther north are mainly remote vacation spots), Collingwood (population 260) has a motor camp, a lodge, a tavern (bistro dinners), tearooms, a post office, a hospital, a small museum, the Courthouse Gallery (arts and crafts), a general store, and a number of vacation homes. Surrounded by mountains and water, with few people but lots of birdlife, Collingwood's distinct appeal in all kinds of weather is guaranteed to bring out the photographer in you.

Collingwood Motor Camp is on the south side of town right along the water's edge on William St., tel. 03/524-8149—you can pull in a fish without leaving your tent flap. It has tennis courts and a boat ramp along with communal facilities. Great tent and caravan sites on a grassy area along the water's edge are $22. If the weather looks ominous (even *slightly* so), fork out for one of the reasonably priced cabins—high winds and a sudden heavy downpour can turn the tent area into a miniature lake. They cost from $38 s or d. The motor camp rents bicycles, canoes, a dinghy, tennis racquets, and gold pans. Another indoor option is **A1 Collingwood Motel,** located right across Haven Rd. from the harbor, tel. 03/524-8224. The self-contained rooms are $70–75 s or d.

Continuing North from Collingwood

If you have your own wheels, driving north to the end of the road is most worthwhile for scenery buffs, wildlife enthusiasts, and bird-watchers. The lonely road takes you along the edge of Golden

Bay through wild rugged scenery chockablock with black swans, Canada geese, ducks, and shore-birds, to Pakawau (motor camp, store, and petrol pump) and Port Puponga. Few homes, buildings, or signs of human life dot the road—local kids attend correspondence school, receiving their daily lessons via the mail bus. From Port Puponga, the road crosses the peninsula to the open ocean, passing **Oldman Rock,** an exposed and weathered cliff "face." At the end of the road, a one-km trail leads steeply over grassy hills and sand dunes to **Wharariki Beach,** where you can view the offshore seal colony of Archway Island through binoculars (largest numbers in winter). Be prepared with insect repellent and, again, if the weather looks ominous, carry appropriate raingear.

Farewell Spit

Known as Onetahua (heaped-up sand) to the Maori, the 26 km of sand dunes and quicksand that make up Farewell Spit are one of the country's most important wading-bird habitats. Protected as a nature reserve by restricted access, the spit is home to banded dotterels, gannets, godwits, and royal spoonbills. A visit to the spit is not just for bird-watchers—the sight of seemingly never-ending sand dunes pushed skyward by the forces of the Tasman Sea and backed by the calm waters of Golden Bay are a sight not soon forgotten.

Because the spit is a protected wildlife sanctuary, the only way to visit it is on a guided tour. These are operated from Collingwood by **Farewell Spit Eco Tours,** tel. 03/524-8257 or 0800/808-257, and **Farewell Spit Nature Tours,** tel. 03/524-8188 or 0800/250-500, and last about six hours. They cost $55–60 pp, which includes lunch. At least one tour runs each day, but departure times (between 6:30 A.M. and 2 P.M.) depend entirely on the tide. Alternatively, for $35 pp you can take a five-hour tour of the lonely north with the **Collingwood Bus Services' mail run** (departs Mon.–Fri. at 10:30 P.M.). Without

a permit, you can freely walk for 2.5 km along the inner beach at the base of the spit or four km along the outer beach; anglers must obtain a permit from a DOC office to fish from the outer beach.

KAHURANGI NATIONAL PARK

If you're in search of relatively undisturbed and spectacular scenery, high mountain lakes, alpine flowers, fishing, rock-climbing, hunting, and great views, head for New Zealand's newest and second-largest (452,000 hectares) national park. The park is best known for the Heaphy Track, but the more accessible **Cobb Valley** is also interesting. Several hiking tracks permit access into the valley, but the short one to Bushline Hut, Lake Sylvester, and Little Sylvester Lake (about two hours one way) is easiest. To get to the Cobb Valley from Upper Takaka, take the road to the powerhouse, and then drive another windy 13 km to the dam. The valley starts 28 km from the Upper Takaka turnoff. Get a good map before you head out, and ask the DOC for advice about the tracks and huts.

> *The 26 km of sand dunes and quicksand that make up Farewell Spit are one of the country's most important wading-bird habitats. Protected as a nature reserve by restricted access, the spit is home to banded dotterels, gannets, godwits, and royal spoonbills.*

Heaphy Track

The 77-km Heaphy Track has always been popular, but is even more so since the proclamation of Kahurangi National Park. You can travel the route in either direction, but most hikers start in the east at Brown Hut (about 35 km south of Collingwood), walk toward the coast, and finish at the Kohaihai Shelter (15 km north of Karamea). The track traverses the park's vast and rugged interior, then follows the Heaphy River to the ocean, continuing south along the coast to the Kohaihai River. Swimming is not advised along the coastal section, but it's fine in the lagoons and the Heaphy River, and the Karamea offers good trout fishing.

On this track you can expect to cross rivers by swing bridge and ford shallow streams; pass through forests, open tussock land, and **Gouland Downs** (lots of wildlife); and finish up walking along a wild, surf-pounded west coast beach. The track takes at least three days, five to six days if you stop and smell the flowers; seven well-equipped huts (heated, gas cookers, bunk beds, and toilets) are situated at regular intervals. You must buy a Great Walks hut or campsite pass before beginning the track. The huts can be crowded at any time of year, but they're most crowded in summer despite the rule of staying no longer than two nights. To be on the safe side, take your own tent, stove, cooking gear, and utensils—camping is permitted around the huts if they're full.

The track is in a high rainfall area so pack for rain and soggy ground. The warm summer months are the most popular time to do the track, but unless you have a good supply of insect repellent, swarms of tiny, pesky sand flies can eat you alive. Many prefer to hike the track in winter when the frosts keep the sand flies and crowds away. The weather can suddenly turn nasty along the track at any time of year, even in midsummer. Take wool clothing, essential wind- and waterproof gear, and a spare pair of tennis shoes or sandshoes; wear comfortable, sturdy hiking boots for the tough terrain. Carry enough food to comfortably last at least five days. Water is readily available along the track, and whatever you do, don't forget that insect repellent! Before you set out, leave your intended date of arrival

with the DOC or reliable friends, and try to find a couple of accompanying hikers (safety in numbers) or at least a person with backcountry knowledge—the track passes through rugged wilderness.

Kahurangi Guided Walks, tel. 03/525-7177, offers a variety of walks along the track. If you just want a taste of park, consider a two-hour walk ($40) or complete the entire track over five days ($800, all inclusive).

Transportation
Kahurangi National Park Bus Services, tel. 03/525-9434, is a scheduled shuttle service running between Nelson and all trailheads along the park's eastern boundary, with stops made at Motueka, Takaka, and Collingwood. The fare between Nelson and the start of the Heaphy Track is $42. At the other end of the track, the **Last Resort,** tel. 03/782-6617, makes pickups on demand at Kohaihai shelter and can arrange onward transportation to Westport.

Information
Head to any of the local DOC offices for information and track passes. Closest is the **Golden Bay Area Office,** 62 Commercial St., Takaka, tel. 03/525-8026. Otherwise try the **Motueka Area Office,** on the corner of King Edward and High Streets, Motueka, tel. 03/528-1810, or **Nelson/Marlborough Conservancy** headquarters, 186 Bridge St., Nelson, tel. 03/546-9335.

Nelson Lakes National Park

Nelson Lakes National Park, a mountainous area with many peaks over 2,000 meters high, lush beech forests, and bush-fringed lakes, lies inland at the northern end of the mighty **Southern Alps.** Off Hwy. 63, approximately 104 km from Nelson and 158 km from the west coast town of Westport, this park is a good place to head if you're looking for a rugged wilderness experience. (If you're on your way to the park from Nelson and you have children with you, make a stop at Wakefield at **Faulkner Bush.** This park has beautiful white pine trees, a picnic area, and a playground with an excellent flying fox.)

The park, with 270 km of hiking trails, can only be truly appreciated on foot. Because of the rough terrain, no roads run through it, but you can still reach a couple of scenic spots by car—the town of St. Arnaud, the two main lakes, and **Rotoiti Lookout** at the end of Mt. Robert Road. Short tracks put the day-tripper close to plenty of beautiful scenery, while long and more difficult tracks challenge the serious hiker. Tricky routes over high mountain passes (where the weather is notorious for rapid and unexpected deteriora-

tion) provide an adrenaline rush for the high-country backpacker and climber. The park has its own ski field where you have to "climb to ski." You can reach quiet, noncommercial **Mt. Robert Ski field** only on foot via a two-hour track from the car park, somehow turning a day's skiing into a one-of-a-kind experience that successfully keeps the hordes and the less energetic at bay. Peaceful and secluded **Lake Rotoroa** is known for good trout fishing; the more visited **Lake Rotoiti** is a mecca for trout fishing, sailing, and boating.

THE LAND

This large wilderness park (102,000 hectares) is sandwiched between Lake Rotoroa and Lake Rotoiti in the north and northeast, the lofty **St. Arnaud Range** on the eastern boundary, the **Spenser Mountains** in the south, and the **Ella Range** in the west. The **Mahanga, Franklin,** and **Travers** Ranges also run through the park, along with several major rivers and their catchment areas—the **Travers River** flowing into Lake Rotoiti, and the **Sabine** and **D'Urville** Rivers flowing into Lake Rotoroa.

The great Alpine Fault runs right through the northern section of the park (welcome to earthquake country), crossing the northern end of Lake Rotoiti, **Speargrass Valley,** and the southern end of Lake Rotoroa. The movement of land along the Alpine Fault, plus glacial erosion, are the two main factors in the formation of the spectacular scenery. Mighty rugged mountains and alpine tarns lie on the southeast side of the fault, and lower forest-covered ranges, ridges, valleys, deep river canyons, and two glacially formed lakes lie on the northwest side.

Flora and Fauna

Lush beech forests are Nelson Lakes National Park's trademark. You can find all four beech species that grow throughout New Zealand here: red and silver beech thrive in the lower areas, hard beech only around Rotoroa, a mixture of silver and mountain beech farther up, and moun-

NELSON LAKES NATIONAL PARK

TO NELSON
BIG BUSH STATE FOREST
TO BLENHEIM
BULLER RIVER
63
ST. ARNAUD
GOWANBRIDGE
6
LAKE ROTOITI
ROTOROA
LAKE ROTOROA
ST. ARNAUD RANGE
BULLER RIVER
NELSON LAKES NAT. PARK
MURCHISON
TO WESTPORT AND GREYMOUTH
0   10 km

© AVALON TRAVEL PUBLISHING, INC.

NELSON AND THE NORTHWEST

tain beech in the high altitude areas (also in lowland low-nutrient soil areas). These trees form a dense, dark canopy and the types of plants found on the forest floor depend on the amount of light that filters through. The high humidity "twilight zone" of the forest floor brings to life an amazingly luxurious assortment of mosses, lichens, ferns, liverworts, fungi, and tree litter, among which all kinds of insects, skinks, and geckos dwell. On a stroll through the bush you're most likely to see fantails, tomtits, robins, grey warblers, riflemen, silvereyes, parakeets, white-bibbed *tui,* bellbirds, and *kaka,* and mice, rats, stoats, and Australian opossums from the lower altitudes up to the tree line.

Apart from the beech forests, *kanuka/manuka* forests survive on the edge of the park in areas of poor soils and harsh climate, where broad-winged moths (their caterpillars have a great "twig" disguise), stick insects, *manuka* beetles, robins, and brown creepers hang out. Also scattered throughout are bogs where the insect-eating sundews thrive, along with several varieties of mosses, red tussocks, blue swamp orchids, weeping *matipo,* and bog pine. Beautiful mixed beech/podocarp forests (native conifers) of *rata, kowhai,* and flax grow in the lower elevations around Lake Rotoroa—home for all kinds of birds including the plump, noisy native pigeon. On the lakes and rivers live many varieties of waterfowl (watch for the beautiful but sadly endangered blue duck). Gulls, shags, herons, kingfishers, oystercatchers, stilts, black swans, and Canada geese are common. Enormous eels (possibly the legendary Maori *taniwha* or lake monsters) thrive in the depths of the lakes, along with large brown trout and a few surviving rainbow trout (see below).

Above the tree line grow tough woody shrubs, colorful tussocks, beautiful alpine flowering shrubs of the snow tussock/herb-field zone, and "vegetable sheep" and herbs of the upper fellfields and scree slopes. You'll see butterflies, bees, moths, beetles, and grasshoppers; rock wrens, riflemen, pipits, *kea,* and many other birds in the upper alpine areas. Large numbers of hares also live in the higher reaches, but only small herds of chamois and the occasional red deer can be seen nowadays—considered pests (their ex-

tensive grazing causes destruction of native forest and erosion), both have been drastically reduced by selective culling in the last 20 years, and the park continues to encourage their eradication (a hunting permit from HQ or Rotoroa Ranger Station is required).

RECREATION
Walks around Lake Rotoiti

Lake Rotoiti, popular with sailors, powerboaters, water-skiers, and anglers, is the most visited area in Nelson Lakes National Park; go to the visitor center in St. Arnaud for pamphlets on all the walks and activities in the area. Several short tracks start near the visitor center and take up to two hours, and longer tracks link to form a circular route around the lake (at least seven hours). For a short but rocky walk to a viewpoint 127 meters above Lake Rotoiti, take the **Black Hill Walk** (90 minutes round-trip), which starts at Rotoiti Lodge. It crosses a *roche moutonnée* or volcanic rock intrusion (where large lizards bask in the sun) and scrublands. If you're not feeling very energetic but enjoy lake views and all kinds of trees, try the easy (90-minute) **Peninsular Nature Walk,** which starts at the western end of the beach at **Kerr Bay** and goes around to **West Bay.** The trees and shrubs along the track have been labeled, and short paths lead off the track to lookouts with views of the lake and the mountains.

Pinchgut Track (1.5 hours one way) starts at the end of Mt. Robert Rd. and climbs through beech forest to the alpine herb fields and the ski field, which offers great mountain views. For a longer hike (five hours round-trip) returning along a different route, walk up Pinchgut Track and return along three-hour **Paddy's Track.** It crosses the open face of Mt. Robert, and ends at a parking area two km down the road. **Lakehead Track** (three hours one way) starts at the eastern side of Kerr Bay and heads down the eastern side of the lake to the far end, passing countless bays likely to lure you off the beaten track and, in summer, into the water. If you plan to go all the way around the lake, ford Travers River near Lakehead Hut (only possible when the water is low enough) or walk from Lakehead

Hut up the valley for at least another hour to the bridge. Return along the western side of the lake via **Lakeside Track.** This track starts in the corner of the lake, west of Coldwater Hut, passes a great view of **Whiskey Falls** en route, and eventually joins **Paddy's Track** to end on Robert Road. Total track time around the lake is about six hours, but it can easily take much longer if you stop to admire the scenery or take a dip or two. If you have the time, stay overnight in one of two comfortable huts at the south end of the lake and make the round-trip an enjoyable and relaxed two-day adventure.

Getting a taste of the rugged St. Arnaud Range is possible from Lake Rotoiti via well-marked **St. Arnaud Track** (five hours round-trip). It starts at the eastern shore of Kerr Bay, climbs through beech forest, and comes out at 1,372-meter-high **Parachute Rocks.** From the top of the range you can see both sides of the divide—allow an entire day for this trip as you'll stop many times to absorb the magnificent scenery along the way.

Walks around Lake Rotoroa

Peaceful Lake Rotoroa is larger, deeper, and less developed than Lake Rotoiti. No powerboats or water-skiers (or anything noisy) are permitted on the lake—sailboats and windsurfers are fine. Head first to the Rotoroa Ranger Station for maps, hiking and hut information, and weather forecasts. If you feel like taking a stroll, try the 10-minute **Flower Walk** starting 100 meters from the lake foreshore (on the eastern side of the Gowan River)—it offers great views of Lake Rotoroa. The **Short Loop Track** is another walk in the same area (20 minutes round-trip); it runs along the lake via Lakeside Track and back to the car park. To get to the beginning, turn left (looking toward the lake) on the road just past the Accommodation House, walk to the end of the road, and continue a short distance along **Porika Track** to the signpost where Loop Track branches off to the right. **Porika Lookout Track** climbs slowly along a ridge to a lookout with excellent views of the lake and the Travers, Ella, and Mahanga Ranges, returning down the hydro track; it takes about three hours.

One of the most beautiful "woodsy" walks in the area is the two-hour **Braeburn Walk.** Start from Braeburn Rd. just down from the ranger station and head south on the western side of the lake. Passing through green arches of beech/podocarp forest full of bellbirds and a wonderland of ferns, the track gradually climbs to a softly cascading waterfall, drops down to the creek, and returns along an old hydro path to Braeburn Road. The area's longest walk (six hours one way), along the eastern side of Lake Rotoroa via **Lakeside Track,** takes you to the far end where the Sabine River enters. It's fairly rough going, but the Sabine Hut awaits you at the end. You will need sturdy boots, warm wind- and waterproof clothing, your own stove (the hut has an efficient fire unit), and a tent in peak periods, as the huts are more than likely to be full. There are no tracks along the western side of Lake Rotoroa.

Hiking Tracks

The many long trails here range from wilderness hikes in river valleys to challenging tracks crossing high alpine passes, and climbing routes to test the most serious mountaineer. The main river valleys are the **Travers, Sabine, D'Urville,** and **Matakitaki,** with huts and campsites at regular intervals. The most popular track, the 80-km Travers-Sabine Circuit, links the lakes, valleys, and passes to form a circular route. Twenty-five huts and a number of shelters are scattered throughout the park, along with many excellent campsites. All the huts have fresh water nearby, and most have a stove or open fireplace (a few have no source of heat at all). During peak periods many huts may be full—it's best to take your own tent, stove, and cooking equipment whether you plan to stay in the huts or not, and extra food in case you're delayed by the weather. Get detailed information on the major tracks, conditions, huts, weather, and maps at the visitor center in St. Arnaud.

The weather is notorious for changing rapidly, and in many of the low-lying areas it's hard to see bad weather coming—the elements are just suddenly upon you! Rain, snow, avalanches, high winds, disorienting mists and fogs, flooded rivers, and, yes, even fine sunny days—Nelson Lakes

National Park gets it all. If you notice high wispy clouds coming from the north followed by a gray haze, expect rain, or snow higher up. The best way to tackle the weather is to hit the tracks prepared for everything; warm clothing, a wool hat, and gloves are essential items no matter what the season.

Fishing

Brown trout are the most commonly caught fish in the lakes and rivers of Nelson Lakes National Park. Rainbow trout are also caught in Lake Rotoroa and the Sabine River, but are less common and are no longer restocked. The most successful angling rivers are the Travers, Sabine, D'Urville, Matakitaki, Buller, and Gowan. The trout season changes year to year but in the rivers it's usually from the first of October to the end of April (11 months a year in the lakes), and you must buy a fishing permit ($15 per day, $30 per week, $75 per year) from the visitor center in St. Arnaud, or from local sporting goods stores. You can use flies, lures, or bait to catch "the big one" and go anywhere you want if you're shore fishing; if you're fishing from a boat, you can fish anywhere other than the areas marked by white poles along sides of rivermouths and outlets. Locals recommend lightly weighted nymphs. The trout share their underwater homes with monstrously large eels (just in case you were thinking of going diving).

Skiing and Snowboarding

You can sample fine downhill and cross-country skiing within park boundaries at the small, quiet **Mount Robert Ski Field** developed by the Nelson Ski Club, tel. 03/548-8336. It provides beginners with gentle slopes and more advanced skiers with steep slopes and a 300-meter vertical drop over 50 hectares of wide east-facing slopes. The season is generally June–Sept. depending on snow conditions (usually driest and most compact from July to mid-September). There are five rope tows, ski and board rentals, and instruction is available. Cross-country skiers head for the popular area along **Robert Ridge.** The unusual thing about Mount Robert is the long walk to the base area. The avid skier or boarder starts at the parking lot at the end of

Mt. Robert Rd. and follows Pinchgut Track all the way up, crossing to the Second Basin (altogether about two hours each way), carrying all gear and necessities; the only alternative is the heli-shuttle (weekends only). This keeps the crowds away and adds to the club atmosphere of this beautiful ski field. Two lodges in the basin provide limited accommodation, but you must book a bed for all weekends and for August and September. A day ticket is $20.

Rainbow Ski Area, tel. 03/521-1861, commercially operated with all facilities, is on the east side of the St. Arnaud Range, just outside the park boundaries (24 km from St. Arnaud), a one-hour drive from Nelson. Well signposted off Hwy. 63, the road to this ski field follows the Wairau River, then branches off to the right following Six Mile Creek—and you can drive to this one! The area has one chairlift, one T-bar, and three other surface lifts that open up 300 hectares of wide, open south-facing slopes. Lift tickets are $47 per day.

ACCOMMODATIONS AND FOOD
St. Arnaud/Lake Rotoiti

If you're looking for comfort and style, **Alpine Lodge** at St. Arnaud, tel. 03/521-1869 or 0800/367-777, website: www.alpinelodge.co.nz, provides a TV and video lounge, a ski room and drying room, a kitchen and tea-making supplies, a ski store, and all meals (main courses $17–25) in the large restaurant. The lodge runs specialized tours (including fishing) and transportation to the ski field; comfortable rooms with lots of exposed wood start at $120 s or d per night. Adjacent to the main lodge is the Alpine Chalet, suited to budget-minded travelers; dorms $18 pp, private rooms $40 s, $45 d. Rental bikes are $20 half-day or $35 full day—but note, bikes are not allowed in the national park. Eight km from Lake Rotoiti is a renovated 1880s cob (mud) hotel called the **Tophouse Farm Guesthouse,** tel. 03/521-1848 or 0800/867-468, where you can savor a home-cooked dinner, stay the night, have breakfast, and enjoy the hospitality of the Nicholls family and their animals (dog, cats, and angora-cross goats) for only $60 pp, meals included. Or just drop in for a Tophouse Tea and check out the hotel's character (note the bullet holes in the ceiling above the verandah). To get there from St. Arnaud, take Hwy. 63 east and look for the road north signposted Tophouse Historic Hotel (it's also a back road to Nelson). Then follow Tophouse Road.

The **Yellow House** in St. Arnaud, only a five-minute walk from Lake Rotoiti, tel. 03/521-1887, website: www.nelsonlakes.co.nz, is a comfortable, laid-back, and inexpensive backpacker lodge, providing basic accommodations and communal facilities for $18–22 pp per night.

At Lake Rotoiti are two well-established camping areas: **Nelson Lakes National Park Camp** at West Bay has communal bathrooms, but in winter the water is mostly turned off and only one toilet and shower are left operating; rates are from $8 pp for tent sites, $9 pp for powered sites. **Kerr Bay Campground,** adjacent to the visitor center at Kerr Bay, provides a shelter with cold water taps, power points, an open fireplace and coin-operated barbecue, toilets, and cold-water basins; same rates as above.

Lake Rotoroa

A member of Small Luxury Hotels of the World and one of the world's great fishing lodges, historic **Lake Rotoroa Lodge** lies on the edge of Lake Rotoroa, tel. 03/523-9121; website: www.rotoroa.co.nz. It provides an elegant Victorian ambience throughout. The eight deluxe suites feature brass beds and feather quilts, while downstairs, guests gather in the restaurant or bar to trade trout-fishing stories. Rates are $475 s, $575 d, inclusive of all meals. Hiring a fishing guide through the lodge costs $625 for two people for the day.

On the Lake Rotoroa foreshore the **Rotoroa Campground** has more limited facilities than the two Rotoiti campgrounds but still provides a shelter, an open fireplace, and toilets; $4 per site.

Food

In St. Arnaud, excellent **Nelson Lakes Village Shop,** tel. 03/521-1854, is run by delightful people and has pretty much everything you need—groceries, hot and cold drinks, gasoline, postal services, fishing licenses and information, lures, mountain-bike hire ($20 per day), and bookings for white-water rafting trips.

If you need a bit of dietary pampering, head for the **Alpine Lodge** in St. Arnaud, tel. 03/521-1869, where a distinct alpine ambience abounds. Dinner selections, such as rack of lamb smothered in freshly prepared mint sauce, run $20–29, or relax with a beer on one of the comfortable sofas around the roaring log fire in the lounge.

TRANSPORTATION

To reach the park from the northwest, take Hwy. 6 southwest from Nelson or Hwy. 61 south from Motueka. From the intersection of these highways at Kohatu, continue southwest toward Murchison and Westport. To get to St. Arnaud (and the main visitor center), turn east off Hwy. 6 at Kawatiri Junction and follow Hwy. 63 to St. Arnaud. To go to Lake Rotoroa instead, take Hwy. 6 a little farther south and turn east at Gowanbridge—the road ends at Lake Rotoroa. To get to the park from Picton or Blenheim, take Hwy. 1 to Blenheim, then Hwy. 63 west to St. Arnaud.

Getting There by Bus

Nelson Lakes Transport, tel. 03/547-5912, operates a twice-daily passenger service between Nelson and St. Arnaud in summer, once a day in winter. **Nelson Lakes Shuttles,** tel. 03/521-1023, connects with ferry arrivals in Picton on Monday, Wednesday, and Friday, making drops at St. Arnaud and Lake Rotoroa. Use this service to travel between St. Arnaud and Lake Rotoroa for $20.

Getting Around

Water taxis operate on both Lake Rotoiti and Lake Rotoroa, providing hikers, fishing enthusiasts, and campers with an alternate way to explore the lakes and their foreshores, or a shortcut to hiking tracks at the far ends of the two lakes. **Rotoiti Water Taxis,** tel. 03/521-1894, provides transportation (minimum four fares) from Kerr Bay to Lake Head for $15 pp, from Kerr Bay to West Bay for $13 pp, from West Bay to Lake Head for $18 pp.

Rotoroa Water Taxi, tel. 03/523-9199, runs to the Lake Head for $25 pp (minimum $60 per trip).

INFORMATION

The main source is the DOC's **Field Centre,** overlooking Lake Rotoiti in St. Arnaud, tel.

03/521-1806. It's open weekdays 9 A.M.–5 P.M., weekends 9 A.M.–noon and 1–5 P.M., for information on tracks, huts, maps, permits, and weather forecasts. For an after-hours emergency, contact the on-duty conservation officer (number posted beside the phone inside the entrance to the Field Centre).

water raft

Buller Gorge

Flowing from Lake Rotoiti to Westport and out into the Tasman Sea, deep, swift **Buller River** churns westward for more than 75 km through scrublands, meadows, and gravel flats, carving its way through rugged bush-clad mountains via the wild and beautiful Buller Gorge. About eight km southwest of **Murchison,** the emerald-green Buller pours between steep cliffs and the forested canyon of Upper Buller Gorge. At Inangahua Junction the Inangahua River joins forces with the Buller; then at Berlins, a historic gold-mining settlement, the water rushes turbulently through the even more magnificent Lower Buller Gorge. The gorge has quite a colorful past—it's been the scene of major earthquakes, mighty landslides and floods, and gold-mining rushes (thousands lived along the banks in the late 19th century), and has been a formidable obstacle for early explorers, coach drivers, and road and bridge builders.

Nowadays Hwy. 6 parallels this mighty river all the way to Westport (less than a four-hour drive from Nelson Lakes National Park), crossing the century-old **Iron Bridge** (which replaced a punt that used to be the only way for coaches and horses to cross the river), and passing by beautiful scenic reserves where you can still fossick for gold, abandoned settlements and relics from gold-mining days, short tracks to waterfalls and rapids, excellent camping spots, and a couple of small towns.

Raft outfitters good cafe

MURCHISON AND VICINITY

This attractive town of 800, 63 km west of St. Arnaud on Hwy. 6, is a popular spot for travelers to

break the 232-km trip between Nelson and Westport. Old-style houses, a peaceful atmosphere, temperatures high in summer and mild in winter, and surrounding lush meadows backed by striking mountains give Murchison a definite appeal. Also, fine trout-fishing rivers flow within a half-hour drive of the town—ask locals for the current hot spots. Despite its unruffled appearance, the town is in an area of active faults and has an exciting geological history. On June 13, 1929, "a dense fog enveloped the town . . . the church

LYELL

In the Upper Buller Gorge, Lyell was a busy gold- and quartz-mining town of 3,000 people in the late 19th century, but today all that remains is the original cemetery, reached by a beautiful track. Where the thriving town once stood is now a historic reserve: read about Lyell's colorful history on the display board, camp for free, or take a walk along **Lyell Walkway** (40 minutes one way). Ten minutes from the trailhead is the fascinating original Lyell cemetery, overgrown and disguised in the bush. The graves, dating from 1870 to 1900, have old-fashioned iron fences around them and trees growing out of their centers. The gravestones tell vivid stories of the difficult lives of the gold dredgers. Don't wander off the main track, as numerous minor tracks lead to old claims, open shafts, and abandoned equipment that could be hazardous. For another perfect camping spot, head across the road from the reserve and down to the river to the small grassy flat suitable for tents.

bell tolled, buildings were hurled from their foundations, and it was impossible to keep to one's feet." The earthquake, with its epicenter close to Murchison, tore the town apart, blocked rivers and roads, and destroyed all telephone communications. It took 21 months to reopen the main road south. Hodgsons General Merchants Store was demolished in the earthquake; rebuilt on the same site, it's open for business to this day. For more intriguing facts, check out the **Murchison District Museum,** 60 Fairfax St., tel. 03/523-9392. It's open most days 10 A.M.–4 P.M.

Sights and Recreation

Make your first stop **Murchison Information Centre,** Waller St., tel. 03/523-9350, where eager volunteers arm you with information on local rafting, horseback riding and trekking, fishing, and pig-hunting opportunities, and suggest scenic sights, walks, and drives; it's open in summer weekdays 9 A.M.–5 P.M. and Saturday 9 A.M.–noon, in winter at variable hours. Whitewater rafting enthusiasts should call **White Water Action Rafting Tours,** 45 Waller St., tel. 03/523-9581.

Accommodations and Food

Options at **Kiwi Park,** 170 Fairfax St., tel. 03/523-9248 0800/228-080, include campsites for $18, basic cabins for $18 s, $30 d, tourist flats for $60–75 s or d, and five motel units for $85–100 s or d. Units at **Mataki Motel,** 34 Hotham St., tel. 03/523-9088 or 0800/279-088, start at $55 s, $65 d ($85 with a kitchen). **Riverview Holiday Park** is on Riverview St. next to the Buller River, almost two km north of downtown Murchison, tel. 03/523-9591. Flat grassy tent and caravan sites are $20 per night, spacious comfortable cabins are $32, tourist flats start at $65 s or d. There's a large living room with TV and pool table, as well as the usual communal facilities.

Murchison has several reasonable places to eat, including **Murchison Tea Rooms,** 48 Waller St., tel. 03/523-9068. At **Stables Restaurant** in the **Commercial Hotel** on Wallace St. (at Fairfax St.), tel. 03/523-9696, tuck into tasty bistro fare (chops, fish, steak) for $12–18; it's open daily 8 A.M.–9 P.M.

To the West Coast and Beyond

From Murchison, Hwy. 6 follows the Buller River for almost 100 km, where it drains into the Tasman Sea near **Westport.** Along the way the road passes through some of the most magnificent gorge scenery. At the small settlement of **Inangahua Junction,** Hwy. 6 crosses the Inangahua River and continues to Westport; Hwy. 69 branches off south—a more direct route to Greymouth.

Not far south of Murchison, Hwy. 65 branches south to Hwy. 7, which crosses over Lewis Pass to Christchurch. For details on this stretch of highway, see the Marlborough chapter.

NELSON AND THE NORTHWEST

West Coast

Introduction

The magnificent West Coast of the South Island (also known as **Westland**), a narrow strip of land squeezed between the Tasman Sea and the Southern Alps, offers a taste of rock, ice, sand, and sea all at once. Although it has the unfortunate reputation for having rainy weather, dull skies, and an abundant summer population of bloodthirsty sand flies, it also has extended periods of blue skies and sunshine (particularly in winter)—all you need is a bit of luck, and insect repellent smothering all exposed areas of your body. Well-maintained Hwy. 6 gives the closest lowland views of the Main Divide and good access to both coastal and mountain activities. Visit the coal-mining and fishing center of Westport in the north, wild and rugged surf beaches, a seal colony at Tauranga Bay, the amazing Punakaiki Pancake Rocks in Paparoa National Park, the West Coast commercial center of Greymouth, and the historic gold-mining town of Hokitika (a good place to browse for greenstone carvings and jewelry). Stop along the highway for a spot of trout fishing in one of several major rivers, or take a photography break at one of the many small lakes that reflect distant snowcapped peaks in their mirror-still waters, then push on south to the lush

Pancake Rocks, Paparoa National Park

rainforests and mighty glaciers of rugged Westland National Park/Tai Poutini.

The best way to see the West Coast is in your own vehicle (you'll want to stop many times along the way), but you can get your share of scenic delights from the bus. Getting to and traveling along the West Coast by public transportation is no problem. Air New Zealand serves Westport and Hokitika airports, the famous TranzAlpine train and many buses run between Christchurch and Greymouth, buses connect Nelson in the north with Westport, Greymouth, and Hokitika, and several bus companies cover all the main West Coast roads (from Karamea to Haast).

A Mountain and Sea Sandwich

WESTPORT

At one time New Zealand's largest coal-exporting town, Westport (5,500) lies at the mouth of the mighty Buller River, 226 km southwest of Nelson and 102 km north of Greymouth.

In the late 19th century gold-mining was an important industry on the Buller between Berlins and Lyell, bringing masses of people to the coast, but the coal industry was what really put Westport on the map. The mines still operate, but the coal is now sent by rail to the east coast for shipping to Japan. The town is nowadays known for its cement manufacturing, tourism, farming, good surf and river fishing (check out all the fishing boats at the wharf), 18-hole golf course, and opportunities to go rafting, caving, abseiling, horse trekking, you name it. The main attractions are the Coaltown Museum on Queen St. featuring the history of the coal-mining industry, good surf beaches, historic Cape Foulwind and the Tauranga Bay seal colony there (see below). If you're going to be in Westport at the end of February, you may want to participate in or watch the start of the **Buller Marathon,** arguably New Zealand's most popular and scenic running race.

Coaltown

This museum and "living piece of the past" on Queen St., tel. 03/789-8204, is Westport's most popular attraction. Inside you'll find room after room of historic displays, all kinds of coal-mining equipment, films on the coal-mining industry (shown every 30 minutes), a room where special effects give the feeling of being underground in a coal mine, and an interesting collection of historic photos. Also see the colonial and mar-

itime wings and the gold-mining exhibition. One of the rooms features a wagon from the famous Denniston Incline, which, after completion in 1880, allowed coal to be lowered in wagons down a very steep hill by gravity—dropping 518 meters over a distance of two km in only 4.5 minutes. The miners and inhabitants of the hill also used the wagons as their only form of transportation down to the railway (what a ride!) in the early years. Coaltown is open daily (varying hours); $7 adult, $3.50 child.

Cape Foulwind and Vicinity

If you have your own transportation, a drive out to **Carters Beach** (five km south of Westport) is a worthwhile sidetrack for a stroll along a sandy beach or a safe plunge in the surf. Then continue to the **Cape Foulwind Walkway** and the **Tauranga Bay Seal Colony** (another 10 km). To get there take Hwy. 6 south out of Westport, cross the Buller River Bridge, then turn right following Carters Beach and seal colony signs.

Cape Foulwind (named by Captain Cook during a fierce storm in 1770) is a rocky promontory of granite bluffs covered in forests, wild grassy downs, and swampy streams and bogs. The walkway starts at the end of Cape Foulwind Rd. (a continuation of Carters Beach Rd.), runs south over the cape's granite bluffs and undulating pasture, passes the Tauranga Bay Seal Colony, and finishes at the north end of sandy Tauranga Beach (the Maori word means Sheltered Anchorage), where you'll find a car park, toilet, and interpretive display at the north end of Tauranga Bay Road. The easy four-km walk (wear light shoes) takes just over an hour each way, and can be done in either direction. From the top of the

W

WEST COAST

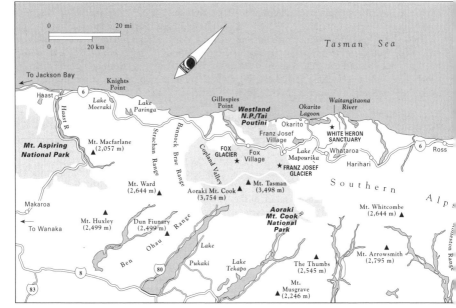

cliffs you get great coastal views and a peek at the Tauranga Bay Seal Colony. The fully protected *Arctocephalus fosterii* seal lives and breeds on the rocky shores around southern New Zealand and on subantarctic islands, and this colony is its northernmost breeding colony—don't climb down and disturb the animals. One of the best times to visit is about January when you can sit at the top of the cliffs and watch the young seals frolic on the rocks, swim gracefully in the ocean, playfully catch waves, or bask with their parents directly below. **Tauranga Beach** is also an appealing place to walk or catch some sun, but resist the urge to catch a wave—the surf can be dangerous for swimming (look for the posted warning signs in summer or ask the locals about recent conditions).

Recreation and Tours

For all sorts of outdoor adventures, including popular "underworld rafting" ($80 pp; allow four hours), contact **Norwest Adventures,** tel. 03/789-6686. **Buller Adventure Tours** on Buller Gorge Rd. (Hwy. 6, six km east of Westport), tel. 03/789-7286, also offers abundant outdoor

activities in the area—jetboating, rafting (its one-day heli-raft Karamea trip for $215 pp is particularly popular), canoeing, horseback riding, gold panning, and more starting at $45; for all the details, call in at their base or book at the Westport Information Centre.

Accommodations

Hotels, motels, and two motor camps provide accommodation, but if you're short of time and want to see as much of the West Coast as possible, continue south to Greymouth, Hokitika, or the glaciers for an overnight break—there's even more to see and do farther south. **Chelsea Gateway Motor Lodge,** a modern two-story motel at the corner of Palmerston and Bentham Streets, tel. 03/789-6835 or 0800/660-033, website: www.goldenchain.co.nz, features spacious self-contained studios, and one- and two-bedroom units for $90–150 s or d.

Looking for a place to pitch your tent or park your van? Do you want a comfortable cabin? **Seal Colony Top 10 Tourist Park,** six km south of town across the road from seemingly endless sandy Carters Beach, tel. 03/789-6732, has tent

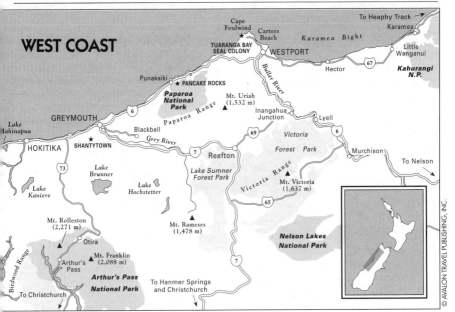

WEST COAST

and caravan sites for $22, spacious cabins for $45 d, modern amenity blocks, and a recreation room. **Westport Holiday Park** on Domett St., tel. 03/789-7043, has tent sites for $16 d, caravan sites for $18 d, shared A-frame chalets for $37 d, cabins for $45 d, and a common room with TV.

Food and Drink

For meat pies, cakes, and pastries, head for **Rainbow Cake Kitchen,** 78 Palmerston St., tel. 03/789-7899. **Bailie's Bar,** 187 Palmerston St., tel. 03/789-7289, serves inexpensive bar meals to a young, active-minded crowd, with Guinness on tap, and Irish music on Friday night. Across the road, the **Black & White Hotel,** 198 Palmerston St., tel. 03/789-7959, serves up similar fare—roasts are about $10.

While Westport's main street offers a variety of convenient dining opportunities, I recommend heading 12 km south from town to **The Bay House** for both its food and wonderful setting. A converted 1929 holiday house, the building blends into the surrounding native coastal bush, while overlooking Tauranga Bay and the wonderful sights and smells of the ocean. The creative menu includes lots of seafood, including scallops poached in a creamy coconut broth and served on a bed of Thai noodles. Dinners range $25–30. It's open Sept.–April daily for lunch from 11 A.M. and dinner from 6 P.M., as well as from 9 A.M. for brunch on weekends. Evening reservations recommended at tel. 03/789-7133.

Transportation

Intercity stops at Craddocks Motors, Palmerston St., tel. 03/879-7819, on each daily service down the west coast from Nelson. Bus service to Nelson is also operated daily by **White Star,** tel. 03/789-6200, and **Westcoast Tours,** tel. 03/789-6658. **East West Shuttles,** tel. 03/789-6251, runs between Westport and Christchurch once daily in each direction.

Information

The excellent **Westport Information Centre** on Brougham St. (off Palmerston, the main drag), tel. 03/789-6658, website: www.Westport.co.nz, features photographic displays on the Buller District, racks of free brochures up for grabs, and enthusiastic staff who fill you in on all the local attractions and book tours, trips, and accommodations; it's open Mon.–Fri. 9 A.M.–7 P.M., Saturday and Sunday 9 A.M.–3 P.M. If it's closed when you hit town, check the map in the window for quick orientation.

KARAMEA

This small beachside community, 100 km north of Westport along Hwy. 67, is a good base for those starting or finishing the Heaphy Track through Kahurangi National Park—and an interesting detour in its own right. Apart from lazing on the beach or fishing, you can tour **Honeycomb Caves,** famous for the discoveries of bones of moas and other extinct birds. Other local attractions include forest walks, intriguing limestone arches formed during the last 35,000 years, rafting, horse trekking (from $50 half-day), scenic flights (30 minutes for $65 pp), mountain bike and canoe rental, and a small museum. You can book all of the above tours at the **Last Resort,** tel. 03/782-6617.

Practicalities

The **Last Resort,** 71 Waverley St., tel. 03/782-6617 or 0800/505-042, website: www.lastresort.co.nz, is a large complex set around a central building that holds a café, restaurant, and bar. Dorm beds are $20, comfortable rooms with shared bathrooms are $50–60 s or d, rooms with private bathrooms are $90, and fully self-contained cottages are $140.

Head to the Last Resort for tourist information, or the DOC **Karamea Information Centre,** Waverley St., tel. 03/782-6652, for local park information; open weekdays 8 A.M.–4:30 P.M.

PAPAROA NATIONAL PARK

A narrow strip of coastline 57 km south of Westport and 47 km north of Greymouth is protected as spectacular Paparoa National Park. Here you can explore spectacular limestone cliffs, several rivers, steep bare-rock canyons, magical creeks

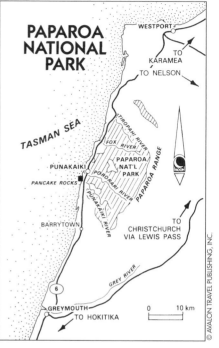

that disappear underground, hills clad in lush ever-so-green ferns and *nikau* palms, numerous underground cave systems, and the Paparoa Range. The Pancake Rocks and the blowholes at Punakaiki are the most well-known features; however, there is much to see inland. You can see some of its lush scenic beauty by driving along the coastal highway, but the best way to appreciate the park (and escape the crowds) is to walk the inland tracks or climb to the top of the granite and gneiss range for spectacular views in all directions.

The Land

The Paparoa Range is not geologically connected with the Southern Alps. It began as an accumulation of Tertiary sand-, mud-, and limestone under the ocean that was uplifted, weathered, eroded, and then reinvaded by the sea. After the range was uplifted again, and eroded by wind, rain, snow, and ice, rivers slashed their way westward to the sea creating deep limestone (karst) gorges and canyons clothed in trees and ferns.

Underground drainage in this limestone region is the most unusual feature of the park—it is this, along with the dissolving action of rainwater on limestone, which sets the karst landscape apart. This is the last area of lowland forested karst left intact and unmodified in New Zealand.

The flora and fauna in the park are varied and diverse. If you explore a lot of the region you'll hike through 26 documented forest types in a very small area, including towering forests of *rimu, totara, rata,* redbeech, *kamahi, quintinia, toro, horopito,* and lancewood. On the forest floor and steep banks along the coastal highway is an incredible conglomeration of ferns, mosses, lichens, and fungi. As you'd expect, all sorts of birds thrive in this green wonderland—bellbirds, fantails, *tui, kaka, kea,* South Island robins, wood pigeons, parakeets, blue ducks, and native falcons, along with great spotted kiwis and the only breeding colony of Westland petrels in the world. Introduced animals and, of course, insects, also hide out in the lush park greenery.

Sights on the Road to Punakaiki

Highway 6 south follows the coastline through a smattering of old gold and coal towns backed by the Paparoa Range, passing through the first coastal section of the park—a lush, bright-green, fern- and *nikau* palm–filled strip. Pull off at signposted lookouts for some of the most stunning coastal views, or wander off along one of the walking tracks signposted from the highway. The scenery along **Truman Track** has a reputation for plenty of eye-opening camera action.

The park's premier attraction is **Pancake Rocks** and the **Punakaiki Blow Holes**—not-to-be-missed natural wonders accessed by a short trail from the small service center of Punakaiki. Made up of layer upon layer of limestone and mudstone, the much-photographed cliffs look like an enormous stack of wafer-thin rock pancakes. To see them, take **Dolomite Point Walk,** a 10-minute stroll from the main highway through a wonderland of tree ferns, *nikau* palms, and northern *rata* to the rocks. On the way you pass a deep surge pool full of waving seaweed and mighty blowholes that in stormy weather boom and roar with the breaking of large waves—often unexpectedly blasting torrents of water skyward to soak startled onlookers with spray. The blowhole performs best when a large southern swell combines with a high tide.

© ANDREW HEMPSTEAD

hiking in Paparoa National Park

WEST COAST

Tracks

Ask at the visitor center for the brochure "Short Walks" and the excellent park map ($11) that has lots of useful information and locations of walks and longer hikes. The brochure covers the equipment you'll need, and safety tips to make the park an enjoyable experience. It also outlines the short **Dolomite Point Walk, Truman Track,** and **Woodpecker Bay Track;** the trails to **Punakaiki, Te Ana O Matuku Caverns,** and **Fox River Caves;** and the longer hiking tracks, **Tiropahi River Track, Pororari River Track,** and **Punakaiki/Pororari Track.** The 25-km two- to three-day **Inland Pack Track** (you need some hiking experience for this one, and take an extra day's supply of food and a map) meanders along the historic inland road built to avoid the rugged Te Miko Coast, through spectacular limestone canyons where deep crystal-clear river pools beckon (take care; the rivers can rise quickly), and past entrances to underground cave systems. If you have time to see only a little of the track, go up the Pororari or Fox Rivers to walk the beginning or end sections. Before setting off along any of the longer tracks, get all the details and a weather forecast from the visitor center at Punakaiki.

Guided Adventures

For those who enjoy exploring the unknown with local experts, **Paparoa Nature Tours** on Hwy. 6, five km south of Punakaiki, tel. 03/731-1826, runs a large number of guided trips to suit all activity levels in and around the park. It offers walking trips (from 40-minute to one-day walks), and bird-watching trips to view some of the 40 native species known to live in or visit this area for breeding or feeding (from $18 pp, minimum five). One of the most popular half-day trips is to the **Westland Black Petrel Colony** to see the breeding grounds during nonbreeding season and then view sooty shearwaters as they return to their burrows in the evening. This trip is suitable for all ages. Guided canoe adventures start at $35 pp per half-day, $60 full day, or you can rent a canoe for an independent adventure for $7 per hour, $14 for three hours. **Paparoa Horse Treks,** tel. 03/731-1839, offers two-hour treks in the Punakaiki Valley, ending up on the beach; rates are $60 pp.

Accommodations and Food

PUNAIKAIKI ROCKS Village

The small village of **Punakaiki** exists only to serve park visitors and highway travelers, but facilities still are limited, so if you're planning to stay overnight in the park, make advance reservations for the following accommodations and don't rely on getting a meal after about 8 P.M.

The pick of the park's accommodations is **Paparoa Park Motel,** overlooking the Punakaiki River and with views to Pancake Rocks from its delightful bush setting south of the information center, tel. 03/731-1883 or 0800/727-276; website: www.paparoa.co.nz. Each of the five spacious, self-contained units is furnished in a simple and practical style, with lots of exposed timber. Rates are $95–105 s or d. More accommodations lie bunched together between Hwy. 6 and the ocean, 500 meters north of the visitor center, including **Punakaiki Beach Hostel,** Webb St., tel. 03/731-1852 or 0800/726-225. It provides dorm rooms for $18 pp, doubles for $23 pp. The modern **Punakaiki Motor Camp,** tel. 03/731-1894, run by the DOC, is near the mouth of the Pororari River (safe swimming; kayak rental available down the street). You'll find access to a wild and beautiful beach—a wonderful spot for walking, and don't forget to take your camera. Protected, grassy, tree-shaded tent sites are $9 pp, caravan sites are $10 pp, bunkroom is $14 pp, and cabins are $32 s or d, $36 with kitchens.

Pancake Tearooms (open daily 9 A.M.–5 P.M.), tel. 03/731-1873, lies along the highway next to the visitor center. For more substantial meals or a quiet beer, head for **Punakaiki Tavern,** on the corner of Hwy. 6 and Oven St., tel. 03/731-1188.

Other Practicalities

Across the road from the walkway to Pancake Rocks is the DOC **Visitor Centre,** tel. 03/731-1895, featuring photographic displays of the area's geology and history, and an audiovisual display. Staff members provide information and maps on the park, including brochures on coastal walks to nearby caves and the most intriguing rock formations in the immediate area. In summer they hold illustrated talks at the center and run scheduled guided walks of varying lengths. The center is open in summer, daily 9 A.M.–6 P.M.; the rest of the year, daily 9 A.M.–4:30 P.M.

Drove through ✱

GREYMOUTH AND VICINITY

Between Punakaiki and Greymouth, Hwy. 6 winds in and out of coastal native bush, passing tall cliffs and gray, sandy beaches; in summer the landscape is sprinkled with colorful wildflowers. Situated at the mouth of the Grey River and originally developed as a port in the 1860s after the discovery of gold, Greymouth grew into the largest town on the West Coast and the main port and commercial center for local coal-mining and sawmilling industries. Greymouth (population 13,000) today is known for good fishing in the Grey River system, and for its many parks and native reserves.

Sights

Shantytown, a historical reconstruction of a West Coast gold settlement of the 1880s, is Greymouth's best-known attraction. Wander through the re-created town with its bank and gold-buying office, store, jail, church, hotel, hospital, printing shop, stables, and fire station. While all the buildings may be replicas, the gold here is real. A high-powered water jet blasts gold-bearing quartz from the hillside, a stamper battery crushes the ore, and then it runs through sluice boxes (or try your own hand at a bit of panning). Another highlight is the steam train, which runs up the valley to an active sawmill and into a claim mined since 1860. Admission is $11 adult, $7 child; gold-panning is an extra $2.50 pp. Off the main highway at Paroa on the road to Marsden, 11 km south of Greymouth, tel. 03/762-6634, Shantytown is open daily 8:30 A.M.–5 P.M.

On the corner of Turumaha and Herbert Streets, **Monteith's Brewing Co.** is open for tours Mon.–Fri. at 10 A.M. and 2 P.M.; the tour ends with a 30-minute all-you-can-drink beer-tasting session. Although Monteith's has been brewing beer for west coasters since 1858, it's

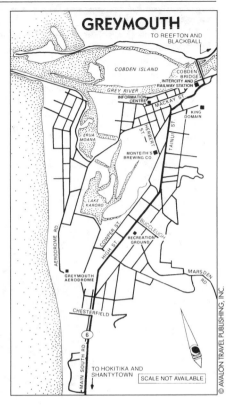

only been the last few years that its classic ales, such as Original, have been available nationwide. Book tours at the information center.

Recreation

Take a bush walk up the hill (near The Gap) through **King Domain** for good views—the track starts on Mount St. near the railway station. Other good walks are along the **Greymouth Flood Wall** for views of the river, town, Fisherman's Wharf, and tidal estuary, and the **Point Elizabeth Walk** from Rapahoe around the headland to the Cobden Beach road end for more spectacular views.

About 15 km beyond the entrance to Shantytown (a gravel road) is the start of the one-km **Woods Creek Walkway,** a 45-minute round-trip track through virgin *rimu* forest that takes

THE TOWN OF BLACKBALL

The historic town of Blackball, which lies on the inland side of the Paparoa Range 40 km northeast of Greymouth (north of Hwy. 7), is one of those out-of-the-way places you occasionally stumble across and never forget. Born as a supply stop during an 1866 gold rush, Blackball later thrived as a coal-mining center, then almost became a ghost town after the last mine closed in 1968. Today its few hundred inhabitants, with no visible source of income, tend to well-kept gardens, while away the time chatting on street corners, and converge on the main surviving business—the local pub. **Formerly the Blackball Hilton** (the unusual name came about after legal problems with an internationally renowned hotel chain with a similar name) on Hart St., tel. 03/732-4705, website: www.blackballhilton.co.nz, is a ramshackle two-story building constructed in 1909. It appears quiet enough at first but is locally known for its raging past. The coal miners used to drink, rant, rave, and party well into the wee hours in this hotel until the mines closed and the miners left in

1968. It has a couple of street-side outdoor tables, but you need to head inside to soak up the history and character of the building and, in turn, the town. Friendly bar staff, a huge fireplace, and antique-lined walls add to the appeal. A few years back, keen local photographers decided to make a photographic record of Blackball and its inhabitants. Ask for the photo albums at the bar—they provide a fascinating glimpse into small-town New Zealand. You'll find much to do around town, including visiting an abandoned mine, fishing, gold panning, horseback riding, or for the more adventurous, hiking the Croesus Track. Ask for details and maps at the Hilton.

The Hilton's upper floor has been renovated, and now offers single and double rooms for $65 pp, which includes bed, breakfast, and dinner (room only, $27.50 pp). Dorm beds are $20 pp, with shared bathrooms, TV lounge, sauna, and spa. There's a communal kitchen, but the pub kitchen is open for meals daily at lunch and dinner.

Formerly the Blackball Hilton

© ANDREW HEMPSTEAD

you past old gold-mine tunnels, shafts (take a flashlight), and other evidence of past gold-mining activities.

Wild West Adventure Co., tel. 03/768-6649, runs a variety of tours, including sight-seeing, nature, rafting, 4WD, and glacier flights. **Sceniclcand Dolphin Watch,** tel. 03/768-9770, can take you out in search of the rare Hector's dolphin aboard a large and stable inflatable boat.

Entertainment

For entertainment, head to any of the hotel bars, the disco at **Railway Hotel,** Mawhera Quay, tel. 03/768-7023, on Friday and Saturday nights, piped music at **Steamers Carvery &**

Bar at 58 Mackay St., tel. 03/768-4193, or movies at the **Regent Theatre,** corner Mackay and Regent Streets, tel. 03/768-5101.

Accommodations

There are plenty of places to stay in Greymouth, from hostels and motor camps to bed-and-breakfasts, motels, and plush hotels. Of the many historic downtown hotels, **Revington's Hotel,** 46 Tainui St., tel. 03/768-7055, is the best choice-and you may end up in the room where Queen Elizabeth II once stayed. All 26 rooms have a private bathroom, but facilities are basic; $70 s or d. Motels around Greymouth are not particularly cheap.

At the lower end of the price scale is **Riverview Motel,** on Omoto Rd. (east of town off Hwy. 7), tel. 03/768-6884 or 0508/807-060, with an outdoor pool, barbecue area, views across the Grey River to the Paparoa Range, and nine self-contained rooms of varying configurations. At $75–80 s or d, this place is an excellent value.

At **Willowbank Pacifica Lodge** on Hwy. 6, three km north of town, tel. 03/768-5339 or 0800/668-355, website: www.pacificahotels.co.nz, choose from two-bedroom studios, two- or three-bed units with kitchens and spa baths, or one- to six-bed units; $85–98 s or d. Guest facilities include a kitchen, laundry, swimming pool, and spa. **Gables Motor Lodge,** 84 High St., tel. 03/768-9991, features 12 well-furnished rooms, each with a fully equipped kitchen and a bath. Town is an easy five-minute walk north. Rates are $95–125 s or d. **Hotel Ashley,** 74 Tasman St., tel. 03/768-5135 or 0800/807-787, website: www.hotelashley.co.nz, is a modern, low-rise complex offering a wide range of facilities, including a large indoor pool, fitness room, spa, sauna, bar, café, and restaurant. Each of the 60 guest rooms is spacious, and many have kitchens. Rates range $100–165 s or d.

For bed-and-breakfast accommodation run by a local family knowledgeable on the area, consider **Rosewood,** 20 High St., tel. 03/768-4674 or 0800/185-748, where the five rooms (three en suite) have comfortable beds, TV, and phone. A full breakfast is included in the rates of $60–80 s, $85–110 d.

The large, well-equipped **Global Village** at the south end of town at 42 Cowper St., tel. 03/768-7272 or 0508/542-636, overlooks a small stream and outdoor sports complex; rates $16 pp dorm, $30 s, $40 d. To get there from Tainui St. (the main street) continue south onto High St., turn right at Buccleigh St., and then turn onto Cowper Street. Funky **Noah's Ark Backpackers,** 16 Chapel St., tel. 03/768-4868 or 0800/662-472, is in a monastery dating from the 19th century within walking distance of town; dorm $17, $22.50 s, $30 d.

The closest motor camp to the city center is **Greymouth Seaside Top 10 Holiday Park** on Chesterfield St. (off the main south highway, about 2.5 km south of Greymouth city center), tel. 03/768-6618 or 0800/867-104. It's next to the beach, has a spa pool, a TV room, a shop on the premises selling basic necessities, communal facilities, and a licensed restaurant, and take-aways within walking distance. Tent sites are $20, caravan sites $22, cabins $36–44 s or d, tourist flats $68 s or d, and motel rooms $80 s or d. The next closest, **Rapahoe Beach Motor Camp,** on the main coast road at Rapahoe, tel. 03/762-7025 or 0508/465-432, is 11 km north of Greymouth, next to a good swimming beach in a small town surrounded by sea and mountains. Sites are $8 pp ($2 extra per site for power), and on-site caravans and cabins range $24–32 s or d.

Food

Many tearooms and coffee bars around town serve snacks and light meals, but if you're looking for something more substantial, try **Jones's Cafe**

© ANDREW HEMPSTEAD

Monteith's, a popular beer throughout the country, is brewed in Greymouth.

WEST COAST

and Bar at 37 Tainui St., tel. 03/768-6468; open daily from 8 A.M. It's small but it has a friendly atmosphere and dinners starting at $15, which includes seven different vegetables. Locally recommended **Cafe Collage Restaurant,** upstairs at 115 Mackay St. (near the station), tel. 03/768-5497, serves seafood crepes, steak, chicken, and spaghetti dishes for about $18–25 in art deco surroundings. It's open from 6 P.M. Mon.–Saturday. The friendly staff at **Bonzai Bakery & Pizzeria** at 31 Mackay St., tel. 03/768-4170, produce tasty pizza ($11–23), steak, chicken, fish, and spaghetti dishes ($15–17.50), a number of desserts ($4.50), and daily lunch specials for $4.50–6.50. Bonzai also stocks 30 varieties of local and overseas beers and red and white wines; it's open Mon.–Sat. 9 A.M. until late. **Arizona's,** Mackay St., tel. 03/768-4577, is a Western-themed restaurant open daily for lunch and dinner. If you're in the mood for dressing up, try **Ashley's Restaurant** in the Hotel Ashley, 74 Tasman St., tel. 03/768-5135, where à la carte selections range $22–31.

Transportation

The nearest airport is 40 km south of Greymouth at Hokitika; a cab between the two costs about $20 pp. Greymouth is the turnaround point for one of the world's great train journeys, the **TranzAlpine** between Christchurch and Greymouth via Arthur's Pass. The trip is popular, so reserve ahead of time at any information center or by calling **Tranz Scenic,** tel. 0800/802-802. It's possible to reach Greymouth from Christchurch and return the same day; the regular fare is $87 round-trip.

Coast to Coast Shuttle, tel. 0800/800-847, follows Hwy. 73 through the same valleys as the rail line on a daily run between Christchurch and Greymouth. **Intercity** provides buses in all directions: north to Westport, east across the Southern Alps to Christchurch, and south to the glaciers. All services leave from the **Greymouth Travel Centre,** near the railway station on Mackay St., tel. 03/768-7080. Many smaller shuttle companies pass through Greymouth, stopping at either the railway station or information center. **Sounds to Coast,** tel. 03/578-

0225, is a thrice-weekly service between Picton and Greymouth.

Car rental agencies in Greymouth include **Avis,** tel. 03/768-0902; **Budget,** tel. 03/768-4343; **Hertz,** tel. 03/768-0196; and **NZ Rent-a-car,** tel. 03/768-0379. For a taxi, call **Greymouth Taxis,** tel. 03/768-7078.

Services

The **post office** is on Tainui St., tel. 03/768-0123. The **public library** is at Mackay and Albert Streets, tel. 03/768-7684, open Mon.–Fri. from 10 A.M. **Greymouth Hospital** is on High St., tel. 03/768-0499. **Mason's Pharmacy** is at 34 Tainui St., tel. 03/768-7470. The **police station** is on the corner of Guinness and Tarapuhi Streets, tel. 03/768-1600.

Information

For general information and more on what to see and do in the area, all the West Coast reading material you could wish for, and a tour and accommodation booking service, go to the **Greymouth Information Centre** in the foyer of the Regent Theatre on the corner of Mackay and Herbert Streets, tel. 03/768-5101. It's open weekdays 9 A.M.–5 P.M., daily 9 A.M.–6 P.M. in summer, and has plenty of pamphlets on the local area and the entire South Island—pick up the handy "Visitor Guide." **Greymouth Field Centre,** Swainson St., tel. 03/768-0427, has all the usual DOC information. The local **AA Centre,** 84 Tainui St., tel. 03/768-4300, offers road maps and accommodation guides.

HOKITIKA

The colorful town of Hokitika (population 3,500) lies beside the Tasman Sea at the mouth of the Hokitika River 40 km south of Greymouth. Backed by the majestic Southern Alps, surrounded by native bush, lakes, and rivers, with architecture reflecting the "golden days" and monuments all over town, Hokitika has character, a special atmosphere, and plenty of things to see and do. Several greenstone factories turn beautiful nephrite jade from nearby mountains and river terraces into jewelry and carvings, and

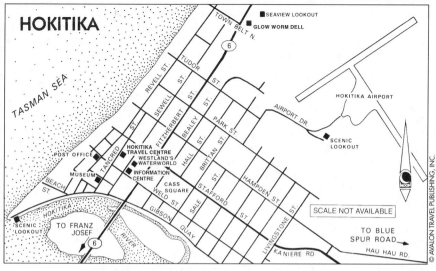

HOKITIKA

TASMAN SEA

SEAVIEW LOOKOUT
GLOW WORM DELL

TOWN BELT N.

6

TUDOR ST
REVELL ST.
SEWELL ST.
FITZHERBERT ST.
BEALEY ST.
HALL ST.
PARK ST.
BRITTAN ST.
HAMPDEN ST.
LIVINGSTONE ST.

HOKITIKA AIRPORT

AIRPORT DR.

SCENIC LOOKOUT

POST OFFICE
HOKITIKA TRAVEL CENTRE
WESTLAND'S WATERWORLD
MUSEUM
BEACH ST.
TANCRED ST.
INFORMATION CENTRE
CASS SQUARE
WELD ST.
GIBSON QUAY
STAFFORD ST.
SALE ST.

SCALE NOT AVAILABLE

SCENIC LOOKOUT
HOKITIKA
TO FRANZ JOSEF
6
RIVER

KANIERE RD

TO BLUE SPUR ROAD →

HAU HAU RD.

© AVALON TRAVEL PUBLISHING, INC.

shops sell gold nuggets and jewelry and outstanding locally produced crafts.

In addition to tourism, dairy farming takes place on surrounding alluvial flats, and Hokitika is also a center for sheep and cattle farming (on the less productive land), and is home to a venison processing plant and a moss-drying factory (sphagnum moss is used in flower arrangements in Japan; it sells for about 50 cents per kg wet or $10 per kg dry).

History

Founded in 1864, Hokitika rapidly mushroomed into the large bustling "Capital of the Goldfields" when gold was discovered in the area a few weeks later. Hundreds of miners flocked to the West Coast from Australia (they called it the "Australian Invasion") and from other parts of the world, and by the end of 1866 up to 50,000 people were living at the various gold diggings in the area (the town itself had about 6,000 residents during the peak gold-rush period). The rivermouth became a busy though treacherous port—many vessels were shipwrecked on the beach—but beachcombers, salvagers, and refloating outfits made out like bandits. Hokitika became a conglomeration of banks, bars, and hotels—more than 100 hotels were hastily built,

most of them on Revell Street. The last real West Coast gold rush occurred in 1867 in the Westport area, and by then more than 1.3 million ounces of gold had been removed. The majority of miners had left for the new goldfields on the Coromandel Peninsula by 1895, but gold remained a major industry along the coast for many years. The last gold dredge on the Hokitika River was dismantled in 1952 and the port was closed in 1954, but plenty of old gold workings, pieces of abandoned equipment, and other relics litter the surrounding district, and of course there's still gold in the local rivers and hills. Gold remains a major industry on the West Coast—locals say 100 or so mines still produce the metal dreams are made of. Pamphlets describing all the places of gold-mining interest are available at the information center.

Sights

If you're interested in finding out more about the gold-rush days, visit the **West Coast Historical Museum** on Lower Tancred St., tel. 03/755-6898, devoted to "Westland's turbulent beginnings." It features displays of old photos and sketches from the gold-mining era, a comprehensive collection of gold-mining equipment, a hall of pioneers, and an original stagecoach.

WEST COAST

Don't miss the Maori artifacts and native birds—some of which are extremely rare and possibly extinct. See the worthwhile 20-minute audiovisual on West Coast life from the discovery of gold till now. The museum is open in summer daily 9:30 A.M.–5 P.M., in winter by arrangement; $3 adult, $1.50 child.

Westland's Waterworld, Sewell St., tel. 0800/242-324, features a number of aquariums filled with saltwater and freshwater critters from along the west coast, including crayfish, whitebait, small sharks, octopus, and massive eels. The eels are fed four times daily. Waterworld is open daily 9 A.M.–5:30 P.M.; $10 adult, $5 child.

For a great view of Hokitika, distant mountains, Hokitika River, and the Tasman Sea, walk along the sandy, driftwood-strewn beach to the south end or along Gibson Quay by the river to the scenic **rivermouth viewpoint.** The view from here is particularly magnificent at sunset, and the weathered remains of an old pier, huge boulders and rocks, and silhouetted fishermen make fascinating photo subjects. The rivermouth is also a popular place for anglers to congregate for some serious salmon fishing and some not-so-serious tale telling. For an even grander panoramic view, head for the **Plane Table Lookout** on the road to the airport (north of town). A pointer and map indicate all the mountain peaks you can see, along with their heights. For fabulous coastal views, head up to **Seaview Lookout** and the historic kauri lighthouse built in 1879; drive north on Fitzherbert St. and turn up the hill toward Seaview Hospital—the lookout is inside the cemetery on the right.

Another free sight well-worth seeing on the north side of town is the **Glow Worm Dell,** beside the main road at the north town boundary—after dark you'll see thousands of tiny lights scattered over the 14-meter banks (take a flashlight to see the path and don't make any noise—noise and bright lights disturb the glowworms and their lights go out). Even if you don't have a flashlight you can easily feel your way up the path in the dark (take someone to hold onto if you're easily spooked)—and keep going; it's more spectacular the farther you go.

Arts and Crafts

Hokitika is renowned for its **greenstone** carvers. Beautiful nephrite jade is converted from lumps of rock into fine handcrafted jewelry of Maori design, with many of the studios open for public viewing. These include **Westland Greenstone,** 34 Tancred St. (by the theater), tel. 03/755-8713; and **Mountain Jade Company,** 41 Weld St., tel. 03/755-8007. At **Jade Experience,** 197 Revell St., tel. 03/755-7612, visitors are invited to spend a full day in a studio, creating a design, then carving their piece under the watchful eye of Gordon Wells. The cost is a reasonable $80. Wells also sells his own carvings, with many of his designs inspired by the ocean.

For gold nuggets and jewelry, try the **Gold Room** on Tancred St., tel. 03/755-8362; or **Ocean Paua,** 25 Weld St., tel. 03/755-6128. Don't miss **Hokitika Craft Gallery,** a cooperative of local artists based at 25 Tancred St., tel. 03/755-8802; it's open daily 8:30 A.M.–5 P.M. Everything is handcrafted—pottery, stunning woven wall hangings, cushion covers, silk scarves, wooden works of art, sweaters, stained glass, paintings, quilts, and jewelry. Another place to check out is **Hokitika Glass Blowing Studio,** also on Tancred St., tel. 03/755-7775.

Recreation

Trout and salmon fishing are popular in the Hokitika region—get your license and free fishing information (ask for the detailed leaflet on trout fishing in the region) from **Aim West Sports,** 20 Weld St., tel. 03/755-8481. Paddleboat enthusiasts may enjoy a peaceful 90-minute cruise up Mahinapua Creek into Lake Mahinapua. Weather permitting, the *Takutai Belle* departs daily at 10 A.M., 2 P.M., and 6 P.M., from just south of Hokitika by the golf course; $30 adult, $15 child. Book through Scenic Waterways, tel. 03/755-7239, or at the Westland Visitor Information Centre.

If you have your own transportation, head east out of town along Blue Spur Rd. (a continuation of Hampden St. and Hau Hau Rd.) to several attractions. Continue to the **Blue Spur New Zealand Forest Lookout**—at the Forest Service notice board turn right and continue for about four km. Tracks lead to old gold workings and abandoned mining equipment, skirt rivers, and reach waterfalls and lakes; the best thing to do is stop at the **Lake Kaniere Reserve** information building (plenty of maps and photos; not staffed) where the river exits the lake and plan your route. This lake (pronounced Canary) and the surrounding area are known for one-stop recreation. The reserve (brochure available at Westland Visitor Information Centre in Hokitika) is about 18 km east of town (no public transportation). Choose from short or long tracks in the forest-clad hills around the lake, see sparkling Dorothy Falls, or hike along the **Kaniere Water Race Walkway** to hydroelectric power stations (four km each way). There's good swimming and fishing in the lake, and campsites at Hans Bay or Geologist Creek. To get there take the main highway south to Kaniere township, then continue straight ahead onto Lake Kaniere Rd. (instead of the main road right over the Hokitika River). Continue to the Landing, where you'll find an information kiosk, mountain peak indicator board, and toilets.

Just south of town, on Hwy. 6, is **Phelps' Gold Mine,** tel. 03/755-7766, which has working machinery on display, as well as gold panning to try in an active mining area surrounded by old workings; it's open daily.

Wildfoods Festival

This unique food celebration has grown considerably in recent times to become the west coast's premier and most popular annual event. A variety of tastings and demonstrations take place throughout the second week of March, culminating on the second Saturday of the month at Cass Square, when a crowd of up to 15,000 gather to eat, drink, and listen to local musicians such as the always-popular Kokatahi Band and their own distinct brand of music. But the highlight is the food. Almost 100 different stands fill the square, offering mainstream New Zealand delicacies such as whitebait, mussels, muttonbird, and venison, but also dishes for the more adventurous, such as "Westcargot," stinging nettle soup, huhu grubs, and earthworms. Although

one of the west coast's best known businesses, Monteith's Brewing Co., is the major sponsor, there's also plenty of more exotic drinks to sample, such as Wild Mountain Moonshine and gorse wine. For details, call 03/755-8321.

Accommodations

Hokitika has a motor camp, backpacker lodgings, a guesthouse, and several hotels and motels. Of the 100-odd hotels in Hokitika, only a few still offer rooms. The nicest of these is the **Southland Hotel,** 111 Revell St., tel. 03/755-8344 or 0800/400-344, website: www.southlandhotel .com, a friendly, family-run place with 23 renovated rooms one block from the oceanfront. Rates are $110–135 s or d. Also centrally located is the bright and breezy **Jade Court Motor Lodge,** 85 Fitzherbert St., tel. 03/755-8855 or 0800/755-885, website: www.jadecourt.co.nz; $85–105 s or d for large rooms with a kitchen. **Fitzherbert Court Motel,** 191 Fitzherbert St., tel. 03/755-5342 or 0800/775-534, offers 18 large, comfortable rooms, all with a well-equipped kitchen. Rates are $80–120 s or d.

The popular **Teichelmanns Bed & Breakfast Inn,** 20 Hamilton St., tel. 03/755-8232 or 0800/743-742, provides bright, cheerful rooms, a comfortable lounge area, and congenial hosts keen to extol Hokitika's virtues. Rates range $60–80 s, $80–110 d, depending on room size and private/shared bathrooms, and include a cooked breakfast. Another B&B option is **Wright Place,** four km south of town on Adair Rd., tel. 03/755-6245, adjacent to a golf course and within walking distance of the beach. Each of the two guest rooms has its own toilet, but the main bathroom is shared; $120 s or d.

Backpackers planning an overnight stay in Hokitika are in for a treat. **Blue Spur Lodge,** tel. 03/755-8445, website: www.bluespur.co.nz, lies in a tranquil bush setting six km east of town, with views extending south to Mt. Cook. All facilities at this purpose-built lodge are of the highest standard, bikes can be used for free, and canoe and kayak rentals are offered. Dorm beds are $19 pp, twin rooms are $42, doubles $46, a double room with en suite is $55, and a self-contained cottage is $110. To get there, take Hampden St. out of town and turn left on Cement Lead Rd., or call from the information center for a pickup. Back in downtown, but with a beachfront location, **Jade Experience Backpackers,** 197 Revell St., tel. 03/755-7612, is home to the Jade Experience (see above). Rates of $17 pp for a dorm and $38 s or d in a private room include free tea and coffee and the use of bikes.

Along the western shores of Lake Mahinapua, 13 km south of town, lies a **DOC campground.** Facilities are basic (water and toilets only), but you're rewarded with great mountain views, hiking trails, and good fishing in the lake; donation requested. The option is **Hokitika Holiday Park** (not really suitable for tents) on Stafford St., tel. 03/755-8172 or 0800/465-436, with the usual facilities (good showers and heat lamps—aah!), plus a game room, trampoline, and adjacent shop selling basic necessities. Sites start at $18, standard and economy cabins range $28–38 s or d, tourist flats are $72, motel rooms $78.

Food

Hokitika doesn't have a large number of restaurants, but many tearooms and coffee lounges serve the usual, as do plenty of take-away bars. It's relatively easy to eat well on a tight budget in Hokitika—most of the eating houses are on Revell, Weld, and Sewell Streets.

For a delicious selection of salads, pies, quiche, light meals ($4–10), pastries, and desserts, and a good variety of teas and coffees, go to **P.R.'s Coffee Shop Bistro,** 39 Tancred St., tel. 03/755-8379; it's open daily 6 A.M.–5 P.M. For relatively inexpensive Chinese meals ($14–21), sandwiches, burgers, and light meals ($11–15), and a buffet Tues.–Sun. nights ($24), locals head for **Millies Place,** 35 Weld St., next to the town clock, tel. 03/755-8128. Eat inside, or outside at the sidewalk tables, or get food to go; it's open daily 6 A.M.–9 P.M. in summer, 6:30 A.M.–8:30 P.M. in winter.

For more of a splurge, consider **Trapper's,** 79 Revell St., tel. 03/755-5133. The rustic decor complements a menu featuring "wild foods" such as whitebait, kangaroo, and crocodile. For ocean views through picture windows, try **Tasman View Restaurant** at the Southland Hotel on Beach St., tel. 03/755-8344 (it's open for dinner 6–9 P.M., $14–23 for a main course, including west coast delicacies such as whitebait), or sample delicious French cuisine at **Cafe De Paris,** 19 Tancred St., tel. 03/755-8933.

Transportation

The West Coast's major airport is two km north of Hokitika, served by **Air New Zealand,** tel. 03/755-8123, from Christchurch three times a day. A taxi to the airport is $6 one way. **InterCity** runs coaches north and south; book at Hokitika Travel Centre, tel. 03/755-8557, on Tancred Street.

For rental cars, call **Avis,** tel. 03/768-0902, or **Budget,** tel. 03/755-7985. For a cab, call **Hokitika Taxis,** tel. 03/755-8437.

Information

Westland Visitor Information Centre is on Hamilton St. (next to the museum), tel. 03/755-6166; it's open in summer daily 8 A.M.–6 P.M., the rest of the year Mon.–Fri. 9 A.M.–5 P.M., Sat.–Sun. 10 A.M.–3 P.M.

HOKITIKA TO THE GLACIERS

Between Hokitika and Westland National Park/Tai Poutini (150 km), Hwy. 6 passes many small lakes, accessible tracks, a few small settlements that once bustled with gold-mining activity, and mighty rivers where you can reel in brown and rainbow trout and the occasional salmon when the water is clear (many of the rivers are cloudy with glacial runoff). Farther south, the road runs by a saltwater forest, swampy areas of marshes and lagoons covered in waterfowl, then lush green paddocks backed by dark-blue mountains. As you get nearer to the town of Franz Josef on the northern boundary of Westland National Park/Tai Poutini, magnificent snowcapped peaks loom into view.

Ross ✓

This small but typical West Coast gold town, 28 km south of Hokitika, has a colorful gold-mining history (kept alive in the local museum), walkways of historic interest, and several tourist attractions. Jones Creek Flat (behind Ross), a stable and productive goldfield in the early 1870s, is where New Zealand's largest gold nugget was found in 1907—nicknamed "the Honourable Roddy" after the local mayor.

The first place to go for information on local walks is the **Ross Information & Heritage Centre,** in the old Bank of New South Wales building, uphill from the Empire Hotel, tel. 03/755-4077; it's open 9 A.M.–6 P.M. Then considering the two loop tracks of the **Ross Historic Goldfields Walkway.** The **Water Race Walk** is two km (steep in parts-allow at least 90 minutes round-trip) starting at the information center. It takes you through an old cemetery where gravestones vividly describe the hard times and tragic accidents of the 1870s (allow extra time for intriguing reading), to lookouts for good views of Ross, and past old coal-mine workings along the disused water race. The **Jones Flat Walk** (90-minutes round-trip), also starting at the information center, winds through regenerating forest along old elevator claim tailings—passing the site of the famous "Roddy nugget."

Tearooms on the highway provide light meals (and a small museum), while around the corner, the **Empire Hotel,** 19 Aylmer St., tel. 03/755-4005, offers pub-style meals, campsites ($10 pp), dorm beds ($15 pp), and basic rooms with private bathrooms ($60 s or d).

White Heron Sanctuary

Continuing south along Hwy. 6, a sanctuary on the northern edge of Okarito Lagoon protects the breeding ground for New Zealand's only colony of white herons, or *kotuku.* These magnificent birds are distinctive for their size, pure white plumage, and elongated necks. The colony currently numbers around 100, with the birds arriving for the breeding season in late winter, hatching one or two chicks per nest, then leaving

Continuing south along Hwy. 6, a sanctuary on the northern edge of Okarito Lagoon protects the breeding ground for New Zealand's only colony of white herons, or kotuku. *These magnificent birds are distinctive for their size, pure white plumage, and elongated necks.*

the following February. In recent years, ocean storms have changed the layout of Okarito Lagoon and its surrounding watershed, making access to the lagoon itself difficult. The best way to visit is with **White Heron Sanctuary Tours,** the only company with DOC permits to visit. Based at Whataroa, the company operates four tours daily late Nov.-late February. Tours begin with a jetboat trip down the Waitangitaona River, then an easy 500-meter walk along a boardwalk through ancient coastal forest to the viewing area. Around 40 minutes is spent at the site. Tour cost is $89 adult, $40 child. White Heron Sanctuary Tours is based at Whataroa, on Hwy. 6, 80 km south of Ross, tel. 03/753-4120 or 0800/523-456. The same company also operates **Sanctuary Tours Motel,** where rooms are $75 s or d, or stay in one of the five adjacent cabins for $35 s or d. Also in town is a store stocked with basic groceries and serving light meals.

√Okarito ~Biked to Beach for lunch~

The Okarito shoreline was the first bit of New Zealand that Abel Tasman saw in 1642. During the gold-rush era of the 1870s, the quiet settlement of Okarito flourished into a boomtown supporting 2,000 people, two banks, and many hotels and stores. Off Hwy. 6, today it's again a peaceful settlement on a typically wild West Coast beach. Several walks for the energetic start here and take you to panoramic views of the mountains, forests, and coastline. You'll find good bird-watching at **South Okarito Forest** and 3,200-hectare **Okarito Lagoon,** New Zealand's largest unmodified wetland, where tidal flats become alive with birdlife at low tide—and you may (if you're lucky) see the rare white heron. Parts of the lagoon are flanked by *kahikatea* forest through which a maze of channels run—a fun place to explore by kayak. **Okarito Nature Tours,** based along the village's main drag, tel. 03/753-4014, rents kayaks; two hours

$30 pp, half-day $40 pp, full day $50 pp. This same company has guided kayak trips from $65. Guided or unguided, the trick is timing your outward trip with the incoming tide for an easy cruise to the lagoon's farthest points. Okarito is also a good base for surf fishing and whitebaiting (seasonal), and for gold mining from the beach or panning in nearby rivers.

Although the small but well-maintained **Okarito Hostel** is an associate of Hostelling International, no one seems to mind if you're not a member—it's $15 pp for everyone (book at 03/753-4124). It's in an 1870s schoolhouse along the main street. Across the road is a pleasant camping area; $3 pp. Buy all your food and supplies and get cash before you head for Okarito. To get to Okarito, turn west off the main highway 12 km north of Franz Josef

and then continue for 13 km along a gravel road, passing The Forks (an old gold-mining center).

Lake Mapourika

About eight km north of Franz Josef, beautiful bush-fringed Lake Mapourika is the largest lake in Westland National Park/Tai Poutini, separated from the main sector of the park by a short stretch of highway. Dark brown from rainwater filtered through the surrounding forest, the lake provides superb reflections, an abundance of birdlife, excellent salmon and trout fishing (get your license at the Franz Josef Store or Park HQ), warm swimming, and boating. It has plenty of shady picnic spots, and a free campground with fresh water and toilets at McDonalds Creek at the north end of the lake.

Westland National Park/Tai Poutini

GREENERY AND GLACIERS ✱

Westland National Park/Tai Poutini was established in 1960, centered around Franz Josef Glacier and Fox Glacier, the two largest glaciers, and the Copland/Karangarua Valleys; in 1982 the coastal landforms and rainforests of Okarito and Waikukupa were added. Highway 6 travels briefly along the northeast boundary of the park, passing through the towns of **Franz Josef** and **Fox,** the two tourist centers in the area and main sources of park information.

Backed by the magnificent mountain peaks of the Southern Alps, Westland National Park/Tai Poutini covers a rugged 70-km-long, 117,547-hectare area of high mountains and glaciers, lakes and waterfalls, hot springs, coastal lagoons, and icy, gray-blue rivers that tumble down through dense forest to the Tasman Sea. The land rises from sea level to peaks more than 3,000 meters high, providing incredible scenery, a diverse range of habitats, plenty of birds and wildlife, and all kinds of recreational possibilities for the masses of visitors that come to this popular stretch of the West Coast each year. Glacier excursions, mountain hikes, forest and beach walks, fishing, mountaineering,

ice-climbing, flightseeing, alpine ski-touring, and ski mountaineering are just some of the activities available. The less adventurous or those in a hurry can appreciate some of the most striking glacier and bush scenery from the road or at the end of short tracks. The best-known features of the park are the stunning Franz Josef and Fox Glaciers, 24 km apart and both flanked by forests and backed by towering snow-covered peaks, yet easily reached by road and tracks, or by ski-plane or helicopter.

The Land

Thirty-km-wide Westland National Park/Tai Poutini, squeezed between the coast and the Main Divide, rises from Gillespies Beach and Okarito at sea level to the 3,498-meter summit of Mt. Tasman (second highest peak in New Zealand). The park is dominated by a massive ice field that sprawls across the top of the Southern Alps. The park's two largest glaciers (out of 60) are Franz Josef Glacier and Fox Glacier, which descend 12 km and 13.5 km respectively from 3,000-meter-high permanent snowfields to dense rainforest only 300 meters above sea level—the only glaciers in the world that descend directly into lowland rainforest.

In the last ice age, 14,000 years ago, even the lowland areas were totally covered in ice. Today, most of the terrain above 1,500 meters is still covered with permanent ice and snow, with high peaks and ridges of frost-shattered rocks where up to 10,000 mm of rain and snow fall per year. The lowland moraines and river valleys are now clothed in alpine grasslands and herbfields, shrublands, and dense coniferous rainforest. Lakes and coastal lagoons nestle in glacially formed hollows, and the entire landscape is riddled with wide gravel beds and mighty glacier-fed rivers.

The Franz Josef and Fox Glaciers cover a combined area of more than 4,000 hectares—an ever-changing landscape of ice and rock. From high in the sky each glacier is a mass of deep blue cracks and fluffy blue-white peaks—"just like pale-blue meringue," claimed one enthusiastic visitor back from a helicopter ride.

Climate

The weather is as varied as the terrain in this area. Westland ("Wetland" to visitors who whiz through the area in search of blue-sky "been-there" snapshots) has the reputation for dull gray skies and rainy days (and accompanying ferocious sand flies) in summer, but the winters are clear and cold and the scenery is dramatic. Be prepared for a downpour and cool temperatures, even in the middle of summer, and you'll be ready to make the most of your surroundings; if you're doing any of the walks in the park, get an up-to-date weather forecast from the Franz Josef or Fox visitor centers before you set off into the wilderness. The average yearly rainfall on the coast is about 3,000 mm; at the townships of Franz Josef and Fox Glacier and at the foot of the mountains, it can be as much as 5,000 mm per year. Up to 10,000 mm of rain and snow are expected above the 1,500-meter level each year.

Flora and Fauna

One of the most fascinating things about Westland National Park/Tai Poutini flora is the way the bare rock surfaces left behind by retreating glaciers are rapidly invaded through a process called "plant succession." In the early years after glacial retreat, windblown grasses and mat plants

colonize the bare surfaces, and within 20 years, various shrubs, such as *tutu* and native broom that fix nitrogen from the air to form soil, have established themselves. Within the next 50 years, dense young forests of *rata* and *kamahi* trees spring up, followed by *rimu* and *miro* trees, forming the canopy of a lush podocarp rainforest. The luxuriant rainforest you drive through on the way to the glaciers also contains *kahikatea, matai,* and *totara* trees, an assortment of small shrubs, and beautiful ferns of all sizes (best appreciated on some of the short walks). Above the *rata* and *kamahi* forests, shrublands and alpine grasslands cover the slopes. Alpine herbs such as edelweiss, buttercups, and hebe grow in the higher reaches of the park, but only lichens survive on the highest rock areas below the snowline. Altogether about 600 species of plants and ferns inhabit the park.

Native birds, such as the *tui,* kiwi, bellbird, pigeon, fantail, tomtit, robin, and parakeet (ears become rapidly accustomed to ever-present rapturous birdsong), and oystercatchers and Caspian terns abound, and you'll see a number of godwits and the occasional crested grebe in the lake areas, wetlands, and coastal lagoons. White herons are prominent during their breeding season, Oct.–February. All kinds of insects creep around in the undergrowth, including termites, *weta,* and *huhu* grubs that feed on fallen trees. Opossums, red deer, chamois, and Himalayan tahr live in the park, and large numbers of fur seals haul ashore at Waikowhai Bluff near Gillespies Beach, west of Fox Glacier, during winter.

FRANZ JOSEF RECREATION

Before you head along the glacier access road for your first glimpse of Franz Josef Glacier, stop by the **Department of Conservation Visitor Centre** (off the west side of the main highway in town) and collect the brochure *Glacier Country.* It has a map showing local attractions, describes some of the short walking tracks, and contains general information on many of the natural features of the glacial valley and glacier itself. Also collect the many brochures on short walks in the area ($1 each). The center has all sorts of fasci-

guided walk is important - 3hrs

nating displays, a stunning photograph/art gallery, all the reading material and maps you could possibly need, friendly staff, and indigenous arts, crafts, pottery, and photographs for sale in the lobby. Don't miss the 25-minute audiovisual on the history of the park; it runs on the hour 9 A.M.–4 P.M. for $3 adult. The center is open daily from December to Easter 8:30 A.M.–6 P.M., the rest of the year it's open daily 8:30 A.M.–noon and 1–5 P.M. Another place to get a taste of glacier country is the Alpine Adventure Centre, where the 20-minute audiovisual *Flowing West* projects onto a massive 13-meter-wide screen. The footage of the glaciers is incredible, and well worth the $10 admission.

To the Glacier

To get to the glacier from the visitor center (six km), head south along Hwy. 6 for about 400 meters, then turn left after the bridge onto the glacier access road. Continue for 5.5 km along this road through lush rainforest to a car park and interpretive shelter to get your first views. Many tracks of varying lengths branch off the glacier access road—look for the signs. The **Lake Wombat Track** is an easy-to-moderate fern-lined trail through *rimu* forest to a small glacial lake where you'll hear all kinds of songbirds and see plenty of waterfowl; 30 minutes one way. The more strenuous **Alex Knob Track** branches off the Lake Wombat Track, climbing steadily through subalpine scrub to alpine grasslands and herbfields for fantastic glacier, mountain, forest, and coastal views. It takes about four hours to climb up, three hours to come down, and you need to take food, water, a raincoat, warm clothes, and a flashlight. Sign the intentions register at the visitor center before doing any of the longer tracks—be sure to sign out again when you return.

Reach the **Roberts Point Track** via a 20-minute walk along the Douglas Track to Douglas Bridge. It climbs up the east bank of the Waiho Valley, crossing slippery rock and side streams to a lookout high above the glacier where you get incredible long-distance views. Classified as a moderate-to-hard forest track, it takes about three hours one way, returning via the same route (don't take a shortcut down from Roberts Point to the glacier track—very unsafe); wear sturdy footwear, and take a raincoat and some energy food.

The **Douglas Walk**, an easy forest walk over glacial landforms formed by advances of the Franz Josef Glacier between 1600 and 1750, starts on the glacier access road. It takes five minutes to Peters Pool (a kettle lake), and about 45 minutes to complete the walk, finishing at a point farther back along the glacier road—altogether an hour round-trip to the original starting point. If you don't have enough time to hike all the way to the glacier, take the short 10-minute climb up **Sentinel Rock** (four km along the glacier access road) for impressive glacier views and many examples of plants that have progressively colonized this huge rock. Keep to the track.

The most popular hike in the area, the **Franz Josef Glacier Valley Walk,** leads to the terminal face of Franz Josef Glacier. Taking about one hour from the car park at the end of the glacier access road (flat and easy at first, more strenuous as you approach the viewpoints), the route crosses riverbed gravel and several small streams, passes impressive waterfalls that cascade down steep glacially carved cliffs, then climbs up and over enormous boulders for great views of the glacier and the Waiho Valley. Stick closely to the marked track, watch out for possible rockfalls, and resist the urge to venture onto the ice without an experienced glacier guide—the front wall of the glacier is unstable. Wear sturdy footwear, take a warm jacket for rest stops (it gets nippy as you approach the ice), and take plenty of insect repellent in summer. The park provides a program of guided walks during the summer vacation period.

Other Walks

The **Terrace Walk** starts opposite the visitor center off Hwy. 6. It's an easy 45-minute round-trip forest walk, zigzagging up the terrace behind Franz Josef to the sluice face (from which a considerable amount of gold was taken), passing old gold-mining relics and finishing on Cowan St. behind Franz Josef village. A 20-minute side-track leads off the main track to scenic Tatare Gorge, where clear water gushes down between enormous boulders. The **Canavans Knob Rainforest Walk** is another short walk/climb for good views. The 20-minute (one-way) track starts on Hwy. 6, two km south of Franz Josef, where the highway makes a sharp left turn.

Guided Glacier Tours 🕊

Franz Josef Glacier Guides, tel. 03/752-0763 or 0800/484-337, offers guided walks up on the glacier. Experienced glacier guides run the 3.5-hour tours up to five times daily from their base beside the Mobil petrol station for $45 adult, $22.50 child. If the ice is stable, the outfit supplies you with glacier boots equipped with spikes and a trekking pole—and before you fully comprehend what's going on, you're in a line of courageous people scrambling up and down ice pinnacles and jumping crevasses (a guaranteed adrenaline rush), with no turning back. The outfit also offers a more challenging full-day walk (five hours on the ice), departing once daily for $90 pp (minimum four). The heli-hike includes two short helicopter rides and a two-hour guided hike in the middle reaches of the glacier; $265 pp (minimum four). For only $32, visitors can joined a guided Terminal Face Walk. It doesn't involve climbing on the ice, but gives plenty of insight into the history and geology of the glacier.

✱ Flightseeing *people thought with $200 – would not*

Several companies based in Franz Josef and Fox Glacier operate a variety of flightseeing glacier experiences, weather permitting, by ski-plane or helicopter. Seeing the glaciers and mountain peaks from the air is unforgettable in fine weather, and although it's expensive, it's worth every cent. But before parting with your cash, shop around for different prices and rides (scenic flights, snow landings, heli-hikes). Book yourself on an early-morning flight (it's worth waiting an extra day to accomplish this)—the skies are most likely to be clear early, rapidly clouding over as the day progresses.

Glacier Southern Lakes Helicopters, with an office on the main road, tel. 03/752-0755, offers a variety of stunning flights ranging from 10 minutes for $135 pp to a 30-minute flight across both glaciers and a quick glacier landing for

$210 pp. For the most fun, take the 20-minute "Snow Landing Scenic Flight" for $120 pp—fly up the glacier to land among spectacular mountain peaks, leave your mark in the ice or frolic in fresh virgin snow, get a spectacular photograph of Mounts Tasman and Cook, and suck in your breath for close-up views of ice peaks and crevasses as the helicopter literally skims the glacier on the way back down. **The Helicopter Line,** tel. 03/752-0716 or 0800/807-767, provides similar flights at similar prices, and a combined flight/glacier walk excursion for $230 pp. Fixed-wing service is offered by **Air Safaris,** tel. 03/752-0716 or 0800/723-274, which offers a 30-minute flight over both glaciers for $150 pp.

FRANZ JOSEF VILLAGE
Hotels and Motels

One block behind the main commercial strip, **Punga Grove Motor Lodge,** Cron St., tel. 03/752-0001 or 0800/437-269, website: www.pungagrove.co.nz, provides comfortable guest rooms decorated in a pleasing mix of natural colors. Each opens to a private balcony surrounded by bird-filled native rainforest. Guests also have use of a spa, pool, and small forest-cloaked conservatory. Rates are $80–140 s or d, with breakfast delivered to your room for a few dollars extra. Also on Cron St., **Alpine Glacier Motor Lodge,** tel. 03/752-0224 or 0800/757-111, is a modern place featuring spacious self-contained units, many with a private spa pool; $150 s or d. Alpine Glacier manages the **Bushland Court Motel,** diagonally opposite; $90–130 s or d.

Glacier Gateway Motor Lodge, 500 meters south of the village, tel. 03/752-0776 or 0800/372-694, website: www.franzjosefmotels.co.nz, is close to the glacier turnoff and provides 23 rooms with kitchens and tea- and coffee-making facilities, as well as a spa, sauna, and barbecue area; $85–135 s or d. **Glacier View Motel,** also on the main highway but 2.5 km north of Franz Josef village in a quiet rural setting with glacier views, tel. 03/752-0705 or 0800/484-397, has similar facilities and charges from $85 s or d for the self-contained units with smallish kitchens.

WEST COAST

If you're on a bus tour, chances are you'll end up at the impressive **Franz Josef Glacier Hotels,** comprising two sections, one at the north end of the village and another (older) wing one km further north, tel. 03/752-0729 or 0800/100-729, website: www.scenic-circle.co.nz; rooms start at $220 s or d and both sections have an in-house restaurant.

Bed-and-Breakfasts

Set on 20 hectares, along Docherty's Creek Rd. between Franz Josef and Fox villages, **Waiho Stables Country Stay,** tel. 03/752-0747, website: www.waiho.co.nz, is an escape from the park's commercialism. The two guest rooms are brightly furnished and feature lots of exposed timber, and each enjoys a rural panorama. Breakfast (including plunger coffee) is served inside or out, and is included in the rates of $225–250 s, $250–275 d.

Surrounded by farmland two km north of the village, **Westwood Lodge,** tel. 03/752-0111 or 0800/741-111, website: www.westwood-lodge .co.nz, offers luxurious guest rooms with king-sized beds and plush duvets, a billiards room, a lounge, and a deck for $320 s, $240 pp d, inclusive of meals.

Backpacker Lodges

Unfortunately, the standard of accommodations for backpackers in the national park is not good. (At Haast, 140 km to the south, Wilderness Backpackers is a great alternative, if you're headed in that direction.) The pick of the bunch is **Glow Worm Cottages,** 27 Cron St., tel. 03/752-0172 or 0800/151-027, where guests enjoy comfortable couches set around a roaring log fire and a hot tub. Dorm beds are $20 pp, or pay $45 s, $50 d for the privacy of your own room. The fully equipped **Franz Josef Glacier YHA,** 24 Cron St., Franz Josef, tel. 03/752-0754, website: www.yha.org.nz, backed by beautiful bush, is also centrally located and has over 100 beds; $20–22 pp. Next door is **Chateau Franz,** 8 Cron St., tel. 03/752-0738 or 0800/472-8568, with large rooms, bike rental, and a video player for rainy days; $19 dorm, $22 double.

Camping

There's nothing quite like climbing out of your tent to the sound of a rushing river and a stunning view of Franz Josef Glacier (but be armed with insect repellent—the sand flies are ferocious in summer). Excellent **Franz Josef Mountain View Holiday Park,** beside Hwy. 6 one km south of Franz Josef, tel. 03/752-0735 or 0800/467-897, offers the above, and more: the kitchen and living area (with TV), and the comfy lounge room are particularly good places to meet fellow travelers; the bathrooms are clean and spacious, with plenty of hot water, disabled facilities, and a baby's bathroom; and there are plenty of coin-operated washing machines and driers. Tent sites are $19, caravan sites are $20, self-contained cabins range $55–65, and motel rooms are $95.

Food

To find a place to eat, just take a stroll through the village—it's small enough that you can easily *see* what's happening. **Fern Grove Food Centre,** on the main road next to the souvenir shop, sells groceries, dairy foods, fruit, and veggies; it's open daily till 8 P.M. **Café Franz,** in the Alpine Adventure Centre, tel. 03/752-0216, is open throughout the day serving up light meals-the perfect place to hang out on a rainy day. It also has public Internet access. **Blue Ice Café,** toward the south end of the commercial strip, tel. 03/752-0707, is a step above the usual tearoom fare and décor. Pizza is the specialty, ranging from $13 for a small Tropicana pizza to $28 for a large Blue Ice Special. At the **Franz Josef Glacier Hotel** (in town, tel. 03/752-0729), you have a choice of good meals at inexpensive prices (lasagna, chicken, and salads from $9.50) in the bistro, or more gourmet dishes at gourmet prices (chicken, steak, lamb, vegetarian, and salads for $18–27.50) in the Fern Room, a dressy à la carte restaurant.

Transportation

Intercity buses to Franz Josef run from Hokitika, Greymouth (with connections from Christchurch), Queenstown, and Wanaka. The bus

CHEEKY *KEA*

A special feature of New Zealand's subalpine environment are the *kea*—unique, dull-green birds with red underwings and large powerful beaks. Not the least bit afraid of mere mortals, they in fact seem to enjoy terrorizing you at times—swooping out of nowhere to land on car or bicycle with a thud. They grab food from your fingers with no encouragement and pose obligingly for photographs, but take particular pleasure in ripping holes in bicycle seats and shredding windshield wipers! They also have a reputation for sliding down the tin roofs of mountain huts during the night, and removing shoelaces from boots left outside—such friendly little critters!

stops outside Glacier Scooter Safaris on the main street, tel. 03/752-0164, with one service daily in each direction. No shuttles run between Franz Josef and Fox Glaciers; instead you must take the Intercity bus.

Franz Josef has no rental cars or taxis, but you can rent a scooter from **Glacier Scooter Safaris,** tel. 03/752-0164. **Kamahi Tours,** tel. 03/752-0699, has regular shuttle between the glacier and town.

Information

For information on Westland National Park/Tai Poutini and Franz Josef, head directly for the **Department of Conservation Visitor Centre,** off the main highway at the south end of town, tel. 03/752-0796. It has all kinds of intriguing displays, intricate models of glaciers, reams of information on the natural and human history of the park (lectures are held in the evenings during summer), and the audiovisual shown on the hour is really worth seeing; $4. The center is open in summer, daily 8:30 A.M.–6 P.M., the rest of the year, daily 8:30 A.M.–noon and 1–5 P.M. You'll find also a historic hut with an audiovisual presentation featured inside at the back of the center; admission free. During vacation periods the staff gives guided nature walks throughout the park—ask what's happening at the recep-

tion desk. Also at the desk buy detailed maps, park handbooks, pamphlets, postcards, and many brochures (small charge) on local walks.

FOX GLACIER RECREATION

To the Glacier

To get to the glacier from Fox Glacier village, take the main highway south about two km, then turn left just before the bridge over the Fox River onto the glacier access road. Continue for about five km to the car park at the end of the road, where the track to the glacier terminal starts. If you want to do some good hikes before you reach the glacier, watch for the sign on the right to **Glacier View Road, River Walk Viewpoint,** 2.5 km along the road. The 30-minute (one way) track takes you over a long, narrow suspension bridge (built in 1929) that literally sways in the breeze (great views of the rushing, icy-cold Fox River far below), and on through *kamahi* forest to meet the south end of **Glacier View Road.** The 40-minute (one way) **Chalet Lookout Track** starts here—till 1930 it was the main glacier access track, nowadays it gives views only of the terminal face and lower icefall. For even better views of the Fox Glacier, branch off Chalet Lookout Walk and take the **Cone Rock Track,** which climbs steeply through forest and up an ice-scraped rock (remnant of a *roche moutonnée),* to eventually rejoin the Chalet Lookout Walk just before Chalet Lookout (two hours up, 40 minutes down, via Chalet Lookout Walk)—the energetic are well rewarded with the view.

Continuing along the main route to the Fox Glacier takes you through green tunnels of overhanging *rata* and *kamahi* trees covered in ferns and mosses; along the icy Fox River past huge potholes in the moraine filled with turquoise water, areas of quicksand (warnings posted), and towering vertical rock cliffs; and eventually to a large gravel car park from where an easy 20-minute (one way) track leads over river gravel to the **terminal ice.** Wear comfortable shoes, keep on the marked track, watch out for rockfalls, and resist the urge to venture onto the ice—unsafe without a glacier guide.

BIRTH OF A GLACIER

A glacier is formed by fresh snow falling on the upper névé or snowfield (up to 300 meters deep), squeezing out air from underlying layers to create firn or soft ice; when most of the air is forced out, dense blue ice is formed. The enormous mass of ice moves downward with the force of gravity (up to five meters a day has been recorded in Westland), creating great pressures deep within the ice as it's crushed against the underlying terrain; the glacier cracks into ravines and crevasses up to 100 meters deep as it spills slowly downward. You can hear its movement at the terminal face—cracking and creaking ice, and rushing glacial melt-off. The glaciers are always either advancing or retreating—the terminal face retreats if the melt rate (due to warm rain) exceeds the snowfall at the head of the glacier, and advances if ice replacement (due to heavier snowfalls or colder temperatures than normal) exceeds melt rate.

In recent years, the west coast glaciers have been advancing, although both Franz Josef and Fox have retreated dramatically overall during the last 200 years (during the last major glacial advance they swept all the way out to the sea), with small advances, totaling 1.8 km, occurring periodically since 1984 (in 1994 the glaciers advanced nearly 200 meters—that's nearly five meters a day). Glaciologists predict this trend will continue for a few more years, even though the long term trend is retreat.

Other Walks

If you enjoy glowworms, take a short nighttime walk along the track to the **Glowworm Grotto,** which starts from Glowworm Forest Lodge on the main highway just south of the village. Another short and easy loop track, the **Minnehaha Walk,** also starts on the main highway just south of the village. This 20-minute round-trip track follows the Minnehaha Stream through typical Westland rainforest chockablock with beautiful ferns—it's a good walk to keep in mind for a wet day, and if done at night (take a flashlight), thousands of tiny glowworms light up the rain-

forest. The rougher **Ngai Tahu Track** (one hour round-trip) branches off the Minnehaha Track to climb beside a waterfall through ferns and *rimu* forest to a kettle swamp at the top of the ridge. Easy **Moraine Walk** starts on Glacier View Rd. (1.5 km from the start), taking 40 minutes round-trip to meander through impressive tree ferns and *rata* forest, showing the effect of glacial advances during the 17th and 18th centuries (another one to keep in mind for wet days). Three km south from Fox Glacier village, just beyond Thirsty Creek, is the four-hour (one way) track to **Mount Fox.** The track climbs steeply through native bush to a viewpoint at 1,022 meters, then up to alpine grasslands and Mt. Fox at 1,337 meters (follow the snow poles) to give impressive views of the Alps, glacier, and coast. Wear sturdy shoes, take warm clothing, food, and water, and leave your intinerary in the book in the Fox Glacier Field Centre.

Guided Hikes and Tours

The best-known and most challenging hike through Westland National Park/Tai Poutini is the **Copland Valley Track,** which crosses from Mt. Cook Village to Hwy. 6. This difficult and demanding track is most often attempted by guided parties.

Much easier are the trails up to and around Fox Glacier. Most popular is the half-day guided hike, with walkers climbing above the glacier, then descending and scrambling across the ice using crampons. This tour departs twice daily (9:15 A.M. and 1:45 P.M.) and costs $42 pp. For the less adventurous, a guided walk to the toe of the glacier costs $25 pp. Other option include a daylong ice-climbing course, heli-hiking, heli-ski touring (spring only), and an overnight trip to a remote Chancellor Hut. For details on all of the above, contact **Alpine Guides Fox Glacier,** based on the ocean-side of Hwy. 6 in Fox, tel. 03/751-0825 or 0800/111-600. Boots, socks, winter coats, and transportation are included in the price of all tours.

Lakes, Beaches, and Seals

If you have your own transportation, a good day trip from Fox village is to take Cook Flat

A small colony of seals makes its home at the north end of Gillespies Beach.

Rd. to beautiful Lake Matheson (a two-hour hike from Fox Glacier village) and on to the historic coastal settlement of Gillespies Beach (22 km from Hwy. 6). **Lake Matheson** is renowned for outstanding reflections (on a calm day) of 3,744-meter Mt. Cook and 3,498-meter Mt. Tasman, and for the beautiful forest walk around the lake. The best reflections are early in the morning before the wind stirs up the surface. The road to Lake Matheson branches off Cook Flat Rd., then a sturdy boardwalk takes you through the forest to the lake (40 minutes round-trip from the parking lot) and around it (90 minutes round-trip from the parking lot); the best views are from the far end. An alternate track leads up to the ancient glacial **Lake Gault** (a farther one and a half-hour climb) and hydropower scheme. Beyond the main trailhead, **Café Lake Matheson,** tel. 03/752-0124, takes full advantage of the famous panorama.

Cook Flat Rd. ends at the settlement of **Gillespies Beach,** where they sand-sluiced for gold (more than 600 people once mined this area) in gold-rush days. A track starts at the bridge near the lagoon mouth. Follow an early miners' track through a cliff tunnel and down to the beach (20 minutes one way), or take a sidetrack at the tunnel for a 10-minute climb to a trig survey marker for superb views. One of the best 1.5-hour (one way) walks is along Gillespies Beach to the **fur seal colony** at the north end, returning through beautiful Waikukupa State Forest. You can get near the seals, but don't disturb them or get between the seals and the sea.

FOX VILLAGE
Hotels and Motels
Several motels and two hotels are in Fox and the surrounding area. The cheaper motels lie along Cook Flat Rd. leading west from the village to Lake Matheson and the coast. The best value of these and closest to the main highway is the **Rainforest Motel,** tel. 03/751-0140 or 0800/724-636, website: www.rainforestmotel .co.nz, comprising 10 self-contained units set on pleasant grassed grounds with a barbecue area off to one side. Rates are $75–85 s, $80–105 s or

WEST COAST

Best Restaurant — Peak ?

d for the studio, one-bedroom, and two-bedroom units. Continuing west along Cook Flat Rd., **Lake Matheson Motel,** tel. 03/751-0830 or 0800/452-243, is still only a short walk back to the services of the village. Rates are $80–90 s or d for modern, fully self-contained units. And a little farther west is **Alpine View Motels,** on the grounds of Fox Glacier Holiday Park, tel. 03/751-0821, which charges $80–85 s or d.

Fox Glacier Resort Hotel, on the corner of Hwy. 6 and Cook Flat Rd., tel. 03/751-0839, website: www.resorts.co.nz, is a historic 1928 two-story lodging with spacious, comfortable rooms in a variety of configurations; $130 s or d. Guests have access to a bar, private lounge, and restaurant.

Te Weheka Inn, opposite the DOC Visitor Centre on Main Rd., tel. 03/751-0730 or 0800/313-414, website: www.weheka.co.nz, opened in 2001 as the park's premier hotel accommodation. Each of the rooms has a contemporary feel, a luxurious bathroom with plush towels and a separate shower and bath, an ironing facility, and a private balcony with comfortable outdoor furniture. Rates are $174 s, $190 d, including a cooked breakfast served in the main lounge area.

Budget Accommodations

Fox Glacier Inn, 39 Sullivans Rd., tel. 03/751-0022, is a modern hostel, one block back from Hwy. 6. Facilities are of a high standard and include a restaurant, bar, bike rentals, and Internet access. Dorm beds are $18 pp, doubles and twins are $22 pp. The other choice for backpackers is **Ivory Towers,** also on Sullivans Rd., tel. 03/751-0838. In several small separate houses, each with two or three dorm rooms, central living area, equipped kitchen, and bathroom, a bed costs $20 pp, doubles and twins cost $25 pp.

The only other budget accommodation in the village is the **Fox Glacier Holiday Park,** 700 meters down the road to Lake Matheson (great views), tel. 03/751-0821. It has communal facilities and a camp store. Tent sites are $10 pp, caravan sites are $11 pp, cabins start at $35 d, tourist flats start at $60, and motel rooms start at $80.

Food and Entertainment

As in nearby Franz Josef, dining opportunities in the village are somewhat limited. Try **Hobnail Cafe,** part of the Alpine Guides complex, tel. 03/751-0005, where you can tuck into good breakfasts and lunches. **Café Neve** on the main road, tel. 03/751-0110, serves café-type fare, toasted sandwiches, pizza, jacket potatoes, and light meals (from $11.50). Buy your meat, groceries, and produce at the **Fox Glacier Store,** tel. 03/751-0829; it's open daily 8 A.M.–6:30 P.M. If you crave a full meal and don't mind parting with some cash, try the restaurants at **Fox Glacier Resort Hotel,** tel. 03/751-0839, for bar meals or fine dining (dinners $18–26.50) or at the **Glacier Country Hotel,** tel. 03/751-0847 (meals from $17).

For evening entertainment during vacation periods, take in the informal slide show and lecture on Westland National Park/Tai Poutini at the visitor center—see the schedule on the door for times and topics, or ask at the reception desk. The only other forms of entertainment are getting to know fellow travelers or dropping in for a quick drink at one of the fancier hotels.

Transportation

Fox Glacier is a turnaround point for Intercity buses, so if you're either northbound or southbound, you must change buses. All services stop at **Alpine Guides** along Hwy. 6, tel. 03/751-0701. By bus, it's four hours north to Greymouth and eight hours south to Queenstown over Haast Pass and via Wanaka.

Information

For information on the national park and the village, visit the **Department of Conservation Visitor Centre,** off the main highway at the north end of town, tel. 03/751-0807. It has a great natural history display featuring the glaciers, lowland rainforests, and wildlife; a lecture hall where slide shows and talks are presented in the evenings; park publications for sale; and a variety of brochures on local walks and activities. The center is open year-round daily 9 A.M.–5, but the building is open till late during vacation periods for slide-show presentations. From mid-December to mid-April the center is open daily 8:30 A.M.–6 P.M.

Over Haast Pass to Wanaka

FOX TO HAAST

Copland Valley Track

Twenty-six km south of Fox, Hwy. 6 runs past the west entrance to the 47-km-long Copland Valley Track (look for the sign 100 meters before Karangarua Bridge). Many people hike the first two sections of this track; you need considerable experience and appropriate alpine equipment to continue over **Copland Pass** (2,148 meters) to Aoraki Mt. Cook Village. February and March are the best months to hike it—attempt it only if you really know what you're doing or have a guide. The huts at Welcome Flat and Douglas Rock have gas cooking, a woodstove, and a limited number of utensils.

The first 20-km section from the main highway to Welcome Flat takes about six hours, starting at the marker on the opposite side of Rough Creek (sign the intentions book there)—if the water's high, a 25-minute walk upstream brings you to a wire crossing. The track wanders through bird-filled bush, crossing several small streams before emerging at Welcome Flat. The natural **hot springs** just beyond Welcome Flat Hut are particularly popular with weary hikers—soak your tired muscles in the soothing water, but remember to keep your head out to avoid contracting amoebic meningitis (a real threat in any hot springs).

The second 10-km section starts at Welcome Flat and wanders through rivers, grasslands, and low forest, climbing gradually to cross several open slips and a suspension bridge before emerging at Douglas Rock Hut; it takes about three hours. The tricky 14-km alpine climb from Douglas Rock to Hooker Hut in Aoraki Mt. Cook National Park takes about eight hours, followed by an easier four- to five-hour walk down the Hooker Valley to end in Aoraki Mt. Cook Village.

Copland Pass is notorious for bad weather and sudden dense fog, and has tricky glacier and rock sections where you need experience and appropriate alpine climbing equipment. Above 1,400 meters elevation the track is only lightly de-

fined. If you're seriously thinking about doing it, get the complete rundown at the DOC visitor centers at either end of the track. If you need a guide, it's cheaper to start at Aoraki Mt. Cook village because you reach the pass more quickly when traveling east to west.

Lake Paringa

Between the mighty Karangarua River and Lake Paringa, Hwy. 6 moseys along the coast through lush tree ferns and forest in almost every shade of green imaginable, passing rugged headlands, desolate pebble beaches covered in driftwood, and the odd lonely farm hacked out of the bush. Surrounded by ferns and forest (in what seems like the middle of nowhere), Lake Paringa is deceptively tranquil but teems with brown trout and quinnat salmon—an angler's paradise. The lake used to be the end of the road before the opening of the Haast route, yet despite the traffic that nowadays whizzes through, it's still a quiet spot for outdoor enthusiasts. **Lake Paringa Lodge** on the main highway at the north end of the lake, tel. 03/751-0894, caters to anglers, with basic cabins for $50 s or d and motel-style units for $80. A boat and guide are available for guests to sample the fishing; rates are $40 per hour. You'll find DOC campsites just off the road south of the lodge.

Lake Moeraki

Lake Moeraki is another beautiful lake known for its distinct glacier-blue color and good fishing. Take the easy 40-minute (one way) bush walk along **Monro's Track** to the coast, where you'll find sandy beaches interspersed with rocky headlands; the track starts near the lake outlet. You'll find a number of pleasing campsites around the lake. Overlooking a fast-flowing stream at the outlet of the lake is the 18-room **Wilderness Lodge Lake Moeraki,** tel. 03/750-0881; website: www.wildernesslodge.co.nz. The lodge, owned by Dr. Gerry McSweeney, a well-known naturalist and one of New Zealand's leading conservationists, provides comfortable accommodations and a riverside restaurant. Rates

[handwritten: We rode our bikes down the pass]

are $320 s, $460 d (winter rates discounted to $230 s, $320 d), which includes three meals prepared using seasonal game such as *cervena* (farmed venison), and accompanied at dinner by fine New Zealand wine. A number of fabulous, guided, outdoor activities can be booked through the lodge: rainforest walks (free), a canoe trip from the lake to the sea ($68 pp), fishing trips (rates on application), and wilderness walks to see seals and penguins ($78 pp). Lodge guests have the free use of canoes, life jackets, and rowboats (rent fishing gear). You also can participate in daily activities (glowworm walks, history and nature talks, and evening stargazing) or explore the network of walking tracks, the lodge library, and all lodge facilities.

Knights Point and Ship Creek

Just southwest of Lake Moeraki is the headland of Knights Point, fringed by golden-sand beaches and rocky bays where seals frolic and fish in the surf. About five km south of Knights Point, 100 meters downstream from the traffic bridge, lies the remains of a ship partially buried in the sand, visible at low tide. It's believed to be the *Schomberg of Aberdeen,* the largest wooden ship ever launched from Britain. It was last sighted off Tasmania in 1885, then disappeared.

Haast *[handwritten: ✱ great sunset on the Beach of sea]*

This town, where the Haast River drains into the Tasman Sea and Hwy. 6 makes a sharp turn away from the west coast, lies just 120 km south of Westland National Park/Tai Poutini, but allow at least two hours for the trip. Haast is worth a stop for the **South West World Heritage Visitor Centre,** tel. 03/750-0809. On December 12, 1990, UNESCO organized the forests, mountains, and coasts of South Westland and Mt. Aspiring National Park into one of the world's outstanding natural heritage sites.

> *On Haast Pass Road there are many one-lane bridges and some narrow stretches with sharp corners and steep drop-offs where it's inevitable you'll meet a large semi-trailer around a blind turn—"a terrible, terrible road," said a man from New York City as he frantically pawed through his luggage for tranquilizers.*

These areas were thereby joined with Fiordland National Park and the two parks to the north to constitute a 2.6-million-hectare **South-West New Zealand World Heritage Area,** also known by the Maori name Te Wahipounamu (The Place of the Greenstone), ensuring integrated, coordinated protection and management. To find out more, make your first stop the impressive, ultramodern, metallic, architectural wonder that appears to rise from a small lake—you can't miss it! This building contains many displays about the entire West Coast. The staff is ready to answer questions and give advice, and you can buy conservation-related books, postcards, T-shirts and sweatshirts, and crafts. It's open daily 8:30 A.M.–7 P.M. from December to mid-April, on weekdays 8:30 A.M.–4:30 P.M. in winter.

The **World Heritage Hotel Haast** at Haast Junction on Hwy. 6, tel. 03/750-0828 or 0800/502-444, website: www.world-heritage-hotel.com, is a 54-room low rise complex with dorm beds for $17 pp, economy rooms with TV and en suite for $59 s, $69 d, and regular motel rooms for $79 s, $89 d. The hotel restaurant has wide-ranging menu that includes traditional roasts such as beef and pork ($15), as well as seafood dishes such as a boneless filet of groper (a type of rock fish common on the west coast) coated in a flower-based seasoning, then lightly grilled ($20). The adjacent bar also serves food and features bands most weekends. *[handwritten: ✱ dinner]*

Wilderness Backpackers is in Haast township proper, three km south of Haast Junction, tel. 03/750-0029 or 0800/750-029. Its spacious, comfortable rooms surround a covered courtyard, and all the facilities are of the highest standard. Dorm beds are $18 pp, private rooms are $32 s, $42 d. **Haast Beach Holiday Park,** 14.5 km south of Haast Junction at Okuru, tel. 03/750-0860, on the Haast

Beach-Jackson Bay Rd., offers tent sites for $16, caravan sites for $18, and cabins from $38 s or d.

Jackson Bay

The road out to Haast Beach Holiday Park continues for another 40 km to Jackson Bay, a small fishing village nestled under Jackson Head. Long sandy beaches and coastal views on one side of the road and dense bush and swampy areas backed by magnificent, steep, tree-covered mountains on the other make an interesting detour from Hwy. 6.

We went south to North

HAAST PASS ROAD ✳

Haast Pass Rd. (Hwy. 6) from Haast to Wanaka is a 146-km route of great beauty. In less than three hours the scenery changes from lush West Coast greenery to the snowcapped peaks and deep river gorges of Mt. Aspiring National Park, the Gates of Haast and Haast Pass (563 meters), mighty lakes with sparkling blue-green water, and open space for as far as you can see. It's best not to drive it at night (you'll miss all the scenery) or when you're in a hurry—most of the road is sealed but a few short stretches are "metal" (gravel), and there are many one-lane bridges and some narrow stretches with sharp corners and steep drop-offs where it's almost inevitable you'll meet a large semi-trailer around a blind turn—"a terrible, terrible road," said a man from New York City as he frantically pawed through his luggage for tranquilizers! If you take time to enjoy the magnificent scenery, stopping at viewpoints and walking along the short tracks to waterfalls, you'll live to tell the tale—even without drugs!

East from Haast

The highway, completed only in 1965, follows the crystal-clear, turquoise Haast River, which is joined by the large Landsborough River; then the road crosses a bridge with fantastic mountain views before passing **Pleasant Flat,** where there's a day shelter and picnic spots. From Pleasant Flat to **Rainy Flat,** Hwy. 6 winds through a small northeast section of **Mount**

Waterfalls abound along the highway over Haast Pass.

© ANDREW HEMPSTEAD

Aspiring National Park. Continue to **Thunder Creek Falls** and take the short forest track—here the water drops an impressive 30 meters from a small notch in the rock. About two km farther along the road at the Gates of Haast bridge, the Haast River roars down a gorge full of enormous schist boulders. **Haast Pass** is the lowest on the Main Divide at 563 meters, and from here to **Makarora Gorge** lies some of the best scenery along the entire route. Rivers meander like silver ribbons in and out of dense bush and hills, through large flats covered in woolly "gorse scrubbers" or "grass cutters" (sheep) for as far as the eye can see.

Makarora

Beyond the pass, Hwy. 6 begins a long and gradual descent to Lake Wanaka, passing through the eastern extent of Mt. Aspiring Na-

WEST COAST

Beautiful Bike Ride

tional Park. As the highway exits the pass, it comes to Makarora, a small service center overlooking the Makarora River Valley. This is also the starting point for a one-day wilderness excursion called the **Siberia Experience,** which includes a 25-minute flight over Mt. Aspiring National Park, a landing in the Siberia Valley, then a three-hour bush walk along a marked track to a jetboat for an exciting return trip to Makarora; $150 pp (minimum three). The adventure is run by **Southern Alps Air,** tel. 03/443-8666, which also offers a number of other flightseeing tours. Also from Makarora, **Wilkin River Jets,** tel. 03/443-8351, offers a one-hour jetboat trip 25 km up the Wilkin River for $65 pp. **Makarora Tourist Centre,** tel. 03/443-8372, includes a shop, tearooms (closes in summer at 7 P.M.), and a swimming pool. It sells petrol and offers cabins for $45 s or d and motel units starting at $70 s or d. **Makarora Field Centre,** tel. 03/443-8365, is a DOC facility for Mt. Aspiring National Park (the main park information center is at Wanaka), open weekdays 8 A.M.–5 P.M. and weekends during summer holidays.

Makarora to Wanaka

The road from Makarora to Wanaka emerges from closed-in Haast Pass to a landscape of wide-open spaces and water, water, water as it first runs along the eastern shores of shimmering bright-blue **Lake Wanaka,** one of the largest southern lakes. Along with good trout fishing, the lakeshores provide many ideal spots for free camping, and generally a good supply of driftwood for campfires; make sure you have an adequate supply of insect repellent before you make camp—in summer, thousands of sand flies alight on your tent in the early hours and attack with passion as soon as you climb out.

The highway crosses The Neck (between Lake Wanaka and Lake Hawea), then parallels the hilly western shores of equally beautiful **Lake Hawea** (known for its excellent trout and landlocked salmon fishing) down to its southern shores and through the small town of Hawea to **Wanaka,** which is covered in detail along with Mt. Aspiring National Park in the Otago chapter. If you plan on heading north to **Aoraki Mt. Cook National Park** after crossing Haast Pass, see the Canterbury chapter.

Canterbury

Christchurch

"THE MOST ENGLISH CITY OUTSIDE ENGLAND"

Largest city on the South Island, capital of the province of Canterbury, and New Zealand's third-largest city (population 330,000), Christchurch conjures vivid images of what are perceived to be some of the best aspects of typical English charm—striking gothic architecture and fine stone buildings, lush green parks and flower-filled gardens, grassy banks and drooping willow trees along the meandering Avon River, and droves of Christ's College schoolboys in black-and-white uniforms and straw boaters cycling home at the end of the day.

Spreading out from the city in all directions lie the flat, patchwork-neat fields of the **Canterbury Plains,** the orderly design broken only by rivers and streams, and the lakes and coastal marshes in the southwest, a favorite hangout for waterfowl hunters. The untamed hills and ragged coast of the **Banks Peninsula** lie due south, and the South Pacific Ocean borders the eastern perimeter of the city.

History

Christchurch was founded in 1850 by the Canterbury Association as a planned Church of England settlement. The first group of settlers started a typically "English" community in the new land. They successfully combined the olde-English aspects they previously enjoyed with the new aspects of a new land—a look and feeling that Christchurch has always retained.

Aoraki Mt. Cook

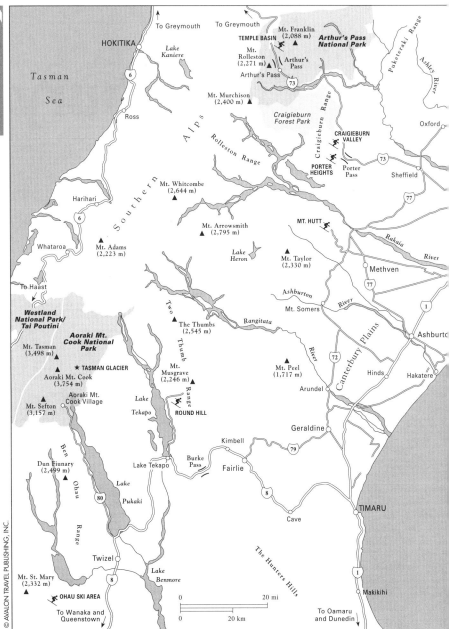

To Greymouth

To Greymouth

Mt. Franklin
(2,088 m)

**Arthur's Pass
National Park**

TEMPLE BASIN

Mt.
Rolleston
(2,271 m)

Arthur's
Pass

Arthur's Pass

73

HOKITIKA

Lake
Kaniere

Tasman

Sea

Ross

Mt. Murchison
(2,400 m)

*Craigieburn
Forest Park*

Puketeraki Range

Ashley River

Oxford

CRAIGIEBURN
VALLEY

Rolleston Range

Craigieburn Range

73

Sheffield

PORTER
HEIGHTS

Porter
Pass

Harihari

Southern

Mt. Whitcombe
(2,644 m)

77

6

Alps

Whataroa

Mt. Adams
(2,223 m)

Mt. Arrowsmith
(2,795 m)

Lake
Heron

MT. HUTT

Mt. Taylor
(2,330 m)

Rakaia

River

Methven

To Haast

**Westland
National Park/
Tai Poutini**

Two

The Thumbs
(2,545 m)

Rangitata

Ashburton

Mt. Somers

River

77

1

Ashburto

**Aoraki Mt.
Cook National
Park**

Mt. Tasman
(3,498 m)

★ TASMAN GLACIER

Aoraki Mt. Cook
(3,754 m)

Aoraki Mt.
Cook Village

Mt. Sefton
(3,157 m)

Thumb

Mt.
Musgrave
(2,246 m)

Range

Lake
Tekapo

ROUND HILL

River

Mt. Peel
(1,717 m)

Arundel

72

Hinds

Hakatere

Canterbury Plains

Geraldine

Ben

Dun Fiunary
(2,499 m)

Ohau

Lake
Pukaki

Kimbell

Burke
Pass

Fairlie

79

Range

Lake
Tekapo

Lake Tekapo

80

8

TIMARU

Cave

Twizel

Lake
Benmore

The Hunters Hills

Mt. St. Mary
(2,332 m)

8

OHAU SKI AREA

To Wanaka and
Queenstown

1

Makikihi

To Oamaru
and Dunedin

0   20 mi

0   20 km

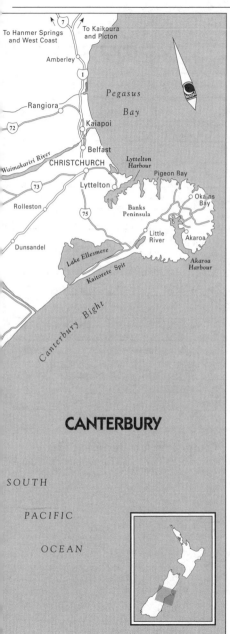

To Hanmer Springs
and West Coast

To Kaikoura
and Picton

Amberley

Pegasus

Bay

Rangiora

Kaiapoi

Waimakariri River

Belfast

CHRISTCHURCH

Lyttelton
Harbour

Pigeon Bay

Lyttelton

Rolleston

Banks
Peninsula

Okains
Bay

Dunsandel

Little
River

Akaroa

Lake Ellesmere

Akaroa
Harbour

Kaitorete Spit

Canterbury Bight

CANTERBURY

SOUTH

PACIFIC

OCEAN

This gives the city its unique atmosphere—one that needs to be felt to be appreciated. Its flat terrain is ideal for walking and cycling, and an excellent public transportation network makes exploring its special nooks and crannies a snap. The central city area bustles with activity, but a short hop from Cathedral Square and you're strolling along a beautiful river with quacking ducks the only sound. Then several blocks later, you're passing house after house with spectacular "English" flower gardens—it's hard to believe you're still in the center of a city (in England, blocks this large would be out in the suburbs). Although the large international airport has made Christchurch the principal gateway to the scenic wonders of the South Island (or "Mainland" according to South Islanders), the city itself (and its many cultural offerings) is a New Zealand attraction that you shouldn't miss.

SIGHTS
Cathedral Square
This large, pedestrian-only plaza with its trees, flower-filled planters, pigeons, and striking cathedral in the heart of the city is the best place to begin your exploration of the city. It's home to the **Christchurch & Canterbury Visitor Centre,** but is also a great place to soak up some of the city's rich heritage, sit and people-watch, dine at surrounding cafes, or just chill out and soak up some sun.

Christchurch Cathedral is the centerpiece and dominant feature of Cathedral Square. Completed in 1904 and built of stone from local Canterbury quarries, topped by a 64.5-meter spire of Australian hardwood and copper, this striking cathedral was quite the pioneer triumph of the day. It's open Mon.–Fri. 8:30 A.M.–8 P.M., Saturday 9 A.M.–5 P.M., Sunday 7:30 A.M.–8 P.M. (Holy Communion is held every day), but the most enjoyable time to visit is during Choral Evensong (during the school term, Friday at 4:30 P.M.) when the Boy Choristers sing—your ears are in for a treat. For a fabulous view of the city (and on a clear day, the distant Southern Alps), climb the 134 nar-

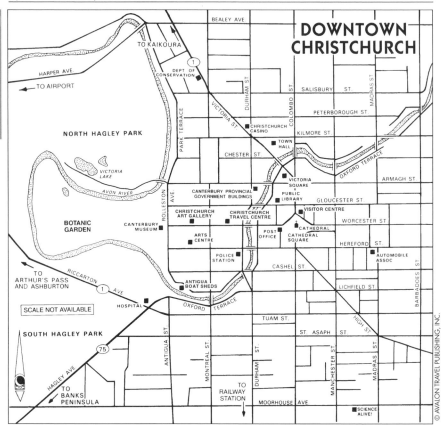

DOWNTOWN CHRISTCHURCH

© AVALON TRAVEL PUBLISHING, INC.

Wed

row stone steps up through the bell chamber to the balconies at the top of the tower ($4). For more information, call 03/366-0046.

The square's most famous resident, orator and self-proclaimed **"Wizard" of Christchurch,** has been making less frequent appearances in recent years. When he does come out, usually weekdays at 1 P.M. (except in June and July, during inclement weather, and when otherwise occupied), he's in front of the cathedral, informing, humoring, annoying, and plain-out manipulating his captivated audience. Grab a quick take-away lunch and a piece of ground in front of the cathedral (stand at the back of the crowd if you don't want to be picked on) and settle back for some free entertainment.

Contrasting Architectural Gems
Canterbury Provincial Government Buildings (or Provincial Chambers) beside the Avon River on the corner of Durham and Armagh Streets are fine examples of Christchurch's Gothic architecture. Until 1876 each province governed itself; the chambers, built between 1858 and 1865, were the main government buildings for Canterbury province. Today the last remaining provincial buildings in New Zealand, they're sources of both historic and architectural interest. Guided tours of the entire buildings are offered Mon.–Sat. 10:30 A.M.–3 P.M., Sunday 2–4 P.M. for a minimal fee, and the Stone Chamber is open Mon.–Fri. 10:30 A.M.–2:45 P.M. (call 03/366-1100 to check times). From Cathedral

Square walk north two blocks along Colombo St., turn left at Armagh St., walk another block, and then cross the river.

For direct contrast, don't miss the modern **Town Hall** on the banks of the Avon River on Kilmore Street. Completed in 1972, it's recognized as one of the finest town halls in the country with its eye-pleasing combination of glass, marble, and still and moving water. You can stroll through weekdays 9 A.M.–5 P.M. From the Provincial Buildings on Armagh St. walk north along the river, passing the attractive **floral clock artwork** on Victoria St. (corner of Chester St. beside the Victoria Square Amphitheatre), until you come to the town hall building.

Canterbury Museum

This museum on Rolleston Ave. at the entrance to the Botanic Gardens, tel. 03/366-8379, had it beginnings as early as the 1870s, when moa bones were traded from local Maori for display. Today the highlight of the museum is the Maori Hall filled with artifacts of early Maori culture from the Moa Hunting era. The museum also features the Hall of Birds (one of the best mounted bird displays in the Southern Hemisphere), Asian art, furniture and fashions throughout the ages, a reconstruction of a colonial Christchurch street from the 19th century, and the fabulous Hall of Antarctic Discovery (pioneer polar explorer Robert Scott visited Christchurch in 1901 and 1910 on his Antarctic expeditions—see his statue standing on the banks of the river at Worcester St.). Another interesting display is the Victoria Museum, a room set up as a museum from the Victorian era. You can have a light meal or snack in the upstairs Museum Café. The museum is open daily 9 A.M.–5:30 P.M. (free admission).

Arts Centre of Christchurch

Formerly the University of Canterbury, the attractive old neo-Gothic buildings at the west end of Worcester St. have become a large cultural and community center, providing entertainment to suit just about everyone. The center is also a working outlet for some of New Zealand's most acclaimed artists and craftspeople. The center's North and South quadrangles, Cloisters, and cob-blestoned boulevards provide the perfect venue for a wide variety of entertainment—from jazz, blues, and classical music to stiltwalkers, jugglers, and street theater. It's the kind of place where you can quickly lose an entire day amidst intriguing entertainment and a variety of shops, eating up a storm at Le Cafe (open daily 7 A.M.–midnight—great espresso), Dux de Lux Restaurant and Bar, or Annie's Wine Bar. There's also plenty of evening entertainment here, all in one relatively small area. The Arts Centre's Visitor Centre is in the Clocktower Building on Worcester St. (near Rolleston Ave.), open for general inquiries and bookings daily 9 A.M.–5 P.M., tel. 03/363-2836.

During the day, stroll in and out of the many crafts, music, book, and wooden-toy shops, and watch the potters, cane and stained-glass workers, and candlemakers creating their works of art. On weekends 10 A.M.–4 P.M., an **Arts, Crafts and Antiques Market** is held at the Arts Centre with all kinds of stalls, buskers (singers, dancers,

AVON RIVER

Gently meandering through the city and particularly noticeable in the city center, the delightful Avon River is Christchurch's dominant natural feature. Grassy daisy-dotted banks, weeping willows and old oak trees, ducks and trout, and small ornate bridges linking the main streets lure office workers and visitors out into the sunshine for tea breaks or lunch, or just to appreciate the peaceful, almost rural atmosphere that permeates the city center. See some of the inner city's most historic and modern buildings, statues, and other items of interest along the Avon River by taking a 90-minute riverside stroll between Cathedral and Victoria Squares.

Enjoy the river from water level on a **punting** trip. Of traditional English design but built locally, punts depart on demand from various points along the river, including the Worcester St. bridge and the Antigua Boat Sheds at the south end of Rolleston Avenue. The cost for a 30-minute ride is $20 for one person, $25 for two. Also at Antigua Boat Sheds, tel. 03/366-0337, you can rent canoes ($6 per hour), paddleboats ($10), and rowboats ($20).

mime artists, and more), and entertainment. In the evenings and on weekends, take in a performance at the Court Theatre, Southern Ballet & Dance Theatre, or Academy Cinema—check here or at the Christchurch & Canterbury Visitor Centre for what's playing. To get to the Arts Centre from Cathedral Square, walk four blocks west along Worcester St. toward the Botanic Gardens; it's on the left.

Art Galleries

At the time of publication, a new **Christchurch Art Gallery** was under construction at the corner of Worcester and Montreal Streets. The finished complex is slated to be four times larger than the old facility, the Robert McDougall Art Gallery, one block west beside the museum.

After selling its permanent collection to the city in the mid-1990s, the **Centre of Contemporary Art** (COCA) at 66 Gloucester St., tel. 03/366-7261, was extensively renovated and now showcases the work of New Zealand artists, including displays of paintings, sculpture, prints, photography, weaving, ceramics, woodcarvings, batik, glassmaking, and jewelry. The Canaday Gallery offers paintings, prints, and weavings for sale; it's open Tues.–Fri. 11 A.M.–5 P.M., Sat.–Sun. noon–4 P.M.; admission free. To get there from the north end of Cathedral Square, walk west along Gloucester St. and cross the river.

Science Alive!

This hands-on science and technology museum, particularly appealing to children (but enjoyed by all ages), has all sorts of working and interactive exhibits. Open Mon.–Fri. 9 A.M.–5 P.M., Sat.–Sun. 10 A.M.–6 P.M.; $7 adult, $5 child. It's in the cinema complex at 392 Moorhouse Ave. (at High St.), tel. 03/365-5199.

International Antarctic Centre

There can be no better location than Christchurch for the world's best Antarctic-related display. After all, Robert Falcon Scott began his ill-fated expedition to the South Pole from here in 1910. Many other Antarctic explorers used Christchurch as a base throughout the years and, in the 1950s, the United States followed suit, basing southbound aircraft and ships here. The International Antarctic Centre primarily serves as an operating base for the New Zealand, United States, and Italian Antarctic programs, but also holds a large public facility incorporating resources collected by the center's programs, along with those of Australia, Russia, Britain, and Japan, to give visitors an insight into all aspects of the continent through the eyes of those who live and work there.

Starting with the exciting human history of Antarctica, the first display, a seven-minute show, gives a feeling of what the earliest Antarctic explorers must have experienced—right down to howling winds and the Southern Aurora. After the show is over, you step inside a realistic simulation of a room at Scott Base, with up-to-date notices, the weekly newsletter, rosters, and weather reports all pinned to the walls (check out the local rules of the base golf course). Then it's on to displays showcasing natural and geological history, flora and fauna, and life today at the various bases—including a re-creation of an Antarctic field camp. The "Great White South," an awe-inspiring 13-minute audiovisual, is a fitting end to the displays.

The newest attraction is the opportunity to ride in a Hagglund, a Swedish-designed vehicle that is the workhorse of all Antarctic bases. A 15-minute jaunt around the base costs $10 pp.

Once back in the main foyer, you can browse through the Antarctic Shop, boasting the world's largest choice of Antarctic-related items, or go to the 60° South Cafe and Bar. Admission to the Antarctic Centre is $18 adult, $15 senior, $9 child. It's open daily, Oct.-Mar. 9 A.M.–8 P.M., the rest of the year, daily 9 A.M.–5:30 P.M. The second Sunday in October is Antarctic Festival Day; most activities take place in the center grounds and across the

If departing and you haven't yet seen the International Antarctic Centre allow time to visit this must-see attraction, a five-minute walk from the International and Domestic Terminals—just follow the painted footsteps.

road at the airport, where Antarctic aircraft are displayed. The Antarctic Centre, at Christchurch International Airport on Orchard Rd., is a five-minute walk from the International and Domestic Terminals—perfect for visiting before a departure, but allow enough time to enjoy it all. For further details, call 03/358-9896.

Christchurch Gondola

A free shuttle bus connects Christchurch Gondola with Cathedral Square, or you can catch a no. 28 Lyttleton bus, or drive out along Ferry Rd. southeast of the city to suburban Heathcote. Why go there? Outstanding 360-degree views of the city, Banks Peninsula, Canterbury Plains, and distant Southern Alps from the Summit Complex, perched on the rim of an extinct volcano. It puts everything into perspective. Also at the top is the Time Tunnel, an easy-to-follow description of the forces that created the surrounding landscape. Various walks, a big-screen audiovisual, two restaurants, and a souvenir shop are other reasons to make the excursion. The cost for the one-km gondola ride is $12 adult, $6 child. For more information, call 03/384-0700.

Air Force World and Vicinity

Airplane buffs should find their way out to Wigram on the south side of the city to feast their eyes and let their spirits soar at Air Force World, on Main South Rd., tel. 03/343-9532. It's open daily 10 A.M.–5 P.M.; $10 adult, $5 child, $25 family—and worth every cent for flying enthusiasts. Aside from studying extensive displays featuring the history of New Zealand aviation, watch a movie on the same in the small theater, marvel at the interactive displays (including an ejection seat), then wander at will around a large number of beautifully displayed aircraft spanning the age of aviation. Adding to the authenticity of Air Force World are the guides—they are all World War II veterans. Allow two hours if you like reading all the details. Access to the museum is from the main highway south (to Timaru), near the Springs Rd. turnoff. By bus take no. 8 from Cathedral Square.

Beside Air Force World, **Dr. Heins Classic Car Collection,** 150 Kilmore St., tel. 03/344-

2222, containing more than 100 cars (many of which are for sale), includes the largest collection of Jaguars in the Southern Hemisphere. It's open daily 10 A.M.–5 P.M.; admission $6.

PARKS AND GARDENS

One hectare in every eight in Christchurch is a public park, reserve, or recreation ground. Lush greenery and gardens abound everywhere you go, always well maintained and usually chock-ablock with flowers—hence the well-deserved title "Garden City." Christchurchians must surely have more green thumbs concentrated in their area than in the rest of the country!

Botanic Garden

One of the best places to appreciate this profusion of vegetation within easy walking distance of the central city is the Botanic Garden, open 8 A.M. until one hour before sunset (a bell is rung at closing time). Stroll through grounds bordered by the gently meandering Avon River, through the rose, rock, and azalea gardens, past an area full of New Zealand native plants, and into all the individual conservatories (open daily 10:15 A.M.–4 P.M.) featuring tropical, flowering, and alpine plants, cacti and succulents, ferns, and spectacular orchids. Seasonal displays feature the most beautiful flowering trees, daffodils, azaleas, rhododendrons, and bedding plants. The **Botanic Garden Information Centre,** tel. 03/366-1701, features displays, horticultural information, botanical books, and souvenirs; it's open Sept.–April daily 10:15 A.M.–4 P.M., May–Aug. daily 11 A.M.–3 P.M. Finish your walk off with morning or afternoon tea or a delicious smorgasbord lunch in the restaurant/tea kiosk, tel. 03/366-5076, on the grounds; it's open daily 10 A.M.–4:30 P.M., smorgasbord noon–2 P.M. Guided tours are available on the "Toast Rack" electric vehicle, which operates (only in fine weather) 11 A.M.–4 P.M., departing from outside the tea kiosk; $4 adult, $2 child. To get to the Botanic Garden from Cathedral Square, walk west along either Worcester St. or Hereford St.—the main entrance is off Rolleston Ave. close to Christ's College and the museum and art gallery.

Hagley Park, the enormous park that borders the Botanic Garden to the north, south, and west, has kilometers of excellent walking, jogging, and cycling tracks, and is a venue for all kinds of organized sports. The park covers an area of about 180 hectares of woods and playing fields (separated from the Botanic Gardens by the Avon River, but bridges allow access), and is divided into two main north and south sections by Riccarton Avenue. If you want a bit of exercise or enjoy watching other people sweat, this is the place. Entrance from the inner city to North Hagley Park is from Rolleston Ave., and to South Hagley Park from Hagley or Riccarton Avenues.

Mona Vale

Built in 1904, this historic mansion is surrounded by 5.5 hectares of traditional English-style gardens. Visitors are invited to stroll through the grounds, absorbing the beauty of conifers, maples, rhododendrons, camellias, magnolias, ericaceous plants (members of the heath family), herbaceous perennials and annual bedding displays, roses, dahlias, fuchsias, herbs, irises, and the Bath House featuring seasonal displays of cool greenhouse plants. The Avon River, home for hundreds of ducks eagerly awaiting handouts, meanders lazily through the gardens, and punt rides are offered from the jetty in front of the homestead. The grounds are open Oct.–March daily 8 A.M.–7:30 P.M., and April–Sept. daily 8:30 A.M.–5:30 P.M. The homestead is open Sun.–Fri. 10 A.M.–3:30 P.M. for morning and afternoon teas and tantalizing smorgasbord lunches; reservations are advised, call 03/348-9660. Entry to Mona Vale is from Fendalton Rd. or Mona Vale Rd., 1.7 km west of Cathedral Square.

Wildlife Parks

Lying 18 km north of downtown is 80-hectare **Orana Wildlife Park,** New Zealand's largest wildlife park, on McLean's Island Rd., Papanui, tel. 03/359-7109. The main reason to venture out here is for the large collection of native birds and tuataras, but you'll also enjoy the many African animals, including giraffes, lions, zebras, and antelopes. The park is open daily 10

Mona Vale

© JANE KING

A.M.–4:30 P.M.; admission of $12 adult, $6 child includes a trip on the Safari Shuttle.

Willowbank Wildlife Reserve, Hussey Rd., Harewood, tel. 03/359-6226, is another large wildlife park specializing in New Zealand fauna. The kiwi house, the largest in the country, is open throughout the day, and the facility stays open after dark, allowing the viewing of kiwis in an outdoor environment. It's open daily 10 A.M.–10 P.M., with dinner available in the Willowbank Restaurant; admission is $11.50 adult, $6 child.

SCENIC DRIVES
Northern Summit Road

For great views of the seaside suburb of Sumner, Lyttelton Harbour, the Seaward Kaikoura Range to the north, Christchurch City, checkerboard Canterbury Plains, and the distant snowcapped Southern Alps, take the 45-km scenic Northern Summit Rd. circuit. From the city center, follow High St. east onto Ferry Rd. heading along the old main road to Lyttelton. Go through Sumner and up Evans Pass, but instead of continuing along the main road down into Lyttelton, turn right (south) onto spectacular Summit Road. Be sure to stop at the **Bridle Path,** the route early colonists took from Lyttelton Harbour over the steep hills to the flat, grassy Canterbury Plains and Christchurch.

Over the hill from Christchurch, **Lyttelton** is a working port, with hilly streets ending at the harbourfront, where many century-old commercial buildings remain. The **Black Cat Group,** 17 Norwich Quay (Jetty B), tel. 03/328-9078, operates the *Black Cat* on harbor cruises—searching out dolphins and viewing natural features around the bay. The two-hour trip is $39 pp.

To return to the city from Summit Rd., turn right at the **"Sign of the Kiwi"** on Dyers Pass Rd. and continue down through Victoria Park with its impressive rock gardens to the **"Sign of the Takahe,"** a fine Gothic building and a great place to stop for morning or afternoon tea or a smorgasbord lunch, on the corner of Dyers Pass Rd. and Victoria Park Rd. (about six km from the city center). From here continue through the attractive suburb of Cashmere via Dyers Pass Rd. or Hackthorne Rd. onto Colombo St., which leads back to Cathedral Square.

Southern Summit Road

Take Colombo St. south from city center, then Dyers Pass Rd. toward Governor's Bay, and at Summit Rd. turn right. This beautiful 52-km-long hilltop road gives spectacular views of Lyttelton Harbour, Governor's Bay, the Canterbury Plains and distant Southern Alps, Lake Ellesmere to the south, and the southern coastline. At Gebbies Pass Rd. turn right down to Motukarara, and turn right again on Hwy. 75 to Tai Tapu and Halswell to return to the city. If you want to explore Banks Peninsula and visit the quaint French-influenced village of Akaroa before returning to the city, turn left on Hwy. 75 and continue to the end.

RECREATION

Beaches

Christchurch has lots of sandy swimming beaches but the tidal currents can be dangerous—it's safest to swim in the patrolled areas between flags,

and with friends. The closest beach, **New Brighton,** is eight km east, reached by a no. 5 city bus. **North Beach** is 10 km east (no. 19 bus); **South Brighton** is also 10 km east (no. 5S bus); and **Sumner** is 11 km southeast (no. 3 bus). **Lyttelton Harbour** has a number of scenic beaches, and **Corsair Beach,** a 15-minute walk from Lyttelton, has excellent swimming. If getting to the beach is part of the fun, consider taking a short 15-minute launch ride from Lyttelton across Lyttelton Harbour to Diamond Harbour and its beach (refreshments available). The launch crosses the harbor several times a day (less frequently on weekends and public holidays—note return times).

Bicycling

One of the most enjoyable and fun ways to discover the flat terrain and lush beauty of Christchurch is on a bicycle—and many roads have special cycling lanes. You can rent all kinds of bikes. **Cyclone Cycles,** 245 Colombo St., tel. 03/332-9588, has good deals for longer term rentals. Twenty-one-speed mountain bikes are $25 for one day, $38 for two days, $50 for three days, plus $10 thereafter per day. Cyclone also rents out double touring bags ($2.50 per day) and helmets ($1.50 per day).

ENTERTAINMENT AND EVENTS

To find out what's on around the city, call in at the Christchurch/Canterbury Visitor Centre, where you can pick up all the free tourist guides and ask locals where the best action is. Daily newspapers have an entertainment page with cinema and theater listings, along with the venues for bands and cabarets, music recitals, and performances. On the back page of the Wednesday and Saturday *Christchurch Press* are all the entertainment venues. Also pick up the free "Christchurch and Canterbury Visitors' Guide," which has an extensive "What's on in Canterbury" section covering art, music, theater, sports, and special events.

Arts Centre of Christchurch

For theater, ballet, cinema, classical, jazz, and folk music, head straight for the Arts Centre at the west end of Worcester Street. The **Visitors Centre** in the Clocktower Building (close to Rolleston Ave.) is the place to make general inquiries and bookings, or call 03/366-0988; it's open Mon.–Fri. 8:30 A.M.–5 P.M. Theater performances ranging from classical Shakespeare to modern playwrights, with special emphasis on New Zealand plays, are put on in the **Court Theatre** continuously throughout the year—enjoy dramas, comedies, tragedies, and farces for about $20; the theater bar and coffee bar in the foyer are open before and after all performances and during intermission. For details see the back of the daily newspapers; book at tel. 03/366-6992. Lunchtime concerts are featured every Friday at 1:10 P.M. in the Great Hall, profiling New Zealand and international musicians from a wide variety of musical disciplines.

The **Southern Ballet & Dance Theatre,** tel. 03/379-7219, performs programs throughout the year at the Arts Centre, along with numerous individual recitals. For retrospective movies, award-winning classics, and foreign films, head for the Arts Centre **Academy Cinema,** tel. 03/366-0167. If you get hungry during all this entertainment, the center has good restaurants, as well as a bakery, bar, and coffee shop.

Cinemas

Cinemas can be found throughout the city, including **Hoyts** complex at 392 Moorhouse St., tel. 03/366-0140; and **Regent on Worcester,** 94 Worcester St., tel. 03/377-8095.

Casino

Christchurch Casino, 30 Victoria St., tel. 03/365-9999, offers gamblers blackjack, roulette, mini baccarat, Sic Bo, stud poker, keno, and more than 300 slot machines. It's open Mon.–Wed. 11 A.M.–3 A.M., 24 hours daily the rest of the week. There's also a dress code—no jeans or T-shirts.

Bars and Nightclubs

You'll find bands in hotels and bars throughout the city almost every night of the week and always on weekends (the better the band, the larger the cover charge). Scan the papers, listen to the radio

for advertisements, or check the information centers to find out current venues and prices. Oxford Terrace holds the main concentration of bars and nightspots. A good place for a quiet beer at any time is the **Tap Room,** 124 Oxford Terrace, tel. 03/365-0547, featuring contemporary décor highlighted by an impressive beer tank behind the main bar. This bar is owned by Monteith's, a West Coast brewer of national repute, and it's this company's "craft beer" that makes the Tap Room a worthwhile stop. Two of the most popular nightclubs are **All Bar One,** 130 Oxford Terrace, tel. 03/377-9898; and **Coyote Street Bar,** 126 Oxford Terrace, tel. 03/366-6055. **Di Lusso,** 132 Oxford Terrace, tel. 03/379-2133, is a New York-style lounge bar, with prices to match. Around the corner, **Baileys Downtown,** 112 Hereford St., tel. 03/379-2515, is another popular downtown bar with bands playing on weekends.

Blues lovers gravitate to the **Southern Blues Bar,** a few blocks southeast of Cathedral Square at 198 Madras St., tel. 03/365-1654. The doors open nightly at 7:30 P.M. and the music starts at 10:30 P.M.

Those who appreciate beer may like to sample a large selection, along with wines, spirits, and cocktails, at the **Loaded Hog,** on the corner of Manchester and Castel Streets, tel. 03/366-6674, a bar with loads of atmosphere in a working natural brewery. It features four beers on tap, including Red Dog Draught, and food, T-shirts, memorabilia, and freshly bottled beer to take away. It's open Mon.–Wed. 11 A.M.–11 P.M., Thurs.–Sat. 11 A.M.–1 A.M., and Sunday noon–10 P.M. Also try beer made on the premises at **Dux De Lux** in the Arts Centre.

Festivals and Events

Music recitals happen regularly in the **Town Hall** (enter from Kilmore St., tel. 03/377-8899; the booking office is open weekdays 9 A.M.–5 P.M., Saturday 10 A.M.–5 P.M.).

In summer the Canterbury Promotions Council arranges all kinds of **"Summertimes"** happenings—such as picnics in the park, country fairs, special exhibitions, kite days, international days, lunchtime entertainment in Cathedral

Square, and rock and jazz concerts in North Hagley Park. The city's biggest summer gathering is the **World Buskers Festival,** tel. 03/377-2365, at outdoor venues such as Cathedral Square, the Arts Centre, and Oxford Terrace over nine days in late January.

Through the middle week of November, Christchurch plays host to the **Canterbury A&P Show,** which is held at the Canterbury Agricultural Park on Curlett's Rd., tel. 03/343-3033. Dating to 1859, this historic gathering includes traditional events such as dog trials, wood chopping, and sheep and cattle judging, but modern agriculture is also catered to, with wine and cheese competitions and exotic animals, such as ostriches, on display. The Friday of the show is a provincial holiday.

HOTELS AND MOTELS
Under $100
Many of Christchurch's old downtown hotels have been knocked down over the years, and those that haven't have been converted for other uses. Therefore, nearly all the hotel or motel accommodations that fall in this price range lie on the fringes of downtown. **Thomas's Hotel** is opposite the Arts Centre at 36 Hereford St., tel. 03/379-2536; website: www.thomashotel.co.nz. Rooms are basic, and most share bathrooms, but all have a TV and phone. Guests have use of a communal kitchen, lounge, and Internet access. Rates are $50–70 s, $55–85 d, with the more expensive rooms having an en suite bathroom.

A few blocks east of Cathedral Square, **Stonehurst,** 241 Gloucester St., tel. 03/379-4620, website: www.stonehurst.co.nz, is set up for backpackers (dorm beds $19), but also has rooms with shared facilities ($40 s, $50 d), en suites ($55–65 s or d), and a few self-contained motelstyle units ($125 s or d). Facilities include a swimming pool, communal kitchens, and an adjacent pub serving meals.

The largest concentration of motels is found northwest of downtown along Bealey Ave. and Papanui Road. Along this strip, you'll find excellent value at the **Southern Comfort Motel,** 53 Bealey Ave., tel. 03/366-0383 or 0800/655-345,

website: www.southerncomfort.co.nz, featuring 21 spacious units, each with a basic but modern kitchen. The Southern Comfort also boasts a swimming pool and barbecue area. Studio units are $79 s, $89 d, with rates rising to $210 for a four-bedroom unit.

In the vicinity, **Avenue Motor Lodge,** 136 Bealey Ave., tel. 03/366-0582 or 0800/500-283, website: www.avenuemotorlodge.co.nz, offers 14 self-contained rooms of a similar standard, some with private patios furnished with outdoor furniture. This property is also within walking distance of numerous restaurants. Rates range $75–155 s or d.

Colonial Inn Motel, close to Hagley Park at 43 Papanui Rd., tel. 03/355-9139 or 0800/111-232, website: www.colonialinnmotel.co.nz, provides comfortable units, each with a sunny bed-living room, kitchen, tea-making supplies, fridge, TV, plenty of space to stretch out, and a community spa; $95–150 s or d.

$100–200
Pavilions Hotel, 42 Papanui Rd., tel. 03/355-5633 or 0800/805-555, website: www.pavilionshotel.co.nz, is northwest of Cathedral Square (within walking distance of the casino). It has 120 simply furnished rooms, an outdoor swimming pool, spa, a small restaurant open daily for a buffet breakfast, and a cocktail bar; rates from $165 s or d.

For travelers arriving or departing Christchurch International Airport, the **Airport Plaza,** directly opposite the airport on Memorial Ave., tel. 03/358-3139 or 0800/100-876, features a large outdoor swimming pool, a restaurant and lounge, 24-hour room service, a laundry, and airport shuttles. Rates start at $170 s or d.

Chateau on the Park, 189 Deans Ave., tel. 03/348-8999 or 0800/808-999, website: www.chateau-park.co.nz, gives the feeling of being miles from the hustle and bustle of downtown Christchurch. In addition to the adjacent botanical garden, the hotel has its own two-hectare garden, including a plot of alpine species and a small planting of pinot noir wine grapes. It features 190 comfortable rooms with garden views starting at $190 s or d (check the website for free upgrades and multi-night discounts), as well as a swimming pool and bike rentals. The Chateau also has an in-house English-style pub and two other dining rooms.

Over $200

Millennium Christchurch, 14 Cathedral Square, tel. 03/365-1111 or 0800/358-888, website: www.millenniumchristchurch.co.nz, is a 179-room, full-service hotel overlooking the city's busiest intersection. Facilities include a fitness room, sauna, business center, currency exchange, and underground valet parking. Rates start at $220 s or d, discounted on weekends to $150.

Overlooking the river, three blocks from Cathedral Square, is **Rydges Christchurch** on the corner of Worcester St. and Oxford Terrace, tel. 03/379-4700 or 0800/654-994; website: www.ridges.com. Rack rates in this European-style lodging are $280 s or d, but call direct or check the Internet for discounted rates.

Fino Casementi All-Suite Hotel, 87-89 Kilmore St., tel. 03/366-8444 or 0800/100-221, the city's finest accommodation, is furnished in the style of Europe's best hotels and with rates to match. Each of the large two-bedroom suites has a full kitchen and private balcony; $280 s or d. At street level is a restaurant and bar. *Worchester Street*

~~Geri~~ ORARI B+B

OTHER ACCOMMODATIONS

Bed-and-Breakfasts

Christchurch has a large number of guesthouses offering bed-and-breakfast. Ask at the information center for all the current listings. One that you may want to try is **Turret House** at 435 Durham St., tel. 03/365-3900, website: www.turrethouse.co.nz, a 10-minute walk from downtown. In one of the city's large old homes (built in 1885) the owners provide spacious, elegant rooms with private bath and a continental breakfast for $70 s, $90–130 d. Get to know the other guests at the evening wine and cheese get-together or at breakfast, or relish complete privacy—whichever you choose. The friendly, flexible owners will even put on a barbecue if the guests request it.

A longtime favorite, 500 meters from Cathedral Square, is the grand old **Windsor Hotel,** 52 Armagh St., tel. 03/366-1503, website: www.windsorhotel.co.nz, offering shared bathrooms, free tea and coffee, a laundry, a full cooked breakfast (6:30–9 A.M.), and a congenial adult atmosphere for $66 s, $98 d. It's often full, so book well in advance (many Antarctic workers use this hotel as a base before flying south).

Next door to the Windsor is the **Grange Guesthouse,** 56 Armagh St., tel. 03/366-2850 or 0800/932-850, website: www.thegrange.co.nz, a historic mansion set back from the road with eight large, tastefully decorated rooms, an attractive guest lounge, and secure off-street parking. Rooms with shared bath are $85 s, $98 d, while rooms with an en suite are $95 s, $115–125 d.

Charlotte Jane, north of downtown at 110 Papanui Rd., tel. 03/355-1028, website: www.charlotte-jane.co.nz, is in an 1891 home built for a sea captain and named for one of the ships that transported Christchurch's early settlers from England. Superbly refurbished without losing any of the original charm, each room features polished timber paneling, a writing desk, a comfortable bed, and a fireplace. Rates of $235 s or d include welcome drinks upon arrival and a full cooked breakfast the following morning.

Hostelling International

Two blocks north of Cathedral Square is **Christchurch City Central YHA,** 273 Manchester St., tel. 03/379-9535; website: www.yha.org.nz. This large, modern hostel lies within easy walking distance of all the downtown sights and many of the best cafés and restaurants. It features more than 160 beds, including many in single and double rooms. A bed costs $22–25 pp.

Adjacent to the Arts Centre, **Rolleston House YHA,** 5 Worcester St., tel. 03/366-6564, website: www.yha.org.nz, is in an old, rambling two-story house with a large common room and kitchen, the usual facilities, and plenty of space to spread out. Its great central location (a couple of blocks from Cathedral Square) makes it handy to all city attractions. The office/shop is open 8–10 A.M., 5–7 P.M., and 8:30–10 P.M.; there is also a detailed information board. Rates are $20–23 pp. To get there from Cathedral Square, head west along Worcester St., cross the river, and continue for two short blocks—the hostel is at the end of the street on the right side.

Other Backpacker Lodges

As with New Zealand's other large cities, what Christchurch lacks in quality backpacker lodges it makes up with the large number of inexpensive beds available. **Foley Towers,** across from the river one km from Cathedral Square, tel. 03/366-9720, is an attractive old guesthouse with well-kept gardens, a stone's throw from the river and a short stroll from city center. It offers a choice of rooms: beds in six-bed dorms are $16, while beds in a bright three-bed room with shared bathroom are $18. A double room with private bathroom is $22 pp. It has a dining room, a comfy guest lounge, luggage lockers, a sunny yard, no TV, and limited off-street parking. Three blocks back toward the city, **Stonehurst,** 241 Gloucester St., tel. 03/379-4620, website: www.stonehurst.co.nz, is a modern backpacker complex with a pool, barbecue area, two communal kitchens, and an adjacent pub; dorm $19 pp, private rooms with shared facilities $40 s, $50 d.

Vagabond Backpackers, 232 Worcester St., tel. 03/379-9677, is another good choice. This small lodge four blocks east of Cathedral Square features comfortable beds, a pleasant courtyard, and a laundry. Dorm beds are $18–24, with most in twin rooms and no room having more than four beds.

Motor Camps

The closest motor camp to city center is **Addington Accommodation Park,** three km southwest of Cathedral Square and a short walk from South Hagley Park, at 47-51 Whiteleigh Ave., off Lincoln Rd., tel. 03/338-9770. It has communal bathrooms, a dining room, kitchen, and laundry. Tent sites are $17 s or d, caravan sites cost $19, and cabins range $35–65. To get there from Cathedral Square, take Colombo St. south, then turn right (west) on Moorhouse Ave., left on Lincoln Rd., and right on Whiteleigh Avenue.

Meadow Park Top 10 Holiday Park, about five km from the city center, at 39 Meadow St.,

off the main road (Hwy. 1 north) near the junction of Cranford St., tel. 03/352-9176, website: www.meadowpark.co.nz, has a sauna, spa, swimming pool, trampolines, a barbecue, and a takeaway food bar. Powered sites are $22 s or d, basic cabins are $40, self-contained cabins are $52, and motel rooms are $90.

Toward the airport, **Russley Park Motor Camp** is opposite Riccarton Racecourse on South Hwy. 73 in the western suburb of Riccarton, at 372 Yaldhurst Rd., tel. 03/342-7021. It has a spa (charge), a TV and recreation room, a trampoline, a pool table, and communal facilities; tent sites are $18, caravan sites are $22, chalets are $39 s or d, and tourist flats are $58 s or d.

If you don't mind being 10 km from city center and prefer to be closer to the ocean, try **South Brighton Motor Camp** on Halsey St. off Estuary Rd., tel. 03/388-9844. With communal facilities, tent sites are $18, caravan sites are $20, cabins start at $33, and tourist flats are $56, all 400 meters from the beach.

If you're approaching from the north, consider staying at Spencerville, 14 km north of Christchurch on the east coast. **Spencer Park Holiday Camp,** at Spencer Park on Heyders Rd. (turn east at Belfast), tel. 03/329-8721, lies adjacent to a sandy beach and has a recreation hall, a TV room, spa, trampoline, miniature golf, and a wildlife park. Grassy tent and caravan sites among the trees are $18–20 d, cabins are $35–45 d, and flats are $55 d. Another choice on the city's northern outskirts is **Pineacres Holiday Park,** about 20 minutes' drive north of the city and north of Kaiapoi along Main North Rd., tel. 03/327-5022 or 0800/746-322. This campground offers tent sites for $10 pp, caravan sites $12 pp, cabins ranging $30–45 d, and tourist flats from $65 d. Facilities include a kitchen, laundry, a large TV lounge and game room, a store, and a licensed restaurant on the premises, often with live music.

FOOD

If you have a particular kind of food in mind, the free *Scenic South* tourist newspaper has an entire page of dining suggestions categorized ethnically. Also grab a free *Christchurch Tourist Times,* which itemizes restaurants and gives you a rough idea of prices. You can find both papers at numerous tourist spots around town, and at the Christchurch & Canterbury Visitor Centre.

Breakfast

The best places to head for breakfast are the cafés and tearooms amply scattered throughout the city, though you're not likely to find many places serving English- or American-style bacon and eggs, or pancakes. For that you need to stay at a hotel or serviced motel, some of which serve breakfast to walk-ins, such as **Thomas's Hotel,** 36 Hereford St., tel. 03/379-9536. **Burnaby John's,** 3 Chancery Lane, tel. 03/379-0501, is a down-home, 1950s café with cooked breakfasts for under $10. A few blocks north of Cathedral Square, **Oxford on Avon,** 794 Colombo St., tel. 03/379-7148, is a pub

---

AFTERNOON TEA

The delightful English tradition of afternoon tea can be enjoyed at locations around the city. Expect fresh scones with cream and jam, finger sandwiches, an array of cakes, and not a tea bag in sight. For beautiful park surroundings, head for **Gardens Restaurant and Tea Kiosk** in the center of the Botanic Garden, tel. 03/366-5076. It's open for lunch and dinner, with Devonshire tea served between meal times.

Mona Vale, west of downtown at 63 Fendalton Rd., tel. 03/348-9660, is a century-old riverside mansion surrounded by immaculate gardens. In this relaxing environment, morning and afternoon tea (from $7 pp) are served daily. Eat in the garden or the gracious homestead dining room with Avon River views. Reservations are advisable.

Another great spot to have morning and afternoon tea, or a mouthwatering smorgasbord lunch (daily noon–2 P.M.; $27 pp), is the **Sign of the Takahe** roadhouse (looks like a castle). It's on scenic Summit Rd., tel. 03/332-4052, in Cashmere; soak up some historic atmosphere and magnificent views while you eat.

---

open for breakfast; expect to pay $10 for bacon, eggs, and toast.

Coffee and Cafés

The coffee scene has improved in recent years. Away from the busiest part of downtown (one block south of Cathedral Square) I had a great cup of coffee at **Café D'Fafo,** 137 Hereford St., tel. 03/366-6083. **Pastels Café,** 77 Hereford St., tel. 03/365-0137, is an older, inexpensive café one block to the west. In the vicinity, the **Arts Centre of Christchurch** has a good selection of casual eateries.

In Cathedral Square are a number of take-away food stands offering foods that cater to just about everyone's taste—good-value lunches on the run. The west end of Cashel St. is another pedestrian-friendly area where you'll find many cafes with lots of outside tables-the perfect place to relax in the sun with a coffee. Around the corner on Oxford Terrace is **Coyote Street Bar,** 126 Oxford Terrace, tel. 03/366-6055, with a cavernous interior decorated Santa Fe style and a few outdoor tables. Next door is **Azure Restaurant and Bar,** 128 Oxford Terrace, tel. 03/365-6088, another trendy café, this one licensed to serve beer and wine.

Pub Meals

For good roasted meats with all the trimmings, and delectable desserts, stop in at the ever-so-popular **Oxford Tavern and Restaurant** on Oxford Terrace. Savor a very filling tasty meal with veggies or salad bar from only $11 in relaxed, pleasant surroundings; it's open Sun.–Thurs. 11 A.M.–9 P.M., Fri. and Sat. 11 A.M.–10 P.M. Two reliable **Cobb & Co.** restaurants are in the city area: one on the southwest side at the **Bush Inn Hotel,** 364 Riccarton Rd., Upper Riccarton, tel. 03/348-7175; and one on the north side at the **Caledonian Hotel,** 101 Caledonian Rd., St. Albans, tel. 03/366-6035. Dated décor aside, these two dining rooms provide excellent value, especially for seniors, who can enjoy a three-course meal for just $15. Two blocks north of Cathedral Square and open daily from 6:30 A.M.–midnight is **Oxford on Avon,** on Colombo St. overlooking the river, tel. 03/379-7148, a pub-style restaurant serving traditional English roast lunches and dinners ($15).

Arts Centre of Christchurch

Le Bon Bolli (french) [handwritten annotation]

The very popular **Dux De Lux** in the Arts Centre at 41 Hereford St., tel. 03/366-6919, is a good place for either lunch or dinner. The menu showcases lots of local produce and is made up almost entirely of vegetarian and seafood dishes. Expect to pay $12–15 at lunch and $19–24 at dinner. The restaurant is part of a larger complex, with an in-house brewery and three different bars offering inexpensive meals. It's open daily 9:30 A.M.–late, with live music in the Tavern Bar some nights. Also in the Arts Centre is **Annie's Wine Bar and Restaurant,** tel. 03/365-0566, offering lots of New Zealand favorites at lunch and dinner daily, along with an extensive range of South Island wines by the glass or bottle. The atmosphere is informal and rustic. Both these Arts Centre restaurants have outdoor dining.

Tourist Favorites

Every evening, a renovated 1926 tram does circuits of the downtown core as the **Christchurch Tramway Restaurant,** tel. 03/366-7511. The menu is necessarily limited, but main courses, such as a rack of lamb basted with molasses and served with minted kumara ($26.50), are relatively well priced. Call for reservations and a schedule. Out of town and with panoramic views is the **Summit Café Brasserie,** at the top of the Christchurch Gondola, tel. 03/384-0700. As you'd expect at this tourist-oriented location, the menu has wide appeal, offering everything from sushi to Caesar salad. Don't let that put you off, though. Many choices ($20–25) have a distinctive Kiwi flair, including a farm-raised venison dish smothered in a thyme and pear cider sauce. Pay at the gondola base to take advantage of package meals from $37.50 pp, including the ride to the top and your choice of two courses from the menu. Dine between 4:30 P.M. and 6:30 P.M. and pay from only $29.50.

A similar distance from downtown as the gondola but farther to the west is **Sign of the Takahe,** Summit Rd., Cashmere Hills, tel. 03/332-4052, a castlelike structure built as a roadhouse in the early 1900s. Although it was never completely abandoned, a massive effort at restoring the grand property has successfully turned this landmark building into a fine restaurant. Open daily for lunch and dinner, enjoy dishes such as a rack of locally raised lamb baked in an apricot and mustard glaze for $29.50. It's open daily 10 A.M.–4 P.M. for lunch and Mon.–Sat. from 6 P.M. for dinner.

Other Restaurants

The city hot spot when I visited on a research trip for this edition was **Cook 'N' with Gas,** 23 Worcester St., tel. 03/377-9166. A fashionable bistro with snappy service and well-informed waitpersons, expect an ever-changing menu that may include such delights as vanilla-seared prawns ($23.50). The wine list is dominated by local and Australian offerings.

For the best chili in town, head for **Zydeco Café,** 113 Manchester St., tel. 03/365-4556. Other Southern classics include jambalaya, gumbo, and blackened fish with a citrus and coriander yoghurt sauce ($20). All starters are $10 (including delicious blackened mussel bites, with a sherry-based dipping sauce), while dinners range $20–25.

For Chinese food, try locally recommended **Chung Wah II Restaurant,** 63 Worcester St., tel. 03/379-3894. Open daily, this large downtown restaurant offers an extensive menu of Westernized Chinese dishes from $8 at lunch and $12 at dinner.

Not Just Desserts!

Those with a sweet tooth shouldn't miss a stop at **Strawberry Fare Restaurant,** 114 Peterborough St., tel. 03/365-4897. Delectable treats such as "Death By Chocolate" that go straight to the thighs range $8.50–15. Just reading the menu is a mouthwatering affair. However, the owners also serve breakfasts (croissants, waffles, and baked goodies) for $6–14, a Parisian breakfast for $14, and savory dishes throughout the day— try their salmon and filo parcel for $19.50, smoked salmon and dill pots for $20, or cheese plate for $15.50 before diving into dessert. Strawberry Fare is open daily 8 A.M.–midnight.

GETTING THERE

Getting to and from Christchurch is easy. An excellent highway network leads to and from the city, it has a bustling national and international airport, and it's well served by major coach companies and by rail from Picton in the north, Greymouth in the west, and Invercargill and Dunedin in the south.

Air

Over four million passengers annually pass through busy **Christchurch Airport,** 12 km northwest of Cathedral Square. The easy 15-minute route to the airport through leafy suburbs with glimpses of beautiful gardens through hedges and white picket fences is well served by airport-city buses and taxis. Within the International and adjoining Domestic Terminals are a bank (open Mon.–Fri. 9:30 A.M.–4 P.M. and for all international flights), a variety of gift and souvenir shops, a bookshop, duty-free shopping (open two hours before every international departure), a florist, showers, various eateries, major car rental agencies, and left-luggage lockers.

When you first arrive at the airport, head for one of the two **Travel & Information Centres;** open 7:30 A.M.–8:30 P.M. in the Domestic Terminal and daily for all international flights in the International Terminal.

The least expensive way to travel between the airport and downtown is with **Canride,** tel. 03/366-8855. Buses depart in both directions, from both terminals and Cathedral Square every half-hour between 6:30 A.M. and 9 P.M. (on Sunday 6:30 A.M.–7:30 P.M.). The downtown pickup point is 65 Cathedral Square (next to the Tower Building); $3 adult, $1.50 child. **Super Shuttle,** tel. 03/365-5655, also offers a door-to-door pickup/return service to all points of the city. The cost is $6–12 pp, depending on the number of passengers. Bookings are essential (for pickup before 7 A.M., book by 10 P.M. the day before). A cab between downtown and the airportcosts $20.

If you're driving to downtown from the airport, take Memorial Avenue all the way onto Fendalton Road, at the park turn left onto Harper Avenue, then keep going straight onto Bealey Avenue. Almost immediately turn right on Victoria Street, then right on Colombo Street, and you're downtown. The route in the opposite direction to the airport is well signposted.

International airlines flying into Christchurch include **Air New Zealand,** tel. 03/379-5200; **Air Pacific,** tel. 0800/800-178; **Qantas,** tel. 03/379-6504; and **Singapore Airlines,** tel. 03/366-8003. Air New Zealand and **Freedom Air,** tel. 0800/600-500, offer direct flights between Christchurch and major centers on both islands.

The **Flight Centre,** 116 Cashell Mall, tel. 03/366-6371, offers the best deals on all international flights and can also book package tours.

Train

Christchurch Railway Station is in the suburb of Addington, three km from the city center (approach from Whiteleigh Ave., then Clarence St.). All services from Christchurch are operated by **Tranz Scenic,** tel. 0800/802-802; website: www.tranzscenic.co.nz. The station is open Mon.–Fri. 9 A.M.–5 P.M. and Sat.–Sun. 7–9:15 A.M.

One of the most spectacular train rides in New Zealand is on the **TranzAlpine** (panoramic windows, onboard commentary) between Christchurch and Greymouth through Arthur's Pass. If you're short on time, take the Arthur's Pass Day Excursion. If you'd rather head north, take the daily **TranzCoastal** to Kaikoura, Blenheim, and Picton. The trip between Picton and Christchurch takes about six hours. Heading south to Dunedin or Invercargill? Take the daily **Southerner** train.

Bus

The **Christchurch Travel Centre** is centrally located at 123 Worcester St., just west of Cathedral Square. It's open daily 6:45 A.M.–7:30 P.M. This is the departure point for all **Intercity** buses, tel. 03/377-0951, including north to Picton, where direct connections are made with the ferry to Wellington. **Newmans,** tel. 03/374-6149, the country's other major coach operator, uses the same depot. The city is also a hub for many smaller shuttle buses. One of these is **Atomic**

Shuttles, tel. 03/322-8883, with services to Picton, Dunedin, and Queenstown. The advantage of Atomic and other small companies is their door-to-door service.

GETTING AROUND
Tram
Trams ran through the downtown streets of Christchurch for the first 50 years of the 1900s and were reintroduced in 1995 on a 2.5-km loop along Armagh St., Rolleston Ave., Worcester St., and through Cathedral Square. It's a good, fun way to experience downtown, but if you need to travel a short distance, walking is much quicker. The trams operate 9 A.M.–6 P.M. (until 9 P.M. in summer) and cost $10 pp (children free) for as long as you're visiting the city. For details, contact **Christchurch Tramway,** tel. 03/366-7830.

Bus
Red Bus, tel. 03/379-4260, contracts all local bus services on behalf of the city. Their bright red buses (called "big reds") seem to go everywhere you want to go, from wherever you are,

regularly, including to the gondola and International Antarctic Centre. In addition, the red **Information Kiosk** in Cathedral Square is an invaluable source of transportation information. The kiosk, open daily and public holidays, is staffed by some of Christchurch's most patient and helpful people. The **Red Bus Day Pass** allows unlimited bus travel on all bus routes for the bargain price of just $5 pp. The pass is sold on board the buses or from the Cathedral Square kiosk. The Shuttle is a free service that operates along a popular downtown tourist route. For all schedules call **Businfo,** tel. 03/366-8855.

Rental Cars
Like Auckland, Christchurch has dozens of car rental agencies. Well-known names include **Avis,** tel. 03/379-6133; **Budget,** tel. 03/358-7489; **Hertz,** tel. 03/366-0549; **National,** tel. 03/366-5574; **NZ Rent-a-car,** tel. 03/358-1358; **Pegasus,** tel. 03/365-1100; and **Thrifty,** tel. 03/374-2357. **Scotties,** tel. 03/338-0997, is one of the local operators (also with an Auckland office) with an inexpensive yet reliable fleet of vehicles. Other local companies include **A1,** tel. 03/349-8022; **Ascot,** tel. 03/377-2621; **Econo-**

Jump aboard the Christchurch Tramway to access all major downtown sights.

© ANDREW HEMPSTEAD

my, tel. 03/359-7410; **Shoestring,** tel. 03/385-3647; and **Stirling,** tel. 03/377-0201.

Taxi

Cab companies in Christchurch include **Advance Taxis,** tel. 03/379-9999; **Arrow Taxis,** tel. 03/379-9999; **Blue Star Taxis,** tel. 03/379-9799; **First Direct Taxis,** tel. 03/377-2789; and **Gold Band Taxis,** tel. 03/379-5795.

Tours

If you have time only for highlights, check at the Christchurch & Canterbury Visitor Centre for tour brochures. Better still, ask one of the staff for suggestions to suit your time frame and budget. **Guided City Walks,** tel. 03/342-7691, have two-hour walking tours departing twice daily from Cathedral Square; $10 adult, $2 child. The information center has a schedule. **Explorer Tourline,** tel. 03/342-5551 or 0800/800-410, offers a variety of sight-seeing bus tours, including a Highlights tour taking in the Antarctic Centre, downtown historic buildings, a wildlife park, and the gondola. The cost is $60 including admissions.

Specialist operator **Canterbury Leisure Tours,** tel. 03/384-0999 or 0800/484-485, offers Morning and Afternoon Sights tours that hit all the main attractions for a reasonable $38 pp. Other options include fishing, horseback riding, and a full day exploring the Akaroa Peninsula.

SERVICES

Trading banks are generally open Mon.–Fri. 10 A.M.–4:30 P.M. (foreign transactions close at 3 P.M.), but a few stay open longer on Friday nights. **American Express Foreign Exchange** is at 773 Colombo St., tel. 03/365-7366. Also downtown is **Travelex New Zealand,** 730 Colombo St., tel. 03/365-4194, and **Interforex,** 65 Cathedral Square, tel. 03/377-1233. The main **post office** is on the southwest side of Cathedral Square. **Vadal Internet Fone Shop,** on Cathedral Square, tel. 03/377-2381, is set up for travelers needing to make national and international phone calls, with rates much lower than public call boxes. It also provides computers for sending and receiving email, as well as a fax service.

Emergency and Medical

Christchurch Hospital is on Riccarton Ave. and Oxford Terrace, west of city center and south of the Botanic Gardens, tel. 03/364-0600. At **High Street Medical Centre** in High St. Mall, 263 High St., tel. 03/366-0235, visitors can get same-day appointments if necessary. Centrally located pharmacies include **Victoria Square Pharmacy,** 748 Colombo St., tel. 03/379-2049; and Hanfins City Pharmacy, 272 High St., tel. 03/366-8071.

The city **police station** is on the corner of Hereford St. and Cambridge Terrace, tel. 03/379-3999.

INFORMATION

Books and Bookstores

Central City Library is on the corner of Gloucester St. and Oxford Terrace, tel. 03/379-6914; it's open weekdays 10 A.M.–9 P.M., Saturday 10 A.M.–4 P.M., and Sunday 1–4 P.M. Internet access is free.

Smith's Book Shop, 133 Manchester St., tel. 03/379-7976; **Whitcoull's,** 111 Cashel St., tel. 03/379-4580; and **Dymock's,** 105 Cashel St., tel. 03/377-8250, are all part of national bookstore chains. Each has a section devoted to New Zealand nonfiction and another to maps. Independent from the chain bookstores is **Scorpio Books,** 79 Hereford St., tel. 03/379-2882, offering a good range of New Zealand fiction and nonfiction. Secondhand bookstore **Pacific Bookshop,** 137 Manchester St., tel. 03/366-8659, features a small collection dedicated to mountaineering in New Zealand.

Information Centers

The main source of information is the **Christchurch & Canterbury Visitor Centre** right on Cathedral Square, tel. 03/379-9629; website: www.christchurch.org.nz. It's open daily 8:30 A.M.–5 P.M. (extended hours in summer). If asked, the staff willingly recommends accommodations and restaurants. Maps of varying sizes and detail (from $3), special-interest brochures (e.g., "Akaroa, Lyttelton and Christchurch, Historic Buildings, Landmarks, and Sights"), and postcards. Christchurch has established sister-city relationships with Christchurch, Dorset (England); Adelaide (South Australia); Seattle, Washington (U.S.A.); Kurashiki (Japan); and Gansu Province (People's Republic of China)—the Center particularly encourages people from these cities to come in and sign the special Sister-City Visitors' Book.

You'll find **Visitor Information Centres** at both the domestic and international terminals of Christchurch Airport. They are open for all arrivals, with efficient, friendly staff booking all sights, tours, and accommodations.

Other Sources of Information

For park and forest information, details of local hiking trails, and detailed maps, visit the DOC's **Canterbury Conservatory** office at 133 Victoria St., tel. 03/379-9758; it's open regular hours Mon.–Friday. To find out if anything's going on in the local parks, call the **Parks and Recreation Department** of Christchurch City Council, tel. 03/371-1999; website: www.ccc.govt.nz.

Banks Peninsula

The remnant of two huge volcanoes attached to the mainland by a gravel plain, rugged Banks Peninsula lies immediately southeast of Christchurch. Trails over craggy peaks and through deep valleys and forest remnants (most take about a day and are best done in summer), good swimming at sandy beaches along the sharply indented coastline, small towns nestled in striking crater harbours, and an overall island-getaway atmosphere make the peninsula an ideal place for a day trip from Christchurch—though you might find yourself staying longer.

If you like getting off the beaten track, get a detailed map of the peninsula and then, in one direction, take roads other than the main route to Akaroa. You'll be traveling narrow (in some places almost one lane), twisty, steep, often gravel roads with fabulous views around every bend, and you'll need a reliable car unless you're a fairly masochistic bicycle rider. On the way back, take the main road, which offers great scenery.

Pigeon Bay

This is just one of the many picturesque little villages waiting to be discovered around the peninsula, reached by sealed road from the main route or by gravel road from the northwest. A campground along the edge of a peaceful bay, a schoolhouse, and a boat club are all you'll find, but it's also the starting point for the five-hour **Pigeon Bay Walkway** that leads to Wakaroa Point.

The track starts by the boat club (parking available); no camping is permitted along the track.

Okains Bay

If you have your own transportation, visit another secluded getaway—the small township of Okains Bay on the northeast side of the peninsula, 83 km from Christchurch but only 25 km from Akaroa. Here you'll find a beautiful sandy beach with lots of shells and safe swimming, boating, fishing, large caves to explore around the bay, scenic walks, and great views. Check out the small campground (no showers), equally small general store, post office, and **Okains Bay Maori and Colonial Museum,** tel. 03/304-8611. Featuring colonial and Maori culture, the museum is open daily 10 A.M.–5 P.M.; $5 adult, $2 child. By car take Hwy. 75 toward Akaroa, but at Hilltop take the Summit Rd. (sealed) instead of the lower road down to Akaroa, and eventually turn left on Okains Bay Road.

AKAROA

This picturesque seaside town on Akaroa Harbour (population 700) has a colonial village appearance with late-Victorian architecture, quaint cottages, narrow streets, cosmopolitan shops, and French and English street signs and place-names. The original Akaroa colonists came over from France in 1840 on the *Comte de Paris*. Once

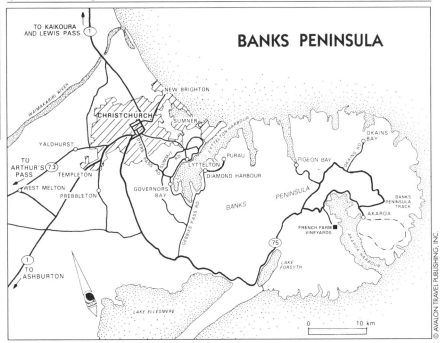

a whaling settlement, Akaroa is now recognized for its plentiful commercial, sport, and recreational fishing. Stroll around town soaking up the atmosphere, dangle a fishing line from the wharf, take a launch ride on the harbor, visit the local museum, or sample sole, grouper, *tarakihi,* crayfish, or gurnard cooked to perfection. Try a variety of fish at the take-away fish shop, or at one of the many restaurants.

Sights

Akaroa is the kind of place you can easily browse on foot. Meander through scenic reserves and waterfront parks where benches have been strategically placed to take best advantage of water and mountain views. Head along the front to the sparkling, whitewashed **Akaroa Head Lighthouse** or through **Akaroa Museum** and **Langlois-Eteveneaux Cottage** on the corner of Rue Lavaud (the main street) and Rue Balguerie, tel. 03/304-7614, to see historical displays, videos, and audiovisuals (open daily 10:30 A.M.–4:30 P.M.; $3 adult, $1 child). Akaroa has many beautiful old buildings dating from the 1840s to 1860s, and even the new buildings have been designed to blend in with the old. Galleries, arts-and-crafts shops, and homes with spectacular gardens along quiet streets or up little alleyways add to Akaroa's general appeal.

Tours and Hikes

Take a variety of cruises on Akaroa Harbour with the **Black Cat Group,** Akaroa Wharf, tel. 03/304-7641. The most popular tour departs daily at 1:30 P.M. (with an extra 11 A.M. departure Nov.–March), heading out in search of seals, dolphins, and sea birds. Stops are made at natural sea caves and a salmon farm. The two-hour cruise costs $33 adult, $15 child. This company also has charter boats for fishing and sight-seeing. Rent sea kayaks from **Banks Peninsula Sea Kayaks,** tel. 03/304-8776, or take a guided tour with them around the calm waters of Akaroa Harbour.

M

Another natural attraction is the **Banks Peninsula Track,** a 35-km (four-day) walkway that winds around the rugged volcanic coastline of the southeast bays, starting and ending in Akaroa. Hikers need to be fit; get all the details before starting out. The track is unique because it is almost entirely on private property, and a limited number of hikers are allowed at any one time. For $150 pp, transportation to the first hut, four nights of hut accommodation, landowners' fees, track registration, and a booklet describing the track are provided. Book at tel. 03/304-7612. On the other side of Akaroa Harbour, and equally spectacular, is the **Southern Bays Walkway.** Also on private property, this 50-km walk winds through the hills and along the rugged coastline of the peninsula. Along the track are four well-equipped huts, each with 12 beds, a hot shower, flush toilet, and modern kitchen. Walking this track costs $100 pp, which includes accommodations and transportation to and from the trailheads. Call 03/329-0007 to make a booking.

Bank of New Zealand building, Akaroa

© ANDREW HEMPSTEAD

Accommodations

Driftwood Motel, 56 Rue Jolie, tel. 03/304-7484 or 0800/928-373, website: www.driftwood.co.nz, enjoys a waterfront location a short walk from downtown Akaroa. The 12 units are modern and well equipped—each has a large kitchen and private balcony, making this accommodation an excellent value at $110–130 s or d. Breakfast delivered to the room is $8–12 pp and kayaks can be rented out front. Opposite the main wharf and above a trendy little café is **L'Hotel Akaroa,** 75 Beach Rd., tel. 03/304-7559. The view from these equally stylish units is also stunning; rates from $120 for a self-contained room.

Chez La Mer is a fantastic budget accommodation in a historic hotel building on the main road, a short walk from the center of Akaroa, tel. 03/304-7024. Offering facilities of a high standard, it features a private garden courtyard, free continental breakfast, and knowledgeable hosts who have plenty of suggestions to keep you on the peninsula at least a couple of days. Rates are $17 dorm, $21 pp in a double.

Akaroa Top 10 Holiday Park on Morgan's Rd., tel. 03/304-7471, provides tent and caravan sites from $18, on-site caravans for $35 d, cabins from $48 d, and tourist flats from $62 d. It can be very crowded in summer, with tents squashed into every spare spot—check out your allocated site before paying. The kitchen and bathrooms are clean, but the showers are the metered push-button type.

Food

Plenty of places to eat lie along the main street, most with their menus conveniently displayed outside. **Akaroa Bakery,** across from the waterfront at 51 Beach Rd., tel. 03/304-8693, sells all kinds of bread, cakes, and pastries, and sandwiches and salads to take away or eat there. It also serves breakfast from $6 with bottomless cups of coffee or tea; open daily 7:30 A.M.–4 P.M. Another inexpensive option is the **Turenne Coffee Shop,** across from the information center and open daily 7 A.M.–6 P.M., tel. 03/304-7005.

Named for an American buccaneer, **Bully Hayes Bar and Café,** 57 Beach Rd., tel. 03/304-7533, is one of Akaroa's best little restaurants,

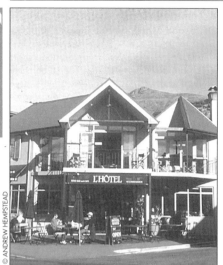

© ANDREW HEMPSTEAD

L'Hotel Akaroa

the main road, **French Farm Winery & Restaurant** has a wine bar and restaurant with alfresco dining on a beautiful terrace overlooking the bay. The winery itself has eight hectares of vines, mostly Chardonnay and Pinot Noir grapes, that thrive on dry, north-facing slopes. The menu is classic French Provincial, but also includes a number of gourmet pizzas and appetizer dishes such as Salmon Tasting Plate ($15). It's open daily 10 A.M.–5 P.M. To get there, turn off at Barry's Bay, signposted to French Farm Valley Road.

Transportation, Services, and Information

Akaroa Shuttle, tel. 0800/500-929, provides twice-daily service between the Christchurch & Canterbury Visitor Centre and Akaroa Information Centre. The rest of the year, trips depart at least once daily; $17 one way, $30 round-trip (pay the driver).

The **post office** is on the corner of Rue Lavaud and Rue Balguerie. The **hospital** and **doctor's office** are on Rue Jolie.

Akaroa Information Centre is along the main road into town on the corner of Rue Lavaud and Rue Balguerie, tel. 03/304-8600. It's open daily in summer from 10 A.M.

although it's not cheap. In keeping with its namesake, a notorious sea captain who sailed into Akaroa in the 1860s, it features a nautical theme. A full cooked breakfast is $14, and main courses the rest of the day range $15–32.

If you're heading back to Christchurch along

Arthur's Pass National Park

ARTHUR'S PASS ROAD

Arthur's Pass Rd. is the highest and most spectacular highway across the Southern Alps—the only crossing over the rugged Main Divide between Lewis Pass in the north and Haast Pass in the south. The 160-km sealed and well-maintained Hwy. 73 (fine for cars and camper-vans, not recommended for caravans) connects the town of Springfield on the western outskirts of Christchurch with the old gold-mining town of Kumara on the West Coast, linking the east and west coasts of the South Island. Apart from passing through a variety of awesome landscapes just to get to the other side, many people travel this route to explore, hike, climb, and ski the mountains of magnificent Arthur's Pass National Park,

which surrounds the highway about 150 km west of Christchurch, 100 km east of Greymouth.

From Christchurch

From Christchurch the road traverses the fertile flatland of the Canterbury Plains, then climbs steeply to the stark and desolate landscape of **Porter's Pass** (945 meters) and **Porter Heights,** closest alpine skiing to Christchurch, tel. 03/318-4002. Located a few km off Hwy. 73, the resort features an impressive 670-meter vertical rise served by five lifts; views from the slopes extend across the Canterbury Plains. Facilities include a café, rentals, and on-hill accommodations. Lift tickets are $46 adult, $22 senior, and $23 child.

Lake Lyndon is a good bird-watching spot in summer and natural skating rink in the frigid cold of July and August. From here the road passes through the lunar landscape of **Castle Hill,** where the background mountains of the **Craigieburn Range** to the west are steep and impressive (see the special topic Craigieburn Valley Ski Area), while the hills closest to the road are round, smooth, and dotted by weirdly shaped limestone formations (some with overhangs covered in Maori charcoal drawings that are thought to be 500 years old).

The scenery changes dramatically as the road enters the mountain beech-covered hills of **Craigieburn Forest Park** (stop at the visitor center for track and general information), then changes yet again as you enter bare eroded hills, passing **Lake Pearson** (known for its great brown and rainbow trout fishing, birdlife, and mountain

reflections) and **Lake Grasmere** (more good trout fishing). Early runholders burnt off much of the natural forest in this high country to clear the hills for grazing. The resulting lack of natural cover accelerated mass erosion of the hilltops and enormous shingle slides that continue today.

Continuing into the mountains, the scenery along Hwy. 73 becomes even more spectacular. The hills give way to tall craggy mountains covered in trees almost to the tops (and snow in winter) as the road curves around the northern end of the Craigieburn Range following the mighty Waimakariri River into **Arthur's Pass National Park.** As you drive through the park, more incredible snowcapped mountains loom above, in front, and beyond, beckoning alpine explorers and nature lovers to pull off the road and

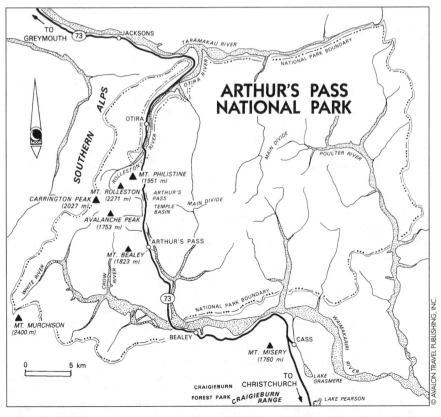

stay for a while. Picnic shelters, camping spots, and walking tracks are clearly signposted as you follow the Waimakariri River into **Bealey,** and then the Bealey River into the township of **Arthur's Pass.** The highway continues through the Bealey Valley to cross Arthur's Pass, where rugged mountains covered in natural bush flank the roadway. Crossing the Otira River, the road takes you through the old railway town of **Otira,** and then the scenery subtly changes yet again as the road joins the Taramakau River. Descending steeply, you soon leave the Southern Alps behind and enter a lush valley with dense natural bush, scrub, and grass typical throughout Westland. Arthur's Pass Rd. finishes at **Kumara Junction,** where it meets Hwy. 6, which runs north to Greymouth or south to the old gold town of Hokitika.

Highway History

The building of Arthur's Pass Rd. and the railway that followed is a vivid piece of New Zealand pioneering history. As you drive this magnificent road, let your mind wander back to the 1860s: imagine the brave mountain explorers who hunted for a suitable pass, colorful gold miners (and the Christchurch merchants who wanted their gold), wild and crazy stagecoach drivers, highly skilled road engineers, and 1,000 courageous men who blasted their way through Otira Gorge in the winter of 1865, with picks, shovels, road drills, and bare hands, to bring the road into reality. Poor food and little shelter forced many to quit, and some even died before the road was completed. The men who went on to build the railroad through Arthur's Pass suffered similar hardships.

In 1864, Arthur Dobson became the first European explorer-surveyor to cross the pass—Kaiapohia Maori used this route (one of several) when they traveled to Westland for *pounamu* (or greenstone). Though at first engineers considered it far too difficult to build a road through, it became known as Arthur's Pass when no better pass was found. The gold rush on the west coast was the original reason for building the road. Would-be prospectors demanded a route from Christchurch to the gold diggings that they could

travel without the distinct possibility of perishing, and Christchurch merchants particularly wanted a route so that successful gold miners would travel back over the mountains to spend their new-found wealth on the east coast. Ironically, the gold never made it back to Christchurch, even after the road was built. It cost too much to carry belongings over the pass, and the gold quickly fizzled out. The following year, however, Arthur's Pass Rd. entered an exciting stagecoach era. In 1866 the first Cobb & Co. stagecoach carrying passengers made the treacherous 170-mile, 36-hour journey over Arthur's Pass (before this crossing, mail had been carried over the pass by coach, pack horse, foot, and boat to Hokitika, taking about 4.5 days). From then on, crossing the pass by stagecoach and overcoming its many dangers became the "in" thing for the wealthy and adventurous men and women "globetrotters" of the times.

Railroad History

At the same time, engineers accomplished some amazing feats as the railroad inched its way from both the east and the west toward the historic underground **Otira Tunnel.** Through the use of air drills and explosives, the railway builders finally joined the two ends of the railroad in the 81.5-km tunnel in 1918, and the first train thundered through in 1923. Stagecoach travel quickly lost its popularity with the completion of the railroad. You can still see the original Cobb & Co. Seddon Coach that ran between Arthur's Pass and the Otira railheads in the 1890s until the tunnel opened; it's on display in the visitor center in the town of Arthur's Pass. While you're there, ask to view the outstanding audiovisual on the history of the road—it brings the rest of your journey across the pass to life. Nowadays the road has regained its popularity as a major coast-to-coast route and as a spectacular access road to the mountain delights of Arthur's Pass National Park.

THE LAND

Straddling the Southern Alps in the center of the South Island, 100,000-hectare Arthur's Pass National Park is the fourth-largest national park in the country, noted for its sharp scenic contrasts and alpine flora. It's a paradise for avid alpine explorers, climbers, skiers, hikers, and naturalists, luring them toward its rugged snow-capped mountain peaks (many over 2,000 meters high) and glaciers, its steep ridges and deep gorges, sheer black cliffs and silver ribbon waterfalls, dense beech forest, bush-covered hills full of birds, flower-filled valleys, and rushing rivers with their wide beds of gravel. Situated at the southern end of the major earthquake zone, Arthur's Pass National Park ranges in altitude from 245 meters in the Taramakau River Valley to the highest peak, Mt. Murchison, at 2,400 meters. At first uplifted by enormous pressures within the earth, the mountainous landscape has obviously been glacially carved, deeply eroded by rivers carrying enormous loads of gravel and shingle, and weathered by an often harsh and unsettled alpine climate.

First impressions can be misleading as you cruise through the low valley floors craning your neck upward. From the highway the "mountains" appear to be steep forest-covered hills with snow-capped peaks behind them, but a full half of the park landscape consists of towering mountains—17 named peaks over 2,000 meters high. The forces that continuously mold the landscape are visible and awesome—mighty rivers in flood tossing huge boulders as though they were pebbles, earthquake-triggered rock falls and landslides careening down cliff faces, and with the heavy snowfalls of winter, avalanches crashing down the mountainsides to line the valleys below. But discovering the park backcountry is safe if you have a good map and keep on the tracks, follow basic safety rules, and have enough food and warm clothing to suit all kinds of weather. One of the park's best features is the easy accessibility from Hwy. 73 to scenic lookouts, short walking trails, longer hiking tracks, and a multitude of spectacular sights for the more energetic. You can enjoy the scenery from car, bus, or train, or on foot from deep within the wilderness—but before you venture out to off-the-road attractions, pick up a detailed map and track brochures, a weather forecast, and general information from the field center in Arthur's Pass township.

Climate

Wet and windy weather generally hits the park from the northwest, dumping the highest amounts of rainfall on the western side of the pass. Though the park is known for long periods of wet and unsettled weather, the rain tends to come in several heavy bursts rather than a continuous miserable drizzle, and you can hit extended periods of beautiful weather if you're lucky. The Otira area has the highest rainfall (about 4,500 mm per year), but it's quickly followed by the central area around Arthur's Pass at 4,000 mm (rain from dense low clouds descends on the pass approximately 160 days per year), Cass on the east side of the Waimakariri River at 1,300 mm, and the Craigieburn Range to the southeast at 1,000 mm. The weather comes in unpredictable cycles. The northwesterlies bring the bad weather, often heralded by cirrus clouds (due to strong winds high in the sky), hog's-back clouds (expect rain in a day or so), or a halo around the sun (ice particles in the air). These are eventually replaced by southerlies that bring periods of fine weather until the next northwesterlies arrive. In winter the park turns into a white, pristine wonderland, with bitterly cold winds from the west and heavy frosts in the shady valleys until October and November, when the snow starts to melt off (the ski season is generally June–September). Around the town of Arthur's Pass the snow doesn't stick to the ground for long.

Flora and Fauna

The flora here is particularly interesting to naturalists: the range in altitude and difference in rainfall from the wetter west to the drier east is apparent in the large diversity of plantlife. On the western flood plains, you'll find podocarp forests of *matai, miro, rimu, kahikatea,* and *kamahi,* clothed in tree ferns and clematis, mosses, and fungi. As you climb higher, *rata* and mountain *totara* become more abundant. Every couple of years in midsummer, the slopes of Otira Gorge are totally covered in the scarlet flowers of the *rata*—a beautiful sight. Beech trees, some covered in parasitic mistletoe, make up the eastern forests, and wild orchids grow on the forest floor. The river gravel beds of the eastern side are home to mat daisies and a variety of ferns, mingling with the prickly shrub *matagouri* in the valley grasslands. The timberline ends abruptly, giving way to subalpine scrub. Up in the rocky alpine areas grows the beautiful white and yellow edelweiss, in the herb fields the anisotomes, alpine daisies, violets, gentians, snowberries, mosses and lichens, and in the alpine bogs, fascinating insect-eating sundews. The subalpine and alpine flowers are best appreciated in their summertime bloom between mid-November and late February.

You'll see and hear many kinds of birds throughout the park. In the river beds and valley flats you'll often see pairs of striking black and white-headed paradise ducks, and banded dotterels, pipits, oyster-catchers, black-fronted terns, and Canada geese. The *tui, morepork* (owl), shining cuckoo, yellowhead, and parakeet dwell in the bush, though you're more likely to see the first two on the western side of the park than the east. The cheeky *kea* lives in the upper forests and high in the mountaintops in summer, and the rock wren also appears in the higher altitudes. You can see even the nocturnal great spotted kiwi in the bush if you have a keen eye and ear and don't mind hunting for it in the middle of the night. The park is also home to extra-large dragonflies and grasshoppers, lots of moths and a few butterflies, and unfortunately, pesky sand flies (go armed with insect repellent). Brush-tail opossums and small numbers of red deer and chamois (all considered pests) live in the park; however, hunting (encouraged but you must have a permit from the Field Centre) has kept their numbers at low levels.

HIKING

Short Walks

Most of the well-marked short trails cover a wide range of scenery, flora, and fauna, and are classified as half-day walks (one to four hours round-trip), or full-day walks (five to eight hours round-trip). For any of the nature walks, pick up the appropriate booklets at the visitor center for lots of interesting information on the flora, fauna, and trails in general, and collect a "Walks in Arthur's Pass National Park" brochure ($1),

which has a brief map showing all the short walks. Remember, the weather can change rapidly in this alpine area—be prepared. Also note that car break-ins are common in parking lots. Keep valuables with you or locked out of sight.

Arthur's Pass Village Historic Walk takes just over one hour, and informative plaques along the trail provide a good introduction to the significance of linking the east and west coasts by road and rail.

One of the most spectacular sights in the park, worth seeing under any weather conditions at any time of year, lies at the end of the short **Devils Punchbowl** trail. The track starts on the east side of Hwy. 73, a half-km north of the visitor center, and takes you 1.5 km (30 minutes) one way to Devils Punchbowl waterfall. These impressive falls plummet down a narrow gorge into a large rock basin more than 100 meters below (avoid clambering on the rocks around the falls). Starting from the same parking lot is a two-km (40 minutes) one-way track to the **Bridal Veil.** It takes you through beech forest to the Bridal Veil Lookout for views of Arthur's Pass village and the Bealey Valley. **Dobson Nature Walk** is a great track to take if you enjoy subalpine and alpine flowers. It starts on Hwy. 73 opposite the Dobson Memorial and takes about 30 minutes for the short loop track, or about 90 minutes for the longer track, which finishes at the Otira Valley car park. **Cockayne Nature Walk** follows Kelly's Creek and takes you through a diverse area of typical west coast plants and flowers. It starts on Hwy. 73 at Kelly's Creek, north of Otira. Another recommended short walk takes you along the Bealey River Valley for an hour or so until you reach a gorge, where avalanche debris thunders down from Mt. Rolleston in the winter—don't go beyond this point unless you're an experienced hiker, and keep in mind that snow avalanches can hit the valley in winter and spring. The track starts on Hwy. 73 opposite Jacks Hut, three km north of the village.

Day Hikes

The easiest way to get into the subalpine environment is on the trail used by skiers to access the ski field in **Temple Basin.** It wanders up the bluffs through subalpine scrub to the alpine grasslands of Temple Basin (the popular ski field is open from June–Sept.) for spectacular views of Mt. Rolleston, Mt. Philistine, Mt. Barron, Phipps Peak, and many other snowcapped beauties; allow one hour each way, plus additional time to explore the bluffs and ridges above the ski lifts. To get to the start of the track, take Hwy. 73 north from Arthur's Pass town for four km to the car park at Upper Twin Creek. Another good track from which to appreciate distinctly different vegetation zones is the **Carroll Hut** track. The climb is fairly heavy going uphill through *rata* and *kamahi* forest and subalpine scrub, onto tussock grasslands that surround the hut, but it's worth the effort. Again allow a full day. The track starts at Kelly's Creek, north of Otira (by Cockayne Nature Walk). Several other full-day walks take you to the top of **Avalanche Peak** and **Mt. Aicken,** up **Mt. Bealey,** and up Mounts **Cassidy** and **Blimit** via the steep and rocky **Cons Track.** Another enjoyable day track takes you over old moraine to the scree-filled head of the **Otira Valley.** For detailed information on these longer walks, call in at the visitor center in Arthur's Pass township. If you leave a vehicle in parking lots at the trailheads, keep valuables with you or locked out of sight.

Backcountry Hikes

Arthur's Pass National Park is a popular mid-South Island area for serious hikers, providing many backcountry tracks with a great variety of scenery to appreciate along the way to the next hut. Eleven major tramping routes are described in a set of guide notes available at the visitor center. Before setting off on any of the backcountry hikes, leave details of your proposed route and expected time of return with someone or on intention cards at the visitor center—cancel the cards at the end of your trip. Huts have been strategically placed along the major hiking tracks throughout the park, and the Carrington, Casey, Goat Pass, Hawdon, and Locke Stream huts have radio contact with Park HQ. They provide bunks and heat—you provide everything else. Take your own stove (stove rental available at the visitor center) and fuel for cooking. A list of the huts and their facilities is given in the *Park Handbook* along with a brief outline of basic backcountry safety procedures. No bookings are accepted; it's first-come, first-served. You must pay hut fees in advance—buy hut tickets and collect maps and route guides at the visitor center before you set off into the backcountry. Each hut also has a visitor's book, in which for your safety it's advisable to enter your name, intended route, and dates of arrival and departure.

OTHER RECREATION
Climbing

The park offers a full range of climbs from easy to challenging on rock, snow, and ice. The most popular climbing areas are the peaks along Hwy. 73, the headwaters of the Waimakariri River (many incline routes on the western flanks of Mt. Rolleston), and the headwaters of the Mingha, Deception, and White Rivers. Although much of the rock is rotten, you'll find solid slabs at The Temple and Speight buttresses. Many experienced climbers come to the park specifically in winter, when some of the climbs become just as exciting and potentially dangerous as those in the Aoraki Mt. Cook region farther south. Climbs up the Otira face of Mt. Rolleston or the Crow Face are dangerous in sudden storms, so many snow or ice climbs are restricted. Potential hazards to climbers (and park users in general) include stonefalls, snow avalanches, unexpected bad weather, and flooded rivers. Get more climbing information at the visitor center; for possible climbing partners and more specialized information, contact the Canterbury Mountaineering Club or the Canterbury Westland section of the N.Z. Alpine Club (ask at the visitor center for contacts).

Skiing and Snowboarding

Most day-trippers from Christchurch head for Porter Heights or Craigieburn Valley, but **Temple Basin,** tel. 03/377-7788, the park's own ski field, also provides skiers and boarders with downhill thrills—that is, those willing to hike up to the ski field itself. Add to the views some excellent downhill slopes (a narrow and steep main run between Mt. Temple and Mt. Cassidy and nurs-

CRAIGIEBURN VALLEY SKI AREA

Alpine regions around the world have their hidden gems, resorts that are talked about in excited tones by expert skiers and boarders alike, places such as Mad River Glen in Vermont, and Red Mountain in western Canada. New Zealand's equivalent is Craigieburn Valley Ski Area, around 100 km west of Christchurch. This private club field with three rope tows has no snowmaking, no grooming, no ski rentals, and no fancy base lodge. In fact it doesn't have much of anything. What it does have is the unchallenged reputation as the country's steepest alpine resort. There are no Beginner or Intermediate runs whatsoever, instead, trail classifications include "Tricky" and "Suicidal," while trail names alone—such as "Plake's Mistake" and "Nun's Rabbit Warren"—are enough to make any self-respecting skier's heart pound. The vertical rise is 560 meters, with 100 hectares of marked terrain spread over two basins. Lift tickets are $38. Dorm accommodation at the on-hill lodge is $45 pp, which includes breakfast and dinner.

Craigieburn Valley is reached by continuing along Hwy. 73 five km beyond the Porter Heights access road, then following an unsealed road for six km to a small parking lot, from where it's a short walk to the base area. For more information or to book accommodation call 03/365-2514.

ery slopes on Mt. Cassidy), three rope tows (highest goes up to 1,800 meters on Temple Col), 320 hectares of patrolled terrain, and a season generally running June–September. To get to the ski field, leave your vehicle at the Temple Basin parking lot, eight km west of the village, then walk the well-graded but steep track (an hour or so depending on track conditions and your level of fitness) the rest of the way—sturdy footwear is essential. During the ski season you can get your equipment and pack carried from the main road up to the basin by Goods Lift. On-hill rentals are available. Tickets are $34 adult, $25 child. Most skiers stay at least one night, in basic bunkroom accommodation that costs $39 pp inclusive of breakfast and dinner.

ACCOMMODATIONS AND FOOD

In summer, finding a bed in the park can be difficult, so book all accommodations as far in advance as possible.

Hotels and Motels

On the main highway through the village, you'll find the **Alpine Motel,** tel. 03/318-9233, which provides seven units with kitchen, private bath, and TV for $75–85 s or d. Also in the heart of the village, **The Chalet,** Hwy. 73, tel. 03/318-9236 or 0800/506-550, website: www.arthurspass.co.nz, offers 10 appealing, comfortable rooms with private facilities and TV for $115 s or d, including continental breakfast.

Backpacker Lodges

Arthur's Pass Alpine YHA, on Hwy. 73 in the center of Arthur's Pass village, tel. 03/318-9230, website: www.yha.org.nz, can accommodate 39 people in two dorms and three double rooms, but during the summer, particularly January, the hostel fills up quickly. Along with the usual communal facilities are a large day room/living area (left open in bad weather) and a relaxed atmosphere; $18–21 pp. Across the road is **Mountain House,** tel. 03/318-9258; website: www.trampers.co.nz. This popular backpacker lodge features friendly owners, a congenial atmosphere, a laundry, barbecue, and a ton of information on local outdoor attractions; rates from $16 pp.

Camping

There are no special camping facilities, but camping at the public day shelter in Arthur's Pass village is $3 per night. Camping is also permitted south of the village at **Klondyke Corner, Hawdon River,** and **Andrews Stream** areas, and north at **Kelly's Creek.** All are signposted along the main highway and have day shelters, toilets, and fresh water, and you can picnic or put up a tent for free in any of these spots. Please note: Car break-ins are common around the camping areas and parking lots. Keep valuables with you or locked out of sight. Hikers will find park huts along the major tracks.

Food

It's best to stock up on supplies in Christchurch or Greymouth, find a place with a kitchen, and whip up your own culinary delights. If you're not in a whipping mood, however, try the **Store and Tearooms** in Arthur's Pass village (good selection of home-baked pies and sandwiches), open daily, or the more expensive licensed **Chalet Restaurant** at the north end of the village, tel. 03/318-9236, serving morning and afternoon teas, lunch 11:30 A.M.–2 P.M. ($14–17), and dinner 6–7:45 P.M. (from $19; bookings advisable). The dinner menu features lamb, salmon, and venison.

TRANSPORTATION

Access to Arthur's Pass National Park is easy by road or train. Highway 73 runs right through the park, giving good access to the mountains.

Train

Tranz Scenic, tel. 0800/802-802, operates the **TranzAlpine** train between Christchurch and Greymouth via Arthur's Pass (see spectacular scenery not accessible by road). After crossing the Canterbury Plains, the train begins to climb, then enters the spectacular Waimakariri Gorge. After passing through a series of tunnels, it stops at Arthur's Pass Village (the center of town is only a short stroll through the subway and right along the main highway from the station), and at Otira (west of Arthur's Pass village). Tranz Scenic offers a variety of one-day and overnight packages from $119–139. The regular fare is $62 one way from Christchurch. The train departs Christchurch daily at 9:15 A.M., and two hours later you're in Arthur's Pass—with five hours to spend before the return train. It is also possible to travel from coast to coast and return in one day.

Bus

The **Coast to Coast Shuttle,** tel. 0800/800-847, operates between Christchurch and Greymouth, stopping at Arthur's Pass along the way. Buses leave Cathedral Square, Christchurch, daily at 8 A.M.

INFORMATION

The main source of park information is the **Department of Conservation Visitor Centre,** tel. 03/318-9211, in Arthur's Pass village on the main highway—an essential first stop before any further exploration. The highlight here is a large room crammed with fascinating displays on the geology, flora, fauna, history, climate, and legends of the park. Read about the discovery of gold in Westland, the resulting construction of the road and railway over Arthur's Pass, and the colorful coaching era. See the original Seddon Coach on display and ask to see the vivid audiovisual about building the road. Don't miss the extraordinarily beautiful panels by John Herbison along the walls of the display room.

Detailed maps of the park are available for $11, and you can pick up pamphlets describing park activities. The center is open daily 8 A.M.–5 P.M., and the amiable staff is one of the most helpful around. During vacation periods, members of the staff offer guided walks in the park and illustrated talks in the lecture hall.

Christchurch to Aoraki Mt. Cook National Park

METHVEN

The alpine resort town of Methven (population 1,000) lies southwest of Christchurch inland from Hwy. 1 across the Canterbury Plains on Hwy. 77 and directly south of Arthur's Pass National Park. As the gateway to one of the South Island's premier ski fields, Methven is busiest in winter, but there's plenty to do year-round. Most summer recreation takes place in the **Mt. Hutt Forest,** west of town, which is laced with hiking trails. Other local activities include jetboating through the Rakaia Gorge, golfing, hot air ballooning, and mountain biking.

Mt. Hutt

The elevation of Mt. Hutt ski field (1,680 meters) is not particularly high, but with modern lifts, views across the Canterbury Plains, and a six-month-long season (longest in the Southern Hemisphere), it's the most popular resort within the vicinity of Christchurch. The resort has a vertical drop of 672 meters and is served by nine lifts, including one quad chair and one triple chair. Snowmaking covers 42 hectares and the longest run is an impressive two km. Lift tickets are $58 per day; lift and lesson packages cost about the same and rentals are from $30 per day. For more information on the resort, call 03/308-5074.

Practicalities

Many local accommodations are only open in winter; the following two are year-round operations. **Brinkley Village Resort,** a few hundred meters north of the main downtown intersection, tel. 03/302-8885 or 0800/161-223, website: www.brinkleyvillage.co.nz, is Methven's premier accommodation. Appealing mostly to the winter crowd, it features 40 modern, self-contained units, as well as a restaurant, bar, hot tub, tennis court, barbecue area, and playground. Studio units are $90 s or d ($125 in winter), one-bedroom units are $120 ($155 in winter), and two-bedroom units with a spa bath are $155

($185 in winter). The resort restaurant has a large outdoor dining area and a reputation for the best food in town. Budget travelers are drawn to **Skiwi House,** 30 Chapman St., tel. 03/302-8772, website: www.skiwihouse.com, for its congenial atmosphere and central location. Dorm beds are $17 pp, double and twin rooms $99 pp.

For maps of the local forest and to book activities, stop at **Methven Visitor Centre,** Main St., tel. 03/302-8955. It's open year-round, daily 9 A.M.–5 P.M.

CHRISTCHURCH TOWARD TIMARU

South of Christchurch, Hwy. 1, the main coastal route, passes through the agricultural plains of South Canterbury and North Otago, linking the two largest South Island cities, Christchurch and Dunedin. Although most drivers complete the 360-km route in less than five hours, Aoraki Mount Cook National Park, to the west, is an inviting detour.

Ashburton

This town, 87 km south of Christchurch and 77 km northeast of Timaru, is a good place to stop, stretch your legs, and grab a bite to eat. Along with the beautiful trees, gardens, and lake of **Ashburton Domain** (on the other side of the railway, off West St. between Willis St. and Walnut Ave.), trees and impeccable gardens are all over the city. The locals take particular pride in their "green" downtown square (Baring Square) with its ornamental tree garden, flower display, and refurbished **town clock** in a specially designed tower. A great number of the historic buildings and churches are made of brick—Ashburton once had a thriving ceramics industry. **Ashburton Visitor Centre** is in the old railway station on the corner of East St. (the main street) and Burnett St., tel. 03/308-1064; it's open Mon.–Fri. 9 A.M.–4:30 P.M., Sat.–Sun. 10 A.M.–2 P.M. Friendly staff will fill you in on all the things to do in the city and farther afield, including several walkways easily accessible to the public and the best places to stay and eat.

Salmon and sea-run trout thrive in **Ashburton River** just south of the city, and many anglers make Ashburton their base while they fish the Rakaia River to the north and the Rangitata River to the south. If you like to hike, fish, and camp out, walk the 19-km **Ashburton Walkway,** which runs along the east side of Ashburton River to the rivermouth and beach at Hakatere. A free camping area with toilets (the river is the only source of water) is halfway along the walk-

way; prearrange a return ride (no public transportation at the coastal end) or be prepared to walk the same route back to town.

TIMARU

On the southern fringes of the Canterbury Plains, 77 km south of Ashburton, Timaru (population 27,000) is one of the country's busiest ports. Before and during the building of the port (beginning in 1877), ships were frequently wrecked as they tried to get close to shore to

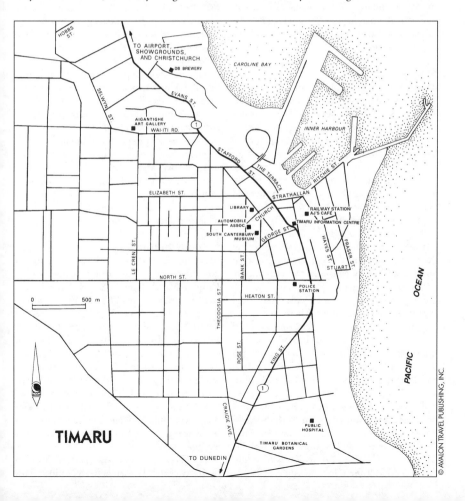

TIMARU

© AVALON TRAVEL PUBLISHING, INC.

transfer cargo through the surf by small boat. Timaru's many local industries include a tannery, brewery, and textiles and milling companies (many give free tours—get more details at the Timaru Visitor Information Centre); many "green spots" scattered throughout the city; and an interesting mixture of modern and traditional architecture (the Landing Service Building, built in 1870, is the oldest of its kind in the Southern Hemisphere). Timaru also produced the famous racehorse, Phar Lap, which won all the major races in Australia and the U.S. in the late 1920s and early '30s (a statue of Phar Lap stands in the paddock at Washdyke where he was born)—Timaru proclaims itself the "Home of Champions."

Sights

At the **port** at the south end of Caroline Bay you can watch the world's largest roll-on roll-off vessels loading and unloading, and an all-weather mechanical conveyor system. Apart from serving a thriving local fishing industry, the port is the largest bulk-storage handler in New Zealand. This is also where live sheep are exported to Saudi Arabia. If you have your own transportation, pick up a map from the information center and take the one-hour scenic drive starting from upper Sophia Street.

All kinds of local Maori artifacts and items relating to the settlement and development of the South Canterbury region are on display at **South Canterbury Museum** on Perth St., tel. 03/684-2212, along with photographs showing the step-by-step building of Timaru's artificial harbor, and information on Maori rock drawings in the district; it's open Tues.–Fri. 10 A.M.–4:30 P.M., Sat.–Sun. 1–4:30 P.M. The **Aigantighe Art Gallery** at 49 Wai-iti Rd., tel. 03/688-4424, has collections of New Zealand and British paintings, and English and continental china; it's open Tues.–Fri. 11 A.M.–4 P.M. and weekends noon–4 P.M.; admission by donation. **Pleasant Point Museum & Railway,** 15 km west of town, tel. 03/614-8323, is home to a restored steam train and the world's only working Model T Ford railcar. Admission is $5 adult, $2.50 child; call ahead for a schedule.

The large **DB Brewery** three km north of downtown on Sheffield St., tel. 03/688-2059, offers tours of the plant Mon.–Fri. at 10:30 A.M.

To absorb some outdoor culture, relax in the greenery around the art gallery and view all the stone sculptures, or head for Timaru's **Botanical Gardens** on the south side of the city (entrance on Queen St., off King St., the main route south), a lush area of bush and flower gardens interspersed with ponds, an aviary, fernery, greenhouses, and an Education Centre.

Recreation

Timaru's most popular attraction, **Caroline Bay,** is a sandy beach with safe swimming, an aviary, miniature golf, tennis courts, picnic spots, and a large expanse of grass along the seafront.

Timaru's most popular festival is the **Caroline Bay Christmas Carnival,** which starts on Boxing Day (day after Christmas) and lasts about two weeks during the peak vacation period. Talent, beauty, and other contests; side shows; and continuous evening entertainment keep the crowds happy, and they whoop it up with a fireworks display and enormous bonfire on New Year's Eve. The carnival attracts masses of people from all over New Zealand and the city quickly fills to its limits—if you plan on being there, book well ahead.

Accommodations

Many motels line Hwy. 1 (Evans St.) north of downtown. One of the least expensive is **Blue Dolphin Motel,** 40 Evans St., tel. 03/684-4589, with 11 smallish one- and two-bedroom self-contained units; rates $68–78 s or d. Adjacent to the park that lines the shore of Caroline Bay is **Baywatch Motor Lodge,** 7 Evans St., tel. 03/688-1886 or 0800/929-828. Rates for the modern rooms range $98–128 s or d. Across the road from the Baywatch, the **Benvenue Hotel,** 16-22 Evans St., tel. 03/688-4049 or 0800/104-049, features 30 brightly decorated units, an indoor swimming pool and spa, restaurant, and bar. Rates start at $110 s or d, $160 for a kitchen-equipped unit.

Both Timaru motor camps are a couple of km from city center. **Timaru Selwyn Holiday Park** on Selwyn St., tel. 03/684-7690 or 0800/242-121, two km north of the post office, has communal facilities, a canteen, TV room, and spa; tent sites set among trees are $18, caravan sites are $20. Lots of small attractive cabins (each with carefully tended flowering bushes outside) start at only $32 s or d, cottages with kitchens $46, tourist flats with private facilities $68. From the north end of town at Evans St. (the main road), turn right on Hobbs St., and then left on Selwyn Street. **Glenmark Motor Camp** on Beaconsfield Rd. at the south end of Timaru, tel. 03/684-3682, has the usual facilities, TV lounge, camp shop, and swimming pool. Tent sites are $16, caravan sites are $18, on-site caravans and cabins cost from $35 s or d, and fully self-contained tourist flats are $80 s or d.

Food

Plenty of cafés, tearooms, and take-aways dish out quick cheap meals and snacks, but for a substantial meal, head for a local pub, most of which serve cheap at-the-counter meals at lunchtime and reasonably priced dinners in the restaurants. One is the always-reliable **Hibernian Hotel** at 4 Latter St., tel. 03/688-8125. It's open Mon.–Thurs. 5 A.M.–9 P.M., till 10 P.M. on weekends; lunch averages $10, dinner $13–19, and there's a Sunday buffet lunch.

You'll find several Chinese restaurants along Stafford St. (along with many take-aways, open late). **Cheng's Chinese Restaurant** at 135 Stafford St., tel. 03/688-8888, next to the information center, offers reasonably priced meals created by experienced chefs from Hong Kong and China, in a tasteful, soothing, Chinese decor. Lunch specials are around $8. At dinner, choose from the à la carte menu (dishes average $16–22) or the eight-course set menu ($32 pp). It's open Mon.–Sat. 11:30 A.M.–1:30 P.M. and daily from 6 P.M. Other restaurants recommended by locals include **Ginger & Garlic,** 335 Stafford St., tel. 03/688-3981 (bay views, healthy menu), and the very popular **Casa Italia** in Timaru's historic Customs Building at 2 Strathallan St., tel. 03/684-5528 (authentic Italian at reasonable prices; open daily for lunch and dinner).

Transportation

Air New Zealand flies daily from Christchurch and Wellington directly to Timaru. **Timaru Taxis,** tel. 03/688-8899, provides a shuttle service from the airport, 10 km north of town, through the city for $10 pp. **Intercity** provides buses to Timaru from Dunedin, Christchurch, and Invercargill ($67 one way), while **Tranz Scenic,** 0800/802-802, offers daily train service between these same three cities. The booking office for both companies is **AJ's Cafe** in the railway station off George St., tel. 03/684-7195.

Car rental agencies in Timaru include **Avis,** tel. 03/688-6240; **Budget,** tel. 03/684-8760; and **Hertz,** tel. 03/684-5199. For a cab, call **Budget Taxis,** tel. 03/688-8779. The **Automobile Association** is on the corner of Church and Bank Streets, tel. 03/688-4189.

Services and Information

Timaru Hospital is at 14 Queen St., tel. 03/684-4000. For less urgent cases, head to the **Dee St. Medical Centre,** 4 Dee St., tel. 03/688-4340. **Central Pharmacy** is at 278 Stafford St., tel. 03/688-0106.

For a city map and general information, drop by **Timaru Visitor Information Centre** at 12 George St. (near the railway station), tel. 03/688-6163; it's open Mon.–Fri. 8:30 A.M.–5 P.M., and during summer every day 8:30 A.M.–5 P.M. An excellent staff is on hand to answer questions and give advice, and you can pick up brochures on local activities, accommodations, restaurants, and destinations farther afield. The website: www.southisland.org.nz has lots of local information.

ASHBURTON TO MACKENZIE COUNTRY

Fairlie

The first town along this route is Fairlie, with pleasant tree-lined streets and a small museum through town to the west. An excellent health food restaurant, the **Sunflower Centre,** tel. 03/685-8258, provides tasty vegetarian meals and snacks and sells homegrown vegetables, bulk health food supplies, and a variety of handicrafts.

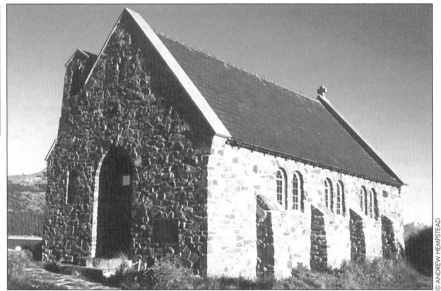

Church of the Good Shepherd, Lake Tekapo

© ANDREW HEMPSTEAD

To Burke Pass

West of Fairlie, Hwy. 8 is lined with bright purple, pink, yellow, coral, and cream-colored lupines. It's an amazing sight when they're all in bloom (January is usually one of the best months for this vivid display). Randall Froude, an internationally renowned artist, has a studio and gallery in **Kimbell,** the last village before Burke Pass. In the vicinity, 19 km from Fairlie, Keith and Margaret Walker operate **Dobson Lodge,** a two-story stone building with a cedar-shingled roof and views to Mt. Dobson. Rates are $60 s, $85–120 d, which includes a cooked breakfast; dinner by prior arrangement is an additional $25 pp.

MACKENZIE COUNTRY

This plateau of high country lies immediately east of the Southern Alps. Highway 8 passes through the heart of the region, passing Lake Tekapo and Twizel on its way to Otago.

Lake Tekapo

Beautiful Lake Tekapo is always a deep milky-blue from "rock flour," finely ground particles of glacial sediment from glaciers high in the Southern Alps. Highway 8 skirts the lake's southern edge, passing through the small lakeside village of Lake Tekapo (population 300), which lies halfway between Christchurch and Queenstown, making it a good overnight stop (and saving the high accommodation prices of Aoraki Mt. Cook National Park, if that's the way you're headed). Wander along the lakefront for views across the water and tussock-covered hills to the snowcapped Southern Alps. The lake is a lot larger than it looks, extending for 32 km to the north and reaching depths of over 120 meters. The simple **Church of the Good Shepherd,** a memorial to pioneer runholders of Mackenzie Country, stands on the lakeshore east of the outlet—the view from its east window is best in the early morning or late afternoon when the light is just right.

If you're interested in guided hiking or cross-country skiing, contact **Alpine Recreation Canterbury Ltd.,** based in town, tel. 03/680-6736. Nearby **Round Hill** ski area has six surface lifts serving over 800 hectares of treeless, gently rolling terrain with views extending down the valley to Lake Tekapo. Facilities include a terrain park, lots of snowmaking, rentals, a ski school, and a special kids' lift for tubing. Lift tickets are $40 adult, $14 child. The resort is seven km north of Lake Tekapo, tel. 03/680-6977.

The main commercial strip through town is lined with a variety of highway services. Separated from the lake by nothing more than tussock grass, **Goodley Resort Hotel,** on the main road, tel. 03/680-6848 or 0800/835-276, website: www.tekapo.co.nz, has a swimming pool, spa, laundry, and three restaurants. Budget rooms are $105 s, $150 d; standard rooms are $145 s, $190 d, and superior rooms range $160–205 s, $180–225; all rates include breakfast and dinner at any of the resort's three restaurants. The other large lakefront lodging is **Lake Tekapo Scenic Resort,** tel. 03/680-6808; website: www.laketekapo.com. Studio rooms are $130 s or d, kitchen equipped family suites are $160, and although the penthouse suite is a long way from luxurious, it does offer a large, modern space complete with a full kitchen and private entrance for $200. **Tekapo YHA,** billed as "the hostel with the million-dollar view," is right on the lakefront west of downtown, tel. 03/680-6857, website: www.yha.org.nz; rates $17–21 pp. In the same vicinity, consider **Lake Tekapo Motels and Motor Camp** along the edge of the lake, tel. 03/680-6825, with excellent showers (and a special baby bath), communal kitchen and dining area, and laundry. Tent and caravan sites with stunning lake-through-the-trees views are $9–10 pp, basic cabins are from $32 d, tourist flats are $58 d, and motel rooms are $80 d.

The **Garden Restaurant** in the Goodley Resort Hotel, tel. 03/680-6848, is the place for hungry diners, open daily from 6:30 A.M. for a buffet breakfast ($14 pp), lunch ($16), and dinner ($29). In the same hotel are a Japanese restaurant and a Chinese restaurant. At nearby **Reflections Restaurant,** in Lake Tekapo Scenic Resort, tel. 03/680-6808, the al a carte menu has wide appeal, ranging from light dishes, such as a salmon and spinach ricotta tartlet for $16, to a roast rack of lamb for $22.50. Bar meals are available in the resort's lounge, which enjoys magnificent views from both inside and out on the lake-facing deck.

Twizel

Beyond the southern end of Lake Pukaki, Twizel (population 1,200) is the gateway to Aoraki Mt. Cook National Park, 60 km to the north.

Originally built as construction housing for the Upper Waitaki Hydropower Development Scheme, Twizel has since grown into the second-largest town in the Mackenzie Basin. The scheme involves the Waitaki, Benmore, and Aviemore Dams; Lakes Tekapo, Pukaki, and Ohau (linked by canals to provide water for power stations); and Lakes Ruataniwha and Benmore (largest earth dam and man-made lake in the country). For detailed information on the hydropower scheme and all the local attractions, visit the **Twizel Information Centre** in the Market Place, tel. 03/435-3118; it's open in summer, daily 8:30 A.M.–6:30 P.M., weekends only 10 A.M.–3 P.M. the rest of the year. At the center you can also book for a DOC **Black Stilt Viewing Hide Tour.** Black stilts are one of the world's rarest wading birds (once widespread, they are now confined to

© ANDREW HEMPSTEAD

Fairlie Museum

the Mackenzie Basin) and this tour gives you the opportunity to view them from hides, built on ridges above the breeding aviaries; tours depart weekdays at 10:30 A.M. and cost $10 adult, $5 child. If you're continuing to Aoraki Mt. Cook National Park and doing your own cooking, Twizel is a good place to stock up on food—prices at the store and restaurants in isolated Aoraki Mt. Cook Village are higher.

Twizel to Wanaka

From Twizel, Hwy. 8 continues its torturous southward journey to Otago and the resort towns of Wanaka and Queenstown; allow three and four hours respectively for this trip.

Stop for the night about four km south of Twizel at enormous **Ruataniwha Holiday Park,** off the main highway along the shores of Lake Ruataniwha, tel. 03/435-0613; tent and caravan sites from $10 pp, cabins from $15 pp. The Canterbury Rowing Championships, held on **Lake Ruataniwha** in February each year, attract a large crowd; book ahead for the event.

Many winter travelers heading south along this route miss a great little alpine resort in the Ben Ohau Range, **Ohau Ski Area.** This small resort has an impressive vertical rise of 425 meters, with three surface lifts over 125 hectares. Lift tickets are $40 adult, $18 child. The base village has rentals, a ski school, and a restaurant. The access road branches off Hwy. 8 south of Twizel, winding through rolling hills and into the alpine over 30 km (the last 10 km are unsealed). At the beginning of the access road and operated by the same people who own the ski field, 75-room **Lake Ohau Lodge,** tel. 03/438-9885, website: www.ohau.co.nz, offers simple yet comfortable lakefront accommodations open year-round. Bunk beds are $18 pp ($50 with breakfast and dinner), while private rooms are $81 s, $92 d. In the new wing, rooms with a view on the upper floor are $105 s, $115 d.

Continuing south, the village of **Omarama** lies in the Waitaki Valley, where Hwy. 83 parallels the Waitaki River for just over 100 km to Oamaru, on the east coast. Highway 8, meanwhile, climbs the bleak tussock-covered hills of 971-meter **Lindis Pass** then descends to the Otago goldfields town of Cromwell and onto Queenstown.

Aoraki Mt. Cook National Park

This park, one of the South Island's major tourist attractions, preserves a spectacular alpine area of great beauty—well worth the 60-km trip off the beaten track by road (or air). With its snow-capped mountains, glaciers, river valleys, and incredibly fresh air, Aoraki Mt. Cook National Park is a popular playground for climbers, hikers, photographers, and skiers who catch ski-planes up to the tops of glaciers for unforgettable experiences in the Southern Alps.

THE LAND

The beautiful Maori word *Aoraki* (High Mountain to the West) is the name of the first-born son of Rakinui, the sky father, and now incorporated as part of the official name of both the mountain and the park. Towering above the surrounding snowcapped mountains and glaciers at 3,744 meters, majestic Aoraki Mt. Cook, when viewed from the south, rises in a perfect pyramid that's both impressive and easily recognized. The mountain was given the European portion of its name by Captain Stokes, who sailed down the West Coast in the survey ship *Acheron* in 1851 and named the mountain in honor of the great English navigator and explorer.

Aoraki Mt. Cook National Park, officially established in 1953 covering 70,013 hectares of the **Southern Alps,** is a long, narrow area of rugged snow-covered mountains and glaciers, 65 km long and only 20 km across at its widest point. Along the Main Divide on its west border lies Westland National Park, stretching from its tall mountain peaks and glaciers to the Tasman Sea. Within the park, the land ranges from river flats at 750 meters to 140 peaks over 2,100 me-

Aoraki Mt. Cook

ters high, including 22 peaks that soar to more than 3,050 meters. New Zealand's three tallest mountains, Aoraki Mt. Cook at 3,744 meters in the **Mount Cook Range,** Mt. Tasman at 3,498 meters, and Mt. Dampier at 3,440 meters in the Main Divide, all lie within a short distance of one another. Because of the high, rugged terrain, more than one-third of the entire park is covered in permanent snow and ice, and huge glaciers are a natural attraction. The gigantic **Tasman Glacier,** 27 km long and up to three km wide, is one of the world's largest glaciers outside the polar regions, and one of the easiest to see (definitely the most photographed)—view it from Hwy. 80 as you enter the park. You can see the other major glaciers, **Mueller, Hooker, Godley,** and **Murchison,** if you're willing to drive or cycle to viewing points or hike the various tracks within the park.

Mount Cook National Park is not completely made up of mountain peaks. Several large valleys occupied by glaciers and rivers separate the mountain ranges: the Godley Glacier, River, and tributaries in the northeast, and the Tasman Glacier, River, and tributaries in the southwest di-

vide the park into two main sections. The only road access is Hwy. 80, which runs up to Aoraki Mt. Cook Village in the southwest, and Ball Hut Rd., near the village up the west side of the Tasman Glacier as far as Husky Flat. The road is closed to vehicles beyond Husky Flat, but you can continue on foot for another 50–60 minutes to reach the old Ball Hut site. Short tracks give further access to many of the major natural attractions, and of course adventurous well-equipped mountaineers can discover it all.

Climate

The climate here is varied and unpredictable. In summer, the area can experience long hot periods of near-drought conditions with temperatures as high as 30°C; in July, sudden snowfalls of up to one meter can stick to the ground for as long as a month. In winter the air temperature can fall as low as minus 8°C during colder years, but in general, the dry cold and clear days make hiking around the village (snow can restrict hiking mid-June to mid-August) and skiing on the glaciers enjoyable experiences. Winter climbing is risky because of abundant snow and frequent avalanches. On the average, Aoraki Mt. Cook Village expects snow on the ground for about 21 days during winter; the average yearly rainfall is 4,081 mm, with up to 8,000 mm of rain and snow falling in higher altitudes.

If you're climbing or hiking in the park, keep an eye out for cirrus clouds racing across the sky, followed by rapid cloud build-up—early warning signs of heavy rain, often accompanied by strong winds from the northwest (which can rapidly rise to gale force) and snow at low levels. Be more than adequately prepared for severe weather with warm, waterproof clothing whenever you're out in the wilderness, and get a weather forecast before you set off.

Flora

Renowned for its variety in alpine flowers, this area literally springs to life in summer (mid-November to the end of February), when flowering plants put on their best show. Most of the alpine flowers are white, blending in with the snow and ice of their harsh environment—

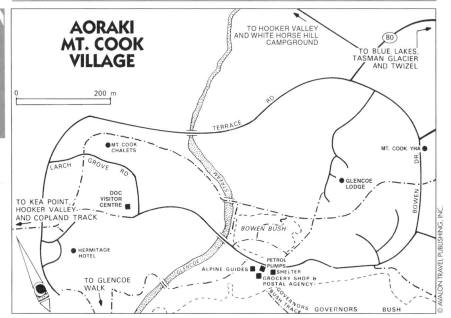

AORAKI MT. COOK VILLAGE

TO HOOKER VALLEY AND WHITE HORSE HILL CAMPGROUND

80

TO BLUE LAKES, TASMAN GLACIER AND TWIZEL

0   200 m

TERRACE RD.

MT. COOK CHALETS

MT. COOK YHA

LARCH

GROVE RD.

STREAM

GLENCOE LODGE

TO KEA POINT, HOOKER VALLEY AND COPLAND TRACK

DOC VISITOR CENTRE

BOWEN DR.

BOWEN BUSH

HERMITAGE HOTEL

GLENCOE

PETROL PUMPS

ALPINE GUIDES

SHELTER

GROCERY SHOP & POSTAL AGENCY

TO GLENCOE WALK

GOVERNORS BUSH TRACK

GOVERNORS   BUSH

© AVALON TRAVEL PUBLISHING, INC.

the most striking is the **Mount Cook lily,** largest ranunculus in the world. It has pure white petals, a yellow center, and shiny saucer-shaped leaves, and although it's called a lily, it's actually an oversized buttercup. In December the mountain daisies put on a terrific display in the alpine scrub and grasslands—58 species are endemic. More than 300 species of native plants have been identified within the park boundaries, from tiny ferns, herbs, mosses, and grasses to shrubs and trees; many grow within a short distance of the village. Only a small area of what was once a large silver beech forest remains at **Governor's Bush** behind Aoraki Mt. Cook Village—in this grove you can also see mountain *totara,* mountain three-finger, broadleaf, and the occasional lancewood; a booklet identifying the trees and plants is available at the visitor center.

Fauna

Birds are everywhere, about 40 species all told: riverbed birds such as black-backed gulls, pied oystercatchers, paradise ducks, and banded dot-terels; bush birds such as native pigeons, tomtits, fantails, riflemen, grey warblers, and *morepork;* and alpine birds such as New Zealand falcons (rare), rock wrens (also rare), pipits, and *kea* or alpine parrots (cheekiest and most familiar). Dull green in color with scarlet underwings and a black heavy-duty beak, the *kea* has a reputation for unlacing boots, tearing holes in bicycle seats, and sliding down tin roofs just for fun—hold onto your food when they're hanging around. Don't feed the *kea*—this encourages their menacing antics, in turn causing many problems for park staff and local residents. If you enjoy identifying birds, ask at the reception desk in the visitor center for a copy of the bird checklist. Also within the park you can find large dragonflies, grasshoppers, a variety of moths and butterflies, alpine *weta* (locally called the Mt. Cook flea), and pesky sand flies, along with chamois and Himalayan tahr—liberated near Aoraki Mt. Cook in the early 1900s, tahr have been drastically reduced in number by control operations and trophy hunters; now only a small number of the wild goats are left.

RECREATION

Short Walks

Though the park has many short walks around the village and along the surrounding valleys to excellent viewpoints and other scenic attractions, it does not provide much in the way of major hiking tracks. Because of the rugged alpine terrain, the park is much more satisfying for serious climbers and experienced mountaineers than for hikers. However, the "short walks" are the only way to grasp a little of the park's natural beauty, varying from a 10-minute bush walk by the village to a 4.5-hour one-way hike through the Hooker Valley for magnificent views of Aoraki Mt. Cook and the Hooker Glacier. Pick up the handy *Walks in Aoraki Mt. Cook National Park* brochure ($1) at the visitor center; it contains a map of the village and brief descriptions and approximate times of each walk. Many of the walks also have individual brochures, which aid in identifying native plants and items of natural history along each route.

If you have your own transportation, head out of Aoraki Mt. Cook Village onto Hwy. 80 and turn left on Ball Hut Rd. (the second road to the left after leaving the village, signposted Tasman Valley Road). This long gravel road (rental cars are not insured for this road!) takes you along the western banks of the mighty Tasman River, passing beech forest, Wakefield Falls, walking tracks, and picnic spots, and continues beside the Tasman Glacier to Husky Flat. At the car park and sign to **Blue Lakes** lookout (about halfway to Husky Flat), take the short, easy walking track to the right. After 15 minutes the uphill track gives you good views of the four colorful Blue Lakes (you can also take a track directly to the lakes—the fourth is particularly popular for swimming and sunbathing in summer). Glacier View Track branches off Blue Lakes Track and continues to the top of the moraine wall for tremendous views of the entire terminal area of the Tasman Glacier, Aoraki Mt. Cook, and Mt. Tasman—it's well worth the short walk; don't forget your camera!

Copland Valley Track

The Copland Valley Track is the most popular alpine hiking route in the Aoraki Mt. Cook area. It involves crossing rugged terrain and a true alpine pass at 2,148 meters exposed to sudden changes in weather and snow conditions; high winds, rain or snow, and poor visibility are common. The track starts at Hooker Hut at the end of the four-to five-hour Hooker Valley Track from Aoraki Mt. Cook Village, crosses the pass (marked only by cairns), then descends through Westland National Park to end on Hwy. 6, 26 km south of Fox Glacier township. Three huts lie along the route: Hooker Hut in this park, and Douglas Rock and Welcome Flat Huts in Westland National Park.

© ANDREW HEMPSTEAD

Kea are found throughout the park.

Pay at the park visitor center or at one of the Westland visitor centers. Only experienced mountaineers with the necessary alpine equipment (ice axes, crampons, rope) or those willing to hire a guide should attempt the pass. **Alpine Guides,** tel. 03/435-1834, based in Aoraki Mt. Cook Village, has most of the necessary equipment for rent at $75 pp per trip (provide your own rope, warm clothes, sleeping bag, and extra food); it also supplies experienced guides for the crossing (basic technical equipment included) at $500 for one person, $700 for two people, and $900 for three people. The office and shop are open daily 8 A.M.–5 P.M., in summer 8 A.M.–8 P.M.

Mountaineering

The first European attempt to climb Aoraki Mt. Cook was in 1882, but it wasn't until 1894 that Clark, Fyfe, and Graham finally conquered the summit. This alpine region is considered one of the best mountaineering areas in the world, offering all levels of climbing possibilities among tall peaks of varying difficulty. High-altitude huts equipped with radios, stoves, cooking and eating utensils, and some blankets lie scattered throughout the park—get more information and pay overnight fees at the visitor center, and before attempting any climb, be sure to first notify park personnel and sign out on leaving the area. **Alpine Guides,** tel. 03/435-1834, provides guided mountaineering services in summer, private instruction, and a School of Mountaineering, and it also hires out most of the mountain-climbing equipment you'd need. If you'd like to read up on the climbing routes in the area, get your hands on the latest edition of *The Mount Cook Guidebook* by Hugh Logan.

Skiing and Snowboarding

The usual season for winter recreation runs from July to early November, depending on conditions. Skiing and boarding in the park is for many a unique experience, but it's also guaranteed to blow your budget unless you've made specific allowances. No commercial ski fields or lifts lie within the park, so you traverse ungroomed, untracked snow between towering peaks on glaciers; ski-planes are the only form of transportation.

The most popular runs are down the long gentle slopes of the Tasman Glacier. The runs are 10-12 km long, "longest runs in the Southern Hemisphere," taking one to two hours each—surrounded by some of the most spectacular scenery imaginable, intermediate and advanced skiers are in for an exhilarating experience. Guides from Alpine Guides patrol the runs. The Tasman hut, standing on a rock outcrop at the head of the glacier, is used as a base for touring and climbing activities in the immediate area.

Advanced skiers can find challenging areas on the Tasman Glacier with a guide, but occasionally prefer the more difficult runs down the Murchison and Mannering Glaciers. The Department of Conservation Visitor Centre is a source of skiing information and up-to-the-minute weather forecasts.

Cross-country skiers mostly head for the Hooker and Tasman river flats when there's enough snow; rent your equipment from Alpine Guides. Lake Tekapo, northeast of Aoraki Mt. Cook Village, is another very popular area for cross-country skiing—for more information contact **Alpine Recreation Canterbury,** Lake Tekapo, tel. 03/680-6736.

If the cost of transportation up to the glaciers is out of your budget, the nearest commercial ski field with a T-bar and platter lift is Ohau Ski field, southwest of Twizel, a 106-km drive from Aoraki Mt. Cook Village.

Flightseeing

All kinds of flightseeing experiences are available by fixed-wing plane or helicopter within the park—most similar to those at Franz Josef and Fox on the west coast, and just as expensive. However, it's the only way to really see this area, so splurge if you haven't already! **Air Safaris,** tel. 03/680-6880 or 0800/806-651, features "The Grand Traverse" from Glentanner Park Centre, a 50-minute flight that takes in Aoraki Mt. Cook, crosses the divide to the famous glaciers and rainforest of the west coast before returning via the Canterbury Plains; $230 pp. **The Helicopter Line,** tel. 03/435-1801 or 0800/650-651, has flights that vary from a 20-minute Alpine Vista for $175 pp to a 45-minute circumnavigation of Aoraki Mt. Cook, the major peaks, and a snow landing for $375 pp, departing from the heli-pad at Glentanner Park, along the access road to the village. The activities desk in the foyer of The Hermitage Hotel in Aoraki Mt. Cook Village makes reservations for many of the flightseeing tours and has all the latest brochures and current prices; call 03/435-1809 and ask for the activities desk.

Tours

The most interesting tour is a bus trip along the rough road to the toe of the Tasman Glacier, with a commentary given along the way and the option of a short walk up on the actual glacier. The tour takes two hours and costs $30 pp. Book through The Hermitage, tel. 03/435-1809. **Glentanner Park Centre,** 22 km south of Aoraki Mt. Cook Village, tel. 03/435-1855, has all kinds of fun tours available: **farm tours** of Glentanner Station (a high-country sheep station) for $25 pp (minimum four), one-hour **4WD excursions** through superb scenery for $40 pp (minimum four), **horseback riding** on Glentanner Station at $45 per hour or half-day treks for $145 pp, and guided **fishing safaris** for brown or rainbow trout or salmon (Oct.–April) at $220 for two hours. Transportation from Aoraki Mt. Cook Village to Glentanner is not included in these prices. Stop by Glentanner Park Centre, or drop by the activities desk in The Hermitage Hotel foyer, Aoraki Mt. Cook Village.

AORAKI MT. COOK VILLAGE

You can't get lost in Aoraki Mt. Cook Village, but the quickest way to orient yourself to your surroundings is to drive to the end of the road. Depending on which route you take, you'll either end up at The Hermitage Hotel, where you can fight your way through the bus tours and collect a free map and brochures from the activities desk in the main foyer, or you'll reach Aoraki Mt. Cook National Park Visitor Centre. The village (population 120) exists primarily to serve tourists; 250,000 visit annually.

Hotels and Motels

Within the village are three hotels/motels all owned and operated by the one company. The flagship property, the **Hermitage Hotel,** has a colorful history, having opened in 1884 and been destroyed twice-once by flooding and once by fire. It boasts one of the finest views of any accommodation in the country and recently underwent $15-million renovations, which included a new foyer aligned toward Mt. Cook, magnificently framed by floor-to-ceiling windows. Also within the hotel are a booking desk, a souvenir shop, an outfitter, two restaurants, a café, and a bar. Each of the 170 rooms is starkly elegant, taking nothing take away from the views. Older rooms are $300 s or d, while rooms in the newer Aoraki Wing range $360–420 s or d, depending on the view. Across from the main hotel complex is **Mt. Cook Chalets,** each with older furnishings, two small bedrooms, and a full kitchen. At $125–155 each they are good value for a small group. Formerly a Travelodge property, the summer-only **Glencoe Lodge** offers 57 standard motel rooms, each with tea- and coffee-making facilities, but no kitchens; $192 s or d. Make bookings for all of the above at 03/435-1809 or 0800/686-800; website: www.mount-cook.com.

Backpacker Lodge

The very popular **Mount Cook YHA,** on the corner of Bowen and Kitchener Drives close to the visitor center and all amenities, tel. 03/435-1820, website: www.yha.org.nz, is open year-round, has excellent facilities including sauna, a log fire, barbecue, facilities for the disabled, and well-stocked shop, and costs $22 pp in a dorm, $31 pp in a double room. From Nov.–May the staff puts on barbecues most nights. Book as far in advance as possible because there are only 72 beds and they fill fast.

Camping

The park-operated **White Horse Hill Campground** is in the Hooker Valley, 1.8 km from the village. It occupies the site of the first Hermitage Hotel, of cob (clay brick) construction, which was destroyed by fire in 1914. The campground and adjacent picnic area have running water and flush toilets in summer, a rainwater tank, pit toilets in winter (a coin-operated shower is available at the Public Shelter in the village), and plenty of space for tents on a grassy hillside; $5 pp per night (self-registration). Note that the campground is exposed to prevailing inclement weather conditions and the normally dry creekbed can become a raging torrent during a storm—if you leave your tent there during the day, be sure it's well staked and not close to the creek. To reach the campground, head out of the village on Hwy. 80 and take the first road to the left.

Glentanner Park Centre

This complex along the park access road, 22 km south of Aoraki Mt. Cook Village, is on a working sheep station overlooking Lake Pukaki, tel. 03/435-1855, website: www.glentanner.co.nz, where the weather (away from the mountains) can be surprisingly better. Along with communal facilities, barbecue, camp store (open 8 A.M.–6 P.M.), and restaurant, the staff arranges all kinds of sight-seeing and adventure tours. Tent sites are $9 pp, powered sites $10 pp, dorm beds $15 pp, basic cabins $50 s or d, and self-contained cabins $70 s or d. A $10 deposit is required to use the communal kitchen, with $5 refunded upon departure.

Food and Entertainment

By far the cheapest way to eat at Aoraki Mt. Cook Village is to cook your own food. The one **food store,** open daily 9 A.M.–5:30 P.M. (8 A.M.–8 P.M. in summer), sells groceries and basic supplies.

The **Coffee Shop,** in the Hermitage Hotel, is now on the upper floor, with a wide-open deck taking advantage of the surrounding mountain panorama. Open daily from 7 A.M., expect to pay $3 for a coffee and $8–12 for a light meal. The hotel's **Alpine Restaurant** is a cavernous, casual dining room; open daily from 6 A.M. Before 9 A.M., a tea/coffee and toast buffet is $9.50 or a continental breakfast buffet is $18. The lunchtime buffet, 11:30 A.M.–2 P.M., is $35 and from 6 P.M., the expansive dinner buffet costs $45. Views from the hotel's more upmarket **Panorama Restaurant,** open in summer only, daily from 6 P.M., are priceless. Dinner choices start at $23, while dishes such as pan-fried salmon

Views from the Hermitage Hotel's more upmarket Panorama Restaurant are priceless.

served on a bed of kumara and accompanied by stir-fried vegetables average $35. Make reservations at 03/435-1809.

Head to the **Chamois Bar** in the Glencoe Lodge to mix with the locals. The setting is rather plain, but dining here is inexpensive. A platter of appetizers is $14, or indulge in the Roast of the Day for $15. In the same lodge, the **Wakefield Restaurant** is a family-style eatery open daily through summer for breakfast (6:30–9:30 A.M.) and dinner (6–9 P.M.).

Transportation

Air New Zealand, tel. 03/435-1848, has direct daily flights to Aoraki Mt. Cook from Christchurch and Queenstown. To catch a bus from The Hermitage Hotel to Mt. Cook Airport, four km from the village, costs $6 each way unless you're going on a scenic flight when the fare is included.

The only road access into Aoraki Mt. Cook National Park is Hwy. 80, which dead-ends in Aoraki Mt. Cook Village. **Intercity** runs a day excursion from Christchurch to Aoraki Mt. Cook Village, as well as regular services from all points on the South Island. On all scheduled Intercity services that make the detour to the park, a one-hour "lunch" stop is made in front of the Hermitage Hotel.

Services and Information

Within Aoraki Mt. Cook Village you'll find a post office (open regular hours, weekdays), a shop selling groceries, supplies (open daily), and petrol, and the Alpine Guides office, tel. 03/435-1834, and store (rental and sales, information on climbing instruction, and guide services, open daily). You can exchange travelers checks at The Hermitage Hotel. You'll find phones at the post office and The Hermitage reception desk.

The **Department of Conservation Visitor Centre,** tel. 03/435-1819, is open daily 8 A.M.–5 P.M. Displays represent a complete record of the park from its creation to modern-day tourism, mountaineering, and skiing activities. The visitor center also has some handy information boards where you can find climbing partners.

Otago

The province of Otago starts at the Waitaki River in the north and extends west to the Southern Alps. The capital of the region is **Dunedin,** 360 km south of Christchurch, renowned for its grand architecture and the nearby natural wonders of the **Otago Peninsula.** From Dunedin, most travelers turn west, to **Queenstown.** Founded after gold was discovered on the Shotover River, the ensuing boomtown could have easily slipped into oblivion, but for one thing-its stunningly scenic location, overlooking a glacial lake and surrounded by the jagged peaks of the Remarkables. In the last 20 years—but particularly in the last decade—Queenstown has made its mark as one of the world's premier resort towns. In addition to old-fashioned adventures such as hiking, fishing, and skiing, Queenstown is a mecca for adrenaline junkies who arrive in the thousands to spend their cash on bungee jumping, white-water rafting, jetboating, and parapenting. A two-hour drive north of Queenstown, **Wanaka** enjoys the same magnificent setting, but without the ritz and glitz of its neighbor.

Hwy. 1 down the east coast is the main route into Otago. This wide, easy-to-drive highway passes through pleasant rural and coastal towns; allow at least four hours (without stops) for the 360-km journey between Christchurch and Dunedin. From Dunedin, it's slower going, traveling the 280 km to Queenstown takes over four hours. Another option from the north is to head inland along Hwy. 79 from north of Timaru. This route passes Aoraki Mount Cook National Park then veers south over Lindis Pass to the resort towns of Queenstown and Wanaka. Finally, if you're approaching Otago from the west coast, there's only one route over the

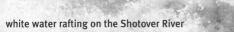

white water rafting on the Shotover River

OTAGO

Southern Alps-Hwy. 6, which leaves the coast at Haast and descends into Otago via Wanaka.

North Otago

OAMARU

Creamy-white stone buildings, wide tree-lined streets named after the rivers of Great Britain, and well-kept gardens give a distinctive air to Oamaru, halfway along the coast between Timaru and Dunedin and main town of North Otago (which begins south of the Waitaki River). This commercial center of 12,000 is a popular base for anglers fishing for quinnat salmon in the Waitaki River. **Oamaru stone,** a white granular limestone, has been used for many of New Zealand's most important buildings, including the customhouse in Wellington and the town halls in both Auckland and Dunedin; Weston, five km west of Oamaru, is the limestone industry center.

Sights

Stroll around town to see some of Oamaru's most attractive historic stone buildings—the courthouse, National Bank, post office on South Thames St., Garden of Memories, and Centennial Memorial Buildings—and stop at the Athenaeum at 58 Thames St. to visit the **North Otago Museum,** tel. 03/434-1652. Displays cover geology, natural history, and Maori and early European settlement of North Otago, and feature the extraction and uses of Oamaru stone; it's open Mon.–Fri. 1–4:30 P.M., admission free.

Oamaru's best-loved natural attraction is the **blue penguin colony.** These blue penguins have made an old quarry in the harbor area at the end of Waterfront Rd. their nesting ground. For years penguins have nested here, but only in recent years have their numbers increased (they are now successfully protected from predators by a surrounding fence). Each night, after the sun has set, they return from a day of feeding on fish to wander up the beach, crossing a lighted area in front of a small grandstand to get to their nesting area. Admission to the colony is $8 pp; check

© ANDREW HEMPSTEAD

main street, Oamaru

with the visitor center for the best viewing time—it varies with the season (best Sept.–Feb.).

Gardening enthusiasts will kick themselves if they don't make time to visit **Oamaru Gardens,** main entrance on Severn St., which date from 1876. Among all the spectacular floral displays are fountains, statues, a summerhouse, the distinctive Japanese Red Bridge, an aviary and peacock house, a wallaby enclosure, and a cactus house. Or tour the gardens in style—in a wagon pulled by a Clydesdale horse—for $3 adult, $1.50 child; rides run every Sunday 1–3 P.M. If you're into geology, walk through from Warren St. to the geological reserves of **Target Gully Shell Pit** and **Hutchinsons Quarry,** where "pillow lava," sub-fossil remains of extinct birds, fossils, and shell deposits have all been found. For good views of Oamaru, the coastline, and the inland mountains, head for **Lookout Point** at the east end of Tamar Street.

Coast Walk

For an enjoyable two-km (30 minutes) one-way walk, take the **Graves Walkway** along a boulder-strewn beach dominated by sheer cliffs. At the base of the cliffs are flows of "pillow lava," unique formations formed when lava cooled quickly upon hitting the ocean. The track starts at the end of Waterfront Rd. (south end of the harbor), but you can hike it only during low tide (look for little blue penguins that often huddle in cliff-face cavities close to the northern access). The second section of the walkway climbs over Cape Wanbrow to beautiful orange-sand and boulder-strewn **Bushy Beach.** Great numbers of seabirds frequent the area, along with a variety of coastal vegetation and sealife on the benches and platforms protected from the pounding surf. At the beach is a colony of **yellow-eyed penguins**—the northernmost breeding colony in New Zealand. You can see (or hear) the penguins almost year-round (except when they're hatching) from the walking track and viewing shelter. The best time to see them coming out of the surf is late afternoon/early evening (slight variation during the year). Ask at the information center about Department of Conservation tours ($5) that allow observers to get closer to the birds than the general public. Don't be caught by the tide—once it covers the rock shelves, it quickly reaches the beach, cutting off access.

Accommodations

The **Ambassador Motor Lodge,** 296 Thames St., tel. 03/437-2146 or 0800/437-2146, is a complex of 11 well-equipped rooms, each with a large kitchen and some with spa baths; $85–120 s or d. One of the many historic buildings in downtown Oamaru is the grand old two-story **Quality Hotel Brydone,** 115 Thames St., tel. 03/434-0011; website: www.qualitybrydone.co.nz. Built in the early 1880s from Oamaru stone, it features 50 comfortable guest rooms, a restaurant, and a bar. Standard rooms are $90 s or d, suites $120–150 s or d.

If you're in Oamaru in summer, the comfortable **Red Kettle YHA,** on the corner of Reed and Cross Streets, tel. 03/434-5008, with swimming pool across the road, has 19 beds for $16–18 pp. It's generally open from mid-Sept. to the end of May.

Oamaru Gardens Holiday Park on Chelmer St., tel. 03/434-7666 or 0800/280-202, has a pleasant location next to Oamaru Gardens; children will love the playground along the street. Aside from the usual facilities, there's a spacious, comfortable TV room, and lots of information on the local area in the office. Tent and caravan sites are $10 pp, and spacious cabins range $32–45 d. From Severn St., the main road from the south, take Cross St., then turn left on Chelmer.

Food

Oamaru has a good number of reasonably priced eateries. **Emma's,** 30 Thames St., tel. 03/434-1165, is a small café popular for its good coffee and cooked breakfasts. For Chinese meals, try **Golden Island Chinese Restaurant,** 243 Thames St., tel. 03/434-8840. Main dishes average $15–20 if you eat in; take-aways average $9 plus rice. Order two dishes and a large rice to go, and you'll have more than enough to feed two healthy appetites. The long narrow dining room in the **Quality Hotel Brydone,** 115 Thames St., tel. 03/434-0011, has an elegant small-town ambience; dinners range $18–28.

Information

Oamaru Visitor Centre is at the western end of Thames St., tel. 03/434-1656; it's open weekdays 9 A.M.–5 P.M. and weekends 10 A.M.–4 P.M.

MOERAKI BOULDERS

Thirty-eight km south of Oamaru, just south of Hampden, Hwy. 1 passes a short gravel road that leads to the boulder-shaped Moeraki Boulders Restaurant. From there various tracks lead down

Moeraki Boulders

to the beach and into unique **Moeraki Boulders Scenic Reserve.** Just to the north, along sandy Moeraki Beach, you come to what at first looks like a group of extra-large turtles washed up on the sand. On closer inspection you find a great number of round, perfectly smooth, gray boulders of varying sizes (up to four meters round) with a cracked design, scattered haphazardly along the sand and sticking out of the cliffs almost as if they're being "born"—some have split apart into several gigantic pieces. Made of carbonate of lime, silica, alumina, and peroxide of iron, the boulders were formed by chemistry on the seafloor about 60 million years ago through the slow accumulation of lime salts around a small core; the cracks are filled with yellow calcite crystals. They "appear" from the beach and cliffs behind as the mudstone in which they lurk is eroded by the sea. According to Maori legend, the boulders were food baskets and water casks from one of the great canoes from Hawaiiki wrecked off Shag Point at the south end of Katiki Beach. These magnificent boulders were once found all over the beaches in this area (volcanic boulders lie on **Katiki Beach** a few km to the south, but they're older and smaller); sadly, most have been carried off as souvenirs—only the largest and heaviest boulders remain, and the area is now protected as a scientific reserve. For a snack, morning or afternoon tea, or light lunch (good salad bar), head to **Moeraki Boulders Restaurant,** tel. 03/439-4827, and enjoy magnificent views of the beach as you munch; it's open daily 8 A.M.–5 P.M., in summer 8 A.M.–8:30 P.M.

Continuing along Hwy. 1 south, you pass the road to the tiny picturesque fishing village of **Moeraki** (Sleepy Sky) where you can often buy fish fresh off the fishing boats, which usually come in about noon–1 P.M. Stay at the **Moeraki Motor Camp** right on the beach, tel. 03/439-4759.

From Moeraki, take Lighthouse Rd. through rolling coastal farmland to **Moeraki Lighthouse.** Built in 1877, it is the perfect place for an enjoyable walk in fresh sea air with good coastal views, and the possible bonus of seeing seals and penguins.

CONTINUING SOUTH

Waikouaiti Beach, originally intended as the place for Otago's major settlement (now Dunedin), is a good place to enjoy some R & R before or after hitting the big city. This small town has a beautiful white-sand beach with safe swimming, surfing, and beachcombing, a good museum, and a wildlife refuge with walkway across the lagoon. **Waikouaiti Motor Camp** is in Waikouaiti Domain, also on Beach St. next to the beach, tel. 03/465-7366. It has communal facilities; tent sites are $16, caravan sites are $19, and on-site caravans are $34 d.

Dunedin and Vicinity

SCOTTISH GATEWAY TO OTAGO

Second-largest city in the South Island (population 110,000) and capital of the Otago region, Dunedin (pronounced Dun-eedin) sprawls around the head of bustling **Otago Harbour** 360 km south of Christchurch. With its well-planned city center, hilly suburbs and harbor views, Victorian-era stone buildings decorated with spires and turrets, stately homes, historic statues and memorials, and well-kept parks and flower gardens, the self-proclaimed "Rhododendron City of the South Island" has plenty of living history, lots to see and do, and a distinct appeal of its own.

Dunedin is also the gateway to the scenic **Otago Peninsula,** northeast of the city center. The peninsula is an enjoyable place to tootle

around for a day—for views, spectacular beaches and towering cliffs, farmland separated by century-old stone walls, and bird-watching. At **Taiaroa Head** (the northeastern tip), the albatross colony and a beach full of yellow-eyed penguins are two Dunedin sights you shouldn't miss.

History

Otago Harbour was a popular whaling ground long before the first European whaling station was officially established at the Maori village of **Otakou** in 1840. In late 1847 the Free Church of Scotland established a Scottish settlement at Otago under the leadership of William Cargill and Rev. Thomas Burns (nephew of famous Scottish poet Robert Burns). The following year **Otago** (the European mispronunciation of Otakou) was chosen as the official name for the settlement, and "New Edinburgh" as the name for the new town—the latter was greatly criticized for its lack of originality and replaced by the Gaelic name for Edinburgh, Dun Edin.

The discovery of gold in Otago in 1861 brought numerous gold diggers, along with bankers, hoteliers, and great wealth to Dunedin, and within a couple of years, public works and enterprises had flourished to the extent that the city became the commercial and industrial heart of the country. It became, in 1882, the first city in New Zealand to set up a freezing works and send frozen meat to England; it was the first city to use kerosene lighting, the first place in the country to use a cable tramway, and the first successful developer of a hydroelectric works (which prompted the government to further develop hydroelectric power throughout the country).

CITY SIGHTS

The Octagon

In the heart of downtown, the attractive eight-sided Octagon is a great place to people-watch (especially around lunchtime). Situated around the Octagon are the **Dunedin Visitor Centre,** art

First Church, Dunedin

© ANDREW HEMPSTEAD

OTAGO

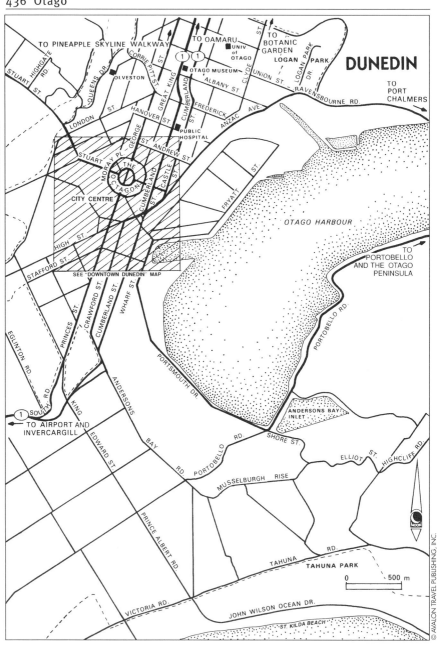

TO PINEAPPLE SKYLINE WALKWAY

TO OAMARU

TO BOTANIC GARDEN

DUNEDIN

UNIV of OTAGO

LOGAN PARK

STUART ST

HIGHGATE RD

QUEENS DR

CORRIE PITT ST

OLVESTON

OTAGO MUSEUM

ALBANY ST

UNION ST

LOGAN PARK DR

RAVENSBOURNE RD.

TO PORT CHALMERS

LONDON ST

HANOVER ST

GREAT KING ST

CUMBERLAND ST

FREDERICK ST

ANZAC AVE

STUART ST

GEORGE ST

ANDREW ST

PUBLIC HOSPITAL

MORAY PL

THE OCTAGON

CUMBERLAND ST

CASTLE ST

FRYATT ST

OTAGO HARBOUR

CITY CENTRE

HIGH ST

STAFFORD ST

SEE "DOWNTOWN DUNEDIN" MAP

TO PORTOBELLO AND THE OTAGO PENINSULA

PRINCES ST

CRAWFORD ST

CUMBERLAND ST

WHARF ST

PORTSMOUTH DR

PORTOBELLO RD.

EGLINTON RD

SOUTH RD

KING EDWARD ST

ANDERSONS BAY RD

ANDERSONS BAY INLET

1 TO AIRPORT AND INVERCARGILL

PORTOBELLO RD.

SHORE ST

ELLIOT ST

HIGHCLIFF RD.

MUSSELBURGH RISE

PRINCE ALBERT RD

RD.

TAHUNA

TAHUNA PARK

0   500 m

VICTORIA RD.

JOHN WILSON OCEAN DR.

ST. KILDA BEACH

OTAGO

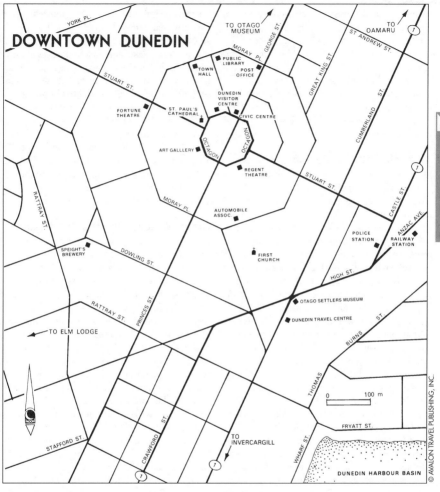

DOWNTOWN DUNEDIN

YORK PL.

TO OTAGO
MUSEUM

TO
OAMARU

ST ANDREW ST.

STUART ST

MORAY PL.

GEORGE ST

GREAT KING ST

ST ANDREW ST.

PUBLIC
LIBRARY

TOWN
HALL

POST
OFFICE

FORTUNE
THEATRE

ST. PAUL'S
CATHEDRAL

DUNEDIN
VISITOR
CENTRE

CIVIC CENTRE

CUMBERLAND ST.

ART GALLLERY

OCTAGON

OCTAGON

REGENT
THEATRE

STUART ST.

CASTLE ST.

ANZAC AVE.

RATTRAY ST.

MORAY PL.

AUTOMOBILE
ASSOC

SPEIGHT'S
BREWERY

DOWLING ST.

FIRST
CHURCH

POLICE
STATION

RAILWAY
STATION

HIGH ST.

RATTRAY ST.

PRINCES ST.

TO ELM LODGE

OTAGO SETTLERS MUSEUM

DUNEDIN TRAVEL CENTRE

BURNS ST.

THOMAS ST.

0   100 m

STAFFORD ST.

CRAWFORD ST.

TO
INVERCARGILL

FRYATT ST.

WHARF ST.

DUNEDIN HARBOUR BASIN

OTAGO

© AVALON TRAVEL PUBLISHING, INC.

gallery, civic center, library, a cathedral, and one block back, the town hall, public library, and post office.

Dunedin Public Art Gallery, tel. 03/477-4000, lies on the west corner of the Octagon. Founded in 1884, the gallery has two claims to fame—first, it's the oldest art gallery in New Zealand, containing an extensive collection of foreign paintings and one of the most important New Zealand collections; and second, it holds the only Monet in the country. The gallery is open weekdays 10 A.M.–5 P.M., weekends 11–5 P.M.

Otago Settlers Museum

This jam-packed museum features photos, costumes, furniture, antique medical and dental instruments (which look like great instruments of torture!), a portrait gallery, a gold-mining exhibit, a pioneer cottage and blacksmith's shop, a penny farthing bicycle, horse-drawn vehicles, a tram, a display devoted to "the forgotten sex and early feminists of New Zealand," and much, much more—it's the kind of place where you can easily spend several hours. The excellent reference library and Research and Reading Room is open to the public during the week. The museum, 220 Cumberland St. (down the road from the railway station), tel. 03/477-5052, is open Mon.–Fri. 9 A.M.–5 P.M., Sat.–Sun. 1–5 P.M.; $5 adult, children free.

Dunedin Railway Station

The Flemish Renaissance architecture of Dunedin's spectacular train station on Anzac Ave. at the east end of Stuart St. is something to see whether you're catching a train or not. When you first see its white Oamaru stone facings, polished granite pillars, covered colonnade and "carriageway," and stunning clock tower, you think you've seen it all. But the highly decorated interior of the main foyer is even more intricate, with a tiled mosaic floor featuring the steam train *Puffing Billy* and the old New Zealand Rail symbol (NZR), Royal Doulton china cherubs frolicking in foliage around the upper walls, and beautiful stained-glass windows with steam trains puffing toward you from every angle. The station was completed in 1907, and the architect, George A. Troup, won the Institution of British Architects Award for this amazing design.

If you'd like to travel on the spectacular **Taieri Gorge Railway,** head to the railway station or call 03/477-4449. Comprising a string of 85-year-old carriages, the rail trip heads west from Dunedin through tunnels, over viaducts, and along a narrow valley for 58 km to Pukerangi before returning to the coast. The four-hour round-trip costs $65 pp.

Olveston

A one-hour guided tour of this stately 35-room home is definitely worth the admission ($12 adult, $4 child) to see all the antique furniture, paintings, and priceless art objects; the gleaming kitchen filled with functional implements, crockery, and silverware; and the maids' and butlers' quarters. You hear the history of the house and its people as you move from room to room. Built

for the Theomins between 1904 and 1906, the perfectly maintained Jacobean-style house was kept in the family until 1966, when they gave it to the city. A tour takes you back to the days of early 20th-century Dunedin, giving you a taste of what it was like to live in style—or *serve* those living in style. Tours start at 9:30 A.M., 10:45 A.M., noon, 1:30 P.M., 2:45 P.M., and 4 P.M.; for current tour times and a reservation (find out which tours to avoid—tour buses always stop at Olveston), call 03/477-3320. The house, at 42 Royal Terrace, is a 20-minute uphill walk from city center. If you'd rather see Olveston as part of an organized tour of Dunedin sights, call Newton Tours at 03/477-5577 or book at the visitor center.

Otago Museum and Discovery World

Museum freaks can spend hours wandering around enormous Otago Museum, with its outstanding collection of Polynesian art (largest collection in New Zealand). Visit the halls on Melanesia, the Maori culture, world civilizations, furniture and ceramics, cameras, coins and medals, lions and primates, birds, small animals, and marinelife. The museum also features a Southern Land, Southern People display and a maritime hall. Visit Discoverer's Den, a hands-on science display that includes various illusions and piano you can play with your feet; $6 adult, $3 child. The museum is open daily 10 A.M.–5 P.M. If you have only an hour or so to explore, pick up the handy "Forty Minutes Of Your Time" brochure in the entrance hall—it directs you to all the highlights. It's on Great King St. across from the university, less than two km north of the city, tel. 03/474-7474; buses run from the Octagon along George St. to one block from the museum.

University of Otago

The university grounds off Cumberland St. (north of city center) are an agreeable place to wander. You'll pass attractive, well-established buildings covered in ivy, as well as modern buildings, green lawns and flower gardens, and Leith Stream, which meanders through to Otago Harbour (follow the creek and you end up at a boat harbor). Call the information center, tel. 03/474-3300, to organize a guided tour. To the north lies Dunedin's beautiful Botanic Garden (see below) and to the east are Logan Park and University Oval.

Brewery Tour

To visit Dunedin's historic **Speight's Brewery,** founded in 1876 and renowned throughout the South Island, call the brewery at 03/477-7697 to confirm a spot on a tour. Departures are from 200 Rattray St. daily at 10 A.M., 11:45 A.M., and 2 P.M.; adult $12, senior $10, child $4.

Connoisseurs of fine whisky can visit **Wilson's Distillers;** it offers tours Mon.–Fri., $5 adult. Bookings are essential through the visitor center, tel. 03/474-3300.

Parks and Gardens

Well-planned Dunedin has no shortage of "green spots" around the city. The large **Botanic Garden** (New Zealand's first) at the north end of George St. features formal lawns interspersed with trees and native bush, magnificent flower displays, trails, an aviary and, in the center, a Visitors Education Centre. The Rhododendron Dell in springtime bloom is a multicolored feast for your eyes—Dunedin is famous for its springtime flowering shrubs. Stop by the Botanica Restaurant next to the Winter Gardens for fruit juice, tea, or a light lunch. The gardens are open daily dawn to dusk. Drive through the gardens via Lovelock Ave. from the south, or Signal Hill Rd. from the north, or catch a bus heading north up George St. from the Octagon to the northwest boundary of the Botanic Garden. All down the west side of the city are parks, gardens, and sports grounds, known as the **Town Belt,** and on the northeast side of the city is **Logan Park.**

Scenic Drive

If you have your own car, follow the one-hour "Know the City" scenic drive, which starts at the post office on Princes St. (look for the signs with a golden arrow on a green background); a free brochure with map and descriptions is available at the Dunedin Visitor Centre. The drive takes you around the city and immediate vicinity to lookout points providing panoramic views of the city, harbor, and peninsula, passing parks

and several city attractions, such as the Moana Swimming Pool complex and Olveston, to name but a few.

OTAGO PENINSULA SIGHTS

Two main roads run along the peninsula: the high Highcliff Rd. (good views) and the low Portobello Rd. along the waterfront (a bird-watcher's delight)—both join at the small settlement of **Portobello** (pub, general store and hot takeaway foods, café, and public telephone). Other than these, the peninsula is relatively noncommercial—buy your lunch, drinks, and munchies in the city before you venture up the peninsula.

To get the most out of the peninsula by car, take the high route first, and after visiting Taiaroa Head, return to the city by the low route. To get to the peninsula from city center, take Hwy. 1 south and turn left on Andersons Bay Rd.,

OTAGO PENINSULA CRUISES AND TOURS

The best way to appreciate the beauty of Dunedin's Harbour and the Otago Peninsula is by boat. A cruise with **Monarch Wildlife Cruises,** tel. 03/477-4276 or 0800/666-272, on the MV *Monarch,* lets you experience the harbor while hearing about its marinelife, folklore, and history. Wildlife often sighted includes seals, penguins, and albatrosses. Boat one way and bus back for $57 adult, $28 child. The longer version (eight hours) takes in all the major sights and includes admissions for $150 adult, $90 child, refreshments and accommodation pickups included. Boats depart from Dunedin Harbour Basin, on the corner of Wharf and Fryatt Streets.

Citibus Newton, tel. 03/477-5577, offers a number of peninsula tours in distinctive red double-decker buses. The fare all the way to Taiaroa Head is $35 adult, $18 child, with stops made at all major attractions along the way. This services runs up to six times daily, picking up from visitor center and Dunedin accommodations. Return from the peninsula with Monarch Wildlife Cruises for an extra $27 pp.

which becomes Portobello Road. Buses to Portobello depart from Centre City New World on Cumberland St. Mon.–Fri. (frequently) and Saturday (considerably less frequently); for times, call 03/477-9238.

Larnach Castle

If you've always wondered what it would be like to live in a genuine castle, wonder no longer. Built in the early 1870s by extravagant banker, businessman, and politician William Larnach, Larnach Castle sits in 15 hectares of bush and gardens, only 13 km from Dunedin city center—a grand and extravagant stone mansion built along Scottish baronial lines, filled with original marble, Venetian glass, plaster, and woodcarvings collected by Larnach from all over the world. Once you pay the $12 adult, $5 child entrance fee, you can wander through the castle and grounds at will, spending as much or as little time as you want; most of the rooms are not roped off so you can actually enter each one and let your imagination run free. Don't miss climbing the narrow stone steps to the top of the tower for incredible views, waltz into the Ballroom Cafe for a Devonshire tea (served till 4:30 P.M.) or lunch, then stroll through the gardens, stopping to check out the stables and dungeon.

The castle, tel. 03/476-1616, is open daily 9 A.M.–5 P.M. in winter, till 7 P.M. in summer, and accommodation is available in a newer building at the back of the castle. If you're any kind of romantic, this is the place to stay—after everyone else leaves, the castle grounds become your own to explore at leisure, and the sunsets are something to write home about. To get there by car from Highcliff Rd., turn left on Camp Rd., following the signs to the castle. To get there from Portobello Rd., turn right on Castlewood Rd., then left on Camp Road. **Citibus Newton,** tel. 03/477-5577, departs four times daily for Larnach Castle; round-trip $30 adult, $15 child.

New Zealand Marine Studies Centre

Operated by the University of Otago, this complex lies on a narrow peninsula near Portobello, tel. 03/479-5826. Primarily a marine education center, it incorporates the Westpac Trust Aquarium, a public facility that allows for a behind-the-scenes look at life under the surrounding waterways. It features the sealife of New Zealand's southern waters, with live specimens, interactive displays, and shallow tanks re-creating the habitat of coastal marinelife. It's open daily noon–4:30 P.M.; $5 adult, $2 child.

Penguin Place

When Howard McGrouther bought a sheep farm on the Otago Peninsula, little did he realize that he would become instrumental in a struggle to save the **yellow-eyed penguin,** the world's rarest penguin. As soon as a small colony began nesting among his grazing sheep, he set out to protect the birds and to ensure that, while they nested on his property, the species would survive. Since the land is devoid of suitable vegetation for nesting, McGrouther constructed special breeding boxes. Predators were trapped, and sick and injured birds were nursed back to health—and now the colony is growing. Today there are at least 36 breeding pairs. To support this private conservation project, the McGrouthers have encouraged visitors to view the penguins. Camouflaged trenches lead to a series of blinds scattered through the colony, allowing visitors to view the penguins at extremely close range without disturbing them. The birds are most active around dusk, on cooler days, and when nesting, but tours with knowledgeable guides are run year-round 10:15 A.M. until 90 minutes before dusk. The tour is $27 adult, $12 child, which includes a 15-minute talk. Bookings are essential at tel. 03/478-0286, or make them through the visitor center.

© ANDREW HEMPSTEAD

yellow-eyed penguin

Royal Albatross Centre

The colony of royal albatrosses at **Taiaroa Head** is an unusual sight—it's the only colony in the world on inhabited mainland. If you're lucky enough, you'll be there when the birds are flying (they need winds of at least 15–20 knots to take off but can land with very little wind). The all-white birds with black wings at Taiaroa are great albatrosses—true seabirds; with wingspans of more than three meters, these large, bulky birds waddle on land but are magnificent fliers. The parent albatrosses (currently around 20 nesting pairs that mate for life) arrive at the colony late in September, build a nest, lay an egg early in November, and share incubation duty for about 11 weeks. The chick hatches by the end of January and the parents take turns guarding it for the first 40 days, feeding it by regurgitation, and caring for it for several months before they bid it farewell and take off to sea. The nine-month-old chick first tests its wings in late September. It takes off in a strong wind with no practice flight, and then it's gone for the next three to four years, during which it circumnavigates the pole—never landing, feeding in flight and on the sea surface.

On arrival at the reception building you're given an informative talk on the albatrosses and their way of life, then taken up a short trail to the observatory and viewing room to see the nests (binoculars help) and the birds flying on windy days (skimming the observatory with great whooshing sounds). You can also see a **Stewart Island shag colony** from the observatory—their nests look like bunches of tiny volcanoes splattered over the rocks. The tour includes a visit to historic Fort Taiaroa, a defense station established in 1885 to protect the port from a Russian invasion that never came. **Pilots Beach** just below the headland is a popular place for **fur seals**—you can walk down to it for close-up views. The best time to visit Taiaroa Head is late afternoon on a windy day when the albatrosses are most likely to be flying, when the shags return to feed their chicks, and when the seals like to hang out on the beach. Access to the colony is restricted September through late November so that the birds are not disturbed during breeding. Tour cost is $27 pp. Other options include just the Fort Taiaroa Tour ($12) or an Albatross Insight Tour ($14), the educational part of the main tour. Buy tickets as far in advance as possible, tel. 03/478-0499.

Southlight Wildlife

Another peninsula attraction for nature lovers is Southlight Wildlife, a penguin and seal colony around the headland from the Royal Albatross Centre. From the parking lot, a trail turns left to a lookout, where you can watch yellow-eyed and little blue penguins climbing out of the surf and heading up to their nests (take binoculars). Another trail to the right leads along rocks where seals bask at very close range (sometimes they bask on the track!). At the end of this trail, you can see spotted shags nesting on overhanging ledges.

Again, you need your own transportation to get there. Stop at the Southlight Wildlife sign just beyond the village of Otakou to get the key to a locked gate, then continue about three km to the Royal Albatross Centre parking lot at the end of the sealed road. Go through the gate, then continue to the end of the road. Entrance fee is $7.50 per adult, children get in free. For further details call 03/478-0287. (Another seal colony inhabits Cape Saunders, on the southeast side of the peninsula.)

Glenfalloch Woodland Garden

Are you a gardening nut, particularly into azaleas, rhododendrons, or fuchsias? Enjoy hand-feeding peacocks and all kinds of semi-tame birds? Then these gardens, originating in 1873 and their pioneer homestead (1871), eight km from the city, are more than worth the request for a donation. The grounds are spectacular in spring; in summer they're noted for colorful fuchsia displays. Take some of the short walks through the trees passing a stream and beautiful woodland gardens. Pottery is made and sold in the Potters Cottage, open 1–4 P.M. Glenfalloch, open daily during daylight hours, is off Portobello Rd., tel. 03/476-1006, and easily reached by the Portobello bus (it runs Mon.–Saturday).

RECREATION

Scenic Hikes

For panoramic views of the city, harbor, and Otago Peninsula, consider hiking the five-km **Pineapple Skyline Walkway.** The track starts at the car park off Flagstaff Whare Flat Rd., takes about two hours (going downhill toward the city), and finishes at the end of Booth Rd. in the northern Dunedin suburb of Glenleith; you can walk it in either direction, depending on whether you want to go uphill or down. For information on public transportation to the track, as well as details of other hiking tracks in the area, head to the visitor center.

Tunnel Beach Walkway is another very popular short walk, starting seven km south of the city off Blackhead Road. Taking about one hour, the walkway meanders down to striking sandstone cliffs, arches, stacks, and caves, and to a stairway through a rock tunnel leading down to Tunnel Beach. Access to the walkway is not permitted during lambing season.

ENTERTAINMENT AND EVENTS

The best sources of entertainment information are the back pages of *Otago Daily Times,* where you'll find a full listing of restaurants and an entertainment guide, and the free *Midweek Weekender* (comes out on Wednesday and Sunday).

On the Town

Bands playing rock 'n' roll, top 40s, and alternative music appear all around Dunedin in the pubs and hotels—just follow your ears. Dunedin is well known throughout New Zealand for its original musical contributions. Two venues feature this particular kind of Dunedin music: the **Crown Hotel,** 179 Rattray St., tel. 03/477-0132; and **Arc Café,** across from the Southern Cross Hotel at 135 High St., tel. 03/474-1135. The latter is the quintessential Dunedin music venue, with a typical student crowd, acoustic jams, and, sometimes, local bands recording live performances for a CD. **Captain Cook Tavern,** near the university at 354 Great King St., tel. 03/474-

1935, has bands playing most nights and gets very crowded. Back toward the city, **Alberta Arms Tavern,** 387 George St., tel. 03/477-2952, is another live music venue, with an Irish house band on Monday night.

The **Regent Theatre** in the Octagon, tel. 03/477-8597, presents a wide variety of local and visiting performers, plays, ballet, and grand opera. At the **Town Hall** on Moray Place, tel. 03/474-3614, you can attend performances by local opera companies and acting groups, and various musical events. Go to the **Fortune Theatre** at 231 Upper Stuart St., tel. 03/477-8323, for professional theater—see the back of the daily newspaper for details or call the box office. Also check out the **Globe Theatre,** 104 London St., tel. 03/477-3274.

Events

At the height of summer, the city springs to life with **Dunedin Festival Week.** All kinds of organized free entertainment and special events happen throughout the city—pick up a free Dunedin Festival newspaper to see what's on and where. All the **movie theaters** show current feature films; see the local newspapers.

ACCOMMODATIONS

Hotels

Dunedin has a fine selection of hotels offering accommodations, many of which have been extensively restored. The **Law Courts Hotel,** centrally located at 65 Stuart St., tel. 03/477-8036, is one such place, with 24 basic rooms scattered around the top three floors of a historic 1880s hotel building. Rates are $60 s, $85 d, with private bathrooms.

A few blocks north of the Octagon (near the Otago Museum) is **Cargills Hotel,** 678 George St., tel. 03/477-7983 or 0800/737-378; website: www.cargills.co.nz. Each of the 50 rooms is large, and comes complete with a selection of plants and a writing desk. The hotel also features a restaurant that opens to a peaceful outdoor courtyard. Rates are $140–225 s or d. If you're in search of a full-facility hotel, complete with 24-

hour café, a fitness center, hairdresser, restaurants, and souvenir shop, try the **Southern Cross Hotel** at 118 High St., tel. 03/477-0752 or 0800/696-963; rooms start at $210 s or d, suites at $300.

Out of town, a cheap hotel is **The Beach Hotel** in the southern suburb of St. Kilda, one block from the beach, on the corner of Prince Albert and Victoria Roads, tel. 03/455-4642; rates from $35 s, $55 d.

Motels

Dunedin's least expensive motels are along Musselburgh Rise, on the way out to the Otago Peninsula. The **Arcadian Motel,** 85–89 Musselburgh Rise, tel. 03/455-0992 or 0508/272-2342, website: www.dunedinmotel.co.nz, charges just $65 s, $75 d for a self-contained room. Similarly priced are **Chequers Motel,** 119 Musselburgh Rise, tel. 03/455-0778, and **Bayfield Motels,** 210 Musselburgh Rise, tel. 03/455-0756. In both cases, all rooms come with a kitchen, and a double costs about $70.

The main concentration of motels is north from the Octagon along George St. **Garden Motel,** 958 George St., tel. 03/477-8251, provides comfortable accommodations in 12 rooms, each opening to a private garden area. Rates start at $65 s, $75 d for a self-contained unit. A larger complex is the **Allan Court Motel,** 590 George St., tel. 03/477-7526 or 0800/611-511, featuring 18 large, kitchen-equipped rooms; $98–128 s or d.

Beyond suburban St. Kilda, and overlooking the long expanse of St. Clair Beach, is the **Esplandade Motel,** 14 Esplanade, tel. 03/455-1987. This motel is fairly basic-you're paying for the view; $105–130 s or d.

Larnach Lodge

The most interesting place to stay when you're in Dunedin is **Larnach Lodge,** tel. 03/476-1616, website: www.larnachcastle.co.nz, on the grounds of this famous castle on Otago Peninsula, 13 km from downtown. Accommodation is in the re-creation of a colonial farm building (12 en suite rooms; $200 s or d) or converted coach

OTAGO

house (six rooms with shared facilities; $95 s or d), and the beautiful 14-hectare grounds become almost your own private garden. Tea- and coffee-making facilities are provided and breakfast is available, as well as full meals in the castle restaurant. For transportation and castle information, see Otago Peninsula.

Bed-and-Breakfasts

For a full listing of Dunedin B&Bs and homestay/farmstay accommodations, visit the visitor center.

Comfortable **Sahara Guest House,** 619 George St. near Otago Museum, tel. 03/477-6662, has a pleasing decor, TV lounge, tea- and coffee-making supplies (dinner available in an adjacent restaurant), laundry, and hospitable owner; rates are $63 s, $84 d (continental or cooked breakfast), or stay in one of the self-contained motel units for $76 s, $80 d.

Built in the early 1900s and recently restored, the **Albatross Inn,** 770 George St., tel. 03/477-2727 or 0800/441-441, website: www.albatrossinn.co.nz, offers accommodation in eight Edwardian-style rooms. Unlike many bed-and-breakfasts, each room in the Albatross has a private bathroom, TV, and telephone. A complimentary breakfast is served in a bright and breezy room on the ground floor. Rates are $75–95 s, $95–135 d.

Backpacker Lodges

Adventurer Backpackers is just around the corner from the Octagon at 37 Dowling St., tel. 03/477-7367 or 0800/422-257, in a historic building once owned by the Salvation Army, now converted into a good city-style backpacker lodge. The large communal area features a small modern kitchen, comfortable lounges, a pool table, and a computer for Internet access. Beds in the large downstairs dorms are $20, while around a balcony that surrounds the main living area are twin and double rooms for $18 pp.

In the same vicinity, **Stafford Gables YHA,** 71 Stafford St., tel. 03/474-1919, website: www.yha.org.nz, is a large Tudor-style building in a handy central location on the south side of the Octagon. It has the usual facilities plus many extras (reading room, music room), and the office

(open all day) sells basic food supplies; rates are $17–21 pp. Take Princes St. south from the Octagon, turn right on Stafford St., and walk two blocks.

Elm Lodge, 74 Elm Row, tel. 03/474-1872 or 0800/356-563, is an excellent backpacker accommodation providing bright cheerful rooms (dorm, single, or double) with views of Otago Harbour, an equipped kitchen, comfy living room with TV, well-kept garden, and barbecue area—all the comforts of a home only a 10-minute walk from the Octagon; rates are $18 pp dorm, $20 pp double or twin. The friendly owners also do bookings for most local activities, rent bikes, and can arrange good-value (and very popular) nature tours of Otago Peninsula and other local sights.

Colonial **Manor House** at 28 Manor Place, tel. 03/477-0484, website: www.manorhousebackpackers.co.nz, is like a home away from home, yet with all the facilities you hope to find: a very spacious and rather grand living room, a modern kitchen, good showers, laundry, and a bush setting. It's a short walk (about five blocks) from city center. Dorm beds are $18 pp, doubles and twins are $20 pp.

Motor Camps

You'll find three motor camps within a reasonable distance of the city center. **Dunedin Holiday Park** on Victoria Rd., St. Kilda (south of the city center), tel. 03/455-4690 or 0800/945-455, is about five km out, but within earshot of the surf on adjacent St. Kilda Beach. It offers the usual facilities, plus TV lounge and pool room; tent sites are $20, powered sites are $22, cabins cost from $36 s or d, and self-contained tourist flats cost $63 s or d.

Aaron Lodge Top 10 Holiday Park, 2.5 km west of the Octagon at 162 Kaikorai Valley Rd., tel. 03/476-4725 or 0800/879-227, is similar, and meals are available in nearby restaurants; tent and caravan sites (mostly gravel) are $20–22, spacious cabins are $35–38 d, tourist flats are $58–70 d, motel rooms are $70 d. Take Stuart St. west from the Octagon and follow it uphill until it becomes Kaikorai Valley Road. Pass the 24-hour petrol station at the top of the hill, then

Kentucky Fried; the motor camp is a little farther on the right.

Leith Valley Touring Park, 103 Malvern St., tel. 03/467-9936, has landscaped grounds bordered by a stream, only three km northwest of downtown. Tent and caravan sites are $22, on-site caravans and cabins from $38.

FOOD

Before treading the streets in search of a bite to eat, pick up a current copy of the *Dining Out Guide,* free from the visitor center. In this you'll find listings of a large variety of restaurants (some with sample menus and prices) and a number of the trendiest entertainment spots.

Light Meals

Around the Octagon and along the main streets radiating in all directions are all kinds of cafés, tearooms, sandwich bars, and restaurants—take your choice. One that's easy to miss is **Café Nova** in the art gallery, tel. 03/477-4000, with a range of simple and inexpensive meals served whenever the gallery is open. Open daily for breakfast, lunch, dinner is **Tip Top Restaurant** on the corner of the Octagon and Princes Street, tel. 03/477-7594. Head here for straightforward meals in a small-town diner atmosphere. For a little more style and choice, **Tangente Café & Bakery,** 111 Moray Place, tel. 03/477-0232, is a good place for breakfast. The Sourdough Extreme, a delicious vegetarian dish topped with a poached egg and hollandaise sauce ($9.50) is a particular treat. The rest of day, healthy choices include a pumpkin-based fettuccini topped with feta and ham ($14.50). Tangente is open daily 8 A.M.–3:30 P.M., and for dinner Friday and Saturday night (no main course over $20). The **Robert Harris Cafe,** for coffee and cakes to eat in or take out, is also just off the Octagon at 43 Princes St., tel. 03/477-2044.

Along Stuart St., downhill from the Octagon, are many trendy little cafés, including **Potpourri Natural Foods,** a vegetarian restaurant at 97 Lower Stuart St. (east side of the Octagon), tel. 03/477-9983. This place serves a large variety of health foods, Mexican meals, fresh salads, light

meals, and desserts (from $11 for lunch or dinner) weekdays 9 A.M.–8 P.M., Sat. 11 A.M.–3 P.M. Continuing down the hill, **Percolator,** 142 Lower Stuart St., has a wide selection of coffee concoctions.

South of the Octagon, across from the Southern Cross Hotel, the **Arc Café,** 135 High St., tel. 03/474-1135, has a bohemian atmosphere and a menu dominated by vegetarian and vegan choices; open Mon.–Sat. from noon.

Pub Meals

For steak, lamb chop, chicken, or fish bistro meals under $10 a plate in comfortable, cozy, Scottish surroundings, head for the **Albert Arms Tavern** on the corner of London St. and George St., tel. 03/477-8035. It's open daily for lunch and dinner. Surrounded by a predominantly tartan decor, enjoy a counter lunch for $6–8 during lunch hours only. On Monday nights, popular Irish bands are the featured entertainment. The Dunedin **Cobb & Co.** is in the Law Courts Hotel at 65 Stuart St., tel. 03/477-8036. It's open daily 7:30 A.M.–10 P.M.; dinners average $14–20 (salad bar extra), and on Sunday it offers a "Sunday Roast" for $18. If you have accompanying children, send them upstairs to the Clown House for active entertainment and supervision by a real live clown while you enjoy a peaceful drink or wait for the meal. In the old Waterloo Hotel at 19 Ruskin Terrace, tel. 03/455-5663, is **Bonaparte's Restaurant.** Meals here are a good value-lunches are $7, while dinners are $14–18.

Other Restaurants

Right in the heart of the action, **Ruby in the Dust,** 6 The Octagon, tel. 03/477-4690, typifies the casual, laid-back atmosphere that pervades throughout Dunedin. The décor—hardwood floors, worn timber furniture, and painted brick walls—belie some serious cooking though. Sample delicious wedges with sour cream and sweet chili ($5.50) or choose a more substantial dish such as chicken kebabs served with a nectarine chutney ($16). Ruby's is open daily 9 A.M. until late.

Just off the Octagon, **Etrusco** at 8 Moray Place (in the Savoy Building), tel. 03/477-3737, is an upmarket Italian restaurant with pastas from $14 and pizzas for two from $20 (closed Monday). Continuing up the hill is **Bennu Café & Bar,** 12 Moray Place, tel. 03/474-5055. In a restored brick building, with original plaster ceilings and a warm European atmosphere, the menu features mainly Mexican and pizza dishes (the antipasto platters are delicious; from $9). It's open Mon.–Sat. for lunch and nightly for dinner. On the other side of the Octagon, at **Café Zambezi,** 480 Moray Place, tel. 03/477-1107, the best choices come from a blackboard menu, with many dishes for the health-conscious.

Excellent **Thyme Out Restaurant** at 629 George St., tel. 03/474-0467, is always packed with locals enjoying a blackboard menu that features many different, innovative ethnic cuisines (meat, fish, and vegetarian). It's open for dinner only Tues.–Sat. from 6 P.M. (book your table); dinners are $16–22. **Abalone Restaurant and Bar,** 44 Hanover St., tel. 03/477-6877, is dominated by a long bar. Best known as a hip drinking spot, the food is also good. Imaginative dishes include roasted venison on kumara mash served with a berry jus and caramelized oranges ($28).

If you're in search of food at an odd hour of the night or early morning, head for the **Southern Cross Hotel,** 118 High St., tel. 03/477-0752. The hotel has a casino with a 24-hour deli. Also in the hotel is the Grand Bar & Café, serving a variety of light meals, including a delicious Thai chicken curry, for $8–15.

TRANSPORTATION
Getting There
Dunedin Airport is about 20 km south of city center. Get there on the **Dunedin Airport Shuttle,** tel. 03/477-6611; $12 pp each way. **Air New Zealand,** tel. 03/479-6594, has direct flights out of Dunedin to Wellington, Christchurch, and Invercargill, with connections to Auckland.

The **railway station** is at the bottom end of Stuart St.; **Tranz Scenic,** tel. 0800/802-802, operates rail service on the Southerner between Christchurch, Dunedin, and Invercargill.

Intercity buses run from Dunedin to Queenstown via Roxburgh and Cromwell; also to

Christchurch, Invercargill, Te Anau, and Milford Sound. Buses terminate at the **Dunedin Travel Centre** at 205 St. Andrews St., tel. 03/474-9600. Many other buses serve Dunedin, often using the information center as a departure point. These include **Catch-a-bus,** tel. 03/453-1480, with one service daily to Queenstown and Invercargill.

Getting Around
Dunedin is a large and hilly city. If you don't have a car, the best way to get around is by **Citi Bus,** tel. 03/477-2224, which leaves from a variety of stops around the Octagon and Princes St.—pick up timetables from the information center.

Buses to Portobello on Otago Peninsula leave from Cumberland St., Mon.–Fri. (frequently) and Saturday (less frequently); for times and fares, call 03/477-9238.

Car rental agencies in Dunedin include **Avis,** tel. 03/486-2780; **Budget,** tel. 03/474-0428; **National,** tel. 03/477-8801; **NZ Rent-a-car,** tel. 03/477-3895; **Pegasus,** tel. 03/477-6296; **Rent-a-dent,** tel. 03/477-7822; and **Thrifty,** tel. 03/486-1993. The **Automobile Association,** 450 Moray Place, tel. 03/477-5945, offers general information on road travel, free maps, and emergency breakdown service for members.

For a taxi to the airport or a variety of sight-seeing tours, contact **Call a Cab,** tel. 03/477-7800; **City Taxis,** tel. 03/477-1771; **Dunedin Taxis,** tel. 03/477-7777; or **Otago Taxis,** tel. 03/477-3333.

Tours
The most popular tours are out to the Otago Peninsula, but **Newton Citibus,** tel. 03/477-5577, offers a 90-minute city tour in an English double-decker bus ($20 adult, $10 child), as well as tours out to the peninsula.

SERVICES
Most of the banks are around the Octagon and along George and Princes Streets. **Thomas Cook Foreign Exchange** (travelers checks and foreign cash exchange) is at 43 Princes St., tel. 03/477-

1532; it's open Mon.–Fri. 8:30 A.M.–5 P.M. The **post office** is on the north side of the Octagon at 251 George Street. Send and receive emails or surf the Internet at the **Arc Café,** 135 High St., tel. 03/474-1135; open Mon.–Sat. noon–11 P.M. **Dunedin Public Library,** Moray Place, tel. 03/474-3690, also has public Internet access.

The staff at **Sudz,** 4 Howe St., tel. 03/477-7421, does complete laundry services for you, or you can do it yourself. A serviced wash is $8 per load. It's open Mon.–Fri. 8:30 A.M.–5 P.M. and Saturday 8:30 A.M.–12:30 P.M. for laundry services, but open every day from 8:30 A.M.–9 P.M. for self-service.

Emergency
Dunedin Hospital is three blocks north of the Octagon at 201 Great King Rd., tel. 03/474-0999. For less urgent cases, head for **After Hours Doctors** at 95 Hanover St., tel. 03/479-2900. It's open 24 hours daily. The **Urgent Pharmacy** is in the same building at 95 Hanover St., tel.

03/477-6344; open Mon.–Fri. 6 A.M.–10 P.M., Sat.–Sun. 10 A.M.–10 P.M. The central **police station** is on Great King St., tel. 03/471-4800.

INFORMATION
Dunedin Visitor Centre, on the north side of the Octagon, tel. 03/474-3300, website: www.dunedintourism.co.nz, is open weekdays 8:30 A.M.–5 P.M. and weekends 9 A.M.–5 P.M. (extended summer hours). The excellent staff happily provides sight-seeing information, city maps, and accommodation and restaurant suggestions; it will book everything but airline tickets. It's one of the best information centers in New Zealand. Headquarters of the DOC **Otago Conservatory** is in Conservation House, 77 Lower Stuart St., tel. 03/477-0677; open weekdays only. **Dunedin Public Library** on Moray Place, tel. 03/474-3690, is open Mon.–Fri. 9:30 A.M.–8 P.M., Saturday 10 A.M.–4 P.M., and Sunday 2–6 P.M.

Spend 3 days here

OTAGO

Queenstown and Vicinity *

Backed by the craggy Remarkables range, Queenstown (population 8,000) nestles along the edge of Queenstown Bay on the northeast shore of **Lake Wakatipu,** 280 km west of Dunedin and 530 km southwest of Christchurch. Beautiful Lake Wakatipu is the second largest of the southern glacial lakes (behind Lake Te Anau) at 77 km long and almost five km wide. Although several rivers feed it (the Rees and Dart are largest), only the Kawarau River drains this always-blue, crystal-clear lake. With a colorful history steeped in gold, outstanding scenery in all directions, and modern-day notoriety as a center for jet-boating, white-water rafting, fishing, backcountry hiking, downhill skiing and boarding, and bungee jumping, Queenstown, the "Adventure Capital of the World," is the most popular and attractive resort in New Zealand.

From all over the world backpackers to businesspeople congregate in this cosmopolitan melting pot, and although tourism is the main

industry, the resort has somehow managed to retain a friendly, small-town atmosphere. Its drawbacks? Irresistible outdoor adventures and heavy-duty nighttime partying require a healthy number of travelers checks on hand (or an understanding credit card company at home)—come here for a couple of days and, time and budget permitting, you're more than likely to stay a couple of weeks.

Accommodations range from motor camps, hostels, and budget backpacker lodges to motels and the ultimate in luxurious top-class hotels. Quick cafés and a great variety of restaurants keep you happily eating out day after day; nightclubs and pubs with live entertainment abound. Alluring shops selling wool sweaters, sheepskin and suede coats, and all kinds of souvenirs line the narrow streets. To complete the picture and remove any last doubts, Queenstown is easily reached by private or public transportation from anywhere in the South Island.

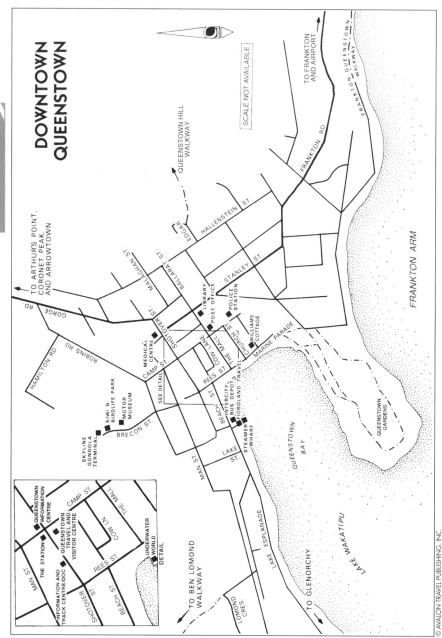

DOWNTOWN QUEENSTOWN

SCALE NOT AVAILABLE

TO ARTHUR'S POINT, CORONET PEAK, AND ARROWTOWN

QUEENSTOWN HILL WALKWAY

TO FRANKTON AND AIRPORT

FRANKTON QUEENSTOWN WALKWAY

FRANKTON RD

FRANKTON ARM

HALLENSTEIN ST

EDGAR

STANLEY ST

LIBRARY

POST OFFICE

POLICE STATION

WILLIAMS COTTAGE

MARINE PARADE

QUEENSTOWN GARDENS

MAGHAN ST

BALLARAT

GORGE RD

HAMILTON RD

ROBINS RD

SHOTOVER ST

MEDICAL CENTRE

CAMP ST

SEE DETAIL

REES ST

COW LANE

THE MALL

CHURCH ST

BEACH ST

INTERCITY BUS DEPOT

FIORDLAND TRAVEL

STEAMER WHARF

MAN ST

LAKE ST

BRECON ST

SKYLINE GONDOLA TERMINAL

KIWI & BIRDLIFE PARK

MOTOR MUSEUM

QUEENSTOWN BAY

LAKE WAKATIPU

LAKE ESPLANADE

TO GLENORCHY

LOMOND CRES

TO BEN LOMOND WALKWAY

DETAIL

QUEENSTOWN INFORMATION CENTRE

THE STATION

QUEENSTOWN TRAVEL AND VISITOR CENTRE

INFORMATION AND TRACK CENTRE/DOC

CAMP ST

MAN ST

THE MALL

COW LN

SHOTOVER ST

REES ST

BEACH ST

UNDERWATER WORLD

OTAGO

© AVALON TRAVEL PUBLISHING, INC.

SIGHTS

artists market on Saturday ↑ Very good

The Waterfront

The best way to appreciate the Queenstown atmosphere is on foot. Start at the waterfront end of the pedestrian-only **Queenstown Mall** (also called The Mall)—a great place to people-watch, listen to accents, and meet fellow travelers. Walk east along Marine Parade into **Queenstown Gardens** (colorful any time but spectacular in autumn) and follow the walkway around the point. Walk back through town and stroll in the other direction along the Queenstown Bay waterfront, passing jetties, the old steamer wharf, and lots of boats—you'll see all the ways you can take to water during the day and evening. An interesting stop along the way is **Williams Cottage.** Built on the shore of the bay in 1864, it was once the home of shipwright John Williams and stayed in the Williams family for more than a century. The house has never had power or water, which is hard to believe after seeing the surrounding commercialism.

From the main jetty at the end of Queenstown Mall you can watch fat trout and enormous eels cruise the clear water below while you feed the large, always-hungry duck population, or enter **Underwater World,** tel. 03/442-8437, ($5 adult, $3 child) and "catch" the action from a viewing lounge five meters underneath; it's open from 9 A.M. *we fished up to the parapet take it —*

Skyline Gondola *★ Beautiful*

To orient yourself to the entire area, hop on the Skyline Gondola on Brecon St., tel. 03/441-0101, for the steep ride up Bob's Peak to an observation deck 450 vertical meters above town for outstanding panoramic views of Queenstown, Lake Wakatipu, and the Remarkables. It operates continuously every day from 9 A.M., and you'll find a coffee shop, restaurant, theater, and souvenir shop on the main observation deck; rates are $14 adult, $5 child. In the theater, sit back and enjoy "Kiwi Magic," a goofy film featuring the spectacular beauty of New Zealand, with more than a splash of Kiwi humor; $8 adult, $4 child. A dry land **luge** run higher up the hill provides a little extra excitement: take the fast track for the thrill (although this is relative in Queenstown) or the slow track for the views. It's $4.50 per ride. For spectacular sunset views, live entertainment, and a huge meal, take the gondola up in the evening for the all-you-can-eat buffet.

Museum and Park *Closed?*

The popular **Queenstown Motor Museum** on Brecon St. (near the bottom of the gondola base terminal), tel. 03/442-8775, displays "marvelous machines and motoring memorabilia"—vintage, veteran, and classic cars, motorcycles, and aircraft—and special exhibitions that change frequently; it's open daily 9 A.M.–5:30 P.M., $8 adult, $4 child. Another well-visited attraction is the three-hectare **Kiwi & Birdlife Park,** also on Brecon St., tel. 03/442-8059, where you can view live kiwis in their nocturnal house and all sorts of New Zealand birds in as-natural-as-possible parklike surroundings; it's open daily 9 A.M.–5 P.M., with feeding at 11 A.M. and 3 P.M. $10 adult, $4 child, $22 family. *Best times*

ARROWTOWN AND VICINITY

Magnificent scenery abounds in all directions from Queenstown, but for an interesting scenic 50-km drive, head north out of Queenstown to Arrowtown. From Queenstown, take Arthur's Point Rd. to Arthur's Point for splendid views of the Shotover River. **Arthur's Point Pub** is a fun place to stop for a drink or a meal, a bit of gold-mining history, and evening entertainment—it does a booming business with the après-ski crowd in winter.

Skippers Canyon

Filled with history from the gold rush days, Skippers Canyon, north of Arthur's Point, is a hub of adrenaline activities but worth visiting in its own right. Gold was first discovered on the Shotover River, which flows through the canyon, in 1862 and was mined until the early 1990s. **Outback New Zealand,** tel. 03/442-7386, offers a great four-hour tour of the canyon. The $90 pp price includes Land Rover transportation taking in Hell's Gate and Heaven's Gate; driving along Pincher's Bluff, the Blue Slip, and Devil's Elbow

OTAGO

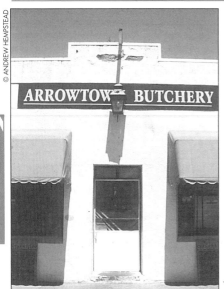

© ANDREW HEMPSTEAD

ARROWTOW BUTCHERY

Arrowtown Butchery

OTAGO

to Bridal Veil Falls; and crossing Skippers Bridge to the site of Skippers township. Also try your hand at gold panning.

Arrowtown

Continue along Malaghan Rd. from Arthur's Point to Arrowtown, which began as Foxes, a wild and unruly gold-mining settlement when gold was discovered in the Arrow River in 1862. A memorial marks the "golden" spot, an 800-meter walk upstream from the present township. The river was soon famous as one of the richest alluvial goldfields in the world, attracting hordes of miners from everywhere.

Today you can still appreciate the original gold-mining character by strolling along the tree-lined streets of miners' cottages, viewing the fine collection of pioneer relics in the **Lakes District Museum** (49 Buckingham St., tel. 03/442-1824; open 9 A.M.–5 P.M., $4 adult, $1 child), the old jail, churches dating from 1873, memorials, and the historic Chinatown site at the west end of town (part of **Otago Goldfields Park**). Shops sell everything from gold-panning equipment to sheepskin coats; cafés and restau-

rants cater to Arrowtown's modern-day industry—tourism.

For an enjoyable hike from Arrowtown, consider walking 13 km up the Arrow River (about 30 river crossings) to the ghost town of **Macetown.** There's not much left, but the three remaining buildings and machinery of a once-thriving gold town are protected as part of Otago Goldfields Park. Allow six to eight hours for the round-trip.

The **Arrow Express,** tel. 03/442-1900, departs five times daily from the top end of Queenstown Mall for Arrowtown; $5 one way.

LAKE CRUISES AND TOURS

The best way to choose among the myriad lake activities is to walk along the waterfront, look at all the boats, and compare trips and prices. Pick up brochures and book any of the various trips at the visitor center, or head down to Steamer Wharf.

TSS *Earnslaw*

One of the most leisurely ways to appreciate Lake Wakatipu is on the historic vintage coal-fired steamship, TSS *Earnslaw,* a Queenstown landmark. Known as "The Lady of the Lake," since 1912 she's carried supplies and stock to shoreside farms, and in recent times, taken visitors on tours. The most popular cruise is to **Walter Peak High Country Farm** on the far side of the lake. This high-country sheep and cattle station offers sheepdog displays, sheepshearing and wool-spinning demonstrations, horseback riding, and viewing of the only fold of highland cattle in the country. This 3.5-hour cruise departs up to four times daily for the farm, passing the spectacular scenery at the head of the lake; rates are $52 adult, $15 child. The TSS *Earnslaw* also departs daily on a 1.5-hour **Midday Cruise** around Queenstown Bay and up Frankton Arm for $34 adult, $15 child. Each night at 6 P.M., the **Evening Cruise** offers the option of tucking into the "Great Kiwi Carvery" at Colonels Restaurant at Walter Peak High Country Farm; $88 adult $44 child. Book all these cruises through **Fiordland Travel,** based at Steamer Wharf, tel. 03/442-7500.

Other Lake Activities

Do-it-yourselfers can rent canoes, kayaks, small catamarans, and personal watercraft from **Water Sport World** on Frankton Beach, tel. 03/442-8665. If a persistent urge to land a rainbow or brown trout necessitates hiring a fishing boat, equipment, and guide, you can find all you need at varying prices along the Queenstown waterfront. Get the current guide rates at the visitor center and a fishing license at sporting goods stores or the DOC.

For a short, thrilling parasailing ride (attached to a parachute, you soar high above the lake behind a jetboat—it's like flying without wings), contact **Paraflight NZ** at the Queenstown Mall Jetty, tel. 03/442-8507; the 10-minute flight costs $65 pp.

RECREATION ON LAND

Hiking

Before you set out on any walks in the Queenstown area, be sure to go to the DOC's **Queenstown Visitor Centre,** tel. 03/442-7933, and the **Information and Track Centre,** tel. 03/442-9708, website: www.infotrack.co.nz, first (both at 37 Shotover St.) and decide whether you need to invest in the book *Wandering in the Wakatipu* ($8.95). Listed below are local short walks in the Queenstown area. For information on the longer Rees and Dart Tracks, the Caples and Greenstone Tracks, and the popular Routeburn Track, see Glenorchy and the Tracks, below.

The three-km (one hour each way) **Queenstown Hill Walk** is a great way to absorb the scenery as you steadily climb to a vantage point for 360-degree views of Ben Lomond peak, the Skyline Gondola, Queenstown, and much of Lake Wakatipu. From the summit you can also see Coronet Peak, the Crown Range, Lake Hayes, Frankton Arm Peninsula, and the bare, craggy Remarkables Range. The track starts at the east end of Edgar Street.

The five-km **Frankton-Queenstown Walkway** wanders along the Frankton Arm shoreline of Lake Wakatipu, with views of the Remarkables and Cecil and Walter Peaks on the far side of the lake, and of Peninsula Hill. The 1.5-hour walk

starts at the east end of Peninsula St. in Queenstown, passing a harbor bustling with boating activity and the fronts of private properties before reaching the north end of Frankton Recreation Reserve on the lakefront (return by bus).

Ben Lomond Walkway is a good 10-km climb through forest and grassland to the 1,746-meter summit of Ben Lomond (snowy in winter). From here you can see Mount Cook in the distant northeast, Mount Aspiring and Mount Earnslaw to the north, the Remarkables and Lake Wakatipu to the southeast, Arrow Flats and Lake Hayes to the east, and Moke Creek and gorge and Moonlight Creek to the north. The track starts and finishes on Lomond Crescent (west end of Queenstown) via Skyline access road and takes about seven hours round-trip; wear sturdy shoes and take a warm jacket for the summit—the weather can change very quickly. On the return trip you can take the sidetrack to the Skyline (signposted) and catch the gondola down for a few bucks.

To get more out of hiking around Queenstown, consider hiking with an experienced local guide. **Guided Walks NZ,** tel. 03/442-7126, offers an easy three-hour guided hike along the shore of Lake Wakatipu, a six-hour hike through the gold-mining areas of Arrowtown, and a full day on the famous Routeburn Track. The hikes cost $75, $85, and $185 respectively, including transportation from Queenstown.

Horseback Riding

Several outfits host guided horseback riding amidst some of the most beautiful scenery. **Moonlight Country,** tel. 03/442-1229, treks are for experienced or inexperienced riders through the Shotover and Moonlight Valleys. A 2.5-hour trek down to the Kawarau River with time for fishing is $99 pp; a full day ride is $150 pp. **Walter Peak High Country Farm,** accessible by the TSS *Earnslaw* from Queenstown, offers horseback riding; contact Fiordland Travel at tel. 03/442-7500 for details. At Glenorchy, **High Country Horses,** tel. 03/442-9915, has a variety of guided horseback rides, with the option of riding unguided for one hour ($35), for two hours ($45), or all day ($70). Transfers from Queenstown are $20 pp.

ADRENALINE ADVENTURES

Booking Agents

For booking the more popular activities detailed below, head to one of Queenstown's many booking agents. The largest is **The Station** on the corner of Camp and Shotover Streets, tel. 03/442-5252 or 0800/367-874. It books most adventure activities, has massive video screens showing footage of jumping, rafting, and jet-boating, and has a row of Internet terminals. Kitty-corner, the **Queenstown Travel & Visitor Centre**, tel. 03/442-4100, the official information center, also makes all bookings, as well as hands out general information. At the same intersection, **Queenstown Information Centre**, tel. 03/442-7319, is another base for a variety of adventure operators.

Bungee Jumping ✯

Bungee jumping is one of the most popular activities in Queenstown and provides thousands of people with unforgettable memories. And once they've "jumped," many come back for more. If *you* relish the idea of diving off a canyon-spanning bridge high above a river, free-falling on the end of an elastic rope, then plunging into icy water before rocketing back toward the bridge for an-

other fall (or two, or three, until momentum subsides), *and* surviving to tell the tale, Queenstown is the place to get your thrills.

The procedure at each of the following jumps is the same. After working out how much rope is needed, experienced operators wrap your ankles with a towel and then with the incredibly springy rope (similar to the rope used by mountain climbers). You're helped out onto a small platform and told to look straight ahead as you dive off, and then a large crowd of not-so-brave onlookers enthusiastically does a community countdown to encourage you to take the plunge. Afterward you're scooped into a boat, released from the life-saving rope, and taken to shore to walk the trail to the top for your designer bungee-jumper T-shirt (you have to jump to get one). Bungee jumping is also a spectator sport. It's almost as much fun to go out to the bridge to watch and listen to the blood-curdling screams, swear words, and shocked silences that occur as the daredevils take the plunge.

New Zealander A. J. Hackett, who started it all, now operates four commercial jumps in Queenstown. His first commercial operation, and the world's first, began in 1988 at the old Kawarau Suspension Bridge spanning the beautiful Kawarau River, about 23 km from Queen-

A SHORT HISTORY OF BUNGEE JUMPING

Bungee jumping originated as a test of manhood on the South Pacific island of Vanutau, where young men would throw themselves off a bamboo tower with nothing more than a vine tied around their ankles. The vine stopped their fall, just centimeters from the ground.

Various daredevils imitated the feat over the years, but it was New Zealander A. J. Hackett and his speed-skier pal Henry Van Asch who got the world's attention by jumping off the Eiffel Tower in the summer of 1987 with only a latex rubber cord separating them from fame and a very public death. The following year, Hackett opened a commercial bungee jumping site on an old suspension bridge over Queenstown's Kawarau River. The enterprise was an immediate suc-

cess and led to the construction of a custom-built bridge over the Shotover River. Today, Hackett also operates a jump from the Skyline Gondola, from a gondola over the Nevis River, and for a time in the mid-1990s from a helicopter over Lake Wakatipu.

Hackett has spread his wings beyond New Zealand and you will see his name on the jump beside Circus Circus in Las Vegas; on Condesa Beach, Acapulco; in tropical Cairns, Australia; and outside Paris, France. Over 1,000,000 otherwise ordinary folk have experienced the adrenaline rush of a lifetime with the Hackett company, and there's no place better to add your name to the list than Queenstown. Or maybe you'd just like to check out his website: www.aj-hackett.com.

stown. At Kawarau you can choose from a "splashdown" (expect to be dipped in the river to your waist) or dry jump (you get close to the surface of the river, but stay dry). The Kawarau jump costs $129, which includes a shirt, video, and transportation from Queenstown. Expanding the notion of bungee jumping as a spectator sport, an underground observation center has been built into the riverside cliffs at Kawarau. Inside is a bungee museum, a big-screen TV with jump demos shown, a café, and an outdoor viewing deck. Another Hackett jump is off the **Skippers Canyon Bridge.** Accessible only by 4WD, this 71-meter-high jump drops into a narrow and spectacular section of the canyon. It costs $110, which includes a shirt and transportation. The latest addition to the jump craze is the **Nevis Highwire,** strung over the Nevis River. This jump, from a glass-bottomed gondola, has a six-second-plus freefall. It also has a unique twist at the end; once you've bounced a couple of times, pull a release pin and swing around and into a sitting position—a perfect way to enjoy the view. This jump costs $149 pp. Finally, and closest to Queenstown, there's **The Ledge,** where daredevils plunge from a platform at the top of the gondola; $85 includes the gondola ride and one jump, $25 each for additional jumps. The actual bungee cord isn't very long (30 meters), but the jump still gets the adrenaline flowing. All Hackett jumps can be booked at the **Queenstown Bungee Centre** in The Station at the corner of Shotover and Camp Streets, tel. 03/442-7122 or 0800/254-225. free for 60+
The fifth Queenstown bungee jump is the **Pipeline,** up Skippers Canyon, tel. 03/442-5455. Named for a pipeline that once carried water to the goldfields, the platform lies more than 100 meters above the canyon floor, making it the world's highest year-round commercial bungee jump. The cost is $150 for the jump and transportation between Queenstown and the canyon.

Jetboating

Jetboat tours from Queenstown combine power, maneuverability in just inches of water, and skilled drivers to provide a thrilling ride through impressive river and canyon scenery. If you

haven't already been on a jetboat, this is the place! Jetboats are operated on the wide, tree-lined, swift-flowing **Upper Kawarau River,** the turbulent and exciting **Shotover River** with its narrow rocky gorge and incredible scenery, and the **Lower Shotover River** with its wide shingle riverbeds, tree-lined narrow sections, and varied terrain. Most trips last 30 minutes to an hour or so; some leave from Queenstown Bay while others provide transportation to launch sites.

The **Shotover Jet,** tel. 03/442-8570, gives you one of the biggest adrenaline rushes for your money, departing every 15 minutes from Arthur's Point and including a ride to the launch site for $89. Operating on the tamer Kawarau River from Queenstown's Town Pier, **Kawarau Jet,** tel. 03/442-6142 or 0800/529-272, was the world's first commercial jetboat operation. Their one-hour trip costs $69 adult, $39 child. **Twin Rivers Jet,** tel. 03/442-3257, also operates on the Kawarau, and trips are longer and less expensive than the Shotover.

If you can afford to spend more, consider one of the concoctions—a jetboat ride and helicopter flight (from $120); or a jetboat ride, white-water rafting trip, and helicopter flight (from $200). You can arrange just about any combination, and there's no lack of booking agents willing to take your money.

If you're looking for a combination of wind-whipping-through-your-hair excitement; outrageously beautiful lake, river, and mountain scenery; and a small, friendly group; and if you have about five to six hours to experience all this fun, look no further than the **Dart River Safaris,** tel. 03/442-9992 or 0800/327-8538. The first 45 minutes is a scenic drive along Lake Wakatipu from Queenstown to the village of Glenorchy, where you board a jetboat and the real adventure begins. Whizzing across the lake, then up the Dart River, the boat performs for the next two hours or more in both deep and surprisingly shallow water with ease, climbing almost 160 meters in altitude. At the end of the trip, the drivers do soak-to-the-skin "Hamilton spins" for a last burst of adrenaline, and then you recover and relive the excitement over a cup of tea and a snack (on the morning trip) or beer at the pub (afternoon trip) at Glenorchy before heading back to Queenstown. All this costs $145 pp; life jackets, windbreakers, and warm woolly hats are provided.

White-water Rafting

Queenstown is the self-proclaimed "Rafting Capital of New Zealand." Rivers are numerically graded from one (easy) to six (unraftable)—in the Queenstown area it's more than likely that, even if you're a total beginner, you'll be rafting a grade four/five river. Trips are on the **Kawarau River** with 15 km of large-volume water and four thundering rapids, and on the **Lower Canyon** of the **Shotover River** with 17 km of grade four-plus roaring rapids, twisting and churning through spectacular rugged scenery to end by shooting 170 meters through the completely dark, narrow-walled Oxenbridge gold-miners' tunnel and down a waterfall—this trip takes guts and is the most popular. Rafting trips take 3.5–4 hours and cost about $85–110; all companies provide helmets, life jackets, and wet suits (a necessity—the water is icy), and you need to wear a swimsuit, wool socks and sandshoes or tennis shoes (some companies provide rubber booties), and a lightweight waterproof jacket. Forget the camera unless it's waterproof and floats.

Queenstown Rafting, 35 Shotover St., tel. 03/442-9792 or 0800/723-8464, has the widest variety of combination trips. The basic Shotover River Rafting is $129 and the Kawarau River Rafting $109. Options include the Shotover River Heli-rafting, $180; the Triple Challenge (rafting, jetboating, and a helicopter flight), $239; and the Crazy Kiwi (the Triple Challenge with a bungee jump), $369. At the completion of all trips you're offered a hot shower and a hot drink at Cavell's Cafe. Another company providing raft trips is **Extreme Green Adventure Co.,** tel. 03/442-8517.

Funyaks

For a fast, 75-minute, jetboat ride to Sandy Bluff on the Dart River followed by a very scenic, guided, paddle downriver in an open, inflatable canoe and a short, guided bush walk, contact **Funyaks,** tel. 03/442-7374 or 0800/386-925.

Operated by Eric Billoud, a former French whitewater kayaking champion, the six-hour trip costs $195 pp, including a gourmet lunch. No previous experience is necessary. If you're walking the Rees and Dart Tracks, you can arrange to canoe the fourth day through Funyaks.

IN THE AIR

Flightseeing

All local flights leave from Queenstown Airport, northeast of town, near Frankton.

Air Wakatipu, tel. 03/442-3148, has a 20-minute flight taking in the lake and surrounding highlights for $55 pp. Air Wakatipu and **Glenorchy Air,** tel. 03/442-2207, have the least expensive flights over Fiordland National Park, costing from $170. **Air Fiordland,** tel. 03/442-3404 or 0800/103-404, provides a number of scenic options, including a 70-minute Milford Sound Overflight for $175 pp and a two-hour Mount Cook Overflight for $380 pp.

The Helicopter Line, tel. 03/442-3034, offers trips from the heli-pad by the airport that range from a 20-minute flight for $160 pp to the "Milford Sound" flight for $545 pp. The local 40-minute flight is most popular. Taking in the Remarkables, Coronet Peak, and Skippers Canyon before following the Shotover River back down to Queenstown, it costs $325 pp. The company also runs flights in combination with other adventure activities. Try the excellent "Crazy Kiwi" for four bursts of adrenaline—a short helicopter flight (as close as you can come to heli-aerobatics!) followed by an exciting jetboat ride, bungee jump, and white-water rafting; $369 pp.

Skydiving

If you'd rather jump out of a perfectly good airplane for kicks, contact **nzone,** 35 Shotover St., tel. 03/442-5867. The basic tandem jump, from 3,000 meters, comprises a 25-second freefall and then up to seven minutes "under the canopy." This costs $245 pp, with an extra charge to have someone freefalling beside you with a still camera ($155) or video ($145). Another option is to have an altitude upgrade. Jumping from a plane is intimidating enough for most people, but in the Queenstown tradition of upping the adrenalin ante, nzone offers a jump from 5,000 meters ($150 extra). From this height, the freefall takes almost a minute and speeds of 200 km per hour can be reached. All Rates include round-trip transportation between Queenstown and the airstrip and a jump certificate.

Hang Gliding

SkyTrek Tandem Hang Gliding, tel. 03/442-6311, New Zealand's first commercial hang gliding operation, offers another way to experience the mountain scenery from above. Once you're at the designated launch site (dependent on wind conditions—usually Coronet Peak or The Remarkables), a short briefing on glider operation is given before your 10- to 30-minute flight. The cost of the flight, $145 pp, includes ground transportation and a photo from a camera mounted on the wing.

Parapenting

Yet another way to take to the sky for a one-way-down flightseeing adventure is by tandem parapenting from the upper gondola terminal. This involves a trip up the Skyline Gondola, a 15-minute walk to the launch area, instruction in the handling of a parapente (a rectangular, very maneuverable parachute that acts like a wing), followed by an airborne plunge off a hill with your guide; $120–145 per jump. Parapenting companies include **Max Air Tandem Parapente,** tel. 025/324-147; **Parapente Queenstown Tandem,** tel. 0800/472-724; and **Flight Park Tandem Paragliding,** tel. 0800/467-325. The latter company uses Coronet Peak ski field as a takeoff point.

WINTERTIME

Queenstown was traditionally a winter resort town, and it has only been in the last decade that its popularity as a year-round destination has grown. Skiers and snowboarders from New Zealand and Australia flock to the slopes of the two local ski fields, with two additional ski fields in nearby Wanaka, and great heli-skiing an added attraction.

Both ski fields rent ski and snowboard equipment, or head to **Queenstown Sportsworld,** 17 Rees St., tel. 03/442-8452.

Coronet Peak

A 30-minute drive north of Queenstown, Coronet Peak, tel. 03/442-4620, is open late June–October. Although there's no on-hill accommodation, it's a very busy, commercial resort suited mostly to beginners and intermediate skiers. One quad and two double chairs along with a variety of surface lifts serve 280 hectares of treeless, rolling slopes. Snowmaking takes over where Mother Nature leaves off, making the season somewhat more reliable than in years past. The spread out base lodge has ski, snowboard, and clothing rentals; a restaurant, self-service cafeteria, and take-aways; and various boutiques. A lift ticket is $68 adult, $38 senior, $34 child. Night skiing is $35, $23, and $20, respectively.

To get to Coronet Peak, take Gorge Rd. north out of Queenstown for about eight km, then turn up Skippers Rd.—it's another eight km or so of sealed road to the sprawling parking lot. The field is also easy to reach by public transportation—**Ski Shuttles,** tel. 03/442-4630, and **Kiwi Discovery** tel. 03/442-7340, run buses throughout the season for the round-trip fare of $25 adult, $18 child.

The Remarkables

Owned by the same company that operates Coronet Peak (multiday tickets are interchangeable), The Remarkables ski field is tucked behind the mountain range of the same name east of Queenstown. Surrounded on three sides by towering jagged peaks, the base area is at 1,730 meters, higher than Coronet Peak, and therefore with somewhat more reliable snow. Three chairlifts and two surface lifts open up 220 hectares and 350 vertical meters of mostly intermediate and easier expert terrain. These statistics don't really give The Remarkables justice as the more experienced skiers and boarders climb or traverse to access surrounding off-piste slopes or take the Homeward Run, which ends along the access road. One thing that you definitely shouldn't miss is the short climb from the top of the Snow Basin chair to a lookout for views over Lake Wakatipu and Queenstown. The field also has two terrain parks. Rentals, clothing, and meals are available in the day lodge. Lift tickets are priced the same as across the valley at Coronet Peak, but The Remarkables has no night skiing. For resort information, call 03/442-4615.

From Queenstown, follow Hwy. 6 through Frankton and around Lake Wakatipu to the signposted access road. From this point, it's 14 km along a steep, winding, and often muddy road to the base area. To save yourself the stress of this trek, use either **Ski Shuttles,** tel. 03/442-4630, or **Kiwi Discovery,** tel. 03/442-7340, to get to the field.

Heli-Skiing and Boarding

For the latest heli-skiing information, contact **Harris Mountains Heli-Skiing,** tel. 03/442-6722, or **Southern Lakes Heliski,** tel. 03/442-6222. You could be whisked away to the Remarkables Range and Coronet Peak, the Thomson Mountains, or the Richardson Mountains, depending on snow conditions. Groups are graded according to ability and matched with suitable terrain. Costs run around $600 pp for a full day (usually three runs) while more experienced skiers and boarders can fit up to seven runs into a day (about $850 pp).

Invincible Snowfields

If you thought a day schussing down the slopes of Coronet Peak or The Remarkables was as far as you could get from the mega-resorts of North America and Europe, think again. High in the remote Richardson Mountains west of Queenstown, where the only access is by helicopter, an entrepreneurial local has built a single 700-meter-long rope tow that opens up 230 hectares of intermediate terrain. Beside the tow is a two-story hut. The lower level holds a kitchen and lounge with open fire while upstairs is reserved for sleeping. It costs $25 pp for the accommodation and $50 pp to use the tow. Transfers are by helicopter from Glenorchy. Call 03/442-9933 for details.

> *Queenstown really hops at night—in summer and during the winter ski season, bands play in pubs and nightclubs around town almost every night, particularly on weekends—just follow your ears.*

ENTERTAINMENT

To find out what's on, pick up the free *Mountain Scene* newspaper and the various pamphlets on Queenstown available at travel centers around town. Also, the friendly young staff at many of the booking centers around town always know where the best action is. Queenstown really hops at night—in summer and during the winter ski season, bands play in pubs and nightclubs around town almost every night, particularly on weekends—just follow your ears.

World Bar, 27 Shotover St., tel. 03/442-6757, is a popular nightspot with daily specials and lots of theme and promotion nights. Toward the lake, **Casbah,** 54 Shotover St., tel. 03/442-7853, offers more of the same, but with a young, international backpacker crowd. Locals head to the **Rattlesnake Room** at 14 Brecon St., tel. 03/442-9995, where a state-of-the-art sound system pumps out everything from pop to country. **Red Rock Bar and Café,** 48 Camp St., tel. 03/442-6850, isn't the most stylish bar in Queenstown, but the beer and food is cheap, especially during happy hour, 4–6 P.M., when a beer is just $2.50. Tucked away on Cow Lane, the **Bunker Room,** tel. 03/441-8030, attracts moneyed locals and anyone else who can find the place. **Pog Mahones,** 14 Rees St., tel. 03/442-5382, has a large two-story deck, packed day and night through summer. Inside, Irish bands play most nights. **Surreal** is an alternative nightclub diagonally opposite at 7 Rees St., tel. 03/441-8492. **Chico's Restaurant and Bar** in Queenstown Mall, tel. 03/442-8439, is very popular and occasionally provides live entertainment.

Two places out of town are often overlooked. The **Skyline Restaurant,** at the top of the gondola, tel. 03/441-0101, has a bar with great views and there's often live entertainment in the main dining area. If you have your own transportation or don't mind taking a taxi, try **Arthur's Point Hotel** along Gorge Rd. at Arthur's Point, tel. 03/442-8007. It's the hot spot après-ski bar in winter.

HOTELS AND MOTELS

You can get anything you want in Queenstown—from basic rooms that share bathrooms to luxurious first-class international-standard hotel rooms. Pick your price range and go from there. **Queenstown Reservations,** tel. 03/442-6340 or 0800/804-111, website: www.queenstown-res.co.nz, is a good place to start looking.

Room rates in Queenstown fluctuate greatly throughout the year. All rates quoted below are for a standard double room in summer (Dec.–Feb.). Rates are higher in busy winter season (late June–late Sept.) and lower the rest of the year. Regardless of the season, use the Internet to find the best rates.

Under $100

Overlooking Steamer Wharf, **Thomas's Hotel,** 50 Beach St., tel. 03/442-7180, website: www.thomashotel.co.nz, is in the heart of the action. It mainly caters to backpackers, but has double rooms with shared bath for $79 s or d. En suite double rooms are $79 s, $94–109 d, with the more expensive rooms enjoying lake views equal to any of the more expensive options listed below. All private rooms have a TV, fridge, and tea- and coffee-making facilities. The hotel also holds a café, laundry, and bike rentals.

Just off Frankton Rd., the **Alpine Sun Motel,** 14 Hallenstein St., tel. 03/442-8482 or 0800/101-914, website: www.alpinesun.co.nz, offers small but comfortable self-contained units and airport transfers, and the hosts will deliver breakfast to your room; from $95 s or d.

A number of other motels, each with kitchen-equipped rooms, lie along Frankton Road. These include **Alpha Lodge,** 42 Frankton Rd., tel. 03/442-6095; **Colonial Village Motel,** 100 Frankton Rd., tel. 03/442-7629 or 0800/226-652; and **Wakatipu View Apartments,** 14 Frankton Rd., tel. 03/442-7463. Rates range $75 s, $95 d.

$100–200

At lakeside **Alpine Village,** five km from downtown at 633 Frankton Rd., tel. 03/442-7795 or 0800/925-746, facilities include three private, open-air spa pools, a tennis court, cocktail lounge, pool table, a restaurant serving breakfast and dinner, and shuttle transportation into town. Rooms start at $110 s or d, lakefront chalets are $140 s or d, and suites are $175 s or d.

Along Gorge Rd. toward Arrowtown, **Cranbury Court,** 19–23 Gorge Rd., tel. 03/442-6483 or 0800/269-666, website: www.cranbury.co.nz, is a French provincial-style motel of 23 self-contained units, each with a private courtyard or balcony and an impressive entertainment system; one-, two-, and three-, bedroom units are $145, $180, and 235 respectively.

Modern and stylish **Novotel Queenstown,** Sainsbury Rd., tel. 03/442-6600 or 0800/655-557, is a self-contained resort on the main road into Queenstown overlooking magnificent Lake Wakatipu. The 148 rooms are fairly standard, but with the views, a large outdoor heated pool, fitness room, two tennis courts, three eateries, and shuttle service to downtown and the airport, it provides good value at $150–180 s or d.

Gardens Parkroyal, downtown on Marine Parade, tel. 03/442-7750 or 0800/801-111, website: www.sphc.com.au, features more than 200 well-appointed rooms surrounding a courtyard filled with gardens and outdoor furniture. The hotel's Promenade Restaurant is open for breakfast and dinner, but in summer it's a barbecue in the courtyard that draws the biggest crowd. Rates start at $160 s or d.

Out of town on the road to Arrowtown is the **Quality Resort Alpine Resort,** Malaghans Rd., tel. 03/442-7850 or 0800/877-999. This low-rise timber and stone lodge features extensive gardens, a swimming pool, restaurant, bar, and courtesy shuttles into town; rates from $160 s or d.

Over $200

Spinnaker Bay, 151 Frankton Rd., tel. 03/442-5050, website: www.spinnaker.co.nz, offers unimpeded views across the lake to the Remarkables and an indoor pool. Each luxurious unit features separate bedrooms, a modern kitchen, and a wood-burning fireplace. Rates range $240–280 s or d.

Millennium, on the corner of Frankton Rd. and Stanley St., tel. 03/441-8888 or 0800/808-228, website: www.millenniumqueenstown.co.nz, is a grand hotel with 220 luxuriously furnished rooms and expansive public areas filled with original art. This upmarket hotel also features a gym, sauna, spa, a large restaurant, and a relaxing bar. It is arguably Queenstown's finest accommodation. Rack rates start at $320 s or d, but check the website for discounted rooms.

Millbrook Resort, 19 km north of Queenstown near Arrowtown, tel. 03/441-7000 or 0800/800-604, website: www.millbrook.co.nz, is one of New Zealand's finest resort complexes. Guests enjoy one of the country's premier golf courses, a fully equipped health club, tennis courts, an indoor swimming pool, and a variety of cafés and restaurants. Accommodation choices include hotel rooms in the Village Inn, each with a private balcony fireplace, and walk-in wardrobe ($320 s or d); spacious kitchen-equipped Villa Suites ($360 s or d); and freestanding cottages ($495 s or d). Check the Millbrook website for multinight packages that include golf and spa services.

Remarkables Lodge

In 1995, the homestead of the Remarkables Station, which lies in the shadow of the famous mountain range, was restored and opened as an upmarket lodge. While none of the building's character was lost during restoration, no expense was spared either, and today guests enjoy a heated swimming pool, hot tub, snooker room, tennis court, library, and comfortable lounge with a log fire. Guests take meals in an elegant dining room that opens to a courtyard and the pool, and the lodge is licensed to serve alcohol. Each of the four rooms are individually decorated, feature twin or king-size beds, and boast luxurious private bathrooms. Rates are from $290 pp per night, which includes a gourmet breakfast, predinner drinks, a three-course dinner, and airport transfers. The lodge is along Hwy. 6 south toward Invercargill (call for directions), tel. 03/442-2720; website: www.remarkables.co.nz. *Boutique*

Bed-and-Breakfasts *Browns Hotel Dale Street*

In **Queenstown House** at 69 Hallenstein St., tel. 03/442-9043, website: www.queenstown-house.co.nz, you'll find a luxurious "homey" atmosphere, and eight bright, individually country-style furnished rooms each with a private bathroom, lake or mountain views, and a king-size bed. In 2002 a new wing with seven additional rooms, some with a private deck, opened off to one side of the original house. Breakfast is a grand affair in the elegant dining room, and each evening, guests can indulge in a complimentary wine and cheese platter. Rooms are $195–250 s or d, including breakfast.

Built back in the 1920s, the **Dairy Guesthouse,** 10 Isle St., tel. 03/442-5164 or 0800/333-393, website: www.thedairy.co.nz, incorporates a dairy (general store) and adjacent house. Converted to a bed-and-breakfast, it offers 11 well-appointed rooms, each with a private bath. The lounge area, complete with log fire, affords stunning lake views. The rates are $215 s, $265 d, which includes a self-serve continental breakfast in the actual dairy itself. *Located Near Browns. Nice Breakfast*

Health Retreat

If you want to be close to Queenstown's action but stay in a beautiful, secluded spot, head for **Bush Creek Health Retreat,** 1.25 km from downtown on Bowen St., tel. 03/442-7260. Stay in the large comfortable house on one hectare, surrounded by gorgeous flower, herb, and veggie gardens, with the constant sound of rushing water from a stream and several waterfalls that cascade naturally through the garden and swimming pool. The friendly owner, Ileen Mutch, does iridology (eye) analysis, nutritional counseling, and reflex massage; sells herbal remedies; and is known for nutritious breakfasts included in the $60 pp room rate (four rooms share two bathrooms). Take Gorge Rd. toward Arthur's Point, then turn left at Bowen St. and follow it to the end.

Backpacker Lodges

The large, modern **Queenstown YHA,** 80 Lake Esplanade, tel. 03/442-8413, is only a short walk along the lakeshore from downtown, with stunning lake and mountain views. Even with 150 beds, the hostel is usually full—especially in winter. Dorm beds are $20, doubles are $26 pp. To get there from downtown, head for the lakefront and follow it around to the west (toward Glenorchy) onto Beach Street. This becomes Lake Esplanade.

Centrally located is **Black Sheep Backpackers,** 13 Frankton Rd., tel. 03/442-7289. As a converted low-rise motel, rooms are large (with up to 10 dorm beds in each). Facilities include a pool room, bar, spa pools, and a communal kitchen; $18 pp for a dorm, $44 d.

Alpine Lodge, a two-minute walk from town at 13 Gorge Rd., tel. 03/442-7220, is a smaller establishment. Reservations are needed here. Dorm beds are $20 pp, doubles and twins are $25 pp. In the vicinity and with great lake views across town, **Hippo Lodge,** 4 Anderson Heights (off Hallenstein St.), tel. 03/442-5785, website: www.hippolodge.co.nz, is probably the pick of the bunch for a quiet night's rest. The beds are comfortable and the atmosphere about as mellow as it gets in Queenstown. Dorms are $20 pp, private rooms are $25 pp or pay $28.50 pp to enjoy an en suite room with its own TV and microwave.

One of the larger backpackers, **Pinewood Lodge,** 48 Hamilton Rd., tel. 03/442-8273, offers good budget accommodation; dorm beds $19 pp, twin or double rooms $25 pp. Along with the usual communal facilities, linen is available, and there is a store, storage, and a good information board, all in a garden setting only a few minutes' walk from town center.

Small, friendly **Deco Backpackers** at 52 Man St. (opposite the entrance to Queenstown Motor Park), tel. 03/442-7384, provides light, clean rooms in a restored art deco home, all the usual facilities, poorly equipped kitchen, and free storage. It's quite an uphill hike from downtown, but courtesy van transportation is available on demand. A dorm bed is $20 pp, a twin or double room is $24 pp.

Motor Camps

Queenstown Holiday Park, one km uphill from downtown, at the west end of Man St., tel. 03/442-7252 or 0800/827-3529, website: holidaypark.co.nz, is a large motor camp with many rules and regulations to keep the crowd in order. Aside from the usual communal bathroom,

kitchen, and laundry, there's a fully stocked shop on the premises. Tent sites are $11 pp, caravan sites are $12 pp. Cabins start at $45 s or d, lodges (each with a toilet and shower) are $60 s or d, flats (with full kitchens) are $70 s or d, and motel units with a separate bedroom start at $95 s or d. From Shotover St. take Camp or Brecon Streets up the hill, then turn left on Man Street.

If you're traveling by camper-van and are looking for a powered site with water and waste disposal, and even TV and phone connections, try **Creeksyde Campervan Park** on Robins Rd. (off Gorge Rd.), tel. 03/442-9447. The sites have been developed around a central building that has modern bathrooms (private ones also available), kitchen, laundry, and spacious lounge with TV and video. Milk, bread, and daily newspapers are available at the office. It costs $25 per van per night. There's also a cottage; for shared facilities but private rooms it's $70 per night. Motel rooms are $90 per night.

Frankton Motor Camp is about five km from Queenstown at the end of Stewart St., Frankton, tel. 03/442-2079. It has communal bath (free showers), kitchen, and laundry; tent and caravan sites are $19 s or d, and cabins range $38–54 s or d. From the main highway at Frankton turn right on Yewlett Crescent, then right on Stewart St., and continue to the end.

FOOD

Café !

Cheap Eats

For reasonably priced take-away Chinese or Mexican meals, or for McDonald's fare, go to the food mall on the lower floor of **O'Connell's Shopping Centre** on the corner of Camp and Beach Streets. Tables and chairs are provided, but it's usually crowded and hard to find a vacated spot to enjoy your meal—take it away! Just across the road is a KFC restaurant. Also in the O'Connell's Shopping Centre, upstairs, is the popular **Lai Sing Thai Food,** tel. 03/442-7881. Expect to pay about $10 for a three-dish Chinese combo (with soup if you get it to go), $14 for the smorgasbord lunch, and $21 for dinner. For cakes, pastries, and meat pies, head to **The Bakery,** 15 Shotover St., tel. 03/442-8698. Around

© ANDREW HEMPSTEAD

OTAGO

Head to the park beside the Steamer Wharf to enjoy a picnic lunch.

the corner on Camp St. **Ken's Noodle Café**, 37 Camp St., tel. 03/442-8628, has inexpensive noodles and sushi. **Habebes Lebanese Takeaways** in Wakatipu Arcade off Rees St., tel. 03/442-9861, has excellent kebabs (meat- and salad-filled rolls) for $6.50–10, and an assortment of other Lebanese delicacies—all tasty, all reasonable in price.

Cafés and Casual

Gourmet Express in the Bay Centre, a small shopping arcade at 62 Shotover St., tel. 03/442-9619, looks like a U.S. diner, complete with chrome furniture and laminated menus listing dishes to suit all tastes. American-style cooked breakfasts start at $9, lunches and dinners range $7–18 (good salad bar), and desserts are about $5; it's open daily 6:30 A.M.–9 P.M. In the same arcade, **Naff Caff**, tel. 03/442-8211, opens early for good coffee, muffins, and cookies. At lunch, a wide range of breads is stuffed with healthy fillings for $5–7.50. In the same vicinity, **Bean to Tea**, 42 Shotover St., tel. 03/442-8969, is a small coffeehouse with a few outdoor tables and an ever-changing blackboard menu of pies, pastries, soups, and sandwiches.

Berkel's Gourmet Burgers, in the Chester Centre at 19 Shotover St., tel. 03/442-6950, is another casual café—this one renowned for its burgers, which start at $5. A cooked breakfast costs $9, which includes bottomless coffee. **Fatz Cat**, 3 Brecon St., tel. 03/442-9828, has a casual, funky atmosphere and a mostly Italian menu. Main courses, such as spaghetti bolognaise, start at $16 or order a pizza to share from $18.

Restaurants *Little India - upstairs Shotover Street*

The small **Cow Restaurant** on Cow Lane (off Beach St.), tel. 03/442-8588, has undoubtedly the best pizza in town, an open fireplace that's very appealing when the evenings get chilly, good music, and a jovial laid-back atmosphere as guests wait around the fire for their turn to sit and tuck in. A large variety of pizza sizes and combinations range $11.95–25, various spaghetti dishes are $12–17, and crisp green salads, homemade soup, garlic bread, and desserts complete your meal. It's open daily noon–11 P.M., has a BYO license (the bottle shop in Cow Lane has a great selection of cold wines and beers), and is very popular with the locals—expect to wait for a table, or go in early (5:30 P.M.), put down your name, and return later. Another great pizza place is **Pasta Pasta Cucina**, 6 Brecon St., tel. 03/442-6762. This long, narrow restaurant offers wood-fired pizza from $19, as well as a wide range of pastas, many prepared using local ingredients.

One of the best places in town is **Avanti**, 20 Queenstown Mall, tel. 03/442-8503. Again, it's so popular with locals *and* visitors alike that you can't just walk in and get a table, but the wait is usually worthwhile. Typically Italian fare and seafood dishes (fresh from the sea on Wednesday) are the specialties, though if you take a look at the desserts you may beg to differ! It's open daily 7 A.M.–10 P.M. Breakfast is $8–12; expect to pay from $12 for a main course at lunch, from $17.50 at dinner. The atmosphere is relaxed and jovial and the service is excellent. The **Stonewall Cafe** just across the mall from Avanti, tel. 03/442-6429, is another busy spot. It's open daily 9:30 A.M.–4 P.M. for delicious lunches ($7–10), sandwiches (from $3.50), and the daily hot special with salad ($11). At dinner it serves fish, game, steak, chicken, a daily vegetarian special, pasta, and salads, with specials about $14, main courses ranging $15–21. Sit inside or outside.

The **Boardwalk Seafood Restaurant** has a magnificent position upstairs in the Steamer Wharf Village, tel. 03/442-5630. The menu changes with the seasons, but there's always a wide variety of starters, such as seafood chowder (from $9.50), and a daily fish special that may be barbecued *hapuka* smothered in a garlic-based mayonnaise ($31). Although the Boardwalk is a touristy, upmarket restaurant, the setting is unpretentious and presentation of food stylish.

Roaring Megs, 57 Shotover St., tel. 03/442-9676, is popular with the locals, serving fine New Zealand cuisine in an original log cabin. Soup starts at $6.50, appetizers are $9.50–14.50, and main courses range from $18.50 for vegetarian to $27.50 for fresh salmon. It's open nightly from 7 P.M.

Like Roaring Meg's, **Gantley's** is in a gold-rush era building, this one seven km north of town on Arthur's Point Rd., tel. 03/442-8999. This elegant dining room features crisp white-linen tablecloths, muted lighting, and attentive service. The food is equally classy; start with the Caesar salad, complete with anchovies and warmed croutons ($13.50) before moving onto mains including Gantley's Breast of Chicken, poached in a coconut-based cream and served with saffron rice and avocado salsa ($28). Gantley's is open daily for dinner.

Above Town and Out of Town

The **Skyline Restaurant** at the top of the gondola on Brecon St., tel. 03/441-0101, holds 300 diners on two tiers, with most tables having fantastic views of Queenstown and its reflections twinkling in the lake far below. The tourist-oriented Taste of New Zealand buffet is $28 pp at lunch and $38 pp at dinner; gondola extra. For something a little less substantial, head for the gondola coffee shop, which opens to a table-filled terrace.

At the **Millbrook Resort,** out toward Arrowtown, tel. 03/441-7000, is Millhouse Cafe. Overlooking a man-made lake and with indoor and outdoor dining, it's open daily for lunch and dinner. Considering this is one of New Zealand's premier resorts, prices are less expensive than you would think, with a warm salad of blackened chicken, for example, costing $15. Also at Millbrook, and overlooking the 18th hole, are the more formal Clubhouse Restaurant and the Sala Sala, a Japanese dining room.

GETTING THERE

Air

Queenstown Airport is nine km east of town at Frankton, flanked by the Remarkables to the south, Richardson Mountains to the north, and Lake Wakatipu to the east. Flying into Queenstown is an unforgettable experience-the approach is awe-inspiring and knuckle-clenching at the same time. **Super Shuttle,** tel. 03/442-3639, is at the airport for all arrivals, charging $8 pp one way into Queenstown. Both are door-to-door services: call ahead for hotel pickups. You can save a few bucks by catching the scheduled **Shopper Bus,** tel. 03/442-6647, which departs the airport six times daily for the top of Queenstown Mall. A cab between downtown and the airport runs about $18.

*Direct **Air New Zealand** flights link Queenstown to Auckland, Christchurch, and Te Anau. The booking office is at 41 Shotover St., tel. 0800/737-000. **Qantas,** tel. 0800/808-767, has direct flights between Sydney and Queenstown, but only in winter. Don't plan to travel between Queenstown and the southern cities of Invercargill and Dunedin by air—these flights are routed through Christchurch. Catch a bus instead.

Bus

To find out schedules and current prices, and to book ongoing transportation, call in at the offices listed below or at the visitor center on the corner of Shotover and Camp Streets. Next door is **Queenstown Travel and Visitor Centre,** tel. 0800/339-966, the booking office for all **Intercity** services. From Queenstown, Intercity has regular buses to Christchurch, via the west coast to Greymouth and Nelson, and through Te Anau to Invercargill and Dunedin. **Great Sights,** tel. 03/442-9445, offer daily transportation between

Christchurch and Queenstown via Aoraki Mt. Cook. More of a tour than a coach service, this cost is $166 pp each way.

Many small shuttle companies provide service to Queenstown. With an extensive timetable is **Atomic Shuttles,** tel. 03/442-8178; its shuttles link Queenstown with Dunedin, Christchurch, Greymouth, and Picton. The **Southern Explorer,** tel. 0800/243-402, departs Queenstown for Te Anau each Monday, departs Te Anau for Milford Sound each Tuesday, and departs Te Anau for Invercargill and Dunedin each Thursday. **Topline Tours,** tel. 03/249-8059, runs daily between Queenstown and Te Anau.

GETTING AROUND

The best way to explore is on foot. The **Shopper Bus,** tel. 03/442-6647, is another good way to get around; it picks up hourly from all major hotels on a loop trip through town ($2 or ride all day for $5). A regular bus service runs between Queenstown and Frankton, and bicycles and rental cars are readily available.

Car Rentals

The main car rental agencies are **Avis,** tel. 03/442-7280; **Budget,** tel. 03/442-9274; **Hertz,** tel. 03/442-4106; **National,** tel. 03/442-5722; **NZ Rent-a-car,** tel. 03/442-7465; **Rent-a-dent,** tel. 03/442-9922; and **Thrifty,** tel. 03/442-8100. A recommended local company is **Queenstown Car Rentals,** tel. 03/442-9220.

Bike Rentals

Queenstown Bike Hire at 23 Beach St., tel. 03/442-6039, is open daily till dark; it rents tandem bikes (from $12 an hour), 10- and 12-speed mountain bikes (from $8 an hour), 21-speed mountain bikes (from $20 for three hours), and scooters (from $45 for four hours, which includes insurance, petrol, and unlimited kilometers).

Taxi

Queenstown taxi companies include **Alpine Taxis,** tel. 03/442-6666; and **Queenstown Taxis,** tel. 03/442-7788.

A more old-fashioned taxi service is offered by **Queenstown's Horse & Carriage,** tel. 025/368-882. Based at Steamer Wharf, it offers a trip across town to Queenstown Gardens for $35 pp, or pay $15 pp per 15 minutes.

Queenstown Water Taxi, tel. 03/442-8665, runs from the Marine Parade wharf to all points of Lake Wakatipu, including the golf course ($20 pp) and Walter Peak ($90 per boat).

SERVICES
General

A shopper's delight, Queenstown has an incredible variety of stores selling handcrafted articles such as sheepskin, wool, leather, and suede goods; local pottery; greenstone jewelry; and Maori woodcarvings. There's also innumerable outdoor clothing and camping outlets, ski and snowboard shops, and all manner of chic boutiques.

The **post office** is on Camp St. near the top of the Queenstown Mall. **Queenstown Library** is at 44 Stanley St., tel. 03/442-7668. Send and receive email at **Budget Communications,** upstairs in O'Connell's Shopping Centre, tel. 03/441-1562.

Emergency

For an **ambulance** call the operator or 03/442-3053; **police** tel. 03/442-7900. For medical care, **Lakes District Hospital,** 20 Douglas St., Frankton, tel. 03/442-3053; and the **Queenstown Medical Centre,** 9 Isle St., tel. 03/441-0500, open Mon.–Fri. 8:30 A.M.–9 P.M.

INFORMATION

Destination Queenstown promotes the town around the world and on the website: www.queenstown-nz.co.nz. Once you get town, head for the excellent **Queenstown Travel & Visitor Centre** on the corner of Shotover and Camp Streets, tel. 03/442-4100; it's open daily 8:30 A.M.–5 P.M., 7 A.M.–7 P.M. in summer. The **Airport Information Centre** is open daily until the last flight, and also does bookings for everything.

For information on Mt. Aspiring and Fiordland National Parks, regional hiking track details (the Rees, Dart, Routeburn, Caples, Greenstone, and Milford Tracks), maps, trail conditions, and hut passes, visit the Queenstown Visitor Centre of the **Department of Conservation** at 37 Shotover St., tel. 03/442-7933; it's open daily 8:30 A.M.–5 P.M., till 8 P.M. in summer. Next door, but still at 37 Shotover St., is the **Information and Track Centre,** tel. 03/442-9708, website: www.infotrack.co.nz, for more of the same plus hiking track transportation information and bookings. Other major booking agents are the **The Station,** tel. 03/442-5252 or 0800/367-874; and the **Queenstown Information Centre,** tel. 03/442-7319, both at the corner of Camp and Shotover Streets.

GLENORCHY

A scenic 50-km drive west from Queenstown brings you to the head of Lake Wakatipu and Glenorchy (population 250), a small village that seems a world away from the commercialism of Queenstown. For outdoor enthusiasts, Glenorchy is best known as the starting point for a number of overnight tramps, but it offers plenty of other activities. The picturesque drive along Lake Wakatipu alone is worth the trip out from Queenstown. Just out of town, **Dart Stables,** tel. 03/442-5688, offers guided trips through high-country farmland with magnificent mountain views and along remote river valleys. A two-hour ride to the delta where the Rees and Dart Rivers drain into Lake Wakatipu is $65 pp, ride for a full day with lunch for $150, or combine a ride with a jetboat trip for $179. **Glenorchy Cruising,** tel. 03/442-9951, has two-hour fishing trips for $75 pp and provides a water taxi service to points around the lake.

Accommodations and Food

Glenorchy Hotel, Mull St., tel. 03/442-9902 or 0800/453-667, provides cheerful rooms with old-fashioned decor, gorgeous views, and a communal TV lounge. Rates are $59–79 s or d, with the less expensive units sharing a bathroom. Backpackers are catered to in comfortable dormitories costing $18 pp per night. You'll find the usual communal facilities at **Glenorchy Holiday Park,** Oban St., tel. 03/442-7171, plus a camp store, storage for hikers doing the tracks, transportation to the tracks, and guided sight-seeing tours. Tent sites are $9 pp, caravan sites are $10 pp, cabins are

Lake Wakatipu from along the road to Glenorchy

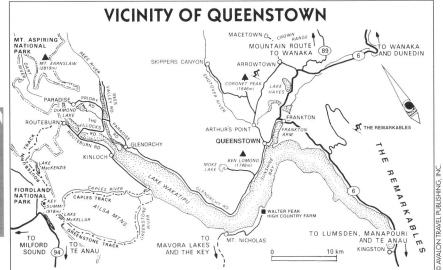

VICINITY OF QUEENSTOWN

© AVALON TRAVEL PUBLISHING, INC.

$30 s or d, and self-contained lakeside cottages are $70 s or d.

Glenorchy Café, Mull St., tel. 03/442-9958, serves cooked breakfasts for $10 and a variety of freshly prepared rolls the rest of the day. The restaurant in the Glenorchy Hotel receives great raves from *everyone* who has eaten there. It offers typical no-frills, hotel-style dining, with hearty portions and friendly service. It's open daily 7 A.M.–8:30 P.M.

Transportation and Information

Many Queenstown tour operators include Glenorchy in their itineraries, or catch the **Backpacker Express,** tel. 03/442-9939. Buses run in either direction at least once every two hours, continuing beyond the village to all trailheads.

Glenorchy Visitor Centre, on the corner of Mull St. and Oban St., tel. 03/442-9937, is open in summer, daily 8:30 A.M.–5 P.M., the rest of the year, Mon.–Fri. 8:30 A.M.–5 P.M.

BEYOND GLENORCHY

Beyond Glenorchy, the road continues 10 km to the **Rees Valley** trailhead for the Rees-Dart Track before dead-ending at the other end of the

track beside the Dart River. Between the two, a side road crosses the Dart River to the beginning of the Routeburn and Caples/Greenstone Tracks. Even if you're not hiking any of these tracks, it's worth driving to the end of the road for the scenery.

If you're planning on hiking in this area, make sure you stop at the DOC **Queenstown Visitor Centre,** 37 Shotover St., Queenstown, tel. 03/442-7933, for hut passes and trail information. Adjacent to the DOC office is the **Information and Track Centre,** tel. 03/442-9708, website: www.infotrack.co.nz, another worthwhile stop where transportation out to the tracks can also be booked. **Kiwi Discovery,** tel. 03/442-7340, serves both ends of the trails detailed below. **Backpacker Express,** operating out of Glenorchy, tel. 03/442-9939, also scheduled runs to all points beyond Glenorchy.

Rees-Dart Track

The Rees and Dart Valleys at the head of Lake Wakatipu are the main hiking routes into the southern sector of Mt. Aspiring National Park. They provide short walks, longer hikes, and a four- to five-day circular hike from one valley to the other (more challenging than the popular

Routeburn Track). They also give access to difficult climbing routes suitable only for experienced climbers—the season is from early November to mid-April. The track parallels the Dart River to its source, crosses Rees Saddle, then descends along the Rees River to Muddy Creek, accessible by 2WD from Glenorchy.

You'll find three huts with wood fires at regular intervals along the Rees-Dart Track. To get to the valleys by car, take the waterfront road from Queenstown west to Glenorchy and on to the head of the lake where the Rees and Dart Rivers enter.

Routeburn Track

This 33-km (three days, two nights) hike, one of New Zealand's finest overnight tramps, begins north of Glenorchy and passes through the southern reaches of Mt. Aspiring National Park and into Fiordland National Park before ending on the road that links Te Anau and Milford Sound. It is detailed in the special topic in the Southland chapter.

In addition to the **Backpackers Express,** tel. 03/442-9939, bus service, the trailhead for the Routeburn can be accessed by boat with **Glenorchy Cruising,** tel. 03/442-9951.

Caples and Greenstone Tracks

The Caples and Greenstone Valleys, around the head of Lake Wakatipu from Glenorchy, have good trails along each river. The tracks connect at both ends, starting from a parking lot at the end of Greenstone Station Rd., south of Kinloch, and finishing by Lake McKellar, just south of the Milford end of the Routeburn Track. You can walk both in either direction. The Greenstone Track is a two-day easy walk following a beautiful river valley, with two huts (coal burners provided; $8 pp per night) en route. The Caples Track is an easy one- to two-day amble along the sparkling Caples River, with comfortable huts (coal burners; $8 pp per night) en route, and plenty of excellent camping spots—camp well away from the track. Take standard backpacking equipment and a fly rod for good trout fishing in both rivers.

QUEENSTOWN TO FIORDLAND NATIONAL PARK

There are three ways to get to Fiordland National Park from Queenstown: via Hwy. 6 to Te Anau; by air to Te Anau or Milford Sound; or, for the adventurous, by foot on the Routeburn Track. If you have your own transportation, take the main road northeast out of Queenstown to Frankton, then Hwy. 6 south between the Remarkables and Lake Wakatipu.

Kingston, at the south end of the lake, is the starting point for trips on the **Kingston Flyer,** tel. 03/248-8848. Pullman green carriages with original wood interiors, black metal and polished brass engine, plume of black smoke, shrill whistle, and staff in period costume take you back to the days of the early 1900s when the Flyer first ran between Kingston and Gore. The train runs Oct.–April, twice daily, along a 14-km-long stretch of track. The fare is $20 adult, $7 child.

Continuing south from Kingston, you come to **Lumsden**—an angler's paradise with five trout-

Parapenting is just one of many adventure activities offered in Queenstown.

filled rivers crisscrossing the countryside within a relatively short distance of town. Just before Lumsden, Hwy. 94 branches west to Te Anau, Manapouri, and Fiordland National Park, and east to Gore.

Along the highway to Fiordland are access roads to several large forests north and south of the highway where there's good hiking, climbing, and fishing. **Mararoa River, Mavora Lakes,** and **Oreti River** in **Snowdon Forest** provide excellent dry fly-fishing, campsites (toilets and fresh water) at the north end of South Mavora Lake, and a long easy hike around the lakes following the Mararoa River into the Greenstone Valley; the Snowdon Forest access road branches north off Hwy. 94 at The Key. Between The Key and Te Anau the highway passes through a bleak yet dramatic "wilderness reserve" established to preserve a unique area of bog pine; as you approach Te Anau, well-stocked deer farms with the standard two-meter-high wire fences line the road.

Fiordland National Park is detailed in the following chapter, Southland.

Wanaka

Encircled by mountains and nestled at the southern end of the crystal-clear, bright-blue waters of **Lake Wanaka,** this four-season resort town (population 3,800) lies 70 km northeast, but seemingly a world away, from Queenstown.

Wanaka has always played second fiddle to its more famous neighbor in the tourism stakes, but the town is in the middle of a mini-boom, with lots of new development and a growing realization that the region has a lot going for it, including the combination of year-round wonderful weather and beautiful scenery. Initially developed to serve the gold-mining industry of Cardrona and vicinity, Wanaka (a corruption of the Maori word Oanaka, the name of a chief who went there to fish) became a commercial center for surrounding farms when the gold ran out.

If kicking back in the sunshine on a lakeshore beach or trying a new sport is your definition of fun, there's lots to do here in the great outdoors department. Though Wanaka is a smaller, more sedate version of tourist-oriented Queenstown (a 90-minute drive southwest), hordes of vacationing New Zealanders and a good number of tourists are attracted to Wanaka in summer for the beaches, boating, water-skiing, trout fishing, and hiking and mountaineering in nearby Mt. Aspiring National Park (the town is packed in December and January). In winter they come to skate on Diamond Lake, ski the uncrowded slopes of Treble Cone or Cardrona, or heli-ski in the spectacular Harris Mountains to the southwest. No shortage of action here!

SIGHTS

Alpine Fighter Collection

New Zealand provided the Allies with the largest number of airmen per capita during World War II, so it's not surprising that the country also holds one of the world's largest collections of air-

The Wanaka lakefront is surprisingly free of commercialism.

© ANDREW HEMPSTEAD

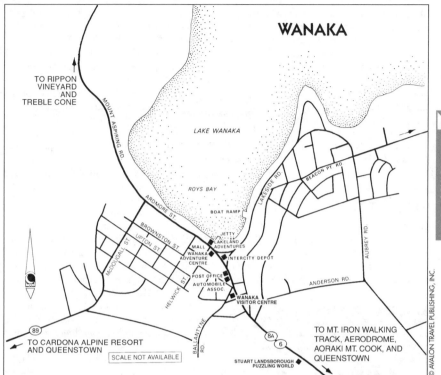

worthy World War II airplanes, housed at Wanaka Airport about 10 km east of town along Hwy. 8. In addition to 50-odd restored planes from both World Wars—complete with colorful descriptions of the pilots who flew them and historical photos of all the action—it shows World War II film footage, has interactive computer programs, holds a roll of honor that remembers each of New Zealand's fighter pilots, and showcases an assortment of military and vintage machines. The airport also hosts **Warbirds over Wanaka** at Easter on even-numbered years; call 03/443-8619. For general information on the collection, call 03/443-7010. It's open daily 9 A.M.–4 P.M.; $7 adult, $2 child.

A Gigantic Puzzle

On the road out to the airport is **Puzzling-World,** two km from town, tel. 03/443-7489.

Stop at this popular local attraction—a 1.5-km, three-dimensional maze of wooden passages, under- and over-bridges, a Tilting House, and a hall of holograms that can tease you from 30 minutes to several hours. At the adjoining puzzle center, all kinds of puzzles are demonstrated and you're encouraged to try them out yourself (and of course, buy them). Illusions Gallery and hologram exhibition, miniature golf, croquet, and Devonshire teas round off the entertainment. It's open daily 8:30 A.M.–5:30 P.M. (until 8 P.M. in summer); admission to the maze is $6 adult, $3.50 child.

Winery

One of New Zealand's most photogenic wineries is **Rippon Vineyard,** developed by Lois and Rolfe Mills on a lakefront sheep farm, four km west of Wanaka off Mt. Aspiring Rd., tel. 03/443-8084.

Otago is the world's southernmost wine-growing region, but a high spring rainfall followed by long dry summer days produces perfect grapes come harvest time. Rippon has 14 hectares of producing vines. The grapes are mostly pinot noir, with chardonnay, sauvignon blanc, and gewürztraminer making up the rest of the planting. Rippon is open to the public Dec.–April, 11 A.M.–5 P.M. and July–Nov., 1–4:30 P.M. (closed May and June).

> *Otago is the world's southernmost wine-growing region, but a high spring rainfall followed by long dry summer days produces perfect grapes come harvest time. Rippon Vineyard has 14 hectares of producing vines.*

SUMMER RECREATION

Hiking

Tracks and walkways around town vary from a short stroll along **Bullock Creek** (the hatchery stream) to a 30-minute (one way) walk to **Waterfall Creek**

Wineries dot the Otago landscape.

© ANDREW HEMPSTEAD

OTAGO

(southwest shore of the lake) starting on the left side of Roys Bay and following the shoreline around to the creek. **Eely Point Walk** starts just past the jetty and follows the shoreline around the right side of the lake to Eely Point (20 minutes one way)—for a longer walk (a couple of hours) continue around the lake to the Clutha River outlet and return to town by Anderson Road. For fabulous panoramic views, climb to the top of **Mount Iron** (527 meters, about 45 minutes one way) in the Mt. Iron Reserve, off the main highway into town. The reserve is known for lizards, abundant birdlife, and semi-arid vegetation. Return along the eastern face for a 1.5-hour round-trip. The more energetic, in search of an even better view, can climb to the top of **Mount Roy** (1,585 meters)—you can see almost the entire lake, its islands, the rivers flowing in and out, plus a spectacular view of Mt. Aspiring and surrounding glaciers and valleys. This eight-km track starts at the base of the mountain on Mt. Aspiring Rd. (closed Oct. 1—Nov. 6); the fit hiker takes about three hours to get to the top. Farther along Mt. Aspiring Rd. is **Diamond Lake.** A signpost on the right side of the road marks the beginning of a short trail (15 minutes one way) to the lake. Continuing beyond the lake, the trail climbs the southern slopes of Rocky Mountain for a panoramic view of Lake Wanaka.

On the Lake

Take a short stroll along the lakefront to shop for all the ways you can view the lake: cruise boats, jetboats, and paraflights high above the lake surface are just a few. Most of these options are offered by **Lakeland Adventures,** in the log cabin beside the main wharf, tel. 03/443-7495. The most popular trip is a three-hour cruise to Mou Waho Island onboard the MV *Paranui* for $50 pp. Mou Waho Island's claim to fame: It's home to New Zealand's largest lake on an island on a lake. Another way to enjoy the lake *and* the Clutha River is onboard the *Clutha River Jet.* The exhilarating 60-minute trip departs daily every hour and on demand; $60 pp. Book through Lakeland Adventures. This company also rents canoes, kayaks, aqua-bikes, small motorboats, and bikes.

Fishing

Before you try to find your own special fishing spot, pick up the excellent guide to about 20 fishing spots on the Upper Clutha River—it covers the area from the outlet to the Lindis River junction, with maps and details on how to get there; put out by the Upper Clutha Angling Club, it will save you time. Lakes Wanaka and Hawea and tributaries boast great rainbow and brown trout fishing, plus landlocked quinnat salmon. Trout and salmon are also abundant in the Clutha and Hawea Rivers (fishability and ease of access to the Hawea River depends on the manipulation of water levels for hydroelectricity), Makarora, Wilkin, Young, Hunter, Matukituki, Motatapu, and Lindis Rivers, and Timaru Creek. The maximum bag is three fish per day from any river flowing into Lakes Hawea, Wanaka, and Wakatipu, and a fishing license is required, available at sporting goods stores and at Lakeland Adventures on the waterfront. Lakeland Adventures, tel. 03/443-7495, also has guides to take anglers to favorite fishing holes around the lake. This costs about $220 per boat for two hours, which includes all the equipment.

Adventure Tours

All kinds of outdoor activities await the adventurous in Wanaka. Sample kayaking down the Motatapu River (calm water and rapids), or go for a more challenging kayak trip, down the Matukituki River from Raspberry Creek to Cameron Flat—previous kayaking experience required. Offered by **Alpine Kayak Guides,** tel. 03/443-9023, these trips cost $120 for a full day, including transportation from Wanaka. **Edgewater Adventures Ltd.,** tel. 03/443-8422, offers a large number of outdoor adventures: a hiking trip to Rob Roy Glacier (Oct.–May), 4WD trips over a high-country sheep farm (Oct.–June), jetboating

on the Clutha River, fishing and cruising trips on Lake Wanaka, and ski packages. **Alpine Biking,** tel. 03/443-8943, takes the hard part out of mountain biking; tours start with a 4WD excursion high above the tree line, then it's onto the bikes and downhill all the way; $165 pp for a full day.

One of New Zealand's newest adventure sports, made popular in France, is white- water sledging—a wild trip through raging rapids gripping nothing more than a small sledge. **Frogz Have More Fun,** tel. 03/443-9130 or 0800/338-737, offers a variety of trips to suit the daring and the not-so-daring, ranging $89 pp for four to five hours.

If you'd like to hike up the Matukituki Valley to Shovel Pass for spectacular views of Mt. Aspiring, and you need a guide, contact Geoff Wayatt of **Mountain Recreation,** tel. 03/443-7330. A three-day low elevation trek costs $595 pp (minimum four) and includes transportation, guiding services, accommodations, and food.

Flightseeing

Aspiring Air, based at Wanaka Airport, tel. 03/443-7943 or 0800/100-943, provides some reasonably priced flights, including short scenic flights over the local area for $70 pp and a spectacular 50-minute flight over snowcapped mountains and glaciers of Mt. Aspiring National Park for $125 pp.

SKIING AND SNOWBOARDING

Wanaka is central to two alpine resorts and New Zealand's premier cross-country skiing facility, as well as a base for heli-skiing. **Wanaka Adventure Centre,** 99 Ardmore St., tel. 03/443-8174, represents both local resorts and takes heli-ski bookings. Next door, **Racers Edge,** tel. 03/443-7882, has ski, snowboard, chain, and winter clothing rentals. Through winter, local radio stations are saturated with snow reports, or call direct.

Treble Cone

Encompassing 550 hectares, Treble Cone, tel. 03/443-9327, is the South Island's largest ski field. Located near Mt. Aspiring National Park,

20 km southwest of Wanaka off Mt. Aspiring Rd., it has open, uncrowded slopes that suit mostly intermediate and advanced skiers and boarders, basins of powder, lengthy natural half pipes, tremendous lake views, and a warm, sunny season generally lasting from late June to the end of September (peak season mid-July to mid-September). Lifts include the Southern Hemisphere's only six-seat detachable quad, as well as one double chair and three surface lifts. Experienced skiers and boarders often climb higher than the lifts, to the 2,000-meter summit, for more diverse and longer runs. Snowmaking is restricted to the beginner's area, while off to one side is a terrain pipe. No on-hill accommodations are provided, but the day lodge has ski and snowboard rentals, a café, and a ski school. Lift tickets are $60 adult, $30 senior and child (under six and over 70 ski for free). The five-day Wanaka Pass, valid at both Treble Cone and Cardrona, is $290 adult, $147 senior and child.

The seven-km Treble Cone access road is notoriously steep, muddy, and generally unpleasant. If you don't feel comfortable driving over this type of terrain (or even if you do), take an **Edgewater Adventures** shuttle, tel. 03/443-8422, from Wanaka for $28 round-trip. From Queenstown, **Johnston's,** tel. 03/442-4630, provides transfers.

Cardrona Alpine Resort

Cardrona, 34 km south of Wanaka off Hwy. 89 (the back road to Queenstown), tel. 03/443-7341, is a lot mellower than its neighbor. With a base area some 300 meters higher than Treble Cone, the snow is somewhat more reliable. Three chairlifts service mostly beginner and intermediate terrain spread over 320 rolling hectares. The resort also has a half pipe, terrain park, ski and snowboard school, and rentals. The access road ends halfway up the slopes, at a massive log day lodge. Meals are available here and in a pizza hut at the resort's furthest point. Lift tickets cost the same as at Treble Cone, as does the five-day Wanaka Pass, valid at both resorts. The season is late June–Oct., with the best snow generally experienced July–September.

Cross-Country Skiing

Waiorau Snow Farm, tel. 03/443-7542, in the Pisa Range about 33 km from Wanaka (just beyond the Cardrona access road) is exactly that-a snow covered farm. The difference between this and the surrounding snow-covered farms is that in winter it is transformed into a world-class cross-country skiing facility. Over 55 km of groomed and ungroomed trails lace the 500-hectare property. The epicenter of the facility is a magnificent timber structure that holds a rental shop, restaurant, bar, and en suite accommodation. Trail passes cost $25 adult, $10 child, inclusive of insurance, which in charming NZ lawyer-speak is "in case something bad happens to you." Ski, boot, and pole rental is $20 pp. **Edgewater Adventures,** tel. 03/443-8422, provides transfers from Wanaka for $24 round-trip.

Heli-Skiing and Boarding

For an unforgettable experience, consider heli-skiing in the Harris, Richardson, or Buchanan Mountains—3,000 square km in total—with **Harris Mountains Heli-ski,** 99 Ardmore St., tel. 03/442-6722. Experienced guides cater to small groups of skiers of all abilities—but strong intermediate skiers get the most out of it. These adventures start at $600 pp for a three-run day. The guides also do a range of alpine ski-touring trips Sept.–Nov., cross-country trips, and the **New Zealand Powder 8's Contest** held annually (about Aug./Sept.) in the Harris Mountains— it's the premier powder-skiing event in the Southern Hemisphere.

ACCOMMODATIONS

Hotels and Motels

Manuka Crescent Motel, 51 Manuka Crescent, tel. 03/443-7773 or 0800/626-852, offers 10 moderately sized units, each with a kitchen, set around pleasant gardens and a small swimming pool; one bedroom $88 s or d, two bedroom $108 s or d. Down the hill toward town, you'll find the **Alpine Motel,** 7 Ardmore St., tel. 03/443-7950 or 0800/822-284, website: www .alpinemotels.co.nz, which charges $85–105 s

OTAGO

or d ($105–165 in winter) for rooms of a similar standard. Facilities here include a pleasant picnic and barbecue area, a laundry, and bike rentals. **Brook Vale Manor,** 35 Brownston St., tel. 03/443-8333 or 0800/438-333, provides studio units (one double bed and one single bed with separate bath and kitchen) and one-bedroom units for $88–98 per night. Guests also have the use of kitchen and laundry, a color TV, and a spa pool.

Wanaka Motor Inn, two km west of downtown along Mt. Aspiring Rd., tel. 03/443-8216 or 0800/624-646, website: www.bestwestern .com, has bright, spacious, timber rooms with private bath, balcony, and breakfast-making supplies. Some have a spa bath, and some have lake and mountain views. The inn also has a laundry and an excellent in-house restaurant. A studio is $149 s or d, a suite with separate bedroom is $175 s or d. Farther west around the lake, **Edgewater Resort,** Sargood Dr., tel. 03/443-8311, has a lively resort atmosphere with tennis courts, putting green, swimming pool, spa, and sauna. Spacious hotel rooms are $160 s or d, self-contained apartments are $250 for up to four guests. The in-house restaurant opens daily for a buffet breakfast and nightly from 6:30 P.M. for à la carte dinners.

Bed-and-Breakfasts

Several private homes around town provide B&B accommodation from $50 s, $70 d—ask at Mt. Aspiring National Park Visitor Centre for all the current listings and rates.

Built of local timber and stone and taking advantage of the surrounding mountain panorama, **Te Wanaka Lodge** at 23 Brownston St., tel. 03/443-9224, website: www.tewanaka.co.nz, is an excellent value. Of contemporary design, the 12 spacious rooms each have a private balcony or verandah and are stocked with plush bathrobes, thick duvets, and a range of toiletries. In the garden, the hot tub takes center stage under an old walnut tree. Rates of $100 s, $110 d include a gourmet breakfast. The Garden Cottage is $185 s or d.

Off Hwy. 6, east of Wanaka, **RiverRun,** Halliday Rd., tel. 03/443-9049, website: www.river-run.co.nz, is an upmarket bed-and-breakfast set on 170 hectares running right down to the Clutha River. The country-style lodge features elegant furnishings, with lots of exposed timber and stylish earthy tones throughout. Each room has a luxurious bathroom, views, robes, and real cotton sheets. A cold and cooked breakfast and non-alcoholic drinks are included in the rate of $280 d.

Backpacker Lodges

The standard of backpacker lodges in Wanaka is considerably better than Queenstown, so if you're looking to kick back for a few days without spending a fortune and yet still be surrounded by the same spectacular scenery, Wanaka is the place to do it. On the other hand, the lodges listed here are small and fill up fast, so book as far in advance as possible. With an alpine ambience, the **Purple Cow,** 94 Brownston St., tel. 03/443-1880 or 0800/772-277, is just two blocks from the lakefront and central to downtown. The dorm rooms have a maximum of four beds, each with a private bathroom, but most of the rooms are doubles or twins. Other features include a pool table, TV room, table tennis, comfortable beds, a modern kitchen, and Internet access. Rates range $20–26 pp. On the same central street is **Bullock Creek Lodge,** 46 Brownston St., tel. 03/443-1265. Like the Purple Cow, all facilities are modern and the views magnificent. A bed in a three-bed dorm is $20 pp, private rooms $32 s, $25 pp d. One block farther back from the lakefront, **Wanaka YHA,** 181 Upton St., tel. 03/443-7405, website: www.yha.org.nz, has the usual facilities in a relaxed setting. Luggage storage is available, and the manager rents out mountain bikes. Only a five-minute walk from the lake, this hostel is popular year-round; rates are $17–21 pp. From the main highway into town, veer left on Brownston St., then left on McDougall St. and right on Upton Street.

Wanaka Bakpaka, 117 Lakeside Rd., tel. 03/443-7837, provides terrific panoramic views of the lake and surrounding mountains from the lounge. This place is popular with hikers and doesn't get the busloads of noisy travelers that the larger lodges do. Rentals are available—mountain bikes ($15 per day), kayaks ($12 per day), and canoes ($24 per day). Transportation to some trailheads is $8–15. Dorm beds are $20, twins and doubles are $24.50 pp.

Motor Camps

The closest motor camp to town is **Wanaka Holiday Park,** 1.2 km from the post office on Brownston St., tel. 03/443-7883. It has good showers, a kitchen, TV room, laundry and drying room, spa, and a boat and caravan park; tent and caravan sites are $10 pp, cabins start at $35 s or d, and tourist flats are $60 s or d. Reservations are essential for all sites and cabins December 20 to mid-January, and for cabins on weekends during the ski season. The next closest is **Pleasant Lodge Holiday Park,** three km west of town on Mt. Aspiring Rd., tel. 03/443-7360. It features TV and game room, swimming pool, indoor spa, barbecue, and shop; tent and caravan sites are $20, cabins start at $35 d, tourist flats range $60–75 d.

If you have your own transportation and don't mind staying out of town, head for the popular **Glendhu Bay Motor Camp** on the lakeside at beautiful Glendhu Bay 11 km from Wanaka on Mt. Aspiring Rd., tel. 03/443-7243, renowned for magnificent views of Mt. Aspiring and attracting large numbers of swimmers, water-skiers, and boaters. It has communal facilities (coin-operated showers), a large kitchen, drying room, shop selling all the basics, and canoe rental; tent sites are $7.50 pp, caravan sites are $8 pp, and cabins start at $28 s or d. Reservations are necessary over Christmas.

FOOD

Wanaka is not renowned for its variety of budget restaurants or lively entertainment—if you're looking for these, head two hours south to Queenstown. However, there are enough delicious choices in the fine-dining category to keep most visitors happy.

Pembroke Village Mall, opposite the lake on Ardmore St., has several food shops and a café, including the **Doughbin Bakery,** tel. 03/443-7290,

serving a large variety of delicious baked goods, and the **Snack Shack,** tel. 03/443-7622, catering to fast-food lovers. If you're in the mood for sandwiches, pies, and pastries, **Kingsway Bar & Cafe,** 21 Helwick St., tel. 03/443-7663, has a large selection, and it's open daily 7 A.M.–5:30 P.M. It has a BYO license—unusual for a tearoom.

Relishes, opposite the lake at 99 Ardmore St., tel. 03/443-9018, is open daily 9:30 A.M.–3 P.M. and 6:30 P.M.–late (closed on Tuesday evenings when it's slow), serving tasty lunches for less than $10, and all dinners (except the venison) for less than $20 in a cozy country-style atmosphere. Delicious pasta, fish, steak, vegetarian dishes, and primo pizzas (eat in the Pizz Sgetti Grotto, or take away) are served at **Te Kano Cafe** at 63 Brownston St., tel. 03/443-1774. It's open from 7 A.M. (main dishes $13–18, pizza $13–26), and the restaurant has a BYO license. **Tuatara Pizza,** 76 Ardmore St., tel. 03/443-8186, is a small specialty pizza restaurant; medium pizzas are $19, but one of these easily fills two hungry diners. It's open for dinner only. **Capriccio,** above the Bank of New Zealand at 123 Ardmore St., tel. 03/443-8579, is another local favorite for Italian cuisine and a friendly casual atmosphere, but you don't have to appreciate pasta to enjoy this restaurant—it also whips up chicken, pork, steak, lamb, and seafood dishes (dinners $16–27), and desserts with an Italian flair (around $10). It's fully licensed, open from 6 P.M. The aptly named **White House,** on the corner of Dunmore and Dungarvon Streets, tel. 03/443-9595, is a casual restaurant with lots of outdoor seating in a courtyard. The Mediterranean-inspired menu uses local produce combined with exotic spices; dinners range $17–26. The **Edgewater Restaurant,** in the Edgewater Resort, tel. 03/443-8311, is open daily for dinner in a casual atmosphere. All dinners are under $30, with the delicious seafood chowder ($8) a great starter.

If you have your own transportation, drive 25 km south along Hwy. 89 (the most direct route to Queenstown) to the **Cardrona Hotel,** tel. 03/443-8153. Built in the mid-1860s during the Otago gold rush, the rustic, slightly decrepit exterior has been deliberately left looking that

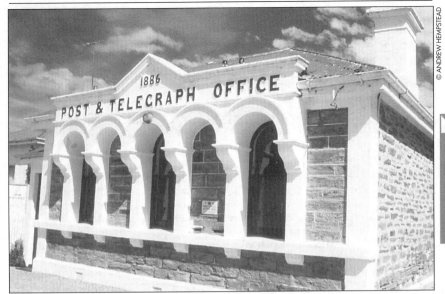
© ANDREW HEMPSTEAD

OTAGO

Heading east out of Wanaka the highway passes many signs of the gold rush era.

way, but the interior has been beautifully restored. Have a drink at the original brass bar, eat inside surrounded by items from the gold-rush days, or enjoy your meal outside in the garden. It's open daily for morning and afternoon teas and lunch (mostly under $10), Wed.–Sun. evenings for dinner (main courses from $16).

TRANSPORTATION
Getting There
The only scheduled flights into Wanaka are from Queenstown with **Aspiring Air,** tel. 03/443-7943 or 0800/100-943. The airport, a hub of flightseeing companies, lies east of Wanaka beside Hwy. 8.

Wanaka is a transportation hub for many bus companies. **Intercity** buses leave from 84 Ardmore St. by The Paper Place (the agent), tel. 03/443-7805. The company provides daily services from Wanaka to Queenstown, up the west coast to Franz Josef and Fox Glaciers, and east to Christchurch. **Wanaka Connexions,** tel. 03/443-9122, links Queenstown and Wanaka via the Crown Range (Hwy. 89).

Getting Around
Wanaka is a compact little town, which makes getting everywhere on foot easy. It's also relatively flat for biking. Rent mountain bikes from **Lakeland Adventures,** on the waterfront, tel. 03/443-7495; $8 per hour, $35 per day.

None of the major car rental agencies have agents in Wanaka. Instead, call **Lakeside Rentals,** tel. 03/443-7495. For **Wanaka Taxis,** call 03/443-7999.

SERVICES AND INFORMATION
Wanaka Post Office is on Ardmore Street.

Wanaka Medical Centre is at 39 Russell St., tel. 03/443-7811. The **pharmacy** is on Helwick St., tel. 03/443-8000. For **police** call 03/443-7272.

Information
On the corner of Ballantyne and Ardmore Streets is the DOC **Wanaka Visitor Centre,** tel. 03/443-7660, also home to the local information center. Inside are all kinds of displays featuring the park—local geomorphology,

geology, vegetation, mounted birds, and history—an audiovisual on birdlife, and an excellent audiovisual on the park (eight minutes long) It's the perfect place to get information before you head for the park. If you're hiking trails in the park, leave your intinerary and date of return here, and sign out when you get back. Also here, **Wanaka Visitor Information Centre,** tel. 03/443-1233, is a good place to collect brochures and buy souvenirs. The complex is open daily 8 A.M.–4:30 P.M., longer hours in summer.

Mount Aspiring National Park

THE LAND

Second-largest national park in New Zealand at 161 km long and 32 km wide, it covers 355,543 hectares of the southern end of the Main Divide. In the center of this alpine park, spectacular **Mount Aspiring** (3,027 meters), a pyramid-shaped peak of snow and ice that the Maori called Tititea (Upright Glistening Mountain) towers above a sea of mighty peaks and more than 50 named glaciers that they called Titiraurangi (Land of Many Peaks Piercing the Clouds). Along the northern boundary are Mt. Brewster and the roaring blue-green Haast River, along the south boundary the Hollyford Valley and Fiordland National Park. Three main valleys allow easy access into the park on foot. This is an area of rugged snowcapped mountains, glaciers, and hanging valleys, with wide rushing rivers and open grassy flats—a wild and untouched paradise for backcountry hikers, mountaineers, climbers, photographers, and bird lovers.

Climate

Conditions in the mountains change quickly—this area has unpredictable weather. The drier eastern side of the park generally receives about 1,270 mm of rain annually, the western side about 5,080 mm, and sudden snowstorms can bring snow down to low levels at any time of year (even midsummer). Storms can suddenly occur—no joking matter when you can't get out of their way in a hurry (and no one else can get in). As usual, be prepared for all kinds of weather when you're in backcountry areas, and take extra food in case you have to wait out a storm. Ask staff at the visitor centers in Makarora, Glenorchy, or Wanaka about the seasonal weather in each region, and get a current weather forecast.

Flora and Fauna

Vegetation varies from dense forest (predominantly silver beech with *rimu, matai, miro,* and *kahikatea* at lower levels on the wetter side west of the divide, and red and mountain beech in the south) to alpine scrublands (snow *totara,* alpine daisies, heaths, hebes, celery pine, Giant Mountain buttercups, mountain flax) and tussock grasslands. Introduced deer, chamois, goats, and hares have had some impact on vegetation. Since deer numbers have been greatly reduced by helicopter hunting, the alpine flora is regenerating.

The park is known for its abundant birdlife. On the valley floors are riverbed inhabitants such as migratory black-backed and black-billed gulls, black-fronted terns, South Island pied oystercatchers, banded dotterels, and spur-winged plovers. You also see skylarks, pipits,

GETTING TO KNOW MT. ASPIRING NATIONAL PARK

The elongated boundaries of Mt. Aspiring National Park allow access from three distinct directions. The main gateway and home of the park's visitor center is **Wanaka.** From Wanaka, the Mt. Aspiring Rd. leads along the southern shore of Lake Wanaka and climbs to the park boundary along the **Matukituki Valley.** Highway 6, linking Wanaka and the west coast, is the only road that actually passes through the park. It traverses the **Makaroa Valley** and climbs to Haast Pass. Access to the southern end of the park is from Glenorchy, and you can only proceed on foot along the famous **Routeburn Track** and the **Rees-Dart Track.**

MT. ASPIRING
NATIONAL PARK

OTAGO

song thrushes, blackbirds, chaffinchs, redpolls, yellowhammers, silvereyes, grey warblers, black shags, grey ducks, mallards, and a large population of striking paradise ducks. In the forests live migratory shining cuckoos, long-tailed cuckoos, yellow-heads, brown creepers, *morepork* and *tui* in the west, bellbirds in the east, and in the far south, yellow-fronted parakeets. The subalpine scrub regions host silvereyes, grey warblers, chaffinchs, redpolls, hedge sparrows, yellow-hammers, blackbirds, New Zealand falcons (quite rare), song thrushes, riflemen, and pied fantails. Considerably fewer birds thrive in the high alpine regions, but you're likely to see cheeky *kea* (alpine parrots),

along with rock wrens, black-backed gulls, New Zealand pipits, and the occasional chukor (an introduced Himalayan gamebird). The rarely seen blue duck has been spotted in some of the park valleys.

MATUKITUKI VALLEY
Hiking
Mount Aspiring Rd. leads from Wanaka past Glendhu Bay (stunning views of the south face of Mt. Aspiring) for 47 km to **Cameron's Flat**—the start of a trail up the east branch of the Matukituki River to Glacier Burn, Junction Flat, and Aspiring Flat. The easy two-hour

(one way) **Glacier Burn Walk** starts at the flat and climbs through beech forests to a saddle with excellent views of peaks and hanging glaciers, and at the head of the valley are impressive bluffs, waterfalls, and lots of birds. The two- to three-hour **East Matukituki to Junction Flat Walk** starts at Mt. Aspiring Station, enters the forest, and follows the river to Junction Flat, where the Kitchener Stream joins the Matukituki (good trout fishing).

Another 6.5 km along the road beyond Cameron's Flat following the west branch of the Matukituki River, you come to the car park at **Big Creek** and the start of a trail—note that you should attempt the road from Cameron Creek by car only in dry weather as it can quickly flood by rain or river. The **Raspberry Creek to Aspiring Hut Walk** is an easy 2.5-hour (one way) hike, leading up the valley along river flats (a popular river-bird habitat), crossing creeks on the way to Aspiring Hut. Using the hut as a base, you can also do many scenic day hikes in this area. Easy and more difficult walks are possible beyond Aspiring Hut (keep an eye on the weather); several climbing routes of varying difficulty beyond Pearl Flat require proper equipment and experience. For a beautiful alpine valley hike and outstanding scenery at the end, sidetrack off the Matukituki Valley Track onto the **Rob Roy Stream Walk.** Cross the Matukituki River on the swing bridge, and follow the track up past the gorge at the stream mouth and through lush fern-filled forest to the valley head, where you can see the south face of Rob Roy (2,606 meters) and its glacier, sheer bluffs, and waterfalls; it's two to three hours one way.

Practicalities

You'll find park huts (charge) along some hiking tracks. The nearest town is Wanaka, with lots of beds, board, and all the regular services.

Information on this central sector of the park is available at the **Visitor Centre** on the corner of Ballantyne and Ardmore Streets, Wanaka, tel. 03/443-7660. In summer, talks are held in the evenings—ask for the current schedule, and watch the short, interesting audiovisual on the park.

To get up the Matukituki Valley from Wanaka, take your own transportation to Big Creek parking lot, or catch the **Mt. Aspiring Express,** operated by Edgewater Adventures, tel. 03/443-8422, to any of the above trailheads ($45 round-trip to Raspberry Creek).

MAKARORA VALLEY

The **Haast Pass Highway,** which cuts across a small section in the northeast to Makarora, links Wanaka and the west coast village of Haast (see the West Coast chapter). A number of short walks are signposted along the highway. To take best advantage of the scenery and walking tracks here, you really need your own transportation.

Just east of the pass, **Makarora** is the starting point for the "Siberia Experience," a day-long adventure put together by local operators. The trip starts with a 25-minute flight over Mt. Aspiring National Park to the remote Siberia Valley. From this point, it's a three-hour walk along a marked track to a jetboat for a fast-paced trip back to Makarora; $150 pp. For bookings call **Southern Alps Air,** tel. 03/443-8666.

Hiking

Various short tracks traverse this northern sector of the park. Take the 20-minute **Makarora Bush Nature Walk** through a forest, starting near the Makarora Visitor Centre. For alpine plant-viewing or a full-day trip and excellent panoramas, start on the Nature Walk track and branch off onto the **Mount Shrimpton Track** (take water in summer). This relatively steep track takes about 3.5 hours (you need to be fit) to climb through silver beech forest to the tree line, and then up to a knob overlooking the Makarora Valley for views of the Southern Alps (two hours back down). If you want to go even farther, it's fairly easy to figure out a way to the top of the McKerrow Range near Mt. Shrimpton (no track)—it's steep, but the view of Mt. Aspiring from the ridge is inspiring.

For an alpine view that takes much less effort than many of the tracks, visit the **Cameron Creek** area (11 km north of Makarora) and take the 10-minute walkway to a lookout. The gradient is easy; all ages can manage this one. Another short walk, starting nine km north of Makarora, leads to the spectacular **Blue Pools** on the Blue River. This easy 15-minute walk meanders through silver beech forest and across the Makarora River by swing bridge.

Another popular walk is on the 1.5-hour (one way) **Bridle Track** from the top of Haast Pass to Davis Flat, following sections of the old Bridle Track, the original link between Otago and Westland. For serious trampers, the four-day **Gillespies Pass** circuit from Makarora provides a great outback experience among high mountains near the Main Divide. Walkers travel two major river valleys—the Young and the Wilkin. Gillespies Pass links the Young with the Siberia Valley, which leads on down to the Wilkin. Huts have been located at strategic places along the route. The Makarora, Wilkin, and Young Rivers offer good brown and rainbow trout fishing, and hunters pursue red deer and chamois within the Makarora catchments. For exciting jetboat trips up the Wilkin River or spectacular scenic flights, drop by the Makarora Tourist Centre in Makarora for more details.

Practicalities

Stay at the **Makarora Tourist Centre** on the main highway, Makarora, tel. 03/443-8372. It has a swimming pool, tearooms, a shop, petrol, and postal facilities; jetboat rides and scenic flights available; and cabins ($45 s or d) and motel rooms (from $70 s or d).

Get park maps and information from the adjacent **Makarora Field Centre,** tel. 03/443-8365, open weekdays 8 A.M.–5 P.M. and weekends during summer holidays.

OTAGO

Southland

Southland, southernmost area of the South Island, is a landscape of hills, lush sheep pastures, plains liberally crisscrossed by trout-filled rivers, large forest parks, and a wild, rugged coastline. Much of the land is protected by **Fiordland National Park,** home to the **Milford Track** and **Milford Sound.**

The main economic and industrial center of Southland is **Invercargill,** the country's eighth-largest city and departure point for traveling across Foveaux Strait to Stewart Island. Bluff, 27 km south of Invercargill, is the region's chief port and harbor. In the remote southeast lies the unspoiled scenic region of the **Catlins.** The central Southland town of **Gore** is the region's second-largest town—its location near many of the best trout rivers makes it an excellent place to kick back and get into some real fishing.

The third and southernmost of New Zealand's main islands, little-developed **Stewart Island** is home to one settlement of island-dwellers, supported mostly by fishing and a growing tourism industry.

windswept coastal bush

© ANDREW HEMPSTEAD

Fiordland National Park and Vicinity

The vast remote Fiordland region in the southwest corner of the South Island is made up of Fiordland National Park and the towns of Te Anau and Manapouri, which lie just outside the park boundary. In a country that has spectacular scenery from top to bottom, Fiordland is one of the most majestic areas—the kind of place where you constantly hear the words "breathtaking," "spectacular," "awesome," and "magnificent." Though you can expect dull skies or endless days of rain and drizzle, keep in mind that the scenery is at its most dramatic after heavy rain. It's a remote area of deep dark fiords and magnificent waterfalls, rugged mountains covered in dense beech forest, large lakes and rivers, and three small settlements that cater to visitors.

If you're an energetic type, some of the best scenery in the country awaits you along the five major hiking tracks in the region—the Milford, Routeburn, Hollyford, Kepler, and Dusky Tracks. For the sightseer, various cruises operate on Lakes Manapouri and Te Anau and launches run the length of Milford Sound; flightseeing companies offer scenic flights from Te Anau and Milford Sound; and the scenic 119-km highway between Te Anau and Milford Sound is the best way to get a taste of the park if you're traveling by car or bus.

If you can spend at least a couple of days in Fiordland, start at Manapouri and see Doubtful Sound, continue north to Te Anau and visit the local attractions and Park Visitor Centre, then travel the impressive road to Milford Sound (take lots of film) starting as early in the morning as possible. The best time to visit Fiordland is June–Aug. when the weather is clear—in summer, be prepared for sand flies (if you think they're bad elsewhere you ain't seen nothin' yet), rain, and more rain—Fiordland is one of the wettest places on earth.

THE LAND

Fiordland National Park covers a remote area of more than 1.2 million hectares of forest-covered mountains, pristine fiords, lakes, enormous waterfalls, and rivers in the southwest corner of the South Island. It's the largest national park in the country (and one of the largest in the world), stretching from Martins Bay and the Hollyford Valley in the north to Preservation Inlet in the south, from the large Lakes Te Anau and Manapouri in the east to 14 fiords along the heavily serrated western coastline. The rocks of Fiordland are among the most ancient in the country, and the mountains you see today were uplifted during the past 15 million years, then carved into sheer valleys, large hollows, and fiords up to 40 km inland during several periods of glaciation—the last ending only 14,000 years ago. After the ice melted, the sea flooded the coastal valleys and the inland hollows, forming the mighty Lakes Te Anau and Manapouri, and Lakes Monowai, Hauroko (deepest known lake in New Zealand at 462 meters), Poteriteri, and Hakapoua. In recent times the ice and snow have been largely replaced by an enormous amount of rain (in this area the people measure meters instead of millimeters); however, after a heavy downpour the scenery is at its best.

The park is a vast region of unspoiled wilderness with areas not yet fully explored. Only superlatives accurately describe the scenery—the deepest lake, finest walk, highest rainfall, second-highest waterfall in the world, and more. Because of the remote rugged terrain, access is limited. Hikers, hunters, and anglers (with pioneer spirit in their blood) take boats to the far sides of Lakes Te Anau and Manapouri to enter the park. The main road access is Hwy. 94 (Milford Rd.), which runs from Te Anau town through the northern section of the park to Milford Sound; other roads enter the park south of Manapouri to the west of Monowai and Clifden. If you're not able to get into the park on foot, the next best ways to appreciate this magnificent landscape are by boat from Milford Sound or Manapouri, or by air from Te Anau or Milford Sound.

SOUTHLAND

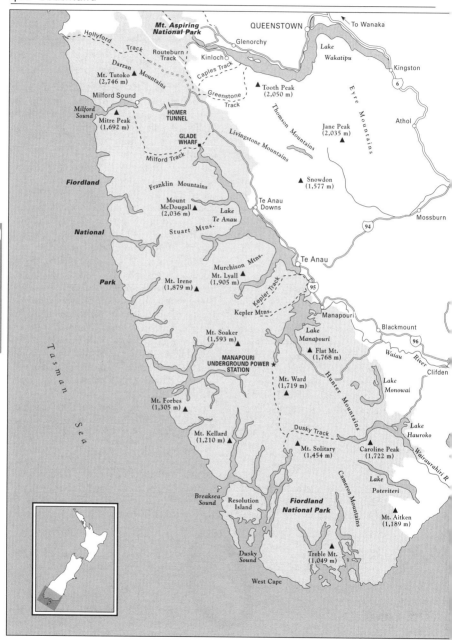

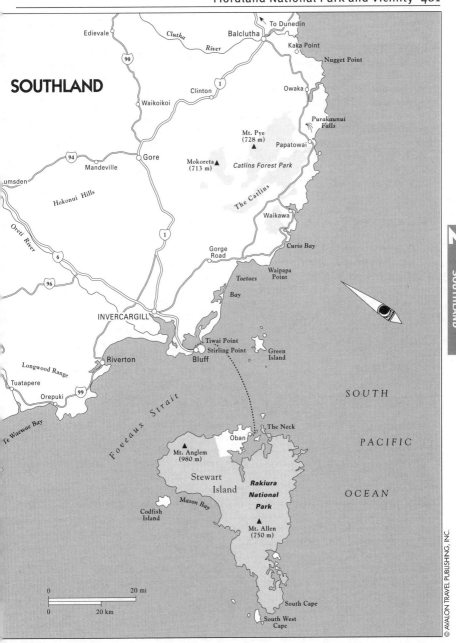

SOUTHLAND

Edievale
Clutha
River
Balclutha
To Dunedin
Kaka Point
Nugget Point

90

Clinton
1
Owaka

Waikoikoi

Purakaunui
Falls

Mt. Pye
(728 m)
Papatowai

94
Mandeville
Gore
Mokoreta
(713 m)
Catlins Forest Park

umsden

Hokonui Hills

Oreti River

The Catlins

Waikawa

1

Curio Bay

Gorge
Road
Toetoes
Bay
Waipapa
Point

6

96

INVERCARGILL

Tiwai Point
Stirling Point
Bluff
Green
Island

SOUTH

Riverton

Longwood Range

Tuatapere

Orepuki
99

PACIFIC

Te Waewae Bay

Foveaux Strait

The Neck
Oban

OCEAN

Mt. Anglem
(980 m)

Stewart
Island

Rakiura
National
Park

Mason Bay

Codfish
Island

Mt. Allen
(750 m)

0   20 mi

0   20 km

South Cape

South West
Cape

SOUTHLAND

Climate

The climate ranges from mild to severe at any time of year. It's generally warm (but never hot) in the lower altitudes, where snow is seldom seen and the rainfall is about 1,200 mm a year (Te Anau), but the entire west coast is battered by gale-force winds (the "Roaring Forties") and some of the heaviest rainfall in New Zealand, more than 8,000 mm a year (up to 250 mm was recorded in one 24-hour period); Milford Sound annually receives more than 7,200 mm. The coldest months (and best time to visit if you're hoping for drier weather) are May–Aug.—frost collects east of the ranges, and the road to Milford Sound is usually open, but the high country beyond the Hollyford Valley is subject to heavy snowfalls and avalanches. The warmest months are Nov.–Feb. (though we have seen the mountains dusted with snow in January) when much of the heaviest rain falls and the sand flies come out in force. Stop first at the Park Visitor Centre in Te Anau or Tuatapere Visitor Centre (in the south) for current weather forecasts, and make sure you're suitably equipped—Fiordland weather should never be taken lightly.

Flora and Fauna

Because of the high rainfall, just about everywhere you look you see flowing water and lush greenery. Rich, dark-green beech forest with a luxuriant understory of prolific ferns, shrubs, mosses, and lichens carpets the landscape. Throughout much of Fiordland, the forest clings precariously to steep rock faces, roots entwined in a thin spongy pad of peat and moss that retains the heavy rainfall and allows understory plants to thrive. Red, silver, and mountain beech are the three dominant species in the forest, with the podocarps *rimu, miro,* Hall's *totara* scattered through the lowland forest, and *matai* and *kahikatea* found in swampier areas. In late spring and early summer the high slopes come alive with flowering alpine shrubs, daisies and buttercups, and other alpine herbs. Above tree line, small mountain lakes (tarns) and bogs surrounded by deep peat, white-flowered donatia, and alpine grasses dot the land.

A large variety of insects lives in Fiordland—the sand flies are worst and most ferocious. These tiny black insects (they hatch in running water) inflict painful bites that swell and itch and cause great discomfort when your sleeping bag warms up at night. They're most annoying in calm weather and around dusk, and insect repellent is at times more of a "must have" for the outdoor enthusiast than food. (Mosquitoes, though present, are not noticeable in comparison.) All kinds of native cicadas live in the park, along with night-flying moths, stoneflies and beetles, and some butterflies.

A great variety of both native and introduced birds thrives here—ask at the visitor center for the pamphlet "Fiordland Birds And Where To Find Them." The most unusual local birdlife are the four kinds of flightless birds. The nocturnal South Island brown kiwi, *weka, kakapo* (a large, nocturnal, yellow-green ground parrot on the brink of extinction), and *takahe* (a large blue and iridescent green bird with scarlet bill and feet, one of New Zealand's rarest birds) all live in Fiordland National Park. You can see a mounted *kakapo* and *takahe* at the visitor center in Te Anau. The Murchison and Stuart Mountains, west of Lake Te Anau, where most of the few remaining *takahe* survive, have been designated as a refuge, with no public access, to ensure that the birds survive in their natural habitat. Another rare bird found in the park is the southern crested grebe. Along the fiords live great numbers of penguins—the Fiordland crested penguin the most predominant—and New Zealand fur seals are common. Stoats, red deer, chamois, pigs, and wapiti (or elk—the Fiordland herd is unique to the Southern Hemisphere) live throughout the park.

HISTORY

The Fiordland coast has a colorful history and is steeped in legend. For many centuries the early Maori made seasonal visits here to fish, hunt, and collect greenstone, evidenced by old Maori campsites discovered in coastal rock shelters. Captain Cook first sailed along the coast in 1770, but was unable to land. He returned in 1773

HIKING IN FIORDLAND NATIONAL PARK

Fiordland National Park is probably the best place in New Zealand for hikers. More than 500 km of developed tracks of varying standards and difficulty crisscross the park. You can walk the five major hiking tracks—Milford, Routeburn, Hollyford, Kepler, and Dusky—either independently (you're called an "independent walker"), staying in basic huts where you provide everything yourself, or with a guided group staying in more comfortable backcountry lodges that include bedding, meals, and hot showers.

Fiordland National Park Visitor Centre

This Department of Conservation facility on the waterfront in Te Anau is the main source of information for all Fiordland Tracks. In addition to a desk dedicated to making and confirming bookings, the center holds displays, carries track and weather conditions, and sells topo maps and various trail guides. For more information, write DOC, P.O. Box 29, Te Anau. For general information call 03/249-7924; to make an actual booking call 03/249-8514. The website, www.doc.govt.nz, has a large section dedicated to all tracks covered in this section.

Milford Track

Often referred to as "the finest walk in the world," the 53.5-km Milford Track starts at the north end of Lake Te Anau and ends at Milford Sound. Hikers here follow in the footsteps of the earliest pioneers, passing through river valleys surrounded by magnificent mountain scenery, climbing up and over 1,073-meter **Mackinnon Pass,** and opting for a sidetrack to breathtaking **Sutherland Falls,** which plunges 580 meters in three cascades—New Zealand's highest waterfall and the world's fourth-highest. The trailhead is Glade Wharf, from where the trail follows the Clinton River to its source, Mintaro Lake, before making a steep ascent to the alpine environment of Mackinnon Pass. The side trip to Sutherland Falls is in this vicinity, then it's downhill all the way, paralleling the Arthur River to Sandfly Point and Milford Sound. The longest day on the trail is the last, when 18 km (5–6 hours) is covered.

The track is strictly regulated: it *must* be hiked south to north, hikers *must* spend one night in each of the three huts (it's a four-day hike and cannot be lengthened or shortened—it's all about crowd control), and no camping is permitted along the track—you must stay in the huts.

The track is so popular that it's usually booked out months in advance. Bookings are taken from July 1 for the following season (late October to mid-April). Numbers are limited to 40 people starting the track each day because this is the number of beds in each hut. Application forms are available from Great Walks Booking Desk, Department of Conservation, P.O. Box 29, Te Anau, tel. 03/249-8514. The booking fee and hut pass cost $105 pp. You must complete the form (one per group) and return it along with total payment. Receipts are sent out, but you must pick up the actual pass from the Fiordland National Park Visitor Centre in Te Anau. Transportation can be booked and paid for on the same form, or see below for details of individual operators.

The total cost for transportation to and from the beginning and end of the track from Te Anau is about $100—a bus/cruise combination or cruise between Te Anau and the trailhead, Glade Wharf, and then a cruise/bus or sea kayak/bus combination from Sandfly Point to Te Anau. After completing the trail, many hikers opt to spend extra time in Milford Sound, which can easily be arranged. If you don't book transportation in conjunction with the Hut Pass (recommended), contact **Deep Water Cruises,** tel. 03/249-7078, or **Fiordland Kayaks,** tel. 03/249-7700.

Milford Track Guided Walk, tel. 0800/659-255, website: milfordtrack.co.nz, offers guided walks along the Milford Track. This option is a much more expensive alternative to independent tramping, but it's perfect for those who want to walk the track but lack the equipment or experience to do it alone; there is also less need to book so far in advance. The cost at $1,690–2,015 pp includes all transportation, four nights in lodge accommodation, and all meals.

(continues on next page)

SOUTHLAND

HIKING IN FIORDLAND NATIONAL PARK *(continued)*

Routeburn Track

The magnificent 33 km (three days, two nights) Routeburn Track passes through high mountain scenery in both Fiordland and Mt. Aspiring National Parks. It runs between the north end of Milford Rd. and Routeburn Rd. at the north end of Lake Wakatipu. Highlights include spectacular Routeburn Gorge, innumerable waterfalls, subalpine lakes, and views from high alpine meadows that extend west across the Darran Mountains. At the trail's high points (up to 1,280 meters), the weather can be severe, and it can snow at any time of year.

Like the Milford Track, huts and campsites must be booked in advance, but unlike the Milford, the Routeburn can be hiked in either direction and there is no limit to the amount of time you can spend on the track. The Great Walks Pass costs $35 pp per night for hut accommodation, while campers pay $12 pp per night. Bookings can be made over the phone, in writing, or by taking your chances and turning up at any local DOC office.

To get to the north end of the track, get yourself to Glenorchy and take the **Backpackers Express,** tel. 03/442-9939, shuttle up a rough track to the trailhead; $15 pp. All buses running between Te Anau and Milford Sound drop hikers at the "Divide," the southern trailhead, including **Fiordland Tracknet,** tel. 03/249-7777.

Hollyford Track

Although a relatively easy walk, the 56-km (four days) Hollyford Track passes through remote territory in the far north of Fiordland National Park. Most hikers begin at the northern trailhead, Martins Bay (accessed only by air), and walk in a southerly direction back to civilization (recommended, as inclement weather often prevents air access to Martins Bay). At Martins Bay, the Hollyford River drains into the Tasman Sea; this river is followed the entire distance, flanked to the west by the snowcapped Darran Mountains and for 15 km

by deep Lake McKerrow. Because the Hollyford is a low-level track, it can be hiked any time of the year. The remote coast around Martins Bay is well worth an extra day's worth of exploration before setting off.

All six huts along the Hollyford are Category 3 ($4 pp per night) and hold up to 20 bunk beds. No bookings are required, but hut tickets must be bought in advance from the Fiordland National Park Visitor Centre in Te Anau.

Hollyford Valley Walks, tel. (03) 442-3760 or 0800/832-226, website: www.hollyford-track.co.nz, offers three-day guided walks, including accommodations and meals at backcountry lodges, and all transportation; $1,290 pp. Independent hikers can book transportation, including flights, through this same company. The southern trailhead, the end of Hollyford Rd. 18 km from the Te Anau-Milford Sound road, can be reached by bus with **Fiordland Tracknet,** tel. 03/249-7777; $30 pp one way.

Kepler Track

This circular 67-km (three to four days) track, which opened in 1988, is the latest to be constructed in the park. Starting between Te Anau and Manapouri at the Lake Te Anau Control Gate, it follows the shore of Lake Te Anau, then climbs past limestone cliffs and above the treeline for panoramic views. From the Mt. Luxmore Hut, the track climbs through stunning alpine scenery, wanders through beech and podocarp forest, and along Lake Manapouri, then meanders along the Upper Waiau River to the original starting point. The full circuit is suitable for hikers with above-average fitness, although everyone can enjoy *some* sections of the track; access has been provided for those wishing to fish and climb. In summer take water for the alpine section (it can be very dry), and be prepared in winter for snow and adverse weather conditions that can close the alpine stretch.

Three serviced huts ($20 pp per night)

equipped with mattresses, water, flush toilets, heating, and gas cooking and lighting lie at regular intervals along the track. The Kepler Track is a Great Walk and, therefore, requires a Great Walks hut pass.

The track officially starts and ends a 45-minute walk from the Fiordland National Park Visitor Centre, but you can catch a boat across Lake Te Anau to Brod Bay ($18 pp one way), cutting just over five km off the total distance; contact **Sinbad Cruises**, tel. 03/249-7106, for a schedule. **Fiordland Tracknet**, tel. 03/249-7777, provides hiker transportation to the control gates, as well as to Rainbow Beach, along the Waiau River, 10 km from the trailhead; $10 pp one way.

Dusky Track
In the south of Fiordland National Park, the Dusky Track links Lake Manapouri to Lake Hauroko. The track traverses long valleys and crosses two alpine passes on its winding route between the two lakes. Most hikers make a 12-km sidetrack to Supper Cove at the head of Dusky Sound, a long fiord that deeply indents the southwest. The track is only suitable for fit, experienced, well-equipped hikers willing to allow up to 10 days to do the track.

Eight Category 3 huts ($4 pp per night) lie along the track. Hikers need to take a stove and fuel (dry firewood is hard to find). To get to the Lake Manapouri trailhead requires a boat trip from Te Anau. Hikers go as passengers on the tour to Doubtful Sound; $30 pp one way. For schedules, call **Fiordland Travel**, tel. 03/249-7416. From the south, **Lake Hauroko Tours**, tel. 03/226-6681, offers a variety of options from Tuatapere, including minibus and launch transportation to the southern trailhead from $60 pp. Rather than walking the entire track, many hikers fly from Te Anau to Supper Cove with **Waterwing Airways**, tel. 03/249-7405, for $150 pp, from where it's a five-day walk back to Lake Manapouri.

and sailed the *Resolution* into Dusky Sound, accurately charting it and describing all the wildlife. From 1792 on, the Fiordland coast went through an intense period of mammal exploitation. Droves of Australian and American sealers slaughtered the New Zealand fur seal almost to extinction, and whaling lasted from 1829 (when whalers bought land from the Maori for a whaling station at inappropriately named Preservation Inlet in the south) to 1838.

During the mid- to late-1800s and early 1900s, pioneer explorers, surveyors, and gold prospectors set out to conquer this virgin wilderness, many of them naming the mountains, passes, and lakes they were the first to see. Quintin MacKinnon discovered the pass over which the famous **Milford Track** crosses, and W. H. Homer found the Homer Saddle in 1889, proposing the tunnel that took 14 years to complete, and which nowadays allows visitors to explore a small section of the park by road. In the 1890s a brief gold rush again brought people to Preservation Inlet to mine or work the sawmill, but the gold ran out quickly, the township was abandoned, and forest reclaimed the land. Now seals, seabirds, and cray fishermen share the Fiordland coast, and the park is the realm of today's pioneering mountaineers, hikers, hunters, and anglers.

TE ANAU

Te Anau (population 1,800), the gateway to Fiordland National Park, is 175 km southwest of Queenstown along Hwy. 6 and then Hwy. 94. Adjacent **Lake Te Anau** is backed by the rugged, glacier-carved mountains of Fiordland National Park and Milford Sound is just up the road. Te Anau is a shortened version of the Maori word Te Ana-au (Caves of Rushing Waters). The caves are on the other side of the lake—rediscovered relatively recently, they've become one of the most visited local attractions. Centrally located with a range of accommodations to suit all budgets, Te Anau is a good base for exploring the many natural attractions of the park, and Milford Sound is less than a three-hour drive through magnificent scenery.

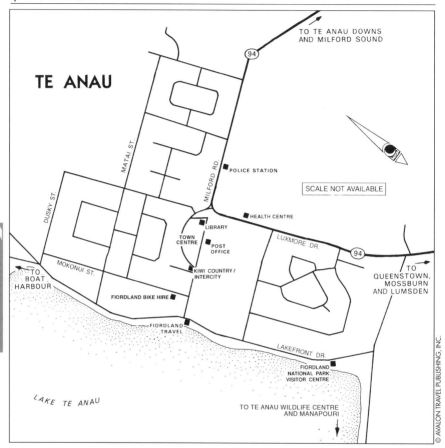

TE ANAU

TO TE ANAU DOWNS
AND MILFORD SOUND

94

MATAI ST.

DUSKY ST.

MILFORD RD

POLICE STATION

SCALE NOT AVAILABLE

HEALTH CENTRE

LIBRARY

TOWN
CENTRE

POST
OFFICE

LUXMORE DR.

94

TO
QUEENSTOWN,
MOSSBURN
AND LUMSDEN

MOKONUI ST.

TO
BOAT
HARBOUR

KIWI COUNTRY /
INTERCITY

FIORDLAND BIKE HIRE

FIORDLAND
TRAVEL

LAKEFRONT DR.

FIORDLAND
NATIONAL PARK
VISITOR CENTRE

LAKE TE ANAU

TO TE ANAU WILDLIFE CENTRE
AND MANAPOURI

SOUTHLAND

© AVALON TRAVEL PUBLISHING, INC.

Sights around Town

A must-see is the excellent **Te Anau Wildlife Centre** just south of Te Anau on the highway between Te Anau and Manapouri. Allow an hour to wander from one enclosure to the next to see some of New Zealand's most colorful and intriguing birds in parklike surroundings—including *takahe* (there are only about 150 of these rare flightless birds left in the wild), *weka,* parakeets, aviary birds, waterfowl, and fish. It's open dawn to dusk; admission is free.

Another place you shouldn't miss is **Fiordland National Park Visitor Centre,** tel. 03/249-7924. Along with the many interesting displays, it shows a very good audiovisual by request.

Local Walks

Tracks just south of Te Anau in Fiordland National Park provide everything from easy day walks alongside Lake Te Anau, the Waiau River, and Lake Manapouri, to the scenic but strenuous four-day **Kepler Track** suitable for the fit hiker, to difficult climbs in the Mt. Luxmore area. To get to the start of the tracks from downtown, take Lakefront Dr. south along the lakefront to the end and turn right on the road to Manapouri following the lake to the control gates. At the lookout and control gates, **Riverside Walk** runs north (1.5 hours) to the Brod Bay nature walk (the more difficult Kepler Track to Mt. Luxmore hut branches off Riverside Walk; it's about five hours one way), or south to Shallow Bay hut (five hours one way) on Lake Manapouri.

Lake Cruises

Start at **Fiordland Travel** on the lakefront, tel. 03/249-7416 or 0800/656-501, for cruise and tour information and tickets, brochures and maps. Be sure to ask about the various discount packages and current "specials" before you hop on a boat. A cruise across Lake Te Anau to the 15,000-year-old "living" limestone caverns of **Te Ana-au Caves** is one of the best cruises for the price; $51 adult, $15 child. The 2.5-hour trip departs several times a day. Operated by Fiordland Travel, the **MV *Tawera*** departs from Te Anau Downs, cruises to the northern end of the lake and allows time for exploring the Glade House area; $38 adult, $10 child.

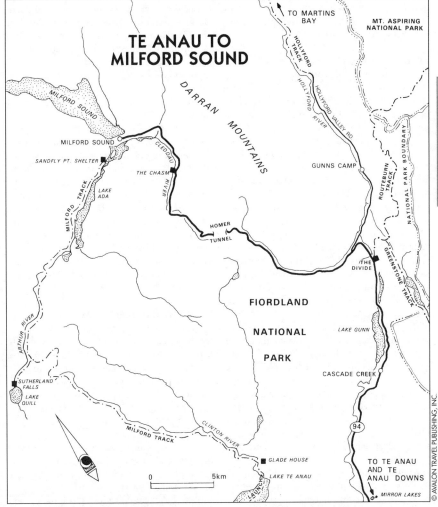

TE ANAU TO MILFORD SOUND

SOUTHLAND

Another way to enjoy Lake Te Anau is on-board the ***Manuska,*** a 36-foot gaff-rigged ketch designed and built by local Murray Cardno, self-proclaimed "Buccaneer of Lake Te Anau." Cardno's plan to take his pride and joy around the Pacific never materialized, and today he operates a variety of lake cruises. A combined cruise and walk is $55 pp, a 90-minute hands-on sailing trip is $45, or join the skipper for an evening cruise with dinner for $65. For bookings wander down to the Main Wharf where it's moored, or call 03/249-7106; the cruises are highly recommended by fellow travelers.

Accommodations

Te Anau has plenty of motel and hotel rooms at the usual high prices—though it's worthwhile checking them out in winter for off-season reductions. **Edgewater XL Motel,** 52 Lakefront Dr., tel. 03/249-7258, is in a central position between downtown and the visitor center. Each of the 16 units has a kitchen, and guests have free use of a canoe; from $85 s, $95 d. In the same prime position is **Campbell Auto Lodge,** 42–44 Lakefront Dr., tel. 03/249-7546, website: www.cal.co.nz, with large self-contained rooms, many with lake views. Rates are $135–155 s or d, with breakfast available for an additional $7 pp. **Village Inn,** Mokoroa St., tel. 03/249-7911 or 0800/249-7911, features large, elegantly decorated rooms, some with kitchens, and a bar and restaurant; $135–180 s or d. Around 200 meters from the lakefront, the **Luxmore Hotel,** Main Rd., tel. 03/249-7526 or 0800/589-6673, has all the modern facilities, plus a coffee shop, bistro, and restaurant. Rooms are $140 s or d. The **Holiday Inn** across from the water at 64 Lakefront Dr., tel. 03/249-9700, has great views, a landscaped pool and barbecue area, private spa pools, a currency exchange, a bar, and a restaurant. Advertised rates are from $190 s or d for the moderately sized rooms, but like Holiday Inn properties the world over rooms are sold in advance under the Great Rates program (from $140 s or d).

Shakespeare House, 10 Dusky St., tel. 03/249-7349 or 0800/249-349, has eight appealing en suite rooms, an bright breakfast room,

a great glassed-in porch that stretches along the front of all the rooms, and tea- and coffee-making supplies. Amiable hosts, the Hendersons, are bound to make your stay enjoyable. The rates are $85 s, $98–112 d.

The modern, well-equipped **Te Anau YHA** is in a new location at 29 Mokonui St., tel. 03/249-7847; website: www.yha.org.nz. Storage is available; rates are $19–23 pp, with some rooms having en suite baths. You can wake up to outstanding lake and mountain views at **Te Anau Backpackers,** right across the road from the lake at 48 Lakefront Dr., a short lakeside walk from downtown, tel. 03/249-7713 or 0800/200-074. Facilities include cozy kitchen, dining room, living room with TV, a laundry, barbecue area, solar-heated pool, off-street parking, and free use of bikes. Uncrowded dorms cost $18 pp, doubles are $22 pp.

Te Anau Holiday Park is beyond the park visitor center on the road out to Manapouri, tel. 03/249-7457. It lies among plenty of trees in a beautiful lakeside setting, one km from downtown. Within the grounds are tennis courts, sauna, volleyball court, comfortable bar and outdoor beer garden, TV, barbecue areas, boat ramp. Vehicles ($65 per day plus 30 cents per km), bikes and golf clubs are available for rent. Tent and caravan sites are $21–23, cabins start at $46 s or d, tourist flats and self-contained units start at $60, and motel rooms are $80. Or stay in the backpackers' section for $20 pp.

Food and Entertainment

Along the main streets downtown are several coffee shops, tearooms, and take-aways. **Redcliffe Cafe,** 12 Mokonui St., tel. 03/249-7431, is a great place to hang out on a sunny day (outside tables are set around a courtyard), while the café's interior is divided into cozy rooms with timber pitched ceilings. The smoked salmon potato pancakes topped in a rich mornay sauce ($13.50) are a particular treat.

The curtains are the same color as the meat at **Settlers Steakhouse,** Town Centre, tel. 03/249-8954, where you get to choose a particular piece of meat and tell the chef exactly how you want it cooked. For the noncarnivores, fish such as cod and salmon from local waters is chosen and cooked in the same manner. Mains range $19–27.

La Toscana, 108 Milford Rd., tel. 03/249-7756, is the place to go for no-frills, reliable Italian fare. Prices are from $14 for spaghetti bolognaise to $24 for a large Quasitutto pizza, and homemade desserts and ice-cream sundaes are all around $6. La Toscana is open nightly from 6 P.M. The **Olive Tree,** 52 Town Centre, tel. 03/249-8496, has a casual atmosphere and few tables on a private terrace. It's open daily for lunch and dinner, with the focaccia bread pizzas ($15–18) shining brightest. **Hollyford Boulevard Bar & Grill,** 63 Town Centre, tel. 03/249-7334, is a huge, modern eatery with dining inside and out and a buffet to suit all tastes. Also on Town Centre, **Keplers,** tel. 03/249-7909, has held the reputation as Te Anau's finest restaurant for many years. The atmosphere is relaxed, almost resortlike, but the service is smart and professional. The menu features traditional dishes, including lots of seafood such as grilled crayfish, and other old favorites such as beef Wellington ($24.50).

Getting There

Air services to and from Te Anau are operated by **Air New Zealand,** tel. 03/249-7516; all flights are routed through Queenstown. Planes arrive and depart from a small airfield seven km south of Te Anau on the road to Manapouri. Shuttle buses meet all flights; $5 pp one way.

Intercity bus services to and from Te Anau leave from Town Centre, on Milford Rd., tel. 03/249-7559. Buses depart regularly for Milford Sound, Queenstown, and Dunedin. The trip to Milford Sound takes just under three hours, with a timetable that allows a two- or four-hour stop in Milford Sound. **Fiordland Travel,** tel. 03/249-7416 or 0800/656-501, operates buses between Queenstown and Te Anau, with services continuing to Manapouri and Milford Sound to link up with the company's various cruises. **Fiordland Tracknet,** tel. 03/249-7777, runs between Te Anau and Milford Sound ($35 one way), stopping at all trailheads. The **Spitfire Shuttle,** tel. 03/249-7505, links Te Anau to Invercargill (via Tuatapere).

Getting Around

For single or tandem bicycle and mountain bike rentals (from $5 per hour, $15 half-day, $25 full day, tandems $10 per hour) head for **Fiordland Bike Hire,** 7 Mokonui St., tel. 03/249-7211.

In addition to a cab service around town, **Te Anau Taxi & Tours,** tel. 03/249-7777, provides drop-offs to all trailheads, to Manapouri, and to Milford Sound.

Services and Information

For unusual designer wool sweaters and a large variety of "bush shirts" (a must for hikers), visit **Kiwi Country** on the corner of Milford Rd. and Miro St., tel. 03/249-7020. The **police station, post office,** and **bank** are all on Milford Road. The **Te Anau Health Centre** is on Luxmore Dr., tel. 03/249-7007; make an appointment Mon.–Fri., open weekends and public holidays for emergencies.

Fiordland National Park Visitor Centre is on the lakefront at the south end of Lakefront Dr., tel. 03/249-7924; it's open daily 8 A.M.–5 P.M., until 8 P.M. in summer.

TE ANAU TO MILFORD SOUND

Scenic Hwy. 94 leads north from Te Anau, ending after 119 km at Milford Sound. With your own vehicle, you can stop for the many scenic points and short hiking trails en-route, but even on an **Intercity** or **Fiordland Travel** bus, the trip to Milford Sound is breathtaking. Many appealing camping spots run by the DOC are marked along the highway. All have toilets and picnic tables. Pay in the honesty box; $4 adult per night.

Stock up on film and insect repellent and set off as early in the morning as possible—the mountains cloud up and disappear as the day progresses, and in summer it's a case of beating the bad weather; allow at least 2.5 hours without side trips. In winter the road may occasionally be closed because of inclemency—get current road conditions from the Fiordland National Park Visitor Centre, Te Anau, or check the sign on the outskirts of Te Anau before continuing.

Te Anau Downs

Te Anau Downs, 27 km north of Te Anau, is the launch departure point for boats transferring hikers to trailhead of the **Milford Track** (see the special topic Hiking in Fiordland National Park). A 10-minute walk from the dock, **Te Anau Downs Motor Inn,** tel. 03/249-7811 or 0800/500-805, website: www.bestwestern.co.nz, has lakefront rooms, each with a kitchen, as well as a restaurant, bar, and public Internet access; $95–117 s or d. This accommodation is closed in winter. Part of the same complex is the excellent **Grumpy's Backpackers,** tel. 03/249-8133 or 0800/478-6797, with dorm beds for $20 pp and private rooms for $48–55 s or d.

North from Te Anau Downs

Beyond Te Anau Downs, Hwy. 94 enters Fiordland National Park then reaches **Mirror Lakes** (55 km from Te Anau), which are worth a stop; a short wooden plank walkway runs through a forest alive with bellbirds, along several small lakes that mirror all that's around them on a still day.

Continuing north, at beautiful **Lake Gunn** you can camp surrounded by trees along the edge of the lake. For the best views of the lake and the Livingstone Mountains, take an early morning hike along the short **Black Lake Track** that runs along the west side of the lake at the south end.

At **The Divide,** lowest east-west pass in the Southern Alps (531 meters), the popular **Routeburn** (see Hiking in Fiordland National Park), **Caples,** and **Greenstone Tracks** lead overland to Lake Wakatipu, and not much farther along the highway, Hollyford Valley Rd. leads off the highway to **Gunn's Camp,** (also known as Hollyford Camp) where Murray Gunn displays a collection of relics that his father accumulated over 50 years of tramping and exploring through the Fiordland wilderness. You can also buy petrol and basic supplies and camp (no facilities). A cabin with a wood-burning stove and hand basin is $29 s or d. With no power or telephone, a night at Gunn's Camp is Southland at its remotest—but waking up to Fiordland songbirds and a fabulous mountain panorama is worth it. Hollyford Valley Rd. ends after 10 km at the southern trailhead of the

Hollyford Track. From Hollyford Valley Rd. to Homer Tunnel, Hwy. 94 veers westward and passes through some of the most magnificent scenery to be found in New Zealand.

The 1.2-km **Homer Tunnel** is another local feat of engineering (built on and off between 1935 and 1954) descending at a grade of one in ten through a mountain to the **Cleddau Portal** on the other side—drive through it with care as it can get foggy and icy inside. Cross the Cleddau River, then look out for a track leading to the **Chasm,** a sight you shouldn't miss; a 10-minute walk takes you to two fascinating viewpoints. From the Chasm to Milford Sound, the road descends steeply through the **Cleddau Valley** between sheer rock walls that become endless waterfalls after a good rain. After several river crossings you pass the local airstrip and the road ends abruptly at the head of Milford Sound.

MILFORD SOUND

Milford Sound (the original Maori name was Piopiotahi meaning Single Thrush, taken from a legend) is actually a 16-km-long fiord—a glaciated valley carved well below sea level, flooded by the sea when the ice melted. The sound is one of New Zealand's best-known attractions, popular for its raw beauty, splendor, and accessibility (reached by road, air, or by hiking the Milford Track). The most famous landmark is pyramid-shaped **Mitre Peak,** a magnificent sheer-faced mountain soaring 1,692 meters straight out of the sea about halfway along the sound on the south side. As in all fiords, the deepest point is at the head rather than the entrance of the sound—in Milford the water plunges 265 meters to sound's deepest point off Mitre Peak. Dolphins, fur seals, an occasional Fiordland crested penguin, crayfishing boats, and tourist launches share the sound's deep dark waters, but you never lose the feeling of being at the bottom of the world.

At the end of Hwy. 94 nestle the few buildings that make up the tourist center of Milford Sound, along with a smattering of fishing boats and sightseeing launches in the small, protected port. It's a busy place throughout the day, with a never-ending stream of buses and cruise boats swapping

© JANE KING

cruising with Fiordland Travel

passengers at the wharf. Early and late in the day, it's a much quieter place. One of the reasons is the lack of places to stay-only lodges, one of which is restricted to hikers coming off the Milford Track.

Weather

The rainfall here is almost unbelievable. More than seven *meters* per year fall on average (the highest recorded fall for one day was 250 mm) and it's one of the wettest places in New Zealand—you can pretty much expect to see Milford Sound in rain or drizzle. However, the scenery is at its most dramatic in stormy weather, particularly during a downpour. Because of the lack of soil, water almost instantaneously cascades down the cliffs, turning into waterfalls up to 100 meters wide, throwing plumes of spray high into the air. The clouds cover the mountaintops, the mist comes down, and you swear the waterfalls are falling straight out of the sky. The sound also has distinct moods that change with the weather—it can be serenely beautiful on a sunny day when the reflections are mirror-perfect (in winter), mysteriously shrouded in low clouds and mist, or downright spectacular in the rain.

Cruises ✳

The best way to see Milford Sound is to take a cruise past some of the main sights while you listen to the skipper's vivid commentary—even in bad weather when you can't see anything. As you slip through the glassy waters craning your neck back to see vertical rock walls soaring 1,500 meters above (and dropping 265 meters below sea level), feeling the spray from torrents of water plummeting straight into the sea, you can understand why Rudyard Kipling described Milford Sound as the "eighth wonder of the world." Pass delicate **Bridal Veil Falls,** come in close to impressive **Stirling Falls,** which the skippers claim they use as a boatwash, and observe fur seals lying on the rocks at aptly named **Seal Point.** Another well-known sight is the two-, sometimes three-tiered **Bowen Falls,** dropping 162 meters from a hanging valley into the sound (see them from the boat or from the foot of the falls; take the short walkway starting at Freshwater Basin wharf)—after a heavy rain, the water arches way out into the Sound, sometimes completely obstructing visibility.

Fiordland Travel, tel. 03/249-7416 or 0800/656-501, offers the greatest variety of cruises. The most popular are aboard the MV *Milford Haven* and MV *Milford Monarch* up the sound and to the Tasman Sea (allow 1.75 hours), with lunch available on the 11 A.M. and 1 P.M. cruises; $55 adult, $15 child. Including coach fare from Te Anau to Milford Sound, the fare is $110 adult, $50 child; from Queenstown the trip costs $170 adult, $85 child. Other optional add-ons include lunch ($12) and admission to an underwater observatory ($20 adult, $13 child).

If sailing is more to your fancy, the **MV *Milford Wanderer*** and **MV *Milford Mariner*** are other Fiordland Travel vessels worth considering. Day cruises depart daily for a 2.5-hour cruise ($60). At the end of every day, these two vessels turn around and head back out onto the sound for an overnight trip. The *Wanderer* has bunk accommodation for 60 passengers ($160 pp) while the *Mariner* also sleeps 60 ($440 s, $500 d), but in private cabins with en suite bathrooms. In both cases, the fare includes dinner, overnight accommodation, and breakfast while you see the sights at a time of day when there's little other boat traffic on the water.

Red Boats, tel. 03/441-1137 or 0800/657-444, offers a 1.75-hour cruise, about nine km to the head of the sound, for $45 adult, $12 child, seven times daily. Twice daily longer options are offered, with a stop made at the observatory; $62 adult, $18 child. Tea and coffee is complimentary with Red Boats, and meal options ranging $13–26 are available if pre-ordered. **Great Sights,** tel. 09/375-4700 or 0800/744-487, provides transportation to Milford Sound that links with Red Boats' cruises. Inclusive of the cruise, the fare from Te Anau is $99 adult, $50 child, and from Queenstown it's $170 adult, $85 child. The Queenstown departure makes for a very long day; therefore the option is given to fly one way and take the coach ($399) or just fly one way ($240).

Sea Kayaking

Milford Sound Sea Kayaks, tel. 03/249-8840, offers fully guided sea kayaking trips along the edge of the sound; $79 for five hours. If you're coming off the Milford Track, you can arrange for kayaks to paddle back into town. The 20-minute paddle is a unique way to finish one of the world's great walks.

Short Walks

Several short walks from Milford provide excellent views of the sound. **Bowen Falls Walk** starts at the rock face by the jetties in Freshwater Basin, follows the shoreline, and comes out at the first view of the falls (which provide the hotel with water and drive a small hydroelectric plant). It's about a 30-minute walk; take a waterproof jacket. **Look-out Track** starts at the west end of the hotel and leads up a steep flight of steps to a lookout for magnificent views of the sound (five minutes); the more experienced can continue up the steep ridge for another hour or so to two more viewpoints. The track then descends to the road that leads to the tourist boat jetties.

Accommodations

Accommodation in Milford Sound is limited to basic backpacker accommodation (unless you're coming off the Milford Track on a guided walk); other options include the campgrounds back toward Te Anau or an overnight stay aboard one of the cruise boats (see above).

Back about one km from the hotel (off the main road down a short road alive with glowworms at night) is **Milford Sound Lodge,** tel. 03/249-8071. Although it's been upgraded in recent years, it's fairly basic. On the other hand, as they have a monopoly on accommodation, prices are fair. Facilities include a communal bathroom and kitchen, guest lounge with cozy open fireplace, sauna, shop with tramping supplies, and restaurant open for breakfast and dinner ($24 for a three-course meal). Rates are $22 pp for a dorm and $50 s or d in the double and twin rooms.

Right on the water, historic **Mitre Peak Lodge** marks the end of the trail for hikers coming off the famous Milford Track with Milford Track Guided Walk, tel. 03/249-7907 or 0800/659-255; website: milfordtrack.co.nz. Although the lodge is now restricted to clients of this company, it is worth a visit for the historical photos in the lobby.

Transportation

Flying into Milford Sound is very weather-dependent. Most people fly into Milford Sound as part of a tour (see Cruises, above) from Queenstown. To get the best out of a day trip to Milford Sound, consider flying one way and catching a bus the other. It's a long day (including a five-hour bus trip) but worthwhile. Expect to pay around $240–285 pp for this trip, which includes a cruise. Flights from Queenstown are provided by **Air Wakatipu,** tel. 03/442-3148; **Glenorchy Air,** tel. 03/442-2207; and **Air Fiordland,** tel. 03/442-3404 or 0800/103-404. Expect to pay around $175 for a 70-minute flightseeing trip over the sound (no landing) from Queenstown.

Intercity, tel. 03/249-7559 and **Fiordland Tracknet,** tel. 03/249-7777, offer scheduled bus service from Te Anau to Milford Sound. **Fiordland Travel,** tel. 03/249-7416 or 0800/656-501, has a variety of options for travel between Queenstown or Te Anau and Milford Sound, including round-trip bus transportation from Te Anau to the sound and a cruise for $110 pp; call for all the other options.

MANAPOURI

The small settlement of Manapouri (population 220), 19 km south of Te Anau, nestles at the mouth of the Waiau River on the shores of Lake Manapouri (corruption of Manawapouri or Lake of the Sorrowing Heart), second-deepest lake in the country at 443 meters and aptly described as "New Zealand's most beautiful lake." In the late 1960s and early '70s the lake was the subject of a large-scale conservation battle when the government proposed raising the lake level 12 meters for a hydroelectric scheme—which would have destroyed its natural beauty. More than a quarter-million concerned New Zealanders (a lot of people when you consider the total population) signed a petition opposing the destruction of the lake, and the incoming Labour Government in 1972 pledged that the lake would be left alone—the power station at West Arm was lowered an impressive 213 meters underground instead.

Backed by the snowcapped **Kepler Mountains,** its crystal-clear waters dotted with forest-covered islands, the lake *is* beautiful, and offers excellent brown and rainbow trout fishing, boating, and swimming. Organized cruises and charter boats cross the lake, and a number of short bush walks lie close to town (on the other side of the river) in adjacent Fiordland National Park. The area's beauty is clear, even on gloomy days when the sky, lake, and bush become ominously dark and mist shrouds the mountains.

Manapouri Underground Power Station

At the far end of the lake, this is the power station that was built in a victory for protesters over 30 years ago. Built over a 10-year period to provide power for the Comalco aluminum smelter at Bluff (south of Invercargill), the entire power station is underground, and no dams are required to drive the massive turbines—just an exceptionally high rainfall—more than 8,000 mm annually. On the lake cruise (see below), you're driven by coach down an eerie two-km spiral tunnel into the heart of a mountain for views of the machine hall carved out of solid granite rock. A guide gives a lighthearted but detailed commentary on power production, the seven turbine-driven generators, and the two 10-km tailrace tunnels that take the water all the way to Deep Cove.

Cruises

Fiordland Travel, on the riverfront at Pearl Harbour, tel. 03/249-6602 or 0800/656-502, offers cruises and guided tours. The most popular tour takes you by boat 30 km to West Arm at the far end of the lake, stopping to visit the Manapouri Underground Power Station, then travels by coach over 700-meter-high **Wilmot Pass** to **Deep Cove,** followed by a cruise to the mouth of remote Doubtful Sound (actually a glacier-formed fiord, misnamed by Capt. Cook). Geographical center of Fiordland National Park, the still waters of the fiord (broken only by penguins, dolphins, and the occasional rock lobster fishing boat), fantastic reflections, sheer 1,500-meter mountain walls, hanging valleys, and tumbling waterfalls combine to make a lasting impression. Allow a day, take your own lunch or buy one of the box lunches available for about $12–25; rates are $185 adult, $55 child, with transfers from Te Anau and Queenstown extra.

Fiordland Adventure, tel. 03/249-6626 or 0800/324-966, offers a more personalized tour along the same schedule as Fiordland Travel, but with sea kayaking and lunch included. It's a full-day trip, departing Manapouri at 7:45 A.M. and not returning until 6:30 P.M. that evening. This tour costs $165 pp, with the option to camp overnight in Doubtful Sound for an additional $30. The company rents camping gear for $40 per night.

Short Walks

Various short walks start across the mouth of the Waiau River from Manapouri. Based in town right across the river from the main trailheads, **Adventure Charters,** tel. 03/249-6626, offers inexpensive transfers across the narrow body of water. The alternative is to rent a rowboat ($20 per day) or canoe ($40 per day) from this company and leave it tied up on the other side. The popular 3.5-hour **Circle Track** follows the shoreline before climbing a ridge to lookouts for excellent views of Hope Arm, Monument, Back Valley, Mt. Titiroa, and Garnock Burn. The three-hour **Pearl Harbour-Hope Arm Track** branches off the Circle Track leading past a lagoon and swamp, and crosses the Garnock Burn to a lakeside beach and hut. The **Back Valley** track takes about three hours, branching off the Hope Arm track to the Back Valley and Garnock Burn. Continue for another hour along Stinking Creek to **Lake Rakatu** for good bird-watching, fishing, and an excellent campsite on the far side of the lake (dinghy provided for public use).

The **Hope Arm-Snow White Track** starts at the hut at the head of Hope Arm, then climbs and descends for longer hikes in the Upper Garnock Burn Valley, where the hunting is good; it's about 3.5 hours one way. You can reach the fairly difficult **Monument Track** only from the beach at the head of the bay (north of Monument in Hope Arm)—get there by boat from Pearl Harbour. The 2.5-hour track climbs steeply to a point above the tree line (be very careful on the crumbly rock and narrow ledges), where you get superb views of Lake Manapouri and the surrounding area; wear sturdy boots and take warm clothing.

Accommodations

Manapouri Lakeview Motor Inn is one km north of the post office on the main road to Te Anau, tel. 03/249-6652; website: www.manapourilake.co.nz. Overlooking the lake, this 55-room complex offers basic yet comfortable rooms. The rooms don't have cooking facilities, but there's a dining room open for breakfast, lunch, and dinner. Rates are from $80 s or d. If you would like to do your own cooking, consider **Manapouri Lakeview Motels and Motor Park,** a couple of hundred meters farther north along the road to Te Anau, tel. 03/249-6624. The eccentric owner has a vast collection of items scattered around the property-everything from a row of Morris Minor autos, to an airplane, to a game room chockfull of working pinball machines from the last four decades. Accommodations here include cabins from $38 s or d, comfortable tourist cabins with kitchens (one has an outrageous lake view) for $60, and motel rooms for $70–95. Camping costs $18. **Manapouri Glade Motel and Motor Park,** tel. 03/249-6623, next to the river and lake, has a spa, TV room, and trampoline. Tent sites are $20, powered sites are $22, cabins are $36, and motel units start at $74.

Don and Joy MacDuff, who once called a remote island on Doubtful Sound home, own **The Cottage,** a delightful accommodation surrounded by English-style gardens and with river views on Waiau St., tel. 03/249-6838. Guests enjoy an en suite bathroom and use of a gas barbecue, outdoor furniture, and laundry for $65 s, $85 d. **Murrell's Grand View House** on Murrell Ave. (look for the sign and the tall hedges across the road from the store), tel. 03/249-6642, website: www.Murrells.co.nz, built in 1889, is the most comfortable accommodation in Manapouri. The old rambling house boasts wide verandas, three homey guest rooms (each with private bathroom), mountain views, and extensive flower gardens. The house is a stone's throw from the beach and only a short stroll from the store and post office. Friendly Jack and Klaske Murrell are the third generation of Murrells to run the guesthouse, and if you want to know anything about the area, talk to Jack. Rates are $230 s, $250 d, including breakfast delicacies such as venison sausages and homemade marmalade (not together).

Food
Manapouri is definitely not a tourist town. The closest town of any size with a number of cafés and restaurants is Te Anau (19 km north). There's a café beside the post office and another under the Fiordland Travel office by the river, or try **Manapouri Lakeview Motor Inn** on the main road to Te Anau, tel. 03/249-6652. Here you'll find a café, restaurant, and a bar with occasional evening entertainment.

Te Anau to Invercargill

SOUTHERN SCENIC ROUTE

The Southern Scenic Route officially begins in Te Anau. It passes through Manapouri, following the eastern boundary of Fiordland National Park to **Tuatapere,** then meanders along a wild stretch of coastline to Invercargill, largest center in Southland. This route is only slightly longer than the inland route (via Lumsden) to Invercargill, but the scenery makes it worthwhile—gentle rural landscapes liberally dotted with sheep, contrasting rugged peaks to the west, access roads to remote lakes and walking tracks in Fiordland National Park, and several small coastal towns seemingly perched at the end of the world.

Borland Road
Just before Blackmount (first community south of Manapouri) is Borland Rd., which leads westward toward Lake Monowai and on to the West Arm Power Station on Lake Manapouri. This road, built during the construction of the power station, is unsealed, very steep in sections, and the only road access into this part of Fiordland National Park. Along the road are many signposted walks. The more adventurous can embark on the **Green Lake/Lake Monowai Track.** For road information and track details, drop by the DOC Field Centres in Te Anau or Tuatapere, or visit the Tuatapere Information Centre where transportation can be arranged.

Clifden and Lake Hauroko
When at Clifden, don't miss the impressive suspension bridge built in 1902 over the Waiau River, and the system of limestone caves nearby. From Clifden, an unsealed road runs west for 30 km to Lake Hauroko, deepest lake in New Zealand. Seventeen km along this road lies an outstanding stand of *totara* trees—including one of the largest known *totara,* believed to be more than 1,000 years old. Lake Hauroko is drained by the Waiau River, which drops 200 vertical meters in its 27-km run to the ocean. **Wairaurahiri Wilderness Jet,** tel. 03/225-8174, provides an exciting ride across Lake Hauroko and down the river to the ocean. The return trip takes four hours and can be combined with a four-hour trek to an abandoned viaduct for $135 pp.

Tuatapere
This small farming town of 700 was once the center of a large timber industry that supported the area for decades (visit the Tuatapere Domain to see what the area *used* to look like). The town is an excellent base for embarking on a number of tracks in the remote southern end of Fiordland National Park—an area that is relatively quiet in comparison with the north of the park.

Rooms are available at the **Waiau Hotel,** 49 Main St., tel. 03/226-6409, for $60 s, $80 d, breakfast included (this is also the best place in town for meals). **Tuatapere Camping Ground** on Peace St., tel. 03/226-6626, provides tent and caravan sites for $15 s or d and a cabin for $32 per night. Other options for campers include the Domain, or, farther out, a DOC campground at Lake Monowai. On the main road is the **Tuatapere Information Centre,** tel. 03/226-6475, where the staff enthusiastically describe everything there is to see and do in the area and help organize transportation to all trailheads. It's open daily 9 A.M.–6 P.M.

SOUTHLAND

From Tuatapere, the Scenic Southern Route continues south to the cliffs high above Te Waewae Bay, following the coast to Colac Bay, an old Maori settlement, and continuing to Riverton and Invercargill. Along the way are stands of macrocarpas bent into strange shapes by prevailing southerlies. To the west and north is **Longwood Forest Park,** with a variety of tracks and good fishing.

South Coast Track

Beginning at Bluecliffs Beach at Te Waewae Bay, this upgraded track traverses a wild bit of coastline to **Port Craig** which, in the 1920s, was the location of New Zealand's largest sawmill. Logs were cut farther west, then brought to the mill along a rough track that crossed four steep-sided valleys over which massive viaducts were constructed. The **Percy Burn Viaduct** was the largest at 125 meters long and a dizzy 36 meters above the valley floor. It has been repaired and redecked, allowing trampers to continue west to the mouth of the Wairaurahiri River (a jetboat service can be organized to Lake Hauroko; call **Wairaurahiri Wilderness Jet,** tel. 03/225-8174) or on to the Waitutu River—a total of 49 km one way. Along the trail are three huts, including the old Port Craig schoolhouse. More detailed information is available from Tuatapere Information Centre, tel. 03/226-6399.

Hump Track

The 35-km Hump Track has been improved to alleviate "overcrowding" on the South Coast Track. It branches north at the end of Bluecliffs Beach, following an old logging road and climbing steadily to a hut just below the tree line. The track then follows a ridge from where you get spectacular views of the national park and Te Waewae Bay before descending to Lake Hauroko. The track can be difficult to follow in bad weather. For track details visit the Tuatapere Information Centre.

Riverton

Historic Riverton, oldest settlement in the south and once the base for sealers and whalers, lies at the mouth of the Aparima River, 38 km west of

You know you're in fishing country when you pass this brown trout.

Invercargill. A popular fishing resort, it has safe sandy beaches and good fishing. Nearby **Riverton Rocks** is another seaside resort with safe beaches. The small **Wallace Early Settlers Museum,** 172 Palmerston St., tel. 03/234-8520, displays items from pioneer days; open daily 2–4 P.M.

The **Riverton Rock,** 136 Palmerston St., tel. 03/234-8886 or 0800/248-886, website: www.riverton.co.nz, offers comfortable and inexpensive lodgings in a historic hotel dating to 1863. The Fireside Forestroom, complete with two beds and a log fire, is $88 s or d; dorm beds are $24, double and twin rooms with communal bathrooms are $35 s, $48 d. In all cases, furnishings and facilities are of the highest standard, and guests have use of a kitchen and lounge, both overlooking the river. **Country Nostalgia Cafe,** 108 Palmerston St., tel. 03/234-9154, serves delicious Devonshire teas. In the Riverton Rock, you'll find a small **information center,** tel. 03/234-8886, open daily 9 A.M.–5 P.M.

HWY. 94 VIA GORE

The most direct route between Te Anau and Invercargill is to take Hwy. 94 to **Lumsden,** then veer south on Hwy. 6 along the Oreti River. But if you're agriculturally minded, have your own transportation, and enjoy scenic sidetracks off the main tourist drag, continue east from Lumsden on Hwy. 94, crossing fertile plains and sheep country to Gore.

Mandeville

Mandeville, 42 km east of Lumsden, is home of the **Croydon Aircraft Company,** tel. 03/208-9755—a must-see for any aircraft enthusiast. They specialize in restoring vintage aircraft, often times from scratch and including rebuilding engines and recalibrating instruments. Visitors are encouraged to wander around the enormous hangar where volunteers patiently work on de Havilland, Tiger Moth, Fox Moth, Dragon Fly, and larger Dominie planes. Adjacent to the hanger and airfield is **The Moth,** tel. 03/208-9662, a historic hotel refurbished with an aviation theme and open Tues.–Sun. for lunch and dinner.

> *The regional urban center of Gore lies on the banks of the Mataura River, reputedly one of the best brown trout rivers "in the world."*

Gore

The regional urban center of Gore (66 km northeast of Invercargill) lies on the banks of the **Mataura River,** reputedly one of the best brown trout rivers "in the world." Wide streets, attractive old-style architecture (dominated downtown by a five-story cereal and flour mill—one of the largest "in the country"), and many parks and gardens give Gore its appeal. The friendly locals (this is not a tourist town) are quite willing to stop and talk to a visitor. Anglers flock from afar to dangle their lines in the Mataura River and its myriad streams and to explore the fishing possibilities of the **Mimihau, Pomahaka, Oreti,** and **Waikaia Rivers** in the surrounding region; get your hot tips and a license at any sporting goods store downtown.

Gore Historical Museum, in the Hokonui Heritage Centre, corner of Norfolk St. and Hokonui Dr., tel. 03/208-7032, is crammed with local history, including one display dedicated to the moonshiners who once plied their trade in the surrounding hills. The museum is open Mon.–Fri. 9 A.M.–5 P.M., Sat.–Sun. 1–4 P.M. About five km west of Gore lies a hilly scenic reserve, **Croydon Bush,** where you can view a na-

M

SOUTHLAND

CATLINS WILDLIFE TRACKERS

Owned and operated by Mary and Fergus Sutherland, Catlins Wildlife Trackers, tel. 03/455-8613, website: www.catlins-ecotours.co.nz, offer numerous options for making the most of the Catlins. Most popular are two- and four-day packages ($275 pp and $550 pp, respectively) that include accommodation at their Papatowai lodge, all meals, and day trips throughout the region, searching out wildlife such as penguins, sea lions, elephant seals, and Hector's dolphins while also hearing about the area's geology, climate, and human history. Travel is by minibus, but most of the time is spent exploring and learning to view nature from a perspective that will be new to all those except the most deeply committed ecotourist.

The Sutherlands also lead an overnight Beach to Beech tramp, with an overnight stay at Mohua Lodge included in the all-inclusive rate of $275 pp. For the more adventurous, pay just $25 pp to hike the Top Track over coastal private property. The cost includes an information kit and an overnight stay in an old trolley bus decked out with bunk beds.

Finally, book sole use of **Kereru Lodge** in Papatowai or **Mohua Lodge** in nearby Tawanui through Catlin Wildlife Trackers. Kereru has ocean views, and full kitchen, and is air-conditioned ($100 s or d) while Mohua is more rustic, yet is private and surrounded by delightful gardens ($80 s or d).

tive flora while wandering at will along tracks through grassland, forest, and valleys crammed with lush ferns. Formal **Dolamore Park,** with its contrasting lawns and flower gardens, lies next to the reserve, and camping ($5 pp; limited facilities) is permitted within the grounds; contact the caretaker at the kiosk, tel. 03/208-9080. **Gore Motor Camp** is on the main road south, 35 Broughton St., one km from downtown, tel. 03/208-4919; it offers communal facilities, tent sites for $16, caravan sites for $18, and cabins for $34. A five-minute walk from downtown, **Riverlea Motel,** 46–48 Hokonui Dr., tel. 03/208-3130, offers clean and comfortable rooms, each with a kitchen and video player. Rates are $85 s, $95 d, which includes a light breakfast.

Gore Information Centre is on Orsdal St., tel. 03/208-9908; open daily 10 A.M.–5 P.M.

THE CATLINS

The alternative to zipping down Hwy. 1 to Invercargill from Gore is to follow Hwy. 1 in the other direction back toward Dunedin, then cut back along the coast to Invercargill on Hwy. 92 through the remote, beautiful Catlins. From Dunedin, the most direct route to Invercargill is via Gore, but if you have plenty of time and like to get off the tourist track, this coastal route will only (without stops) add two hours to the journey. Meander through the nine podocarp-hardwood forests that make up **Catlins Forest Park,** getting tempting glimpses of isolated sandy beaches and rugged coastal scenery; side-tracks to the coast are worthwhile (especially **Cannibal Bay** north of Owaka and **Jack's Bay**—cliffs, grassy hills, a perfect golden-sand

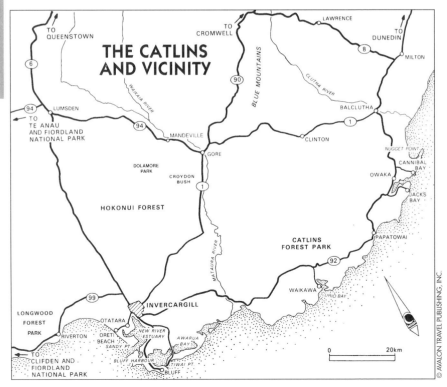

© AVALON TRAVEL PUBLISHING, INC.

© ANDREW HEMPSTEAD

Hooker's sea lions often drag themselves
ashore along the Catlins coast.

surf beach, and a 30-minute track to 55-meter-
deep Jack's Blowhole in the middle of clifftop
pastures—south of Owaka). Birds abound in
the Catlins, the rivers provide all types of trout
fishing and whitebaiting in season (get your license at local sporting goods stores), and sea-
fishing for blue cod is popular along the coast.
Historic, scenic, and recreational reserves line
the road—most providing short scenic nature
walks, lookouts, campgrounds (limited facilities)
or picnic areas, and toilets and fresh water.

Balclutha to Papatowai

The first worthwhile detour is to **Nugget Point.**
To get there, turn off Hwy. 92 seven km south of
Balclutha and follow the road for 21 km, passing
through the picturesque seaside community of
Kaka Point. For the last one km, the road climbs
steeply to a parking lot, from where an exposed
walking track leads to **Nugget Point Lighthouse,**
built in 1869. Bird- and sealife abound around
the point. Southern fur seals bask year-round on

the rocks below, elephant seals and Hooker's sea
lions frequent the area, penguins breed here, and
gannets, shags, and shearwaters nest and feed
around the point.

Back on Hwy. 92, between Owaka and Papatowai, keep your eyes peeled for the sign to
Purakaunui Falls, a great little track for stretching your legs. A five- to 10-minute stroll from
the flat, grassy, camping area takes you to a viewing platform overlooking these pleasingly asym-
metric falls.

Papatowai Motor Camp, 30 km southwest of
Owaka on Hwy. 92, tel. 03/415-8500, has tent
sites for $7 pp, caravan sites for $8 pp, cabins
for $32 s or d, the usual facilities, tearooms/store
(all the basic foodstuffs plus handmade sweaters,
and gasoline) at Papatowai (great yellow-sand
beach with plenty of shells and a picnic area by
the parking lot). For a more private hideaway in
the trees, consider staying at **Tautuku Lodge** in
550-hectare Lenz Reserve, about six km south
of Papatowai beside the Fleming River, tel.
03/415-8024. Owned by the Royal Forest and
Bird Protection Society Inc., facilities include a
six-bed lodge with bathroom and well-equipped
kitchen; a bathroom block; an attractive four-
bed cabin with kitchen, lounge, and large deck;
and a tiny, two-bed, A-frame cabin with basic
kitchen. Several walks and tracks of varying
lengths start at the lodge. It's signposted on the
main road, but because it's understandably popular, it's best to book with the caretaker. Rates
start at $20 pp per night.

Continuing along toward Invercargill on Hwy.
92, stop at **Florence Hill Lookout** to appreciate
stunning, panoramic views of **Tautuku Bay.**

Continuing West from Papatowai

As the road leaves Papatowai, it passes through
Catlins Forest Park, with all the coastal and scenic
reserves and walking tracks well signposted. The
first worthwhile stops are **Waipati Beach** and
Cathedral Caves; from the parking area it's a
15-minute walk to the beach, a 25-minute walk
through native bush and along the beach to impressive caves that resemble an English cathedral (accessible only at low tide; tide-tables are

© ANDREW HEMPSTEAD

lighthouse along the Catlins coastline

posted at the turnoff from Hwy. 92). About seven km farther along the road, watch for the sign to **Chaslands Farm Motor Lodge** on Waipati Rd., tel. 03/415-8501—one of the best accommodation deals in the Catlins. For only $55 s, $65 d, you get a motel unit that's like a small home-away-from-home in a farm setting. You may find large, woolly sheep mowing the grass by the swings or snoozing under the trampoline. Each unit has bedrooms with linen and towels provided, a bathroom, a fully equipped kitchen with refrigerator (bring your own food), and a living room with TV. The friendly owners provide a free bottle of milk, and plenty of information on the Catlins.

Curio Bay and Vicinity

Turn off the highway 35 km west of Papatowai and drive through Waikawa to reach Curio Bay, one of the highlights of the Catlins. This bay is protected from the prevailing southerly winds by high cliffs to the south. From the end of the road, the high headland provides a panoramic view across the bay (scan the bay's calm waters for dolphins, which often frolic near the shore). To the south, the cliffs drop dramatically to a wide ledge and the raging southern ocean. Follow the cliff line westward and you'll come across Petrified Forest signs, leading to **Curio Bay Scientific Reserve,** where there are a lookout, interpretive boards, and wooden stairs that lead down to a flat rock platform cluttered with petrified tree stumps. If it's low tide, don't just stop at the lookout. You need to be actually on the rocks to really appreciate all the petrified tree logs and stumps that make up one of the world's best examples of a Jurassic Fossil Forest.

When the weather permits, **Koramika Cruises** offers tours aboard *Dolphin Magic* in search of Hector's dolphins, the world's smallest and rarest dolphins. Tours depart a couple of times daily and cost $50 pp. A 2.5-hour Twilight Cruise is $70 pp. Get all the details and arrange pickups at the Dolphin Information Centre, on the main road through Waikawa, tel. 03/246-8444.

You can camp along the clifftop at Curio Bay, but facilities are limited (no showers or kitchen; $5 pp per night) and the weather can deteriorate rapidly. A better option is **Waikawa Holiday Lodge,** on the main road through Waikawa, tel. 03/246-8552. It's small with just three rooms, but the lounge is cozy (with a log fire) and the communal kitchen well equipped. Rates are $18 for a dorm bed, $40 s or d for the twin room, and $40 for the double. The hosts live elsewhere in the village, so call ahead and they'll meet you at the lodge, show you around, and tell you everything there is to do and see in the region.

Information

Balclutha has a seasonal information center, but a better source of information is the DOC **Southland Conservancy** office at 33 Don St., Invercargill, tel. 03/214-4589. There's so much to see in this relatively small area that it's best to get the entire rundown beforehand. The DOC puts out excellent pamphlets, "Walks and Tracks in the Catlins," "Catlins Birds," "Catlins Trout Fishing," and "Southern Solitude" (information about the Catlins region).

Invercargill and Vicinity

Invercargill, largest city of Southland and one of the world's southernmost cities, is a well-planned metropolis of 49,000. Originally settled by Scottish people, Invercargill has wide tree-lined streets named after Scottish rivers, many beautiful parks and reserves (the acreage of parks per population is highest in New Zealand), and plenty of reasonable places to stay, though it's not the place to come for titillating tourist attractions or exciting nightlife. The main at-

traction is nearby **Stewart Island,** across Foveaux Strait.

Intensive farming is practiced on the plains stretching inland from the city—this productive and obviously prosperous region produces more than six million lambs a year, 36 million kg of wool, two million bushels of wheat, 6,000 tons of potatoes, and 5,000 tons of cheese. The bulk of the region's wealth comes from more than eight million sheep, though the dairy factories, small

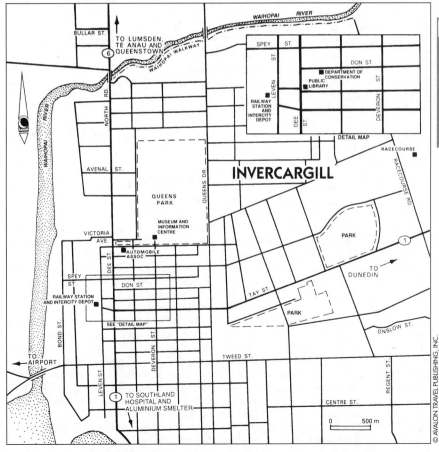

seed producers, timber mills, fertilizer, cement, and freezer works, a paper mill, a coal mine, and an aluminium smelter are all major contributors.

SIGHTS
Parks
Eighty-hectare **Queens Park** on Queens Dr. is a peaceful green spot in the central city, the perfect place to while away some time, especially on the weekend when everything closes. Wander past perfect lawns under all kinds of native and exotic trees; visit the large aviary, statuary, gardens, and duck ponds; and if you're feeling energetic, follow the fitness trail. You'll also find beautiful lawns, gardens, and native bush in **Anderson Park** around the **Art Gallery,** eight km north of the city center.

Southland Museum and Art Gallery
Near the entrance to Queens Park, this museum has been rebuilt in the shape of a pyramid. In fact, it's the largest pyramid in the Southern Hemisphere, standing 26 meter high with a 50-meter base. The biggest attraction within this distinctive structure is the gallery dedicated to Antarctica, featuring the "Beyond the Roaring Forties Subantarctic Experience," a stunning 25-minute audiovisual on the islands ($3), a subantarctic garden, and a historical display.

The museum also features items from the province's early days, a collection of Maori artifacts, and a fascinating "tuatarium," one of the only places in the country where you can see live *tuatara* in a closely simulated native environment. The *tuatara* looks like a lizard but is actually the only surviving species of the Sphenodontia order of reptiles, once widespread but now found only on about 30 islands off the northeast coast of the North Island and Cook Strait (they're featured on the New Zealand five-cent coin). Described as New Zealand's "living fossil," the *tuatara* has an

> *Described as New Zealand's "living fossil," the* tuatara *has an undetermined life span but it's believed that it lives to be at least 100 years old. This tuatarium is the only place in the world with a regular captive breeding program.*

undetermined lifespan but it's believed that it lives to be at least 100 years old. This tuatarium is the only place in the world with a regular captive breeding program. If you watch the *tuatara* for quite some time, you may actually see one of them move—maybe Henry, who is more than 115 years old, or Lucy, who is over 50 years old! The museum is open Mon.–Fri. 10 A.M.–5 P.M., Saturday 1–5 P.M., Sunday and holidays 1–5 P.M.; admission is by donation. For more information, call 03/218-9753. Also in Queens Park is the Astronomical Observatory, open Wednesday evenings 7–9 P.M. April–October.

Anderson Park
Originally a farm, Anderson Park, tel. 03/215-7432, features 20 hectares of native bush that has remained virtually unchanged and a garden of exotic trees. The original farmhouse is now an art gallery open Tues.–Thurs. and Sat.–Sun. 2–4 P.M. The park lies seven km north of Invercargill.

RECREATION
Short Walks
Before Invercargill was built, the entire area was natural bush—see how it used to be in **Waihopai Scenic Reserve,** 34 hectares on the city's northern outskirts, with a 2.8-km walk along the Waihopai River (it starts on Hwy. 6 at Gladstone Terrace and finishes on Racecourse Rd.; one hour one way), and 120-hectare **Seaward Bush** southeast of Invercargill.

Sandy Point Reserve, west of the city along **New River Estuary,** is another good area for short bush walks with views of the estuary, Invercargill, and several protected beaches. Get information and brochures on walking tracks around the city and the region at the DOC Field Centre in the State Insurance Building, Don St., tel. 03/214-4589.

Oreti Beach, 9.5 km west of the city along the shores of Foveaux Strait, is a long sweep of sand excellent for walking; on a clear day, you can see Stewart Island. The water is warmer here than along many South Island beaches, thanks to a warm current from Australia.

Flightseeing

Stewart Island Flights, based at Invercargill Airport, tel. 03/218-9129, provides daily scheduled flights to Stewart Island and complete package weekend holidays; call for more information, bookings, and prices.

Entertainment

Invercargill is not the most exciting place in New Zealand for evening entertainment—unless you enjoy drinking in the many hotel bars around town, or attending the trots (horse races) or greyhound races at local racecourses (see the newspaper for dates and times). All the hotels and bottle stores in the city are operated by Invercargill Licensing Trust, a local authority founded in 1944 when liquor licensing was re-established after 38 years of prohibition, with members elected by the community; all profits are used to remodel the hotels or for community projects. The **Embassy,** 112 Dee St., tel. 03/214-0050, Invercargill's premier nightclub, has a huge dance floor. For something a bit tamer, call the **Invercargill Musical Theatre,** 176 Don St., tel. 03/218-9601, and see what's on.

Invercargill Summer Festival

In summer (usually early February) the city springs to life for the annual Invercargill Summer Festival. Parades, competitions, races, a rodeo, gymkhanas, and live music happen all over town for about a week straight.

ACCOMMODATIONS

Hotels and Motels

A few old downtown hotels offer rooms. Dating to 1896, **Gerrard's Hotel,** opposite the railway station and the bus stop on the corner of Esk and Leven Streets, tel. 03/218-3406, website: www.gerrards.co.nz, has 20 bright rooms, but no kitchen or laundry, and a decent restaurant. Rates, including breakfast, are $40 pp in a single or double room with shared facilities, and $75 s, $90 d for a room with a bathroom.

Montecillo Lodge, 240 Spey St., tel. 03/218-2503, is an attractive house built in 1895. The rooms in the original building, along with a dining room and lounge, are appealingly old-fashioned. They are $80 s, $100 d, which includes breakfast. Adjoining the old house are four newer motel rooms costing $70 s, $85 d, with no breakfast. One block farther east (away from downtown), the **Ashlar Motel,** 81 Queens Dr., tel. 03/217-9093, charges $78 s, $90 d, for its four self-contained units. **Tower Lodge Motel,** 119 Queens Dr., tel. 03/217-6729 or 0800/802-180, offers 10 one- and two-bedroom units, each with a kitchen in a central location (within walking distance of downtown and the museum). Rates are $88–105 s or d.

The **Ascot Park Hotel** is a sprawling complex just under four km east of the city along Hwy. 1 at the corner of Tay St. and Racecourse

Climb to the top of this water tower, on Leet Street, for city views.

SOUTHLAND

Rd., tel. 03/217-6195. It's designed mainly as a conference center but has a heated pool and spa, landscaped gardens, a restaurant, and a bar. Accommodations are in spacious self-contained motel-style rooms ($105 s or d) or in more luxurious hotel rooms ($155–170 s or d).

Backpacker Lodges

Southern Comfort, 30 Thomson St., tel. 03/218-3838, is one of New Zealand's finest backpacker accommodations—it's full most of the time. In one of the city's many leafy suburbs, it's an easy walk to the museum and downtown. All the usual facilities are provided, everything is modern, the building is immaculately clean, and guests have free use of a few bikes. Dorm beds are $19 pp, doubles and twins are $21 pp.

The world's southernmost YHA property, **Invercargill YHA,** 122 North Rd., Waikiwi, tel. 03/215-9344, website: www.yha.org.nz, is fairly basic but modern, one km north of the city boundary on the main highway to Te Anau—a 40-minute walk or a short bus ride from the stop opposite the railway station to the suburb of Waikiwi; rates are $16–20 pp.

Motor Camps

Invercargill offers several motor camps. The most central is **Invercargill Caravan Park,** on Victoria Ave. off Dee St. (the main highway north), tel. 03/218-8787. One km north of city center, it's next to a track where greyhounds are trained some mornings (free entertainment) and raced two evenings a month. The camp has communal facilities, TV lounge, and general store. Tent sites in the large, grassy camping area are $8 pp, caravan sites are $10 pp, comfortable cabins start at $28 (definitely worth the extra bucks when it's raining), and a few bunk beds are $12 pp. Also next to a racecourse, the **Coachmans Inn,** just over four km east on the main highway to Dunedin, 705 Tay St., tel. 03/217-6046 or 0508/426-224, has a number of tent and powered sites for $18 and cabins for $32 s or d. The adjacent inn has a restaurant and bar.

Beach Road Motor Camp is one km from Oreti Beach (beyond the airport), eight km from city center but close to the beach, tel. 03/213-

0400. Tent sites are $7 pp, powered sites are $9 pp, cabins are $16 s, $28 d, and tourist flats are $45 s or d.

FOOD

Light Meals

Oyster lovers *must* sample Foveaux oysters—the region's delicacy. Try **Cod Pot Seafood,** 136 Dee St., tel. 03/218-2354, for oysters in season (March and April), fresh blue cod, and cooked mutton birds (another delicacy with a unique taste that you'll either love or hate). If you can't get them fresh, buy canned oysters in the local shops.

Colonial Bakery, at 297 Dee St., tel. 03/218-2376, sells delicious baked goods. **In a Pickle,** 16 Don St., tel. 03/218-7340, serves up sandwiches, rolls, and wraps throughout the day. A good place for a light meal is **Tillermans Café Bar,** 16 Don St., tel. 03/218-9240, a health food restaurant. Sit in an airy room surrounded by elegant antique furniture while you munch on sandwiches and mixed salads, the hot dish of the day (whole foods, vegetarian, seafood, chicken), sushi, or fresh fruit salad; $7–12 for light meals, $14–19.50 for main dishes. It's open weekdays for lunch, Tues.–Sat. for dinner, with live music (from classical to blues) most weekends. The **Zookeeper Café,** 50 Tay St., tel. 03/218-3373, is a popular eatery with standard and well-priced city-style staples.

Dinners

The best place in town for seafood is **Kings HMS Restaurant** at 82 Tay St., tel. 03/218-3443. In a very nautical atmosphere—lots of wood, portholes filled with shells, knotted rope, and life preservers—tuck into a tasty seafood meal. Dishes average $22 (the Fisherman's Platter for $24 has a good selection of deep-fried seafood), and the portions are enormous. In March and April savor oysters fresh from the sea. It's open weekdays 11:30 A.M.–9:30 P.M., Sat-Sun. 5–9:30 P.M. Many hotels and taverns around town serve meals seven days a week.

Most folk dine out so they *don't* have to cook, but doing so can be fun also. At **Big Willy Rustlers Bar & Grill,** in the Newfield Tavern on Centre St., tel. 03/216-7313, choose your meat of choice and cook it yourself on the large barbecue Tues.–Sat. from 4:30 P.M. ($14–18 including extras such as potato and salad).

Attractive **Molly O'Grady's** restaurant, upstairs in the Kelvin Hotel building on the corner of Esk and Kelvin Streets, tel. 03/218-2829, is very popular with businesspeople. It serves seafood, steak, and salads, and you can expect to pay about $11–14 for a light meal, $16–27 for main dishes. The **Cobb & Co** on the corner of Avenal and Dee Streets, tel. 03/218-8944, does a roaring business. Expect to pay about $16–18 for a main dish or $12 for a late supper snack and coffee on Friday and Saturday nights 10 P.M.–midnight. It's open weekdays 11 A.M.–2 P.M. and 5–10 P.M., Friday and Saturday till midnight.

TRANSPORTATION

Getting There

The airport is 2.5 km from the city center. Inexpensive transfers between the airport and downtown are provided by Spitfire Shuttles, tel. 03/214-1851; $3 each way. **Air New Zealand,** tel. 03/214-4737, flies from Invercargill to Dunedin and Christchurch direct. Flights to all other points are routed through Christchurch. The **Air New Zealand Travelcentre** is at 46 Esk St., tel. 03/215-0000. Invercargill is also the gateway to Stewart Island. **Stewart Island Flights** provides the link; tel. 03/218-9129 or 0800/843-475.

Invercargill is the southern terminus of the **Tranz Scenic,** tel. 0800/802-802, Southerner, which takes nine hours to run down the coast from Christchurch via Dunedin; the railway station is on Leven Street.

Intercity, tel. 03/214-0598, provides regular bus services from Te Anau, Queenstown and Lumsden, Dunedin and Gore to Invercargill, terminating at the Invercargill Travel Centre in the railway station on Leven Street. Shuttle services around Invercargill include **Spitfire Shuttles,** tel. 03/214-1851, which runs to Te Anau, and **Catch-a-bus,** tel. 03/214-5652, which runs to Dunedin.

Getting Around

The main way of getting around Invercargill is by **Invercargill Passenger Transport,** tel. 03/218-7108. Buses depart from opposite the old post office on Dee Street; $1.20 will get you anywhere in the city.

suburban Invercargill

Car rental agencies with offices in Invercargill include **Avis,** tel. 03/218-7019; **Budget,** tel. 03/218-7012; and **Hertz,** tel. 03/218-2837.

You can reach **City Cabs** at tel. 03/214-4444, or **The Taxi Co** at tel. 03/214-4478.

SERVICES AND INFORMATION

Services

The **post office** is at 51 Don St., tel. 03/214-7700; it's open Mon.–Thurs. 9 A.M.–5 P.M., till 8 P.M. on Friday. **Invercargill Public Library** is on Dee St., tel. 03/218-7025; book ahead for public Internet access.

Southland Hospital is on Kew Rd. in Kew, a suburb south of city center, tel. 03/218-1949. **Invercargill Urgent Doctor,** 103 Don St., tel. 03/218-8821, is open Mon.–Fri. 5–10 P.M., weekends and public holidays 8 A.M.–10 P.M., For the **police station** call 03/211-0400.

Information

For information on Invercargill, Southland in general, and Stewart Island, call in at the **Invercargill Visitor Information Centre** in Southland Museum near the entrance to Queens Park, tel. 03/214-6243. It's open Mon.–Fri. 9:30 A.M.–5 P.M., Sat.–Sun. and holidays 1–5 P.M. The **Tourism Southland** website is www.southland.org.nz. For information on Fiordland National Park, all the Southland forest parks, reserves, hiking trails, and outdoor activities, stop by the DOC **Southland Conservancy** office in the State Insurance Building, 33 Don St., tel. 03/214-4589. Open weekdays 8 A.M.–5 P.M., it has a library of pamphlets and brochures and sells books and topographical maps. The **Automobile Association** is at 47 Gala St., tel. 03/218-9033.

BLUFF

At the end of Hwy. 1, 27 km south of Invercargill, lies Bluff, the South Island's largest port, and home base for fishing fleets that cruise the south and west coasts for fish, crayfish, and delicious Foveaux Strait oysters (commonly called Bluff oysters). The Maori called Bluff Motu-Pohue or Island of Pohue, after a giant white convolvulus that flowers yearly on Bluff Hill. At the *very* end of Hwy. 1 (or at the beginning—Cape Reinga, north of Auckland, lays claim to being the "end" of Hwy. 1) is **Stirling Point**—and an often-photographed sign giving distances to far-flung destinations around the world. For panoramic views of the harbor, Foveaux Strait, Stewart Island, and the New Zealand Aluminium Smelter, head up to the top of **Bluff Hill** (265 meters) to the lookout—particularly enjoyable in the evening when the waters far below are dotted with fishing boats on their way home.

Sights

New Zealand Aluminium Smelters Ltd. at Tiwai Point, 26 km south of Invercargill, is the largest aluminium smelter in the Southern Hemisphere (no, not a spelling error—"aluminum" is a trademarked North American bastardization of the proper spelling), eighth largest in the world, and a vital part of Southland economy. It offers free tours weekdays at 10 A.M., lasting about two hours, but you need to book a space (tel. 03/218-5999), have your own transportation out there, and wear a long-sleeved shirt, long pants, and closed-toe shoes; look in the newspaper service section for details. Although the smelter is at Bluff, access is along Tiwai Rd., which branches off Hwy. 1 eleven km south of Invercargill.

Walks

Two good walks around Bluff together make up the **Foveaux Walkway.** The 1.5-km Glory Walk starts at the "Gunpit" site at the end of Gunpit Rd., meanders through a scenic reserve, and finishes at the Stirling Point-Ocean Beach Track; it takes about 30 minutes one way. The 6.6-km Stirling Point-Ocean Beach Track follows the coastline around Bluff Hill for magnificent views of beaches and offshore islands, crossing small gullies into open pasture with views of farmland and the coastline. The track starts at Stirling Point and finishes near the Ocean Beach Freezing Works on the main highway; it's about 2.5 hours one way. Take a windbreaker and something to drink, and wear sturdy shoes.

Practicalities

Bluff has no motels. Instead, consider **Land's End New Zealand,** overlooking the ocean from a hilltop position right at the very end of Hwy. 1, tel. 03/212-7575; website: www.landsend.net.nz. This white, two-story lodge has six guest rooms, each with a private bathroom. Rates are from $85 s, $115 d, which includes breakfast in a downstairs cafe. Adjacent, the **Drunken Sailor**

Cafe, tel. 03/212-8855, has stunning views over Foveaux Strait. Seafood features prominently with chowder ($8) and fish dishes, such as battered flounder ($12.95), are reasonably priced. The menu even includes an American Sandwich ($10), which is basically a BLT—just what you've traveled to the end of the road at the opposite side of the world for. The Drunken Sailor is open daily at 10 am. for lunch and weekends for dinner.

Bluff Information Centre is in Foveaux Souvenirs 74 Gore St., tel. 03/212-8305.

Stewart Island

Stewart Island is the third and most southerly of New Zealand's main islands, separated from the South Island by shallow, 24-km **Foveaux Strait.** Called Rakiura (Land of the Glowing Skies) by the Maori, it became known as Stewart Island after William Stewart, an officer on the ship *Pegasus,* visited and charted Paterson Inlet in 1809. This peaceful, secluded island's appeal lies in its virtually untouched bushland, well-maintained tracks, and lack of population. It's known for lingering twilights—a "heavenly glow" (in summer it's light until 10 P.M.), and spectacular sunsets. **Oban** (population 400), the only settlement, home of fishermen, vacationers, and island devotees, lies nestled along the protected shores of Halfmoon Bay on the east side of the island; it's reached from the mainland by boat or plane.

A thriving fishing industry (blue cod, crayfish, and *paua*) and three fish- processing factories support most of the population; deer hunting and tourism bring an increasing number of visitors to the island each year. Going to Stewart Island is like taking a giant step back in time—the locals depend on rainfall for water, a few depend on individual generators for electricity, and there are few roads. It's not the place to go for lively evening entertainment—residents and visitors alike tend to go to bed early so they can make the most of the daylight for outdoor activities. Go there to revel in scenery and solitude, to hike

through bush and along endless sandy beaches, and to cruise remote inlet waters.

THE LAND

Including outlying islands, Stewart Island covers an area of 1,746 square km. The island, almost triangular in shape, stretches about 65 km from north to south, 40 km from east to west, and its deeply indented coastline is about 755 km. It

STEWART ISLAND

SOUTHLAND

lies between latitudes 46 and 47 degrees south—probably the closest that most people ever get to Antarctica. Most of the island is mountainous and hard to penetrate, with short, sheer gullies and steep ridge systems, but it's fringed with bays and sandy beaches. In the north the rugged highlands rise to 979-meter **Mount Anglem,** highest peak on the island. **Paterson Inlet,** the main inlet with an average width of four km, has three main arms and an indented coastline, and extends 16 km westward across the central part of the island, almost dividing it in two. Of the total 174,600 hectares of forest and bush, about 93 percent is designated as Crown Reserve to protect native flora and fauna, Maori land, or Scenic Reserve.

Climate

Stewart Island has mild temperatures throughout the year, and relatively high rainfall ranging from 1,500 mm in coastal areas (such as Oban) to 5,000 mm in the high country. Frosts are rare, but snow lies on the highest peak, Mt. Anglem, for short periods. Westerly gales are common (cold from the southwest, warm from the northwest), and low clouds occur frequently—even though there can be fairly long periods without rain (the islanders welcome rain as they depend on it for their water supply). The locals are only too willing to admit that the weather is for the most part unpredictable, and it's quite possible to experience four seasons in a single day! Go prepared for everything and you'll be comfortable.

Flora and Fauna

The high rainfall, mild winter, and fertile soil have resulted in dense forest and native bush. Though the vegetation has been modified by introduced deer and possum, it remains a unique forested wilderness of native *rimu, miro, totara,* ferns, mosses, scented native orchids (30 species), and a wealth of native plants. Stewart Island is a bird sanctuary to several rare birds and many seldom seen on the mainland. *Kaka,* parakeets, Stewart Island robins, fernbirds, dotterels, Stewart Island brown kiwis, the almost extinct *kakapo* (a flightless nocturnal parrot found only here),

pied shags, Stewart Island shags, and yellow-eyed penguins all live on the island. The forest abounds with bush birds—*tui,* bellbirds, pigeons, parakeets, cuckoos, *kaka,* brown creepers, fantails, tomtits, grey warblers, and finches. Along the shores you find oystercatchers, herons, black-billed gulls, blue penguins, Hookers sea lions, and fur seals. Muttonbirds or sooty shearwaters breed on the offshore islands and islets, the largest breeding ground of muttonbirds in New Zealand (descendants of Rakiura Maori have sole rights to the April capture of young muttonbirds). Introduced white-tailed deer, red deer, and possums, and native long-tailed bats live here; native short-tailed bats live only on the offshore islands.

SIGHTS

Oban is the principal settlement, nestled along the sandy shores of Halfmoon Bay. Most of the island's 400 residents live at Halfmoon Bay (half the residences are permanently occupied, the rest are holiday cottages), and the 50-boat fishing fleet is anchored here. A variety of short tracks start in Oban, and several beautiful beaches lie within walking distance of town.

Around Oban

If you're able to spend only a day on Stewart Island (not long enough), you'll find lots of things to do in and around Oban. Your first stop should be the **Stewart Island Visitor Centre** on Main Rd., tel. 03/219-1218. In the same building is a DOC Field Centre, tel. 03/219-1130, which has general island information, hiking trail brochures, and displays (don't miss the mounted *kakapo,* a rare native parrot). The **Rakiura Museum** on Ayr St. houses a fascinating collection of historic relics relating to the island's whaling, sealing, timber milling, and pioneering past; Maori art; and information on the island's modern fishing industry. It's open Mon.–Sat. 10 A.M.–noon, Sunday noon–2 P.M., and admission is a worthwhile $1.

Many short tracks in the area lead through beautiful bush to places of scenic or historic interest, and to lookouts with spectacular views. Don't miss the view from **Observation Rock,** particularly splendid at sunset.

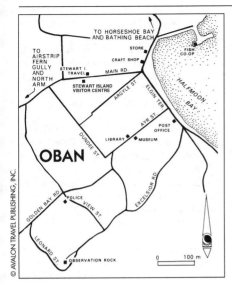

OBAN

© AVALON TRAVEL PUBLISHING, INC.

RECREATION

If you're on the island for at least a couple of days, walk the many several-hour tracks (such as the 1.5-hour track to **Horseshoe Bay**), search for shells along beautiful beaches, or if you're a well-equipped hiker, head off into the backcountry along well-maintained tracks. Take a launch ride to isolated areas of the island totally inaccessible on foot, or to the island's newest industry of salmon farming, historical whaling sites, and beautiful **Ulva Island** in Paterson Inlet. Extended seafaring trips and fishing charters are also available; get all the options at the information center.

Hiking

Find out where all Stewart Island's tracks lead by picking up *Stewart Island Day Walks* at the visitor center ($1). It's packed with useful information, and has directions and descriptions for all the day tracks close to Oban.

Well-maintained tracks take you into some of New Zealand's most beautiful bush. Locals say that as long as you can hike with a pack for at least four hours nonstop, you're fit enough to do the tracks on Stewart Island. Tracks in the northern sector of the island are especially intended

for experienced hikers, winding along the picturesque shoreline and deep into the dense interior. The most popular walking track, the **North-West Circuit,** meanders along the northern coast of the island, taking 7–10 days to complete—add several extra days if you sidetrack to Mason Bay on the west coast. Note well: This is not a suitable track for beginner hikers! The first four days can be summarized by hills, tree roots, and mud; the rewards are rainforest beauty and birds, birds, birds. Shorter tracks lead to Port William, Bungaree, and Christmas Village. The latest to be developed is the 36-km **Rakiura Track,** which takes three days. Buy a detailed map and get all the details from the DOC staff, and be more than adequately prepared for the elements.

Cruises

All manner of cruises can be taken from Oban, with **Ulva Island,** in Paterson Inlet, the most popular destination. The island is predator-free and has been a bird sanctuary since 1922. Hiking trails lead to all corners of the island, and the habitat remains natural. Water taxis run over to the island regularly (about $20 pp round-trip), or take a guided tour. Typically, a cruise includes a stop at the island and a visit to a salmon farm. If you want to spend more time on the island, ask to be left behind and you get picked up on the boat's return from the farm. All trips leave from the wharf at south end of Golden Bay Road. One recommended operator is **Thorfinn Charters,** tel. 03/219-1210. Thorfinn specializes in nature trips, searching out sea birds and marine mammals, such as seals and dolphins (half day $55 pp; full day $70 pp), and also offers bed-and-breakfast accommodation. If you'd like to see kiwis feeding in their natural environment, try one of the popular evening cruises. You go by boat to the Neck in Little Glory Bay, then walk through the bush to Ocean Beach to spot kiwis that feed on washed-up kelp. Take a warm coat, wear sturdy shoes or boots, and carry a flashlight; a hot drink and cake are provided on the boat. Leaving every alternate night, the tour costs $55 pp. The glass-bottomed *Seabuzzz,* tel. 03/219-1282, offers something a little different.

The main booking agents for the above tours are **Adventure Centre,** down on the wharf, tel. 03/219-1134; **Oban Tours and Taxis,** tel. 03/219-1456; and **Stewart Island Travel,** tel. 03/219-1269.

Sea Kayaking

The calm waters of Paterson Inlet are perfect for sea kayaking. The inlet lies a couple of kilometers by road south of Oban, offering endless opportunities for a wilderness trip with its convoluted shoreline, many small islands, and a number of DOC huts. **Stewart Island Sea Kayak Adventures,** tel. 03/219-1080, rents single and double kayaks for $30 pp per day and can arrange drop-offs anywhere around the inlet.

Golfing

On the outskirts of Oban, **Ringa Ringa Golf Course** boasts just six holes, but the fact that it's farther south than any other golf course in the world makes it a popular attraction. Rent clubs ($10) and buy balls ($2 each) at Stewart Island Travel, tel. 03/219-1269. Green fees are $12.

ACCOMMODATIONS AND FOOD

Accommodations on the island are limited, so make bookings before arriving. That said, they span the entire length of the price spectrum.

Hotels and Motels

Built in 1927, the rambling old **South Sea Hotel,** tel. 03/219-1059, website: www.stewart-island.co.nz, overlooks Halfmoon Bay and has 16 guest rooms with shared bathrooms. Rates are $60 s, $80 d ($90 with water views). Adjacent are more modern if smallish motel rooms for $120 s or d. In the main complex is a restaurant and bar. The **Rakiura Motel** lies just over one km north of Oban on Horseshoe Bay Rd., tel. 03/219-1096. Each of the five rooms is self-contained; $95 s or d.

Bed-and-Breakfasts

Centrally located **Jo and Andy's B&B,** tel. 03/219-1230, is good value at $25 pp for a bed in a double and twin room, which includes a cooked breakfast. Kitchen and bathroom facilities are shared.

Best known for their nature cruises, **Thorfinn Charters** also rent two rooms in their modern home on Horseshoe Bay Rd., tel. 03/219-1210; website: www.thorfinn.co.nz. Overlooking Butterfield Beach, a short, private stretch of sand where guests can dig for clams, the atmosphere is laid-back and the price right—$75 s, $100 d including breakfast. Book through Thorfinn for two nearby houses that can be rented in their entirety for $100 s or d.

A modern home overlooking Halfmoon Bay, **Goomes B&B,** tel. 03/219-1057, has three rooms sharing two bathrooms. Rates are $65 s, $120 d, which includes a cooked breakfast and pickups from the airport or ferry dock.

Port of Call, Leask Bay Rd., tel. 03/219-1394, website: www.portofcall.co.nz, is a modern bed-and-breakfast operated by sixth-generation islanders. Running right down to the ocean, the 20-hectare property is surrounded by bird-filled bush and encompasses an 1870s stone cottage. Guests are encouraged to mingle in the comfortable lounge with an open fire and plenty of local literature. Rates are $180 s, $240 d, which includes a light breakfast and complimentary hot drinks, fruit, and cookies throughout the day.

Backpacker Lodge

Stewart Island Backpackers, just up the hill from the harbor, tel. 03/219-1114, has dorm beds ($18 pp), basic rooms with shared bathrooms ($24 s, $40 d), as well as a couple of rooms made up with linen ($36 s, $60 d). Facilities include a communal kitchen, barbecue area, TV room, game room with pool table, and Internet access.

Camping

Free camping is available throughout the island—you'll find a particularly nice campground at the end of the popular North-West Circuit track by a huge old apple tree; toilets and fresh water are provided. Ask for campground locations at the DOC Field Centre.

Food

If you like fresh fish, Stewart Island is a culinary delight. The residents live off the sea, and although a thousand sheep graze the backcountry and deer are widespread, crayfish and blue cod are the main sources of income and diet. At **Anchor Merchants General Store,** tel. 03/219-1069, you can buy just about everything you need, but as supplies are sent over from the mainland by ferry or plane, prices tend to be high; it's open Mon.–Fri. 9 A.M.–5:30 P.M., weekends and holidays 10 A.M.–noon.

Justcafe, 1 Main Rd., tel. 03/219-1422, has good coffee, a range of cakes and pastries, and other homemade goodies, such as quiche. **Church Hill Café** offers fantastic views from its elevated location at 36 Kamahi Rd., tel. 03/219-1323. Open daily from 10:30 A.M., seafood dominates the menu.

South Sea Hotel, tel. 03/219-1059, offers surprisingly good food to be enjoyed at the bar, in the dining room, or at tables out front. Start with the seafood chowder ($9), and then choose a local specialty, such as battered blue cod with tartar sauce ($19) or roasted muttonbird ($25). Less adventurous seafood treats, such as chowder, oysters, and mussels, are good for a lighter meal. A separate bar menu is less expensive but offers many of the same choices. Meals are served daily noon–2 P.M. and 6–8 P.M.

TRANSPORTATION

There are two ways to get to the island—by a 20-minute flight from Invercargill or a one-hour catamaran crossing from Bluff. If you can afford the time and expense, ferry one way and fly the other for a broader experience.

Getting There by Air

Until 1980, when an island airstrip was developed, seaplanes landed right in Oban Bay. Today, **Stewart Island Flights,** tel. 03/218-9129 or 0800/843-475, offers three scheduled flights daily between Invercargill Airport and the island; bus transfers to Oban are included in the airfare. The one-way fare runs about $80, but

discounts are offered for seniors, students, YHA members, or those prepared to go standby; call to find out the best deal. Packages offered by Stewart Island Flights include a same-day return fare, including a 90-minute bus tour, a boat trip, and lunch combined with flights for $190 pp. The baggage allowance on all flights is just 15 kg pp.

Getting There by Ferry

Stewart Island Marine, tel. 03/212-7660, website: www.foveauxexpress.co.nz, operates two small passenger-only catamarans between Bluff and the main wharf at Oban, departing Bluff Mon.–Sat. at 9:30 A.M. and 5 P.M. and on Sunday at 5 P.M. only (reduced winter sailings). The crossing takes an hour; $45 one way, $84 round-trip. If you need vehicle storage in Bluff, it's available for $5 per day. Buses leave from the Invercargill depot to connect with ferry departures and arrivals at Bluff; $12 each way. (The Strait is very shallow and can become extremely rough at a moment's notice. The ferry makes crossings, weather permitting, but it can still get uncomfortably rough. If you're susceptible to seasickness, take drugs.)

Getting Around

Stewart Island has only 32 km of roads, and in the village of Oban everything is within walking distance of the harbor, so getting around is not a problem. **Oban Taxis,** tel. 03/219-1456, and **Sam & Billy the Bus,** book through Stewart Island Travel at 03/219-1269, offer short island tours along the road system for $20 pp. Highly recommended, these are a great introduction to the island. As the name suggests, Oban Taxis also runs a cab service around the island's short road system. **Stewart Island Travel,** tel. 03/219-1269, has a couple of small cars that they rent for $50 per half-day and $70 per full day. For transportation around the island by boat, see Cruises, above.

SERVICES AND INFORMATION

In the re-creation of a fisherman's cottage, **The Fernery,** tel. 03/219-1453, is crammed with island souvenirs emphasizing the natural history of

Stewart Island. It's the place to buy living ferns, souvenirs, cards, books, delicate silk scarves, dressing gowns, and prints—all with a fern theme. **Halfmoon Bay Library** on Ayr St. is open Wednesday 2–3:15 P.M. and Fri.–Sat. 11 A.M.–noon.

Stewart Island Health Centre is on Argyle St. (near the information center), tel. 03/219-1098. It's open daily 10:30 A.M.–12:30 P.M., and a nurse is on call 24 hours.

Information

Up Main Rd., 200 meters from the wharf, **Stewart Island Visitor Centre,** tel. 03/219-1218, has general information on the island, listings of budget accommodations, a list of launch operators willing to run you to remote areas, fishing and hunting charters and permits, interesting displays, a video guide, maps, and booklets on short walks and the major back-country tracks. In the same building, the **DOC** operates a field center, the place to get information on the island's natural wonders and details of all the hiking trails. It also holds interesting displays on local flora and fauna, including an aquarium. You can store excess baggage at the center for a small fee and leave passports and valuables in the safe. The center is open year-round daily 8 A.M.–5 P.M., until 7 P.M. in summer. Across the road, **Stewart Island Travel,** tel. 03/219-1269, sells souvenirs and provides local sight-seeing tours. Another booking agent is **Stewart Island Adventure Centre,** on the wharf, tel. 03/219-1134.

Resources

Glossary

Common New Zealand Words and Phrases

Aussie: an Australian

barbie: barbecue

bastard: usually an endearment, but sometimes used as an insult

bathroom: literally the room with bath and basin—the toilet is usually separate

beaut: beautiful

Beehive: the main government building in Wellington

big smoke: city

bike or **motorbike:** motorcycle

biscuits: cookies (scones resemble American biscuits)

bloke: a guy or man

bludger: someone who "borrows" something but does not necessarily give it back; e.g., "May I bludge a cigarette?" Also, someone who is lazy

bonkers: a bit crazy

bonnet: the hood of a vehicle

boot: the trunk of a vehicle, or footwear

Boxing Day: 26 December—a national holiday

brolly: umbrella

bush: the wild, untouched areas of native forest and woodland

BYO: restaurants are either "licensed" or BYO-bring your own beer or wine

caravan: a small, mobile house-trailer generally used for vacations

carpark: parking lot

cheesed off: mad at something or someone

chemist: pharmacy

choppers: teeth; e.g., "Sink your choppers into this, mate!"

ciggies: cigarettes

clothes pegs: clothespins

coach: long-distance bus

"Come again!": "Repeat what you just said, please."

cordial: a bottle of concentrated fruit-flavored juice, which is reconstituted into a drink by adding water

crook: ill, not feeling well

cuppa: usually refers to a cup of hot tea

dairy: small shop selling basic groceries, snack foods, and newspapers; often open when everything else in the area is closed

date: Note that in New Zealand, the day comes before the month, followed by the year; e.g., June 11, 1956, is written 11/06/56

deli: delicatessen, a more expensive version of a dairy

(on the) dole: unemployment benefits

domain: a well-tended public park with lots of flowers and trees

dressing gown: bathrobe

dustbin: garbage can

dustmen: garbage collectors (they also call themselves "garbologists!")

eiderdown: a warm quilt, most often filled with feathers

entree: an appetizer, eaten before the main course of a meal

"Fair dinkum": either means "Honestly, it's true," or asked in a questioning tone means "Is that true?"

"Fair go": "Give me a chance."

fortnight: two weeks

fridge: refrigerator

flat: apartment

flicks: the movies or cinema

footie/football: rugby league; American football is called "gridiron."

footpath: sidewalk

gallon: The New Zealand imperial gallon is bigger than an American gallon.

"G'day": a greeting meaning good day, or hi! The Australian version sounds more like "geday."

go for a burn: go for a fast ride in a car

"Good on yer, mate": "Good for you, pal."

greengrocer: fruit and vegetable (veggie) shop

ground floor: first floor (street level)

gumboots: everyone has a pair of these rubber boots for rainy days

hire: rent

hotel: any accommodation licensed to serve alcohol

jumper/jersey: sweater

kiwi: a flightless bird; the national symbol of New Zealand; many New Zealanders also like to call themselves "Kiwis."

laundrette: laundromat or laundry

left luggage: an area in a railway station, airport, etc., where you can safely leave your baggage, usually for a small fee

letter box: mailbox

licensed: as in a restaurant licensed to serve alcohol

lift: elevator

loo: toilet, usually in a room of its own

mate: friendly way of addressing someone, be they friend or stranger; e.g., "G'day mate, how ya goin'?"

metal surface: the road surface is gravel, not paved

milk bar: a shop selling dairy products, hot snack foods, some canned food, sweets, and candy bars; open longer hours than most shops and on weekends

motor camp: a safe, clean place to stay inexpensively, with tent and caravan sites, cabins and tourist flats, and communal bathroom, kitchen, and laundry

motorway: freeway/highway/autobahn

mozzies: mosquitoes (their bite is not as bad as that of sandflies)

muckin' around/muckin' about: fooling around

nappies: diapers

ocker: a derogatory way of describing a person from Australia

paddock: a field

pavement: sidewalk

peckish: a bit hungry

petrol: fuel/gas

petrol station: gas station

piss: beer (don't be offended if a Kiwi invites you to "come over and drink some piss")

postman/postie: mailman

prang: car or bike accident

pushbike: bicycle

return ticket: a roundtrip ticket, to destination and back

rubber: an eraser

rubbish: garbage

rubbish bins: garbage cans

sandfly: a tiny biting insect (the bite leaves an itchy welt that when persistently scratched leaves a small scar) that can drive you bonkers unless you're armed with strong insect repellent

sandshoes: tennis shoes/gym shoes/sneakers

school: primary and secondary school, or junior and senior high; does not apply to college or university education

sealed road: paved road

"She'll be right": everything will be okay (heard often)

skifield: alpine resort, regardless of its size.

stirrer: a troublemaker or person who likes to joke around

takeaway: food to go, to take out

tea: has various meanings—can be a cup of tea, a light evening meal, or dinner, depending on the context (it's always best to confirm the exact meaning before you show up at someone's place!)

telly: television

toll call: a long-distance telephone call

torch: flashlight

tramp/tramper/tramping: hike/hiker/hiking

trundler: shopping cart

tucker: food

varsity: university

wee: small (or early, as in "early hours")

whinge: whine; e.g., "He's a bit of a whinger."

woolies: usually means long underwear or outer winter wear

Yank: an American

Yank tank: slang for a large American-made car

z: In New Zealand (and Britain and Australia), the letter Z is pronounced "zed."

Common Maori Words and Phrases

ao: cloud

aotearoa: Land of the Long White Cloud (one of several translations)

atua: god

awa: river, valley

haere mai: welcome

haera ra: farewell

haka: a war dance and chants performed by the men

hangi: a Maori feast where the food is cooked/steamed in an earth oven

hau: wind

Hawaiiki: legendary homeland of the Maori

kia ora: good luck

kumara: sweet potato

makomako: bellbird

mana: prestige

manu: bird

maunga: mountain

moana: sea or lake

moko: tattoo

motu: island, or anything that is isolated

pa: fortified village

pakeha: foreigner, white person, European

po: night

puna: spring of water

rangi: sky

roto: lake

rua: two; e.g., Rotorua: two lakes

tapu: sacred

utu: retribution

wai: water

whanga: bay, stretch of water, inlet

whare: house

whenua: land

Some Common Misunderstandings

- **French fries** are called hot chips, potato chips are just called chips.
- And if you like **ketchup** with your fries, ask for tomato sauce (ketchup also exists but it's completely different from American-style).
- **"Tea"** can mean a cup of hot tea, or a complete dinner—confirm the exact meaning before you accept an invitation.
- **Napkins** are called "serviettes."
- **A cultural note on cuisine:** Beetroot (red beets) is slapped in almost everything, including all hamburgers. If you don't want it, be sure to specify "no beetroot."

Suggested Reading

All the books listed below can be found at major bookstores throughout New Zealand or in major libraries throughout the country, unless otherwise noted.

History

Best, Elsdon. *Polynesian Voyagers.* Dominion Museum Monograph No. 5. New Zealand: A.R. Shearer, Government Printer, 1975. 54 pages. A compact history of the Polynesian deep-sea navigators, explorers, and colonizers—the Maori voyage from their ancient homeland, Hawaiiki, to Aotearoa, New Zealand.

Buck, Sir Peter. *The Coming of the Maori.* New Zealand: Whitcoulls Publishers, 1950. 574 pages. Maori ethnology; the exciting adventures of early Polynesian Pacific navigators.

Howard, Basil. *Rakiura.* New Zealand: A.H. and A.W. Reed. The history of Stewart Island.

Pope, Diana, and Jeremy Pope. Mobil New Zealand Travel Guides: *North Island* and *South Island.* New Zealand: Reed Publishing, (North) 1996, 326 pages; (South) 1995, 326 pages. Detailed geographic travel guides to the North and South Islands, with emphasis on local history.

Reed, A.H. *Historic Bay of Islands.* New Zealand: A.H. and A.W. Reed, 1960. 48 pages. Beautifully illustrated history of the Bay of Islands in an easy-to-read format.

Geography

Egmont National Park Track and Hut Guide. New Zealand: The Department of Conservation, 1988. 40 pages. Along with mountaineering, tramping, and skiing tracks and routes, this handy guide outlines the park's history, volcanology, weather, vegetation, and flora and fauna.

Gage, Maxwell. *Legends in the Rocks.* New Zealand: Whitcoulls Publishers, 1980. 426 pages. A comprehensive, illustrated, layperson's guide to the geology of New Zealand.

Land of the Mist: The Story of Urewera National Park. New Zealand: The Department of Lands and Survey, 1983. 111 pages. The natural and human history of the park, along with recreational opportunities, Maori legends, and Maori place-names and their meanings.

The New Zealand Automobile Association. *AA Book of New Zealand National Parks.* New Zealand: Lansdowne Press, 1983. 176 pages. Another good souvenir book on New Zealand's national parks loaded with recreational information and color photographs.

Potton, Craig. *The Story of Nelson Lakes National Park.* New Zealand: Department of Lands and Survey and Cobb/Horwood Publications, 1984. 160 pages. An illustrated geography, flora and fauna, geology, and history of the park, with comprehensive sections on outdoor activities—tramping, mountaineering, fishing, skiing, and hunting.

Reader's Digest. *Wild New Zealand.* New Zealand: Reader's Digest, 1990. 335 pages. A detailed guide to the less-inhabited, off-the-beaten-track areas of the country, packed with geographical information and spectacular photography. Much more than a coffee-table book—an invaluable New Zealand souvenir.

The Restless Land: Stories of Tongariro National Park. New Zealand: The Department of Conservation, 1996. 160 pages. The geography, history, flora and fauna, climate, and myths and legends of the park, along with sections on skiing, climbing, huts, and services.

Flora and Fauna

Chambers, Stuart. *Birds of New Zealand Locality Guide.* Arun Books, 1989. 115 pages. Listings of all of New Zealand's native birds along with their favored habitats and locations.

Poole, A.L., and N.M. Adams. *Trees and Shrubs of New Zealand.* P.D. Hasselberg, Government Printer, 1980. 400 pages. A complete coverage of all the native trees and shrubs in the country, with illustrations.

Soper, M.F. *Birds of New Zealand and the Outlying Islands.* New Zealand: Whitcoulls Publishers, 1984. All you want to know about New Zealand birds, and more.

Turbott, E.G. *Buller's Birds of New Zealand.* New Zealand: Whitcoulls Publishers, 1967. 280 pages. New Zealand's native birds in color.

The Great Outdoors

DuFresne, Jim. *Tramping in New Zealand.* Australia: Lonely Planet, 1995. 320 pages. An easy-to-read backpacking guide to all the major hiking tracks in the country.

Forrester, Rex. *Trout Fishing in New Zealand.* New Zealand: Whitcoulls Publishers, 1979. 208 pages. Find out how, when, and where to catch New Zealand's fighting trout, then learn how to smoke them.

Gould, Peter. *The Complete Taupo Fishing Guide.* Auckland: William Collins Publishers Ltd., 1983. 240 pages. A detailed guide to all the major fishing spots in the Taupo area, with advice on what to use, weather, fishing etiquette, and entertaining fishing yarns.

Gould, Rex. *50 Top New Zealand Golf Courses.* Auckland: Reed Books, 1995. Beginning each chapter with general sightseeing information and continuing with the statistics and descriptions of 50 golf courses, this book is a must-have for those planning a golfing holiday in New Zealand.

New Zealand Automobile Association. *AA Guide to Discovering New Zealand.* Lansdowne Press, 1995. 252 pages. Loaded with interesting facts about all the places you'll see along the major roads throughout the country, with plenty of color photographs—a good souvenir book.

Rushton, Nigel. *Pedaller's Paradise.* Lake Tekapo: Dab Hand Publishing, 1996. Two in-depth volumes (one to each island) to major highway routes, alternative routes, connecting roads, and scenic routes of tourist interest, plus terrain, distances, gradients, surface, road conditions, and location of accommodations along each route.

Sharpe, Marty. *A Guide to the Ski Areas of New Zealand.* Random House NZ, 1995. 368 pages. Describes every skifield in the country, giving details of lifts, runs, and the facilities in each area. The first chapter is a good introduction to the unique conditions that apply to skiing Downunder.

Shutt, Peter. *Fishing NZ for Trout and Salmon.* Timaru, New Zealand: self-published, 1992. 240 pages. A well-written guide to trout and salmon fishing, loaded with handy tips and detailed information for major rivers, lakes, and less-fished locations.

Smith, Rodney. *A Guide to the Skifields of New Zealand.* New Zealand: A.H. and A.W. Reed Ltd., 1981. 130 pages. A guide to most of New Zealand's commercial and club skifields, with terrain and run descriptions, facilities, suitability for beginner or pro, how to get to each field, and brief accommodation, food, and entertainment information.

Temple, Philip. *Shell Guides to the Great New Zealand Walking Tracks* series. New Zealand:

Whitcoulls Publishers. Pocket-sized guides to the major tracks of both North and South Islands, including track history, detailed descriptions, information, advice, and maps.

Turner, Brian, ed. *The Guide to Trout Fishing in Otago.* Dunedin, New Zealand: Otago Acclimatisation Society, 1984. 103 pages. A guide to all the main fishing rivers and lakes of Otago.

General Interest

Bowden, Beth. *Parliament and The People.* P.D. Hasselberg, Government Printer, 1984. 64 pages. Written primarily for children and for visitors to Parliament, this illustrated book describes New Zealand's constitution and explains its development.

Gallen, Rodney, and Allan North. *Waikaremoana: A Brief History of the Lakes of the Urewera National Park.* Te Urewera National Parks Board, 1977. 64 pages. A souvenir booklet of Waikaremoana, Wairaumoana, and Waikareiti, covering the history of the lakes, the people, and the land.

Ihimaera, Witi. *Maori.* Wellington: A.R. Shearer, Government Printer, 1975. 45 pages. A brief historical insight into the Maori from Hawaiiki to modern-day New Zealand.

Jungowska, Maria. *Livingston's Auckland Explorer.* David Livingston of Scarab Publishing, 1984. 193 pages. A handy pocket-sized book packed with everything a traveler could want to know about Auckland, with maps.

Leland, Jr., Louis S. *A Personal Kiwi-Yankee Dictionary.* U.S.A.: Pelican Publishing Company, 1990. 120 pages. An entertaining pocket-sized guide to the English language and colloquial New Zealandisms written specifically for Americans.

New Zealand Automobile Association. *AA New Zealand Road Atlas* (Classic Edition). Auckland: Hodder Moa Beckett, 1999. This invaluable companion for those driving around New Zealand divides the country into 15 double-page maps, with city maps making up the back pages.

Accommodation Guides

Budget Backpacker Hostels. *BBH Backpacker Accommodation New Zealand.* Updated twice annually with input from more than 200 backpacker lodges as well as travelers, this small booklet is invaluable for backpackers. It lists prices, facilities, and a unique "rating" system to help ease accommodation choices. It's available from all lodges listed as well as most information centers.

Greening, Mark, and Elizabeth Greening. *Baches and Holiday Homes to Rent.* Nelson, N.Z.: Mark and Elizabeth Greening, 1999. An excellent guide to New Zealand homes and retreats available for rent, with descriptions and tariffs.

Jason Publishing Co., Ltd. *Jasons Motels and Motor Lodges.* Updated annually, a guide to motels and motor lodges throughout the country.

New Zealand Automobile Association. *AA Accommodation Guide.* Updated annually, this guide to New Zealand's hotels, motels, and motor camps is worth its weight in gold. It is available from all AA offices and many bookstores.

Thomas, James. *The New Zealand Bed and Breakfast Book.* Moonshine Press. A comprehensive guide to bed-and-breakfasts, homestays, and farmstays throughout the country, including a short description of each one, what to expect from the hosts, and rates that are updated annually.

Youth Hostel Association. *YHA New Zealand Accommodation Guide.* This free pocket-sized handbook tells you the locations of all the YHA hostels throughout New Zealand, local sights, outdoor recreational information, and services and discounts available to members.

Internet Resources

Accommodations

Accor: accorhotels.com.au

Best Western: www.bestwestern.co.nz

Budget Backpacker Hostels New Zealand: www.backpack.co.nz

CDL Hotels: www.cdlhotels.co.nz

Copthorne Hotels and Resorts: www.copthorne.com.au

Department of Conservation: www.doc.govt.nz

Golden Chain: www.goldenchain.co.nz

International Youth Hostel Federation: www.iyhf.com

Jasons Accommodation Directory: www.jasons.co.nz.

Mainstay: www.mainstay.co.nz

Manor Motor Inns: www.manorinns.co.nz

New Zealand Bed and Breakfast Book: www.bnb.co.nz

Pacifica: www.pacificahotels.co.nz

Top 10 Holiday Parks: www.top10.co.nz

Tourism New Zealand: www.purenz.com

VIP Backpackers: www.vip.co.nz

YHA New Zealand: www.yha.org.nz

Transportation and Tours

Air Canada: www.aircanada.ca

Air New Zealand: www.airnz.co.nz

Fiordland Travel: www.fiordlandtravel.com

Flying Kiwi: www.flyingkiwi.com

Freedom Air: www.freedomair.co.nz

Fullers: www.fullers.co.nz

Great Sights: www.greatsights.co.nz

Intercity: www.intercitycoach.co.nz

Interisland Line: www.interislandline.co.nz

Kiwi Experience: www.kiwiexperience.com

New Zealand Automobile Association: www.nzaa.co.nz

New Zealand Nature Safaris: www.nzsafaris.co.nz

Newmans: Newmanscoach.co.nz

Qantas: www.qantas.com.au

Stewart Island Marine: www.foveauxexpress.co.nz

Tranz Scenic: www.tranzscenic.co.nz

United Airlines: www.ual.com

Car and Campervan Rental

A1 Rent-A-Car: a1rentacar.co.nz

Adventure Deluxe Motorhomes: www.nzmotorhomes.co.nz

Britz: www.britz.com

Avis: www.avis.com

Budget: www.budget.com

Easy Car Rental: www.easyrentals.co.nz

Hertz: www.hertz.com

Ideal Rentals: www.ideal-cars.co.nz

Kea Campers: www.keacampers.com

Maui: www.maui-rentals.com

Metropolitan Rentals: www.metropolitan.co.nz

National: www.nationalcar.com

New Zealand Rent-a-car: www.nzcars.co.nz

Scotties: www.scotties.co.nz

Thrifty: www.thrifty.com

Government and Tourism

Christchurch City Promotions: www.christchurch.org.nz

Department of Conservation:
www.doc.govt.nz

Destination Lake Taupo:
www.laktauponz.com

Destination Queenstown:
www.queenstown-nz.co.nz

Dunedin Tourism:
www.dunedintourism.co.nz

Fish and Game New Zealand:
www.fishandgame.org.nz

Hawke's Bay Tourism:
www.hawkesbaytourism.co.nz

Latitude Nelson: www.nelson.net.nz

New Plymouth Online:
www.newplymouthnz.com

New Zealand Government: www.govt.nz

New Zealand Historic Places Trust:
www.historic.org.nz

New Zealand Immigration Service:
www.immigration.govt.nz.

New Zealand Mountain Safety Council:
www.mountainsafety.co.nz

Pacific Promotions: www.pacpro.net.nz

Totally Wellington: www.wellingtonnz.com

Tourism Auckland: www.aucklandnz.com

Tourism Eastland:
www.eastland.tourism.co.nz

Tourism Industry Association of New Zealand: www.tianz.org.nz

Tourism New Zealand: www.purenz.com

Tourism Rotorua: www.rotorua.co.nz

Tourism Southland: www.southland.org.nz

Tourism Waikato: www.waikatonz.co.nz

Index

Churches/Houses of Worship

Gardens

Geothermal Sites/ Hot Springs

Great Walks

Index

Historic Houses

The Maori

Scenic Views

Wine/Wineries

U.S.~Metric Conversion

1 inch	=	2.54 centimeters (cm)
1 foot	=	.304 meters (m)
1 yard	=	0.914 meters
1 mile	=	1.6093 kilometers (km)
1 km	=	.6214 miles
1 fathom	=	1.8288 m
1 chain	=	20.1168 m
1 furlong	=	201.168 m
1 acre	=	.4047 hectares
1 sq km	=	100 hectares
1 sq mile	=	2.59 square km
1 ounce	=	28.35 grams
1 pound	=	.4536 kilograms
1 short ton	=	.90718 metric ton
1 short ton	=	2000 pounds
1 long ton	=	1.016 metric tons
1 long ton	=	2240 pounds
1 metric ton	=	1000 kilograms
1 quart	=	.94635 liters
1 US gallon	=	3.7854 liters
1 Imperial gallon	=	4.5459 liters
1 nautical mile	=	1.852 km

To compute celsius temperatures, subtract 32 from Fahrenheit and divide by 1.8. To go the other way, multiply celsius by 1.8 and add 32.

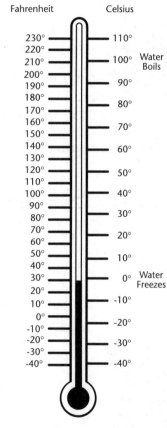

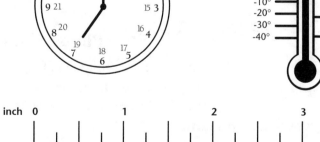

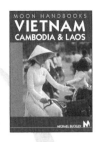

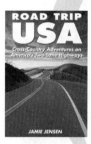